TENNESSEE CONVICTS

Early Records of the State Penitentiary

Volume 1
1831-1850

By
Charles A. Sherrill
and
Tomye M. Sherrill

JANAWAY PUBLISHING
Santa Maria, California

Copyright © Charles A. Sherrill, 1997

ALL RIGHTS RESERVED.
No part of this publication may be reproduced, stored in a retrieval system, or transmitted in any form or by any means whatsoever, whether electronic, mechanical, magnetic recording, or photocopying, without the prior written approval of the Copyright holder or Publisher, excepting brief quotations for inclusion in book reviews.

Originally published
Nashville
1997

Reprinted and Published by:

Janaway Publishing, Inc.
732 Kelsey Ct.
Santa Maria, California 93454
(805) 925-1038
www.janawaygenealogy.com

2007, 2015

ISBN: 978-1-59641-074-9

Made in the United States of America

TABLE OF CONTENTS

Introduction: *Life in the Penitentiary* .... Pages i - xxiv

Convict Record Book 1831-1850 .... Pages 1 - 163

This section of the book includes complete transcription of volume 45 of the Tennessee State Penitentiary records (Record Group 25) at the State Library and Archives. Volume 45 provides detailed descriptions and biographies of 600 inmates from 1831-1842. Entries were transcribed verbatim, with some changes in punctuation and abbreviations for clarity. <u>Underlining</u> has been added to confirm peculiar spellings, and [brackets] indicate text supplied by the transcriber, with question marks added where the original was illegible. Not every prisoner in the penitentiary merited an entry in volume 45; it is uncertain what the criteria for inclusion may have been.

Also included in this section of a book is a transcription of the first pages of volume 87 of the Tennessee State Penitentiary records, comprising the entries made from 1845 to 1850. Volume 87 and volume 45 are similar, though the entries in the later volume are generally more brief, and a smaller percentage of inmates are represented.

Comments written in the margins of these two volumes, usually relating to the prisoner's discharge, have been italicized.

Convict Ledger 1831-1850 .... Pages 165 - 313

This section of the book is a complete transcription of the prisoner data in volume 86 of the Tennessee State Penitentiary records. The original volume is in columnar format and the data has been rearranged for this publication. Volume 86 includes information on all 1,176 inmates, and was used by the Keeper of the Penitentiary to compile reports and statistics for the Legislature.

Index of Places .... Pages 315 - 320

Indexes names of counties mentioned in the transcription. Where only a state is given and no county, the state alone was not indexed in the case of Tennessee, North Carolina and Kentucky. Place names mentioned without a county (ie Shelbyville, Tenn.) have generally been indexed under the name of the county (ie Bedford County) and not the town.

Index of Names .... Pages 321-350

Tennessee Convicts: Records of the State Penitentiary

LIFE IN THE PENITENTIARY

The records of the Tennessee State Penitentiary can be viewed in two ways. A casual approach reveals a body of historical records of fascinating and valuable detail. But on closer reflection, the misery and evil reflected in the records will send a chill down the spine of the imaginative reader.

Most people shrink from thinking much about prisons. But the process of dealing with crime and criminals in 19th-century Tennessee resulted in the creation of a huge body of records. They range from the minutes and case files of the local courts to the records of gubernatorial pardons. For both the historian and the genealogist, these records are well worth investigating.

The purpose of this book is to provide both historical and genealogical information based on the earliest records of the Tennessee State Penitentiary. The impetus for the work came from the discovery of several ledgers maintained by the Keeper of the Penitentiary, who kept a careful record of each prisoner. These records, housed at the Tennessee State Library and Archives, provide fascinating glimpses into the identities of the inmates of the Penitentiary during its first two decades.

The world these records represent can never be completely understood by modern minds, but a study of the laws providing for punishment and of the rules and procedures of the Penitentiary helps shed some light on them.

* * *

Tennessee Convicts: Records of the State Penitentiary

When George W. Cook walked through the brand new gates into the Tennessee State Penitentiary on Jan. 21, 1831, he became the first of thousands of Tennesseans to spend years of their lives in captivity there. Cook, a 21-year-old tailor, spent two years in the prison. His nights were endured in a dank cell only 18" longer than his 6-foot frame. He was forbidden to speak to any of the 78 other thieves, liars, murderers and counterfeiters who joined him there during his stay. His family could not visit or write to him; he was entirely cut off from the world "outside."

Cook, found guilty of stabbing by a jury in Jackson, may have considered himself fortunate to be sent to the Penitentiary. Several years earlier, the punishment for his crime could have included whipping and branding as well as incarceration in a local jail. Before the penitentiary was built, harsh punishments were imposed for most crimes in Tennessee. Hanging, branding, cropping and whipping were commonly meted out to criminals. The courts served as instruments of retribution, and shaming or frightening the criminal into submission was the only form of rehabilitation. However, this changed in 1829 when the legislature voted funds to build a penitentiary and revised the criminal code so that crimes other than first degree murder were punishable by imprisonment.[1]

There was a celebratory mood in Nashville on the day the prison opened. Proud to have been chosen over Knoxville as the site for the new institution, local citizens had given the $2,500 needed to purchase the property. It was located well out of town, about a mile from the Davidson County courthouse, in the area now between Church and Charlotte west of 15th Avenue. The building was paid for

View of Nashville, ca. 1834, by Matthew Rhea

---

[1] State of Tennessee, General Assembly, <u>Acts passed at the stated session of the eighteenth General Assembly of the State of Tennessee, 1829</u> (Nashville: Hall & Heiskell, 1829) chapters 5 and 6.

ACTS

PASSED

AT THE STATED SESSION

OF THE

EIGHTEENTH GENERAL ASSEMBLY

OF THE

STATE OF TENNESSEE,

1829.

PRINTED BY AUTHORITY.

ALLEN A. HALL & FREDERICK S. HEISKELL,
PRINTERS TO THE STATE.

In 1829 the 18th General Assembly voted to build the Penitentiary in Nashville with state funds, and the local papers boasted that it was more economically constructed than any similar prison in the country. Cook's arrival marked the culmination of years of effort, and the exulting *National Banner and Nashville Whig* went so far as to take a rather jovial view of his crime, saying the conviction was the result "the too free use of his dirk."[2]

As the winter of 1831 continued, Cook was joined by several other convicts. In April, Cook saw the prison's fifth inmate join the unhappy community. Alexander Spears was a convicted horse thief and had good reason to appreciate the revised list of punishments. Several years earlier he would have been hanging by the neck in the courthouse square at Winchester, Tennessee, following his guilty verdict there. Horses were prized and valuable possessions on the frontier, and the state's early criminal code reflected this, as the crime of horse stealing was punishable by death even on the first offense.[3] Spears, at 21, had many years of life to look forward to even after serving his six-year term. However, almost exactly two years after his release in 1837 Spears re-entered the prison. He had been found guilty of grand larceny by a Bedford County jury.

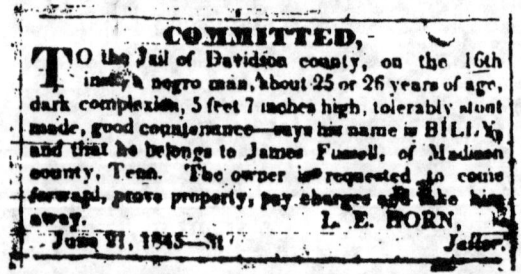

Prisoners were held in county jails until sentencing. Those found guilty of fines punishable by imprisonment were then sent to the Penitentiary

---

[2] National Banner and Nashville Whig, Jan. 24, 1831.
[3] State of Tennessee, General Assembly, Acts passed at the first session, third General Assembly of the state of Tennessee... 1799 (Knoxville: Roulstone & Wilson, 1799) chapter 20.

Tennessee Convicts: Records of the State Penitentiary

The first perjurer to enter the Penitentiary was James Wilson, who joined Cook, Spears and the others in November of 1831. According to the laws in force as late as 1822, perjury convictions required the prisoner to "stand in the pillory one hour, having his ears nailed during the whole time, and at the expiration of said hour, both ears of the offender to be cut off and severed from the head leaving them nailed to the pillory, until the setting of the sun."[4] Wilson, with a mere four-year sentence, may have thought he was getting off lightly.

None of these prisoners were allowed to talk to each other. They were confined in separate cells, and when outside the cell were always under the supervision of a guard. Occasionally guards would speak to prisoners to give orders, but the rules forbade any casual conversation. The restrictions on communication from outside the prison were just as strict. As set out in the 1829 laws governing the prison, they read:

> The convicts shall receive no letters or intelligence from or concerning their friends, or any information on any subject out of the prison; nor be permitted to write letters themselves. No relative or friend shall be allowed to speak to a convict except in some extraordinary case, where the condition of his property or family imperiously requires it, and then only in the presence of the Agent.[5]

In their solitary cells at night the prisoners in the summer of 1833 listened to each other retching and sobbing, as one in four of them died during a cholera epidemic. James Wilson, the perjurer, died that summer.

One of the guiding principles of the Penitentiary was to make a profit. Indeed, some of the early political rhetoric about the need for a prison to insure more humane punishments is overshadowed by the emphasis given to profit-making immediately upon the opening of the institution. "Even

---

[4] Edward Scott, Laws of the State of Tennessee ... now in force .... (Knoxville: Heiskell and Brown, 1821) I:156.

[5] State of Tennessee, General Assembly, Acts passed at the stated session of the eighteenth general assembly ... 1829, (Nashville: Hall & Heiskell, 1829), chapter 38, section 22:4.

Tennessee Convicts: Records of the State Penitentiary

NAME.	WHEN RECEIVED.			CRIME.	FROM WHAT COUNTY.
William Cassells	Feby	23	1833	Horse Stealing	Madison
Isham Conner	"	"	"	Stabing	Gibson
Robt C Brogan	March	7	"	Forgery	Knox
Hazard Kesterson	"	8	"	Petit Larceny	Anderson
Peter Seals	"	10	"	Asslt & Battery with intent to kill	Dickson
John B Wright	"	21	"	Larceny	Davidson
William Hamilton	April	10	"	Passing Counterfeit money	Rutherford
John Yates	"	18	"	Asslt with intent to murder	Marion
George W Morris	"	19	"	Forgery	Henderson
John N Chapman	May	5	"	Petit Larceny	McMinn
Bennett A James	"	15	"	Horse Stealing	Wayne
Jackson J Swaggirty	"	25	"	Petit Larceny	Monroe
William Tinsley	July	6	"	" "	Davidson
Hyram Johnson	Augt	21	"	" "	Williamson
Hatchford Valentine	Sept	8	"	Murder 2d Degree	Shelby
John Brandon	"	10	"	House Breaking	Lawrence
William Clipp	Oct	2	"	Petit Larceny	Carter
John J Brazeal	"	22	"	Asslt & B intent to kill	Henderson
Hamilton Goddett	"	28	"	Horse Stealing	Rutherford
Archibald Porter	"	"	"	" "	Hamilton
John Milton	Nov	6	"	Petit Larceny	Wilson
James W Duncan	"	8	"	Horse Stealing	McMinn
George Corbin	"	10	"	Stabing	Maury
William Walton	"	"	"	Forgery	"
Francis McCaspin	"	"	"	Grand Larceny	"
Samuel Cooxey	Decr	10	"	Petit	Henry
William Brown	"	12	"	Forgery	Monroe
Green White	"	17	"	Stabbing	Davidson
John Brown	"	26	"	Horse Stealing	
Ira Olive	Jany	14	1834	Stabbing	Tipton
Henry Cook	"	"	"	Passing C Bank Notes	"
Henry K Redman	"	"	"	"	"
Joseph Collins	"	28	"	Horse Stealing	Franklin

Entries in this convict record book (vol. 86) run across two pages

Tennessee Convicts: Records of the State Penitentiary

AGE.	OCCUPATION.	SENTENCE. Years.	Mos.	WHERE BORN.	WHEN DISCHARGED.		BY WHAT AUTHORITY.
27	Labourer	3		Tennessee	Feby	16	1836	Conduct Very Good
41	"	2		S Carolina	March	27	1835	" Exceptionable
27	Hatter	3		Kentucky	May	16	1836	
52	Labourer	1		Virginia	June	"	1833	Died of Cholera
37	"	10	8	"	May	4	1843	Pardoned by Gov. Jones
31	"	3		Tennessee	Augt	17	1835	Died of a Fit X
29	Cab. maker	3		Georgia	Sept	06	1836	Conduct Exceptionable
34	Waggon maker	3		N Carolina	June	10	1833	Died of Cholera
35	Labourer	3		S Carolina	April	19	1836	Conduct Good
21	"	1		" "	May	15	1834	" Generally Good
35	Blk Smith	3		Tennessee	June	"	1836	" " "
25	Labourer	1	3	"	Sept	3	1834	" " "
26	Cabinet maker	1		Kentucky	Sept	29	"	" Exceptionable
30	Shoe maker	1		New York	Novr	18	"	" Good
34	Labourer	10		N Carolina	May	5	1843	Pardoned by Gov. Jones
17	"	3		Tennessee	July	1	1835	Died of Cholera
47	"	2		N Carolina	Novr	25	"	Conduct Bad
41	"	21		Tennessee	"	19	1838	Pardon
20	"	0		" "	"	17	1836	Conduct Good
21	"	4		N Carolina	July	2	1835	Died of Cholera
25	"	2	6	Tennessee	June	5	1836	Conduct Good
25	"	8		S Carolina	Augt	12	1841	Pardoned by Gov. J. K. Polk
37	Blk Smith	2		Virginia	Novr	10	1835	Conduct Good
21	Labourer	8		"	April	8	1834	By Court of Appeals
17	"	3		Kentucky	June	30	1835	Died of Cholera
18	"	1	6	Virginia	April	"	1836	Conduct Bad
27	"	3		Tennessee	Decr	29	"	" Good
21	"	5		Kentucky	July	5	1835	Died of Cholera
28	Blk Smith	3		N Carolina	Decr	25	1836	Conduct Good
40	Labourer	2		" "	Jany	14	"	" "
25	"	3		" "	" "	"	1837	" "
52	Blk Smith	3		Virginia	Feby	26	"	" Generally Good
28	Labourer	6		S Carolina	Sept	15	1835	Died of Cholera

Notice the "Occupation" column on this page

the early reformers, however, never intended for the convicts to be idle: as they were paying their debt to society by their incarceration, they were expected to contribute to their own upkeep through forced labor."[6] Reports of the Agent and Keeper to the legislature nearly always began with an account of the profit and loss statement of the prison workshops.

As prisoner number one, George Cook helped get the prison workshop program off to a good start. He was an experienced tailor, and thus brought a useful trade to the prison. Prison records show that among his first duties was the making of his own uniform.[7] Cook was the first employee in the "tailor's department." He was soon paired with another tailor, Barbee Beasley from Giles County, who was to serve a 20 year term for shooting. Cook was released at the expiration of his term in 1833, and Beasley fell victim to the cholera epidemic a few months later.

Although Cook was the first inmate and Beasley the fourth, the prison was not blessed with another experienced tailor until the arrival of David Gawley six years later. Over the years, prison officials bemoaned the fact that too many men without any useful skills were sent to the penitentiary. A great effort was made to teach each man a trade, so that he could at least earn his own keep. The Inspectors in 1833 even went so far as to suggest to the legislature that penitentiary terms of one year were not long enough, as "the time is too short ... to learn a trade."[8]

Because of this emphasis on constructive labor, one of the critical pieces of information entered into each prisoner's record was his occupation. The vast majority of prisoners were described as "laborers." As Tennessee's economy was almost entirely agricultural, it is logical to assume that these men had been farm laborers before their imprisonment.

---

[6] Larry D. Gossett, "The keepers and the kept : the first hundred years of the Tennessee State Prison system, 1830-1930," diss., Louisiana State U., 1992, (Ann Arbor: University Microfilms International, 1994) 47-48.

[7] Gossett 36.

[8] State of Tennessee, House of Representatives, Journal of the House of Representatives ... eleventh general assembly, appendix, 3. (Knoxville: Heiskell & Hall, 1833) 112.

Tennessee Convicts: Records of the State Penitentiary

OCCUPATIONS REPORTED BY INMATES 1831 - 1850
listed by number of inmates

Occupation	#	Occupation	#	Occupation	#
laborer	647	counterfeiter	2	machine maker	1
farmer	68	distiller	2	manufacturer	1
blacksmith	57	engineer	2	miller	1
blank or none	57	ferryman	2	moroed(?) dresser	1
shoe maker	46	fisherman	2	moulder	1
boatsman	28	loafer & thief	2	painter turnerge(?)	1
tailor	24	machinist	2	potter	1
carpenter	22	overseer	2	preacher	1
wagon maker	15	saddle tree maker	2	printer	1
hatter	12	stone mason	2	quack doctor	1
cabinet maker	10	waggoner	2	race rider	1
cooper	10	whore	2	raftsman	1
school teacher	9	abolitionist	1	ran rules	1
sailor	9	artist	1	rigger	1
painter	7	bookbinder	1	rough carpenter	1
saddle maker	7	bookkeeper	1	seaman	1
tanner	7	bricklayer	1	shoe/boot maker 1	1
loafer	7	brickmaker	1	silversmith	1
stage driver	6	brickmason	1	smelter	1
thief	6	constable	1	soldier and printer	1
soldier	5	ditcher	1	spinner	1
gun smith	5	doctor	1	stealing	1
harness maker	5	dyer	1	steamer doctor	1
mail carrier/rider	4	ex sheriff	1	stone driver	1
stone cutter	4	gambler	1	store keeper	1
clerk	4	general mechanic	1	tinner	1
peddler	4	grocery keeper	1	upholsterer	1
butcher	3	grog shop keeper	1	vagabond	1
plasterer	3	hammerer	1	wagon painter	1
merchant	3	house carpenter	1	well digger	1
cabin boy	2	house painter	1	wheelright	1
cobbler	2	jailer	1	wool carder	1
cook	2	lawyer	1		

However, a remarkable number of the convicts reported some other skills. The table on the following page shows the general occupations reported for all the prisoners admitted through 1850.

According to the 1840 census of Tennessee 90 percent of the men in the state were farmers. Yet in the penitentiary, even if all "laborers" are considered farmers, nearly 40 percent of the inmates had non-farm occupations. Several interesting possibilities are suggested by these figures. Does this indicate that farmers were far less likely to commit crimes than other people? Or could it show that men in crafts and trades were often drifters by necessity, without strong community ties, and more likely to be severely punished by the courts when caught in crime? Certainly many of the prisoners were tried and arrested across the county line from where their family lived. One example is Robert Brogan, a hatmaker convicted of forgery in Knox County, while his father and wife lived in Anderson County. Another, further from home, was Alexander Cohen of Tuscaloosa, Alabama, a "renovater and dyer" who was found guilty of second-degree murder in Fayette County.

Of those 462 convicts with non-farm occupations, twenty might be considered professional criminals of one sort or another. Among the criminal class was counterfeiter Benjamin Foster. Although making money was listed as Foster's occupation, he was in prison on charges of bigamy from the Hickman County Circuit Court. There were 51 other inmates convicted of making or "passing" counterfeit bank bills. This crime seems to have reached a peak in 1847, when eleven men were brought in with that charge against them. A group of five from Davidson County all came in January, perhaps the result of a "bust" by local law enforcement.

One prisoner gave his life in the Civil War, a decade before the war started. Richard Dillingham (erroneously recorded as Dillionham in the ledger) was a Quaker schoolteacher from Cincinnati who had been "persuaded by some colored people there to go to Nashville to get some of their relations from a 'hard master.'" He was caught at the Cumberland River bridge with three slaves in his closed carriage, and arrested on December 5, 1848. At his trial, Dillingham said that he alone was

Tennessee Convicts: Records of the State Penitentiary

Jackson J. Swaggerty was received in the Penitentiary on the twenty-fifth of May one thousand eight hundred & thirty three he is five feet & nine inches & a half in height, weighs one hundred & eighty five pounds light hair blue eyes dark complexion & strongly built twenty five years of age. Born in Cocke County Tennessee brought up there where his father, mother three brothers & seven sisters now reside he has two sisters married one to ____ now living in Monroe County about five miles from John McGee ____ Swaggerty's parents residence is about six miles above ____ on the Greenville road he had a wife & two children they reside at ____ one of his other sisters is married to ____ Sloat his residence not known he has several scars on the forefinger of the left hand where it joins the hand the little finger of this hand is crooked he had several scars on the shins & one running up & down on the inside of the left leg this leg has been broken a scar on the left side of the forehead had generally followed Farming was found guilty of Petit Larceny at the Circuit court of Monroe County & sentenced to Fifteen Months Imprisonment in the Jail & Penitentiary House of the State of Tennessee.

Detailed descriptions of convicts, like this one of Jackson Swaggerty, were often beautifully penned in this convict record book (volume 45) "responsible for the error into which his education and his feelings of philanthropy led him."[9] He entered the penitentiary April 16, 1849, to serve a three year sentence. The prison keeper listed his occupation as "abolitionist." This noble idealist died June 30, 1850, of cholera while still incarcerated.

Nineteen other prisoners were at the Penitentiary on charges of "negro stealing," although it is unlikely that they were abolitionists like Dillingham. John Murrell of Madison County was the first of these, imprisoned in 1834. Murrell was perhaps the most famous person to "do time" in the Tennessee State Penitentiary. His entry in *Who was Who in America* lists his profession as "outlaw" and states:

> Led life characterized by stealing and gen. illegal activities before 1826; leader of a large band of outlaws who terrorized Southwest territories, 1826-34; especially known for his acts of Negro stealing for which he was caught by Virgil A. Stewart, 1834.[10]

A biography of Murrell published in 1847 describes in flowery terms his entrance into the Penitentiary:

> The convict entered the portal of the prison.... His insolent composure faltered as he touched the threshold; there was a trepidation in the step, before so confident and bold; and as the closing gate creaked a malicious mockery on his ear, his heart sank, his lips turned white and faint....[11]

This biographer relates Murrell's assignment to the blacksmith shop on the Penitentiary grounds, and alleges that Murrell and his associates learned to signal each other "by means of his digital alphabet." Using

---

[9] Chase C. Mooney, Slavery in Tennessee (Bloomington: Indiana U. Press, 1957) 60, 61, 218.
[10] Who was Who in America, Historical Volume 1607-1896 (Chicago: Marquis Who's Who, 1967) 444.
[11] Augustus Walton, The Life and Adventures of John A. Murrell (Philadelphia: T.B. Peterson & Brothers, 1847) 122.

these hand signals, Murrell is supposed to have organized continuing crimes.[12] An escape, apparently, was not among them, as he served most of his 10-year sentence. Murrell's several biographers would have done well to consult the Penitentiary records, as Murrell gave the prison officials detailed information about his birth, early life and family of which these writers were unaware. Information about Murrell's career after his release from prison in 1844 is also incomplete, but some writers claim he died in Bledsoe County just a few years later.

A handful of inmates came from more conventional backgrounds, and the harsh conditions at the prison must have been a shock to them. Nine school teachers, three merchants, three doctors (one of them, however, described as a "quack") and a lawyer all came to the penitentiary during this early period. Richard Pruett, a former member of the Indiana State Legislature, was caught stealing a horse in Franklin County and sent to the prison for seven years. He sickened and died after only a year, at the age of 41.

The prison was obviously designed to keep people in, not to make them comfortable. Two hundred cells and other buildings were contained in an area about 350 feet square, all enclosed by a wall 20 feet high and four and a half feet thick.[13] Each cell was tiny, only seven feet six inches long, three feet six inches wide, and seven feet high. This was barely large enough for a grown man to lie down.[14] Certainly no furniture was provided, and very little air. Physicians at the prison frequently complained that even the small vents leading into the cells were blocked with construction debris, creating unhealthy (not to mention uncomfortable) conditions.

In this situation contagious disease could run rampant. Fast-acting cholera was a major threat. Dr. Felix Robertson described the prison's first cholera epidemic in his 1835 report to the legislature:

---

[12] Walton 122.
[13] Eastin Morris, Tennessee gazetteer or topographical dictionary... (Nashville: Hunt & Co., 1834) 221.
[14] Nashville Republican and State Gazette, Dec. 7, 1830, page 3, column 1.

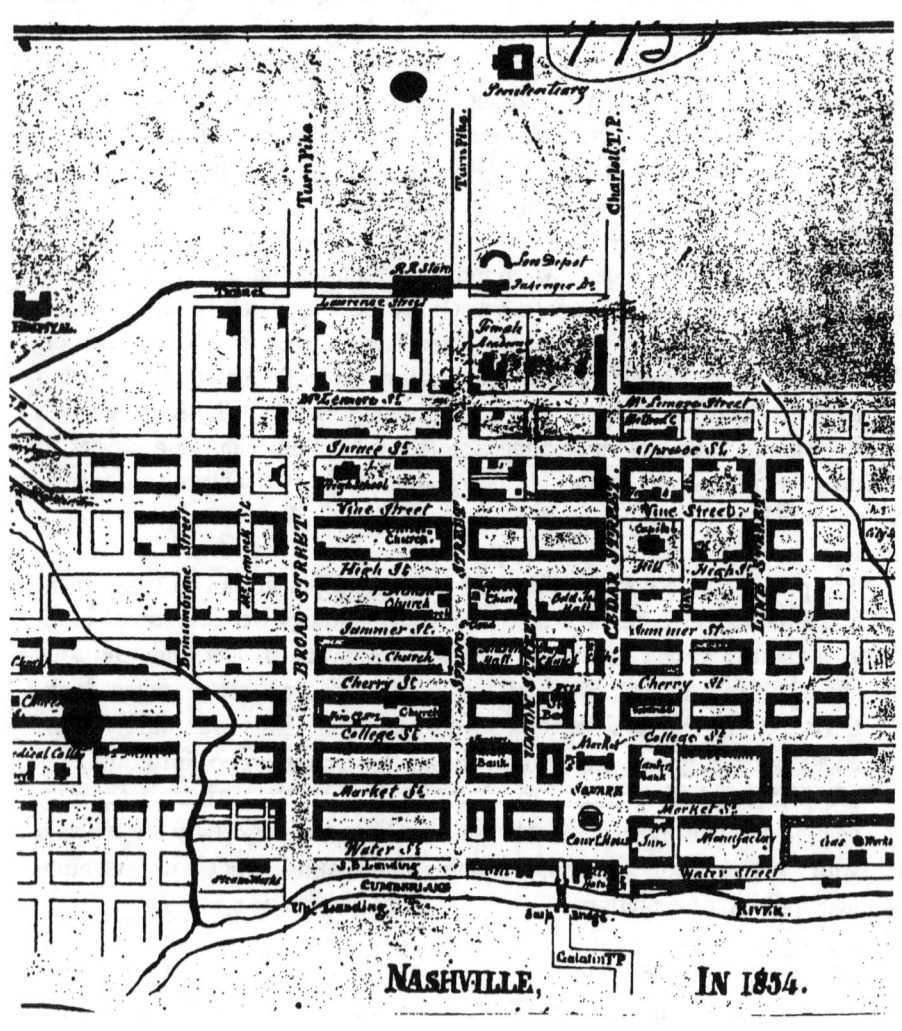

An 1854 map of Nashville shows the Penitentiary far away from the main part of town, but as the city grew its citizens wanted the facility moved still farther away.

Tennessee Convicts: Records of the State Penitentiary

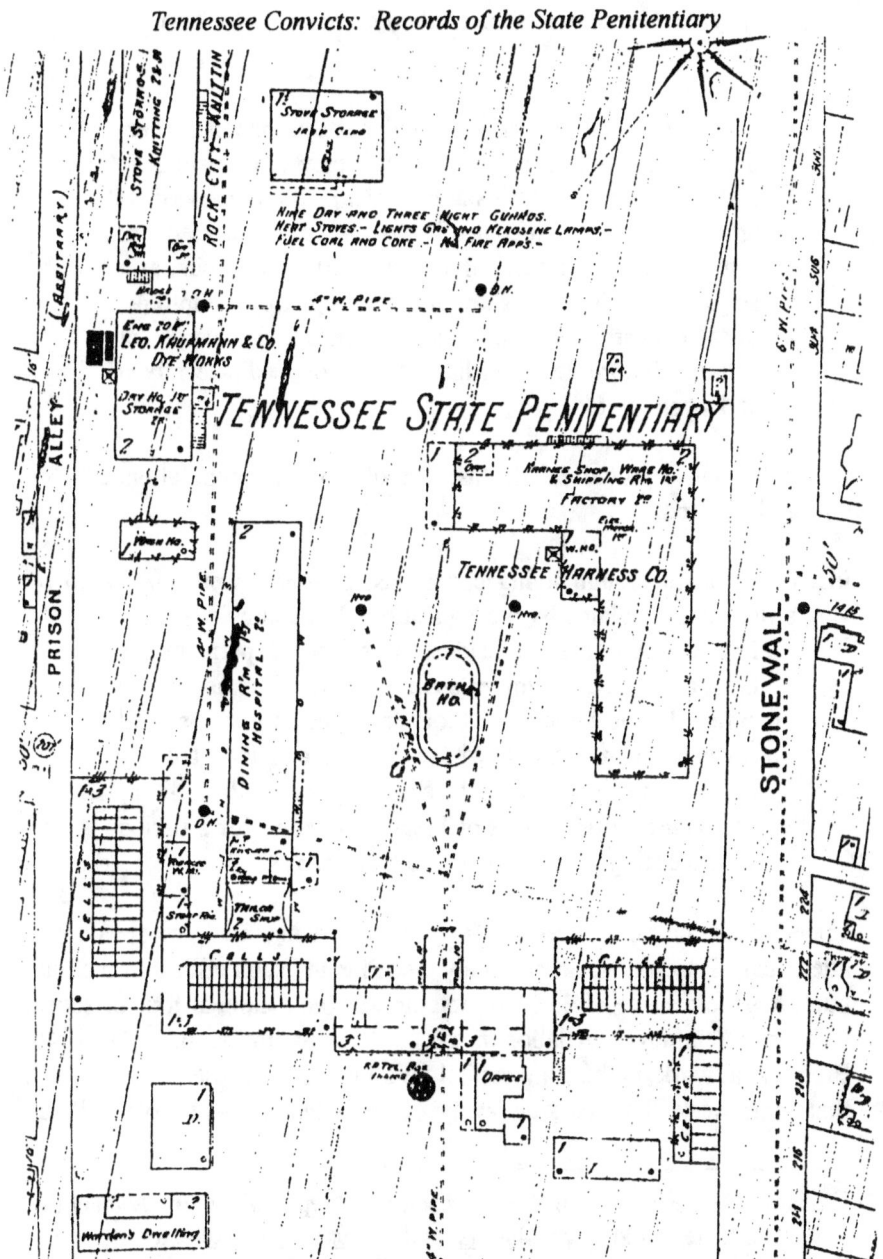

The 1898 Sanborn-Perris "Insurance Map of Nashville" shows the prison buildings just before they were demolished. Some of the workshop buildings had been leased to private industries

> Many were still laboring under the effects of [an earlier] fever, when, about the first of July, they were visited by that fell destroyer, the Asiatic Cholera. It commenced its attack on the enfeebled, but it soon ceased to discriminate, prostrating the most healthy and robust at a single blow. It rarely showed the premonitory symptoms, but frequently prostrated its victim to the verge of collapse before he could have a dose of medicine mixed and swallow it.[15]

Dr. Robertson reported 30 deaths, out of a prison population of 165, during the period.

In addition to the rough living conditions, prisoners were oppressed by very strict rules mandated by the legislature. For example:
> If any prisoner shall neglect or refuse to perform the labour assigned to him, or shall willfully injure any of the materials, instruments or tools entrusted to him, or shall engage in conversation with any other convict either by words, gesture or signs ... he shall be punished by solitary confinement upon a diet of bread and water, for a period not exceeding thirty days for each offence....[16]

Under such circumstances, it is not surprising that escapes were attempted. Prison officials probably nipped many such efforts in the bud, but a few were successful. Most notable was the escape of four prisoners who were "employed at labor in the city" on Saturday, June 21, 1845. Probably at work on the state capitol building, as the cornerstone was laid that same week, the men stole away. One of them, 25-year-old William

---

[15] State of Tennessee, House of Representatives, "Report of the Physician of the Tennessee State Penitentiary," Journal of the House of Representatives ... at the twenty-first general assembly... (Knoxville: Ramsey & Craighead, 1836) 52.

[16] State of Tennessee, General Assembly, Acts passed at the stated session of the eighteenth general assembly ... 1829, (Nashville: Hall & Heiskell, 1829), chapter 38, section 24:5.

Swaney, was drowned as he tried to swim across the Cumberland River. Swaney was only three months away from completing an 18-month sentence for killing a bull. The Keeper ran an ad in the newspaper offering a $50 reward for each man.[17] William Ferguson was, at 43, the oldest of the escapees, and he was recaptured along with Abraham Briley. James Gaddy, the youngest at 19, made his escape good. Interestingly, the prison ledger merely shows him as having been "discharged" on the date of the escape.

> **Two Hundred Dollars Reward.**
>
> THE following described Convicts of the Tennessee Penitentiary, made their escape on Saturday, 21st instant; for the apprehension and delivery of whom the above reward will be paid, or **Fifty Dollars** for either of them, viz:—
>
> **William Ferguson,** from Grainger county.— He is 45 years old, 5 feet 10 inches high, black hair, roman nose, and some defect in his front teeth, down look, somewhat stoop-shouldered and thin visage—weighs 160 pounds.
>
> **William Swaney,** 26 years old, 5 feet 9½ inches high, dark hair and dark heavy beard, grey eyes, large full features, and weighs about 170 pounds; has a scar running with the jaw-bone on the left side, commencing about ¼ of an inch from the centre of the chin and running back about two inches. The finger next to the little finger on the left hand has a scar running to the first joint, which leaves the nail imperfect. His right great toe has been cut with an axe, commencing near the root of the nail on the outside, and running across to the next toe and up the foot about 1½ inch. He is from Claiborne county.
>
> **James Gaddy** is 21 years old, 6 feet high, weighs 180 pounds, dark hair, blue eyes and dark skin. The fore-finger of his left hand has been cut off at the root of the nail. He is from Lincoln county.
>
> **Abraham Briley,** from Henry county, 25 years of age, 5 feet 6½ inches high, weighs 154 pounds, dark brown hair, dark complexion, heavy made, with rather a good countenance.
>
> H. I. ANDERSON, Agent and Keeper Penitentiary of Tennessee.
>
> Nashville, June 21, 1845—tw3t&wlt

---

[17] *Tri-Weekly Nashville Union,* June 24, 1845, 2:1; June 26, 1845, 3:1.

The construction of the beautiful state capitol building, still gracing Nashville today, was made possible in large part by "free" prison labor. Constructed of Tennessee marble, the job required a large number of laborers to work with the stone. The prison report of 1847 shows that 56 inmates were employed in cutting stone, 12 in carrying it, 30 in sawing it and 13 others assisting the stonecutters in various ways.[18] By 1851 the number of convicts deployed to work with stone for the Capitol had increased to 133.

Other trades plied in the prison workshops included carpentry, wagon making, blacksmithing, hat making, coopering, shoe and harness making and painting. The tailor's shop, in which the first inmate had been put to work, was out of business by 1845. In 1846 a chair shop and the task of "hacking shucks" (perhaps for mattresses) were added.[19]

Any group of historical records reveals interesting patterns in names. The computer data-base allows us to learn that of the people in the penitentiary during this period, the most common name was, of course, John (152), followed by William (121) and James (108). But some of the more unusual names stand out. That there were two men named Davenport seems odd: Davenport Wiseman from North Carolina and Davenport Romines born in Virginia. Two others were named Paris. Foreign influences are evident in names like Nickolas, Ermando and Francisco. Francisco was Cuban-born, Nickolas and Ermando were Southern boys from Virginia and North Carolina. Odd names were popular, then as now; including Meflin (Hannum), Mizay (Hazlett), Murdock (Bullard) and Osenberry (Harrison). The Bostick family of South Carolina, apparently quirky with names, produced a Littleberry and an Orlonzo, both criminals.

---

[18] State of Tennessee, Senate, "Report of the inspectors and agent of the Tennessee Penitentiary," Senate journal for the first session of the twenty-seventh General Assembly... (Nashville:J.G.Shepard,1848) appendix 413.

[19] State of Tennessee, House of Representatives, "Report of the Keeper of the Penitentiary," Journal of the House of Representatives ... twenty-sixth General Assembly... (Nashville: W.F. Bang, 1846) appendix 306.

Tennessee Convicts: Records of the State Penitentiary

Some boys seem to have been destined for a life of crime, having been saddled with a name that required a tough exterior. One of these was poor Weakley Chick from Alabama, who grew up to become a robber. Craven Butts was another. Ake Johnson, with his painful name, stole a beehive and ended up in the penitentiary at age 15.

The record of Lewis de St. Leger reveals a man with a violent past. At only 29 years old, he bore bullet marks on his cheek, shoulder, hip and arm, and scars on his face from the bite of a man. His conviction was for assault with intent to kill. In a letter to the governor regarding St. Leger's application for a pardon, State Representative Austin Miller commented, "He has led a dis[s]ipated life and has frequently been in broils and quar[r]els, threatening and attempting to take the lives of his adversaries."[20] This image of a hardened criminal is belied by his occupation: Lewis was a portrait painter!

In 1839 and 1841 prison officials conducted surveys of the inmates, perhaps in an effort to help determine the causes of crime. Of 177 inmates in the latter survey, 84 of them (47 percent) admitted to being constantly drunk "when they could procure the means." Thirty of these alcoholics claimed a "tolerably fair education." Twenty more said they could read and write and had been morally brought up. Of 15 who said they did not drink at all, only two said they had been morally brought up and educated. According to the report, "They all seemed to deplore the want of correct instruction in their youth, and the intemperate course of life it gave rise to" and blamed their criminal nature on these root causes.[21]

Regarding literacy, the number of prisoners who could read and write in 1839 was 81. The Agent qualified this by stating that a large number of

---

[20] Recommendations for Pardon, Gov. James K. Polk Papers, Tenn. State Library and Archives, Nashville, box 3, folder 4.

[21] State of Tennessee, House of Representatives, "Report of the Inspectors and Agent of the Tennessee Penitentiary," <u>Journal of the House of Representatives ... twenty-fourth General Assembly...</u> (Knoxville: E.G. Eastman, [1841]) appendix 6.

them could do so "only indifferently." Nineteen, or 12 percent, were categorized as "wholly destitute of learning."[22] Census figures on literacy are not available until 1850, but in that year about 20 percent of native-born adults in the South were illiterate. It is interesting that inmates appear to have had a higher rate of literacy than the general population.[23]

By 1850 Chaplain John P. Sledge had been appointed to the Penitentiary. Mr. Sledge was either very well received or inclined to exaggerate the positive. He reported:

> It is but just that I should say, they have been uniformly clean, cheerful and comfortable in their appearance. Their apartments [!] also seem to be kept neat and clean. And I would further say, the Prisoners have always seemed anxious to listen, and have given the best attention.

The prisoners had each been provided with a volume of the New Testament and the Psalms, "with print big enough for them to read in their cells." The chaplain concluded:

> Nineteen have confessed they believe the Truth, and have been immersed. How they will conduct themselves, only time will prove. But I hope they, with us, may prove faithful unto death, and then we shall receive the promised reward.[24]

---

[22] State of Tennessee, House of Representatives, "Report, Superintendant of the Tennessee Penitentiary...," Journal of the House of Representatives ... twenty-third General Assembly... (Knoxville: Gifford & Eastman, 1839) 934.
[23] J.B. DeBow, Statistical view of the United States... (Washington: A.O.P. Nicholson, 1854) 153.
[24] State of Tennessee, Senate, "Report of the Keeper of the Penitentiary," Senate Journal of the first session of the twenty-ninth General Assembly... (Nashville: Bang, McKennie, [1852]) appendix 120.

Tennessee Convicts: Records of the State Penitentiary

Laws of the period permitted even very young offenders to be imprisoned. The youngest person found in these records was 13-year-old Jesse Puckett, convicted of grand larceny in Warren County. He served all of his three-year term. There were three 14-year-olds and ten 15-year-olds, all boys. These young prisoners may have been hardier than the others, as none of them died during their confinement.

On the other end of the spectrum, the oldest prisoner was Simon Williams, a black man convicted of arson. Williams told the Prison Keeper that he was 80 years old when he arrived at the penitentiary. He served his two-year sentence, with time off for good behavior, and left on Jan. 12, 1847. Five men came to the penitentiary in their seventies, and three of them died there. Seventy-one-year-old Arthur Davis, a murderer imprisoned for life in 1843, died of old age after serving about eighteen months.

Even during the construction of the penitentiary, it was understood that men and women, whites and blacks, would be incarcerated there. Separate quarters were mandated by the legislature, but the punishment of women, even in this age of many biases, was strictly equal to that of men. During its first ten years of operation, the penitentiary was strictly a men's establishment. But nine women can be identified in penitentiary records from 1841 to 1850, as shown on the accompanying chart. Mehala Brewer (also listed as Melinda) returned for a second sentence in 1848, after a two-year respite.

WOMEN IN THE PENITENTIARY 1841-1850

Name	Crime	Age	Occupation	Notes
Mehala Brewer	petit larceny	18	nothing	conduct good
Priscilla Childress	larceny	17	whore	pardoned by Gov. Jones
Mary Finney	larceny	33	labourer	conduct good
Elizabeth Henderson	larceny	22	nothing	pardoned by Gov. Polk
Narcissa Lemon	petit larceny	17	nothing	conduct good
Nancy Ann Smith	larceny	20	labourer	col[ore]d, pardoned
Eliza Williams	bigamy	36	whore	pardoned by Gov. Jones
Lucy Witcher	barn burning	20	sailor [?]	pardoned - act of 1836
Francis Shropshire	petit larceny	32	farmer	to lunatic asylum

The pitiful story of Frances Shropshire is related in the Keeper's report of 1851, as follows:

>...James Shropshire and his wife were received in Penitentiary as Convicts from Hawkins County.... She was in a state of pregnancy when received, and very early thereafter becoming deranged, gave birth to her child while in that condition. It lived some few months and died. Ascertaining that the Governor was willing to pardon her, I used every exertion to learn whether she had any relations who would receive her, but failed in my enquiries. I then endeavored to get her placed in the Lunatic Asylum, and although I proposed paying her board, was refused her admission. And thinking it improper to turn her loose on the community, in a deranged condition, and her refusal to leave the Prison if discharged, has induced me to still retain her, although it is not a suitable place for a Lunatic."[25]

The records show that Frances (alias Vicca) Shropshire was eventually accepted into the state Lunatic Asylum. Her husband, James, served his full six-year sentence in the Penitentiary.

During the penitentiary's first five years pardons were very rare. In fact, most inmates served several weeks or months beyond the date of their original sentence because of penalties for misbehavior. Death was the only way to get out early, and many took it.

There were, however, three pardons granted during those first five years. John B. Coleman, convicted of horse stealing in 1832, was pardoned by Governor William Carroll the day after his arrival at the penitentiary. John Gill, a blacksmith from Giles County, was sentenced for three years on an assault charge. Carroll granted him a pardon after he had served half of his sentence. Carroll, one of the prison's board members and probably the individual most deserving of credit for having it built and

---

[25] State of Tennessee, Senate, "Report of the Keeper of the Penitentiary," Senate Journal of the first session of the twenty-ninth General Assembly... (Nashville: Bang, McKennie, [1852]) appendix 102.

His Excellency William Carroll Governor in and
the State of Tennessee
                The petition of the undersigned Citizens
of Franklin County would respectfully represent to
your Excellency that David Lewis is now confined in
common jail of White County under the sentence of the
Supreme Court for the crime of manslaughter, and without
the interposition of Executive Clemency will have to
remain for eleven months & 20 days. We therefore
beg suggest to your excellency the propriety of a pardon
we humbly believe that said Lewis is a fit subject for
Clemency & for a more minute statement of the facts
and circumstances in relation to the commission of
said offence we would refer you to a former petition on
ding ... and as the policy of the country has changed and
the heretofore punishment now inflicted on Mr Lewis
has been abolished and a more ...
substituted in its place we would respectfully
... and earnestly request that said Lewis
may be pardoned & set at liberty, as we believe that
the cost & other punishment which he has received is an
ample punishment for his crime, and will ensure a reform-
tion on the part of said Lewis –
                                James Brittain
                                Jonathan Clayton
                                A V ...
John I. ...
R. C. ...
Thomas Williams   ... Bostic

Petition for pardon from Franklin County.
Many signatures appeared on the accompanying pages.

funded, was apparently reluctant to offer pardons. The third pardon was issued by Carroll's successor, Governor Newton Cannon, just a month after taking office. This was for John Minor, convicted of manslaughter and sentenced to eight years. Cannon pardoned Minor after less than a year's imprisonment.

In 1836 the Tennessee State Legislature passed the nation's first "good conduct" law.[26] Known to prison officials as the "Act of 1836" it provided that Governors should reduce sentences by two days for every month in which the prisoner conducted himself "with industry and propriety."[27] This act was frequently invoked by Newton Cannon and his successors in office. The papers of these governors, on file at the State Library and Archives, often include petitions of citizens requesting that a prisoner from their neighborhood be pardoned.

In the years following 1850 the prison population continued to grow, and additions were made to the building. The Civil War brought military rule to Nashville and the prison was crammed with political prisoners and captured Confederates. After the war convict leasing programs led to the development of branch prisons close to the mines where prison labor was needed. These and other changes are reflected in later records of the Tennessee State Penitentiary, but the personal details in records of the first twenty years are what make them unique.

---

[26] Gossett 57.
[27] State of Tennessee, General Assembly, Public acts passed at the first session of the twenty-first General Assembly... 1835-6 (Nashville: Nye & Co., 1836), chapter 63, section 4.

Tennessee Convicts: Records of the State Penitentiary

CONVICT RECORD BOOKS 1831-1850
Tennessee State Penitentiary

Morris Artist from Madison County. Crime: shooting. Sentence: three years from 4 May 1840. Received: 4 May 1840. He is 18 years old, 5' 10" high, weighs 177 lbs. He was born in North Carolina, brought up in West Tennessee five miles north of Jackson, Madison Co., where his father, mother, four brothers and three sisters live with John Morrin [Mornin?]. He is black, has had three fingers of the right hand cut which makes the middle fingers stiff, the thumb nail of the left hand is injured. [Ledger 45, p. 1]

Jacob L. Anderson from Fayette County. Crime: larceny. Sentence: four years from 20 May 1840. Received: 9 June 1840. He is 24 years old, weighs 140 lbs., 5' 8" high. Born and brought up in Cumberland Co., Virginia, six miles north of Cumberland Court house. He has dark hair, blue eyes and fair skin. Said Anderson has a wife and two children at her father's, Wm. May, six miles south of Somerville near the road leading to Lagrange on Wolf River within two miles of Dan'l Johnson's mill. [Ledger 45, p. 1]

Martin Armington from Stewart County. Crime: horse stealing. Received: 13 Nov. 1840. Sentence: eight years from 4 Nov. 1840. For particulars of him refer to former description, this being his second conviction. [Ledger 45, p. 1]

James Arnett from Davidson County. Crime: passing counterfeit money. Sentence: three years from 1 Feb. 1841 when he was [received?]. He is 42 years old, 5' 8" high, weighs 165 lbs. Born in Henrico Co., Virginia, has brother in said county. He has dark gray hair, hazle eyes, tolerable fair skin. Has a scar on the instep of the right foot near the ankle. [Ledger 45, p. 1]

John Armstrong from Davidson County. Crime: larceny. Sentence: three years from Jan. 27, 1842. He is 54 years old, 5' 7" high, weighs 170 lbs. Born and brought up in Montgomery Co., Maryland, in the county town. He has a wife and 3 children in Caldwell Co., Kentucky., 2.5 miles below Eddyville on a piece of land of his own. He is a cooper. Served his apprenticeship in the City of Baltimore. He has, he says, less [lost?] the use of his left eye and wears green spectacles. Has been a regular under Gen. Brown. He has a scar just above the left knee caused by a musket ball at the Battle of Plattsburg. Has dark gray hair, blue eyes and fair skin. [Ledger 45, p. 2]

Tennessee Convicts: Records of the State Penitentiary

George W. Allen from Hamilton County. Crime: larceny. Sentence: one year from 5 Apr. 1842. Received: 12 Apr. 1842. [Note: page torn; words missing shown with dashes]. -- years old, 6 ft. high, weighs 148 lbs. Born --- in Fayetteville, North Carolina, his father is --- [m]other married to a man by the name --- and lives near to the above named --- . [H]as dark hair, blue eyes and dark skin. --- the tailoring business. [Ledger 45, p. 2]

Beasley Barbee was received into the Penitentiary 9 April 1831. He is about 20 years old, 5' 9 $^{1}/_{2}$" high, weighs about 165 lbs., dark skin and hair, eyes gray. The little finger on his left hand has been broke. Scar on the middle finger of the same hand, scar on the left side of the left leg below the knee. Born in Orange Co., North Carolina, and brought up in the counties of Marion, Giles, and Hardin, Tennessee. Has a brother living in Louisiana on the Mississippi River near the Arkansas line, and a sister married to John Garner near Pulaski, Tenn. Was found guilty of maliciously shooting N.J. [or N.G?] Nye at the Circuit Court of Giles County, and sentenced to four years and eight months confinement in the Jail and Penitentiary House of the State of Tennessee. *Beasley Barbee [died] of Cholera on the [17th?] of June 1833.* [Ledger 45, p. 3]

William Baldwin was received into the Penitentiary 30 September, 1831. He is 24 years old, weighs 166 lbs. He is 6' 6" high, blue eyes and fair skin, has a small scar on the left hand between the thumb and four finger, the left leg has a large scar on the shin, also as remarkable scar in the left groin. He was born and brought up in Barren Co., Kentucky, where his mother now lives. She was marrried to a man by the name of Miller who has since deceased and left her again a widow. He has one sister married to a Mr. Quinn near Pikeville, Kentucky, and he has a brother near Bowling Green, Kentucky. He has served two years in the Kentucky Penitentiary, and has worked at hemp hackling and spinning. He was found guilty of horse stealing at the Circuit Court of Overton County and sentenced to four years confinement in the Jail and Penitentiary House of the state of Tennessee. *William Baldwin died of Cholera on the 10th day of June 1833.* [Ledger 45, p.3]

John Batchellor [also Batchelor] was received into the Penitentiary 27 November 1831. He is 40 years of age, 5' 11" high, weighs 140 lbs., has black hair, hazel eyes, dark skin. Born and brought up in Franklin Co., North Carolina, where some of his relations now live. Has lived 22 years in Tennessee in Bedford, Sumner and Maury Counties. Has a wife and nine children near Columbia, on his own farm, two miles distant. He is a farmer. He has a mark on his right shoulder scattering over several inches and has the appearance of strawberries, a scar on the left foot half way between the big toe and ankle bone. Also on the left hand their are several scars. Found guilty of perjury at the Circuit Court of Maury County and sentenced to six years confinement in the Jail and Penitentiary of the State of Tennessee. *John Batchelor was discharged the 29th day of November 1837.* [Ledger 45, p.3]

Charles T. Broughton was received into the Penitentiary 23 January 1832. He is 5' 7 ¹/₂" high. Common weight 170 lbs., blue eyes, fair skin, dark hair, round face, good countenance. Born and brought up in the state of New York, Delaware Co., where his father and mother now live. He has one brother living in Shenango Co., New York, two sisters single when he left home. His relations generally live in New York. His wife lives with her mother in Bedford Co., Tenn. She is a daughter of the widow Perry, living near Smith Mill on the north fork of Duck River, 12 miles from Shelbyville. He has a small scar on the right hand between the thumb and four finger , ³/₄" long. Also a scar on the left hand just where the fore finger and thumb joins the wrist joint. A scar on the inside of the ankle bone of each foot, that on the left foot running up and that on the right across the bone. Found guilty of petit larceny at the Circuit Court of Franklin County and sentenced to two years confinement in the Jail and Penitentiary House of the State of Tennessee. *Charles T. Broughton was discharged March 30 1834, he was detained 66 days for bad conduct.* [Ledger 45, pp. 3 and 4]

James Barker was received into the Penitentiary on the 18 March, 1832. He is 17 years old, 5' 5" high, weight 116 lbs., blue eyes, fair hair and skin. He has a large scar on the left knee, on the cap. A great number of scars on the right knee caused by biles. The big toe and the next toe to it, on both feet, have grown together about half way from the foot to their ends. His countence bad, he says his right name is Barker [Basker?]. He was born and brought up in Jackson Co., Tenn., where his father and mother now live, on the head of Indian Creek, four or five miles from Gen'l Simpsons Mill. All of his relations live in the same neighborhood, except one sister who is married to[Vernon?] Willis and lives in Smith Co., Tenn., 15 miles from Carthage on Peytons Creek. Found guilty of grand larceny at the Circuit Court of Roane County and sentenced to three years confinement in the Jail and Penitentiary House of the State of Tennessee. *James Barker was discharged by expiration of sentence on the 9th day of June 1835. Detained 83 days for bad conduct.* [Ledger 45, p.4]

Joel Blackwell was received into the Penitentiary on 6 June 1832. He is about 31 years old, 6' ¹/₂" in height, weight 160 lbs. Born in Abbeville District, South Carolina, and brought up in Monroe County, East Tenn., where his mother is now living. He has also a wife and two children in Monroe County. His wife's name, before marriage, was Loftes. He has one uncle living in Ray

[Rhea?] County near India Noochee old fields on the bank of big Tenn. River. He has dark hazel eyes, large nose and high cheek bones. He has a scar over the left eye 3/4" long, running into the eyebrow. He has also a scar on the left cheek. He has a small scar on the chin. The middle finger of the left hand is crooked from a bite. Found guilty of concealing stolen horses at the Circuit Court of Monroe County and sentenced to three years confinement in the Jail and Penitentiary House of the State of Tennessee. *John Blackwell was discharged by expiration of sentence on the 30th day of July 1835. Detained 55 days for bad conduct.* [Ledger 45, p.4]

Jacob Bradley was received into the Penitentiary on 8 June 1832. He is 5' 9 1/2" high, weight 158 lbs., 45 years of age. Black hair, dark skin and blind of the left eye, the other eye is black. Born and brought up in Halifax Co., Virginia. He has lived some time in the county of Wilson in Tenn., where he has two brothers and three sisters now living. Two of his sisters are married to John & Robert Ware, the other one to William Trout. He has a small scar on the left side of the under lip, also one on the chin, a scar across the right eye near the corner. Carpenter & wagon maker by trade, has served four years in the Kentucky Penitentiary. Found guilty of petit larceny at the Circuit Court of Davidson County and sentenced to two years and six months confinement in the Jail and Penitentiary House of the State of Tennessee. *Was discharged by expiration of sentence on the 12th of Jan.1835. He was detained 35 days for bad conduct.* [Ledger 45, p.5]

Cornelious Butram was received into the Penitentiary 3 October 1832. He is 5' 5" in height and weighs 134 lbs. He is 24 years of age, has dark eyes and hair, roman nose, tolerable heavy beard. Born in the state of Virginia and brought up in Wayne Co., Kentucky, where his father and mother now reside about 16 miles from Monticello on the little south fork of Cumberland River. He has a wife and one child living in Rhea Co., Tenn., with John Lock Miller [Lockmiller?] on the waters of [Little Looey?] near Medlock's Mill. He has a small scar where the little finger joins the left hand and one on the ball of the fore finger and several on the back of the same. One scar on the instep and another on the great toe of the left foot caused by a cut from an axe. He was found guilty of horse stealing in the Circuit Court of Rhea County and sentenced to three years confinement in the Jail and Penitentiary House of the State of Tennessee. *Cornelius Butram was discharged on the 17th of Nov. 1835. Detained 45 days for bad conduct.* [Ledger 45, p.5]

Robert C. Brogan was received into the Penitentiary on the 7th of March 1833. He is 6' 1". in height and weighs 160 lbs. Dark hair, blue eyes, dark complexion, 27 years of age. Born in Kentucky, brought up in Anderson Co.,

Tenn., where his father now resides on Clinch River. His wife and three children, likewise, live in the same County in the Big valley about 10 miles from Clinton. Her maiden name was Whitton. Her mother is now married to a man named Wm. Bremmit and resides in Campbell Co., Tenn. He has a brother living in Anderson and one in Claiborne Co., Tenn. The small finger of the right hand is crooked, a scar running across from the little toe of the right foot towards the instep and a small one where the hand joins the wrist. He has served an apprenticeship to the hatting business in Blount Co., Alabama. Was found guilty of forgery at the Circuit Court of Knox County and sentenced to three years confinement in the Jail and Penitentiary House of the State of Tennessee. *Robt. C. Brogan was discharged the 16th of May, 1836, having been detained 70 days for bad conduct. Returned Jan. 18, 1837, for horse stealing. Sentence 6 years. From Maury County. Died July 2, 1837.* [Ledger 45, pp. 5-6]

John Brandon was received in the Penitentiary 10 Sept. 1833. He is 5' 10" in height and weighs 132 lbs. Light hair, blue eyes, fair complexion, and 17 years of age. Born in Giles Co., Tenn., and brought up there. His Mother, one sister and one brother still reside there, on the line between the counties of Giles and Lawrence, about 11 miles from Lawrenceburgh. He has one brother married and living in Indiana, two uncles living in Giles Co. about 6 miles distant from each other, near the waters of Richland Creek. Their names are Stephen Gardner and Jonathan Ford. He has a scar on the end of the little finger of the left hand, near the nail and a large scar on the back part of the right thigh. Likewise a large mole in the center of his breast. Has followed farming. Was found guilty of house breaking, at the Circuit Court of Lawrence County and sentenced to three years confinement in the Jail and Penitentiary of the State of Tenn. *John Brandon died of cholera on the 1st of July 1835.* [Ledger 45, p. 6]

John J. Brazeal was received in the Penitentiary 22 Oct. 1833. He is 5' 8 3/4" in height and weighs 169 lbs. Dark hair and eyes and tolerably fair complexion, 41years of age. Born in Knox Co., Tenn. Has no knowledge whether his parents or connections are living, not having seen them for 12 years. He has a wife and 5 children living about 10 miles east of Lexington in Henderson Co. His wife's maiden name was Essray. He has a scar caused by a stab in the right nipple and one on the bottom of the calf of the right leg, where the leg appears to be somewhat shrunk. He has a scar from an axe on the same leg and one on the instep of the right foot, and a scar running between the toes, in the center of them, on the same foot. Likewise, a scar on the finger of the left hand next the little one. He has generally followed farming. Was found guilty of assault and battery with intent to kill and sentenced at the Circuit Court of Henderson County to 21 years confinement in the Jail and Penitentiary

Tennessee Convicts: Records of the State Penitentiary

House of the State of Tennessee. *Pardoned by Gov. Cannon Nov.19, 1838, and discharged.* [Ledger 45, pp. 6&7]

William Brown was received in the Penitentiary 12 Dec. 1833. He is 5' 8 ½" in height. Weighs 147 lbs., brown hair, blue eyes, fair complexion and 27 years of age. Born in Grainger Co., Tenn., and brought up there. His parents reside in Roane Co., Tenn., about ¼ mile from Patty's mill on the waters of Paint rock. He has three brothers and one sister, all married except one brother, residing in the same neighborhood with his parents. His sister married Joseph Dennis and one of his brothers Miss Dennis. The other brother married Miss Taylor. Brown has three uncles living in Grainger Co.: William, Isaac, and Thomas Dyer. He has a remarkable scar on his head on the right side, caused by a rising when a child. A scar over the right eye touching the eyebrow, a scar in the center of his forehead. A scar near the left corner of the mouth on the under lip caused by a fall. A scar on each of the two middle fingers of the left hand, between the first and second joints from cuts with a reap hook. A scar between the two joints of the thumb of the left hand and a scar on the left knee from a bile. Has generally followed farming. Was found guilty of forgery at the Circuit Court of Monroe County and sentenced to three years confinement in the Jail and Penitentiary House of the State of Tennessee. *William Brown (Hatter) discharged 20th of Dec. 1835. Detained 8 days, conduct good.* [Ledger 45, p. 7]

John Brown was received in the Penitentiary 20 Dec. 1833. He is 5' 10 ¼" in height. and weighs 150 lbs. Dark hair, blue eyes, fair complexion, heavy beard, well made, about 28 years of age. Born in Randolph Co., North Carolina, and brought up in Jackson, Jefferson Co., Georgia. His father is dead, his mother resides in Carroll Co., Georgia. He has one brother (living), Wm. Brown in Watson Co., Georgia, and two uncles, Benjamin and Britt Fuller, residing in Randolph Co., North Carolina. He married Miss Malinda Kearney, who now resides with her father, William Kearney, about 12 miles from Nashville on Little Marrowbone, about 1 ½ miles from the road leading from Nashville to Clarksville and four miles from the Cumberland River. He is remarkably clear of scars, having only one, on the thick part of the inside of the left arm, occasioned by a burn. He is a blacksmith by trade, served his apprenticeship with William Greeter, partly in Raleigh, North Carolina, partly in Augusta, Georgia. Was found guilty of horse stealing at the Circuit Court of Davidson Co. and sentenced to three years confinement in the Jail and Penitentiary House of the State of Tenn. *John Brown's clothes were , by his request, given to [D?] Wiseman on his discharge, the 20th of March, 1835. John Brown was discharged 25th. Dec., 1835. Conduct generally good, detained 5 days.* [Ledger 45, pp. 7-8]

Francis Booby was received in the Penitentiary May 24, 1834. He was born on the Island of St. Dominga and brought up there. He is of French extraction, of a bright mulatto colour, with bushy hair, about 53 years of age. He has lost one leg considerably above the ankle and the other from just below the knee, the thumb and fore finger of the right hand and the little finger, with the adjoining one of the left hand, all of which had been amputated from a frost bite, whilst in Jail. He has lived for a short period on the Island of Jamaica, New Orleans, Pensacola and Alabama, where he has a wife residing, and the western district of Tenn. Was found guilty of receiving stolen goods at the Hardeman Circuit Court, which judgement was confirmed by the Supreme Court at Jackson in Madison County and sentenced to three years confinement in the Jail and Penitentiary House of the State of Tennessee. *Died of consumpton on the 9th day of May, 1835.* [Ledger 45, p.8]

Joseph Blackwell was received June 26, 1834. 5' 11 ½" in height and weighs 150 lbs. 36 years of age, a man of colour of rather a yellowish cast. Born in Nash Co. and brought up in Johnson Co., North Carolina. He has resided in Shelby Co., Tenn., principally, for the last six years and cohabitated with a free woman of colour, named Grace Kincaid, in the town of Memphis. He has a scar on the wrist of his right hand from holding the hock. He has a scar on the right arm, on the thick part above the wrist, from the bite of a dog. Two scars on the left arm, about 3" from the elbow, rather under the arm. A scar on the left foot, running from the joint of the great toe and a scar running along the toe where it had been split open by a cut from an axe. He is a plaisterer by trade. Was found guilty, on two indictments, of petit and grand larceny and sentenced to four years confinement in the Jail and Penitentiary House of the State of Tennessee, at the Circuit Court of Shelby County. *Was discharged July 28, 1838, having served his sentence of 4 years 1 month and 2 days for improper conduct.* [Ledger 45, pp. 8-9]

Basil Bunch was received in the Penitentiary 26 June,1834. He is 5' 8 ¾" in height and weighs 181 lbs., blue eyes, light hair, fair complexion, 23 years of age. Born in Lexington, Kentucky, and brought up in Pope Co., Illinois. He has one brother and four half brothers, his mother's name is Perowe[?]. He has a scar on the top of the right foot, a scar on the right cheek bone, a scar on the back of the left hand, and a remarkable one on the small bone of the wrist of the left arm. He has generally followed boating. Was found guilty of having and passing counterfeit money at the Circuit Court of Shelby County and sentenced to three years confinement in the Jail and Penitentiary House of the State of Tennessee. *Was discharged July 1, 1837. Detained 5 days for violation of prison rules.* [Ledger 45, p. 9]

James Brown was received in the Penitentiary Dec.11, 1834. He is 22 years of age, 5' 7" high and weighs 167 lbs. Blue eyes, light hair, fair complexion, broad face and stout built, no remarkable scars. Served an apprenticeship at the shoemaking business in Bedford Co., under a negro belonging to Henry Davis of said county. Born in Knox, and brought up, principally, in Giles Co., Tenn. Father dead. Mother, Betty Brown, and five children living on Molly's Creek, Bedford Co., Tenn. He intermarried with Zelpha Green, daughter of Bethel Green, who resides on Molly's Creek, Bedford Co., with her father. He was found guilty of petit larceny at the Circuit Court of Bedford Co. and sentenced to one year and six months confinement in the Jail and Penitentiary House of the State of Tennessee. *Was discharged June 11, 1836. Conduct good.* [Ledger 45, p.9]

Nicholas Browder was received in the Penitentiary 24 Sept. 1834. He is 21 or 22 years of age, 5' 7." or 8" high and weighs 140 lbs. He was born and raised in Brunswick Co., Virginia. His Father and Mother now reside in the same county four and 1/2 miles from Richard Edmund's Mill on Great Creek, two miles from Piney Grove Meeting House, and four miles from Red Oak Church. Black eyes, dark complexion, light hair and sharp nose. A large scar on the left side of his head, one on his left elbow, and one on the left side. All of which were occasioned by a burn when a child. He has chiefly followed waggoning, was found guilty of petit larceny at the Circuit Court of Washington County and sentenced to two years confinement in the Jail and Penitentiary House of the State of Tennessee. *Nicholas Browder died of cholera on the 11th day of July, 1835.* [Ledger 45, p.10]

John Bond was received in the Penitentiary 14 Oct. 1834. He is 24 years of age, 5' 10" or 11" in height and weighs 180 lbs. Dark hair, fair complexion, hazel eyes, long projecting chin, short nose, low forehead, broad face and very stout built. His father and mother reside in Callaway Co., Kentucky. He was born and raised in Caldwell Co., Kentucky. Was married to a Miss Bone in McCracken Co., Kentucky, whose parents live in Perry Co., Tenn., near Tennessee River, not far from Stringers Mill on Roanes Creek. He has a remarkable scar on the small finger of the right hand (running from the center of the nail to the second joint) occasioned by a cut from a reap hook. He has chiefly followed farming. Was found guilty of petit larceny at the Circuit Court of Perry County and sentenced to one year's confinement in the Jail and Penitentiary House of the State of Tennessee. *John Bond died of cholera 2 July 1835.* [Ledger 45, p.10]

Tennessee Convicts: Records of the State Penitentiary

Thomas Butcher, a coloured man, was received in the Penitentiary 25 March 1835. He is 38 years of age, 5' 5" or 6" high, and weighs 156 lbs. Prominent cheek bones, thick neck, black eyes. Hair a little gray on the top of his head. A knot about the size of a pa[r]tridge egg near the root of the thumb of the right hand. A scar on the middle joint of the fore finger and one near the end of the middle finger of the left hand; a scar on the instep of the left foot. By occupation a plaisterer. Born and brought up in Dinwiddie Co., Virginia, but lately moved to Washington Co., Tenn., where he kept as a wife a negro woman belonging to Joseph Young, who lives about five miles from Jonesborough. He was found guilty of Petit Larceny at the Circuit Court of Washington County and sentenced to one year's confinement in the Jail and Penitentiary House of the State of Tennessee. *Thomas Butcher died of cholera 3 July 1835.* [Ledger 45, p. 10-11]

Micajah Brummet was received in the Penitentiary 6 April 1835. He is 31 years of age, 6' high, and weighs 165 lbs. Blue eyes, auburn hair, fair complexion, bald head and long face. Two scars on the back of the left hand, one on the first joint of the little finger of the same hand, and one about 3" in length on the inside of, and running parallel with, the left shin bone. Labourer. Born and brought up in Washington Co., Tenn. A wife and four children living in said county, on Cherokee Creek, about four miles from Jonesboro, who will probably move, agreeable to his request, to Sullivan Co., Tenn., to live with an uncle of his named John Bowman, who lives in that county near Rockholt's Post Office. His wife's maiden name was Norris, daughter of Thomas Norris, who deceased in Washington Co. on the waters of Chucky River, about 15 miles from Jonesboro. The greater portion of her relations have emigrated to Illinois. He was found guilty of horse stealing at the Circuit Court of Carter Co. and sentenced to four years confinement in the Jail and Penitentiary House of the State of Tennessee. *Discharged May 11, 1839.* [Ledger 45, p.11]

Thomas Biggs was received in the Penitentiary on 21April 1835. He is 17 years of age, 6' 2" or 3" and weighs 140 lbs. Black eyes, dark hair, dark complexion. A scar between the second and third joints of the left thumb, one on the third joint of the fore finger of the left hand, and a few small scars on the back of the same hand. A scar on the back of the right hand caused by a burn and a very large one on the outside of the left leg just above the ankle. Labourer. Born and brought up in Hawkins Co., Tenn. Father (Thos. Biggs) dead. Mother (Polly Biggs) a widow resides near Rogersville, Hawkins Co., Tenn. One brother (Jno. Biggs), carpenter, married and living in Rogersville. Four sisters, married, one living in Gra[i]nger Co. and three living in Hawkins Co., near Rogersville. He was found guilty of voluntary manslaughter at the

Tennessee Convicts: Records of the State Penitentiary

Circuit Court of Hawkins County and sentenced to one year's confinement in the Jail and Penitentiary House of the State of Tennessee. *Thomas Biggs died of cholera June 30,1835.* [Ledger 45, p.11]

David Brunson was received in the penitentiary on 4 June 1835. He is 37 years of age, 5' 9" or 10" high, and weighs 175 lbs. Black hair, mixed with grey, brown or yellow eyes and straight dial nose. Several large scars on the shin-bones of each of his legs, one on the middle joint of the fore finger and one near the end of the middle finger, of the left hand. Labourer. Born in Edgefield District, South Carolina, and brought up in Stuart Co., Tenn., on the waters of Cumberland River, Deer Creek, in the neighbourhood of Jno. Lee, Justice of the Peace. His late residence was in Henry Co., Tenn., but his wife and four children live in Callaway Co., Kentucky, with her brother (Jas. Rotteree) who now resides in the Wells neighbourhood, where she expects to remain until the return of her husband. Her and his relations (principally) reside in Henry Co., Tenn. He was found guilty of petit larceny at the Circuit Court of Henry County and sentenced to two years' confinement in the Jail and Penitentiary House of the State of Tennessee. *David Brunson was discharged June 14,1837, conduct generally good, detained 10 days.* [Ledger 45, p.12]

Samuel J. Brockwell was received in the Penitentiary 23 Aug. 1835. He is 37 years of age, 5' 7" or 8" high and weighs 180 lbs. Stout built. Blue eyes, auburn hair, heavy beard, and fair complexion. His left leg has been amputated a few inches above the ankle, and he now has a wooden leg, which is fastened on at the knee. Labourer. Born in Orange Co., North Carolina, and brought up in Giles Co., Tenn. He has a wife and six children, who are residing in Alabama, about twenty miles from Pulaski, Giles Co., Tenn. He married a woman named Stokes, who had, when he married her, four children, three of whom are now living with their mother, which makes the number of children in family nine. He was found guilty of forgery at the Circuit Court of Giles Co. and sentenced to three years' confinement in the Jail and Penitentiary House of the State of Tennessee. *Samuel J. Brockwell died of a rupture of a blood vessel 13 Dec. 1835. His conduct was very good.* [Ledger 45, p.12]

George W. Cook was received in the penitentiary 21 Jan. 1831. He is 6' high, light hair, blue eyes, fair skin and by profession a taylor. Was born in the state of Kentucky and brought up in and near Nashville, Tenn., where most of his relatives now live. Has a scar on his left thumb about 1" long, Is about 21 years of age. Was found guilty of stabbing at the Circuit Court of Madison Co. and sentenced to two years' confineme nt in the Jail and Penitentiary House of the State of Tennessee. *George Washington Cook was discharged by* expiration of sentence 21 Jan. 1833. Conduct very good. First man ever brought to the Penitentiary. [Ledger 45, p.13]

William H. Crawford was received in the Penitentiary April 6, 1831. He is 5' 8 3/4" high, about 21 years of age, dark hair and blue eyes. Blind of the right eye, with a scar over the left. Also a scar on the middle finger of the left hand, also one on the fore finger of the same hand. Common weight about 130 lbs. Born in Natchez and brought up in Pennsylvania. His father lives in Rogersville, East Tenn., and he has two uncles by the name of Crawford living near Pittsburgh. A brick layer by profession. Was found guilty of feloniously stealing bank bills at the Circuit Court of Rhea Co., and sentenced to three years confinement in the Jail and Penitentiary House of the State of Tennessee from 31 Mar. 1831. *William H. Crawford was discharged July 4,1834. He was detained 89 days for bad conduct.* [Ledger 45, p.13]

James Counce was received in the Penitentiary 11 May 1831. He is 5' 7 1/2" high, weighs about 170 lbs. Stout and well formed, complexion and hair dark, pleasant countenance, hazel eyes. Born and brought up in Shanandoah Co., Virginia, where he has two brothers residing and a married sister. He has an uncle living in Gra[i]nger Co., East Tenn. A scar on the left knee, forming a cross. The toe next to the large one on the left foot off at the first joint. A scar on the instep of the right foot, also one on the little finger of the right hand. Large nose and yellow eyes. By profession a hatter. Was found guilty of feloniously stealing tea spoons to the value of one dollar, before the Circuit Court of Maury Co., and sentenced to two years confinement in the Jail and Penitentiary House of the State of Tennessee. *James Counce was discharged by expiration of sentence on 11 May 1833. His conduct was generally good.* [Ledger 45, p.13]

Wilson Coats was received into the Penitentiary 23 Feb 1833. He is 6' 5" in height and weighs 175 lbs. Light hair, blue eyes, and fair complexion, 37years of age. Born in Robinson [*sic*,, Robertson] Co., Tenn., and brought up in the same. His father, a Baptist preacher, resides near the Chalk level in Humphries Co., Tenn. One sister married to a man named Rheuminger living in the same neighborhood. One brother living on Cahawba river, Alabama. Coats married Elizabeth Hokimer, who is now living with her father at the mouth of Sugar Creek, Garret[t] Co., Kentucky. His left hand has been broken and the fore finger at the point has been injured by a burn. His left eye has been gouged out. He has a scar on the right and left foot on the outside of each caused by cuts from an axe. A scar running up and down the shin about 4" long, from the cut of a tomahawk at the Battle of the Horse Shoe. A scar very near this, on the inside of the leg. A mark from a spent ball on the inside of the arm, a little above the bend of the elbow. A dent on the left side of the crown of the head caused by the falling of the limb of a tree. He has worked at blacksmithing, shoemaking, and flax and cotton wheel making. He was found guilty of murder at the Circuit Court of Woodford Co. [Kentucky?], which sentence was confirmed by the Supreme Court at Jackson, Madison Co., and sentenced to be hanged, which sentence was commuted by the Governor into 21 years confinement in the Jail and Penitentiary House of the State of Tennessee. *Wilson Coats died of chronic diarrhoea 17 July 1833.* [Ledger 45, p.13-14]

Isham Conner was received in the Penitentiary 23 Feb. 1833. He is 5' 11 ¼" in height and weighs 196 lbs. Fair hair, greyish blue eyes, fair complexion, 41 years of age. Born in Chester Co., South Carolina, and brought up partly there and partly in Jackson Co., Tenn. His parents are dead. He has two brothers, Jacob and Isaac Conner. One residing in Hamilton and one in Franklin Co., Illinois. He has a wife and eight children. His wife resides in Weakl[e]y Co., Tenn. One daughter married named Ross living in Weakl[e]y Co., Tenn. He has a large dent on the top of his forehead caused by a blow from a stone. The middle joint of the little finger of the right hand is stiff. A scar on the inside of the right thigh caused by an axe. Generally followed farming. Was found guilty of stabbing at the Circuit Court of Gibson Co., which was confirmed by the Supreme Court at Jackson, Madison Co., and sentenced to two years confinement in the Jail and Penitentiary House of the State of Tennessee. *Isham Conner was discharged by expiration of sentence 27 Mar. 1835. Detained 35 days for bad conduct.* [Ledger 45, p.14]

Abraham Conly and Sylas Conly were received in the Penitentiary Aug. 29 ,1831. Abraham is 5' 6" high, 21 years of age, common weight 130 lbs., dark hair and skin, gray eyes. Born in Hawkins Co., Tenn., brought up in Knox Co., where he has a wife, now living with her father, John Haskins, three miles from Campbells Station. A small scar on the thumb and one over the left eye. Silas is 25 years of age, 5' 5" high, common weight 130 lbs., dark hair, fair skin, and blue eyes. Has worked at the gun smith business. Born in North Carolina and brought up in Hawkins Co., Tenn. His wife is at her father's, Harris Ryon [Ryan?], in Campbell Co., 10 miles from Jacksboro. A large scar on his right side occasioned by a blister plaster. Abraham and Silas were both found guilty of stealing bacon at the Circuit Court of Knox County and sentenced to one years imprisonment in the Jail and Penitentiary House of the State of Tennessee. *Discharged by expiration of sentence, Abraham Conly, Aug.29, 1832. Abraham Conly's conduct was good. Silas Conly was discharged by expiration of sentence Sept.23, 1832, he was detained for bad conduct 25 days. Silas Conly's conduct was exceptionable.* [Ledger 45, p.15]

Tennessee Convicts: Records of the State Penitentiary

David Cole was received into the Penitentiary Oct. 3, 1831. He is 5' 7 ½" high, 38 years old, and weighs 145 lbs. He has fair skin, dark hair and blue eyes. He has a scar on the left side of the face, cut with a knife, commencing just above the ear and running entirely across the face, stopping about the center of the under lip. Also one on the right side of the face just at the lock of the jawbone caused by cutting out a wen [?]. A cut over the left eye near the edge of the hair, besides others not neccesary to name. Cole is not a mechanic of any kind. He was born in Sullivan Co., East Tenn., raised in Wilson Co., West Tenn., where he has a wife an[d] five children now living, seven miles from Lebanon and three miles from Cumberland River and near Davis' Mill. His mother lives near the road leading from Nashville to Lebanon, six miles from the latter place. A brother in the same neighborhood and a sister, married to a man of Word [perhaps "by the name of Word"?] 15 miles the other side of Lebanon, near Clopton's Mill. Two brothers in the Western District of Tenn., near Brownsville. His wife's relations in the same neighborhood with his wife. Sentenced to five years imprisonment in the Jail and Penitentiary House, from Lincoln [Co.] Circuit Court. *David Cole died of cholera July 6,1835.* [Ledger 45, p.15]

Edwin Clark was received in the Penitentiary Oct.16, 1831. He is 5' 7 ½" high, 37 years old, common weight 141 lbs., fair skin, blue eyes, his hair a little inclined to be sandy. He has lost two of his lower front teeth, a small scar above the left eye and one on the back of the right hand near the wrist, caused by a burn. Also one on the inside of the left wrist, caused by a burn. He was born and raised in the state of New Jersey. By profession a hatter. He has two sisters in the City of New York. One uncle living near Princeton, New Jersey. Found guilty of petit larceny at the Circuit Court of Robertson County and sentenced to two years imprisonment in the Jail and Penitentiary House of the State of Tennessee. *Edwin Clark was discharged Jan.5, 1834. He was detained 81 days for bad conduct.* [Ledger 45, p.15-16, see also John Moore on Ledger 45, p. 115]

Elisha Cole was received in the Penitentiary Oct.31, 1831. He is 6' high, 42 years old and commonly weighs 140 lbs. He has fair skin, blue eyes, a little inclined to be bald headed. A scar on the first joint of the small finger of the left hand, large nose, round face, good countenance. He was born and raised in the State of Tenn., has a wife and three children living in Wilson Co. near to his mother,in the same county. One brother in the Penitentiary before him. His wife's maiden name was Anderson. Her father lives in Wilson Co. also, seven miles from his wife. He lived within two miles of Big Cedar Creek Meeting House. Found guilty of stealing promissory notes at the Circuit Court of Wilson Co.and sentenced to three years imprisonment in the Jail and

Penitentiary House of the State of Tennessee. *Elisha Cole was discharged by expiration of sentence Nov.1, 1834. His conduct was exceptionable.* [Ledger 45, p.16]

Riley Chappell was received in the Penitentiary Nov. 27, 1831. He is 34 years old, 5' 8 1/4" high, weighs 140 lbs., rather dark complexion, light hair, grey eyes. Small scar above the left eye, scar on the outside of the calf of the left leg, caused by a bile. Hollow eyes and prominent nose. He was born in Wake Co., North Carolina, lived in Georgia two years, in Green and Monroe counties. He has two sisters living in Hickman Co., Tenn. He has a wife and two children living in Hickman Co., Tenn., with her father, James Lawson. Found guilty of stabbing at the Circuit Court of Maury Co. and sentenced to two years confinement in the Jail and Penitentiary House of the State of Tennessee. *Riley Chappell was discharged by expiration of sentence Nov. 27, 1833. His conduct was good.* [Ledger 45, p.16]

David Claxton was received in the Penitentiary Dec. 12, 1831. He is 30 years old, 6' 1" high, weighs 179 lbs. Dark hair, blue eyes, fair skin. A small scar on the right point of the fore head, a remarkable scar on the right hand, caused by the cut of a knife. His right leg has been broken and is generally sore. Born in Wilson Co., Tenn., and raised in Smith [and] Bedford Counties, Tenn. He has a wife and two children in Bedford Co., Tenn., seven miles this side of Shelbyville, also six brothers and one sister in said county. Lived three years in Gallatin Co., Illinois, 18 miles below Shawneetown. His father and mother living in Bedford Co., Tenn. Found guilty of passing counterfeit money or bank bills at the Circuit Court of Bedford County and sentenced to three years confinement in the Jail and Penitentiary House of the State of Tennessee. *David Claxton was discharged by expiration of sentence Jan.15, 1835. Detained 35 days for bad conduct.* [Ledger 45, p.16]

John B. Coleman was received into the Penitentiary Mar. 15, 1832, and liberated by the pardon of the Governor on the 16th of March 1832. He was sentenced by the Circuit Court of Warren County for horse stealing to three years confinement in the Jail and Penitentiary House of the State of Tennessee. [Ledger 45, p.17]

Willis Clement was received into the Penitentiary Aug. 24, 1832. He is 6' 3 1/4" in height, weighs 164 lbs., 30 years of age, black hair, blue eyes, fair skin, heavy beard and tolerable good countenance. Born in the state of Georgia and brought up chiefly in Spencer Co. in Kentucky, but has lived in several counties in that state. His father, mother and three brothers and two sisters now reside within two miles of Cornersville in Giles Co., Tenn. And an uncle named

Clements living in Hart Co., Kentucky. Has a scar on the knee cap and one on the shin of the left leg. One on the right leg, about 4" above the ankle joint, occasioned by a bite from a dog. He has generally followed farming. Was found guilty of passing counterfeit bank bills at the Circuit Court of Giles County and sentenced to three years confinement in the Jail and Penitentiary House of the State of Tennessee. *Willis Clement died of Chronic Diarrhoea 26 Oct. 1833.* [Ledger 45, p.17]

Gibson Cate was received in the Penitentiary Nov. 11, 1832. He is 5' 11 1/2" in height, weighs 165 lbs., 32 years of age, dark hair and eyes, sallow complexion. Born and brought up in Jefferson Co., Tenn. His father and mother reside in McMinn Co., about three miles from Athens, near Metcalf's Carding and Spinning Factory. Likewise, one sister living at this place married to a man by the name of Witt. One brother, married and living in Jefferson Co. He has a wife and six children living on Mouse Creek, about six miles from Athens and within two miles of Wm. Cates's Mill and Mr. Baxter's Plantation. His wife's name was Benton, all of whose family reside on Mouse Creek. He has a scar below the right nostril, one on the first joint of the third finger of the left hand occasioned by a cut from a reap hook. One on the instep of the right foot about 1 1/4" long, and one on the center of the shin 1 1/2" long. He has generally followed farming. Was found guilty of assault with intent to kill, at the Circuit Court of McMinn County and sentenced to nine years confinement in the Jail and Penitentiary of the State of Tenn. *Gibson Cate died of cholera on the 17th day of June 1833.* [Ledger 45, p. 17]

James Campbell was received in the Penitentiary Dec. 5, 1832. He is 6' in height, weighs 170 lbs., 22 years of age, blue eyes, brown hair, fair skin somewhat pockmarked, sandy beard, slender built to his height. Born in Lancaster Co., Pennsylvania, where his father, mother, two brothers, two sisters and the remainder of his connections now reside. He has several scars on the shin of the left leg. Has generally followed farming. Was found guilty of petit larceny at the Circuit Court of Davidson County and sentenced to one year and six months confinement in the Jail and Penitentiary House of the State of Tennessee. *James Campbell was discharged on the 28th day of Aug. 1834. He was detained 85 days for bad conduct.* [Ledger 45, p.18]

William Cassels was received into the Penitentiary Feb. 23, 1833. He is 6' in height and weighs 175 lbs., light hair, blue eyes, fair complexion, round face and well formed. Born in Robinson [*sic*,, Robertson] Co., Tenn. His father, mother, four brothers and two sisters all reside in Madison Co., Tenn. He has one sister, married to a Mr. Chambers, living within six miles of Lancasters Mills, on the Forked Deer River. He has an half uncle, named Turner, near this place, in Wilborn's neighborhood. He has a scar on the inside of the fore finger of the left hand, occasioned by a cut, also two moles on his neck, the one on the left side nearest the jaw. He was found guilty of horse stealing at the Circuit Court of Madison County and sentenced to three years confinement in the Jail and Penitentiary House of the State of Tennessee. (From the 16th day of Feb. 1833.) *William Cassels was discharged Feb. 16, 1836, agreeably to sentence. His conduct was good.* [Ledger 45, p.18]

John N. Chapman was received in the Penitentiary May 5, 1833. He is 5' 9" in height, weighs 172 lbs., hair dark, blue eyes, fair complexion. Born in Pickens Co., South Carolina, and brought up in Smith Co., Tenn. Married Sarah Lemans, who is now residing with her father on Big Sowee [Sewee?] Creek, 16 miles from Athens, in McMinn Co., Tenn. He has a large scar on the instep of the left foot and one on the inside of the ankle of the right foot, both caused by cuts from an axe. One on his left wrist and several on his left thumb, one on the back of his head caused by a cut from a hoe and one near the left temple. Has generally followed farming. Was found guilty of petit larceny at the Circuit Court of McMinn County and sentenced to one year's confinement in the Jail and Penitentiary House of the State of Tennessee. (21 years of age.) *John N. Chapman was discharged May 15, 1834. He was detained 10 days for bad conduct.* [Ledger 45, p.18-19]

George Corbin was received in the Penitentiary Nov. 10, 1833. He is 5' 8" in height and weighs 143 lbs., grey eyes, hair rather light, fair skin, long nose, and tolerable good countenance, 37 years of age. Born in Culpepper Co.,Virginia, and brought up there. He thinks his parents are dead. He had three brothers and five sisters, they were all living at the Kenahaw[?] Salt Works, except one brother who resides in Ohio. He has not seen any of them for 17 years. He has a wife and six children, living about five miles from Mt. Pleasant in Maury Co., Tenn., where he has resided for the past 10 years, but expects his wife to move to her fathers [blank space left for father's name] residing in Bedford Co. He has a scar on the fore and middle fingers of the left hand, near the middle joint, and the top of the fore finger has been taken off by a bone felon. He has a remarkable dent at the point of the fore finger and the little finger is crooked at the first joint, on the right hand. Two scars on the outside of the left leg, one above and the other below the calf, occasioned by biles, and a scar on the back part of the neck. He is a blacksmith by trade. Was found guilty of stabbing at the Circuit Court of Maury County and sentenced to two years confinement in the Jail and Penitentiary House of the State of Tennessee. *George Corbin was discharged by expiration of sentence the 10th day of Nov. 1835. Conduct good. Good blacksmith.* [Ledger 45, p.19]

Tennessee Convicts: Records of the State Penitentiary

Francis McCarpin was received in the Penitentiary Nov. 10, 1833. He is 5' 6" in height and weighs 134 lbs., hazel eyes, dark hair, fair skin, round face, 19 years of age. Born in Logan Co., Kentucky, and raised in Maury Co., Tenn. His mother is dead, his father resides in Alabama. He has one sister and four brothers, they all reside near Franklin, Williamson Co., Tenn., except one brother, younger than himself, who lives in Logan Co., Kentucky. His three brothers who reside in Williamson are bricklayers by trade. One of them married a daughter of William Blackburn, who resides nine miles from Franklin. He has a very remarkable scar covering the knee and part of the thigh of the left leg. He has two moles on the breast and several round the neck. Was found guilty of grand larceny at the Circuit Court of Maury County and sentenced to three years confinement in the Jail and Penitentiary House of the State of Tennessee. *Francis McCarpin died of cholera on the 30th day of June 1835.* [Ledger 45, p.19-20]

Samuel Cooxey was received into the penitentiary Dec. 10, 1833. He is 5' 5" in height and weighs 119 lbs. Blue eyes, red hair, fair freckled complexion, rather inclined to be cross eyed, about 18 years of age. Born in Virginia and brought up in Henry Co., Tenn. His father resides somewhere in Illinois, having abandoned his family about five years ago. He is a millwright by trade. Cooxey's mother resides about three miles from Paris, Henry Co., Tenn. He has three brothers and three sisters. One of his brothers is married to a Miss Fiddler. He has been frequently bound out, but always absconded from his employer. Once to Capt. Roberts Tanner[?] and once to Alexr. McCorkle, blacksmiths. Those gentlemen reside in the neighborhood of Paris. He has a scar under the chin about ¾" long, a scar on the joint of the thumb of the left hand where it joins the hand. A very long scar on the outside of the calf (on the top) of the left leg caused by a horse running him against the corner of a fence. He has several specks on the inside of the left arm, marked by powder. He was found guilty of petit larceny at the Circuit Court of Henry County and sentenced to one year and six months confinement in the Jail and Penitentiary House of the State of Tennessee. *Samuel Cooxey was discharged 30th April 1836 having been detained 325 days for bad conduct.* [Ledger 45, p. 20]

Henry Cook was received in the Penitentiary on the 14th of January 1834. He is 5' 8 ¼" in height and weighs 171 lbs. Dark hair, blue eyes, fair complexion, 25 years of age. Born in Buncom [Buncombe] Co., North Carolina, and brought up there. His mother, one brother, and three sisters still reside there, on Reim's[?] Creek about one-half mile from Weaver's mill. One of his sisters married a Mr. Davis and one a Mr. Wagoner. He has a scar on the heel of the hand caused by a bone felon. He has a remarkable scar on the cap of the left knee and a blemish in the left eye. Has generally followed farming. Was found guilty of passing counterfeit bank bills and sentenced to three years confinement in the Jail and Penitentiary House of the State of Tennessee at the Circuit Court of Tipton County. [Ledger 45, p. 20]

Joseph Collins was received in the Penitentiary 23 January 1834. He is 5' 8 1/4" in height and weighs 161 lbs. Blue eyes, sandy complexion, dark hair and 28 years of age. Born in Richland district, South Carolina and brought up in Blount Co., Tenn., on Baker's Creek near Wallis's mill about 11 miles from Maryville where his father and family now resides. He has a wife now living with her father, Richard Jones, in the above neighborhood. He has a scar above the left eye, the little finger of the left hand is crooked, and a small scar on the joint occasioned by a cut from a sickle. He has a thick short neck and round face, a small scar over the right eye. He has generally followed farming. Was found guilty of horse stealing at the Circuit Court of Franklin County and sentenced to 6 years confinement in the Jail & Penitentiary House of the State of Tenn. *Joseph Collins died of Fever 15th Sept. 1835.* [Ledger 45, page 21]

Young Chumley was received in the Penitentiary 18 February 1834. He is 5' 9 1/2" in height and weighs 162 lbs. Hair rather dark, grey eyes, fair complexion, 27 years of age. Born in Tenn., Davidson County, on White's Creek and brought up in Maury County, Tenn., where his father, mother, two sisters and two brothers now reside on Duck River about three miles from Columbia. He has one sister married to Thomas Richards, overseer for John Pointer, living on the road leading from Nashville to Columbia about two miles from the latter place. Chumley has a wife and one child, they are now residing with his father. Her maiden name was Aikens. She has some cousins of that name in Nashville. He has a small scar on the temple (left), a scar below the cap of the knee running across, a scar on the inside of the shin of the right leg, a scar on the upper part of the calf of the left leg caused by a cut from the end of a rail. His right arm has been broken near the wrist. A scar running round the middle finger of the left hand caused by a cut. He has generally followed farming. Was found guilty of larceny at the Circuit Court of Giles County and sentenced to three years confinement in the Jail and Penitentiary House of the State of Tennessee. *Young Chumley was discharged 20th March 1837. Detained 30 days for breach of rules.* [Ledger 45, page 21]

Samuel Chamberlain was received in the Penitentiary June 17th, 1834. He is 5' 7 1/2" in height, and weighs 155 lbs. Dark hair, grey eyes, fair complexion, hands and face much freckled, 35 years of age. Born and brought up partly in Hawkin[s] County, East Tenn., and partly in Rutherford. His parents reside in Wilson County about four and a half miles from Lebanon in the neighbourhood of Horton's mill and Spring Creek Meeting House. He has three children living in Giles County. The little finger of the left hand is crooked, a small scar on the forefinger of the right hand. He has no remarkable scars. He has generally followed farming but has been engaged as [a] teamster for some years past. Was found guilty of petit larceny at the Circuit Court of Davidson County and sentenced to one year's confinement in the Jail and Penitentiary House of the State of Tennessee. *Samuel Chamberlain was discharged by expiration of sentence on the 20th day of June, 1835. His conduct was good.* [Ledger 45, page 22]

James Courier was received in the Penitentiary 16 September 1834. He is 15 years of age, 4' 4" or 5" high, and weighs 115 lbs. Blue eyes, fair hair, dark complexion, small short forehead and cross eyes. Born and raised in Albemarle Co., Virginia, where his mother now resides. He was brought to this country by Lane Overton. Has a scar on the thumb of the left hand where it joins the hand, and one near the second toe of the right foot. He was found guilty of petit larceny at the Circuit Court of Overton County and sentenced to one year's confinement in the Jail and Penitentiary House of the State of Tennessee. *James Courier was discharged by expiration of sentence on the 22nd day of Sept. 1835. He was detained four days for ill conduct. His conduct was generally bad.* [Ledger 45, page 22]

Elijah Crosen was received in the Penitentiary on 7th day of November, 1834. He is 39 years of age, 5' 7" in height, and weighs 140 lbs. Dark eyes, dark hair, dark complexion, short forehead and short nose. The nales [sic,] of the ring and small fingers of the left hand have been injured by a tiller[?], and he has a scar on the inside of the left leg, just below the knee, caused by a bite from a dog [hog?]. He is a tolerable country shoemaker but has chiefly followed farming. He was born in Prince William Co., Virginia, brought up in Hawkins and Murry [Maury] counties, Tenn.. Has been living in Murry Co. until the time of his sentence. On Flat Creek (where his wife and five children now reside) in the neighbourhood of Hart Cross Rodes [sic,]. Has a brother John Crosen living in Monroe Co., Mississippi, a sister married to John Sweet (a farmer living in the neighbourhood of his family), and another sister married to Meshac Morris (a farmer) living in Hamilton Co., Illinois. He was found guilty of having aided in murder, at the Circuit Court of Murry County and sentenced to two years confinement in the Jail and Penitentiary House of the State of Tennessee. *Elijah Crosen was discharged 12 Dec. 183[6?], detained 35 days for bad conduct.* [Ledger 45, page 22]

George W. Cross was received in the Penitentiary 5 December, 1834. He is 20 years of age, 5' 7" high, and weighs 164 lbs. Fair hair, gray eyes, fair complexion, full cheaks [sic,] and face and stout built. Has a small scar on the left leg just below the knee. Has chiefly followed farming. Born in White Co., Tenn., near Sparta. Mother dead; father (Wm. Cross) two brothers and one sister living together on Big Creek, four miles from Madisonville, Monroe County. One of the brothers (Elihu Cross) is married. He has also another brother (Alfred Cross) living in Bartholomew Co., Indiana. A wife but no children living with her mother (Nancy McDaniel) at the Boat Yard on Holston River in Blount Co. He was found guilty of petit larceny at the Circuit Court of Monroe County, and sentenced to 14 months confinement in the Jail and Penitentiary House of the State of Tennessee. *George W. Cross was discharged 24th day of February, 1836. Was detained 20 days for improper conduct.* [Ledger 45, page 23]

Samuel Childress was received in the Penitentiary 4 December 1834. He is 23 years of age, 5' 7" high, and weighs 166 lbs. Heavy built, brown hair, blue eyes and sandy beard. Has a small scar above the left eye, another on the instep of the left foot and another near the big toe on the same foot. Chiefly follows farming. Born in Lawrence Co., South Carolina, and brought up in Greenville Co. in the same state. His mother, six sisters and one brother reside in Lumpkin Co., Georgia. Four of the sisters married as follows, viz: to William Taylor, James P. Neal, Thomas Burns and Thomas Goff. Also a brother (Wm. C.) residing near Lem Childress' mill in the Cherokee Purchase of Tenn.. He has a wife and three children living with her father (Wm. Gray) on Ball Play Creek, Monroe County, Tenn.. He was found guilty of forgery at the Circuit Court of Monroe County and sentenced to three years confinement in the Jail and Penitentiary House of the State of Tennessee. *Died 22 Nov. 1835 of chronic direah [sic,].* [Ledger 45, page 23]

Owen Collins was received in the Penitentiary on the 17th day of January, 1835. He is 45 years old, 6' 1" high, and weighs 150 lbs. Dark hair, blue eyes, dark skin and slender made. A slender scar running from the crown of his head to the top of his forehead, about 4" in length; two scars nearly together on the inside of his left thigh just above the knee; a scar on the second joint of the right thumb, and one on the ball of the left thumb. His mother, wife (who was a daughter of Lewis Collins) and eight [children?] are all living near Tazewell, Claiborne Co., Tenn.. He was born in Guilford Co., North Carolina, but brought up in the above named county in Tenn.. Has chiefly followed farming. Was found guilty of "assault and battery with intent to kill" at the Circuit Court of Claiborne County and sentenced to three years confinement in the Jail and Penitentiary House of the State of Tennessee. *Owen Collins died of chronic diarhea [sic,] Sept. 19, 1837.* [Ledger 45, page 24]

Tennessee Convicts: Records of the State Penitentiary

William Cox was received in the Penitentiary 11 June, 1835. He is 28 years of age, 5', 7" or 8" high, who weighs about 165 lbs. Sandy hair, hazel eyes, long thin nose, low forehead and fair complexion. A very large scar on the inside of the right leg, the lower and largest part of which is above, and partly upon, the upper edge of the ankle bone. The middle part forms a small sink in the flesh, and the upper part, which is near the edge of the shin bone, forms a sink in the flesh about an inch in length. The whole length of the scar is about 5". Labourer. Born in Carter County and brought up in Bedford County, Tenn.. His father, Isaac Cox, resides in Bedford County, Tenn., on Sugar Creek about seven miles from Shelbyville. He married Susan Culps, daughter of Adam Culps, who resides in Bedford County, on Duck River, about six miles from Shelbyville. His wife and children (two) reside on a part of her father's (the above named Adam Culps') plantation. He was found guilty of petit larceny at the Circuit Court of Bedford County and sentenced to two years confinement in the Jail and Penitentiary House of the State of Tennessee. *William Cox died of cholera on the 1st day of July, 1835.* [Ledger 45, page 24]

Burwell Clark was received 11 May 1835. He is 5' 10" high, weighs 145 lbs., is 18 years old. Born in Georgia and the last eight years has lived in Madison Co., Tenn., where his father John Clark now lives on land belonging to Edmund Childers. Fair skin, sandy hair, thin beard, blue eye (the right one out and the pupil nearly obscured, occasioned by fever) his mouth small, full face. Was found guilty of forgery and sentenced to three years confinement in the Jail and Penitentiary of Tennessee at the Madison County Circuit Court, April Term, 1836. *Burwell Clark was discharged June 13th, 1839, by expiration of sentence after having been detained 33 days for misconduct (Tailor).* [Ledger 45, page 25]

Alexander Cohen from Fayette County, Tenn., was received 3 June 1836. He is 5', 5" high, weighs 195 lbs. Is 50 years old, large and full face, large and full blue eyes, large nose, bushy sandy eyebrows, heavy stout form, thick neck. His family lives in Tuscaloosa, Alabama. By occupation a renovater and dyer. He was born in Cork, Ireland. He lisps a little, fond of talking and full of good humour. Has three warts on his right eyebrow. Found guilty of murder second degree and sentenced to 21 years imprisonment at hard labour in the Tenn. Penitentiary. [Ledger 45, page 25]

Ezekiel Collins from Hawkins Co., East Tenn.. Was received August 24, 1836. Offense: hog stealing Sentence: three years. He is 34 years old, weighs 141 lbs., is 5' 8" high, dark complexion, black hair and eyes. Born and raised in Hawkins Co, East Tenn. [Ledger 45, page 25]

Tennessee Convicts: Records of the State Penitentiary

Andrew Collins from Hawkins Co., East Tenn.. Brother of Ezekiel, same offense and sentence. Received August 24, 1836. He is 28 years old, weighs 160 lbs., is 5', 10" high. Dark complexion, black hair and eyes. Born and raised in Hawkins County, where their father now resides. [Ledger 45, page 25]

Joseph Doan from Sullivan County. Offence grand larceny, sentence three years. Was received December 25, 1836. He is 18 years old, 5' 7" high, weighs 140 lbs. Has dark hair, grey eyes, dark skin, good countenance. A scar on the bone of the small finger of the right hand say 2" from the wrist joint. One on the back of the fore finger of the same hand, one also on the brow of the right eye, all small but plain. Born and raised in Washington Co., Virginia. Parents dead. His relations reside in said county, Virginia. [Ledger 45, page 26]

Gilford Cook from Dickson County, Tenn.. Offence: larceny. Sentence: three years from 18 February 1837. Was received 19 February 1837. He is 48 years old, 6' 2 1/2" high, and weighs 180 lbs. Has dark hair, grey eyes. Born and raised in Franklin Co., North Carolina, where he married Sarah Bass. Says he has lived in Wilson Co., Tenn., near Richard Drake, and moved to Dickson Co., Tenn., in 1833, where his family now lives near Kendrick Myatt's on the old Natches [sic,] trace 15 miles from Charlotte. *Pardoned by Gov. Polk, January 8th, 1840. Conduct good.* [Ledger 45, page 26]

Uriah Cummings from Knox County, Tenn.. Offence petty larceny. Sentence two years and six months. Was received March 3, 1837. He is 27 years old, 5' 7 1/2" high, and weighs 152 lbs. Has black hair, hazle eyes and dark skin, a scar on the left thumb running from the nail to the last joint and then across. One on the calf of the left leg occasioned by the bite of a dog. A scar from a scald as large as the hand on the outside of the right arm beginning at the elbow. Born in Virginia and resided in Knox Co., Tenn., where he married a daughter of John N[?] Smith. His father lives in Knoxville. *Discharged September 4th, 1839. Conduct good. Returned May 24th, 1841, from Monroe County. Crime larceny, sentence 21 months.* [Ledger 45, page 26]

Jacob Calhoun from Montgomery County, Tenn. Offence: murder in the second degree. Sentence: 20 years. Received 26 September 1837. He is 40 years old, 5', 8" high, weighs 162 lbs. Dark grey hair, black eyes, very heavy black beard, dark skin. Was born in Edge Comb [sic., Edgecombe] Co., North Carolina, and brought up in Montgomery Co., Tenn., 12 miles from Clarksville and six miles from Port Royal where his brother Lemuel Calhoun now lives. He has two sisters married, one to Robert Bryan who lives on the Elk fork of

Red River two miles from Williamson's mill. The other sister married a man by the name of David Holland and lives ¼ of a mile of Lemuel Calhoun. He has generally followed farming. He is crippled in both shoulders. He was sentenced by the Circuit Court of Montgomery County to the Jail and Penitentiary House of the State of Tennessee. [Ledger 45, pp. 26-7]

William Kennedy from Morgan County. Offence: larceny. Sentence: one year. Received 29 November 1837. He is 18 years of age, 5' 6" high, weighs 155 lbs. Dark hair and skin. Born and brought up in North Carolina, Caswell Co. He has two sisters married and living in North Carolina. One is married to a man by the name of Swan. The other to a man by the name of Martin. His mother and other relations live in Missouri some where on the Osage River. He has worked at the shoe making business, he says. Sentenced by the Circuit Court of Morgan County to one year's confinement in the Jail and Penitentiary house of the State of Tennessee. *Wm. Kennedy was discharged December 6th, 1838, having been detained five days for improper conduct.* [Ledger 45, p. 27]

David S. Cloppe from Carroll County. Offence: voluntary manslaughter. Sentence: five years. Received Nov. 23, 1837. He is 19 years old, 5' 8 ½" high, weighs 135 lbs. Born in Guilford Co., North Carolina. Brought up in Bedford Co., Tenn. His father lives in Lewisburg, Marshall Co. [and] works at the carpenter's business. Black eyes, fair skin. He has several moles on his face, one directly over his right eye brow. He has had the white swelling in the left hip. He has some relations living near Shelbyville, Tenn. He is a tailor. Sentenced by the Circuit Court of Carroll County to five years confinement in the Jail and Penitentiary House of the State of Tennessee. [Ledger 45, p. 27]

Joseph Carr from Monroe County. Refer to letter D. [Ledger 45, p. 27]

John S. Crocker from Knox County. Sentenced by the Circuit Court of McMinn [County] for forgery. Sentence three years from 16 June 1838. He is 25 years old, 5' 7" high, weighs 152 lbs. Born and brought up in Madison County, State of New York, in the town of Carnovia, where his father now lives. He says [he] has clerked in the City of New York for the House of Cambel and Smith, 132 Water Street. He enlisted in the Florida Campaign. He has dark hair, blue eyes and fair skin. He has a scar on the ankle bone of the left foot on the inside. Has worked some at the carpenters business. [Ledger 45, page 28]

Robert Chappel from Hickman County. Offence: grand larceny. Sentence: one year from the time of his reception. Received July 16, 1838. He is 25 years old, 5'. 6" high, weighs 130 lbs. Born in North Carolina, brought up in Tenn.,

Hickman County. His father, Ansel Chappel, lives in said county on the waters of Spring Creek. He has nine sisters, two of which is married and lives in the same settlement. One to Eli Chappel the other to Cain Clamer. His wife and child is living with her father James Rigsby on Piney [Creek?]. The thumb of his right hand is off to the middle joint. He says it was cut off with the saw of a cotton gin. Their [sic,] is also a scar where the piece of thumb joins the hand about an inch long. *Robert Chappel discharged by order of the Governor of this State on 16th of April 1839.* [Ledger 45, page 28]

Michael Corley from Davidson County. Offence: forgery. Sentence: three years. Was received into the Penitentiary 3rd day June 1839. He is 26 years old, 5' 9" high, weighs 160 lbs. Born and brought up in Ireland. He has a mother and two brothers living in the City of New York. Said Corley has lived in Nashville about three years. Has lived with a woman by name Martha Minor; not married to her. Sandy hair, grey eyes, large head. Tolerable countenance. He has generally followed Pedling [sic,] before he came to Nashville, where he kept a livery stable on Market Street. See p letter **R**. [Ledger 45, page 28]

John Dougan was received in the Penitentiary 27 January 1831. He is 45 years of age, 5' 10" high. Dark hair, somewhat gray, dark complexion and gray eyes, weighs about 180 lbs. Scar on the inside of the left foot and one on the right hand. Was born in Randolph County, North Carolina, and brought up in Warren County, Kentucky, on the waters of Gaspers [sic,] River. His father, mother and wife live in Franklin County, Tennessee. One brother in Dickson County and an other [sic,] in Fayette County in this state. Was found guilty of man slaughter [sic,] at the Circuit Court of Franklin County and sentenced to ten years confinement in the Jail and Penitentiary House of the State of Tennessee. *John Dougan died of cholera on the 14th day of June 1833. First from Franklin Co.* [Ledger 45, page 29]

John Delk was received into the Penitentiary 4 May 1832. He is 40 years of age, 5' 8 ½" in height, weighs 148 lbs. He was born in Green[e] County, Tenn., brought up in Buncam [Buncombe] County, North Carolina. Has lived in Campbell County for many years in the neighborhood of Chambers Mill, where his family now lives, consisting [of] a wife and nine children. His relations live in the same neighborhood, that is a mother, three brothers and three sisters. One by the name Adkins and one by the name of Owens and one by the name of Sowders[?]. He has grey eyes, dark skin and heavy beard. He has a scar over the right eye next the nose, also one over the left corner of the left eye, they were both caused from bites. He has a scar on the thumb of the left hand, on the back part of the thumb running from one joint to the other.

The little finger of the left hand has been broken, and leaves a knot on the middle joint and is somewhat crooked. He has a scar on the right leg say middle of the leg about three or four inches long, running from the shin a little down. Was found guilty of hog stealing at the Circuit Court of Campbell County and sentenced to one years confinement in the Jail and Penitentiary House of the State of Tennessee. *John Delk died of cholera on the 20th day of June 1833.* [Ledger 45, page 29]

James R. Dickenson was received into the Penitentiary 17 April 1832. He is 5' 9" high, weight 154 lbs, 26 years of age. Born and brought up in Charlotte Co., Virginia. He has lived in Smith Co., Tenn., for the last eight years Where he has a wife and two children living within two miles of Hagens[?] Creek Meeting house and four miles from Carthage. His wifes relations live in the same neighborhood. He has dark hair and skin, yellow eyes, long sharp nose round full breast. A small scar on the inside of the left knee, very clear of scars otherwise. He has worked at shoemaking a little. Was found guilty of petit larceny at the Circuit Court of Smith County and sentenced to one years confinement in the Jail and Penitentiary House of the State of Tennessee. *James R. Dickenson was discharged on the 21st of April 1833. His conduct was generally good.* [Ledger 45, page 29]

James W. Duncan was received in the Penitentiary 8 November 1833. He is 5' 8" in height and weighs 150 lbs. Dark hair, grey eyes and rather dark complexion, 25 years of age. Born in Kershaw District, South Carolina, and brought up there. His parents reside either in Jackson or Jefferson County, Missouri. He has five brothers and six sisters. Three of his brothers and four of his sisters are married. One brother resides in Rhea County, E. Tenn., on Tennessee River five miles from Kellis[?] ferry, and one brother living in Montgomery County, Alabama. The remainder reside in Missouri. He has no remarkable scars except one on the first joint of the middle finger of the right hand caused by a bite. He has generally followed farming . Was found guilty of horse stealing at the Circuit Court of McMinn County and sentenced to eight years confinement in the Jail and Penitentiary House of the State of Tennessee. [Ledger 45, page 30]

James Denton was received in the Penitentiary 15 April 1834. He is 5' 10" in height and weighs 136 lbs. Grey eyes, light hair and fair complexion, prominent features, 24 yrs of age. Born in Jackson Co. and brought up in Perry Co., Tenn. His father is dead, his mother resides in Wayne Co. about fifteen miles from Waynesboro and three miles from David Bicknells[?] mill on Possum Creek a branch of Buffalo River. He has five brothers, five half brothers and eight sisters. Seven of his brothers are married and all his sisters.

They are scattered in White, Jackson, McNairy and Perry counties. He has a wife and two children, her maiden name was Spence. She now resides on Cedar Creek in Perry County about five miles from Col. Dickson's Steam mill and twelve from Perryville, but expects to move on South Harper River, Davidson County, where she has two sisters living, they are married to Lewis Jones and Isaac Joy[?]. He has a remarkable scar on the finger next the little finger of the left hand, running along the back of the hand, caused by a chop from an axe. He has three small scars on the thumb of the right hand showing the mark of three teeth, a small scar on the back of the same hand caused by a drawing knife. One side of his breast bone is considerably lower than the other, having been crushed in by a kick from a horse, he has scars on each of his knees, not very visible. Denton has generally followed farming. Was found guilty at the Circuit [Court] of Perry County of petit larceny and sentenced to two years confinement in the Jail and Penitentiary House of the State of Tennessee. *James Denton died of cholera on the 4th day of July 1835.* [Ledger 45, page 30-31]

Charles T. Daviss [*sic,*, also written *Davis*] was received in the Penitentiary August 15, 1834. He is 5' 5" in height and weighs 135 lbs. Dark hair, dark hazel eyes and fair complexion. Well formed to his height, twenty years of age. Born in Pittsylvania Co., Virginia, brought up partly there and partly in Madison Co., Kentucky. His father is dead, his mother and one sister still resides there, about twelve miles from Richmond and three from the waters of Silver Creek and the round top Meeting House and near Whites Mill. He has a scar on the forefinger of the left hand forming the letter Y, and one on the forefinger of the right hand where the finger joins the hand. A mole on each side of the throat about ½" apart. A small scar over the right eye about one-third of the distance from the hair to the eye, and a scar on the inside ancle[?] of the right [*sic,*]. He has worked some little as a Painter. Was found guilty at the Circuit Court of Giles County of horse stealing and sentenced to three years and six months confinement in the Jail and Penitentiary House of the State of Tennessee. *Charles T. Davis escaped on Friday Night, 12th day of June 1835.* [Ledger 45, page 31]

John A. Dean was received in the Penitentiary 8 November 1834. He is 27 years of age, 5' 9" high and weighs usually from 150 to 156 lbs. Black hair, black eyes, dark complexion, tolerable full face and good countenance. Has a scar near the out corner of the left eye and one on the left side of his face, between the ear and the cheak bone. Was born in Huntingdon and raised in Chambersburg, Pennsylvania, where he served an apprenticeship at the shoemaking business which has ever since been his occupation. His father lives in Chambersburg, Penn. He has a brother (a Phasician) residing in Harrisburg, and a sister married to Wm.R.Hewling (an Attorney) residing in Chambersburg. He had been living in Cambell Co., Tenn., about six months, when he was found guilty of petit larceny at the Circuit Court of that County, and sentenced to three years confinement in the Jail and Penitentiary House of the State of Tennessee. *Died of cholera on 27 June 1835.* [Ledger 45, page 31]

George W. Dyer was received in the Penitentiary 3 March 1835. He is 24 years of age, 5' 7" or 8" high and weighs 150 or 160 lbs. Black eyes, black hair, thin beard and fair complexion. A scar about ¾" in length just above the left corner of the mouth, and one on the under lip near the same corner of the mouth. Served an apprentiship at the saddleing business in New Market, Jefferson Co., Tennessee. Born in Savierville, Savier Co. Father dead, mother who afterwards intermarried with a Mr. Dickey (who is also dead), one sister (Patsey), and one brother (Stewart), neither reside in the same place (Savierville), another sister (Polly) married to Hopkins Anderson living near the same place. Wife (daughter of Abner Frazer) and three children are residing in New Market, Jefferson Co. He was found guilty of petit larceny at the Circuit Court of Knox County and sentenced to one year's confinement in the Jail and Penitentiary House of the State of Tennessee. *Geo. W. Dyer was discharged 3d March 1836. Having served the term of sentence. Conduct good.* [page 32]

James Wiley Davis was received in the Penitentiary 2 November 1835. He is in his 17th year, 5' 7 ¾" high and weighs 140 lbs. Auburn hair, hazle eyes, heavy brow and common complexion. A scar on his lower lip, one on his right jaw. All of his right hand fingers much scared, a large scar near where his thumb joins the hand, a large scar just above left knee cap, several scars on the same and a large [one] on his right knee cap. He was born and raised in Maury Co., Tenn. He has worked some little at hoe making. His father, mother, one brother and three sisters live in Lawrence Co., Tenn. near Calvin McCrackens store about four miles from Esq. Jno. McCrackens and about one mile from Davis Hughes' (who is his maternal uncle) Mill. He was found guilty of petit larceny at the Circuit Court of Maury County and sentenced to one years confinement in the Jail and Penitentiary House of the State of Tennessee. Neither reads nor writes. *James W. Davis was discharged 13 Dec. 1836 having served 41 days for breach of Prison rules.* [Ledger 45, page 32]

William M. Duke was convicted of horse stealing at the Perry County Circuit Court May Term 1836 and sentenced to five years imprisonment in the Jail and Penitentiary of the State of Tennessee. Was received 13th day of April 1836. He is full 5' 9" high. Stout form, healthy appearance, dark hair, dark blue eyes, heavy beard, arched eyebrows, broad forehead, broad face and rather flat, common complexion. Has a scar on the left wrist caused by a stab, one on the shin nearly the size of a quarter dollar, a mole on the left breast smoothe with the skin, also a projecting mole on the left side of the neck. Aged about 24 years. Says he was born in Barren Co., Kentucky, and raised in in Madison Co., Alabama. His father lives in Fayette Co., Alabama, on his own land. One brother a shoe and boot maker living in Hickman County. The other a farmer living in Georgia, and one sister married to a Mr. Reeder, a gun smith, living in Giles Co., Tenn. *Gave his coat to John Forgus 6 May 1837.* [Ledger 45, page 32-33]

Edmond Davis convicte[d] of petit larceny at the Grainger Circuit Court April Term and sentenced to one year imprisonment in the Penitentiary. Received 3 May 1836. He is 6' and ½" high. Bony form, light hair, dark grey eyes. Long under jaw, short upper jaw. Long face, nose falling on his under lip. When his mouth is shut it would be supposed he had lost all his upper front teeth. He has not lost any of them. Says he was born in Henry County, Old Virginia, and that he is 42 years old, appears to be older. *Edmond Davis was discharged June 6th 1837. Conduct generally good, detained one month and three days for Violation of Prison Rules.* [Ledger 45, page 33]

Joseph Doan from Sullivan county. Offence: grand larceny. Sentence: three years. Was received Dec. 25, 1836. Refer to letter C for description. *Joseph Doan was discharged January 16,.1840, being detained 21 days for bad conduct.* [Ledger 45, page 33]

William Dean from Bedford County, Tenn. Offence: murder. Sentence: 15 years Was rec'd April 18, 1837. He is 45 years old 5' 9" high, weighs 159 lbs. Has red hair , blue eyes , fair skin, hair turning grey. A scar on the nose running towards the left eye and one from that ¾" long running down the nose likewise, nearest the left eye. Several slight scars on the left side. A scar on the right side rather below the corner of the right eye and one on the chin. The scar down the nose was caused by a blow with a stone and can be felt on the bridge of the nose plainer than seen. Born in South Carolina. Raised in Bedford Co., Tenn., where his father now resides. [Ledger 45, page 33]

George W. Anderson, alias G. W. Dyer. Offence: petit larceny. Sentince: one year. Was received June 18, 1837. Has been here on a former sentence, from Knox County, for petit larceny. He is now sentenced by the Circuit Court of White County to one years confinement in the Jail and Penitentiary House of the State of Tenn. For discription refer to his former sentence. [Ledger 45, page 34]

John Dowinng [sic,] from Maury County. Offence: horse stealing. Rec'd Jan. 22, 1838. Sentence: five years. He is 38 years old, 5' 6" high, weighs 159 lbs. Born and brought up in Burtee [Bertie] Co., North Carolina. Has dark hair, blue eyes, heavy brows, coarse features. Has a scar between the eyebrows, one in the lower eye lash of the left eye. Has had the end of the middle finger of the right hand bit and shows a scar. Has had his left arm broken and it is crooked and stiff. He has worked at the cabinet business and carriage making some. Has a wife and five children living in Wickley [Weakley] Co. 10 miles north east of Dresden. W.M.I. [Ledger 45, page 34]

Isaac Dale. Received February 5, 1838. Crime: murder in 1st degree. Sentenced to be hanged by the Circuit Court of Giles Co. Appealed and sentence of the Circuit Court confirmed by the Supreme Court at Nashville. Sentence of death com[m]uted by Gov. N. Cannon to imprisonment for life in the Penitentiary. He is 62 years old, 5' 7" high, weighs 148 lbs. Born and brot up in Pitt County, N. Carolina. He has dark grey hair, dark eyes and skin. He has one brother, Abel Dale, living in Grainger Co., Tenn. He has the middle finger of the left hand stiff in the joint nearest the finger end. *Isaac Dale died of rheumatism April 27, 1839.* [Ledger 45, page 34]

Joseph Carr from Monroe County. Offence: petit larceny. Rec'd May 24, 1838. Sentence: one year. He is 15 years old, 5' 7" high, weighs 125 lbs. Born in North Carolina and brot up in Monroe Co., Tenn., near Philadelphia where his father, Danl. Carr now lives. He has dark hair, blue eyes, fair skin. He has a scar on the forefinger of the left hand, between the [k]nuckle joint and hand, also a scar on the instep of the left foot, a scar on the top of the head two inches long. [Ledger 45, page 35]

Perry Daniel from Overton County. Offence: petit larceny. Sentence: one year. Rec'd July 3, 1838. Sentence to commence the fourth day of July, 1838. He is 27 years old, 5' 7 ½" high, weighs 172 lbs. Born in S. Carolina, Marrion County, near the Pedee River. Bro't up in Overton County four miles north of Monroe, where his mother, Dicy Daniel, now lives. Wm. Daniel, his uncle, lives in the same settlement and has a mill on the waters of Eagle Creek. Has two brothers and one sister in Sequatchee Valley. Boath his shins is filled with scars caused by cuts and burns. *Perry Daniel was discharged July 4th, 1839. Detained only one day.* [Ledger 45, page 35]

Josiah Dayton from Shelby County. Offence: grand larceny. Sentence: five years. Rec'd Oct. 18, 1838. He is 24 years old, 5'.5 ¼" high, weighs 146 lbs. Born and brot up in Montgomery Co., Pennsylvania. He has one brother, two sisters and one uncle in said county. He has dark hair, grey eyes with an umber colored spot or speck in the blue part of the right eye. His left hand has had the little finger and the one next it shot of[f]. The middle finger of the same hand is stiff and sticks out straight. He says he is a boot fitter. W.M.I. [Ledger 45, page 35]

Charless I. [or J?] Donald from Hamilton County. Offence: petit larceny. Sentence: one year from 30 Nov. 1838. Rec'd Dec.7, 1838. He is 22 years old 5' 10 1/2" high, weighs 142 lbs. Born and brot up in France in the city of Paris. Has been a resident of the United States five years Has a great many images and c[h]aracters on his arms if they have not been extracted. He has dark hair, blue eyes, sallow complexion. Tolerable good countena[n]ce. Professes to be a confectioner baker and a regular bred physian [*sic,*]. [Ledger 45, page 36]

John Dennis from McNairy County. Crime: grand larceny. Sentence: three years. Rec'd 20 Dec. 1838. He is 34 years old, 5' 8" high, weighs 153 lbs. Born and brot up in G[u]ilford County, N. Carolina. Has a wife and seven children living nine miles north of Purdy in McNairy Co., Tenn. He has dark hair, blue eyes, fair skin, very heavy beard. [Ledger 45, page 36]

Andrew Duncan from Marshall County was received into the Penitentiary June 13, 1839. He is 33 years of age, weighs 167 lbs. 5' 10" high. Born and brought up in Ierdale [*sic,,* Iredell] County, North Carolina. Has a wife and seven children living in Marshall Co., north corner, where Murray, Marshall, Bedford and Williamson counties join. His wife was a Duval. She has one brother in Call<u>o</u>way County, Kentucky, seven miles south of Wadesboro. His wife is living on her own land. He has dark grey hair, fair skin, blue eyes. He has a scar in the left eye brow formed thus [drawing of a "T" shape]. Gunsmith by trade. The said A. Duncan was convicted by the Circuit Court of Marshall Co. of the crime of making and passing Base Coin and sentence[d] to undergo confinement in the Jail and Penit[entiar]y House of this State from [*sic,*] the term of four years commencing from this day. [Ledger 45, page 36]

Daniel Doxey from Marshall County. Rec'd into the Penit'y June 13, 1839. He is 33 years of age, weighs 153 lbs., 5' 10 1/4" high. Born and brought up in North Carolina, Johnson C[oun]ty. Has a wife and six children living 12 miles north of Lewisburg near McLains Mill on Duck River in Marshall Co. He has dark hair, haz<u>z</u>le eyes, rough features, ve<u>rr</u>y bad countenance, sallow complexion. His wife was a Miss Hicks. Sentenced to confinement in the Penitentiary for the space of two years. [Ledger 45, page 36]

John H. Davis from Bradley County. Rec'd into the Penitentiary 9 Sept. 1839. He is 50 years of age, weighs 135 lbs. 3' 9" high. Born and brought up in South Carolina. He has a wife and nine children living in Blou[n]t Co., luckyatuckey[?] cave on little River 16 miles east of Meryville. His father and mother are both living in the same county. Has five brothers and three sisters all living in Blou[n]t County. He has black hair, very grey beard, grey eyes, sallow complexion, a good countenance. Two fingers on the left hand have been marked which makes them crooked. A farmer by occupation. Said John H. Davis was found guilty of horse stealing in the county of Bradley and sentenced to undergo confinement in the Jail and Penitentiary House of this State for the space of four years [Ledger 45, page 37]

James Dalton from Robinson [*sic,*, Robertson?] County. Crime: larceny. Sentence: one year from 8 Jan. 1840. Rec'd January 12, 1840. He is 29 years old, 5' 10" high, weighs 152 lbs. Born in Rockbrid[g]e County, Virginia, and bro[ugh]t up in Norfolk. He has sandy hair, hazle eyes, fair skin. [Ledger 45, page 37]

Benjamin Dennis from Davidson County. Crime: horse stealing. Sentence: three years from 14 Oct. 1840. Rec'd 14 Oct. 1840. He is 38 years old, 5' 6"high, weighs 165 lbs. Born in Sumpterville District, South Carolina, and brought up in the town of Nashville ,Tenn. His grandfather Danl. Dennis is living with Timothy Gillman the uncle of the above named Dennis. He has a wife and 2 children living on the old Huntsville Road, near the widow Buchanan's. He has red hair, fair skin, blue eyes, stout made. Has had his right arm broken near the joint, which makes it stiff. [Ledger 45, page 37]

Wm. R. Doss from Robertson County. Crime: bigamy. Sentence: two years from 11 Oct. 1841. Rec'd 13 Oct. 1841. He is 36 years old, 5' 8 ½" high, weighs 145 [lbs]. Born in Pittsylvania Co., Virginia, bro[ugh]t up in Adair Co., Kentucky,in the town of Columbia. Has followed wool carding and cotton spinning. His first wife has one brother in Marshall Co. by the name of Philip Doss, one in Rutherford Co. in Rock Creek. _S Dr/S[?] The above named Doss has carded wool for Blackman Hayes in this county, where he and his first wife parted. He then carded for Garrett on White's Creek. He then went to Squire R.B Mitchell's of Rober[t]son Co. and married the daughter of Lawrence Morris, Mary Ann Morris. Said Doss has dark hair, black eyes,dark skin. He has a scar on his left foot running from between the little toe and the one next it, 3" up his foot. [Ledger 45, page 38]

Tennessee Convicts: Records of the State Penitentiary

George M. Dickey from Lawrence County. Crime: incest. Sentence: 15 years from 20 Oct. 1841, when he was received. He is 56 years old, weighs 176 lbs., 6' 1 ½" high. Born and brought up in Orange County, North Carolina. Has one daughter married to a man by the name of F.W. King and lives in Giles County near Cornersville. Has two other daughters in the same settlement, one at the Widow Johnston's, the other, don't know where. Has one in Lawrence with his wife. Said Dickey has grey hair, hazle eyes and dark skin. Has worked at coopering and waggon making, but is not a proficient in either. [Ledger 45, page 38]

Thomas Daniels from Davidson County. Crime: maiming. Sentence: two years, from 24 March, 1842. Rec'd 26 March 1842. He was born at Nashville, Tenn., where his mother now lives. He is about 23 years of age, 5' 10 ½" high, weighs 165 lbs., has dark hair and eyes and fair skin. Has been shot in the left arm above the elbow, which makes a large scar and the slugs parting makes two smaller ones where they came through on the inside of the arm. The finger next the little on the right hand has been bit, rather above the last joint, which makes it stiff and bends considerably to the little finger. There is a small scar above and one inch to the right of the right corner of the mouth caused by a burn[?]. By occupation boatman[?]. [Ledger 45, page 38]

Joel Doolin from McNairy County. Crime: larceny. Sentence: five years from September 15, 1841. Received September 15, 1841. He is 19 years old, weighs 155 lbs., 5' 9" high. Born and brought up in Wayne Co., Tenn. His father, Rice Doolin, is a bricklayer and lives five miles south of Pinhook in the above named county. He has fair hair, hazle eyes and fair skin. Has several small cuts on his left hand, which he says were done with a razor when he was a child. [Ledger 45, page 40]

Theodore Deming from Monroe County. Crime: larceny. Sentence: four years from May 21, 1842. Rec'd May 21, 1842. He is 32 years old, 5' 5 ½" high, weighs 136 lbs. Born and brought up in Troy, New York, Ransalier [sic,, Rensselaer] County. He has a wife and two children in Murray County, Georgia, about three miles from Red Clay Post Office, near Mitchell P. Varnum's[?] . His wife's maidin name was Sarah Russel. She has some relations living in Floyd County, Georgia, by the name of Shugart[?] and a family of the Reeces living near Rome [Georgia]. Said Demming has dark hair, hazle eyes and fair skin, heavy beard, he has two scars below the knee of the left leg, one of which is on the inside of the leg. [Ledger 45, page 40]

William Estep was received in the Penitentiary 2 Oct. 1833. He is 5' 4 ¼" in height and weighs 151 lbs. Dark hair and eyes and tolerable fair complexion,

47 years of age. Born in Ash[e] Co., North Carolina, and brought up there. His mother, three sisters and four brothers all reside in Carter Co., Tenn. He has one brother living in Monroe Co., Tenn. Two of his sisters are married, one to John Oliver, the other to Martin Kilburn [or Hilburn?], residing near his mother, about four miles from Elizabethton. Estep has a wife and six children, her maiden name was Duncan. She is now living about two and one-half miles from Elizabethton, Carter Co. He has a stammering in his speech. The finger next the little on the left hand is quite flat, where it joins the hand, occasioned by being mashed during a fit [*sic,*], a scar on the left jaw caused by a bite, a scar on the right eyebrow from a blow and one on the left side of the upper lip. He has generally followed farming. Was found guilty of petit larceny at the Circuit Court of Carter County and sentenced to two years confinement in the Jail and Penitentiary House of the State of Tenn. *Estep was detained 55 days for bad conduct. Discharged 25 Nov. 1835. Conduct very bad, lazy and hipocritical.* [Ledger 45, page 41]

Alfred Ellis was received May 6, 1834. He is 5' 9 ½" in height and weighs 166 lbs. Dark hair, grey eyes, and tolerably fair complexion, thick nose, large face, short forehead, 19 years of age. Born and brought up in Claiborne Co., Tenn. His mother resides at Sharp's Furnace, Grainger Co., Tenn. He has one brother, married, living in Sullivan Co., Tenn. An uncle named Furry, living at Crocket's Iron Works in Claiborne Co., Tenn. Another uncle, Isaac Suthert[?]living near McHenry's ferry on Powell's river, about eight miles from the town of Tazwell. He has a scar on the ball of the left thumb. The toe next the great toe is crooked and the next appears to ride upon it, he is very clear of scars. [He] is a moulder of castings by trade. Was found guilty of voluntary manslaughter at the Circuit Court of Claiborne Co. and sentenced to five years confinement in the Jail and Penitentiary House of the State of Tenn. *Alfred Ellis was discharged by expiration of sentence May 6, 1839.* [Ledger 45, page 41]

Thomas Ely was rec'd in the Penitentiary on 5 Nov. 1834. He is 29 years of age, 5' 10" or 11" high and weighs 177 lbs. Blue eyes, dark hair, fair complexion, tolerable sharp nose and face, and stout built. Has several small scars on the middle finger of the left hand, several small moles about the centre of the breast and one on the right side of the neck about 2" below the ear. Has chiefly followed labouring. Was born and raised in Lee Co., Virginia. Served a sentence of two or th[re]e years in the Kentucky Penitentiary. His father, three brothers and one sister now reside together in Lee Co., Virginia, on a little creek called Sugar Run, about eight miles from Jonesville. He also has a sister married to George Scott (a farmer) who lives in the same neighbourhood. He was found guilty of horse stealing at the Circuit Court of Claibourne Co.

and sentenced to six years confinement in the Jail and Penitentiary House of the State of Tenn. *Thomas Ely gave his coat to Wm. Cassels, 16 Feb. 1836, in the presence of Alfred Stewart and G. Whitson.* [Ledger 45, pages 41-42]

James Edwards was rec'd in the Penitentiary 21 March 1835. He is 30 years of age, 5' 9" or 10" high and weighs 169 lbs. Black hair and beard, dark eyes, large face and fair complexion. Two scars between the first and second joints of the thumb of the left hand. A scar on the ring finger of the left hand, between the second and third joints, one on the knuckle of the little finger of the same hand and one between the second and third joint of the same finger. Left arm very crooked at the elbow and smaller than the right arm. Served four years in the Kentucky Penitentiary, under the name of James E. Fanning, where he learned the wagon making business. Born in Maryland and brought up in Loudo[u]n, Co., Virginia, about three miles from Leesburg. Found guilty of horse stealing at the Circuit Court of Roane County and sentenced to five years confinement in the Jail and Penitentiary House of the State of Tenn. [Ledger 45, page 42]

John Elkins was rec'd in the Penitentiary on 27 July 1835. He is 23 years of age, 5' 8" or 9" high and weighs about 150 lbs. Light hair, blue eyes, and fair complexion. Three scars on the cap of the right knee, and one on his face, under the left corner of his nose. Labourer. Born and brought up in Cocke Co., Tenn. Father dead, mother married to a man named Elijah Fox, who resides in Cocke Co., on the Chucky River [Nolichucky?] about five miles from Newport. A wife and one child living in Cocke Co. on a piece of land near Jas. Dunn's plantation, on the head waters of Bear Creek, about eight miles from Newport. He was found guilty of petit larceny at the Circuit Court of Cocke County and sentenced to one years confinement in the Jail and Penitentiary House of the State of Tenn. *John Elkins was discharged Aug.30, 1836, detained 34 days for bad conduct.* [Ledger 45, page 42-43]

Beuford Easly from Fayette County, Tenn. Was received 3 June 1836. He is 30 years old, 5' 8" high, slender made, weighs 140 lbs. Black hair, dark skin, large ha<u>zle</u> eyes and large ears, which stand off from his head more than common. Thin face, high thin nose, dark full eyebrows, full forehead and bad countenance. His family lives in Tipton Co., Tenn., nine miles from Randolph, on the road to Covington, with her mother, Barbary A. Parker. Was found guilty of negro stealing and sentenced to six years imprisonment in the Penit'y. *Beuford Easly died 4 August 1836. Swo<u>len</u> legs and feet and fever. Was sick about 19 days.* [Ledger 45, page 43]

Parker Everett from Grainger County. Offence: malicious stabbing. Sentence: five years. Received July 3, 1837. He is 46 years old, 5' 10" high, weighs 159 lbs, dark grey hair, yellowish black eyes, dark skin, heavy brow. Born in Maryland, bro[ugh]t up in East Tenn., Knox Co., 10 miles from Knoxville, at a place known by the name of Grassy Valley. Has had two wives, they are bo<u>a</u>th dead. He has two children at the Widow Thornburg's, Jefferson Co., near New Market. The other two are with his brother, Sylvanus[?] Everett in Knox Co., seven miles east of Knoxville. Has a scar above his right eye brow. A hatter by profession. Sentenced by the Circuit Court of Grainger Co., Tenn. [Ledger 45, page 43]

Enoch Estep from Bl[o]unt County. Offence: horse stealing. Sentence: five years. Rec'd Oct 15, 1837. He is 32 years old, 6' high, weighs 175 lbs., dark hair, haz<u>le</u> eyes, light beard. Born and bro[ugh]t up in Ash[e] Co., North Carolina. He has seven brothers and three sisters, six of which is married. They all live in the counties of Carter and Blount. His mother lives in Blount Co., within one mile of John Stratin's Mill. He has a wife and 4 children living in Carter Co., one-half mile north of Elizabeth[ton]. He has a small scar across his right eye brow, also one on the right side of the upper lip, his nose turns to the left. Sentenced by the Circuit Court of Bl[o]unt County [to] ----- [blank] years confinement <u>to</u> the Jail and Penitentiary House of the State of Tenn. [Ledger 45, page 43]

Squire Estep form Bl[o]unt County. Offence: horse stealing. Sentence: five years. Rec'd Oct. 15, 1837. He is 35 years old, 5' 7" high, weighs 175 lbs. Born and bro[ugh]t up in Ash[e] Co., North Carolina. Sentenced by the Circuit Court of Bl[o]unt County to five years confinement in the Jail and Penitentiary House of the State of Tenn. He has dark hair and eyes, ver<u>ry</u> heavy black beard and stutters a little, as rather a stoppage in his sp<u>ea</u>ch. [Ledger 45, page 44]

Harris Evans from Rhea County. Offence: malicious sta<u>b</u>ing. Sentence: two years from 11 Nov. 1837. Rec'd 17 Nov. 1837. He is 42 years old, 5' 6" high, weighs 150 lbs. Born in South Carolina, Pendleton County. Bro[ugh]t up in Knox Co., Tenn. He has dark grey hair, blue eyes, fair skin, black beard. Has a small scar in his right eye brow, one on his forehead, one on his nose. His right arm is the finger longer than the left arm, it was caused by white swelling. His father lives in Wrightsville, at the mouth of Iron[?] Creek, Roane Co. He has a wife and four children at his brother-in-law's, in White Co., Clayton McCormick[?], on Cane Creek, 12 miles from Sparta. Sentenced by the Circuit Court of Rhea County to two years confinement in the Jail and Penitentiary House of the State of Tenn. *Discharged Nov. 18, 1839. Conduct good.* [Ledger 45, page 44]

Wm. Edwards from Washington County. Offence: involuntary manslaughter. Sentence: one year. Rec'd 29 March 1838. He is 37 years old, 5' 5 ¼" high, weighs 109 lbs. He has dark grey hair, grey eyes, long nose, thin visage. Born in Granville Co., North Carolina. His mother, Delila Edwards, lives 4 miles from Jonesborough in Washington County, E. Tenn. He has generally followed farming. He has one brother, Drewry Edwards, living in West Tenn. on the waters of Forked Deer River. [Ledger 45, page 44]

Peyton Elkins from Knox County. Offence: grand larceny. Sentence: three years from 14 June 1838. Rec'd July 1, 1838. He is 36 years old, 5' 7" high, weighs 135 lbs. Born and bro[ugh]t up in Gra[i]nger Co., Tenn. Has a wife and four children in Knox Co., living on Sam'l Fraziers land, nine miles from Knoxville on the Beaver Crick Road. He has two brothers living in Hardeman Co., West Tenn., 10 miles from Boliver. He has dark hair, grey eyes and dark skin, has lost one of his front teeth. [Ledger 45, page 45]

Wm. Merrill alias Edwards. He is 16 years old, 5' 5" high, weighs 120 lbs. Born in Williamson Co. Brought up in Galloway, about 20 miles distant from the Tennessee River. Wm. Edwards is an illegitimate son of Kitty Edwards. She is now married to Merrill, who lives in Henry County 18 miles from Paris. They have 5 children living with them. He has light hair, blue eyes, fair complexion, a large scar on his left middle finger, also one on his left big toe. He is a common Labourer. The said, Wm. Mirrell was found guilty of stealing money and sentense to undergo confinement in the Jail and Penitentiary House of this State, commencing from the day of reception July 8, 1839, for three years. [Ledger 45, page 45]

Leonard Edins from White County. Rec'd Feb. 18, 1840. Sentence: two years. Offence: murder. He is 25 years old, 5' 10" high, weighs 162 lbs. Born in Smith Co., Tenn. Bro[ugh]t up in the Counties of White and Warren. His mother, Elizabeth Edins, lives in DeKalb Co., near the corner of said county, 12 miles west of Sparta, White County, where his wife and one child now is. His wife's name, before marriage, was Sarah Riggs. Said Edins has fair hair, blue eyes, and fair skin. Has a small scar ¾" long on his upper lip. The finger next the little finger of the right hand is crooked or half shut, caused by rising or fellon. [Ledger 45, page 45]

Cleveland Estep from Carter County. Sentence: three years from 20 March 1841. Rec'd March 20, 1841. He is 19 years old, 5' 7" high, weighs 146 lbs. Born in North Carolina, brought up in Tenn. He is an illegitimate child. His mother was Susan Estip, his father John Lane. His mother has also another child by a man named Ale'r Scott, but has since been married to a man named Wakeller[?], who is dead. She is now living on Stony Creek in Carter County. Said Estep has dark skin, blue eyes, black hair, stout made. [Ledger 45, page 46]

Daniel Estep from Carter County. Crime: grand larceny. Sentence: three years from 23 July 1841. Rec'd July 23, 1841. He is 40 years old, 5' 7" high, weighs 188 lbs. Born and brought up in Nash County, North Carolina. Has been married and has one child. His wife is dead, his son about 14 or 15 years old is at his grandfather's, Jesse Triplett's, in Wilk[e]s Co. near Wilksborough. Said Estep has dark grey hair, black eyes, dark skin, has had the left thumb of the left hand out of place, which still remains out. He has had three brothers convicted, two of whom are still in prison, their names are Squire, Enoch and William. [Ledger 45, page 46]

John Finley was received in the Penitentiary 12 Dec., 1831. He is 5' 8 1/2" high, 41 years old, weighs 157 lbs. Born and raised in Mecklenburg Co., North Carolina. Lived two years in Union District, South Carolina, Packolet River, where he married his wife, who was a Miss Garner, and where her relations now live. She has a brother near Farmington, Tenn. His wife is dead. He has six children in Bedford Co., Tenn., near Farmington. He has a half-brother (Richard White) in Union District, South Carolina. He has light thin hair, a little grey, fair skin, blue eyes, scar on the cap of the left knee, caused by the cut of an axe, round full face. Found guilty of petit larceny at the Circuit Court of Bedford County and sentenced to 12 months confinement in the Jail and Penitentiary House of the State of Tennessee. *John Finley was discharged 24 Feb. 1833. He was detained 74 days for bad conduct.* [Ledger 45, page 47]

Daniel Fulwood was received into the Penitentiary 11 June 1832. He is 5' 3 1/2" high, weighs 127 lbs. Born in Onslow Co., North Carolina. He has three uncles now living in Sumner Co., Tenn, also a grand father in Sumner Co. Their names air Binder. His mother is married to a man by the name of Brooks, now living in Nashville, Tenn. He is about 21 years old, has dark hair, grey eyes, round face and dark skin. Has a scar in the corner of the left eye, 3/4" in length. He has a mark on the right cheek about the size of a twenty five cent piece, it is darker than the rest of the skin. He has worked a short time at the tailoring business. Found guilty of petit larceny at the Circuit Court of Davidson County and sentenced to two years confinement in the Jail and Penitentiary House of the State of Tenn. *Daniel Fulwood was discharged by expiration of sentence June 11, 1834. His conduct was good.* [Ledger 45, page 47]

Tennessee Convicts: Records of the State Penitentiary

John Forgus was received in the Penitentiary on 21 April 1834. He is 5' 10" in height and weighs 185 lbs. Blue eyes, dark hair, tolerably fair complexion, heavy built and about 30 years of age. Born in Cabarras Co., North Carolina, and brought up in Union District, South Carolina. His parents reside in the State of Mississippi. He has an uncle, John Forgus, residing in Cabarras Co., North Carolina, at Kirksville Post Office on Toby's Creek. Forgus has a wife and two children, he has chiefly lived in Franklin and Muscogee Counties, Georgia, but supposes his wife has removed to Meriwether County. He has a scar on the inside of the middle finger of the left hand near the first joint, a small scar in the right eyebrow and a small scar near the corner of the right eye, about the shape and size of a grain of wheat. About the middle of the inside part of the arm, apparently caused from the breaking of a sinew, about 3" from the elbow. There appears to be a <u>wen</u> on the same arm. Two moles on the left side of the neck, one much lighter colour than the other. Three scars on the right leg, one just under the knee, and the other two on the shin, in a direct line with each other. A scar on the left leg, rather inside, below the cap of the knee, about an inch long. He has worked a short time as a house carpenter. Was found guilty of having and concealing counterfeit bank bills and sentenced to three years confinement in the Jail and Penitentiary House of the State of Tenn. *John Forgus was discharged May 6, 1837. Detained 15 days for breach of prison rules. Gave his shirt and pants to Henry Cook 14 Jan. 1837. Left a hat for Brandon.* [Ledger 45, page 47-48]

Wm. E. Felter, Davidson County, was received 7 June 1836. He is 25 years old, 5' 6 1/4" high and weighs 147 lbs. Full round face, slightly pitted with small pox, yellow eyes, dark hair, lower front tooth on the left side, broken off nearly even with the gum. A scar on the inside of the left arm, above the wrist, caused by a burn. Square, compass, pillars visible and arch scarcely visible and badly put on the left arm, on the inside of the elbow. The same on the right arm with the addition of the letter G and three burning tapers, below the elbow. A scar running from the jaw bone up to a mole on the right cheek bone. A small mole about an inch to the right of and level with the right corner of the mouth. Thick stout neck and well formed. A shoe and boot maker by trade. He has spent several months with Brown and others in their circus. His mother lives 9 1/2 miles from West Point in Newberg[h], Orange Co., New York. His brothers and sisters, two each, lives in Shenango County, New York. Found guilty of horse stealing and sentenced to hard labour in the Tennessee Penitentiary for the term of three years. *Wm. E. Felter was delivered to F.R.Rains, D. S. of Davidson County, 12 Dec. 1836. See order of the clerk 12 Dec. 1836. Filed with clerks transcripts 1836.* [Ledger 45, page 48]

Tennessee Convicts: Records of the State Penitentiary

William Felts from Roane County, Tennessee. Offence: petty larceny. Sentence: one year from 29 Oct. Was received Nov. 14, 1836. He is 36 years old, 5' 9" high, weighs 158 lbs. Dark hair, haz<u>el</u>e eyes, dark skin, heavy beard, full forehead, no scars. Born and raised in ~~Roane Co., Tenn.~~ Wilkes Co., North Carolina. Has a wife and children living in Roane Co., Tenn. *William Felts was discharged November 6, 1837. Conduct good.* [Ledger 45, page 48]

Joseph G. Fogg from Giles County, Tennessee. Offence: forgery. Sentence: three years. Was received January 20, 1837. He is 27 years old, 5' 5" high, fair skin, weighs 146 lbs., dark hair, dark blue eyes and fair skin. Born in Boston, Massachusetts, and raised in the District of Columbia. Learned the black smiths trade with Dan'l Hutchinson, in the city of Richmond, Virginia. Says he has been on the River several years and has traded with the fire King. [Ledger 45, page 49]

Ernando Frasier from Shelby County. Offence: horse stealing. Sentence: three years. Was received Jan. 21, 1838. He is 25 years old, 5', 8", weighs 165 lbs. Fair hair and skin, grey eyes, full face. He has had his left arm broke and it is crooked. He was born and brought up in Wake Co., North Carolina, 18 miles from Ra<u>w</u>leigh, where his mother now lives. He has one brother living in Natche<u>s</u>, a dry goods merchant. Has a sister, married to William James, living in Carrolton, Mississippi. [Ledger 45, pages 49 and 74]

Daniel Foust, sent from Anderson County. Was received into the Penitentiary July 20, 1839. He is about 55 or 60 years of age, 5', 6" high, weighs 160 lbs. Born in North Carolina, br<u>ot</u> up in Knox and Anderson counties. Has a wife and seven children living six miles from Clinton, on the Jacksboro Road. Offence: house burning. Has fair skin, grey eyes. He is a cooper, wheel and chair maker. Has one brother, Lewis Foust, living in Middle Tennessee. Sentence: two years at hard labour, in the Jail and Penitentiary House of this state from the date of his reception. *Pardoned by Governor Cannon September 25, 1839.* [Ledger 45, page 49]

Joseph Freeland was received in the Penitentiary 15 April 1840, from Hawkins County. He is 21 years old, 5' 9 $^{1}/_{2}$" high, weighs 158 lbs. Bornd and brought up in Orange Co., North Carolina, about 16 miles from Greensbor<u>ough</u>, where his mother, three sisters and two brothers now lives. He has fair hair and fair skin and blue eyes. A little inclined to be stoop shoulderd. Sentence: three years from the above date. He was found guilty of horse stealing. [Ledger 45, page 49]

Isaac Fullerton from McNairy County. Crime: larceny. Sentence: one year from January 12, 1842. Rec'd: January 12, 1842. He is 30 years old, 6' 4" in height, weight 186 lbs. Born near Hartford, Vermont, bro[ugh]t up in Pennsylvania 18 miles west of Pittsburg[h]. Has a wife and two children 18 miles n.w. of Purdy at her brother's by the name of Sam'l[?] Elkins. Said Fullerton has been a keel boat hand on the Ohio River for 10 or 11 years. Has dark hair, black eyes & skin off the same piece. [Ledger 45, p. 50]

James Foster from Bledsoe County. Crime: grand larceny. Sentence: five years from 15 July 1842. Rec'd: 15 July 1842. He is 27 years old, weighs 138 lbs., 5' 9" high. Born in Rhea and bro[ugh]t up in Bledsoe Co., Tenn. His mother Rachel Foster with two of her children now lives one mile from Pikeville in the last named county. He has seven sisters married and lives in the neighborhood of Pikeville. Their names are Walker, Lawson, Hart, Jones, Lawrence, Whitsell and Parker. Said Foster has dark hair, black eyes, dark skin. Has worked at the harness making business in Nashville with R. Savage. Has two hair moles in front of his left ear about one inch apart. Was in the Ky. Prison under the name of Robinson. [Ledger 45, p. 50]

James Gibbons was received in the Penitentiary August 1, 1831. He is 18 years of age, 6' high, common weight 155 lbs. Dark skin and hair, blue or gray eyes. A scar on the forefinger of the left hand and one on the thumb of the right hand. Two scars on the left knee and one on the great toe of the left foot. Also one on the instep of the right foot. Has a wife living with her father John Sarton [or Sorton?] near Dandridge, East Tenn. Was found guilty of passing base coin at the Circuit Court of Jefferson Co., and sentenced to three years imprisonment in the Jail and Penitentiary of the State of Tenn. Born in Jefferson Co., Tenn. *James Gibbins was discharged August 25, 1834. He was detained 25 days for violation of rules. His general conduct was good.* [Ledger 45, p. 53]

John Gill was received in the Penitentiary August 27, 1831. He is 6' 4 ½" high, 42 years of age, weighs 186 lbs. Born and brought up in Chester Co., South Carolina, where two of his brothers resides. Has an uncle living in Hardin Co., Tenn. Black hair, dark skin and blue eyes. A scar over each of his eyes. A number of scars between his left shoulder and breast is badly ruptured. Was found guilty at the Circuit Court of Giles County of an assault with the intent to kill and sentenced to three years imprisonment in the Jail and Penitentiary House of the State of Tenn. *Pardoned March 30, 1833. Conduct very good.* [Ledger 45, p. 53]

John J. Green was received in the Penitentiary 11 Nov. 1832. He is 22 years of age, 5' 9" in height, weighs 156 lbs. Dark hair & skin, grey eyes, heavy brow. Was born in With [Wythe] Co., Virginia, and brought up in Washington Co. in the same state. He has four brothers & one sister. His sister is married to John Moore in Washington Co., and an uncle living in With [Wythe] Co., Virginia, named Joseph Green. He has been residing at the Gold Mines in North Carolina. He likewise lived about two years in Sevier Co., Tenn., with one Augustus Lee, Tinner, having served an apprenticeship to that business in Abingdon, Virginia. He has a cut on the left side of the chin bone and a large scar on the left arm about 10" long running round the arm caused by a burn. One on the big toe of the left foot at the first joint. Was found guilty of stealing bacon at the Circuit Court of McMinn County & sentenced to two years confinement in the Jail and Penitentiary House of the State of Tenn. *John J. Green was discharged by expiration of sentence 1 Jan. 1835. He was detained 40 days for bad conduct.* [Ledger 45, p. 53]

Oliver Griffith was received in the Penitentiary on 31 Dec., 1832. He is 5' 4 1/2" in height, weighs 128 lbs. Auburn hair, blue eyes, fair skin, 31 years of age. Born in Baltimore County, State of Maryland, his relatives by the name of Lane live in Reestown[?], Maryland. Those by the name of Griffith reside in the city of Philadelphia. His left arm is marked with India ink as follows **OG with two stars above. There is a scar of an oblong shape on this arm between this mark & the wrist. He has served an apprenticeship to a Cabinet Maker in the City of Baltimore, likewise two sentences in State Prisons, one in Maryland & the other in Kentucky. He is a good loom & shuttle maker in fact a general Mechanic. Was found guilty of grand larceny at the Circuit Court of Shelby Co. and sentenced to four years & six months confinement in the Jail & Penitentiary House of the State of Tenn. *O. Griffith's coat, hat & vest were by his request given to Hiram Johnson on his discharge Nov. 18, 1834. Oliver Griffith was discharged Dec. 4, 1837, having served his sentence of four & a half years, and five months and three days for bad conduct.* [Ledger 45, p. 54]

Hamilton Gossett was received in the Penitentiary on 28 Oct. 1833. He is 5' 8 1/2" in height, weighs 168 lbs., blue eyes, light hair, fair complexion and pleasing countenance, 20 years of age. Born in Wilson Co. and brought up in Rutherford Co., Tenn. His parents live in Hickman Co., Tenn. He has three brothers and five sisters. They all reside in the neighborhood of his parents except one sister married to Henry Gossett and residing on Mill Creek near Capt. Bates's mill in Wilson Co., Tenn. He has a remarkable scar on the right side of the right foot caused by a cut from an axe. The end of the toe of the one next the great one is cut of[f]. A large scar on the instep of the left foot. A scar on the inside of the shin on the left leg. The little fingers of each hand are crooked, the left one more so than the other. He was found guilty of horse stealing at the Circuit Court of Rutherford County and sentenced to three years confinement in the Jail and Penitentiary House of the State of Tenn. *Hamilton Gosset was discharged 17 Nov. 1836, having served 20 days for breach of prison rules. Conduct generally good.* [Ledger 45, p. 54]

Robert Gollihorn was received in the Penitentiary August 18, 1834. He is 5' 4 ¼" in height and weighs 143 lbs. Black hair, grey eyes, dark complexion, black beard, about 33 years of age. Born in Buckingham Co., Virginia, and brought up in Jefferson Co., Tenn. His mother resides in Green[e] Co., Tenn., on the waters of Lick Creek about three miles from Perkins[?] mill and ten miles from the town of Greenville. He has a wife and six children in Blount Co. residing on Jere Hameltre's[?] land near the town of Morganton. Her maiden name was Massy, her father lives in Orleans, Orange Co., Indiana. He has a brother living in Cocke Co., Tenn., and another in Jackson Co., Illinois, and a sister in Arkansas named Smith. He has a scar on each knee at the lower part of the calf, the one on the right knee very perceivable from a cut from a drawing knife. One on the fore finger of the left hand just below the nail. He is a silversmith by trade. Was found guilty of counterfeiting coin at the Circuit Court of Blount County and sentenced to three years confinement in the Jail and Penitentiary House of the State of Tenn. *Robert Gollihorn discharged 23rd September 1837.* [Ledger 45, p. 54-55]

John Gage was received in the Penitentiary on 14 Oct. 1834. He is 5' 10" in height, and weighs 160 lbs. Light sandy hair, grey eyes and long face, beard heavy and very much mixed with grey hairs. He has a scar under the left eye which has a blue appearance and a remarkable one above the wright eye running paarallel with the eye-brow an inch in length, occasioned by a blow from a rock. Also a ccar on the thumb of the wright hand between the middle joint of the hand. Tolerable stout built, 46 years of age. Born in Rutherford Co., North Carolina, brought up in Warren Co., Kentucky, and moved when about 14 years old to Normans Settlement, Rutherford Co., Tenn. He married a Miss Maryan Arbaugh. His wife and eight children are now living near Purdy, McNairy Co., Tenn. His parents live in Hardy [sic,, Hardin?] Co., Tenn., and his wife's parents live in Arkansas Territory near Little Rock. He was found guilty of passing a counterfeit bank note at the Circuit Court of Perry County and sentenced to three years confinement in the Jail and Penitentiary House of the State of Tenn. *Died 14th March 1836.* [Ledger 45, p. 55]

Jeremiah George was rec'd in the Penitentiary on 28 May 1835. He is 17 years of age, 5' 6" high, and weighs 135 lbs. Black hair, grey eyes, fair complexion, square face. Second joint of the fore-finger of the left hand very much scarred. Labourer. Born in South Carolina and brought up, principally, in that state and the State of Tennessee. The residence of his father not known. His mother resides on Caney fork, two miles from Rock Island, in White Co., Tenn. An uncle (Cherry George) residing in Sparklingburg [*sic*,, Spartanburg] Co., South Carolina, seven miles from the Court House, on Pacolet river. He was found guilty of petit larceny at the Circuit Court of Monroe County and sentenced to four years' confinement in the Jail and Penitentiary House of the State of Tenn. [Ledger 45, p. 56]

John S. Gilbert was rec'd in the Penitentiary on 6 June 1835. He is 32 years of age, 5' 7 or 8" high, and weighs about 150 lbs. Blue eyes, fair complexion, fair hair, tolerable long sharp nose and good countenance. A scar on the underside of the right wrist, and one on, and one immediately above, the cap of the right knee. Born in North Carolina, has lived in East Tenn.; in Kentucky near the Crab-Orchard; on the waters of White river, state of Indiana; on Red river, near Cheak's Tavern, Sumner Co., Tenn.; on Swan creek, near Mt. Pleasant, Maury Co., Tenn., (where he worked three summers for Samuel Jennings); in Hardin Co., Tenn.; on Tennessee river in Lotterdale [*sic*,, Lauderdale] Co., Alabama; near Shannonsville, Perry Co., Tenn.; and in Henderson Co., Tenn., where he married Elizabeth Innman. He moved thence to Tipton Co., Tenn., on the north side of Hatchie river, near Durhamsville, at which place his wife died. He then returned to Henderson Co. amongst his relations, and married Mary Hart, daughter of Thos. Hart of that county. His wife and four children (one hers, and three by his first wife) are residing in the edge of Hardin Co., seven miles from Hawkin's Store, and four miles from Squire Cater's. Labourer. Found guilty of petit larceny at the Circuit Court of Hardin County and sentenced to one years' confinement in the Jail and Penitentiary house of the State of Tennessee, which sentence was confirmed by the Supreme Court held at the Court house of Hickman County at the June term for 1835. *John S. Gilbert was discharged 14 August 1836, detained 69 days for improper conduct.* [Ledger 45, p. 56]

James T. Gorham, convicted of burglary at the May term 1836 for Robertson County and sentenced to confinement in the Penitentiary for the term of five years from the 5 May, 1836. He is 18 years old, 5' 11 $1/4$" high, grey eyes, dark hair, common complexion, slender form, weighs 140 lbs. Large wrist and hand, hand unusually long. Has had a fellon on the ball of the left thumb which has left a scar dented in. A small scar on the forehead just above the nose. Two small bumps on the right buttock caused by a shot about 2 $1/2$" apart. Two small scars on the inside of the left knee and two above the cap of same knee, besides some other scars on each knee. A scar on the right arm just below the elbow 1" long, ½" broad. His father now lives in Springfield, Robertson Co., Tenn., where the s[ai]d James was born and raised. Has worked some at tanning. Has a sister who married a Mr. Braden with whom lives his younger brother learning the tailor's trade. His grandfather lives nine miles from Springfield, two miles from Suttles[?] Camp ground near the Kentucky line of the name of Gunn. Some uncles in the same neighborhood. His Grandfather Gorham did live four miles beyond Lexington, Kentucky. Has four uncles of the same name and in the same neighborhood, and one aunt, the widow Pearson, living at the 4 Mile House. One uncle, Thornton Gorham, living 12 miles from Indianapolis, Indiana. *James F. Gorham discharged, conduct generally good.* [Ledger 45, p. 57]

Isaac George, from McMinn County, for stealing bacon, was received August 20, 1836. Sentence three years from 4 Aug. 1836. He is 40 years old, 5' 11" high and weighs 175 lbs. Blue eyes, fair hair, dark complexion, a homely man [last remark is underlined]. Is a tolerable shoe maker. Was born and raised in Stokes Co., North Carolina. (No scars perceivable, has lost an upper front tooth.) Has lived in McMinn Co., has a wife and five children now there near Athens. *Isaac George discharge[d] August 6, 1839, having been detained two day[s]. Conduct generally good.* [Ledger 45, p. 57]

Richard Gaither, from Rutherford Co., Tenn. Offence: horse stealing. Sentence: three years. Was received Oct. 28, 1836. He is 23 years old, 5' 6" high, weighs 157 lbs. Light hair, blue eyes, rather dark skin, small face, no remarkable scars. Says his parents live in Madison Co., Alabama, where he was born and raised. *Richard Gaither was discharged on 28 Oct. 1839 by expiration of sentence. Conduct good.* [Ledger 45, p. 57]

Russell Goforth from Hamilton Co., Tenn. Offence: petty larceny. Sentence: one year. Was received Dec. 10, 1836. He is 37 years old, 5' 8 ½" high, weighs 145 lbs. Blue eyes, fair hair, dark skin. The wrist of the right arm has been put out of joint and now shows crooked. A small scar in the right brow. Was born in Barren Co., Kentucky, and raised in Sevier Co., Tenn. His father now lives in Jackson Co., Ohio. His wife and children live in Hamilton Co., Tenn. *Russell Goforth was discharged Dec. 10, 1837. Conduct good.* [Ledger 45, p. 58]

David Gawley from Gibson County. Offence: stabbing. Sentence: four years. Received July 10, 1837. He is 36 years of age, 5' 8" high, weighs 155 lbs., dark hair, black eyes, fair skin, rough features. Has a scar on his right hand running from the third finger into the hand. Born in South Carolina within 12 miles of Abbeville Court house. Served an apprenticeship to the tailoring business in Charlestown, South Carolina, with a man by the name of J. L. Roach. He has worked at his trade with McCutcheon in Murfreesboro, Tenn. Also with Thomas Taylor in Old Jefferson. He is a cripple in his left knee caused by a fall from a horse which nocked his knee cap on the out side of his knee. He has one uncle on Green River 14 miles from Bolingreen [Bowling Green], Kentucky. He has two brother near Gallatin in Sumner Co., Tenn. Also one brother in Gibson Co. (Jas. Gawley) lives four miles east of Trenton on the road leading from Trenton to Huntington. Was sentenced by the Circuit Court of Gibson County to four years confinement in the Jail and Penitentiary house of the State of Tenn. [Ledger 45, p. 58]

Wm. Gragson [or Grayson?] from Morgan County. Offence: [blank] Sentence: [blank]. He is 30 years old, 5' 8", weighs 137 lbs. Born in Ireland, bro[ugh]t up in Russle Co., North Carolina, where he served an apprenticeship to the tailoring business. He has a wife but no children. She is in Knox Co. 10 miles west of Knoxville with Dennis McCahin. He has a small scar on the middle joint of the fore finger. He has dark hair, hazle eyes, fair skin, heavy beard, has several moles on his breast. He has carried on the tailoring business in Newmarket in Jefferson Co., [and] Louisville, Bl[o]unt Co.. Sentenced by the Circuit Court of Morgan Co. to [blank] years confinement in the Jail and Penitentiary house of the State of Tenn. [Ledger 45, p. 58-9]

Levi Goens from Hamilton County. Offence: larceny. Sentence: three years from 30 March 1838. Recd. 4 Apr. 1838. He is 38 years of age, 6' ½" high, weighs 194 lbs., dark sandy hair, black eyes, Roman nose, well made. Born and bro[ugh]t up in Gra[i]nger Co., Tenn. He has a wife and five children in Hamilton Co. six miles east of Dallas near Robt. McCreath and Wm. Clift's mill. He has generally folloed farming but was once bound to the shoemaking [trade], but is not a proficient at the business. He has two visible scars in the left hand, the one nearest the rist forming a simicurcle [sic,]. He has also a scar on the bottom of his left foot caused from the cut of a drawing knife. [Ledger 45, p. 59]

George Gallimore from Roane County. Sentence: three years from 30 June. Rec'd July 8, 1838. He is 19 years old, weighs 130 lbs., 5' 8" high. Born and bro[ugh]t up in Roane Co., Tenn. His father and mother lives near Emerys gap on the Cumberland mountains. He has red hair, black eyes and dark skin. He has a mark of an ovel shape and brown colour on his right side about half way from the hip to the arm pit. Found guilty of a false token[?] for the purpose of obtaining articles illegally. [Ledger 45, p. 59]

Tennessee Convicts: Records of the State Penitentiary

Baylum M. Gillespie from Williamson County. Offence: horse stealing. Sentence: 7 years and 6 months. Rec'd July 20, 1838. He is 22 years old, 5' 8 ¼" high, weighs 148 lbs. Born in North Carolina, brought up in Maury Co., Tenn., near Mount Pleasant. His father Patrick Gillespie lives in Warren Co., Kentucky, eight miles from Franklin in Simpson [County]. He has five brothers and four sisters. One of his sisters is married to a man by the name of Joshua Pearce and lives near her father. He has a wife and two children living with her uncle in Lawrence Co. seven miles from Lawrenceburg. Her uncls name is James Kelly. He has a grist mill and distilery on Big Creek. He has sandy hair, dark eyes with heavy brows and bad countenance. He has a small scar on the rist of the right hand caused by his rist being broke. Also a scar on the inside of the left hand. [Ledger 45, p. 60]

Joseph B. Gilbert from Warren County. Offence: murder. Sentence: 2 years. Rec'd Dec. 31, 1838. He is 17 years old, weighs 150 lbs., 5' 7" high. Born in Virginia, bro[ugh]t up in McMinn [County], Tenn. He has dark hair, black eyes, dark skin, good countenance. Has lost one of his upper teeth. Has a cut on the left leg directly above the ancle say 2" or 3" long. Has a small scar on the big toe of the left foot. A farmer. *Pardoned by Governor Polk, January 29, 1840.* [Ledger 45, p. 60]

James W. Gray from McMinn County. Was received into the Penitentiary July 4, 1839. He is 50 years old, weighs 204 lbs., 5' 11 ¾" high. Has dark grey hair, hazle eyes, rough features. Has a scar on his left chin cut, he says, by a stone pitcher. Has had his wright leg broken just above his ankle which makes it shorter than the other and leaves a large scar. It was broken by a man named Arthur Henry[?] in Randolph Co., Alabama. He has a wife and six children living in McMinn Co. two miles east of Calhoun. He has two half-brothers by the name of Wolfe living in the same neighborhood. Has lost the first joint off the fore finger of the right hand. Has worked at shoe making business and blacksmithing but generally followed farming. His wife lives on Wolfe[?] land. Sentence: three years. Crime: felony. [Ledger 45, p. 60]

Benjamin F. Glanton from Tipton County. He is 18 years old, 5' 10" high, weighs 136 lbs. Born in South Carolina, Abbeville District. Bro[ugh]t up in the counties of Giles and Tipton, Tenn. His mother Margaret, who has married a man by the name of Roddey, who lives in Jackson Co., Arkansas, about 25 miles south of Elizabethtown. He has fair hair, fair skin, blue eyes. He is slightly crosseyed. Offence: horse stealing. Sentence: three years. Rec'd Oct. 26, 1839. [Ledger 45, p. 61]

Tennessee Convicts: Records of the State Penitentiary

James R. Gray from McMinn County. Crime: felony. Sentence: three years from 16 April 1840. Received 26 April 1840. He is 18 years old, 5' 10" high, weighs 154 lbs. Born in Hall Co., Georgia. Brought up in McMinn Co., Tenn., one mile from Calhoun where his father Jeremiah Gray now lives. Said Gray has two brothers and two sisters at his father's. He has fair hair, hazle eyes, dark skin, cross eye'd. The little finger and the one next to it in the right hand is crooked. He has a small scar below the corner of the left eye. Has some uncles by the name of Jones (James M. and W. Jones) in Overton Co.. [Ledger 45, p. 61]

James Grooms from Shelby County. Crime: grand larceny. Sentence: three years from 16 June 1840. Rec'd 16 June 1840. He is supposed to be 75 or 80 years old, 6' high, weighs 144 lbs. Born and brought up in Charleston, South Carolina, has a wife in Ringley, Shelby Co., Tenn. Said Grooms has fair hair, black eyes and fair skin. [Ledger 45, p. 61]

James Graham from Jefferson County. Crime: felony. Sentence: three years from 25 Dec. 1840. Rec'd 11 Jany. 1841. He is 20 years old, weighs 165 lbs., 5' 9" high. Born in South Carolina, brought up in Jefferson Co., East Tenn., on the waters of Beaver Creek, 13 miles north of Dandridge. He has three brothers and two sisters at home with his father. One sister married to a man by the name of Thos. Wilson some where in Virginia. Has three uncles at the foot of Cumberland mountain where the turnpike road crosses. [Ledger 45, p. 62]

David George from Davidson County. Crime: horse stealing. Sentence: four years from 29 May 1841. Rec'd 17 June 1841. He is 25 years old, 5' 8" high, weighs 159 lbs. Born in South Carolina, brought up in Louisiana. He has belonged to three men by the names of Howard, Hughes and Allnut. He run off from them and has since been living as a free man. He says he was born free, is a bright mulatto and a smart boy. Has a wife living in Wilson Co. on Sugar Creek 12 miles this side of Lebanon. Has followed the River in the capacity of cook, has been on the *Josiah Nichol*, left her last Christmas. [Ledger 45, p. 62]

William Goff from Bledsoe County. Crime: passing counterfeit money. Sentence: three years from 16 July 1841. Rec'd 23 July 1841. He is 46 years old, 5' 9" high, weighs 149 lbs. Born in Henry Co., Virginia, brought up in Roane Co., Tenn. His father Ambrose Goff lives in Bledsoe Co., Tenn., 5 ½ miles from Pikeville on the road leading to Sparta. He has a wife and six children in the same settlement with his father. His wife was the daughter of Tho. Wollen of White Co. He says he owns a farm of his own on which his wife lives. He has three sons that are near men grown, they are at home with their mother. He has dark hair, blue eyes, dark skin. He has a small scar on the side of the nose and upper lip. [Ledger 45, p. 62]

Thomas Gaddys from Overton County. Crime: petit larceny. Sentence: one year from 11 March 1842. Rec'd 10 Mar. 1842. He is 19 years old, 6' 1" high, weighs 177 lbs. Born in White Co., brought up in Overton Co.. He has a wife and one child in Jackson Co. at her (Temperance Hicks) mother's about ½ mile from Whitaker's mill on Roring River. His father, Wm. Gaddys, lives in Overton Co. on the Hurrican fork of Spring Creek. [Ledger 45, p. 63]

Thomas Haines was received in the Penitentiary 6 Oct. 1831. He is 5' 11" high, weighs 151 lbs., and is 41 years of age. Fair skin, dark hair, blue eyes and grey beard. He was born in Washington Co., Virginia, and brought up in Jefferson Co., Tenn. His wife lives in Rhea Co. with Jeremiah Haines on Muddy Creek near Rogers Mill on Pine Creek. His father now lives in E -- [blank] Co., Indiana. He has a scar on the left ear which was cut through and has grown together. Found guilty of petit larceny at the Circuit Court of Rhea County and sentenced to one years imprisonment in the Jail and Penitentiary house of the State of Tenn. *Thomas Haines was discharged by expiration of sentence on 6 Oct. 1832. His conduct was good.* [Ledger 45, p. 65]

John W. Hill was received into the Penitentiary 28 Dec. 1831. He is 27 years old, 5' 11 ½" high, weighs 188 lbs., has fair hair and skin and blue eyes. He has a scar on the ball of the thumb of the left hand caused by a cut, and some small scars on the fingers of the same hand. A scar on the instep of the right foot, near the leg, and one on the foot near the toes running from the large toe across the foot extending to two or three toes. He is by profession a cabinet maker. He was born and brought up in Adams Co., State of Ohio, near West Union on the waters of Eagle Creek. His mother now lives near Foster's Mill in the same neighborhood. He has one brother traveling and working at the business. Found guilty at the Circuit Court of Fayette Co. for breaking open the Jail and letting out one James Powel who [was] confined therein on a charge of murder, and sentenced to five years confinement in the Jail and Penitentiary house of the State of Tenn. *John W. Hill discharged 28 Dec. 1836. Conduct good.* [Ledger 45, p. 65]

John B. Howard was received into the penitentiary April 16, 1832. He is 31 years old, 5' 10 ½" high, weight 206 lbs. Fair hair, hazle eyes and tolerable fair skin, pail [sic,] complexion. Born in the state of Georgia, brought up in Allen Co., Kentucky. Lives now in Gibson Co., Tenn., where he has a wife and four children. His father-in-law lives in Allen Co., Kentucky, where he was married to a Miss Pilchford. Her father lives in Allen Co. on Long creek six miles from Scottsville. All his relations live in the same county. He has a scar on the right foot caused by a cut with an axe rather between the large and second toes. He has also a cut just below the inside of the left ancle bone, about 2" long. He has no trade but has worked at the blacksmith's business a little. He was found guilty of grand larceny at the Circuit Court of Robinson [sic,, Robertson?] County and sentenced to four years confinement at hard labour in the Jail and Penitentiary house of the State of Tenn. *John B. Howard was discharged 7 July 1836. Detained 82 days for bad conduct.* [Ledger 45, p. 65]

George Herndon was received into the Penitentiary 23 July 1832. He is 5' 6 1/2" in height and weighs 122 lbs. 37 years of age, grey hair, grey hollow eyes, short face and light beard. Born in Pittsylvania Co., Virginia, where his father, mother, brother and two sisters now reside. Has lived in Lincoln Co., Tenn., for the last five or six years where his family now lives, consisting of a wife and eight children. He has a scar on the forehead directly over the nose. The forefinger of his right hand has been broken. Has no trade, generally worked at farming. Was found guilty of altering a cotton receipt and sentenced at the Circuit Court of Franklin County to three years confinement in the Jail and Penitentiary House of the State of Tenn. *George Herndon was discharged by expiration of sentence, on 22 July 1835, conduct good.* [Ledger 45, p. 66]

Henry Horn was received in the Penitentiary on 22 Oct. 1832. He is 5' 9 1/2" in height and weighs 147 lbs. Light hair, blue eyes, dark complexion, 17 years of age. Born in the State of Georgia, brought up in Smith Co., Tenn., where his mother now lives within four miles of Liberty and near Fite's Mill on Smith's fork of Cumberland River. She is married to a man by the name of Ethridge, Horn being the only child by her first marriage. He has a scar a little below the elbow of the left arm, one on the middle joint of the fore finger of the left hand making a knot, a small one on the back of the wrist of the right hand, one on the shin of the right leg about 6" below the knee cap, one on the left leg of a similar appearance just below the cap of the knee on the left side, a mole on the left eyebrow and a small scar between the corner of the left eye and nose. Was found guilty of stealing a $5 bank bill at the Circuit Court of Smith County and sentenced to three years confinement in the Jail and Penitentiary House of the State of Tennessee. *Henry Horn was discharged 24 Feb. 1836, having been detained 125 days for bad conduct.* [Ledger 45, p. 66]

Robert Hare was received in the Penitentiary on 7 Dec. 1832. He is 5' 9" in height and weighs 201 lbs. Dark hair, light blue eyes, fair complexion, 21 years of age. Born in Barren Co., Kentucky, and brought up in Giles Co., Tenn., where his father now resides about 1 1/4 miles from Cornersville on the road to Pulaski. He has two uncles living in Barren Co., Kentucky, by the name of Charles and Alexander Coulter. He married a Miss Smith who is at present living with her mother in Warren Co. four and [one] half miles from McMinnville on the road leading to Sparta about one and a half miles from Roland's Mill. He has a scar on the under part of the nose caused by a bite, one on the middle finger of the right hand, one on the fore finger of the left hand where the finger joins the hand, a small one on the first joint of the great toe on the right foot, and one across the cap of the left knee. He has generally followed farming. Was found guilty of horse stealing at the Circuit Court of Bedford County and sentenced to three years and six months confinement in the Jail and Penitentiary House of the State of Tennessee. *Rob't Hare was discharged 18 June 1836, conduct good.* [Ledger 45, p. 66-67]

Redding R. Hall was received into the Penitentiary 8 Jan. 1833. He is 6' in height, weighs one hundred and [blank] lbs. Dark hair, hazel eyes, dark complexion, 38 years of age. Born in Pendleton Co., South Carolina, near Pearce's ford on Saluda river. He has a wife and four children living in Crittendon Co., Arkansas. His wife's maiden name was Tafflestreet whose connexions reside in Allen Co., Kentucky. His brother Carter T[?] Hall live[s] near Gallatin, Tennessee. He has a scar on the inside of the nose near the right eye caused by a blow from a stick, a scar just above the wrist of the left arm, and one very near this rather on the outside of the arm, one on the outside of the right foot about three inches in length caused by a cut from an axe, a dimple on his chin. He has generally followed farming. Was found guilty of passing counterfeit bank bills at the Circuit Court of Tipton County and sentenced to three years confinement in the Jail and Penitentiary House of the State of Tennessee. *Redding R. Hall died of Cholera on the 14th day of June, 1833.* [Ledger 45, p. 67]

William Hamilton was received 10 Apr. 1833. He is 5' 10 ¼" in height and weighs 170 lbs. Light hair, hazel eyes, fair complexion, well formed, 29 years of age. Born in Columbia in the State of Georgia and brought up there. He has two sisters living there, one married to Marmaduke Mendenhall and one to Jacob Thompson. He has a scar on the ball of the thumb of the right hand and one on the left hand near the wrist, one on the left cheek, one over the left eyebrow, one on the instep of the right foot running from the second toe up the foot. The nail of the great toe of the right foot has been split open. A cabinet maker by trade. Was found guilty at the Rutherford [County] Circuit Court of passing counterfeit money and sentenced to three years confinement in the Jail and Penitentiary House of the State of Tennessee. *Wm. Hamilton was discharged 6 Sept. 1836, detained 149 days for bad conduct.* [Ledger 45, p. 67-8]

Tennessee Convicts: Records of the State Penitentiary

Richard Hankins was received in the Penitentiary 5 June 1834. He is 5' 9 ½" in height and weighs 168 lbs. Dark hair, blue eyes, broad face, large nose, thin beard, tolerably fair complexion, 34 years of age. Born in Jefferson Co., Tenn., and brought up there. His parents still reside there on Holstein [Holston] river about two miles from Richland Meeting House near Robin Stouts[?] mill. Hankins has five children, four by his first wife and one by his present wife who is his niece, the daughter of Thomas Nations[?] who resides on Babb Creek in Monroe Co.. He has a scar on the inside of the wrist on the right arm caused by a bite, a scar on the left arm about 2 ½" long, the large part downward, not far from the wrist, caused by a cut in getting corn tops[?]. A scar on the end of the ball of the thumb of the left hand, a mole on the outside of the right arm about 3" from the wrist, and one on the right side of the nose. When employed has worked at farming. Was found guilty of incest at the Circuit Court of Monroe County and sentenced to five years confinement in the Jail and Penitentiary House of the State of Tennessee. *Pardoned.* [Ledger 45, p. 68]

James Harris was received in the Penitentiary on 7 Nov. 1834. He is 35 years of age, 5' 10" high, and weighs 178 lbs. Blue eyes, fair hair, fair complexion, large full round face and stout built. A scar on the forehead just above the right eye, beard tolerable heavy but lays principally under his chin. He was born in Lancaster Co., Pennsylvania, where he was brought up, and served an apprenticeship at the blacksmith's business, which has since been his occupation. Was married in Pulaski, Tenn., to a Miss Charlotte Morris. Resided and carried on the blacksmith's business for some time in Florence, Alabama, and afterwards carried on the business in Rogersville, Lotterdale [*sic*,, Lauderdale] Co., Alabama. He expects his wife and two children are now residing in the neighborhood of the same place with her sisters. He was found guilty of grand larceny at the Circuit Court of Murry [*sic*,, Maury] Co. and sentenced to three years confinement in the Jail and Penitentiary House of the State of Tennessee. *James Harris died of Cholera on the 1st day of July, 1835.* [Ledger 45, p. 68-9]

Hugh Hoy was received in the Penitentiary 1 July 1835. He is 35 years of age, 5' 7" or 8" high, who weighs 174 lbs. Black hair, heavy black beard and blue eyes. A small scar on the forehead just above the root of his nose; one about an inch below the left eye; one of the edge of the palm of the left hand near the wrist; a large one about 2" below the elbow on the right arm; a small one just above the elbow on the same arm, and one about 2" in length running from the edge of the back of the right hand to the joint of the wrist. By trade a baker. Born and brought up in Entram Co., in the north of Ireland. Wife and children residing in York, Upper Canada. He was found guilty of grand larceny at the

Circuit Court of Shelby County and sentenced to three years confinement in the Jail and Penitentiary House of the State of Tennessee. *Hugh Hoy was discharged 20 Sept. 1838, being detained two months and twenty days for misconduct.* [Ledger 45, p. 69]

Jacob K. Horton was received in the Penitentiary on 20 July 1835. He is 31 years of age, 5' 10 or 11" high, and weighs about 170 or 180 lbs. Dark hair, blue eyes and thin beard. Left hand very much scar[r]ed with small scars; a scar about an inch in length running across the left arm, half way between the elbow and the wrist. By trade a gun smith. Born and brought up in Cincinnati, Ohio, where his mother, Margaret Horton, a brother-in-law, James Saffarans, who, he says, is Marshall of that City, and two other brothers-in-law, Charles C. Ross and Benjamin Smith, now reside. He has a brother living in Limestone Co., Alabama, named Andrew P. Horton. He was found guilty of grand larceny at the Circuit Court of Carroll County and sentenced to three years confinement in the Jail and Penitentiary House of the State of Tennessee. *Discharged Oct. 16th, 1838. Detained 86 days for misconduct.* [Ledger 45, p. 69]

Robert Henderson was received in the Penitentiary on 30 Aug. 1835. He is 21 years of age, 5' 5" in height, and weighs 142 lbs. Fair hair, blue eyes, short forehead, swarthy complexion, stout built. Thick short small hand and remarkably short fingers. A scar on the fore finger of the left hand, between the first and second joint. A small scar between the thumb and fore finger of the same hand. A mole just under the left ear, about an inch distant from it. His left shoulder has been mashed or injured, which seems to have enlarged it, it now projects somewhat farther than the right shoulder. He says it was occasioned by an accidental fall of a rock, in blasting. Labourer. Born in Washington Co., Pennsylvania, and brought up in Jefferson Co., Kentucky. His father, John Henderson, resides in Jefferson Co., Kentucky, 3 miles from the mouth of Salt River, on the road leading therefrom to Louisville. Two uncles residing in Jefferson Co., Kentucky, of the name of Henderson, namely, Hamilton Henderson residing about five miles and Henry Henderson residing about nine miles from the said John Henderson's. He says that Doct'r Jacob Allen of Louisville is his Grandfather. He married Elizabeth Williams, daughter of James Williams, who resides about seven miles from Lawrenceburg, Lawrence Co., Tenn. He was found guilty of grand larceny at the Circuit Court of Lawrence County and sentenced to four years and six months confinement in the Jail and Penitentiary House of the State of Tennessee. *Discharged 2 March 1840. Conduct exceptional.* [Ledger 45, page 70]

Tennessee Convicts: Records of the State Penitentiary

Jones Humes was received in the Penitentiary on 5 September 1835. He was born and raised in Grainger Co., Tenn., and raised principally to farming, but has worked a little at the tailoring business. He is 5' 10 ½" high, aged about 21 years. Of a yellow complexion, short round face, wide mouth. A large scar on his right foot, beginning at the little toe and running to the ancle bone, weighs [blank] lbs. His mother, brother, and sister live in Grainger County, near Lee's Mill on Richland Creek, one-half mile from Esqr. Campbell, on the road leading from Knoxville to Blains[?]. He was found guilty of petit larceny at the August term 1835 of the Circuit Court of Knox County and sentenced to undergo confinement in the Jail and Penitentiary House of the State of Tennessee for 1 year. *Jones Humes was discharged 11 October 1836 by expiration of sentence. Detained 25 days for bad conduct.* [Ledger 45, page 70]

Moses Tredway Hopkins was received in the Penitentiary 21 Sept. 1835. He was born in Buckingham Co., Virginia. Served an apprenticeship to the wagon making business with Genl. William Simpson in Newbern, Virginia. He lived some years in North Carolina and has been living in this state about three, in Carter County, with Col. James N[?] Taylor, about five months at Bells Forge on Harpeth River. Worked a short time at Bartons Creek Forge for Massly[?] & Taylor in Hickman County, where his wife "departed this life." He is 45 years of age, 5' 5 ½" and weighs 135 lbs. Black hair, beard and eyes and dark skin, thin visage and eyes sunk considerably in his head. Has lost one fore and several jaw teeth. A scar on his chin occasioned by the kick of a horse. He has a son two years old living with a Mr. Gamble, near Anthony Vanleers Furnace in Hickman County. He is a cousin of Christopher Brooks of Nashville and of William Brooks, an innkeeper on the Nashville & Murfreesborough Turnpike, about 11 miles from Nashville. He was found guilty of horse stealing at the Sept. term of the Hickman County Circuit Court and sentenced to eight years and six months confinement in the Jail and Penitentiary House of the State of Tennessee. [Ledger 45, page 71]

Mizay Hazlett convicted at the Circuit Court of Davidson County "of having received stolen goods knowing them to have been stolen" and sentenced to three years confinement in the Jail and Penitentiary House of the State of Tennessee, was received in the Penitentiary 16 Dec. 1835. He was born in [blank] County, South Carolina and bred a shoe and boot maker in Nashville, Tenn., where his mother, one brother, a sister and his wife (Nancy, daughter of [blank] Duprice[?], near Kimbro's Store, Rutherford Co., Tenn.) now reside. His sister is the wife of Richard Mchord [McChord?] a carpenter, in Nashville. He is 25 years old, 5' 8 ½" high and weighs 151 lbs. Hazle eyes, dark hair and common complexion. He has a large scar in the middle of his left jaw, one on his third finger right hand, several on his forehead, one on his left temple bone, a scar on his left knee cap and a large scar, occasioned by the bite of a dog, on his right thigh, remarkably clear of scars. He has a brother in Texas and one somewhere in the "Western District." *Mizay Hazlett was discharged Dec. 17, 1838.* [Ledger 45, page 71]

Patrick Hare [also written Here] convicted of grand larceny at the Williamson County Circuit Court March term and sentenced to three years confinement in the Penitentiary of Tenn. from 11 April 1836. He is 5' 3 ¼" high, stout built, weighs [blank] lbs. Dark hair and beard, light complexion, large blue eyes, heavy brows, large ears, thick lips, a small scar over the left eyebrow, has lost one upper front tooth. Figures and hierogliphicks on the right arm, [thus?] **60055** [drawing shows a house with a **G** inside and a Masonic symbol below, with the letters **P H** underneath]. And on the left arm, the representation of a horse and rider - below the horse **S K W**, and below the elbow, a ladder, level and a star with long rays. Says he was born in Ireland and has the a little of the brogue. Further states he has a family living in Hopkinsville, Kentucky, say[s] a wife and three children. Has brothers and sisters living in Philadelphia, Pennsylvania. *Patrick Hare was discharged by expiration of sentence after being detained 40 days for breach of prison rules.* [Ledger 45, pages 71-72]

Nimrod Hooper from Shelby County. Offence: negro stealing. Sentence: 15 years. Was received 16 Nov. 1836. He is 49 years old, 5' 8" high, weighs 155 lbs. Has blue eyes, dark hair, sandy beard, good countenance, full chest. His right hand was caught in a mill wheel and left some scars. Two large scars on the right leg, from biles [*sic,*]. A bullet passed into his right arm, just below the elbow and remains in the lower part of the arm, where it can be seen and felt. Also a small scar on the same arm, up and down the arm. He was born and raised in Davidson Co., Tenn., on Whites Creek. Wife dead, children lives in this county. [Ledger 45, page 72]

Thomas Hudson from Bedford County. Offence: burglary and larceny. Sentence: three years. Was received Dec. 12, 1836. He is 18 years old, 5' 9" high, weighs 145 lbs. Has black hair, grey eyes and dark skin. A scar on the outside of the right leg, half way between the knee and the ancle. A scar on the back of the left leg near the ham. Born and raised in Maury Co., Tenn. His father and mother now live in Bedford County. *Thomas Hudson pardoned November 8, 1838. Conduct very good.* [Ledger 45, page 72]

Samuel Halliday from Tipton County. Offence: voluntary manslaughter. Sentence: five years. Was received March 6, 1837. He is 37 years old, 5' 6" high and weighs 120 lbs. Has dark hair, hazle eyes, small features, nose

Tennessee Convicts: Records of the State Penitentiary

inclines to the right. Born in Greene County, North Carolina. His family lives in Tipton County, three miles from Covington east. *Samuel Holliday was pardoned July 8, 1839, by N. Cannon.* [Ledger 45, page 72]

Isaac Hamilton from Lawrence Co., Tenn. Crime: rape and incest. Sentence: seven years and six months. Was received March 19, 1837. He is 50 years old, 5' 7 1/2" high, and weighs 158 lbs. Has dark hair, grey eyes, fair skin, bad teeth, which injures his speech. A scar on the finger next the little one of the left hand, an inch long. The little finger of the right hand has been broken or crooked at the last joint. His family lives in Lawrence Co., Tenn., 10 miles from Lawrenceburgh on Sugar Creek. [Ledger 45, page 72 and 73]

Wm. Grayson [Gragson?] from Morgan County. Offence: malicious Stabbing. Sentence: five years from 22 Nov. 1837. Received Nov. 29, 1837. He is 30 years of age, 5' 8" high, weighs 137 [lbs]. Born in Ireland, brought up in Raughleigh, North Carolina. He has dark hair, hazle eyes, fair skin, heavy beard and has several moles on his breast. He has a wife, but no children. She is living with her father, Dennis McChaughin[?] 10 miles west of Knoxville in Knox Co. He has a scar on the midle joint of the fore finger, also a small scar across his forehead. Is a tailor by proffession and has carried on the tailoring business in New Market in Jefferson County and Louisville in Bl[o]unt counties Tenn. [Ledger 45, page 73]

Joseph Hullett from Sumner County. Offence: grand larceny. Received 25 Oct. 1837. Sentence: three years from 25 Oct. 1837. He is 23 years old, 5' 10", weighs 147 lbs. Has the scald head, light hair, blue eyes, fair skin. His father, William Hullett, lives on Whites Creek, about two miles above McGavock's Mill. Sentenced by the Circuit Court of Sumner County to [blank] year confinement in the Jail and Penitentiary House of the State of Tennessee. *Pardoned by Governor Polk, September 3, 1840. Conduct Good.* [Ledger 45, page 73]

James Henry from Bl[o]unt County. Offence: grand larceny. Received 2 Nov. [1837]. Sentence: three years and six months from 31 Oct. 1837. He is 31 years old, 5' 6" high, weighs 135 lbs. Has dark hair, hazle eyes, dark skin, verry heavy beard. Born in Lincoln Co., North Carolina. Bro't up in Bl[o]unt Co., Tenn., on the waters of Nine Mile Creek three miles from Dan'l Boss Mill and two from John Henry Mill, where his father now lives. He has had a wife, she is dead and left two children, who are with their grandfather, Matthew Cooper, in Spartanburg Co., South Carolina. He has a scar on the ancle bone of the right foot 1 1/2" long. [Ledger 45, page 73]

55

Tennessee Convicts: Records of the State Penitentiary

Sterling Hindman from Perry County. Offence: larceny. Sentence: three years. Received Dec. 13, 1837. He is 23 years old, 5' 7 ½" high, weighs 131 lbs. Red hair, blue eyes, fair skin, thin visage. Has a small scar in the edge of each eyebrow, he says caused by buckshot at the battle of St. Jacinto in Texes. Born and bro't up in the state of New York, Dutchess County. Has acted as clerk for Ezra Scofield, White & Co. Has followed sc[h]oolteaching in Tenn. Was found guilty and sentenced by the Circuit Court of Perry County, to three years confinement in the Jail and Penitentiary House of the State of Tennessee. [Ledger 45, page 74]

Blake Huskey from Shelby County. Offence: arson. Received Jan. 21,1838. Sentence: four years, five months. He is 32 years old, 5' 10" high, weighs 175 lbs. Born and brought up in Brumsey [sic,, Brunswick?] Co., Virginia. Has a wife and seven children near Morning Sun Post Office, Shelby County. Has one brother living in Brumsey[?] Co., Virginia. He has fair hair, blue eyes, heavy eyebrows, sleepy look. Has a small scar on the cap of the left knee. Has worked at the mill [w]right business, but not a professed workman. [Ledger 45, page 74]

John Huffman from Fayette County. Offence: horse Stealing. Received January 26, 1838. Sentence: three years. He is 19 years old, 5' 10" high, weighs 156 lbs. He was born in Pittsylvania Co., Virginia. He has black hair, grey eyes, good countena[n]ce. He has a small scar on the inside of the left leg, between the knee and ancle. His father, Michael Huffman, lives in Carroll Co., Tenn., nine miles from Huntington, on the Rosses Ferry Road. He has seven sisters and six brothers, all single but one, she is married to Tho's Bates and lives on her fathers plantation. [Ledger 45, page 74]

Thomas K. Henson from Perry County. Offence: murder or voluntary manslaughter. Sentence: four years. Received April 10, 1838. He is 30 years old, 5' 8" high, weighs 157 lbs. Born and bro't up in Jackson Co., Tenn. He has a small scar near the corner of the left eyebrow, also one in edge of the hair of the right. He has dark hair, blue eyes and fair skin. His father, Samuel Henson, lives in Giles Co., Tenn. He has seven brothers and eight sisters. They are all married, two in Illinois, near the Saline Lick. His wife and six children are living in Lauderdale Co., Alabama, 15 miles below Florence, near Colberts Reserve. His left arm has been out of joint at the elbow. He also has some scars on the right hand. He has worked at the blacksmiths trade and has foll[ow]ed pegg[?] shoe making. [Ledger 45, page 75]

Caleb Holley from Rutherford County. Offence: petit larceny and receiving stolen goods. Sentence: three years from 6 July 1838. Received July 16, 1838.

Tennessee Convicts: Records of the State Penitentiary

He is 27 years old, 5' 7" high, weighs 142 lbs. Born and bro't up in North Carolina, Granville County. He is a bright Molatto [sic,]. His wife and three children lives in Williamson Co., Tenn., on Wayne Murphys land. He has the end of his fore finger of the left hand mashed, which disfigures it. Has worked at the shoe making business. Also a scar on the top of the right foot, caused by the cut of an ax. [Ledger 45, page 75]

Charles J. Donald from Hamilton County. Sentence one year from 30 Nov. 1838. Offence: petit larceny. Received December 7, 1838. He is 22 years old. [No further information.] [Ledger 45, page 75]

William Hearvy[?] from Monroe County. Sentenced: four years. Received Sept. 21, 1838. Offence: horse stealing. He is 32 years old, 5' 9" high, weighs 173 lbs. Born and bro't up in Washington Co., Tenn. His father, Geo. C. Hearvy[?], is living in Bradley Co., four miles from Cleveland, on the old Alabama Road. He has a wife and six children living in Bl[o]unt Co., on the Shaws Ferry Road seven miles from Merryville. Has five brothers, two in Washington Co., three living near his father. He has dark hair, blue eyes, dark skin. Has had the lower part of his right ear bit off, the left bit so as to leave scars. He has a scar over the right eye in the edge of the hair, a small scar under the chin. [Ledger 45, page 76]

Thomas Howerton[?] from Cannon County. Offence: manslaughter. Sentence: three years. Sentence confirmed by the Court of Appeals. Received Dec. 20, 1838. He is 28 years old, 5' 8" high, weighs 156 lbs. He has dark hair, blue eyes, fair skin. Was born in Buckingham County, Virginia. Bro't up in Gilford Co., North Carolina. He has a wife and six children living in Cannon Co., Tenn., 15 miles from McMinnville, on the road leading to Murfreesboro. Has a large scar on each shin bone caused by a white swelling. The toe next the little toe of the right foot has the nale [sic,] nail cut off of it. [Ledger 45, page 76]

Henry Hood from McMinn County. He is 19 years old, weighs 152 lbs, 5' 9" high, dark hair, hazel eyes, fair skin. Born and bro't up in Roane Co., Tenn. He has a wife, living in Monroe Co., with her mother and step father, John Morris, on Natchez Creek, three miles south of Madisonville. Also one brother, married and living in Knox County, three miles south of Knoxville. Received 28 Dec. 1838. Offence: felony. Sentence: three years from 17 Dec. 1838. *Hood gave his overcoat to Richard Trimble on his discharge.* [Ledger 45, page 76]

Tennessee Convicts: Records of the State Penitentiary

Thompson Jones was received in the Penitentiary 24 Dec. 1831. He is 55 years old, 5' 7 ½" high, weighs 175 lbs. Black eyes, his hair grey and thin on the top, round full face, large nose. Has the likeness of a woman and child on the left arm, put in with india ink or powder and at the feet of them the letters **T.J.J. A.M.J.** He has a large scar on the under side of the left arm, caused by a cut. He was born near Fredericksburg, Virginia and raised in Caswell Co., North Carolina. Has lived nine years in Tennessee. He has a wife and five children now living in Williamson Co., Tenn. One brother living near Cincinnatti, Ohio. Found guilty of horse stealing at the Circuit Court of Davidson County and sentenced to three years and eight months confinement in the Jail and Penitentiary House of the State of Tennessee. *Thompson Jones died of Cholera on the 15th day of June, 1833.* [Ledger 45, page 77]

Bennet A. James was received into the Penitentiary 15 May 1833. He is 6' and ½" in height, weighs 200 lbs, dark hair, grey eyes, dark complexion, 35 years of age. Born in Sullivan Co., East Tenn., and brought up in Hamilton Co., Ohio. His wife's maiden name was Mackey, she is deceased, has left one son, who is now living with Bennet's father in Lawrence Co., Tenn. His wife's connections live in McNairy Co., Tenn. Bennet is clear of scars, with the exception of one in the center and one on the left side of his forehead. He is a blacksmith by trade. Was found guilty of horse stealing at the Circuit Court of Wayne County and sentenced to three years confinement in the Jail and Penitentiary House of the State of Tennessee. *Bennet A. James was discharged 15 June 1836. Detained 30 days for misconduct. Conduct generally good.* [Ledger 45, page 77]

Hiram Johnson was received into the Penitentiary 21 August 1833. He is 5' 6 ½" in height and weighs 143 lbs, dark hair, hazel eyes, and fair complexion, 30 years of age. Born in the City of New York and brought up there. His father, mother, and one brother now reside there. He has no remarkable scars. He is a shoemaker by trade. Was found guilty of petit larceny at the Circuit Court of Williamson County and sentenced to one years confinement in the Jail and Penitentiary House of the State of Tennessee. *Hiram Johnson was discharged by expiration of sentence on the 18th day of Nov. 1834. Detained 90 days for bad conduct.* [Ledger 45, page 77]

James B. Ivey was received in the Penitentiary June 5, 1834. He is 5' 11 ½" in height, weighs 157 lbs, light hair, blue eyes, long slim nose, fair complexion, 33 years of age. Born and brought up in Grainger Co., Tenn. He has a wife and four children residing in Monroe County on Tellico river, near the Corn Tassell Meeting House, on Allen D. Gentry's plantation. He has a scar on the wrist of the left hand, caused by a burn, a scar from a cut on the instep of the right foot, about ½" long, a scar just below the elbow and one <u>on in</u> the fleshy part of the forearm (right), several small scars on the left arm and a scar on the ball of the thumb. A mole on the right jaw, about midway between the chin and ear, one just under the left ear about 1 ¼" from the ear. A mole on the nose, near the corner of the left eye and one just above the eyebrow nearly paralell [sic,] with that on the nose. He has generally followed farming. Was found guilty of forgery at the Circuit Court of Monroe County and sentenced to three years confinement in the Jail and Penitentiary House of the State of Tennessee. *James B. Ivey died of cholera on the 7th day of July 1835.* [Ledger 45, page 78]

John Jackson was received in the Penitentiary on 24 March 1835. He is 35 years of age, 5' 8" or 9" high and weighs 160 lbs. Sandy hair, grey eyes, thin visage, nose sharp and a little inclined to the left. A small scar near the point of the chin, one on the point of each the little and ring fingers of the left hand; a knot on the instep of the left foot and a scar near the small toes on the left side of the left foot. A blacksmith by trade. Served two years in the Kentucky Prison under the name of John Gibney. Born and brought up in Jessamin[e] Co., Kentucky. Married Nancy, daughter of Samuel Hunter, who then lived near Nicholasville, Jessamine Co., Kentucky, they having separated before he was put in the Kentucky Prison. He, shortly after his discharge, married Sarah Wildman of Rutherford Co., Tenn., who, he says, ran away from Memphis, to which place he had removed her, with Doct'r. Tucker of that place. He was found guilty of "grand larceny" at the Circuit Court of Humphreys County and sentenced to three years confinement in the Jail and Penitentiary House of the State of Tennessee. *(Called inside John Gibney) Conduct good. Discharged Feb. 17, 1838. The balance of his sentence having been remitted by N. Cannon Gov'r [of] Tenn.* [Ledger 45, page 78]

Joseph Jackson was rec'd in the Penitentiary 6 June 1835. He is 36 years of age, 5' 8 or 9" high and weighs about 150 lbs. Blue eyes, light hair a little mixed with grey, fair complexion and good countenance. A scar just under the left eye, and one near the inside ankle bone of the left foot. Labourer. Born in East Tennessee and brought up in Clinton Co., Ohio, 16 miles from Wilmington C[ourt] H[ouse] and near the road leading from Hillsboro to Lebanon. He there married Nancy Hart, daughter of Thomas Hart, who now lives in Henderson Co., Tenn. Lived one year at the head waters of White River in the state of Indiana. Has been living in the neighbourhood, on and near the line between Perry and Henderson counties, Tenn., for 10 or 11 years. His wife and children (5) now reside in the same neighbourhood, on the waters of Hurricane Creek. He was found guilty of petit larceny at the Circuit Court of Hardin County and sentenced to one years confinement in the Jail and

Penitentiary house of the State of Tennessee. Which sentence was confirmed by the Supreme Court, held at the Court House in Hickman County, at the June term for 1835. *Joseph Jackson was discharged 14 Aug. 1836. Detained 69 days for improper conduct.* [Ledger 45, p. 79]

Asbury Jolly was rec'd in the Penitentiary 11 June 1835. He is 24 years of age, 5', 10 or 11" high, who weighs about 170 lbs. Dark hair, grey eyes, and dark complexion. The little finger of the left hand is very much scarred and very crooked, and there is a large scar on the inside of the right leg, near the shin bone, about halfway from the ankle to the knee. Blacksmith. Born in Kentucky and brought up, partly in Franklin Co., Tenn., and partly in Jackson Co., Alabama. He married Nervazene Bridges, daughter of Wm. Bridges, formerly a resident of Jackson Co., Alabama, now deceased, whose widow, Mrs. Bridges, resides in Bedford Co. about a mile and 1/2 west from Rowsville [*sic,*, Roseville?]. He has no children. His wife lives with his father, Stephen Jolly, who resides in Bedford Co., Tenn., about two miles east from Rowsville [*sic,*, Roseville?]. He was found guilty of grand larceny at the Circuit Court of Bedford County and sentenced to three years confinement in the Jail and Penitentiary House of the State of Tennessee. *Asbury Jolly was discharged July 15, 1838. Was detained 35 days for improper conduct.* [Ledger 45, p. 79]

Henry Johnson, convicted of horse stealing and sentenced to three years imprisonment in the Jail and Penitentiary from 31 March 1836, at the March term, Lincoln County. Was received 6 April 1836. He is 5' 4 1/2" high, weighs about 150 lbs. and is about ___ [blank] years old. Dark hair, blue eyes, sandy beard, round full and florid face, fair complexion. Has the letters H. J. on the left arm a little above the elbow, also a dot between the thumb and forefinger of the left hand, apparently made with powder or india ink. Several blister marks on the right arm and abdomen and a few of the same sort on the left arm. Three marks of nature on the back part of the left shoulder, shaped like islands or lakes. Several scars on the left arm, such as inoculation for small pox leaves, but more scattered. A painter by profession. Says he was born in New Jersey, Salem County. Father living in Philadelphia. Has a wife and child living with her father, Wm. Hynes, in the same city. One brother in Europe and one in Philadelphia, the latter a merchant or grocer. *Pardoned and discharged on 1st day of March 1839. Gave his clothes to Slaughter and Hamilton.* [Ledger 45, p. 80]

Jeremiah Johnson from Wilson County. Offence: petty [*sic,*] larceny. Sentence: one year. Was received November 21, 1836. He is 20 years old, 5' 11" high, weighs 165 lbs., blue eyes, dark hair, and skin. A scar over the left eye, over the forehead. Was born and raised in Wilson County, where his mother now lives. His relations (generally) live in Sumner County. By profession, a farmer. *Jeremiah Johnson was discharged 24th of November 1837. General conduct very good.* [Ledger 45, p. 80]

Aaron F. Jones from Wilson County. Offence: horse stealing. Sentence: three years from 20 March 1837. Was received 21 March 1837. He is 33 years old, 5', 8" high and weighs 155 lbs. Has dark hair, hazel eyes, dark skin and sallow complexion. Both arms have been broken just above the wrist joint, which may be perceived sooner by feeling than seeing. A scar 1" long over the right eye, running toward the nose. On the left side about 8" below the arm pit is the mark of a bullet, and about 2" back of the left ear and a little above is a dent in the scull. Was born in Virginia. Has a wife and five children in Cannon County, where his father and brother reside. Professes general mechanism. *Discharged 12th May 1840. Conduct bad. Sent Aron F. Jones law book to his family by Wm. Bond by Jones request. November 10, 1837. C. S. Anderson.* [Ledger 45, p. 80]

Wm. P[?] Jacobs from Franklin County. Offence: forgery. Sentence: three years from 30 November. Rec'd Dec. 7, 1837. He is 21 years old, 5' 8" high, weighs 150 lbs. Born and bro't up in Orange Co., Virginia, on the waters of Mine Run, five miles from Zoar meeting house, one mile of Gibsons Mill, where his father Nathaniel Jacobs now lives. Has one uncle, on his mothers side, in the state of Ohio, by the name of Reuben Strong. Has one sister, married to Ambrose Smith, living in Culpepper Co., Virginia. He has light hair, blue eyes, fair skin. A scar near the collar bone of the right side, a scar on his cruper bone on the rump, the size of a dollar. Sentence by the Circuit Court of Franklin County to three years confinement in the Jail and Penitentiary House of the State of Tennessee. [Ledger 45, p. 81]

Allen Jarnagin from [blank] County. Offence: malicious stabbing. Sentence: three years. Rec'd 12 Dec. 1837. He is 58 years old, 5' 7" high, weighs 126 lbs. Born and bro't [up] in Johnson Co., North Carolina, near Smithfield. Has a wife and two children living in Coffee Co., Tenn. Has six children married and living in the same county. Has dark grey hair, blue eyes, and a large Roman nose. Has had the finger next the little finger of the left hand broke. Has generally followed farming, but is a cooper by profession. [Ledger 45, p. 81]

Nathan S. Johnson from Maury County. Rec'd 21 Jan. 1839. Sentence: three years. Offence: horse stealing. He is 22 years old, weighs 172 lbs., 5' 10 ½" high. Born and bro't up in Maury Co., Tenn. He has six sisters but no brothers. Two of his sisters are married, one to a man by the name of Dickson

Sellers, the other to a man by the name of Gofourth. They boath live in Yellow Bushy [Yalobusha] Co., Mississippi. He has dark hair, blue eyes and dark skin and heavy eyebrows. He is [a] stout well made man. He has a scar extending from one eyebrow to the other across between his brows. He has also a small scar on the left hand where the fingers joins the hand. Also a scar on the big toe of the left foot. [Ledger 45, p. 81]

William Imes from Shelby County. Was received into the Penitentiary June 22, 1839. He is 21 years old, 5' 10" high, weighs 140 lbs. Born in Sumner Co., Tenn. Bro't up in Shelby, where his father now lives (John Imes). Has one uncle near Bledsoes Lick, by the name of William Imes. He has a wife and one child in Shelby County, 12 miles from Memphis, on the Pigeon Roost Road. He has dark hair, dark skin, hazel eyes, has a small scar near the outside corner of each eye. Has a scar running from the joint of the thumb near the joint of the [w]rist, also a scar across the joint. The above scars are on the left hand. Also a scar on the middle joint of the thumb on the right hand. By occupation a farmer. Was found guilty of larce[n]y by the Circuit [Court] of Shelby County and sentence[d] to undergo confinement in the Jail and Penitentiary House of this state for from years, commencing from the day of his reception. [Ledger 45, p. 82]

James Joyce from Marshall County. Was received into the Penitentiary Oct. 14, 1839. He is 66 years of age, 5' 11" high, weighs 155 lbs. Born in Henry Co., Virginia. Bro't [up] in Georgia, has resided in what is now called Marshall Co., Tenn., 34 years, on the waters of Spring Creek, within six miles of Duck River, near the road leading from Huntsville to Nashville, near the fishing ford. He has two sons in Hickman Co., Kentucky. The rest of his connexion [sic,] are in Marshall County. Had one cozin [sic,] married to a Miss Blackman, died, and she married again. He has grey hair, fair skin, blue eyes, and good countenance. Sentence two years and six months. Offence: shooting. [Ledger 45, p. 82]

James Jones from Sullivan County. Sentence: three years. Rec'd Dec. 9, 1839. He is 16 years old, 5' 5 1/2" high, weighs 130 lbs. Born and bro't up in Washington Co., Virginia. His father James Jones lives in Sullivan Co., Tenn. He has sandy hair, light eyebrows, blue eyes, fair skin. Has some scars on the outside of his right leg and thigh, caused by a burn. His fingers are all croocked, he said he was born with his fingers in the form they are. [Ledger 45, p. 82]

Noel K. Johnson from Madison County. Offence: larceny. Sentence: one year from 21 Jan. 1840. He is 24 years old, 5' 7" high, weighs 140 lbs. Born in

South Carolina, Bro't up North Carolina. He has fair hair, grey eyes, sallow complexion, very long crooked nose. A labourer. [Ledger 45, p. 83]

William Jones from Jefferson County. Crime: grand larceny. Sentence: three years from 19 August 1841. Received 30 Au. 1841. He is 22 years old, 5' 10" high, weighs 131 lbs. Born and brought up in Jefferson County on Dumplin Creek, about two miles from Bethlehem meeting house. He has three brothers and six sisters, all living in the above county. Said Jones has dark, dark skin and hazle eyes. Has had the little finger of the left hand split open, also some cuts on the finger next to it. [Ledger 45, p. 83]

Reuben Johnson from Lincoln County. Crime: remaining in the state over 20 days. Sentence one year from 21 Feb. 1842. Rec'd 21 Feb. 1842. He is 40 years old, 5' 4" high, weighs 140 lbs. Born and brought up in Rockingham Co., Virginia. He is a black boy of good countenance. Has had his right leg broke below the knee. Has followed waggoning and striking in a blacksmiths shop. [Ledger 45, p. 83]

Talton Johnson from Van Beuren County. Crime stealing a bee hive. Sentence two years from 30 April [1842?], when received. He is 67 years old, 5' 8" high, weighs 129 lbs. Born and brought up in Darlington County [South Carolina], 24 miles from ___ [blank]. He has dark grey hair, blue eyes, and sallow complexion. [Ledger 45, p. 83]

Ake Johnson. He is 15 years old, 5' 1 1/2" high, weighs 92 lbs. Born in Blount Co., Tenn. He has fair hair, hazle eyes and fair skin. [Ledger 45, p. 83]

George Johnston from Obion County. Crime: petit larceny. Sentence: one year five months, from 30 June 1842. Rec'd 30 June 1842. He is 39 years old, 5' 9" high, weighs 152 lbs. Born and brought up in Bennington, Vermont. Has travelled with show men, has worked, or pretended, at several trades. Has dark hair, blue eyes, fair skin. Has a small scar under the chin and has been shot in the back, by accident. [Ledger 45, p. 84]

William Left Johnson from Rhea County. Crime: passing counterfeit money. Sentence: three years from Nov. 20, 1842. Rec'd Nov. 20, 1842. Said Johnson is 26 years old, 6' high, weighs 180 lbs. Born and bro't up in McMin[n] County by one Jacob Johnson, he being left at his house an infant about eight days old. His mother is supposed to be by the name of Caldwell and lives in Madison Co., Kentucky. Has a wife and three children living and one dead. He married the daughter of Nancy McCrary, but her mother has since married a man by the name of James Tyson, who is also dead. He has dark hair, fair skin, hazle eyes. Has a scar above his left eyebrow. Has two scars on his head caused by strokes with a stick and the one above the eye caused by the kick of a horse. [Ledger 45, p. 84]

Samuel Kerr was received into the Penitentiary 13 June 1832. He is 54 years old, 5' 9" ½" high, weight 143 lbs. Born and brought up in Sullivan Co., East Tennessee. Has one sister married to a man by the name of Alexander, living in Hawkins Co., East Tennessee on the waters of the Holston. He has a wife and five sons, living at Bledsoes Lick, Sumner County, and two sons grown living 100 miles above Natchez. Has a large scar on the left arm, between the shoulder and elbow. Dark gray hair, gray eyes, and dark skin. Found guilty of having and concealing counterfeit bank notes at the Circuit Court of Davidson County and sentenced to five years confinement in the Jail and Penitentiary House of the State of Tennessee. *Samuel Kerr died of cholera on the 18th day of June 1833.* [Ledger 45, p. 85]

Hazard Hesterson was received into the Penitentiary 8 March 1833. Grey hair, hazel eyes, fair complexion, 52 years of age. Born in Amherst Co., Virginia, and brought up in Augusta Co., Virginia. He has a wife and 10 children, seven of which and his wife reside in Anderson Co., Tenn. He has two children married and living in Virginia, a daughter and son. The daughter married James LeMar. He has two brothers in Virginia, Benjamin and Willis, residing near Augusta and one in Anderson Co., Tenn., Sylvanus Hesterson. He has a scar on the top of the left knee, caused by a cut from an axe, and one on the ancle bone of the right foot. He has generally followed farming. Was found guilty of petit larceny at the Circuit Court of Anderson County and sentenced to one years confinement in the Jail and Penitentiary House of the State of Tennessee. *Hazard Hesterson died of Cholera June 16, 1833.* [Ledger 45, p. 85]

John King was received March 11, 1833. He is 5' 8" in height and weighs 156 lbs. Light hair, blue eyes, fair complexion, 31 years of age. Born in Tennessee and brought up there in Fentress County. He has a wife and seven children, 4 boys and three girls. Her father, Smith Ferrell, resides in Overton Co., Tenn., near Wolf Meeting House. He has a small scar in the edge of the hair, near the center of the forehead. A scar near the instep of the right foot. A scar on the forefinger of the right hand, running across the finger, from the cut of a Tomahawk. He has generally followed farming. Was found guilty of petit larceny at the Circuit Court of Fentress County and sentenced to one years confinement in the Jail and Penitentiary House of the State of Tennessee. *John King was discharged by expiration of sentence on the 15 day of Mar. 1833. Detained one day for bad conduct.* [Ledger 45, p. 85]

Alfred B. King from Knox County, Tenn. Offence: larceny over $50. Sentence: three years. Was received 28 Oct. 1836. He is 19 years old, 5' 6" high, weighs 125 lbs. Blue eyes, light hair, fair skin, no scars perceivable. His parents dead. He was born and raised in Hawkins Co., Tenn., where his relations live, say a brother, sister, uncles, aunts and etc. on the waters of Holston (Dodsons Creek) near Esquire Reynolds. A. B. King discharge[d] Dec. 2, 1839, b[e]ing detained 35 days for bad conduct. [Ledger 45, p. 86]

James Kyle from Madison County. Offence: violating the mail of the United States. Sentence: six calendar months from 15 Sept. 1837. Rec'd 15th [Sept.] 1837. He is 15 years old, 5' 1/2" high, weighs 103 lbs. Born in Hawkins Co., East Tenn. Bro't up in White County. Has one uncle in Wayne County, 26 miles from Waynesboro at Furgesons Furnace. He has fair hair, blue eyes, and fair skin, down look when spoken to. [Ledger 45, p. 86]

Lewis Kirk from Harden County. Rec'd April 7, 1839. Sentence: one year. Offence: hog stealing. He is 42 years old, weighs 120 lbs. Born in Mecklin Burg [sic,, Mecklenburg] Co., Virginia. Bro't up in North Carolina. He has a brother in Maury County, near Mooting Mills on Duck River. He has a wife and seven children in Hardin County, 12 miles west of Savannah. He has dark hair, grey eyes, dark skin, thin visage and heavy beard. [Ledger 45, p. 86]

Jessee Killian from Hamilton County. Offence: receiving stolen horse. Sentence: four years from 30 Nov. 1839. Received December 5, 1839. He is 34 years old, 5' 11 1/2" high, weighs 180 lbs. Born in North Carolina, bro't up in Bledsoe Co., Tenn. He has a wife and eight children, living in Hamilton Co., Tenn., on the waters of Grasshopper Creek. He has dark hair, hazle eyes, fair skin, has a scar in his left eyebrow. A batch[?] shoemaker and blacksmith. [Ledger 45, p. 87]

William Kilbuck from Maury County. Offence: grand larceny. Sentence: three years. He is 23 years old, weighs 170 lbs., 5' 10" high. Born and bro't up in Sumner Co., Tenn., where his mother, Patience Kilbuck, now lives, five miles from Galitan [sic,, Gallatin], on the road leading to Springfield. Has one brother in Galitan, an apprentice to John Stewart, to learn the carpenters trade. He has black hair, dark heavy brows, black eyes, dark skin. Stout and well made, a hatter to trade. [Ledger 45, p. 87]

Elvin Kirk from Anderson County. Offence: malicious stabbing. Sentence: two years and three months from 14 March [year not given, ca. 1840]. He is 24 years old, 5' 9" high, weighs 177 lbs. Born and brought up in Anderson Co.,

Tenn., eight miles east of the County Seat of said county. He has a wife and two children with her father, R. Dew, on Buffalo Creek in the above named county. Said Kirk has fair hair, blue eyes, fair skin. A saddle tree maker, by trade. Has a small scar on the top of the thumb, of the right hand. [Ledger 45, p. 87]

Henry Kelley from Hawkins County. Offence: petit larceny. Sentence one year. Received 9 June 1840. He is 20 years old, weighs 145 lbs., 6' 2" high. Born and bro't up in Hawkins Co., Tenn., 1/4 of a mile of Williamson Cages Mill, on Big Creek. Said Kelley has dark hair, hazle eyes, dark skin and thin visage. Labourer. [Ledger 45, p. 87]

Haywood Keith from Marshall County. Sentence: three years from October 6,1840. Received October 6,1840. Crime: horse stealing. He is 25 years old, 5' 6 1/4" high, weighs 136 lbs. Born in North Carolina, brought [up] in Bedford Co., Tenn., 9 miles east of Shelbyville. His father, Britton Keith, now lives in Lawrence County, seven miles north of Lawrenceburg, near the camp ground known by the name of Pleasant Grove. He has black hair, black eyes, sallow complexion. Has had the ankle bone of the left leg on the inside cut off. He has one brother by the name of John Keith living in Gibson County in the town of Trenton. A farmer. [Ledger 45, p. 88]

Philip Kasler from Madison County. Crime: larceny. Sentence 5 years from 4 May 1842. Rec'd 4 May 1842. He is 38 years old, 5' 4 1/2" high, weighs 137 lbs. Born and brought up in Germany. Has one brother in North Carolina, a tinner. He has fair hair, blue eyes, and fair skin. He has followed razor and scissor grinding and tinning. He has a scar in each cheek bone, his nose is crooked. [Ledger 45, p. 88]

William Lefever was received in the Penitentiary July 19, 1831. He is 5' 10 1/2" high, common weight about 175 lbs., 28 years of age, gray eyes, fair hair and skin, red beard. Born in Sparklinburg [*sic,* Spartanburg], South Carolina and brought up in Burke Co., North Carolina, where most of his relatives now live. He has a brother living in Warren Co., Tenn., and another in Missouri. He has a wife, living with her friends in Sequatchee Valley. A number of scars on his left hand, nose sharp and a little turned to the right. He has worked a little at the blacksmith business. Was found guilty of forgery at the Circuit Court of Franklin County and sentenced to three years imprisonment in the Jail and Penitentiary of the State of Tennessee. *William Lefever was discharged by expiration of sentence on the 1st November 1834. Detained 106 days for bad conduct.* [Ledger 45, p. 89]

Tennessee Convicts: Records of the State Penitentiary

Garland G. Lucas was received into the Penitentiary 12 April 1832. He is 5' 7 ¾" high, 42 years old, weight 152 lbs. Born in Orange Co., Virginia, and brought up in Amherst. Moved to Sullivan Co., East Tenn., 12 years ago. He has lived in Hawkins Co., Tenn. He has a wife living with H. Churchil on Holston River, near Lynns Boat Yard, in Sullivan County, 16 miles from Bluntsville [sic,, Blountville], on the road leading from Nashville to Abington, Virginia. He has blue eyes, dark hair inclining to gray, dark skin, sharp nose, countenance good. He has followed waggoning, has been a soldier in the Virginia line, in Colonel Freemans Regiment. His relations live in Amherst Co., Virginia, consisting of one sister and three brothers. He has a scar over the right eye 1 ½" long, but narrow. Also a scar on the middle finger of the right hand, on the inside of the finger near the middle joint, and a small round scar on the left leg, 4" above the inside ancle bone. Was found guilty of grand larceny at the Circuit Court of Sullivan County and sentenced to three years imprisonment in the Jail and Penitentiary house of the State of Tennessee. *Garland G. Lucas died of cholera on the 11th day of June 1833.* [Ledger 45, p. 89]

Josiah Landers was received in the Penitentiary 23 Oct. 1832. He is 5' 7 ¼" in height, weighs 153 lbs., blue eyes, fair skin, dark hair, small nose. Born in Wilson Co., Tenn. His mother lives in Hickman County, about ¼ mile from Bear Creek Meeting House. He has an uncle, named Landers living in Maury, and one in McNairy Co., Tenn., and one in Guilford Co., North Carolina. He has a scar on the inside of the right arm, about 2" from the wrist. One on the inside ancle bone of the right foot caused by a cut from an axe and two small scars above the cap of the left knee. Has generally followed farming. Was found guilty of breaking open a grocery store and stealing therefrom, money and promissory [sic,] notes, at the Circuit Court of Carroll County and sentenced to three years confinement in the Jail and Penitentiary House of the State of Tennessee. 21 years of age. *Josiah Landers died of Chronic Diarrhoea on the 11th October 1833.* [Ledger 45, pp. 89-90]

Henry A. Luzenbury was received in the Penitentiary 23 Nov. 1832. He is 6' in height, weighs 170 lbs., 22 years of age, light hair, blue eyes, prominent nose, short chin and fair skin. He was born Iredale [sic, Iredell] Co., North Carolina. Brought up in Lincoln Co., Tenn., where his mother and part of his brothers and sisters now reside. He has one brother living in Iredale Co., North Carolina, and one in McNairy Co., Tenn. He has a mole near the right ear, no scars perceivable. Has generally followed farming. Was found guilty of biting of[f] part of David T. Ross's nose and sentenced at the Circuit Court of Hardin County to two years confinement in the Jail and Penitentiary House of the State

Tennessee Convicts: Records of the State Penitentiary

of Tennessee. *Was discharged 10th day of January 1835. He was detained 52 days for bad conduct.* [Ledger 45, p. 90]

Isaac Lowrance was received into the Penitentiary 23 Feb. 1833. He is 5' 6 ½" in height, weighs 135 lbs., black hair, yellowish eyes, dark complexion, and heavy beard, 27 years of age. Born in Lincoln Co., North Carolina, where his brother John Lowrance now reside[s]. His father and mother live in McNairy Co., Tenn., within seven miles of the town of Purdy and 1 ½ miles from Booths Mill on Huggins's Creek. He has a brother, Peter Lowrance, living in Lawrence Co., Indiana. He has a scar on the ball of the thumb of the right hand, a scar on the outside of the left thigh, caused by a cut from a knife. He was found guilty of larceny at the Circuit Court of McNairy County, which was confirmed by the Supreme Court held in Jackson, Madison County, and sentenced to three years confinement in the Jail and Penitentiary House of the State of Tennessee. *Isaac Lowrance was discharged 24th March 1836. Detained 50 days for bad conduct.* [Ledger 45, p. 90]

Hugh Lenox was rec'd in the Penitentiary 16 Jan. 1835. He is 25 years of age, 5' 9 or 10" high and weighs 172 lbs., blue eyes, dark hair, fair complexion, good countenance, a remarkable scar on the chin, caused by a cut from a whip saw. Born and brought up in Cocke Co., Tenn., near Hollands Ferry on French Broad River, by a man by the name of Leonard Marbury. Has a wife and two children living with her father (John Maxwell) in Haywood County, near Salem Meeting House in a settlement formerly called "Murphreys Settlement." He was found guilty of horse stealing at the Circuit Court of Haywood County and sentenced to three years confinement in the Jail and Penitentiary House of the State of Tennessee.
Hugh Lenox died of Cholera on the 9th day of July 1835. [Ledger 45, pp. 90-91]

Michael Lynch was convicted of petit larceny at the March term for Lawrence Co., Tenn., and sentenced to one years imprisonment in the Jail and Penitentiary. Was received 8 March 1836. Born in Ireland, County Waterford. Aged 55 years, 5' 3 ½" high, light form, weighs 118 lbs. Thin swarthy face, long nose, light grey beard, hazle eyes and dark hair. Has a knot or wen about the size of a marble on the side of his head and near the top. A mark of nature on the left arm, yellow and about 2" long. Says he has a family in Ireland. *Michael Lynch was discharged 9th March 1837. Conduct good.* [Ledger 45, p. 91]

Tilman Lovell from Sumner County. Offence: stab[b]ing. Sentence: two years, commencing from 24 Oct. 1837. He is 24 years old, 5' 9" high, weighs 165 lbs. Born and bro't up in Sumner Co., Tenn., near Fountain Head Meeting House, where his father, Cyrus Lovell, now lives. He has a wife and two children with his father. He has one uncle, on the waters of Mill Creek, by the name of Henry McClure. His thumb of the left hand has been put out of joint and cured[?] out, which makes it stiff. Sentenced by the C<u>u</u>ircuit Court of Sumner County to [blank] years confinement in the Jail and Penitentiary House of the State of Tennessee. <u>He is a cooper by profession.</u> [underlined in original] *Tilman D. Lovell pardoned by the Gove[r]nor, Sept. 13th, 1839. Conduct good.* [Ledger 45, p. 91.]

James M[?] Lively. From Wilson County. Offence: mare stealing. Sentence: five years. Rec'd Nov. 20, 1837. He is 29 years of age, 5' 8" high, weighs 158 lbs., dark red hair, black eyes, fair skin. Born and bro't up in Nelson Co., Virginia, seven miles from Livingston, one mile from New Market, where his mother now lives. He has two brothers and three sisters. His brothers, William and Robert, are bo<u>a</u>th married and live in the same county, near their mother. He has a wife and three[?] children living with her father in Rutherford County on the waters of Bradleys Creek, within two miles of Milton. One uncle in Missouri, Pike County, four miles from Pikeville on the road to St. Louis. He has a small scar on the right side of his forehead, in the edge of his hair, a scar on the right che<u>a</u>k, a scar on the outside of the [w]rist of the left arm. Has the ends of the small finger and the one next it scar[r]ed from a bite, a scar on the cap of the right knee. He was found guilty of horse stealing at the C<u>u</u>ircuit Court of Wilson County and sentenced to five years confinement in the Jail and Penitentiary House of the State of Tennessee. He has generally followed farming. His father in laws name is Eli Harrell. [Ledger 45, pp. 91-2]

Addison Leath. From Anderson County. Offence: stabbing. Sentence: three years from reception. Rec'd 24 Nov., 1837. He is 25 years old, 6' high and weighs 175 lbs. Fair hair, greyish eyes, fair skin, good countenance. Has a scar on his fore finger of the left hand 1 ½" long. Born and bro't up in Anderson Co.; Tenn., seven miles south of Clinton on Clinch River, three miles from Scarryberrys Mill. He has seven brothers and five sisters. One sister married to Larkin Hackwell. His relations all live in the same county. His father, Willis Leath, lives in Anderson County, seven miles south of Clinton. Was found guilty at the C<u>u</u>ircuit Court of Anderson County and sentenced to three years confinement in the Jail and Penitentiary House of the State of Tennessee. *Addison Leath was pardoned by Gov. Polk, Nov. 29, 1839. Conduct good.* [Ledger 45, pp. 92-93]

J. Lewis. From Montgomery County. Sentence three years. Offence: horse stealing. Received May 24,1839. Sentence to commence from 23 May 1839. Said Lewis is 24 years old, 5' 9" high, weighs 157 lbs. Born in Virginia, bro't up in Warren Co., Kentucky. He has dark hair, grey eyes, fair skin, and good countenance. He has a wife and one child at her father's, Lewis Matheny, 13 miles below Clarksville, within two miles of New York. He has three sisters and one brother. His sisters are with their grandfather, Jackson Walters, six miles from Bowling Green, two miles off the road leading to Nashville. He has one uncle, W. Walters. He keeps the bridge at Red River. [Ledger 45, p.92]

Thomas Lamsing[?] was received into the Penitentiary 4 June 1839. He is 24 or 25 years of age and weighs 139 lbs. 5' 2 1/2" in height. Born and brought up near Shigo in Ireland and in the city of New York. Has no relations in the United States. His hair is of a sandy [color], fair skin, blue eyes, heavy brow, full face. Has had the small pox. Has a down look, which may be called a bad countenance. Short chin, light beard. The middle finger of the left hand has a deformed nail. Was found guilty of stealing money by the Circuit [Court] of Davidson County held at Nashville, and sentenced to the Jail and Penitentiary house for one year. [Ledger 45, p.93]

John Lavendar was received into the Penitentiary in the year 1839, June 4th, 1839. He is 31 years old, weighs 196 lbs., 6' 1" high. Born in Oldham Co., Kentucky, and brought up in Murry [Maury] Co., Tenn., 1/2 mile west of Spring Hill, where his father, Pickens Lavendar, now lives. He has three brothers and four sisters, one of whoom is married to Ovin Hopkins and lives on the same farm. Dark hair, hazzle eyes, dark skin. Has had both arms broken in 2 places, the fingers of the left hand are crooked. Said John Lavendar has followed stage driving on the Florence line, from Spring Hill to Columbia. Likewise from Spring Hill to Franklin. Has had the small pox. The said John Lavendar was convicted by the Circuit Court of Davidson County of the crime of forgery, and sentenced to undergo close confinement in the Jail and Penitentiary House for the space of three years. [Ledger 45, p.93]

John Lawrence. From Wilson County. Offence: grand larceny. Received June 14, 1839. Sentence eight years. Said Lawrence is 47 years old, 5' 9 " high, weighs 143 lbs. Born and bro't up in the city of Philadelphia, Pennsylvania. He is a bright mulatto. He has a crusifix on his left arm and the images of two persons shaking hands on the right. Is a barber, has worked in Nashville, in several shops. Has follow[ed] the river as a steward and cook on steam boats.

Is a smart boy, quick spoken. Was bro't from Philadelphia, he says, by the Zeatmans, has waited about houses. [Ledger 45, p.94]

Moses Lowe. From Bledsoe County. He is 47 years old, weighs 150 lbs. 5' 10" high. Born in Washington Co., Tenn., and bro't up Bledsoe Co., Sequatchie Valley. Has a wife and seven children in said valley, about 15 miles from Pikeville, near Tolletts Mill, on a tract of land owned by his son, John William D.F. Lowe. Said Lowe has light grey hair, blue eyes, fair skin. His right hand has been injured by the fever, which makes it crooked. Has worked at shoe making. Sentenced two years. Rec'd July 17, 1839. Offfence petit larceny. Has made a profession of religon, of the Methodist order. [Ledger 45, p.94]

Ellmore Lindsey. From Williamson County. Offence: horse stealing. Sentence: three years from Nov. 23, 1839. Received 28th instant. He is 30 years old, 5' 9" high, weighs 145 pounds. Born in Rutherford Co., Tenn., and bro't up in Williamson. He has a wife and two children living in the last named county, on the Fishing Ford road, within half a mile of Riggs X Roads, on the land of Thomas Willson, her brother in law. His father, William Lindsey, lives in Park[e] Co., Indiana, on the waters of Little Rackoon[?] Creek, eight miles east of Rockville. He has one brother, that is a sadler and works in Naplis[?] in Park[e] County. His mother's connection[s] lives in North Carolina, Orange County. He has fair hair, fair skin, hazle eyes, large nose and what the most of persons would call a good countenance. *Clothes given to J. Duncan. J. Duncan gave them to John Rhea.* [Ledger 45, p.94]

Edward Land. From Overton County. Crime: grand larceny. Sentence: three years from 1 July 1840. Received 1 July 1840. He is 32 years of age, 5' 9" high, weighs 155 lbs. Born and brought up in Buckingham Co., Virginia. Has a wife and two children in Clinton Co., Kentucky, eight miles west of Albany, on the road leading from Burksville to Covington. Has one uncle, by the name of Williamson, living in the Western District. Has overseed for old Col. Ward, is now overseeing for McNeely. His father and all of his other connections live in Clinton, Cumberland Co., Kentucky. Said Land has dark grey hair, dark and black beard. Has a scar on the calf of his left leg, say 4" or 5" long, caused by the cut of a scythe blade. [Ledger 45, p.95]

Samuel Larkey alias Refe Matlock. From Shelby County. Crime: larceny. Sentence: three years from June 26, 1841. Rec'd June 26, 1841. He is 30 years old, 5' 8" high, weighs 139 lbs. Born in Smith County near Dixins [Dixon] Springs on the road to Carthage. His mother, Susan Matlock, is now living at the Eagle Tavern on the road leading from Nashville to Lebanon. Has one brother, Gideon Matlock, now living on the Turnpike Road from Nashville to

Lebanon, about 16 miles from Nashville. Said Matlock has fair hair, blue eyes, dark skin. Has a scar across the eye brow of the left eye, caused by the kick of a horse. Has worked at shoe making, say, one year. Has lived in Illinois at Lockport on the canal and was employed writing[?] in the canal office, in the employ of Col. Jacob Fry, who married a cousin of his. His wife was a Miss Turney, sister of the Hon. Hopkins L. Turney. [Ledger 45, p.95]

Robert Myers. From Monroe County. Crime: manslaughter. Sentence: two years from 28 Sept. 1842. Rec'd 28 Sept. 1842. He is 22 years old, weighs 173 lbs., 6' high. Born in Washington Co., Virginia, and bro't up in Monroe Co., Tenn., three and one half miles north of Madisonville. He has two sisters married, one to Robt. Reed, the other to Peter Brakeville. Also two single sisters and two single brothers, all living in Monroe County. He has dark hair, hazle eyes, and dark skin. Has had twp cuts in the instep of the left foot, say 2 $1/2$ " long. [Ledger 45, p.96]

Charles Lapier. From Davidson County. Crime: larceny. Sentence: one year from 7 Sept. 1842. Rec'd 7 Sept. 1842. He is 21 years old, weighs 156 lbs., 5' 6 $1/2$" high. Born and bro't up in Montreal, Lower Canada. Has been a sea farer ever since he was eight years old. Has a mother and two sisters living in the above named place. He has blue eyes, dark skin, and dark hair. Has 11 spots running across each wrist and 15 on the back of each hand, with a heart and anchor and a heart on his right arm and seven letters on his left. Right side peppered with shot. [Ledger 45, p.96]

Blackwood Lyons. From Gibson County. Crime: petit larceny. Sentence from Nov. 17[?] 1842, one year. Rec'd Nov. 17, 1842. He is 21 years old, 5' 9" high, weighs 161 lbs. Born and bro't up in White Co., Tenn., and in Gibson. His mother, Sally Lyons, lives about two miles from Trenton, on the Lexington Road, and one mile from Alexander Coopers. Said Lyons has dark hair, blue eyes, and fair skin. Has one sister, married and lives 18 miles from Memphis, Tenn., on the Sommerville road. She is married to a man by the name of Overall Landerson. [Ledger 45, p.96]

David May was received in the Penitentiary 19 April 1831. He is about 5' 7" high, about 130 lbs. in weight, dark hair, good countenance and hazel eyes. His father and mother are dead and he has no knowledge of the residence of his living relations. A scar on the instep of the left foot and one on the ancle of the same foot. The two small fingers on his right hand are badly deformed. Was found guilty of petit larceny at the Circuit Court of Robertson County and was sentenced to one years imprisonment in the Jail and Penitentiary of the State of

Tennessee Convicts: Records of the State Penitentiary

Tennessee. *Remarks: Discharged April 19, 1832. Conduct very good.* [Ledger 45, p.97]

John Marsh was received in the Penitentiary Sept. 4, 1831. He is 5' 7" high, 31 years of age. Common weight 156 lbs., black hair, blue eyes, dark skin. Born in North Carolina and brought up in Powells Valley, Tennessee. His wife resides 10 miles from Sparta. His father and mother reside in White Co., Tenn., and his brother in Wayne Co., Kentucky. Three small scars on the back of the neck and two or three moles on his breast. Was found guilty of petit larceny at the Circuit Court of White County and sentenced to one years confinement in the Jail and Penitentiary of Tennessee. *John Marsh was discharged on 23 December 1832. He was detaied 100 days for bad conduct.* [Ledger 45, p.97]

Hugh Moore was received in the Penitentiary 16 September 1831. He is 6' 2 ½" high, weighs 161 lbs., but is now in bad health. His common weight is 220 lbs. Grey hair, blue eyes, fair skin, thin beard, a small mole on the chin, no scars perceivable. Born and raised in Spartanburg District, South Carolina, on Thickety[?] Creek, waters of Broad River, 10 miles from the court house and three miles from Pacolet Springs, where his family now lives, consisting of a wife, five sons and two daughters. Also a son, married and lives in the same [neighbourhood]. He is 58 years old. He has no trade, but is a farmer and has preached for 30 years, of the Baptist persuasion. Found guilty of forgery at the Circuit Court of the United States at Nashville for the district of West Tennessee and sentenced to five years imprisonment in the Jail and Penitentiary House of the State of Tennessee. *Hugh Moore died of cholera on the 15th day of June, 1833.* [Ledger 45, p.97]

Wm. B. McCracken was received in the Penitentiary 27 September 1831. He is 23 years of age, 6' high, weighs 166 lbs. He has blue eyes, fair skin, dark hair, and good countenance. A scar of a bile[?] and cut just above the instep of the left foot. Also a scar of a bile[?] just above the cap of the right knee. Also a small scar on the little finger of the right hand, running from the finger nail to the knuckle joint. Very small teeth. A small wen just above the forehead, the size of a marble. His father is dead. His mother lives in Randolph Co., North Carolina, on the waters of Caraway Creek, near Ashboro. He has two brothers. He has two sisters married, one to a Mr. Chalmes and one to a Mr. Hill. He has no trade. He has pedled and taught school in Randolph Co., North Carolina. Found guilty of forgery at the Circuit Court of Maury County and was sentenced to three years confinement in the Jail and Penitentiary House of the State of Tennessee. *Wm. B. McCracken died of cholera on the 14th day of June 1833.* [Ledger 45, p.98]

Tennessee Convicts: Records of the State Penitentiary

Henry P. Morgan was received into the Penitentiary 18 May 1832. He is 5' 6" high, weighs 124 lbs. He is 17 years of age. Born in Fairfield District, South Carolina. His father is living in Monroe County in Tennessee, three miles and a half from Hughes Mill and 10 miles south of Madisonville. He has also one uncle living in Monroe County and a brother in Fairfield District, South Carolina. Morgan has lived in McMinn Co., Tenn., one year or upwards. He has dark skin, grey eyes, short round face and a tolerable good countenance. He has a scar on the middle finger of the left hand 3/4" in length. He has also a scar over the nose, running up into the hair and a mole on the neck under the ear. He has a small scar between the middle toe and the one next the big toe. Found guilty of forgery at the Circuit Court of McMinn County and sentenced to three years confinement in the Jail and Penitentiary house of the State of Tennessee. *Henry P. Morgan was discharged by expiration of sentence on the 10th day of June 1835. Detained 43 days for bad conduct. His conduct, generally, was good.* [Ledger 45, p.98]

Peter Mitchell coloured man was received in the Penitentiary 23 November 1832. He is 5' 7 3/4" in height, weighs 173 lbs. 21 years of age, very large mouth. Born in South Carolina and brought up in Maury Co., Tennessee. He has a low forehead and short flat nose. He has resided, chiefly, with Martin Harding, about two miles from Columbia, ever since he has been capable of labour. When convicted he was living with Watkins Harding, near the town of Savannah and about three miles from Hardins Ferry on Tennessee River. Has been employed principally in taking care of horses. Was found guilty of burglary at the Circuit Court of Hardin County and sentenced to 5 years confinement in the Jail and Penitentiary House of the State of Tennessee. *Peter Mitchell was discharged January 20, 1838. His conduct was exceptionable. Hence he was detained.* [Ledger 45, p.98-9]

John Morrison was received in the Penitentiary 6 December 1832. He is 5' 8 1/2" in height, weighs 190 lbs. Black hair, hazel eyes, and good countenance, 54 years of age. Born in North Carolina and brought up in Blount Co., Tennessee. He has three daughters living near the Tellico Plains, Monroe Co., Tennessee. One married to Richard Miller, one to Martin Thomson and one to Robert Bohannon. Morrison is stout built. He has a scar on the middle finger of the right hand and one on each knuckle of the two middle fingers of the left hand, and one on the left cheek. Has generally followed farming. Was found guilty of voluntary manslaughter at the Circuit Court of Monroe County and sentenced to two years confinement in the Jail and Penitentiary House of the State of Tennessee. *John Morrison died of cholera on the 14th day of June, 1833.* [Ledger 45, p.99]

George W. Morris was received in the Penitentiary April 19, 1833. He is 5' 9 3/4" in height and weighs 145 lbs. Fair hair and complexion, black hollow eyes, long chin, 35 years of age. Born in South Carolina and brought up partly in Mecklenburgh Co., North Carolina, and Williamson Co., Tenn. He has a wife and four children. They are now residing with her father and mother 1 1/2 miles from John T. Hatch & Sons Mill on Griffins Creek in Henderson Co., Tenn. Her maiden name was Spain. He has a scar over the left eye near the brow, one on the middle finger and thumb of the left hand, one on the shin of the left leg running outside the leg, one on the back of the neck where it joins the body. Was found guilty of forgery at the Henderson Circuit Court and sentenced to three years confinement in the Jail and Penitentiary House of the State of Tennessee. (followed farming) *George W. Morris was discharged 19 Apr. 1836, conduct good.* [Ledger 45, page 99]

John Melton was received in the Penitentiary 6 Nov. 1833. He is 5' 9" in height and weighs 170 lbs., grey hollow eyes, light hair and complexion, long nose, hooked chin and tolerable good countenance. 25 years of age. Born in Tenn. and brought up in Wilson County. His father and mother reside at present in Pope Co., Illinois. He has five brothers and four sisters. One brother resides in Mississippi and four near Yelconda[?], Illinois, all married. He has one sister married to Oliver Sutton, they reside about three miles from Lebanon, Tenn. He has no remarkable scars. A few scars on the forefinger of the left hand and one on the left knee caused by a bile. He has generally followed farming. Was found guilty of petit larceny at the Circuit Court of Wilson County and sentenced to two years and six months confinement in the Jail and Penitentiary House of the State of Tennessee. *John Melton was discharged 5th June 1836. Detained 30 days for bad conduct.* [Ledger 45, p. 100]

William Morgan was received in the Penitentiary 5 Feb. 1834. He is 6' 1/2" in height and weighs 177 lbs. Dark hair, blue eyes and fair complexion. 22 years of age. Born in Hanover Co., Virginia, about 25 miles from Richmond on the three Chops[?] road, and brought up there. His parents, four brothers and two sisters still reside [there]. His grandfather John Morgan resides near Lexington, Kentucky; and three uncles, John, Robert and Stephen Williams [are] living in Powhatten Co., Virginia. He has a scar under the left arm near the elbow caused by a ball passing thro[ugh] the flesh. A small scar on the heel of the right hand, a scar on the small part of the left leg just below the shin caused by a cut from an axe. He has worked a little at the wagon making business. Was found guilty of horse stealing at the Circuit Court of Madison County and sentenced to three years confinement in the Jail and Penitentiary

House of the State of Tennessee. [Ledger 45, p. 100-101] *William Morgan died of consumption Jan. 24th at 11 O['clock] p.m., 1836.*

William Miller was received Mar. 28, 1834. He is 6' ½" in height and weighs 147 lbs. Dark hair, dark hazel eyes and tolerably fair complexion. 19 years of age. Born in Knox Co., Tenn., and brought up partly in Roane and Monroe counties. He has three brothers, Mark, Robert and Moses, and two sisters, one of them married to Thomas Giles. They all reside on Pond Creek, Roane Co., near Esqr. Gamble about 15 miles from the town of Kingston. Miller has a scar on the centre of the forehead near the edge of the hair, one on the end of the right eyebrow nearest the nose, and one on the right knee at the upper edge of the cap. He has generally followed farming. Was found guilty of larceny at the Circuit Court of Roane County and sentenced to four years confinement in the Jail and Penitentiary House of the State of Tennessee. *Died of cholera on the 30th day of June, 1835.* [Ledger 45, p. 101]

Franklin McCullouch was received in the Penitentiary May 3, 1834. He is 5' 11" in height and weighs 149 lbs. Light hair, yellowish eyes and fair complexion, 18 years of age. Born and brought up partly in Rutherford Co., Tenn. His father [and] mother reside in Wilson Co., Tenn., (he has six brothers and six sisters) about two miles from Spring Creek, six miles from the town of Jefferson and 14 miles from Lebanon and six miles from Ridley's mill. He has one brother, a blacksmith, Henry McCullouch residing in Lebanon. He has three sisters married: Polly, Martha and Eliza, to <u>John</u>, James and <u>John</u> Sanders. They all reside in the same neighborhood or nearly so with their parents. McCullouch has a scar where the forefinger joins the hand and one on the joint next the nail, all on the left hand. He has several moles on the neck and breast. A scar about midway between the right eye and hair. The great toe of the right foot has been split. A scar on the instep of each foot and a scar on the inside of the left leg about two thirds of the distance between the ancle and the knee. He has worked a little at blacksmithing. Was found guilty of negro stealing at the Circuit Court of Wilson County and sentenced to five years confinement in the Jail and Penitentiary House of the State of Tennessee. *Franklin McCullough was discharge[d] May 3 by expiration of sentence. Conduct generally good.* [Ledger 45, p. 101-102]

John Mowry was received in the Penitentiary 5 June 1834. He is 5' 11" in height and weighs 152 lbs. Grey eyes, dark hair, slim face, long nose, heavy beard, rather dark complexion and 43 years of age. Born and brought up in Knox Co., Tenn. His father resides near Peary's[?] mill on Flat Creek. Mowry has a wife and eight children living on Stekey[?] Creek near Johnson's mill. He has a daughter married to Solomon Stephens residing on the beforementioned creek in Roane County. Mowry's wife's maiden name was McCluer. Her conne<u>x</u>sions reside in Jefferson County near the town of New<u>m</u>arket. He has a remarkable scar below the cap of the knee of the left leg, and one on the toe next the small toe where the toe joins the foot. He has no other scars of note. Has generally followed farming. Was found guilty of petit larceny at the Circuit Court of Monroe County and sentenced to one year and three months confinement in the Jail and Penitentiary House of the State of Tennessee. *John Mowry died of cholera on the 1st day of July 1835.* [Ledger 45, p. 102]

Lutin McGee was received in the Penitentiary June 7, 1834. He is 6' 1" in height and weighs 158 lbs. Light blue eyes, fair hair, thin beard, fair complexion, 21 years of age. Born and brought up in Stewart Co., Tenn. His parents are now residing near the head of Hurricane Creek. He has one sister married to Henry Milam living on Long Creek. He has two uncles Adam and Thomas McGee residing on Cumberland River about two miles above the town of Dover. All the above mentioned places are in Stewart County, Tenn. He has a small scar in the forehead about midway between the corner of the left eyebrow and the nose, and another about midway between that scar and the hair on the left temple. A scar on the first finger of the left hand on the joint where the finger joins the hand, and one about midway between the next two joints. The nail of the finger next the little finger of the left hand has been much disfigured by the end of <u>the end of</u> [*sic.*, underlined in original] the finger being mashed. He has generally followed farming but the past year has been under the instruction of Joseph P.[?] Lisle, Carpenter, of Paris, Henry Co., Tenn. He was found guilty of burglary at the Circuit Court of Henry County and sentenced to five years confinement in the Jail and Penitentiary House of the State of Tennessee. *Pardoned and discharged April 1st, 1839. Conduct good.* [Ledger 45, p. 102-3]

John A. Murrell was received in the Penitentiary Aug. 17, 1834. He is 5' 10 ½" in height and weighs from 158 to 170 lbs. Dark hair, blue eyes, long nose and much pitted with the small pox. Tolerably fair complexion, 28 years of age. Born in Lunenbur<u>gh</u> Co., Virginia, and brought up in Williamson Co., Tenn. His mother, wife and two children reside in the neighborhood of Denmark about nine miles from Jackson, Madison Co., Tenn. His wife's maiden name was Manghan [or Maugham?]. Her conne<u>x</u>ion reside on the waters of South Harpeth, Williamson Co., Tenn. His brother Wm. S. Murrell, a druggist, resides in Cincinnati, Ohio. He has another brother living in Sumptersville, South Carolina. He has a scar on the middle joint of the finger next the little finger of the left hand, and one on the middle finger of the same hand. A scar on the inside of the end of the finger next the little finger of the right hand. Has generally followed farming. Was found guilty of negro stealing at the Circuit Court of Madison County and sentenced to 10 years confinement in the Jail and Penitentiary House of the State of Tennessee. *See order of court of Errors & Appeals at Jackson filed with convicts rec'd, 1834. Returned April 26th, 1837, by order of Court of Appeals.* [Ledger 45, p. 103-104.]

Robert McCall was received in the Penitentiary 8 Sept. 1834. He is 6' 2 ½" in height and weighs 191 ½ lbs. Dark hair, blue eyes and tolerably fair complexion. 43 years of age. Born in North Carolina and brought up in Jefferson Co., Tenn. His wife and six children reside at present on the waters of Wolf River near the town of Moscow in Fayette Co., Tenn. His parents and one brother reside in Limestone Co., Alabama. He likewise has one brother living in the same neighborhood his family reside in. His wife's parents are citizens of Warren Co., Tenn. He has a piece bit out of his right ear and a scar running round the right thumb from a bite. Has worked as a millwright, wheelwright, wagon maker and cooper. Was found guilty of voluntary manslaughter at the Circuit Court of Fayette County and sentenced to two years confinement in the Jail and Penitentiary House of the State of Tennessee. *Robt. McCall was discharged Oct. 18th, 1836, by expiration of sentence, being detained 40 days for bad conduct.* [Ledger p. 104]

Henry Minor was received in the Penitentiary 27 Sept. 1834. He is 4' 5" in height and weighs 109 lbs. Has light hair, fair complexion and light blue eyes, 15 years of age, born in Maury County and brought up in Lincoln County. He has two sixters (one single, and the other married to William Hignen) and three brothers, all of whom are residing together in Lincoln County near Findlay's Horse Mill, about two miles from Cane Creek on a Plantation in the neighborhood of Major Caruthers, belonging to Old Mr. Findlay. There is a scar on the cap of his right knee and a small one below the same knee, both of which were occasioned by biles. He, together with his father, was found guilty of voluntary manslaughter at the Circuit Court of Lincoln County and sentenced to eight years confinement in the Jail and Penitentiary House of the State of Tennessee. *Henry Minor was pardoned Oct. 4th, 1838, by Gov. Newton Cannon.* [Ledger 45, pp. 104-5]

John Minor was rec'd in the Penitentiary 22 Sept. 1834. He is 56 years of age, 5' 9 or 10" high, and weighs usually (when in good health) from 150 to 160 lbs. Blue eyes, gray hair and fair complexion. Born and brought up in Halifax Co., Virginia. Has had his left arm broke just below the elbow. He, together with his son Henry Minor (above described), was found guilty of manslaughter at the Circuit Court of Lincoln County and sentenced to eight years confinement in the Jail and Penitentiary House of the State of Tennessee. ~~Pardoned Feb'y 21, 1835. Conduct very good.~~ [Text crossed out.] *Conduct bad.* [Ledger 45, p. 105]

John W. Moore was rec'd in the Penitentiary 21 Oct. 1834. He is 26 years of age, 5' 4 or 5" high, and weighs 140 lbs. Black eyes, black hair, dark complexion and prominent forehead. The forefinger of the left hand is crooked and stiff at the first joint from the end, caused by a bite, and the same finger of the right hand has had the end bit off. He has chiefly followed farming. Born in Richmond Co., North Carolina. Partly brought up there and partly in Chesterfield Dist., South Carolina. His father (Wm. Moore) and mother reside in Muscova [*sic,*, Muscogee] Co., Georgia. Has three brothers and four sisters. One brother (a tailor) living in McDonough, Henry Co., Georgia. A sister married to George Hamilton (a phasician) living in Decalb Co., Georgia, and an uncle, (Travis [?] Moore) a Baptist preacher residing on Cumberland River near Dover in Stewart Co., Tenn. He was found guilty of forgery at the Circuit Court of Henderson County and sentenced to three years confinement in the Jail and Penitentiary House of the State of Tennessee. *Jno. W. Moore was discharged Nov. 14th, 1837. Detained 24 days for misdemeanors. Conduct of course exceptionable.* [Ledger 45, p. 105]

Avery Mayfield was rec'd in the Penitentiary 10 Feb. 1835. He is 24 years of age, 5' 9 or 10" high, and weighs 173 lbs. Hazle eyes, dark hair, large face and fair complexion. Two scars about an inch apart, on the instep of the right foot, and one on the inside of the right leg, just below the knee. Born in Savierville, Savier Co., Tenn. Bound an apprentice to the hatter's business and removed to Alabama by William Bromly when 14 years of age. Has been living in Warren County for some time past. Married Elizabeth Dotson, daughter of James Dotson, then of Marion Co., Tenn., but who now lives in the Cherokee Nation. His wife and four children are now residing in Warren County three[?] miles from Webb's Mill on Rocky River. Mother resides on Collins River in the same County seven miles from McMinnville. He was found guilty of larceny at the Circuit Court of Warren County and sentenced to one year and six months confinement in the Jail and Penitentiary House of the State of Tennessee. *Avery Mayfield died of Cholera on the 30th day of June 1835.* [Ledger 45, p. 106]

Jared B. Milsap was rec'd in the Penitentiary 17 Feb. 1835. He is 25 years of age, 5' 7 or 8" high, and weighs 150 lbs. Grey eyes, dark hair and beard, sharp nose and fair complexion. Forefinger of the left hand very much scar[r]ed. A scar on the middle finger of the same hand, between the first and second joint. One on the forefinger of the right hand between the second and third joint.

Tennessee Convicts: Records of the State Penitentiary

One of an ovel form on the back of the right arm about halfway between the [w]rist and elbow, and one on the right foot about an inch in length running length ways of the foot, commencing between the second and third toes. Born on Cosby's Creek, Cocke Co., Tenn., and brought up in Haywood Co., North Carolina, on Tuckaseige River, four miles from Gibson's Mill (on Crooke's Creek), where his father (Edward Milsap), eight brothers and three sisters now reside. He married Jane Rolston, daughter of Polly Rolston, who lives on Sweet Water Creek in McMinn Co., Tenn. His wife and two children are living with Mrs. Winniford Smith in Blount Co., Tenn., on Little River, near Levi Dann's Mill and Mount Zion Meeting House. Has chiefly followed farming but professes to be a tolerable wheel wright. He was found guilty of grand larceny at the Circuit Court of Blount County and sentenced to three years confinement in the Jail and Penitentiary House of the State of Tennessee. *Jared B. Milsap was discharged February 22nd, 1838. Conduct generally good, detained five days for breach of prison rules.* [Ledger 45, p. 106]

George Madden was rec'd in the Penitentiary 21 Apr. 1835. He is 62 years of age, 5' 9" high, and weighs 137 lbs. Blue eyes, grey hair and beard and high forehead. A scar on the edge of the right hand between the little finger and the wrist. Labourer. Born and brought up in Shenandoah Co., Virginia. Married Katharine, daughter of John Liford of Lee Co., Virginia. Afterwards settled in Hawkins Co., Tenn., on Clinch River near Wallen's Bend 16 miles from Rogersville, where he has resided ever since. Has nine children. One daughter married to a man named Crigmore, another to Thomas Holland, and one son (John) married Betsey, daughter of Moses Johnson. All living in the aforesaid neighborhood on Clinch River near Wallan's Bend. He was found guilty of "stabbing" at the Circuit Court of Hawkins County and sentenced to two years' confinement in the Jail and Penitentiary House of the State of Tennessee. *George Madden died of chronic diarhea 1st Nov. 1835. Conduct good.* [Ledger 45, p. 107]

William McNeeley was rec'd in the Penitentiary 11 May 1835. He is 5' 10" high, 30 years of age and weighs 157 lbs. Black eyes, black hair and beard and dark complexion. Two small scars on the forehead, one between the eye-brows, and one in the edge of the hair on the left side, and a scar on the forefinger of the left hand near the third join. Born in Pittsylvania Co., Virginia, and brought up in Campbell Co., Tenn. His father (William McNeely) and family reside in Campbell Co., Tenn., on Powell's River in Trammell's Rent, five miles from Glade Spring Meeting House. Married Sarah Hetherly, daughter of John Hetherly, who also lives in Trammel's Rent in Campbell County. His wife and children (five) are residing on the same plantation with his father. He was found guilty of petit larceny at the Circuit Court of Campbell County and sentenced to one year's confinement in the Jail and Penitentiary House of the State of Tennessee. *William McNeeley died of cholera on the 4th day of July 1835.* [Ledger 45, p. 107]

William J. May was received in the Penitentiary 5 Sept. 1835. He was born in Hampshire Co., England, whence he removed to the United States about 23 years ago. He was raised principally to farming. Since he has been in the United States he has been manufacturing and merchandiseing. Aged 43 years. Weighs about 175 lbs., about 5' 5" high and heavy built. Large nose and it has the appearance of a drinking man's. Light hair, blue eyes, dark heavy bea[r]d. No remarkable scars visible. He has no near relations in the United States to his knowledge. He served a sentence in the Kentucky Penitentiary for two years for forgery. A man of mild manners and good sense. He was found guilty of horse stealing at July term 1835 of Roane County and sentenced to three years confinement in the Jail and Penitentiary House of the State of Tennessee. Sentence to commence from 22 July 1835 from which said judgment of Roane Circuit Court he appealed to the Supreme Court of the State of Tennessee held at Knoxville the Sept'r following. Judgment confirmed. *William J. May died Augst. 29th, 1837.* [Ledger 45, p. 108]

Daniel McCarty was received in the Penitentiary 28 Oct. 1835. He is 27 years of age, born and raised near Watson's Iron Works on Yellow Creek, Montgomery Co., Tenn. 5' 6" high, weighs 151 lbs. Blue eyes, hair rather light, heavy black beard, dish face and dimple chin, eyes considerably sunk in his head. He has some small scars on the forefinger of the left hand. A large scar on the left knee, one on the under [underlined in original] side of his right jaw[?]. A large scar on the right side of his head occasioned by falling from a horse. He was brought up to the blacksmith's business and worked principally while and apprentice with Hiram McElyea in Humphreys Co., Tenn. He has worked some at his trade in Louisville, Kentucky. He has traveled a good deal in Indiana, where he has a brother and two sisters, one married to Joshua Phillips, the other single, [and] an uncle, Jno McElyea, all of whom reside in Orange County. Also an uncle Henry McElyea who lives in Carter Co., Tenn. He was found guilty of petit larceny at the Circuit Court of Hamilton County and sentenced to one year and three months confinement in the Jail and Penitentiary House of the State of Tennessee. ("so mote it be") yet in a state of "single blessedness" *Daniel McCarty was released 8th March 1837. Detained 38 days for breach of prison laws.* [Ledger 45, p. 108]

William McCluskey, convicted of manslaughter at the March term for Lincoln Co., Tenn., and sentenced to imprisonment at hard labour in the Penitentiary two years and three months from 1 Apr. 1836. He was born in South Carolina and raised in Franklin Co., Tenn. 45 years old. Black and heavy beard. Is getting bald. Dark grey eyes, black hair and a heavy coat of black hair on the breast. A scar on the thumb of the left hand where it joins the hand. 5' 10" high, says his parents are living 10 miles south of Fayetteville on the West fork of Flint River. Has a wife and nine children living on his father's land. Two oldest daughters married and live in the same neighborhood, one to James McCoun, the other to James J. Jones, near Haney's Mill. *William McClusky was discharged July 10th, 1838. Conduct good.* [Ledger 45, p. 109]

Jess_ee_ Moore was convicted of stealing a mare at the March term 1836 for Lincoln Co., Tenn. Was received 6 APR 1836. Sentenced to three years imprisonment in the Jail and Penitentiary House of Tennessee from 31 Mar. 1836. He was born in South Carolina, Lawrence [*sic,*, Laurens] District. _____ [blank] high, weig[h]s 160 lbs. Blue eyes, dark hair, sandy beard, small slim nose, upper forteeth [*sic,*] broken, head stoops a little forward, several moles on the breast, a scar near the knee of the left leg, 42 years old. Says he has a wife and nine children living in Lincoln Co., Tenn., on Alexander Gray's land near the head of Flint River. His mother, two brothers and two sisters live in Lawrence District, South Carolina. Two sisters married and living in Jackson Co., Alabama, one to Jerry Collins, the other to Thomas Scurlock. *Discharged by order of the Governor, March 7th 1839. Conduct generally good.* [Ledger 45, p. 109]

James Miller from Knox Co., Tenn. Was received 1 July 1836. He is 23 years old, 5' 4 3/4" high, weighs 145 lbs. Dark hair, dark hazl_e_ eyes, dark skin, short full face, rather hollow eyes, small ears. Has an uncle named Jas. Baker in Edgecom_b_ Co., North Carolina. His father Jonathan Miller lives in Madison Co., Tenn. He was born in Bertie Co., North Carolina. Was found guilty of larceny, horse stealing, and sentenced to six years imprisonment in the Tennessee Penitentiary. [Ledger 45, p. 109-110]

Thomas Morrison from Fayette Co., Tenn. Offence: pett_y_ larceny. Sentence: three years. Was received 30 Sept. 1836. He is 16 years old, 5' 5" high, weighs 140 lbs., has blue eyes, dark hair, fair complexion, large nose, appears confused when spoken to. Was born in state of Georgia. Says his parents are dead. He has traveled with a circus company. *Thomas Morrison discharged.* [Ledger 45, p. 110]

James McNees_e_ from Giles Co., Tenn. Offence: assault with intent to kill. Sentence: three years from 2 Nov. 1836. Was received Nov. 6, 1836. He is 28 years old, 6' 3 ½" high, weighs 175 lbs. Blue eyes, fair hair, fair skin, light beard. The middle finger of the left hand has been bit off near the end. A small scar above the wrist of the left hand on the back of the arm. Born in Maury and raised in Giles Co., Tenn. His parents now reside in Giles Co., Tenn. Has no family. *James McNeece was discharged Jan. 17th, 1840, being detained two months and 13 days for bad conduct.* [Ledger 45, p. 110]

James Miller from White County, Tenn. Offence: horse stealing. Sentence: three years. Was rec'd Feb. 19, 1837. He is 18 years old 5' 8" high and weighs 135 lbs. Has auburn hair, blue eyes, fair skin and boyish look, no beard, is fond of talking. Was raised in Overton Co., Tenn. His father lives on Sidwell Creek near Gen'l. Harrisons. *James Miller died of [blank] July 12th, 1837.* [Ledger 45, p. 110]

Samuel Moran from Bedford Co., Tenn. Offence: larceny. Sentence: one year from 18th Apr. 1837. He is 5' 8 3/4" high, weighs 155 lbs. Dark hair, grey eyes, fair skin. Has a wife and one child living in Bedford Co., Tenn. His father John Moran lives in Wilson Co., Tenn., near Statesville. [Ledger 45, p. 111]

Thomas Mills. Offence: receiving stolen goods. Sentence: one year. Rec[eive]d 16 May 1837. He is 32 years of age, 5' 8" high, weighs 163 lbs. A bright mulatto. He was born in Georgia, brought up in Georgia. Sentenced by the Cuircuit Court of Shelby County to one years confinement in the Jail and Penitentiary House of the State of Tennessee. [Ledger 45, p. 111]

William Moore. Offence: murder. Sentence: 14 years from 26th May 1837. He is 58 years old, 5' 8" high, weighs 135 lbs. Dark grey hair, fair skin, thin visage. Was born in Amherst Co., Virginia. Brought up in York District, South Carolina, where he has a sister living married to Edmond Kindrick. He has one brother living in Clayburn Co., Mississippi, near Port Gibson. He has but one child. She is married and lives in Carroll Co., Tenn. Was sentenced by the Cuircuit Court of Fayette County to the Penitentiary House of the State of Tennessee. *Thomas Mills was discharged by expiration of sentence.* [Ledger 45, p. 111]

Sam'l Moore. From Maury County. Offence: grand larceny. Sentence: three years from reception. Received Sept. 11, 1837. He is 40 years old, 5' 7" high, weighs 135 or 140 lbs. Black hair, hazle eyes, light beard, rough features. Has been powder burnt in the face. Born and bro[ugh]t up in Burtee [sic,] Co., North Carolina, four miles east of Windsor. Sentenced by the Cuircuit Court of Maury County to three years confinement in the Jail and Penitentiary House of the State of Tennessee. [Ledger 45, p. 111]

Tennessee Convicts: Records of the State Penitentiary

Curtis Manley. From Henderson County. Offence: assault and battery with intend to kill. Sentence: three years. Rec'd: Dec. 6, 1837. He is 25 years of age, 5' 8" high, weighs 162 lbs. Born in Wayne Co., North Carolina. Bro't up in Henderson Co., Tenn., near Independance. Where his father Elcany[?] Manley now lives. He has two sisters married, one to Council Holmes, the other to Henry Holmes. He has a wife and one child at her father's, Thomas Crawford, near Independance. He has fair skin, blue eyes, light hair. Has generally followed farming. [Ledger 45, p. 112]

Hiram B. McCrory. From Davidson County. Received: 10 Mar. 1838. Sentenced: three years. He is 18 years old, weighs 165 lbs., 6' 2 ½" high. Born in Alabama, bro't up in Maury and Davidson counties, Tenn. His mother lives in Davidson on Little Harpeth near Stockets[?] Meeting House. He has one uncle living in the same settlement, by the name of Samuel Nothern[?]. His father's brothers all lives in Alabama. He has dark hair, fair skin, blue eyes. He has a small scar over his right eye. [Ledger 45, p. 112]

Geo. Measel. From Haywood County. Received 12 Oct. 1838. Sentence: three years for horse stealing. He is 32 years old, 5' 9 ½" high, weighs 158 lbs. He has dark hair, hazle eyes, a scar on the cap of the right knee. Born and bro't up in Burtee [sic,] Co., North Carolina. He has a wife and three children living with her brother Henry Gaskin six miles east of Brown[s]ville on the road leading from Brown[s]ville to Jackson. He has two brothers and three sisters married and living in Burtee Co., North Carolina. He lived with John Hunter one year as overseer on the road leading from Brownsville to Fulton. He also overseed [sic,] two years for Robt. C. Scott on said road. [Ledger 45, p. 112]

Mark Manus. From Henderson County. Sentence: three years. Rec'd Dec. 8, 1838. Offence: grand larceny. He is 22 years old, 5' 9" high, weighs 133 lbs. Born and bro't up in Moore Co., North Carolina. His mother, Maloney Manus, lives in Henderson Co., Tenn., six miles west of Lexington on Pina[?] Creek, one and a half miles from Criders Mill. He has light hair, hazle eyes, large nose. Has had the under eye-lid of each eye tore in the corner next his nose. He has two sisters, one living near his mother. The other is married to a man by a the name of Elija [sic,] Brewer and lives in Rhea County. He has a scar imediately bolow the ancle bone of the left foot. [Ledger 45, p. 113]

Joshua Mullins, Johnson County. Crime: petit larceny. Sentence: two years. Received 29 Dec. 1838. He is 45 years old, 5' 9" high, weighs 157 lbs. Born and bro't up in Johnson Co., Tenn., where his father, William Mullins, now lives one mile east of Tailorsville on the Abington Road. He has light hair, hazel eyes, fair skin. Has two scars on the right jaw. Has one sister married to

Tennessee Convicts: Records of the State Penitentiary

Henry Morefield and works at Ward Iron Works or Furnace. He has been burned in the left hand which keep[s] all the fingers of this hand half shut. [Ledger 45, p. 113]

Obediah May. From Madison County. Rec'd Jan. 15, 1839. Offence: murder. Sentence: during his natural life. He is 60 years old, 5' 8 ¼" high, weighs 153 lbs. He has dark hair, blue eyes, fair skin. Born in Virginia, bro't up in Logan Co., Kentucky, by his mother's brother Absalum Chism who has kept the tavern at Shakertown or South Union for many years. He was married to Obediah Chism's daughter by whom he had two children. They then parted. Since that time he has been married to a Miss Stewart by which he had three children. He then murdered her, for which he was sentenced. His last children are with the Stewarts, his wife's brothers. He has one brother living in Hardeman Co., Tenn., near Mattemora [sic,]. Said May is a laborer. [Ledger 45, p. 113]

John McGrew. From Franklin County. Offence: horse stealing. Sentence: three years. Rec'd Jan. 24, 1839. He is 19 years old, 6' high, weighs 178 lbs. Born in Georgia, bro't up in Maury Co., Tenn. He has fair hair, hazle eyes, fair skin. He has one uncle living in Lincoln Co., Georgia, by the name of John Haws. His mother is dead; he has neither brother nor sister. His father he says he does not know where he is. [Ledger 45, p. 114]

Matthew Murphey. From Wayne County. Offence: larceny. Sentence: three years. Rec'd Mar. 26, 1837[?]. He is 28 years old, weighs 167 lbs., 5' 10" high. Born and bro't up in Lawrence District., South Carolina. His father John Murphey lives in Lauderdale Co., Alabama, 13 miles north of Florence. His wife and one child is living with his father. He has four brothers and four sisters, the[y] all live in Lauderdale Co., Alabama. He is a farmer by profession. [Ledger 45, p. 114]

Wm. Martin. From Hamilton County. Sentence: one year from 29 Mar. 1839. Offence: larceny. He is 29 years old, 5' 10" high, weighs 148 lbs. Born in South Carolina, bro't up in Tennessee in the counties of Roane and Hamilton, where his mother, Elizabeth Martin, now lives 10 miles below Dallas on Chickamaugy [sic,] Creek near its mouth. He has a wife and five children which live within one half mile of Mrs. Martin's. He is quite grey for one of his age. He has blue eyes, dark skin. He has a scar on the right cheek bone caused by a blow. He is a labourer. *William Martin discharged.* [Ledger 45, p. 114]

William Miles. From Franklin County. Offence: grand larceny. Received May 23, 1839. Sentence: three years. Said Miles is 32 years old, 5' 10" high, weighs 162 lbs. Born in Jackson Co., Tenn., and bro't up in Franklin. Said William Miles has a wife and six children ten miles east of Winchester near Branan's [sic,] Meeting House. His wife was a Miss Timms[?] before marriage. He has fair blue eyes, fair skin. Has a scar in his forehead caused by a fall when a child, say 1 ½" long. [Ledger 45, p. 114]

Jesse J. McLeod. From Fayette County. Was received into the Penitentiary 7 July 1839. He is 23 years old, 5' 10" high, weighs 136 lbs. Born in North Carolina, Montgomery County. Brought up in Carroll Co., Tenn., where his mother, four sisters and one brother now live in the neighborhood of Bledsoe Mill. Has one sister married to Ambrose Hadley and lives in Murrey [sic,, Maury] County near Duck River. Has three sisters in Carroll County married, one in Missouri married to a man by the name of John Phillips. He has fair skin, grey eyes, brown hair. His finger appears to have a natural crook at the knuckle joint. He has followed well diggin[g]. The said J.J. McLeod was convicted in the county of Fayette of the crime of horse stealing, and sentenced to undergo confinement at hard labour in the Jail and Penitentiary house of this state for three [years] commencing from the day of his reception. [Ledger 45, p. 115]

John Moore. From Sullivan County. Wash [sic,] rec'd into the Penitentiary 14 Apr. 1839. Crime: grand larceny. Sentence to hard labour in the Jail and Penitentiary House of this State for three years. For further particulars refer to former sentence (under the name of Edwin Clark). [Ledger 45, p. 115]

John Mahaffe. From Bradley County. Crime: petit larceny. Sentence: one year from 29 Apr. 1840. Received 7 May 1840. He is 23 years old, 5' 9" high, weighs 160 lbs. Born and brought up in Rhea Co., Tenn. Has a wife and three children in Bledsoe County. He has fair hair, blue eyes, fair skin. [Ledger 45, p. 115]

William Mercer. From Carroll County. Crime: malicious stabbing shooting. Sentence: two years from 13 May 1840. Rec'd 13 May 1840. He is 24 years old, about 5' 8" high, weighs 140 lbs. Born and brought up in Pitt Co., North Carolina. He has lost the use of his left leg by a white swelling. [Ledger 45, p. 116]

Wesley McGuire. From Franklin County. Crime: petit larceny. Sentence: one year from July 29, 1840. Rec'd July 29, 1840. He is 21 years old, weighs 148 lbs., 5' 8" high. Was born in White County near the Blue Spring Cove, brought up in Alabama, Jackson County. Has a wife and one child on the waters of Flat Creek living near her father Elijah Oozele. Said McGuire has light hair, blue eyes and fair skin. [Ledger 45, p. 116]

Jackson McGuire. From Franklin County. Crime: petit larceny. Sentence: one year from July 29, 1840. Rec'd July 29, 1840. He is 24 years old, weighs 120 lbs, 5' 4" high. Born in White County, Tenn., and brought up in Jackson Co., Ala. Has lived in Bedford Co., Tenn. He has been married, his wife died and left him one child. It is in Bedford County with its grandmother, Nancy Beard. Said McGuire has dark hair, hazle eyes, fair skin, generally clear of scars. [Ledger 45, p. 116]

Daniel McCarty. From Bradley County. Crime: larceny. Sentence: two years from 1 Jan. 1841. Rec'd 11 Jan. 1841. Second conviction. See former description when before rec'd on 28 Oct. 1835. [Ledger 45, p. 117]

Henry A. Manley. From Fayette County. Crime: petit larceny. Sentence: one year from 8 Feb. 1841. Rec'd 8 Feb. 1841. He is 27 years old, ____ [blank] high, weighs 180 lbs. Born and brought up in Halifax, North Carolina. Has a wife and three children in Fayette County, belonging to Wilson Carter, about five miles from Somerville on Little Muddy near the Covington[?] and Randolph Road. He is a bright mulatto with very curly hair. Has a small scar on the upper lip. [Ledger 45, p. 117]

Isaac Mahaffy. From Wilson County. Crime: murder. Sentence: 10 years from 2 Feb. 1841. Rec'd 8 Feb. 1841. He is 34 years old, 5' 8" high, weighs 154 lbs. Born in Carhow [sic,] Co., South Carolina, on Hanging Rock Creek. Brought up in Wilson Co., Tenn., at or near Jesse Holt's mill. Has a wife and four children in the poor house in Wilson County. Four other children bound out. Said Mahaffy has sandy hair, fair skin, blue eyes. Has a small scar on the first joint of the forefinger of the left hand, also the middle finger of the same hand is stiff in the joint nearest the end of it. Has three cuts on the instep of his left foot. Has a small scar on the underpart of the right foot near the big toe. [Ledger 45, p. 117]

Alexander McClellan. From Hamilton County. Sentence: five years from 24 Mar. 1841. Rec'd 4 April 1841. Crime: burglary and larceny. He is 28 years old, 5' 11 1/2" high, weighs 157 lbs. Born and brought up in Moore Co., North Carolina, on Cape Fear River near the Buckhorn falls. Has one sister married to a man by the name of John Lawrence, and lives in DeKalb Co., Georgia. Also one married to a man by the name of Jos. [Jas.?] Mangrum and lives in

Coosa Co., Alabama, near Wetumpka. He has fair hair, blue eyes and fair skin. His nose a little crooked. [Ledger 45, p. 118]

Abel L. Middleton. From Monroe County. Crime: horse stealing. Sentence: four years from 24 May 1841. Rec'd 24 May 1841. He is 19 years old, weighs 158 lbs., 5' 8" high. Born and brought up in Jefferson Co., Tenn., six miles n.e. of Dandridge. Has two sisters in Cannon Co., Tenn., both married, one to man by the name of Saml. Cannon and the other to a man by the name of John Vasser[?]. Said Middleton has fair hair, blue eyes, fair skin. [Ledger 45, p. 118]

John McBride. From Shelby County. Crime: counterfeiting. Sentence: eight years from 26 June 1841 when he was received. He is 39 years old, 5' 8" high, weighs 155 lbs. Born in Knox Co. and brought up in Maury Co., Tenn. Has one brother in Benton Co. nine miles from Mason's Ferry on the Tenn. River, by the name of Zekiel McBride. One in Wayne Co. by the name of And'w Jackson McBride, he is living on the waters of Balter's[?] Creek. Also one living in Hardeman Co. on Hatchee River about 12 miles above Bolivar, a gun smith by trade. Has but one sister and does not know where she lives. Said John McBride married the daughter of John Hodges who now lives 16 miles east of Memphis, one on the state line road and within three miles of Germantown. Said McB has hazle eyes, dark hair a little grey, fair skin, quiet spoken. Has had a cut on the little finger of the right hand. [Ledger 45, p. 118]

Joshua Morgan. From Green[e] County. Crime: larceny. Sentence: 21 months from June 29, 1841. Rec'd: June 29, 1841. He is 17 years old, 5' 7 3/4" high, weighs 139 lbs. Born in Carter County, left there when 10 years old, has lived since that time in Green County two miles from Green[e]ville where his father James Morgan now lives. He has four brothers and three sisters. One brother and one sister married, live in Green Co. near his father's. He has red hair very freckled, fair skin and blue eyes. [Ledger 45, p. 119]

Aaron Mobley. From Grainger County. Crime: murder. Sentence: 21 years from Sept. 13, 1841. Received Sept. 13, 1841. He is 27 years old, 5' 7" high, weighs 117 lbs. Born and brought up in Chatham Co., North Carolina, where his father James Mobly now lives about 14 miles north of Pittsborough. He has fair hair, blue eyes and fair skin. He has a wife and three children living in Chatham Co. with his father. Her name before marriage was Sally Coggins. She was brought up in the same county that he was. [Ledger 45, p. 119]

Tennessee Convicts: Records of the State Penitentiary

John Collins. Riley H. Melton. [crossed out in original] From Wayne County. Crime: petit larceny bigamy. Sentence: two years from 14 Oct. 1841 when he was rec'd. He is 48 years old, weighs 145 lbs., 5' 7 ½" high. Born and brought up in South Carolina. Has lived in Smith Co. near Liberty, also in Warren Co. near Shell's ford on Collins River. He has a wife and three stepchildren in Wayne Co. on Harden's Creek, 10 miles west of Waynesboro. He has grey hair, has a small lump in the corner of his left eye near his nose, hazle eyes and dark skin. [Ledger 45, p. 119]

Riley H. Melton. From Wayne County. Crime: petit larceny. Sentence: two years from 14 Oct. 1841. Rec'd 14 Oct. 1841. He is 19 years old, weighs 117 lbs., 5' 6" high. Born in Bedford Co. 12 miles from Shelbyville, three miles from the Fishing Ford on Duck River. His father John Melton now lives in Wayne Co. 12 miles from Waynesboro on the Florence Road. He has fair hair, blue eyes and fair skin, tolerable good countenance. [Ledger 45, p. 120]

Francis McAllister. From Henderson County. Crime: larceny. Sentence: three years from 9 Dec. 1841. Rec'd 9 Dec. 1841. He is 30 years old, weighs 154 lbs, 5' 8" in high[t]. Born in Rutherford Co., brought up in Henderson Co. Has a wife and three children living on the waters of Spencer's Creek with her mother, Sarah D. Strain. He has sandy hair, blue eyes, fair skin. Has two brothers, one a painter and lives in Fort Pickering on the Miss. Has three sisters, one in the Cherokee Nation, two in Henderson Co., one married to Rich'd Hamlett, one to John Tyler. [Ledger 45, p. 120]

Anderson Masters. From Carroll County. Crime: grand larceny. Sentence: three years from 13 Jan. 1842. Rec'd 13 Jan. 1842. He is 17 years old, 5' 5" high, weighs 123 lbs. Born in Overton Co. Has been bound to Judge Totten for five years. He is a smart boy, a mulatto. His hair is very straight for a boy of his color. [Ledger 45, p. 120]

Robert L. Montgomery. From Lincoln County. Crime: involuntary manslaughter. Sentence: one year from 21 Feb. 1842. Rec'd 20 Feb. 1842. He is 22 years old, 5' 4" high and weighs 122 lbs. Born in Lincoln County and brought up in said county on Norris' Creek where is father Hu Montgomery now lives. He has fair hair, blue eyes and fair skin. Has worked at the blacksmith's trade 10 or 12 years [Ledger 45, p. 121]

Lemuel J. Mills. From Lincoln County. Crime: counterfeiting. Sentence: three years from 21 Feb. 1842. Rec'd 20 Feb. 1842. He is 42 years old, 5' 9" high, weighs 153 lbs. Born in Sumner County on Bledsoe's Creek near the mouth of said creek. Has a wife and six children in Lincoln [County] near

Phelps Mill on Mulberry Creek. Has one daughter married to a man by the name of M. Lee and lives on Big Creek in Giles Co. about four miles from Bootenhammer's Mill, it is on a Spring branch. He has dark hair, black eyes and dark skin. Has several scars on the fingers of both of his hands. Has had the big toe of the right foot split which leaves a scar. Is a blacksmith. [Ledger 45, p. 121]

James E. Murray. From Knox County. Crime: malicious stabbing. Sentence: two years from 14 Mar. 1842 when he was rec'd. He is 22 years old, 5' 6" high, weighs 142 lbs. Born and brought up in Knoxville where his father Thomas D. Murray now lives. He is a sad[d]ler. Has one sister married and lives in Holly Springs, her husband's name is J. Vestal, a cabinet workman. Has one brother in Napoleon, Arkansas, a doctor. Has a wife living with her mother, Christenia Johnston, in Knoxville. He has blue eyes, fair skin and light hair. [Ledger 45, p. 121]

John McNeal. From Davidson County. Crime: larceny. Sentence: three years from March 1842. Rec'd March 1842. He is about 26 years of age, 5' 8" high, weighs 145 lbs. Black hair and dark beard, haz<u>l</u>e eyes and dark eyebrows. Born in North Carolina, Walker County. The two upper front teeth one much damaged near the gum and the one to the<u>ir</u> right is rotted and half gone. He has a scar 1" long between the thumb and forefinger and rather more on the back of the hand. On the back of the little finger, same hand, there are several small scars and one on the next finger made by a reap hook. His hands are small and short fingers. [Ledger 45, p. 122]

John Maxfield, alias John Wyatt. From Hamilton County. Crime: malicious stabbing. Sentence: two years from 4 Apr. 1842. Rec'd 12 Apr. 1842. He is 28 years old, 5' 9 1/4" high, weighs 174 lbs. Born and brought up in Grainger Co., Tenn. He has six brothers and six sisters. His mother's name was Dicy Wyatt. She was never married but had 13 children, seven by a man named James Blair and six by a man named Isaac Maxfield. He has a brother and one sister in Wayne Co., West Tenn. Said Wyatt has blue eyes, dark skin and dark hair. Has a scar on the left cheekbone about 4" long, one on the upper lip near the corner of his mouth. [Ledger 45, p. 122]

Clements Manning. From Stewart County. Crime: manslaughter. Sentence: two years six months from 2 July 1842. Rec'd 4 July 1842. He is 20 years old, weighs 154 lbs., 5' 9" high. Born and brought up within 1 1/2 miles of Dover where his father, John Manning, now lives. Has four uncles in the same settlement. Has four uncles in Obion County by the name of Moody. Said Manning has dark hair, haz<u>l</u>e eyes, dark skin, has a scar just below each knee cap across the leg, he says caused by cuts from falling on iron on board a boat. He has followed boating as cook, fireman and deck hand. [Ledger 45, p. 123]

Robert Myres. From Monroe County. Crime: manslaughter. Sentence: two years from 28 Sept. 1842. Rec'd 28 Sept. 1842. He is 22 years old, weighs 173 lbs., 6' high. Was born in Washington Co., Virginia, [and] bro't up in Monroe Co., Tenn., 3 ½ miles north of Madisonville. He has two sisters married, one to Robt. Reed, the other to Peter Brakeville. Also two single sisters and two single brothers all living in the above named county of Monroe. He has dark hair, hazle eyes and dark skin. Has had two cuts on the instep of the left foot, size about 2 ½" in length. [Ledger 45, p. 123]

John Calving Manning. From Stewart County. Crime: manslaughter. Sentence: two years from 2 Oct. 1842. Rec'd Nov. 8, 1842. Said Manning is 18 years old, weighs 144 lbs., 5' 6" high, and has a blemish in his right eye. For other particulars see description of his brother Clements Manning, this page. [Ledger 45, p. 123]

John Mitchell. From Williamson County. Crime: grand larceny. Sentence: three years from 30 Nov. [18]42. Rec'd 30 Nov. 1842. Said Mitchell is 26 years old, 5' 7" high, weighs 157 lbs. Born and bro't up in Lancastershire, England. Has two cousins in Philadelphia working at calico printing, but does not know by whom they are employed. He has sandy hair, fair skin, blue eyes. Has a scar on his nose crosswise, about ⅔ from the point to where it joins the forehead. Has a scar on his left thigh just above the knee. He has worked with Loads & Co., New Orleans, steam boiler making. Also worked a short time in the Franklin Factory, Franklin, Tenn. [Ledger 45, p. 124]

Ambrose A. Norris was received in the Penitentiary 31 Dec. 1832. He is 5' 11" in height, weighs 153 lbs., dark hair, blue eyes, heavy brow, tolerable fair skin, well formed and intelligent, 25 years of age. Born in Bourbon Co., Kentucky, brought up in Cincinnati, Ohio. His mother, brother and two sisters reside in Preble Co., Ohio, near Newton's Mills on Seven Mile Creek, 35 miles from Cincinnati below the town of Dayton. The above mentioned mills are owned by his stepfather whose name is Newton. He has one brother, John Norris, living in the town of Oxford, Butler Co., Ohio. He has a small scar over the right eyebrow, a small one about an inch from the left corner of the mouth running up and down the face, one on the instep of the right foot, one on the left foot between the great toe and second. He is a cabinet maker and painter by trade. Was found guilty of petit larceny at the Circuit Court of Shelby County and sentenced to two years and six months confinement in the Jail and Penitentiary House of the State of Tennessee. *Ambrose A. Norris was discharged 21st of*

April 1836 having been detained 296 days for bad conduct. [Ledger 45, p. 125]

Moses A. Nelson was received in the Penitentiary 25 Jan. 1834. He is 5' 9 ½" in height and weighs 163 lbs. Light hair, blue eyes, fair complexion, 34 years of age. Born and brought up in Washington Co., Tenn., where his mother still resides, about three miles south of Brownsborough. He has seven brothers and one sister. His brothers reside in Missouri. His sister, who is a widow named (Hickson), in Indiana. He cannot tell what county in either state. He has an uncle John Hughes living in Seqachee [sic,] Valley and a wife and nine children now residing in Hamilton County but expects to remove to ____ [blank]. His wife was the daughter of Adam Gann, dec'd, of Jefferson Co., Tenn. He has a scar on the inside ancle and one on the instep of the left foot, a scar on the inside ancle of the right foot, a scar just below the knee of the right leg, and a small mole on the left breast. He has generally followed farming. Was found guilty of petit larceny at the Circuit Court of Cocke County and sentenced to one years confinement in the Jail and Penitentiary House of the State of Tennessee. *Moses A. Nelson was discharged by expiration of sentence on the 24th day of January 1835.* [Ledger 45, pp. 125-6]

Henry Norwood. From Carroll County. Crime: buggery. Sentence: five years from 12 May 1841. Rec'd 12 May 1841. He is 16 years old, 6' ½" high, weighs 148 lbs. Was born in Madison Co., Tenn., and brought up in Carroll Co. on Blunt Creek, 12 ½ miles from Huntingdon and one mile from Sandy, where his father Wm. Norvell now lives. He has three sisters and two brothers married, one brother in Texas, one in Arkansas at Little Rock, also one sister married to a man by the name of John Nandin and lives on Birdsong Creek, Benton Co., Tenn. Has dark hair, hazle eyes, fair skin and somewhat freckled. [Ledger 45, p. 126]

Obadiah Norris. From Claiborne County. Sentence: three years from Feb. 5, 1842. Crime: manslaughter. Rec'd Feb. 5, 1842. He is 25 years old, 5' 8" high, weighs 174 lbs. Born and brought up in Gra[i]nger Co., Tenn., on Bull run, 2 miles from John Chesney's mill. Has a wife and one child living at Boon Creek Forge in Claiborn[e] County. He has sandy hair, black eyes, fair skin. Has worked three years at Boon Creek Forge in the employ of J. Frazier. [Ledger 45, p. 126]

Jesse Norris. From Dickson County. Crime: larceny. Sentence: three years from Feb. 24, 1842. Rec'd Feb. 26, 1842. He is 46 years old, 5' 6 ½" high and weighs 128 lbs. Born in Georgia and brought up in Dixon Co., Tenn., on Yellow Creek. He has a wife and four children living on the road leading from

Tennessee Convicts: Records of the State Penitentiary

Charlotte to Mason's Ferry on Tennessee River, four miles from Charlotte. Has two sisters on the waters of Yellow Creek, one by the name of Nancy Dillihay, the other Eleanor Spence. Said Norris has dark gray hair, sandy beard, blue eyes and dark skin. [Ledger 45, p. 127]

Wm. Nun. From Claiborne County. Crime: petit larceny. Sentence: one year from May 29, 1842. Received May 29, 1842. He is 53 years old, 5' 11" high, weighs 180 lbs. Born in old and brought up in New Virginia, Wythe County, on Reed Island Creek. He has a wife and six children on a creek called Coney about 1 ½ miles from James Carpenter's mills. Said Nun has dark hair, hazle eyes and fair skin. He has a scar on his breast cut with a cradling scythe. [Ledger 45, p. 127]

Ira Olive was received in the Penitentiary 14 Jan. 1834. He is 5' 8 ¾" in height and weighs 158 lbs. Light hair, blue eyes, sandy complexion and 40 years of age. Born in Chatham Co., North Carolina, brought up in Davidson Co., Tenn. His parents are dead. He has a wife and four children residing in Stewart Co., Tenn., at his father in law's, George Bruton, about eight miles from Dover Furnace. There is a remarkable scar on the shin caused by a kick from a stallion. He has a mark of nature from the left hand up nearly to the shoulder and speckled over the arm from the elbow (called by himself a mark of wine). A scar near the hair over the right eye from a blow with a rock. He has worked a little at shoemaking and saddling. Was found guilty at the Circuit Court of Tipton County of stabbing and sentenced to two years confinement in the Jail and Penitentiary House of the State of Tennessee hazle. *Ira Olive was discharged this 14th day of January 1836 having served his term without censure from any of the officers.* [Ledger 45, p. 129]

James Orr. From Marshall County, Tenn. Offince: horse and money stealing. Sentence: three years. Rec'd 2 Dec. 1836. He is 22 years old, 5' 11" high, weighs 200 lbs. Blue eyes, fair or light hair, fair skin, round full face. Two scars on the fore finger of the left hand, a small scar in the fore head. Born in Maury County, Tenn. Has lived in Alabama and Illinois, where his father now lives. *James Orr discharged Dec. 4, 1839. Conduct generally good.* [Ledger 45, p. 129]

Jeremiah Oakley. From Maury County. Rec'd Jan. 21, 1839. Sentence: two years. Offence: hog stealing. He is 39 years old, 5' 10", weighs 187 lbs. Born and bro't up in Orange Co., North Carolina. He has dark grey hair, hazle eyes, fair skin. Has had his left ancle injured from a cotton bale falling on it. He has a wife and two children living in Maury County about 1 ½ miles from Jordan's

[Gordon's?] ferry on Duck River. Has followed shoemaking. [Ledger 45, p. 130]

David Ozment. From Haywood County. Crime: felony. Sentence: three years from 21 June 1840. Rec'd 21 June 1840. He is supposed to be 40 years old. Weighs 133 lbs, 5' 9 3/4" high. Born in Guilford Co., North Carolina, where he was partly brought up. His father Saml. Ozment then moved to Wilson Co., Tenn., where he lived 15 or 16 years within eight or ten miles of Lebanon. Worked at gun smithing with his cousin by the name of W.M. Swain in the Richmond settlement. Has one brother in Wilson County. Has one sister living in Brownsville, Haywood County, her husband follows gunsmithing, his name is James [surname left blank]. Said Ozment has a wife and seven children, seven miles from Brownsville near the key[?] corner road. Said Ozment is a gunsmith by trade. [Ledger 45, p. 130]

Patrick O'Brien. From Davidson County. Crime: horse stealing. Sentence: three years from May 29, 1841. Rec'd May 29, 1841. He is 19 years old, 5' 6" high, weighs 128 lbs. Born in Spain in the city of Madrid and brought up in New York City where he has two brothers and four sisters all living. He has red hair, fair skin, black eyes, quick spoken. Has what some people would call a good countenance. Has had the small pox which left one pock on his left cheek. He has a red mark in his left hand, he says on the full moon it is very red. [Ledger 45, p. 131]

James H. Oney. From Giles County. Crime: horse stealing. Sentence: three years from 30 June 1841. Rec'd 30 June 1841. He is 23 years old, 5' 5" high, weighs 135 lbs. Has dark hair, blue eyes, dark skin. Has worked at wagon making and blacksmithing. Has one sister in Smith Co., Virginia, she is married to a man by the name of Ralph M. Stafford. He has lived in Giles County where he followed driving a wagon. Said Oney was born and bro't up in Wythe Co., Virginia. [Ledger 45, p. 131]

Spencer Oliver. From Washington County. Crime: grand larceny. Sentence: three years from 4 Nov. 1842. Received 29 Nov. 1842. The above S. Oliver is 33 years old, weighs 167 lbs., 5' 9" high. Born and bro't up in Washington County. Has one brother in Roane Co., Tenn., and one in Scott Co., Missouri. Has four sisters in Washington County about 1 1/2 miles from Jonesboro on John Elliston's land. He has fair skin, dark hair, eyebrows dark and heavy. Has had his right thigh broken. Has a scar on his nose caused by a kick from a horse. [Ledger 45, p. 132]

Tennessee Convicts: Records of the State Penitentiary

Jackson Pannel was received in the Penitentiary 16 June 1831. He is 6' 2" high, dark hair, gray eyes, heavy beard and weighs about 175 lbs. A small scar on the upper lip, and one on the left arm occasioned by a burn. Dark complexion. Born and brought up in Northampton Co., Maryland. Has resided in Fayette Co., Kentucky, for the last seven years, lived at Thomas Hughes'. Has no trade. Was found guilty of horse stealing at the Circuit Court of Davidson County and sentenced to eight years confinement in the Jail and Penitentiary House of the State of Tennessee. *Pardoned by Governor Cannon January 22nd, 1839. Conduct good.* [Ledger 45, p. 133]

Baxter A. Powell was received into the Penitentiary 18 Jan. 1832. He is 5' 11 ¼", weighs 146 lbs., is 20 years old, dark hair, grey or hazle eyes. Born and raised in the State of Tennessee, Davidson County, on Big Harpeth River. Raised partly in Humphreys County. He has a small scar between the middle fingers of the right hand, and a small scar on the outside of the left leg, and on the same side of the right a little higher up the leg than that on the right [*sic,*], caused by a bite. Generally very clear of scars. He has one brother in the United States Army and one living, the last he heard of him, in McNairy Co., Tenn. He was convicted of burglary at the April term of the Robertson Circuit and sentenced to be hanged. By an act of the General Assembly of the State of Tennessee, passed at Nashville 19 Dec. 1831, and of an act passed on 20 Dec. 1831, the Governor is vested with full power and authority and commutes the punishment of death of the said Baxter A. Powell to 15 years hard labor in the Jail and Penitentiary House of the State of Tennessee. [Ledger 45, p. 133]

Abram Powel was received in the Penitentiary 15 Dec. 1832. He is 5' 11" in height, weighs 187 lbs., dark hair, hazel eyes, rather dark complexion, 27 years of age. Born in Orange Co., North Carolina, and brought up there. His father, mother, three brothers and four sisters now reside in Guilford Co., North Carolina. He has two brothers in this country, their residence not known. One of his legs has been injured by a log rolling on it, leaving a large scar below the shin. It is on the right leg. Has generally followed farming. Was found guilty of petit larceny at the Circuit Court of Henry County and sentenced to two years confinement in the Jail and Penitentiary House of the State of Tennessee. *Abram Powell died of cholera on the 16th day of June 1833.* [Ledger 45, p. 133]

Archibald Porter was received in the Penitentiary 29 Oct. 1833. He is 5' 10" in height and weighs 151 lbs. Blue eyes, dark hair and complexion, high forehead and prominent nose, about 21 years of age. Born in North Carolina and raised in Blount Co., Tenn., by his uncle Archibald Murphy. He has a sister living in Hamilton Co., Tenn., married to James Wilson. Their residence is about 11 miles from the town of Dallas and about one mile from the residence of Daniel Henderson, Esqr. Porter has a scar on the inside of the wrist of the right arm, occasioned by a burn. A scar just above the right eye, a scar on the lower part of the shin of the left leg, a scar on the toe next the great one on the right foot, and five moles on the right side of his neck. He has generally followed farming. Was found guilty of horse stealing at the Circuit Court of Hamilton County and sentenced to four years confinement in the Jail and Penitentiary House of the State of Tennessee. *Archibald Porter died of cholera on the 2nd day of July 1835.* [Ledger 45, p. 134]

William Phillips was received in the Penitentiary June 13, 1834. He is 5' 4 ½" in height and weighs 140 lbs. Light hair, blue eyes, dark complexion, large nose, stout built and 47 years of age. Born and brought up in Richmond, Virginia. He has a wife and seven children residing in Lincoln Co., Tenn. He has been a seaman for 16 years. Was present at engagement between the Constitution and Java frigates during the late war. He has a scar from a boarding pike on the right side of the forehead, and two scars from cuts of a cutlass in the act of boarding. He has the letters **G C N N** [?] on the left arm. Was found guilty of burglary at the Circuit Court of Bedford County and sentenced to five years confinement in the Jail and Penitentiary House of the State of Tennessee. *William Phillips was discharged June 17th, 1839.* [Ledger 45, p. 134]

John D. Padgett was rec'd in the Penitentiary 16 Sept. 1834. He is 5' 9 ¼" in height, weighs 194 lbs., 31 years of age. Light hair, b[l]ue eyes and fair complexion. Born in Cocke Co., Tenn., and partly brought up in Cocke and Overton counties. His father and mother reside on Obys River, Overton County, near Esq. McClellen's mill in the neighbourhood of Esq. Paris. He has a wife (whose made name was [blank]) and one child. His [*sic,*, her?] parents live on Wolf River in [blank] County in the neighbourhood of Genl. John Rogers. He has resided some time in Nashville. A scar above the right eye occasioned by a blow from a rock. A scar on the edge of the forehead and one on the right thigh, very remarkable, in the shape of a slanting *T* . He has generally followed shoemaking. Was found guilty of petit larceny at the Circuit Court of Overton County and sentenced to one year confinement in the Jail and Penitentiary House of the State of Tennessee. *John D. Padgett died of cholera on the 30th day of June 1835.* [Ledger 45, p. 135]

Culverson Phillips was rec'd in the Penitentiary 5 Nov. 1834. He is 5' 8" in height, 21 years old, and weighs 175 lbs. Bl[ac]k eyes, black hair, and dark complexion. Very full, broad face and stout built. Has a scar about the centre of the left eye brow. Was born in Mecklenburg Co., North Carolina, and brought up in Bunkum [sic,, Buncombe] County in the same state. His father and mother reside in Campbell Co., Tenn. He was found guilty of petit larceny at the Circuit Court of Claibourne County and sentenced to one years confinement in the Jail and Penitentiary House of the State of Tennessee. *Culverson Phillips was discharged by expiration of sentence December 9th 1835, being detained 35 days for misconduct. Conduct generally good.* [Ledger 45, p. 135]

Moses Parks was rec'd in the Penitentiary 16 Dec. 1834. He is 20 years of age, 5' 8" high, and weighs 165 lbs. B[l]ue eyes, dark hair, fair skin, well formed, heavy built, slightly hair-lip[p]ed under the left side of the nose but not so as to injure his speech. A small scar at the upper end of his nose, in the centre of the same and precisely between the eyes. The small finger of the right hand is crooked at the first joint. A scar about 2" in length running across the right hip occasioned by a stab, and a scar above the left eye in the edge of the hair caused by a blow from a stick. Has chiefly followed boating. Born in Barren Co., Kentucky, and brought up in Nashville, Tenn., where his parents now reside. One sister married to Thomas Corder and three sisters living with their parents. Two brothers (John and William), one (John) living in Nashville who chiefly follows boating, and the other (William) is in the lower country rafting timber to New Orleans. He was found guilty of "assault and battery with intent to kill" at the Circuit Court of Davidson County and sentenced to three years confinement in the Jail and Penitentiary House of the State of Tennessee. *Discharged by expiration of sentence 24 Dec. 1837, detained 9 days for bad conduct.* [Ledger 45, pp. 135-6]

Samuel D. Pugh was rec'd in the Penitentiary 23 April 1835. He is 31 years of age, 5' 10" or 11" high and weighs 168 lbs. Black eyes, dark hair, heavey beard, large nose and thin visage. A scar between the second and third joints of each, the middle and fore finger of the right hand. By occupation a cabinet maker. Born and bred in Green[e] Co., Tenn. Married Mildred Reid, daughter of James Reid of Pendleton District, South Carolina. His wife and children (four) are residing on Sequache [sic,, Sequatchie] River in Sequache Valley, five miles from Jasper. He was found guilty of petit larceny at the Circuit Court of Marion County and sentenced to one years confinement in the Jail and Penitentiary House of the State of Tennessee. *Samuel D. Pugh died of cholera on the 30th day of June 1835.* [Ledger 45, p. 136]

Thomas Prewett. For description see letter R. [Ledger 45, p. 136]

Tarleton Poindexter. Convicted of grand larceny and sentenced to three years imprisonment by the Hawkins County Circuit Court, April term. Was received

27 April 1836. He is 6' 2" high, stout form, not incumbered with flesh, weighs 197 lbs. Narrow, high, oval forehead, short peaked nose, short chin, light hair and beard. A scar on the right thumb on the joint that joins the hand, shaped like a fish hook, and one on the fore finger of the same hand thus, *J*. And a scar between the finger and thumb of the left hand. A scar above the right eye brow ¾" long. Fair skin. Says he was born in Hallifax Co., Virginia. Is 19 years old. Parents live in Hawkins Co., Tenn., in the Blair and Stubblefield neighborhood near the county line meeting houses. One sister married to John Bays, the other to Peter Badget, who live in Pittsylvania Co., Virginia. Badget owns land in said county. *Talton Poindexter [was released] June 4th 1839, having been detained 38 days for misdemeanor.* [Ledger 45, p. 137]

John Petty. Convicted of grand larceny at the April term 1836 of the Ci[r]cuit Court of Franklin Co., Tenn., and sentenced to four years confinement in the Penitentiary. He was received 6 May 1836. He is 5' 7" high, a stout and good form, weighs 152 lbs. Light hair, grey eyes, common complexion, good countenance, deep in the head, under teeth juts in, small mouth. On the outside of the arm and just above the rist of the right arm a cluster of scars (say three) of irregular shape and close together, sunk below the skin. A black mole in the centre of the breast and smoothe with the skin. Both fore fingers curve considerably towards the other fingers. A scar on the left hand ¾" long and cloudy appearance. Says he was born in Franklin Co., Tenn., and raised by his Grandfather Petty, who resides within one mile of Coldwell's Bridge on the road leading from McMinnville to Bellfonte, 31 miles from the former. His wife lives with Mr. Long in the same neighborhood. She was of the name Hedgecock. Her mother lives in Lincoln County 1 ½ miles from Lynchburgh. His mother is married to a man named Jonathan Armstrong who lives on the waters of Black Warrior. Says he has not lived with his mother since he was two years old, is now about 21 years old. [Ledger 45, p. 137]

Azariah Parks. From Haywood Co., Tenn. Offence: negro stealing. Sentence: 10 years. Was rec'd Mar. 11, 1837. 29 years old. He is 5' 8" high, weighs 161 lbs., auburn hair, grey eyes, fair skin, slightly pitted with the small pox. He has had a blow rather to the left side and above his fore head which broke the skull. Another under the chin, left side, cut with the point of a knife. Says he was born in Caswell Co., North Carolina, and moved to this state in 1826 or 1827. Lived in Blount County six years, worked with John Montgomery, Jno. Eagleton, George Hootzell three years and then went in 1834 to Haywood County where his mother lives, nine miles from Brownsville near Mr. Byers. He was employed by Picker Wilson as overseer in 1836. He lived with Henry S. Williams on Hatchee seven miles this side of Covington. [Ledger 45, p. 138]

Tennessee Convicts: Records of the State Penitentiary

Samuel West Pew. Offence: grand larceny. Sentence: five years from 22 June 1837. He is 5' 6" high, weighs 140 lbs. Born and bro't up in Pittsylvania Co., State of Virginia, where he has two cozens John West and William Trainer. He has dark grey hair, grey eyes, dark skin. He has a scar on the right side of the upper lip. Was sentenced by the Cuircourt [sic,] of Lincoln County to five years confinement in the Jail and Penitentiary House of the State of Tennessee. [Ledger 45, p. 138]

W.W. Perry. From Stewart County. Offence: rape. Sentence: 12 years from 17 July 1837. Was received July 24, 1837. He is 58 years old, 5' 8" high, weighs 180 lbs. Dark hair, blind of the left eye, he says it was cut out with a knife, dark heavy beard. Born in North Wales. Has followed the seas. Says he is a sailor. Has worked at farming and has worked at shoemaking. Family lived in Montgomery Co., Kentucky, with a man by the name of McCormic. Sentenced by the Cuircuit Court of Stewart County to 12 years confinement in the Jail and Penitentiary House of the State of Tennessee. [Ledger 45, p. 138]

Jacob Parkerson. From Smith County. Offence: pettit larceny. Sentence: one year. Received Dec. 29, 1837. He is 24 years old, 6' high, weighs 170 lbs. He has fair hair, grey eyes and fair skin. Born and bro't up in Smith County on the Caney Fork five miles from Alexandria. He has a wife and four children with her father in Cannon County on the waters of Smith's Fork, Holton's Creek, within two miles of Clapingers [Clopingers?] Mills. Found guilty at the Circuit Court of Smith County and sentenced to one years confinement in the Jail and Penitentiary House of the State of Tennessee. [signed] W. McIntosh. *Jacob Parkerson discharged by expiration of sentence.* [Ledger 45, p. 139]

Eli Peck. From Jefferson County. Offence: larceny. Sentence: 18 months. Rec'd Jan. 26, 1838. He is 36 years old, 5' 7" high, weigh[s] 145 lbs. Born in Litchfield Co., Connecticut, bro't up in Oneida Co., New York. Has dark grey hair, black eyes, good countenance. Has worked at carpenters business. Has a small scar over the right eye. *Eli Peck discharge[d] July 20th, 1839, having been detained three days for misconduct.* [Ledger 45, p. 139]

John Posey. From Lawrence County. Offence: receiving stolen goods and rendered infamous. Sentenced four years. Received Mar. 19, 1838. He is 56 years old, weighs 179 lbs, 5' 9" high. He has grey hair, full face and black eyes, fair skin. Born and bro't up in South Carolina, Spartenberg District. He has been twice married and has five children, one son in Alabama. His wife's relations live in Rutherford County. He says his mother Sarrah Ann Posey lives near Winchester, Tenn. He has a scar on his breast caused by a stab of a knife, also a scar on his ancle of the right foot. [Ledger 45, p. 139]

Alexander Plunket. From Hickman County. Offence: bigamy. Sentence: two years. Rec'd July 16, 1838. He is 23 years old, 5' 9" high, weighs 135 lbs. Born in North Carolina, bro't up in Hickman Co., Tenn. His supposed father, now the husband of Dicy Plunket, is now living in Hickman County near Centerville. He has blue eyes, fair skin, dark hair, verry heavy eye brows, good countenance. He has a scar on the instep of the right foot caused by the cut of an ax. Also on the same foot commencing at the big toe and runing 2" or more towards the heel. He has a small scar on the right hand about 1" long, it runes across the vain of the arm that extends down to the thumb. [Ledger 45, p. 140]

Lacy W. Pickett. From Hardin. Offence: murder in second degree. Sentence: 21 years. Rec'd Aug. 4, 1838. He is 25 years old, 5' 9" high, weighs 152 lbs. Born in Smith County, bro't up in Wayne Co., Tenn., near Carrollville on the road leading from the above named town to Waynesboro, where his father David Picket now lives. He has four brothers and three sisters. One of his sisters is married to a man by the name of Wily Dicus, he is a wood chopper at the Marine Furnace in Hardin Co., Tenn. He has one uncle, Wm. Pickett, living in the Kentucky Purchase near Island No. 1, also one in Illinois and one in Jefferson County near where his father now lives. [signed] W.M.I. *General pardon by Gov. Wm. B. Campbell, January 16th, 1852.* [Ledger 45, p. 140]

Wm. Peoples. From Bradley County. Crime: incest. Sentence: 10 years from 27 Dec. 1838. He is 42 years old, 5' 9 1/2" high, weighs 165 lbs. Born and bro't up in Mecklenburg Co., North Carolina. He has sandy hair, blue eyes, fair skin. He has a wife and eight children living in Bradley Co., Tenn., on Candi[e]s Creek, 5 1/2 miles east of Cleaveland. A farmer. [Ledger 45, p. 140]

James Powers. From Madison County. Offence: larceny. Sentence: three years. Received Jan. 21, 1840. He is 20 years old, 5' 7" high, weighs 139 lbs. Born in Jasper Co., Georgia, 10 miles east of Monticello on the Augusta road. His mother Sarah Powers lives in Alabama, Tallapoosa County, near the town of Deadville, the county seat of said county. He has five brothers, all married and live in the above named county. He has dark hair, hazle eyes, dark skin. Has had the end of the finger of the left hand next to the little finger has been cut, which leaves a scar and leves the end of the finger crooked. He has worked at the tailoring business two years with a man by the name of Rucker in the town of Forsythe County [crossed out in original], Alabama. [Ledger 45, p. 141]

James W. Payson, alias James W. Lewis. From Maury County. Offence: larceny. Sentence: three years from Jan. 20, 1840. Received Jan. 21, 1840. He is 30 years old, 5' 7" high, weighs 160 lbs. Born and bro't up in the city of Philadelphia. He has been married, his wife is dead and left one child which is with its grandfather, W.W. Amos, in Bloomington, Indiana, or James W. Kanaby. He has one brother in St. Louis, a hatter by trade. He has fair hair, fair skin, good countenance. Is a hatter by profession. Has worked in Nashville, Tenn. He has done business for himself in St. Louis, Missouri, but failed in trade, in other words broke. [Ledger 45, p. 141]

Guilford Payne. From Marshall County. Crime: grand larceny, stealing bills of exchange, notes, etc. Sentence: four years from 5 Oct. 1840. Rec'd 5 Oct. 1840. He is 27 years old, 5' 6 ½" high, weighs 175 lbs. Born and brought up in Robertson Co., Tenn., on Red River, 15 miles above Springfield, near which place he has three uncles by the names of Warren, John and Simpson Payne. His father Dudley Payne lives in Rutherford County about four miles from a little town called Middleton. Said Payne says he has lived in Texas since 1835. He has dark greyish blue eyes, fair skin, heavy black beard, appears to stutter slightly. Has a small scar on his right eye brow running across it. Has a scar on the wrist of the right hand running across it. Also a scar on the skin of the left leg, say 2" long, running up and down the leg. [Ledger 45, p. 141]

Robert Pendergrass, Sr. From Monroe County. Crime: larceny. Sentence: three years from 25 Jan. 1841. Rec'd 24 Jan. 1841. He is 52 years old, 5' 8" high, weighs 170 lbs. Born in Chester Co., South Carolina. Has a wife and five children with his sons in [blank] County, North Carolina. He has grey hair, hazle eyes and fair skin. [Ledger 45, p. 142]

S.L. Pearson. From Wilson County. Crime: forgery. Sentence: four years from 4 Oct. 1841. Rec'd 11 Oct. 1841. He is 18 years old, weighs 144 lbs., 5' 9" high. He was born and brought up in Wilson County about eight miles from Lebanon in the northern part of the county. His relations generally live in Wilson, all but one uncle who lives in Hartsfield, Sumner County, his name is J.W. Locke. Said Pearson has dark hair, dark skin and grey eyes. Tries to be hard of hearing. Has worked at the tailoring business four or five months. [Ledger 45, p. 142]

John Perdew. From Sullivan County. Crime: petit larceny. Sentence: two years from 9 Dec. 1841 when received. He is 20 years old, weighs 129 lbs., 5' 5" high. Born and brought up in Sullivan Co., Tenn. His father Wallace Perdew now lives on the road leading from Blountville to Buchanan's mill on Beaver Creek. He is copper color and smart for a boy who can neither read nor write. [Ledger 45, p. 142]

John Perdue. From Davidson County, appeal from Coffee County. Crime: passing counterfeit money. Sentence: three years from Dec. 22, 1841. Rec'd Dec. 22, 1841. He is 33 years old, weighs 150 lbs., 5' 7" high. Born in Virginia, bro't up in Wayne Co., Kentucky, on the waters of Otter Creek near Turner's old mill. He has a wife and two children in Franklin [County?] on Mud Creek about one mile from Simpson's mill and at or near Mud Creek meeting house with her father, Timothy Ruark. He has fair hair, blue eyes and fair skin. [Ledger 45, p. 142]

Richard C. Pruett. From Franklin County. Crime: horse stealing. Sentence: seven years from March 30, 1842. Rec'd March 29, 1842. He is 40 years old, 5' 10" high, weighs 173 lbs. Born in Albert Co., Georgia, and brought up in Lincoln Co., Tenn. Has two brothers, James and John, living in Tishomingo Co., Mississippi, in the town of Farmington, one a merchandizing [sic,], the other had a farm rented adjoining town and was farming. He has a wife and eight children living 13 1/2 miles west of Winchester and three miles from Salem. He has lived in Park[e] Co., Indiana and carried on blacksmithing and wagon making in the town of Romeville on Big Racoon Creek. He also lived in Vigo County on the road leading from Terre Haute to Greencastle, there he farmed and sold goods. He was a member of the Legislature from the County of Park in the State of Indiana in 1830 and 1831. Said Pruett has fair hair, blue eyes and fair skin. When he lived in Indiana he says he did not make use of his middle name, but he says he does not know what the letter C stands for unless it is Colbert. [Ledger 45, p. 143]

Jesse L. Puckett. From Warren County. Crime: g[rand] larceny. Sentence: three years from 18 May 1842. Rec'd 18 May. 1842. He is 13 years old, 5' 1" high, weighs 99 lbs. Born and brought up in Trigg Co., Kentucky, where his mother Sarah Puckett now lives within 1 1/4 miles of Cadiz, Kentucky. His mother has 12 children (six girls and six boys). Three of the daughters are married. One of her sons is dead, his name was Stokes. One by the name of Sandford Folly, Geo[rge] Dempsey, all living in Trigg County in the neighbourhood of Cadiz. He has no trade but race riding. Has fair hair, blue eyes, fair skin. Has a small scar on the joint of the middle knuckle of the left hand. He is a boy of good countenance. [Ledger 45, p. 143]

James Perry. From Hamilton County. Crime: forgery. Sentence: three years from 6 Dec. [18]42. Received 14 Dec. 1842. Said Perry is 26 years old, 5' 5" high, weighs 156 lbs. Born in North Carolina and bro't up in Sullivan Co., Tenn. His relations all live in Sullivan County. He has three brothers and three sisters, two uncles by the name James and Isaac Eades living in the above county, near the Virginia line. He has dark hair, black eyes and tolerable fair skin. No trade. [Ledger 45, p. 144]

Elvis Bevil. From Grainger County. Crime: horse stealing. Sentence: four years from 30 April 1840. Received 12 May 1840. He is 24 years old, 5' 9" high, weighs 168 lbs. Born and brought up in Wythe Co., Virginia, three miles east of Wytheville. His father Howell Bevil lives in Monroe Co., Kentucky, and has five sons and one daughter at home with him. Said Bevil has a wife and two children with her father Moses Pentigrass one mile from Wythe Court house. He has a large connection in Virginia by the name of Fulks. He has fair hair, blue eyes, fair skin. Has a large scar on his right foot between the ankle and bottom of the heel on the inside of his leg. [Ledger 45, p. 146]

John Busbee. From Henderson County. Crime: murder. Sentence: two years from 10 Aug. 1840. Rec'd 10 Aug. 1840. He is 21 years old, 5' 8" high, weighs 146 lbs. Born in Dixon[?] County and brought up in Henderson Co., Tenn. His father Cayce Busbee lives five miles east of Lexington on the waters of Haley Creek, three miles from Harman's mill on Harman's Creek, to the left of the Perryville road. Said Busbee has dark hair, blue eyes, fair skin. Has had the toe next the big toe of the left foot cut off, or nearly so, which makes it stiff in the middle joint. His relations live in the late purchase had of the Cherokees. [Ledger 45, p. 146]

William Brumley. From Marion County. Crime: murder. Sentence: ten years from 24 July 1840. Received 30 July 1840. He is 25 years old, weighs 143 lbs., 5' 4" barefooted. Said Brumley was born in Knox Co., Tenn., and brought up in Marion. His father is dead, his mother Margaret Brumley is living on Tellico River seven miles from Jasper near the Suck. She has one daughter and two sons home. Said Brumley has two sisters married, one to James Craig and lives in the same settlement with his mother, the other to a man by the name of James Scrimpter[?] and lives in Monroe County. He has fair skin, fair hair, blue eyes. Has two uncles by the names of James and William Mason living in Monroe County, six miles from Madisonville. Said Brumley has a wife and no children. She is with his mother in Marion, he thinks. He has two small scars directly between the eyes, say ½" long. Also one on the right cheek bone caused by the kick of a musket. [Ledger 45, p. 146]

Frederick Branstutter was received into the Penitentiary 14 Aug. 1839 from Sullivan County. He is 28 years of age, weighs 180 lbs., 5' 10" high. Born and bro't up in Sullivan Co., Tenn., ten miles east of the boat yard on Holston

He has dark hair, dark skin and black eyes. His wright arm at the elbow is out of joint, which makes it crooked. He is a common labourer by profession. Crime: petit larceny. Sentence to confinement in the Jail and Penitentiary House of this state for two years. [Ledger 45, p. 147]

Henry Blalock. From Roan[e] County. Crime: bigamy. Sentence: two years from 28 Feb. 1840. He is 37 years old, 5' 7" high, weighs 157 lbs. Born and brought up in Brumsey [sic,, Brunswick?] County, Virginia. Said Blalock has a wife and one child in Roane County two miles from Kingston with her mother Polly Bledsoe. Has fair hair, grey eyes, fair skin. Has a flesh mole on the right cheek. [Ledger 45, p. 147]

Murdock Bullard. From Gibson County. Crime: grand larceny. Sentence: 18 months from 18 Mar. 1840. He is 15 years old, 5' 6" high, weighs 116 lbs. Born and brought to what he is in North Carolina, Mulberry District. Said Bullard has black hair, black eyes and dark skin. His relations live in Alabama and North Carolina. His father lives in Weakl[e]y County. [Ledger 45, p. 147]

James H. Brown. From Carroll County, Tenn. Offence: grand larceny. Sentence: three years. Was rec'd Mar. 21, 1837. He is 24 years old, 5' 8" high, and weighs 175 lbs. Has large blue eyes, full face, florid complexion, dark hair, stout built, good countenance. A scar on the back of the little finger of the left hand. Some signs of scaldhead. Says he was born and raised in Whitley Co., Kentucky, where his parents now live. *Pardoned by Gov. Polk, 28th January 1840. Conduct good.* [Ledger 45, p. 148]

William Bunch. From Grainger County. Offence: petit larceny. Sentence: one year from 15 Aug. 1837. Was received Sept. 6, 1837. He is 16 years old, light hair, blue eyes, fair skin, weighs 112 lbs. Born and bro't up in Grainger County, nine miles from Rutledge where his step father now lives, his name is John Yates. *William Bunch was pardoned 11th of August 1838 by Newton Cannon. Conduct generally good.* [Ledger 45, p. 148]

John Brown. From Montgomery County. Offence: larceny. One years sentence from 15 Sept., rec'd 26 Sept., 1837. He is 24 years old, 5' 7" high, weighs 148 lbs. Was born in Pennsylvania seven miles from Philadelphia. Brought up in Schuylkill County where his father, Jacob Brown, now lives. (Said Brown is slightly pock marked.) Is a hatter but has followed pedling dry good in Maryland and Pennsylvania. He has had the ends of the two middle fingers mashed, which leaves scars on them. [Ledger 45, p. 148]

Jonas Brown. Was rec'd into the Penitentiary Nov. 18, 1837. He is 22 years old, 5' 9" high, weighs 159 lbs. Red hair, blue eyes, fair skin. Born in Kentucky, bro't up in Wilson Co., Tenn., where his father, Reubin T. Brown, now lives 12 miles from Lebanon off the road leading to Old Jefferson. He has five brothers and three sisters at home with his father. One brother married and lives in Franklin County on Mulbary Creek six miles from Finches mill. He has a wife but no children, she is living with her father John Singleton in Gibson County on the road leading from Trenton to Lexington near Scott's upper mills on the north fork of Forked Deer River. He has a scar in the edge of his hair on the right forehead caused by a burn. Has some small scars on his four and midle fingers of the left hand. He has a scar on the great toe of the left foot nearly forming the letter V. Was found guilty of felony at the Cuircuit Court of Gibson County and sentenced to three years confinement in the Jail and Penitentiary House of the State of Tennessee. *Sent all his clothes to his father's, by his brother, 11th Dec. 1837.* [Ledger 45, p. 149]

Sherwood Brake. From Bledsoe County. Offence: hog stealing. Sentence: three years from 18 Nov., rec'd 23rd [Nov.], 1837. He is 57 years old, 5' 8" high, weighs 144 lbs. Light grey hair, bald headed, yellowish grey eyes, verry heavy grey beard. He has a wife and two children living 16 miles north east of Pikeville. He has one daughter married to William Cartright and lives in Sequchey [sic,, Sequatchie] Valley near James Schuylfields. Sentenced by the Circuit Court of Bledsoe County to three years confinement in the Jail and Penitentiary House of the State of Tennessee. [Ledger 45, p. 149]

Craven C. Butts. From Dyer County. Offence: petit larceny. Sentence: two years. Rec'd July 4, 1838. He is 26 years old, 5' 8", weighs 145 lbs. Born and bro't up in Green[e] County, North Carolina. Has lost his right leg and half of his thigh. Has dark hair, dark eyes and skin. Has worked at the shoe making but is not a workman. Found guilty and sentenced by the Cuircourt [sic,] of Dyer County, West Tennessee. [Ledger 45, p. 149]

Jack Brown. From Williamson County, a free boy of color. Crime: larceny. Sentence: three years from 13 July 1838. Rec'd 20 July 1838. He is 14 years old, 5' high. Born in Florence, Alabama. Bro't up in Williamson Co., Tenn. He is moon eyed or in other words he cannot see when the sun shines in mid day. [Ledger 45, p. 150]

John A. Berry. From Shelby County. He is 25 years old, 5' 11 ½" high, weighs 182 lbs. Has light hair, thin eyebrows, greyish blue eyes, fair skin. He has a scar on the cap of the right knee, has been powder burnt above and below the right eye. Born in Prince Edward Co., Virginia, bro't up in Cumberland County near the Appomattoc River about three miles from James Town. Found guilty of grand larceny at the Cuircuit Court of Shelby County and sentenced to five years confinement at hard labour in the Jail and Penitentiary House of the State of Tennessee. *Clothes given to John Rhea.* [Ledger 45, p. 150]

Robert Bullington. From Knox County. Received into the Penitentiary July 24, 1839. He is 28 years of age, weighs 140 lbs., 5' 9" high. Born in Union, bro't up in Sparters-burg [sic,, Spartanburg] counties, N.C. [sic,, South Carolina], where his mother now lives 13 miles from Spartenberg. Has one brother in Washington Co., Alabama. He has dark hair, hazle eyes, sallow complexion, has a scar above the left eye caused by a fall [from] a carriage. Has a tolerable countenance. A house painter by trade, served his apprenticeship in Tuscaloosa, Alabama, with a man by name (Martin Goodman). Was found guilty of larceny at Knoxville in Knox County and sentenced to undergo confinement in the Jail and Penitentiary House of this state for the space of three years. [Ledger 45, p. 150]

Washington Rayborn Rogers was received in the Penitentiary Aug. 27, 1831. He is 5' 10 ¾" high, 32 years of age, common weight 175 lbs. Fair hair, light complexion, blue eyes. By profession a shoe maker. Born in Boutetort [sic, Botetourt]Co., Virginia, brought up in Knoxville, Tenn., where his mother now lives. Has an uncle residing in Abington, Virginia. A scar on the wrist of the left hand, also a scar occasioned by a rifle ball on the right arm between the elbow and shoulder. A scar from branding on the left hand. Was found guilty of horse stealing at the Circuit Court of Giles County, and sentenced to five years and six months imprisonment in the Jail and Penitentiary House of the State of Tennessee. *Washington R. Rogers died of cholera on the 11th June 1833.* [Ledger 45, p. 151]

Henry K. Redman was received in the Penitentiary 14 Jan. 1834. He is 6' 2 ½" in height and weighs 204 lbs. Black hair, dark eyes, good countenance, stout made, 32 years of age. Born in Greenbriar Co., Virginia, and brought up in Brown Co., Ohio, where his mother still resides about eight miles from Ohio River near the Redoak Meeting House. He has one sister married to Wm. Dyer and residing in the above neighborhood, one brother residing in Morgan Co., Illinois, and two brothers in Cincinnati, Ohio. Redman has a wife and three children. Her maiden name was Davis. She now lives at the lower end of No.

35 Island in the Mississippi River on Pecan Point. He has a scar on the inside of the right thumb, five moles on the right side of the neck nearly under the jaw, a small scar just in the edge of the hair over the left eye, two scars on the instep of the right foot just above the ancle bone. Has generally followed blacksmithy and gunsmithing. Was found guilty of passing counterfeit bankbills at the Circuit Court of Tipton County and sentenced to three years confinement in the Jail and Penitentiary House of the State of Tennessee. *Henry K. Redman was discharged 26 Feb. 1837. Detained 43 days for bad conduct.* [Ledger 45, p. 151]

John Rodes. Was rec'd in the Penitentiary 4 Dec. 1834. He is 24 years of age, 5' 9 or 10" high, and weighs 155 lbs. Dark hair, blue eyes and fair complexion. A scar running from the instep to the hollow of the left foot, another on the right foot about an inch in length, running lengthways of his foot and terminating near the two middle toes, and another running through the brow of the left eye. Born and brought up in Wilk[e]s County, North Carolina, where his father (John Rodes), six brothers and three sisters now reside. Two of his brothers (Elijah and William) and two of his sisters (Elizabeth and Nancy) are married. He has a wife and two children living in Monroe Co., Tenn., on the waters of Chastowa ten miles from her father (Jarvis Smith) who resides on Tellico River near Tellico Plains, Monroe County. He has mostly followed farming. Was found guilty of petit larceny at the Circuit Court of Monroe County and sentenced to one years confinement in the Jail and Penitentiary House of the State of Tennessee. *9 days detained for bad conduct. Discharged 19th Jan. 1836, having served the term of sentence and time charged for misdemeanors.* [Ledger 45, p. 152]

James Roberts was rec'd in the Penitentiary 15 Apr. 1835. He is 49 years of age, 5' 8" high, and weighs 155 or 160 lbs. Hair formerly black, now grey, beard of the same colour and very heavy, grey eyes, thin visage, fair complexion. A piece off each ear, both of which he says were bit off. Born in Halifax Co., Virginia, and brought up in Pendleton District, South Carolina. Married Delila, daughter of James Wood of Roane Co., Tenn. Resided in Dixon [*sic,*] Co., Tenn., on Harricane Creek, on the road leading from Charlotte to Reynoldsburg, near Jno. Johnson's mill, until about two years ago when he removed to Perry County and settled on Tom's Creek near Welch's Mill, where his wife and four children now reside. Two sons labouring at different places in the neighborhood, a son married to Patsey, daughter of Thos. Graves, and a daughter married to Dempsey Hooper, in all eight children, all of whom reside in or about the last described neighbourhood. He has chiefly followed farming. Was found guilty of "keeping in his possession counterfeit coin" at the Circuit Court of Perry County and sentenced to three years confinement in the Jail and Penitentiary House of the State of Tennessee. *James Roberts died of cholera on the 30th day of June 1835.* [Ledger 45, pp. 152-3]

Thomas Prewett (Pruett) was rec'd in the Penitentiary 21 Apr. 1835. He is 5' 9 or 10" high, 57 years old and weighs 162 lbs. Black eyes, hair once black but now grey, beard grey and very thick on his chin and upper lip. A large scar near the root of the thumb of the right hand. Badly ruptured. Labourer. Born and bred in Granville Co., North Carolina. Married Sarah, daughter of Thomas Willis of Nash Co., North Carolina, who died in Roane Co., North Carolina, leaving five children. He does not know where his children now reside. He was found guilty of petit larceny at the Circuit Court of Hawkins County and sentenced to one years confinement in the Jail and Penitentiary House of the State of Tennessee. *Thomas Pruett died of cholera on the 5th day of July 1835.* [Ledger 45, p. 153]

John Ransum was rec'd in the Penitentiary 4 June 1835. He is 23 years of age, 5' 5 or 6" high and weighs about 150 lbs. Mulatto, black eyes, black nappy hair, short flat nose, square face and stout built. A scar about 1" in length in the edge of the hair on the right side of the front part of the head, one in the edge of the hair on the left side of the same part of the head, one on the back part of the head about 2" above the left ear, one on the shin bone of the right leg about half way between the knee and ankle, and one on the left shin bone just below the knee. Labourer. Born and bred in Davidson Co., Tenn. Has lived, the most of his time, in Nashville, and has sometimes worked on board of a steam-boat as fireman. His mother, a free mulatto woman named Huldia, generally called Huldia Ransom, resides on John Cockrell's plantation about a mile from Nashville. Two sisters living with his mother. One [sister] living on Brent Spence's plantation, married to a free man of colour named George King (blacksmith). One [sister] living in Nashville, and one living in Cincinnati. A brother (Jas. King) living in Louisville, Kentucky, whose principal occupation is that of steward on board of a steamboat. He was found guilty of murder in the second degree at the Circuit Court of Davidson County and sentenced to 20 years confinement in the Jail and Penitentiary House of the State of Tennessee. [Ledger 45, pp. 153-4]

Nathaniel Rye (alias Jacob Bradley). Convicted of horse stealing and grand larceny at the May term 1836 for Maury County and sentenced to four years imprisonment in the Penitent'y. Received 17 May 1836. (For descriptions see Jacob Bradley.) [Ledger 45, p. 154]

Tennessee Convicts: Records of the State Penitentiary

Robert Ramey. From Henry Co., Tenn. Was received 9 June 1836. He is 48 years old, 5' 7 ½" high and weighs 170 lbs. Has black hair, grey eyes, heavy beard, hairy, stout man. Short hands and fingers, the right little finger a little crooked. A slip of the right ear and the left mashed up to the head at the upper part, but not much deformed. A scar across the front of the left thigh where a ball was cut out. A small scar back of the left corner of the left eye. His family lives in Johnson Co., Illinois, 14 miles from Vienna and four miles from the Ohio River. His son Jesse lives in Wilson Co., Tenn., near the Rutherford line in the neighborhood of Rhodes. Was found guilty of assault and battery with intent to kill and sentenced to three years imprisonment in the Tenn. Penit'y at hard labour. *Rob't Ramey discharge[d] June 13th, 1839, by expiration of sentence.* [Ledger 45, p. 154]

Asa S. Ricker. From Bradley County, Tenn. Offence: petty larceny. Sentence: one year. Was received Jan. 19, 1837. He is 31 years old, 5' 6 ¾" high, weighs 172 lbs. Dark hair, grey eyes, a large scar on his right leg occasioned by a burn, and on the shin a cut. It all resembles a scald. Born in Newberry Port, Massachusetts and served his apprenticeship to the hatting business in Boston. *Asa S. Ricker was pardoned by Gov. Cannon in consideration of his good behaviour while in prison 22 days or 2 days for each month. Discharged Dec. 27th, 1837.* [Ledger 45, p. 154]

John Rhea. From Washington County. Offence: b[u]ying stolen goods. Sentence: three years. Received July 3, 1837. He is 30 years of age, 5' 8" high, weighs 145 lbs. Dark hair, eyes bluish cast, fair skin. Born and bro't up in Green[e] Co., Tenn., where his father Samuel Rhea now lives. He has a wife and two children at his father's. His wife is a daughter of John Oliver. He has three brothers: Thomas, Ezekiel and James. The two latter lives in Green[e], the other in Grainger. Was sentenced by the Cuircuit Court of Washington County to three years confinement in the Jail and Penitentiary House of the State of Tennessee. *John Rhea discharge[d] April 25th, 1840, by pardon of J.K. Polk.* [Ledger 45, p. 155]

Smith Roberts. From White County. Offence: petit larceny. Sentence: one year. Rec'd July 3, 1837. He is 5' 7" high, weighs 131 lbs. Fair hair, blue eyes, fair skin, down look. Born and brought up in White Co., Tenn., 10 miles south of Sparta where his mother now lives. He has two brothers and two sisters with his mother. He has a scar on his left foot run[n]ing from between his mid[d]le and third toes upwards. Sentenced by the Cuircuit Court of White County to one year's confinement in the Jail and Penitentiary House of the

State of Tennessee. *Smith Roberts was discharged June 29, 1838.* [Ledger 45, p. 155]

Wm. Randolph. From Stewart County. Offence: horse stealing. Sentence: four years from 15 Nov. 1837. Rec'd 26 Nov. 1837. He is 43 years old, 5' 7" high, weighs 147 lbs. Verry dark sandy hair, yellow eyes with the sight of the right eye more than as large again as the left, and he says he cannot see out of the large sight. Heavy beard. Has a scar above the elbow on the under side of the right arm 2" long and ½" wide. He says it was caused by a ball from a gun accidentally going off. He has a scar on the thumb of the left hand where it joines the hand. Born in Tiger[?] Valley, Virginia, and lived their [sic,] until he was 16 years old. Went then to Fayett[e] Co., Kentucky, two miles east of Lexington. Then to Hawkins Co., Tenn., two miles from Rogersville on the road leading to Jacksonville, Georgia. He had one brother and two sisters. He says his brother was killed by a man by the name of Robertson in Nashville. His mother and sisters he thinks are in the District west of the Tennessee river. He has two uncles in Georgia, their names are Peter and Robert Thomas, one lives in Wilk[e]s County, the other in Lawrence County. He has three uncles some where in Virginia, David, John and James Randolph. He has been married, his wife is dead. He has five children living with his cozen [sic,] Richard Johnson in White County. He has generally followed farming, but has worked some at wagon making. Was sentenced by the Cuircuit Court of Stewart County to four years confinement in the Jail and Penitentiary House of the State of Tennessee. [Ledger 45, pp. 155-6]

[The following entry is marked through with an X]
Smith Roberts. From White County. Offence: pettet larceny. Sentence: one year from 18 June 1837. He is [blank], hight 5' 7", weighs 131 lbs. Fair hair, blue eyes, fair skin, down look. Born and brought up in White Co., Tenn., 10 miles south of Sparta where his mother now lives. He has two sisters and one brother with his mother. He has one brother in West Tennessee. He has a scar on his left foot running from between the mid[d]le and third toes upwards. Sentenced by the Cuircuit Court of White County to one year's confinement in the Jail and Penitentiary House of the State of Tennessee. [Ledger 45, p. 156]

Samuel Rogers. From Washington County. Offence: stabbing. Sentence: two years. Rec'd Dec. 6, 1837. He is 21 years old, 5' 11" high, weighs 163 lbs. Born and bro't up in Washington Co., Tenn., 1 ½ miles from Elija[h] Embrees Rol[l]ing Mill and Nail Factory, where his father Reuben Rogers now lives. He has once uncle who lives in Indiana on the waters of White River, also one in Clayburn [sic,] County, Powells Valley, Tenn. He has black hair, dark skin and

Tennessee Convicts: Records of the State Penitentiary

eyes. Good countenance. He has a scar in the left eye brow, a mole on his right cheak, a scar on the back part of the left hand. Has worked at blacksmithing business. [Ledger 45, p. 156]

John Randolph. From Fayette County. Offence: larceny. Sentence: two years. Rec'd June 9, 1838. He is 22 years old, 6' high, weighs 176 lbs. Born and bro't up in Jackson Co., Georgia, 11 miles from Jefferson on the old Federal Road. His father Peyton Randolph lives in Vans Valley, Floyd Co., Georgia. He has six children yet at home with him. He has one uncle by the name of Randolph in Jackson Co., Georgia. He is well made, good countenance, light red hair, grey eyes, fair skin. [Ledger 45, p. 157]

James Reed from Knox County. Offence: grand larceny. Sentence: four years. Rec'd Oct. 28, 1838. He is 42 years old, 5' 7 1/2" high, weighs 148 lbs. Born and bro't up in State of Rhodisland [sic,], Providence. He has dark hair, grey eyes, fair skin. He has a scar on the shin of the right leg just above the ancle joint. He is a shoe and boot maker by profession. Also some scars in his forehead. His relations all live in Bellingham in State of Massachusetts. [Ledger 45, p. 157]

Richard Ridgeway. From Davidson County. Sentence: three years. Rec'd Dec. 14, 1838. Offence: grand larceny. He is 21 years old, 5' 8" high, weighs 162 lbs. Born in Georgetown, District of Columbia. Bro't up in the City of Baltimore where his mother, Henrietta Ridgeway, now lives. He has a scar on the left cheak near 3" long. He has fair hair, blue eyes and fair skin. He has worked at house and sign painting with Danl. Pope in the City of Baltimore say two years. [Ledger 45, p. 157]

Drury Reed. From Bedford County. Offence: horse stealing. Sentence: three years and eight months from 12 Dec. 1838. Rec'd 25 Dec. 1838. He is 20 years old, 5' 10" high, weighs 171 lbs. Born and bro't up in Rutherford County. He has sandy hair, blue eyes, fair skin. Has a wife living with her step father John Dunlap, 10 miles from Shelbyville on the Columbia road. His father William Reed lives about two miles from Dunlap. He has some small scars on his middle finger of the left hand. He has a small purple spot behind his left ear. By profession a farmer. [Ledger 45, p. 158]

Devenport Romines. From McMinn County. Offence: felloney [sic,]. Sentence: three years. Rec'd Dec. 28, 1838. He is 20 years old, 6' 1" high, weighs 170 lbs. Born and bro't up in Prince Edward Co., Virginia. He has dark hair, hazle eyes and dark skin. His father lives in Clark Co., Illinois. A saddler by profession. [Ledger 45, p. 158]

Smith Roberts. From Marion County. Offence: grand larceny. Sentence: three years from 20 Mar. 1839. For particulars of whom refer to former sentence. [Ledger 45, p. 158]

Joshua Cresong. From Bradley County. Offence: horse stealing. Sentence: three years from 26 Dec. 1839. Received Jan. 8, 1840. He is 19 years old, weighs 138 lbs., 5' 6" high. Born in Rowan Co., North Carolina, bro't up in Roane Co., Tenn., where his mother Polly Cresong now lives within the vicinity of Kingston. He has dark hair, hazle eyes, fair skin and good countenance, and he stutters verry bad at some words and at others speaks fluently. [Ledger 45, p. 158]

John D. Robinson. From Madison County. Offence: larceny. Sentence: three years from Jan. 21, 1840. He is 20 years old, 5' 8" high, weighs 145 lbs. Born in Maury Co., Tenn., and brought up in Madison County. His father, Benjamin Robinson, lives on the lower Brownsville Road, 12 miles from Jackson near Squire Pentigross. He has dark sandy hair, blue eyes, fair skin. He has a scar or mark on the heel part of the right hand. No other scars perceivable.

Godfrey R. Romines. From Henry County. Offence: assault with intent to kill. Sentence: five years from 1 Feb. 1840. He is 50 years and seven months old, 5' 6" high, weighs 196 lbs. Fair skin, blue eyes, light hair, sandy beard and full face for his age. He was born and brought up in Cocke Co., East Tenn. His left eye brow has been mashed by a rock. Under the same eye he has two flesh moles, and under the right eye has a scar about 1 ½" long. Has a large flesh mole near the lower end of his breast bone, and a large scar on his left instep. He married a Miss Nancy Parker in Stewart County, she is his second wife, by whom he has had two twin children (a son and daughter). She is now living at Mills Point on the Mississippi River. He married his first wife in Cocke Co., East Tenn. Her name was Anna Collins, she died in Stewart County and left two children, a son and daughter. He married her (Anna C.) at Thomas Cheatham's in Benton County. His father lives in Ray [sic,, Rhea] Co., East Tenn. His mother is dead. He has one brother living in Alabama, one sister in South Carolina, near Pendleton Court house. [signed] J. Ayres [Ledger 45, p. 159]

Tennessee Convicts: Records of the State Penitentiary

Henderson K. Richards. From White County. Offence: bigamy. Sentence: three years. He is 20 years old, 5' 8" high, weighs 168 lbs. Born in Severe [sic,, Sevier] Co., Tenn., bro't up in the counties of Overton and White. His father, Isaac Richards, is living in White County near Stinson[?] meeting house which is near the three forks of Obeds River. He has been twice married, his first wife was a Miss Narcissa Daniel, the other Mary Graham. She has scince married a man by the name of Hunter. Said Richards has three sisters and two brothers. He has dark hair, yellow hazle eyes, fair skin, good countenance. [Ledger 45, p. 160]

William N. Ross. From Shelby County. Crime: robbery. Sentence: five years from 25 Oct. 1840. Received 25 Oct. 1840. He is 19 years old, 5' 11 $^{1}/_{2}$" high, weighs 147 lbs. Born in Surry Co., North Carolina. Brought up no where but left his father Benjamin Ross living 10 miles south of Knoxville, Knox Co., Tenn., about five years since. He has dark hair, blue eyes and fair skin. He has had a large cut on the shin of the left leg and almost as knock legged as J. George Harris, the present Editor of the Nashville Union. [Ledger 45, p. 160]

Joseph Fuller. From Rutherford County. Crime: forgery. Sentence: three years from 21 Nov. 1840. Rec'd 30 Nov. 1840. He is 23 years old, 5' 7 $^{1}/_{2}$" high, weighs 160 lbs. Born and brought up in Rutherford Co., Tenn., 11 or 12 miles from Murfreesboro near Joseph Kimbrough, and 1 $^{1}/_{2}$ miles from Rock Spring meeting house, and about 5 $^{1}/_{2}$ miles from Nolensville. His step father John Foster now lives near Burnett's Camp Ground in the above named county. Has one brother and three sisters and two half brothers. Their names are Foster, all living with his step father. He has fair hair, blue eyes and fair skin. [Ledger 45, p. 160]

Joseph C. Cook. From Franklin County. Crime: forgery. Sentence: three years from 26 Nov. 1840. He is 23 years old, weighs 140 lbs., 5' 9" high. Born in Warren Co., Tenn., brought up in Franklin, nine miles north of Winchester on Elk River at Jones Ford where his mother and step father, Allen Young, now lives. His mother has had three husbands, has had nine children: by her first five, by the second two, by the third two [underlining in original]. He has fair hair and yellowish grey eyes, dark skin, hair and eye brows. Has one sister married and lives near him. [Ledger 45, p. 161]

James Claxton. From Davidson County. Crime: murder. Sentence: five years from Dec. 21, 1840. Rec'd Dec. 21, 1840. He is 21 years old, 5' 9 $^{1}/_{2}$" high, weighs 167 lbs. Born in Sumner and brought up in Davidson County. Has generally followed race riding until too large. Since then he has followed the

River as deck hand, fireman and cabin boy. Said Claxton has black hair, hazle eyes, dark skin. Has had his right arm broken in the elbow joint which makes it crooked. Has a scar at the top of his forehead, one just above the left eye, also one on the left cheek bone, and a dark scar on the shin bone of the left leg. A cut on the left arm. Has been shot in the left arm and leg. His grandmother lives seven miles from Madisonville, Kentucky. Two uncles on Duck River. His father Joshua Claxton lives nine miles from Charlotte in Dixon [sic,] Co., Tenn. His mother keeps a house of ill fame in or near Nashville (Vinegar Hill). He has a brother in Arkansas about 40 miles from Memphis, Tenn. [Ledger 45, p. 161]

John Calvin. From Henry County. Crime: larceny. Sentence: three years from 24 Jan. 1841 when he was rec'd. He is 20 years old, 5' 8 ½" high, weighs 145 lbs. Born and brought up in Madison Co., Missouri, within 12 miles of Frederick about two miles from St. Francis River. Has two brothers, one named Alfred, the other Lewis Calvin. He has black hair, black eyes, very dark skin. Has followed the River as steward. His brothers both follow the River, one as pilot the other as engineer. He is related to the French [underlined in original]. [Ledger 45, p. 161]

Willis Carlisle. From Davidson County. Crime: horse stealing. Sentence: five years from 5 Feb. 1841. Rec'd 5 Feb. 1841. He is 43 years old, 5' 11 ½" high, weighs 170 lbs. Born and brought up in Lincoln Co., Georgia. His relations live in Lincoln Co., Georgia. Said Carlisle has sandy hair, blue eyes, fair skin. Has a mole on his right cheek. Has had his left arm broken which keeps it from turning as the other does. Has been branded in the left hand, and the brand cut out, which leaves a scar. He has also had the right hand injured, which makes one of the fingers stiff (the finger next the little finger), also leaves a scar on the same hand. He has very short thick fingers. [Ledger 45, p. 162]

Leslie Clark. From Wilson County. Crime: perjury. Sentence: three years from June 4, 1842. Rec'd June 6, 1842. He is 19 years old, 5' 8" high, weighs 132 lbs. Born in Logan Co., Kentucky, about six miles from Russelville on the Bowling Green road. His mother is married to a man named Wm. Carney and lives on the above named road. He has black hair, grey eyes and dark skin. Has a scar on the part of the foot near the middle toe. [Ledger 45, p. 162]

Fielding Churchwell. From Wayne County. Crime: grand larceny. Sentence: three years from 14 June 1842. Rec'd 15 June 1842. He is 24 years old, 5' 8" in height [sic,], weighs 162 lbs. Born and brought up in Wayne County about eight miles from Mount Jasper Furnace and 15 miles northeast of Waynesboro. He has a wife and two children living with her father Jos. [Jas.?] Stagg two miles from Jasper Furnace on the waters of 40 Mile Creek. He has two sisters in Hardin County about six miles from Savannah near the road leading to Purdy. One married to a man by the name of Blanton, the other to a man by the name of Brumby [Brumley?]. [Ledger 45, p. 162]

John Clasure [Closure?]. From Shelby County. Crime: grand larceny. Sentence: three years from 6 July 1842. Rec'd 6 July 1842. He is 53 years old, 6' high, weighs 168 lbs. Born in Fayette and brought up in Henry Co., Kentucky, 1 ½ miles from New Castle. Has a wife and six children living on the road from Vincennes to St. Louis, 14 miles from Maysville. He has dark hair, grey eyes, dark skin, and [is] a farmer. [Ledger 45, p. 163]

Isaac Collins. From Lincoln County. Crime: horse stealing. Sentence: three years from 13 Oct. 1842. Rec'd 13 Oct. 1842. He is 17 years old, 6' ¼" high, weighs 140 lbs. Born and bro't up in Coffee Co., Tenn. His father, W. Collins, is now living five m[ile]s south of the old stone fort on the road leading from Nashville to Winchester. His wife is with her father, Peyton Strong, who lives in the same settlement with his father. Says he has worked some at the blacksmith business. Has fair hair, hazel eyes and sallow complexion. [Ledger 45, p. 163]

John Cornwell. From Greene County. Crime: keeping and concealing counterfeit money. Sentence: three years from 28 Oct. 1842. Rec'd 28 Oct. 1842. He is 40 years old, weighs 165 lbs., 6' 2" high. Born and bro't up in Faquier Co., Virginia. Has a wife and six children now living in Monroe Co., Kentucky, 10 miles from Tompkinsville on the right hand side of the Bowlinggreen road, on Scruggs' Creek, but thinks she will go to her father's, John Wheelock, in Washington Co., East Tenn., on Kendrick Creek 10 miles from Jonesboro on the Snapps Ferry road. He has fair hair, blue eyes and fair skin. Has a large scar on the under part of the right thigh. [Ledger 45, p. 163]

Ayres Childress. From Madison County. Crime: larceny. Sentence: three years from Jan. 21, 1840. He is 22 years old, 5' 8" high, weighs 132 lbs. Born in Knox Co., East Tenn. Bro't up in the counties of McNairy and Madison. He has a wife but no children. His wife is with her mother, Mrs. Phillips, five miles east of Purdy in McNairy County. He has one brother by the name of Loten Childress in Nashville, Davidson Co., Tenn., a merchant. [Ledger 45, p. 164]

Tennessee Convicts: Records of the State Penitentiary

William Clark. From White County. Offence: petit larceny. Sentence: one year. Received Feb. 18, 1840. He is 19 years old, 5' 8" high, weighs 132 lbs. Born in Gates Co., North Carolina. His father, Reuben Clark, lives in Overton County near the White Plains. He has three brothers and two sisters at home with his father, all younger then himself. He has dark hair, blue eyes and fair skin. [Ledger 45, p. 164]

Wm. Carter. From Rhea County. Crime: horse stealing. Sentence: three years from July 7, 1841. Rec'd July 15, 1841. He is 19 years old, 6' 1" high, weighs 164 lbs. Born in the State of Indiana, brought up in Hamilton and Rhea counties. Has a sister married to a man by the name of Louis Elliston and lives in Missouri but he does not know what part. He has three uncles living in Alabama by the names of John, William and Solomon Gay. His mother, Polly Carter, lives about 16 miles above Dallis on the Tennessee River, about a mile below Hutchinson's Ferry, formerly Bligh's[?] old ferry. He has dark hair, fair skin, blue eyes. Has had the little toe of the left foot cut off. [Ledger 45, p. 164]

William Campbell. From Shelby County. Offence: pettit larceny. Sentence: two years. He is 33 years old, weighs 155 lbs., 5' 6" high. Born in Scotland in the town of Glasgow. Bro't up on the seas as a sailor. Has been on the steam boats. He has sandy hair, grey eyes, fair skin. [Ledger 45, p. 165]

William Childress. From Knox County. Offence: grand larceny. Sentence: three years. Received Nov. 4, 1839. He is 30 years old, 5' 11" high, weighs 145 lbs. Born and bro't up in Knox Co., Tenn., nine miles west of Knoxville. He has a wife and two children living with his mother at the above named place. He has one uncle living in Alabama by the name of John Childress. Said Childress has dark hair, hazle eyes, fair skin and heavy sandy beard. Has no trade but has generally followed farming. [Ledger 45, p. 165]

Chas. C. Mitchell. From DeKalb County. Offence: hog stealing. Sentence: one year. Received Dec. 16, 1839. Sentence to commence from 13th instant. He is 28 years old, weighs 160 lbs., 5' 9" high. Born in Warren Co., Kentucky. Bro't up in Rutherford Co., Tenn. Has one uncle by the name of James Wilkinson living in Rutherford County near the mouth of Cripple Creek. Said Mitchell has a wife and two children living near Smithville in DeKalb County with her father, John Bevirt[?]. He has dark hair, fair skin, hazle eyes. [Ledger 45, p. 165]

Tennessee Convicts: Records of the State Penitentiary

Andrew Curtis. From Maury County. Crime: larceny. Sentence: three years from 12 Sept. 1842. Rec'd 12 Sept. 1842. He is 20 years old, 5' 10" high, weighs 165 lbs. Born near Raleigh, North Carolina. Has an uncle living near Fort Smith, Arkansas. His father E. Curtis, with his wife, three sons and two daughters, live[s] in Panola Co., Mississippi, 20 miles east of the town of Panola, the county seat of said county. He has worked at the tailor's trade. Has dark skin, haz<u>le</u> eyes and dark hair. Has a scar on the shin extending up to the knee. Also two scars on the thumb of the left hand, and one on the fore finger same hand. Has a mole on the left side of his chin just below the corner of his mouth, and a small one on the right side of his upper lip just above the corner of his mouth. [Ledger 45, p. 166]

George Bean. From Hamilton County. Crime: murder second degree. Sentence: 21 years from 2 Dec. 1842. Rec'd 14 Dec. 1842. He is 32 years old, 5' 7 $^{1}/_{2}$" high, weighs 168 lbs. Born in Grainger and bro't up in Hamilton Co., Tenn. He has a wife but no children living with her brother-in-law in Ocoa [sic,, Ocoee] Dis't on the Tennessee River about five miles from Blythes ferry, his name is Moses Atchela. Has three brothers and five sisters living in the above county. He has three children by his first wife living with his brother-in-law in the same settlement that his wife lives in. Said Bean has dark hair, haz<u>le</u> eyes and dark skin. Has an uncle by the name of Jesse Bean living near where the counties of Wayne and Fentress join<u>s</u> Kentucky. Has also an uncle by the name of Edmond Bean who did live in Nashville, a blacksmith by trade. He has a scar on the instep of the left foot cut by an axe. [Ledger 45, p. 166]

John E. Ray. From Williamson County. Crime: horse stealing. Sentence: three years and three months from 30 Nov. 1842. Rec'd 30 Nov. 1842. John E. Ray is 18 years old, 5' 10" high, weighs 161 lbs. Born in Davidson County and bro't up in Williamson and Bedford where his father John Ray now lives, about four miles on this side of Doolittle about $^{1}/_{2}$ a mile from the Nashville road. He has a wife and one child at his father's. Her father is by the name of David Lamb and lives about one mile from John Ray's. His grandfather lives in Wesleys bend of the Cumberland River. Has an uncle in Williamson County about five miles from Hardeman's X [Cross] Roads. [Ledger 45, p. 168]

James H. Richards. From Lauderdale County. Crime: larceny. Sentence: four years from 12 Feb. 1841. Rec'd 12 Feb. 1841. He is 22 years old, 6' high, weighs 165 lbs. Was born and brought up in Stewart Co., Tenn. He has blue eyes, fair skin, light hair. His father John Richards formerly carried on a small shop in Stewart County at Dover. [Ledger 45, p. 169]

Wm. Roach from Hardeman County. Crime: larceny. Sentence: three years from 23 May 1841. Rec'd 23 May 1841. He is 24 years old, weighs 142 lbs., 5' 6" high. Was born and brought up in Madison Co., Tenn., three miles north of Richmond. Has one brother and mother in Cass Co., Illinois, 1 1/2 mile from Beardstown on the Illinois River. Said Roache has dark hair, blue eyes, dark skin. Has a small scar on his forehead with shows by being whiter than the other flesh. His right shin has a large dark scar on it caused, he says, from fever and ague. [Ledger 45, p. 169]

William Roberts. From Bradley County. Crime: larceny. Sentence: three years from Aug. 27, 1841. Received Sept. 10, 1841. He is 37 years old, weighs 140 lbs., 5' 9" high. Born in Jefferson Co., Tenn., and brought up in Jefferson and Bradley counties. He has a wife and seven children in Madison Co., Alabama, about 15 miles east of Huntsville and about three miles [no direction given] of Summerville on Flint River. He has dark hair, blue eyes and fair skin. Has lost a piece of his right ear. [Ledger 45, p. 169]

Alexander Spears was received in the Penitentiary 18 Apr. 1831. He is about 21 years of age, 5' 10 3/4" high. Dark skin and hazel eyes. A scar about an inch long on the out side of left eye, and one near the wrist of the right hand. Born in North Carolina, brought up in Jefferson Co., Alabama, and resided for some time in Cumberland Co., Kentucky, 12 or 15 miles from Burksville. His father and mother live near the Chickasaw Bluffs. Has a sister by the name of Gaines residing in Jefferson Co., Alabama. Weighs about 175 lbs. and is by profession a laboror. Was found guilty of horse stealing at the Circuit Court of Henderson County and sentenced to six years confinement in the Jail and Penitentiary House of the State of Tennessee. *Alexander Spears was discharged April 18th, 1837. Conduct good. Learned the blacksmiths business.* [Ledger 45, p. 171]

William Sexton was received in the Penitentiary 29 Sept. 1831. He is 25 years of age, 5' 7" high and weighs 144 lbs. He has a yellow or hazle eye, hair rather light, fair skin. Has two scars on the under side of the right arm, about equal distance above and below the elbow joint. Has blowed and struck a short time at the blacksmith's business, but has generally worked at farming. He was born in Burke Co., North Carolina, and raised in Roane Co., East Tenn. His mother lives in Munroe Co., Tenn., and a brother and sister lives with his mother. He has one sister in Roane County who is married to Jacob Frits, and lives near Daniel Mosses Mill, which is on Hickory Creek, the waters of Clinch River. His mother lives in three miles of Tellico, the seat of justice of Monroe County. His wife and one child lives on the same farm with his mother. His mother-in-law and brother-in-law lives in Roane County 13 miles from Kingston and one and a half miles from Clabey's[?] Mill. Was found guilty of horse stealing at the Circuit Court of Roane County, and sentenced to three years confinement in the Jail and Penitentiary House of the State of Tennessee, from the verdict of the jury. *William Sexton was discharged Oct. 18th, 1834. He was detained 20 days for bad conduct. Lernt [sic] the wagon bisness [sic] while in prison. Conduct generally good.* [Ledger 45, p. 171]

William Swafford was received in the Penitentiary 1 Dec. 1831. He is about 30 years of age, 5' 11" high, common weight 167 lbs. Blue eyes, light hair a little inclined to be sandy, not very fair skin, heavy and sandy beard. He was born in Pendleton Co., North [sic,] Carolina, and raised in Jackson and Bledsoe counties, Tennessee. His wife lives now in Bledsoe County five miles from Maddisonville clost [sic,] to Utters Mill. His mother lives in Bledsoe Co., Tenn. One brother in Tomkinsville, Monroe Co., Kentucky. He has two brothers in Sequatchie Valley, Tenn. He has two scars, one over each eye, the one over the left nearly perpendicular. Two scars on the inside of the right leg on the calf, and one on the left leg caused by a bile or biles, all on the inside of the leg. Has some knowledge of the blacksmiths business. Found guilty of concealing stolen horses at the Circuit Court of Monroe County and sentenced to three years confinement in the Jail and Penitentiary House of the State of Tennessee. *William Swofford was discharged by expiration of sentence on the 1st day of Jan. 183 [page torn]. He was detained 30 days for bad conduct.* [Ledger 45, p. 171]

Francis Smith was received in the Penitentiary 29 Feb. 1832. He is 5' 9 1/4" high, weighs 146 lbs. Dark hair, black or dark yellow eyes, swarthy complexion. He has a scar on the left cheek bone, and one in the left eye brow, running up from the eye. A small scar just below the left knee. He was born and raised in Franklin Co., Tenn., is 22 years old. His father now lives in Franklin Co., Tenn.; his mother is dead. He has one brother and one sister with his father. He has some half brothers and sisters in Alabama, on the Alabama River near Independance Town. He was found guilty of grand larceny at the Circuit Court of Williamson County and sentenced to three years confinement in the Jail and Penitentiary House of the State of Tennessee. *Francis Smith was discharged by expiration of sentence on the 28 day of Feb'y 1835. Conduct very good.* [Ledger 45, p. 172]

Andrew Stephens was received into the Penitentiary 13 Feb. 1832. He is 5' 4 1/2" high, 18 years old, weighs 130 lbs. Blue eyes, fair hair and skin, his face inclined to freckle. He has a small mole on the left side of the nose, near a half inch from it. A small scar on the middle joint of the thumb of the left hand, and one the middle joint of the fore finger of the same hand. Has had a cut on the left foot running from the toe next the big toe up the foot, about 2" long. One also on the right foot, from the great toe up the foot about the same length. He was born in Sevier Co., Tenn., and raised in Monroe Co., Tenn. One brother a tanner living in south Alabama. Two brothers living in Monroe Tennessee. One who is a taylor [sic,] living in Philadelphia Tennessee, the other a farmer near the same place. One uncle on Little Tennessee River, Blount County, by the name of McCain, an uncle in Sevier County on Little Pigeon River name Joseph Sutton. He was found guilty of grand larceny at the Circuit Court of Blount County and sentenced to three years confinement in the Jail and Penitentiary House of the State of Tennessee. *Andrew Stephens was discharged by expiration of sentence on the 21st day of October 1835. He was detained two hundred and fifty days for bad conduct ("so mote it be").* [Ledger 45, p. 172]

Thomas Sherod was received in the Penitentiary 12 Apr. 1832. He is 5' 10 ³/₄" high, 23 years old, weighs 172 lbs. Blue eyes, fair skin and hair, prominent nose and a tolerable good countenance. He was born in Sullivan and brought up in Knox Co., Tenn., where his father and mother now lives, 10 miles east of Knoxville near Jno. McMillen, Esq. His father's name is Henry Sherod. He has also one uncle in the same neighbourhood. He has worked some at the carpenter business. He has a small scar on the second joint of the thumb of the left hand, forming the letter T or nearly so. Also a small scar on the back of the middle finger of the same hand, near the nail. The finger next the little finger has been mashed, leaving a small scar on the end of it. He was found guilty of passing counterfeit bank bill at the Circuit Court of Sullivan County, and sentenced to three years confinement in the Jail and Penitentiary House of the State of Tennessee. *Thomas Sherrod was discharged by expiration of sentence on the 21st day of July 1835. Detained 110 days for bad conduct.* [Ledger 45, p. 172]

William Standifer was received in the Penitentiary 11 Nov. 1832. He is 5' 7 ¹/₄" in h[e]ight, weighs 154 lbs. 18 years of age, dark hair, grey eyes, full fat face and tolerable good countenance. Born in Lee Co., Virginia, where his mother now resides. Brought up in McMinn Co., Tenn., with Thomas Burton about eight miles from Calhoun on Hiwassee River, one mile and a half from Dotson's and the same distance from Rucker's mill. He has three brothers and two sisters. His right wrist is out of place, his left arm has been broke[n] about one and a half inches above the wrist. Has a small scar on the chin just under the lip, one below the cap of the left knee, and a scar from a cut on the first joint of the fore finger of the left hand. Has generally followed farming. Was found guilty of stealing a pair of pantaloons at the Circuit Court of McMinn County and sentenced to three years confinement in the Jail and Penitentiary House of the State of Tennessee. *Discharged Nov. 21, 1835. Detained 10 days for improper conduct. His conduct generly [sic] good. Lernd [sic] the tailoring bisness [sic] whilst in prison.* [Ledger 45, p. 173]

Peter Seals was received into the Penitentiary 10 Mar. 1833. He is 5' 11 ¹/₂" in h[e]ight and weighs 155 lbs. Dark curling hair, blue eyes, fair complexion, light sandy beard, 37 years of age. Born in Virginia and brought up in Dickson Co., Tenn. He has a wife and eight children who reside on the middle fork of Barton's Creek about 10 miles from the town of Charlotte, Dickson Co., Tenn. His wife's maiden name was Evans. Her connections likewise reside on Barton's Creek. He has two brothers, John and William Seals, who likewise live on the same creek together with the above mentioned persons, all within seven miles of Judge Humphery's mill. The fore finger of the left hand is crooked at the first joint and is very remarkable, caused by a cut. He has a scar rather above the instep of the right foot and two small scars near each other on the forehead. He has generally followed farming. Was found guilty of assault and battery with intent to kill at the Circuit Court of Dickson County and sentenced to ten years and eight months confinement in the Jail and Penitentiary House of the State of Tennessee. [Ledger 45, p. 173-4]

Jackson J. Swaggerty was received in the Penitentiary 25 May 1833. He is 5' 9 ¹/₂" in height and weighs 185 lbs. Light hair, blue eyes, dark complexion, heavy built, 25 years of age. Born in Cocke Co., Tenn., and brought up there where his father and mother, three brothers and seven sisters now reside. He has two sisters married, one to Jessee Van living in Monroe County about five miles from John McGee, Esqr. Swaggerty's parents residence is about six miles above Newport on the Greenville road. He has a wife and two children, they reside at Jessee Van's. His other sister is married to James Shoat, his residence not known. He has several scars on the forefinger of the left hand where it joins the hand. The little finger of this hand is crooked. He has several scars on the shin and one running up and down on the inside of the left leg. This leg has been broken. A scar on the left side of the forehead. Has generally followed farming. Was found guilty of petit larceny at the Circuit Court of Monroe County and sentenced to 15 months imprisonment in the Jail and Penitentiary House of the State of Tennessee. *Jackson J. Swaggerty was discharged Sept. 3rd, 1834. He was detained 10 days for bad conduct.* [Ledger 45, p. 174]

Tennessee Convicts: Records of the State Penitentiary

Charles Spears was received in the Penitentiary March 31, 1834. He is 5' 9" in height and weighs 173 lbs. Dark hair, dark blue eyes and tolerably fair complexion. 25 y[ear]s. Born in Pendleton District, South Carolina, and brought up partly in Maury and Lincoln County, Tenn. His mother, four brothers and two sisters reside in Perry Co., Illinois. He has a wife now living with her brother-in-law, John Winston, who resides about two miles from Esqr. Claiborne's and near the Widow Driver's Horse Mill and 16 miles from Fayetteville, Lincoln Co., Tenn. Her maiden name was Wall. Spears has a remarkable scar on the forehead about 1 $^{3}/_{8}$" long, running from the hair to the eyebrow in rather a horizontal direction. A scar on the upper lip near the right nostril, a scar on the inside of the second finger of the right hand. The nails on both great toes has been disfigured by cuts from an axe. He has generally followed farming. Was found guilty of petit larceny at the Circuit Court of Lincoln County and sentenced to two years and six months confinement in the Jail and Penitentiary House of the State of Tennessee. *Charles Spears was discharged 24th Nov. 1836. Served 55 days for breach of prison rules. Conduct generally good. Returned for horse stealing Dec. 9th, 1836.* [Ledger 45, pp. 174-5]

John Slaughter was rec'd in the Penitentiary 19 Dec. 1834. He is 28 years of age, 5' 7" high, and weighs 150 lbs. Red hair, grey eyes, fair complexion and high forehead. A remarkable crook in the rist of the left arm, caused by having it broken, the bone projects out and accasions a large knot. A scar about an inch in length on and running lengthways of the back of the left hand, and one on the inside of the right leg occasioned by a shot from a rifle gun. Chiefly followed stage driving. Born in Greene Co., Tenn., and brought up in Limestone Co., Alabama, on Limestone Creek four miles from Tennessee River, where his father (Wm. Slaughter), one sister (Ann) and one brother (James) now reside. Also two sisters (Elizabeth and Sarah) married to Edwin Owens and Woodson Huddleson living in the same neighbourhood. One brother (Branson) residing near Florence in Lotterdale [*sic,*, Lauderdale] Co., Alabama. He was found guilty of maiming at the Circuit Court of Fayette County and sentenced to two years confinement in the Jail and Penitentiary House of the State of Tennessee. *John Slaughter was discharged 20 Dec. 1836. Detained one day. Conduct good. (Carpenter).* [Ledger 45, p. 175]

Francisco St. John (Spaniard) was rec'd in the Penitentiary 1 July 1835. He is 26 years of age, 5' 4" or 5" high, and weighs 135 lbs. Black hair, black eyes and dark complexion. He professes to be a Roman Catholic. Has the representation of the cross inscribed on the left arm above the elbow, and a double heart crossed by an arrow with the initials of his name above and two Es below it inscribed on the right arm above the elbow. A scar just above the outside corner of the right eye, a scar on the back part of the left wrist, a scar on the back of the left hand, and a scar about 2" in length running lengthways with the arm, on the left arm just below the elbow. Tailor. Born and brought up on the Island of Cuba. He was found guilty of grand larceny at the Circuit Court of Shelby County and sentenced to nine years' confinement in the Jail and Penitentiary House of the State of Tennessee. [Ledger 45, p. 175-6]

Samuel Surber was received in the Penitentiary Oct. 15, 1835. He is 39 years of age [blank] feet [blank] and weighs 161 lbs. Born in Ireland and while yet an infant his father, desireing to get rid of paying tythes and etc., moved to this "the asylum of the oppressed and home of the brave." But it pleased divine providence to deprive Samuel of his father (at an early age), who then resided at Abington, Virginia. Here he learned the weaver's business with Peter Ritchie and Samuel Harley, and of "late years" he has drove a wagon for Capt. Samuel Preston near Abington. About a year since, Samuel took it into his head to seek his fortunes in the "far west" and removed to Sullivan Co., Tenn. Shortly afterwards he took to wife Lavicy, daughter of Mrs. Andrews, who lived in the "Horn settlement" near Holston River and in the vicinity of Burton Childress' mill, where he has lived ever sin[c]e. He left his "rib" together with a "pledge" about three months old with his mother-in-law but thinks it quite probable that they will leave that neighborhood soon. Dark eyes, hair and complexion and dish face, which expresses little or nothing [underlined in original]. A scar beginning near the centre of his nose and running forhedwise [sic,, underlined] near the extremity of the lip. One on the right side of the chin. One on the shin just above the ancle joint. Two scars below the knee of the same (left) leg, all occasioned by the white swelling which has also made him lame in the same leg. A scar on the fore finger near the hand occasioned by the cut of a swingling knife, one on the same (left) hand between the small finger and the one next it. Nature has been spareing in her intellectual gifts with Sam. He was found guilty of "an assault and battery with intent to kill" at the Circuit Court of Sullivan County and sentenced to three years confinement in the Jail and Penitentiary House of the State of Tennessee. (Sens[?] facit) *Samuel Surber died on the 14th day of Oct., 1838 of [blank].* [Ledger 45, p. 176-7]

Eli Sartin, convict from Jefferson County, January term, for assault and battery with intent to kill, and sentenced to imprisonment at hard labour th[r]ee years. Was received 2 Feb. 1836. He was born in North Carolina and raised in Jefferson Co., Tenn. He is 5' 6 ½" high, 23 years old, blue eyes, fair hair, round face, light beard. Weighs about 145 lbs. He has a remarkable scar under the left eye resembling small clear warts connected, a mole under the chin and one on the left side of the neck, and one near the right nipple. Parents living near Dandridge, Jeff[erso]n Co., Tenn. Two sisters and three brothers, one of the sisters married to Joseph Wise. *Eli Sartin was discharged by expiration of sentence Feby. 6th, 1839.* [Ledger 45, p. 177]

Reddick Sanders was convicted of grand larceny at the Bedford County Circuit Court, April term, and sentenced to three years confinement in the Penitentiary of the State of Tennessee, commencing 9 Apr. 1836. (Received 12 Apr. 1836.) He is 5' 9 ½" high, weighs [blank] lbs., dark skin, dark hair, blue eyes, short thick nose, short under jaw and chin, and talks with his teeth closed. His hands and fingers are unusually long. Has a scar across the joint of the right thumb, and marks similar to small pock [sic,] pits on the left side of the neck and running up into the beard. Says he is 28 years old (his appearance indicates it). His mother lives on land of her own seven miles from Old Jefferson in Wilson Co., Tenn., on the waters of Dry Hurricane Creek. Has a wife who stays with her brother Daniel Doxey. *Reddick Sanders was discharged 29 Apr. 1839. Detained 20 days for breach of prison rules.* [Ledger 45, p. 177]

Stockley D. Swaggarty. From Knox County, Tenn. Was received 1 July 1836. He is 36 years old, 5' 8 ¼" high barefoot, and weighs 145 lbs. Born in Knox Co., Tenn. Blue eyes, fair skin, light hair, long thin face, deep hollow eyes. He has a wife and six [children] in Blount Co., Tenn., near Henry's Store. Short hand[s] and remarkably short wide nails on his fingers. Found guilty of receiving stolen goods and sentenced to one year imprisonment in the Tenn[esse]e P[enitentiar]y from 16 June 1836. *Stockley D. Swaggerty was discharged by order of N. Cannon, Gov. of Tenn'e, 25th March 1837.* [Ledger 45, pp. 177-8]

Jesse Smith. From Bledsoe Co., Tenn. Was received 19 July 1836. Found guilty of horse stealing and sentenced to three years imprisonment in the Jail and Penitentiary House [crossed out in original] from 14 July 1836. He is about 35 years old, 5' 10 ½" high, com[m]on weight 150 lbs., fair skin, light blue eyes, beard and hair half grey. High nose and rather large. High forehead, nearly bald to the crown of the head. Left ear large and stands off from the head, and [has a] slip off of the right, commencing at top and cutting down to the centre of [the] back part. The thumb of the left hand has been badly mashed about the last joint, which makes it crooked and inclines it to double in and lay across the palm of the hand. A scar on the left instep running with the leaders, and one just below, verry large, extending down to the hollow of the foot, cut with an axe. He married Peggy, daughter of Alexander Johnson of

Tennessee Convicts: Records of the State Penitentiary

Bledsoe Co., Tenn. His family now lives in Hamilton Co., Tenn., on Tennessee River, two miles above the mouth of Possum [underlined in original] Creek. [Ledger 45, p. 178]

Lewis D. S. Leger. From Shelby County. Offence: assault to kill. Sentence: three years. Was received Jan. 17, 1837. He is 29 years old, 5' 11 ½" high, weighs 173 lbs. Has dark hair, hazel eyes, fair skin. Many scars, viz. 1 ½" below the left ear made by a bullet which came out about the same distance below the cheek bone, scarcely visible, and between the two a scar from the bite of a man. One across each thumb running across the last joint diagonally, between the two joints. A scar on the back of the thumb of the left hand which cut the sinew. A scar on the point of the left shoulder and one below through the muscle of the right arm where bullets had entered. They were extracted under the arm which leaves a scar. A scar on the right hip bone occasioned by an ounce ball. By profession a portrait painter. *Gave one hat, one shirt, one vest and one pr pants to John Forgus. 6th May 1837.* [Ledger 45, p. 178; pardon papers show his name as Lewis de St. Leger]

Lewis Sexton. From Meigs Co., Tenn. Offence: larceny. Sentence: one year and six months from 18 Apr. 1837. Was rec'd April 24, 1837. He is 5' 9 ½" high, weighs 183 lbs., and is 25 years old. A stout made man, florid complexion, dark hair and grey eyes. A corner broke off the right front too[t]h above, and the one next to it is broke off even with the gum. His lower teeth rather irregular. Was raised in Hamilton Co., Tenn., where his father now lives. His wife and three children lives in Bradley Co., Tenn. By profession a farmer. *Lewis Sexton was discharg[ed] by expiration of sentence, Oct. 25th, 1838.* [Ledger 45, p. 179]

Thomas B. Staley. Offence: pettit larceny. Sentence: one year. Was rec'd 25 Apr. 1837. He is 22 years of age, 5' 7" high, weighs 155 lbs. Born and brought up in Craven Co., North Carolina, on the road leading from Newburn to Washington, where his mother now lives. He has fair hair, blue eyes and fair skin. He has two brothers and one sister in the same county. He also has one uncle by the name of David Whitford in the same county. He has a scar on the right side of the lower jaw caused by a wen. Was sentenced by the Cuircuit Court of Hawkin[s] County. [Ledger 45, p. 179]

John Shepherd. From Washington County. Offence: receiving stolen goods. Sentence: three years from 3 July 1837. He is 37 years old, 5' 7" high, weighs 184 lbs. Fair hair, blue eyes, fair skin, full face and inclined to be corpulent. He has a wife and two children living about eight miles north of Jonesborough,

Washington County, East Tennessee. His wife is a daughter of John Huffines of North Carolina. He was born and bro't up in Stokes County, North Carolina. His father, mother and two sisters live͟s in Washington, one mile from Jonesbor͟o on the road to Elizabethtown. He has one uncle living near Lynchburg, Virginia. The fore and middle fingers on͟e boa͟th hands bends outwards. Sentenced by the C͟uircuit Court of Washington County to three years confinement in the Jail and Penitentiary House of the State of Tennessee and confirmed by the Circuit Court at Knoxville, Knox County. [Ledger 45, pp. 179-180]

James Sampson. From Stewart County. Offence: stabbing and sh͟uting. Sentence: two years from 12 July 1837. Received July 24, 1837. He is 30 years old, 6' high, weighs 187 lbs., fair hair, greyish blue eyes, fair skin. Born in Kentucky, bro't up in Williamson Co., Tenn., on the waters of West Harper [*sic,*], four miles from Franklin. Has had a wife and three children, they are all dead. His wife was a daughter of Ephriam Russell, now living at Springhill between Franklin and Columbia. He has a scar on the top of the head caused by the kick of a mule (scar 2" long). Has a scar on his upper lip and one on the right side of the under part of the chin. Sentenced by the Circuit Court of Stewart County to two years confinement in the Jail and Penitentiary House of the State of Tennessee. [Ledger 45, p. 180]

Warren Smith, alias Warren Graham. From Anderson County. Offence: pettit larceny. Sentence: one year. Rec'd Nov. 24, 1837. He is 18 years old, 5' 6" high, weighs 156 lbs. He has fair hair, blue eyes and fair skin. Has two small scars on his forehead. Born in Anderson County about two miles from Clinton on Clinch River. His mother is married to a man by the name of Benjamin Graham. He has two uncles living in Bl[o]unt County, A[l]ex Smith, Calton Keeland. They live within two miles of M͟erryville. Found guilty and sentenced by the C͟uircuit Court of Anderson County to one years confinement in the Jail and Penitentiary House of the State of Tennessee. [signed] W. McIntosh. *Warren Smith was discharged Dec. 5th, 1838, having been detained 11 days for improper conduct.* [Ledger 45, p. 180]

Benjamin Springs was rec'd in the Penit'y June 19, 1838. Sentence: three years. From White County. Crime: grand larceny. He is 22 years of age, 5' 10 $^{1}/_{2}$" high, weighs 140 lbs. Straight and well formed, dark hair and eyes, fair complexion, long nose rather thick at the end. Has a scar above and commencing at the inner end of the right eye brow, a small one on the left side of the nose. A large scar under the right arm about half way between the elbow and wrist joints, by a cut with a drawing knife. A scar on each fore finger between the hand and middle joint, and one on the left foot. He was born and raised in Wilson Co., Tenn., where his uncle Abner Springs now resides. His mother lives 2 ½ miles from Sparta near the Knoxville road. He followed stage driving in different parts of the state and latterly in and near Sparta. [Ledger 45, p. 181]

Andrew Swisegood. From Knox County. Offence: horse stealing. Sentence: three years. Rec'd July 1, 1838. He is 20 years old, 5' 7" high, weighs 140 lbs. Born and bro't up in Davidson Co., North Carolina, six miles west of Lexington where his father, Andrew Swisegood, now lives. He has two brother uncles living in Pike Co., Indiana, by the name of Snider. Two brothers in Pike Co., Illinois. He has red hair, black eyes, fair skin but freckled. Has a scar on the instep of the left foot. Has a scar on the thigh 6" or 8" above the knee, also a small scar near the left corner and just above the corner of his mouth. Found guilty by the Cuircuit Court of Knox County. [Ledger 45, p. 181]

Anthony G. Smith. From Monroe County. Offence: horse stealing. Rec'd Jan. 30, 1839. Sentence: five years. He is 50 years old, 5' 10" high, weighs 160 lbs. Has light grey hair, blue eyes, fair skin, long Roman nose. Born in Cumberland, Virginia. Bro't up in Buckingham Co., Virginia. He has one brother in Hawkins Co., Tenn., also two in Knox Co., one in Green[e]. Their names are as follows: John [and] Sterling in Knox; Thomas in Green; Robert in Hawkins. He has a wife and one child in Monroe County. He has one son in Indiana, Bush County. Also two daughters in Rhea Co., Tenn., and one daughter in Hawkins married to a man by the name of Bird Smith. [Ledger 45, p. 182]

Parham Strange. From Davidson County. Offence: manslaughter. Sentence: seven years. Rec'd Feb. 11, 1839. He is 46 years old, 5' 10 ½" high, weighs 178 lbs. Born and bro't up in Hallifax Co., Virginia. Has lived on Harper Ridge for 13 years, 13 miles from Nashville on the Charlotte road. He has been married to a woman by the name of Milly Long, but they parted and he returned to his old mate with whom he has lived about 26 years. He is a man of bad countenance. He has one brother in Kentucky by the name of Bird[?] Strange, one at Harris' on Harper Ridge. He has light grey hair, blue eyes, fair skin. Has worked a[t] the carpenter's trade. [Ledger 45, p. 182]

Hezekiah Satterfield. From Bl[o]unt County. Sentence: two years. Rec'd Feb. 12, 1839. Offence: petit larceny. He is 23 years old, weighs 160 [lbs.], 5' 10" high. Born in South Carolina, bro't up in Blunt Co., Tenn. His mother is married to a man by the name of Dan'l Delany and lives in said county 12 miles south of Merrysville [sic,, Maryville] near Baker Creek meeting house. He has dark hair, hazle eyes, dark skin, has worked at the cabinet business and mill righting [sic,]. [Ledger 45, p. 182]

McDaniel Smith. Was received Feb. 20, 1839. He is 24 years old, 5' 8 ½" high, weighs 150 lbs. Born and raised in Wilk[e]s Co., North Carolina. His father, Joseph Smith, lives in Georgia at the Pigeon Roost gold mines, follows merchandizing and owns a 40 acre lot of gold mine, who also has a store in Clarksville, Habersham Co., Georgia. He has one brother who is a Methodist sircuit preacher. Has been engaged on board of steam boats as fireman. Has dark hair, hazle eyes, fair skin, good countenance. Is entirely clear of marks or scars of any notoriety. Has a wife, but no children, living in Wilson County. His wife has several uncles living in s[ai]d county by the name of Richmond. He was found guilty of bigomy and sentenced by the Sircuit Court of Wilson County and sentenced to four years confinement in the Jail and Penitentiary House of the State of Tennessee. [Ledger 45, p. 183]

Alexander Spears. From Bedford County. Was received April 17, 1839. Sentence: four years. Offence: grand larceny. For discription, refer to former sentence. [Ledger 45, p. 183]

P.L. Smith. From Wilson County. Offence: receiving stolen negro. Received June 14, 1839. Sentence: four years. He is 27 years old, 5' 11 ½" high, weighs 163 lbs. Born and bro't up in Wilson Co., Tenn., where the most of his relations still live. He has a wife, but no children, living in Benton, Saline Co., Arkansas. She was a daughter of Jacob Shook of Washington in Hempstead Co., Arkansas. Said Smith has been merc[h]andising in Benton in co[mpany] with his uncle Keesee, and [with] Covant [who is] said Keesee['s] soninglaw [sic,, son-in-law]. Smith has dark hair, dark skin and hazle eyes. Is generally clear of scars, good countenance, pleasing manners. Has a scar on the back of the left hand between the size of nine pence and 25 c[en]t piece. *Gregory note sent to Rev'r R. Davis, Benton, Saline County, Arkansas, one for $200 and other for $500.* [Ledger 45, p. 183]

William Sparks. From Anderson County. Received Nov. 25, 1839. Offence: pettit larceny. Sentence: 15 months. He is 35 years old, weighs 141 lbs., 5' 9" high. Born in North Carolina, bro't up in Tennessee, Claiborne County. He has a wife and five children living in the above named county eight miles west of Tazwell on the land of Timothy Norvell. Said Sparks has dark hair, black eyes, dark skin. Has a mark [on the] side of the head just above the right ear. A labourer. [Ledger 45, p. 184]

Nancy Ann Smith. From Bledsoe County. Crime: larceny. Sentence: three years from 11 July 1839. Received June 14, 1840. She is 20 years old, 5' 5 ³/₄" high, weighs 130 lbs. Born and brought up in Bledsoe Co., Tenn. Her mother Nancy Smith lives in Siquoidshee [sic,, Sequatchie] valley, one mile below Pikeville. Said girl is a bright mulatto, her mother is white and her father a coloured man. [Ledger 45, p. 184]

Martin Scott. From Bledsoe County. Crime: petit larceny. Sentence: one year from 15 July 1840. Rec'd 23 July 1840. He is [blank] years old, 5' 6" high, weighs 140 lbs. Dark complexion, yellow eyes, dark hair. His left arm has been broken at the elbow, some of the bone has come out on the underside and left a large scar. He has a scar on his right thigh near the knee. Born and brought up in Cumberland Co., Kentucky. He has a wife and three children in Bledsoe County (two girls and one boy). His wife Cynthia lives a mile north east of Pikeville near R. Brown's. Said Scott's father and mother died when he was quite young. He has three brothers and three sisters in Cumberland County, they live 12 miles from Burksville in the fork of Cumberland and Obey's River. [Ledger 45, p. 184]

William Summerville. From Wilson County. Crime: stealing notes, papers and records. Sentence: three years from 3 Oct. 1840. Received 3 Oct. 1840. He is 25 years old, 5' 7" high, weighs 130 lbs. Born in Fleming Co., Kentucky, brought up in Illinois, Edgar County, 10 miles north of Paris at which place he has two uncles, one named John, the other Alex'r. Has no connexion else where. He is a shoe maker by trade. He has dark hair, fair skin and hazel eyes. Has had the wrist of the left hand scalded which left a scar. [Ledger 45, p. 185]

Charles Sherman. From Giles County. Crime: stealing a slave & etc. Sentence: five years from 30 Oct. 1840. Received 30 Oct. 1840. He is 26 years old, weighs 132 lbs., 5' 4 ¹/₄" high. Born and brought up in the town of Barry, State of Vermont. He has red hair, blue eyes and fair skin. Has had his left thigh broke which makes his toes turn more out than the other foot. Said Sherman has drove stage from this[?] to Franklin and from thence to Columbia, and drove the team in to Pulaski. He says he first drove in Kentucky. *Gave his clothes to Devenport Romines.* [Ledger 45, p. 185]

James Scott. From Davidson County. Crime: negro stealing. Sentence: five years from 15 Dec. 1840. Rec'd 15 Dec. 1840. He is 38 years old, 5' 9 ¹/₂" high, weighs 180 lbs. Born in Lincoln Co., North Carolina, brought up in Overton Co., Tenn. He has been twice married, had two children by his first wife, one of whom is dead, the other is married to a man by the name of George Hill and lives on Crow Creek in Franklin County. His second wife lives in the round cove in the last named county near her father Wm. Wilkinson, four miles s[outh] w[est] of Shumacher's meeting house. Has one uncle in Franklin County by the name of Perry Hill. Two in Hardeman County by the names of Quiller Nearing and John Piles near Bolivar. Said Scott has dark gray hair, hazle eyes and dark skin. Has had a small piece bit off his right ear, has several scars on the middle finger of the left hand caused by a bite. Has worked at shoe making. [Ledger 45, p. 185]

Henry Smith. From Fayette County. Crime: horse stealing. Sentence: five years from 8 Feb. 1841. Rec'd 8 Feb. 1841. He is 20 years old, 6' high, weighs 144 lbs. Born and brought up in South Alabama in Marengo County where his mother, Martha Smith, now lives about 16 miles s[outh] e[ast] of Demopolis near Dodsy[?] mill. He has dark hair, blue eyes, fair skin. Has a scar on his right eye brow. Has one sister married and lives near the mouth of the Ohio River in McCracken Co., Kentucky. [Ledger 45, p. 186]

Stephen Snell. From Henderson County. Crime: forgery. Sentence: three years from 23 Apr. 1841. Rec'd 23 Apr. 1841. He is 41 years old, 6' 1 ½" high, weighs 160 lbs. Born in North Carolina, brought up in Davidson Co., Tenn., in the settlement of John Harding. When there he was engaged in carrying the mail on horse back for Polk and Walker. He has a farm on the head waters of Beach River near the Trenton road. His left hand has two stiff fingers caused by a blow, has a scar on the under part of the left side of the jaw bone. He has dark grey hair, dark skin, blue eyes and a good countenance. [Ledger 45, p. 186]

Lewis Shepherd. From Davidson County. (Alias W.A. Holcomb) Crime: grand larceny. Sentence: five years from 28 Sept. 1841, when he was rec'd. He is 26 years old, weighs 155 lbs., 5' 7" high. Born and brought up in the town of Westfield, Hampden County, [Massachusetts?]. His mother, two sisters and one brother now reside in [blank] County, Ohio, in the town of Revena [sic,, Ravenna], about 35 miles from Cleveland. Said Shepherd has various emblems, or coats of arms. On his right arm is a monument with the American, English and one other flag placed on each side of it. He has on his breast the American Coat of Arms. On his left arm he has two hearts connected by three darts. Also a small monument on same arm just above the hearts. He has a scar 2" long on his right temple. Has black hair, black eyes and dark skin. [Ledger 45, p. 186]

Seth Sears. From Stewart County. Crime: larceny. Sentence: two years and six months from Nov. 3, 1841. Rec'd Nov. 8, 1841. He is 33 years old, 6' 1" high, weighs 188 lbs. Born and brought up in Meigs Co., Ohio, Setart[?] Falls. He has a wife and one child living in Dover, Stewart Co., Tenn. Said Sears has black hair, hazle eyes, dark skin, has a scar in the right side of his upper lip caused by the kick of a colt. [Ledger 45, p. 187]

John Sasseen. From Knox County. Crime: taking a letter from U.S. mail. Sentence: four years from 22 Oct. 1841. Rec'd 31 Oct. 1841. He is 19 years old, weighs 151 lbs., 6' 1" high. Born in Virginia and br[ough]t up in Jefferson and Cocke counties. His mother, Elizabeth Sasseen or Eliz. Thompson is now living in Dandridge, her husband is a tanner. Has a sister married to a man by the name of Jos. Henderson. He is a farmer and has followed boating apples, flour and such articles down the river. Has fair hair, grey eyes, fair skin. Has had the big toe of the right foot cut with a foot adze. [Ledger 45, p. 187]

Wm. Shadden. From Jackson County. Crime: perjury. Sentence: three years from 30 Nov. 1841. Rec'd 30 Nov. 1841. He is 49 years old, weighs 159 lbs., 5' 11 1/2" high. Born and bro't up in East Tennessee in the counties of Knox and Jackson. Has been married three times. Two of his wives are dead. He has dark blue eyes and fair skin. [Ledger 45, p. 187]

James Sartin. From Davidson County. Appeal from Coffee C[ount]y. Crime: murder. Sentence: six years from 17 Dec. 1841. Rec'd 17 Dec. 1841. He is 44 years old, 6' high, weighs 147 lbs. Born in Georgia, brought up in Franklin Co., Tenn. Has a wife and five children living in Coffee County on Elk River, four miles above Caldwell's bridge. Her name was Simmons[?] and was bro't up in Robertson County. Has dark grey hair, black eyes and dark skin. [Ledger 45, p. 188]

Samuel Smith. From McMinn County. Crime: horse stealing. Sentence: five years from 17 Dec. 1841. Rec'd Jan. 10, 1842. He is 22 years old, weighs 152 lbs., 5' 8" high. Born in Craven Co., North Carolina. Born and bro't up in the same counties and towns as his brother (see his description below). Has dark sandy hair, black eyes and fair skin. [Ledger 45, p. 188]

Hardy Smith. From McMinn County. Crime: horse stealing. Sentence: four years from 17 Dec. 1841. Rec'd Jan. 10, 1842. He is 21 years old, 5' 10" high, weighs 190 lbs. Born in Craven Co., North Carolina, and brought up in White Co., Tenn., four miles from Sparta on the waters of Calf Killer, near Simpson's mill. His mother lives in Bradley County on Hiwassee near Perry Ackerson's ferry. He has fair hair, fair skin, haz<u>le</u> eyes. His left side, leg, foot and face is larger than the right. Has a great many connections in West Tennessee but does not know where. [Ledger 45, p. 188]

John Simpson. From Shelby County. Crime: grand larceny. Sentence: four years from 26 Feb. 1842. Rec'd 26 Feb. 1842. He is 24 years old, 6' ½" high, weighs 160 lbs. Born and brought up in the City of New York. Has a wife with his mother Jane Simpson in ~~New York~~ Newark, New Jersey. Has fair hair, grey eyes and fair skin. Has no scars or marks. [Ledger 45, p. 189]

James Shelton. From Anderson County. Crime: petit larceny. Sentence: one year from 25 Mar. 1842. Rec'd 25 Mar. 1842. He is 22 years old, 5' 11" high, weighs 170 lbs. Born and brought up in Anderson County eight miles west of Clinton, four miles from Poplar Creek meeting house. He has dark hair, haz<u>le</u> eyes and dark skin. [Ledger 45, p. 189]

Abraham Spears. From Shelby County. Crime: murder 2nd degree. Sentence: 21 years from Oct. 24, 1842. Rec'd [blank]. He is 20 years old, 5' 9" high, weighs 143 lbs. Born and bro't up in Fayette and Shelby countys. He has a wife and one child with her brother, Thomas Simmons, about 16 miles from Raleigh on the road leading to Lagrange. His mother in law Jane Simmons lives in Rutherford County near Murfreesboro. He has black hair and black eyes and dark skin. <u>Strait</u> and well made. His relations generally live in Alabama and North Carolina, the counties he does not recollect. [Ledger 45, p. 189]

Jeremiah <u>Barney</u>. From Fayette County. Crime: horse stealing. Sentence: five years from 8 Feb. 1841. Rec'd 8 Feb. 1841. He is 17 years old, 5' 7" high, weighs 159 lbs. Born and brought up in Claiborne Co., Tenn. His father Benj. <u>Bordine</u> now lives 10 miles south of Bloomington, Indiana, within four miles of Col. Ketchem's mill on Clear Creek. He has dark hair, blue eyes, fair skin and what might be called a good countenance. [Ledger 45, p. 190]

John Bordine. From Tipton County. Crime: larceny. Sentence: three years from 8 Mar. 1841. Rec'd 8 Mar. 1841. He is 27 years old, 5' 7 ½" high, weighs 172 lbs. Born in Virginia and brought up in Marybone[?], Ohio, 18 miles from Dayton on the Franklin Road, where his father John Bordine now lives. Has one brother, William, lives in Indiana near Terre Haut[e]. Said Bordine has followed the river on steam boats as deck hand. He has light hair, hazle eyes, fair skin, moles on his face, one on each cheek and one near the left corner of his mouth. Has a light beard. [Ledger 45, p. 190]

Archibald Bradfute. From Warren County. Crime: horse stealing. Sentence: three years from June 2, 1841. Rec'd June 2, 1841. He is 16 years old, 5' 7" high, weighs 125 lbs. Born and brought up in Nashville. His father, Rob. Bradfute, is a bricklayer and lives in Nashville, and is thought to be an honest man. Has an uncle by the name of J[?] H. Bradfute who is Prefrecter[?] of the Race Course at Tuscumbia, Alabama. He has fair hair, hazle eyes and fair skin. His mother was by the name of Vascer[?] before marriage, he does not know where her relations live. [Ledger 45, p. 190]

Burrel Bradley. From Davidson County. Crime: horse stealing. Sentence: three years from 7 June 1841. Rec'd 7 June 1841. He is 17 years old, weighs 147 lbs., is 5' 8" high. Born in Monroe Co., Tenn., and partly brought up in said county, and then his father Isaac Bradley moved to Davis Co., Kentucky. He has one brother, Isaac Bradley, living in Roane Co., Tenn., near King's Iron Works. All the rest of his connections live in Missouri, he does not know the name of the county. He has fair hair, hazle eyes, dark skin. Has a scar about 1" or 1 1/4" long on the joint of the wrist of the right hand. Also one between that and the first joint of the thumb on the same wrist, looking somewhat like warts. [Ledger 45, p. 191]

Robert Brooke. From Washington County. Crime: petit larceny. Sentence: one year from 14 July 1841. He is 39 years old, 5' 9 1/2" high, weighs 160 lbs. Born and brought up in Washington Co., Tenn., on the head waters of Middle Limestone, two miles from Leesburg. Has a wife and two children, the property of Richard[?] Dickens. The above named boy has a scar on the right side of the fore head caused by a lick with a rock. He has had his right thigh broken, which makes that leg the shortest. A negro. [Ledger 45, p. 191]

Robert Boyle. From Marshall County. Crime: manslaughter. Sentence: six years from Feb. 1, 1842, when received. He is 60 years old, 5' 8" high, weighs 140 lbs. Born and brought up in Iredale Co., North Carolina. Has a wife and one child at the head of Richland Creek near Wm[?] Cook's mill. Said Boyle has grey hair, black eyes, fair skin. [Ledger 45, p. 191]

Bailey Brooks. From Madison County. Crime: manslaughter. Sentence: two years from 21 Apr. 1842. Rec'd 21 Apr. 1842. He is 68[?] years old, 6' 2" high, weighs 166 lbs. Born and brought up in Amherst Co., Virginia. He has grey hair, blue eyes, and fair skin. Has a lump in the palm of his left hand. [Ledger 45, p. 192]

John B. Benham. From Greene County. Crime: passing counterfeit money. Sentence: four years from 28 Oct. 1842. Rec'd 28 Oct. 1842. He is 41 years old, weighs 146 lbs., 5' 7" high. Born and bro't up in Greene Co., Tenn. Has a wife and five children in Monroe Co., Kentucky, about 10 miles from Hopkinsville on the Bowlinggreen [sic,] road. Has dark grey hair, black eyes, dark skin. Owns the land on which his wife lives about 3/4 mile from Cowins horse mill. [Ledger 45, p. 192]

Thomas Bragg, Sr. From Fayette County. Crime: murder 2nd degree. Sentence: 18 years from 9 Oct. 1842. Received 9 Oct. 1842. He is 53 years old, 5' 7 1/2" high, weighs 130 lbs. Born and bro't up in Lunenburg Co., Virginia. Has a wife and five children living in Fayette County, seven miles south west of Sommerville near the north fork of Wolf River. Has one daughter married to a man by the name of J[?] B. Smith, who is now living with a man by the name of Creed B. Halley, four miles s.w. of Sommerville. S[ai]d Bragg has grey hair, blue eyes and fair skin. Has a scar above each knee, one round, the other about 1 1/2" long. Had a sister in Lincoln Co., Tenn., about six years since but is not certain whether she is there now or not. [Ledger 45, p. 192]

Thomas Bragg, Jr.. From Fayette County Crime: murder 2nd degree. Sentence: 18 years from 9 Oct. 1842. Rec'd 9 Oct. 1842. He is 23 years old, 5' 6 1/2" high, weighs 130 lbs. Born and brought up in Lunenburg Co., Virginia, and brought up in Fayette Co., Tenn., where his mother now lives. He has fair hair, dark skin and blue eyes. Has a scar above each eye, say 1 1/2" long. The one above the right eye runs across the eyebrow. [Ledger 45, p. 193]

Robert Bragg. From Fayette County. [No other information given.] [Ledger 45, p. 193]

George Boatman. From Grainger County. Crime: incest. Sentence: five years from Sept. 9, 1842. Rec'd Sept. 9, 1842. He is 70 years old, 6' 3" high, weighs 157 lbs. Born in Virginia, bro't up on the Holston River in Grainger Co., Tenn. Has a wife and 10 children living in the above named county, six of whom are married. He has yellowish blue eyes, fair skin and white hair. Has had his leg broke by the kick of a horse. [Ledger 45, p. 193]

Jackson C. Thomas was received into the Penitentiary 6 Dec. 1831. He is 18 years of age, 6' high, weighs 154 lbs. His complexion a little yellowish. A small scar in the left eye brow, one large and remarkable scar over the left eye, running into the hair. A scar between the chin and under lip running crosswise. A small scar on the right corner of the right eye brow. A scar across the middle finger of the right hand. A small scar on the cap of the left knee. Can write his own name, and read a little. Stout scar on the back of the head nearest the left year [sic,]. Was found guilty of petit larceny at the Circuit Court of Davidson County, and sentenced to three years confinement in the Jail and Penitentiary House of the State of Tennessee, from 6 Dec. 1831. *Jackson C. Thomas died of cholera on the 9th of June, 1833.* [Ledger 45, p. 197]

Thomas Terrell was received into the Penitentiary 27 Nov. 1831. He is about 35 years of age, 5' 7" high, weighs 145 lbs. Born and raised in Etonderry, Ireland, Kings County. He has no relation in the United States. Married a daughter of Alexr. Law of Columbia, Tennessee, where his wife is now living with her father. His wife has one brother and two sisters grown. The brother married and living in Shelbyville, Tennessee. He is a hatter by trade. He has a hard rising on the nose between the eyes. He is a Catholic in his religion, has the sign of the cross and etc. on his right arm between the elbow and wrist, with the letters T T at the lower part of the same. He has large scars on both sides of both of his legs. Complexion fair than otherwise, sandy hair approaching to red, blue eyes. Was found guilty of stabbing at the Circuit Court of Maury County and sentenced to two years confinement in the Jail and Penitentiary House of the State of Tennessee. *Thomas Terrell was discharged by expiration of sentence 29th Nov. 1833. His conduct was good.* [Ledger 45, p. 197]

James Richardson Tarlton, alias James Richerson Tarlton alias James Tarlton was received into the Penitentiary 18 Mar. 1832. He is 31 years old, 5' 6 ½" high, weighs 156 or 160 lbs. Dark skin, blue eyes, dark hair which is very thin and a little grey. Born and raised in Iredale Co., North Carolina, lived in Buncomb[e] Co., North Carolina, where his father now lives. One brother in Green[e] Co., Tenn., where his wife lives, 12 miles from Greenville on the road leading from Carolina to Kentucky near the Chucky river in the house with her father (Henry Varner). His eyes are a little crossed if closely examined. Dark beard, tolerable good countenance. A small scar on the middle finger of the right hand, near the hand. One scar on the same hand between the thumb and the wrist joint, caused by a bile. A large scar on the left foot, running from the big toe across the foot, cut with an axe. One on the left knee, and two on the right knee, one from a bile and one from a cut with a knife, the one from the bile above the other. He was found guilty at the Circuit Court of Green County for grand larceny and sentenced to three years confinement in the Jail and

Tennessee Convicts: Records of the State Penitentiary

Penitentiary House of the State of Tennessee. *James R. Tarlton was discharged by expiration of sentence 29th day of June 1833. He was detained 104 days for bad conduct.* [Ledger 45, pp. 197-8]

Joseph Thompson was received into the Penitentiary April 16, 1832. He is 25 years old, 5' 5 ¼" high, weight 148 lbs. He was born and brought up in Hartford, Ohio County, Kentucky, where he passed by the name of Joseph T. Ward, which he says is his right name. He is stout made, handsome faced, smart turned. Has dark hair and curley, black eyes and fair skin, and a tolerable good countenance. His father lives on the road leading from Elizabethtown to Frankfort, Kentucky. He has an uncle living near Frankfort by the name of Charles Thompson, one also in Louisville by the name of Dunn. He says his father is a Baptist preacher. He has a mark on the left arm put their with India ink, between the elbow and rist in the form of an eagle with liberty wrote on it with some spriggs or leaves below it, and a breast plate, and the following letters **J. & M. W.** He has on the right arm the likeness of a woman with the letters **M. P. S.** over her head and **J. W.** below her feet. She is holding a flower in her left hand. His arm has been broken above the rist of the left arm. He has a scar over the right eye in the hair, say 2" long. He says he has a wife in Washington Co., Pennsylvania, and one child. She is living with her father three miles from the town of Washington, her father's name is Chappell, where the stage stops. Thompson has no trade but has worked a little at the tailoring. He was found guilty of petit larceny a[t] the Circuit Court of Robinson [*sic.,* Robertson] County, and sentenced to three years confinement at hard labour in the Jail and Penitentiary House of the State of Tennessee. *Joseph Thompson was discharged on the 23 day of April 1835. Conduct exceptionable.* [Ledger 45, p. 198]

William Tinsley was received into the Penitentiary 6 July 1833. He is 5' 11 ½" in height and weighs 174 lbs. Dark blue eyes inclining to hazel, light hair and tolerably fair complexion. 26 years of age. Born in Fleming Co., Kentucky, and brought up there. His parents are dead. He has one sister living in Fleming. He has a scar from a cut on the ball of the thumb on his right hand, and one on the instep of the left foot caused by a bruise from a stone. Served an apprenticeship in Cincinnati, Ohio, to a cabinet maker. Was found guilty of petit larceny at the Circuit Court of Davidson County and sentenced to one years confinement in the Jail and Penitentiary House of the State of Tennessee. *William Tinsley was discharged Sept. 29th, 1834. He was detained 60 days for bad conduct.* [Ledger 45, pp. 198-9]

Tennessee Convicts: Records of the State Penitentiary

John Turner was received Aug. 19, 1834. A good looking boy about 15 years of age. Dark hair, dark eyes and complexion. Born and brought up in Cocke Co., Tenn., where his mother and a large family of illegitimate children live. Her name is Mary Turner, still resides on the land of Absolam Fox on the waters of Neeley Creek, a branch of Chucky River, and ten miles from the town of Centreville. He has a scar over the left eye and a scar across the knuckles where the fingers joins the hand, caused by a severe cut from a switch. His left thigh has been broken and he has several scars on each knee. Was found guilty of grand larceny at the Circuit Court of Jefferson County and sentenced to three years confinement in the Jail and Penitentiary House of the State of Tennessee. *Discharge 4th Sept. 1837.* [Ledger 45, p. 199]

Henry Townsend was rec'd in the Penitentiary 9 July 1835. He is 32 years of age, 5' 9" or 10" high and weighs 160 or 170 lbs. Black hair, heavy black beard, black eyes and tolerable handsome. A scar on the back of the right hand. Blacksmith. Born in Baldwin Co., Georgia, and brought up in Madison and Marion counties, Alabama. A wife and one child living with his mother, who resides in Fayette Co., Tenn., on Wolf River. He married Mary Davis, daughter of Moses Davis, who once lived in Fayette Co., Tenn., now dec'd. He was found guilty of "assault with intent to kill" at the Circuit Court of Tipton County and sentenced to three years confinement in the Jail and Penitentiary House of the State of Tennessee. [Ledger 45, p. 199]

James Tipper was rec'd in the Penitentiary 23 Aug. 1835. He is 21 years of age, 5' 9 or 10" high and weighs, generally, about 160 lbs. Hazle eyes, auburn hair, fair complexion. A scar on the inside of the middle finger of the left hand, between the second and third joint. A scar on the outside of the forefinger of the same hand, between the second and third joint. A tolerably large scar on the outside of the left leg, about 6" above the ankle. Several small scars on the cap of the right knee, and a scar about 2" in length 4" or 5" above the right knee. Born in White Co., Tenn., and brought up partly in Bedford and partly in Giles Co., Tenn. His father (Kinchy Tipper) now resides in Giles Co., Tenn., eight miles from Pulaski. One sister (Sarah) married to Wm. Johnson, who resides about a mile and a half from said Kinchy Tipper's. He married Dicy Ferrell, daughter of Wm. Ferrell, who resides near Kimbro's Mill on Agnews Creek, seven miles from Pulaski, Tenn. His wife is now living with her father. Labourer. He was found guilty of horse stealing at the Circuit Court of Giles County and sentenced to five years and six months confinement in the Jail and Penitentiary House of the State of Tennessee. *James Tipper died April 29th, 1839, in the morning, of chronic inflammation of the heart and dropsy of the p[e]ricardium.* [Ledger 45, p. 200]

Reuben Tims was rec'd in the Penitentiary 5 Oct. 1835. He is 4' 10 3/4" high, 25[?] years of age, weighs 116 lbs. Dark hair, hazl̲e eyes, thin visage, long nose and chin, thin beard and chiefly on his upper lip. A small scar begin[n]ing near the corner of the left eye and passing up to his forehead, occasioned by the bite of a horse. A little bowleg[g]ed. The great toe on each foot is much shorter than the one next it. About 6" above the ancle joint there is a scar on the ankle bone about the size of a "four pence." He is remarkably clear [of] scars. Born in Pendleton District, South Carolina, principally raised in Franklin County. His father lived within two miles of Winchester and oversees for a Mr. Wiggins. He afterwards removed nine miles from Winchester down Elk River to the "Rich Hill" neighborhood where he lived five years. From the[re] he removed to Madison Co., Tenn., within three miles of Jackson, where he lived five or six years. He (Reuben Tims) there married Nancy, daughter of John Matthews, and lived near Jackson one year and on Clover Creek, Madison County, near where his father now lives, two years. His mother has two brothers by the name of Golden whoe̲ live in the vicinity of Jackson, Tenn. He moved in January last to McCracken Co., Kentucky, lived in the "Loveless Settlement" where he has resided ever since resided [sic,] and where his wife and child were when he left them, but presumes that they will go to his father. He has two paternal aunts by the names of Russell and Tilley[?] who live in the same vicinity in which he resided in Kentucky. He is a laborer. Found guilty at the Circuit Court of Stewart County of horse stealing and sentenced to five years confinement in the Jail and Penitentiary House of the State of Tennessee. [Ledger 45, pp. 200-1]

Larkin Tims (brother of the above described) has lived pretty much the same life as his brother and generally in the same neighborhood, and whilst in Kentucky lived with his aunt Tilley[?] near Paducah (Kentucky). He is about 20 years of age, 5' 6" in height, weighs 135 lbs. Bl[ac]k hair, hazl̲e eyes, common complexion and a countenance not indicative of the confirmed rascal. He has two small scars on his right arm about 1 1/2" apart and about midway from the elbow to the shoulder. A small scar about 1 1/2" above the right knee cap. Boil marks about his left knee and remarkable for having but few scars. He was tried at the same time and place for the same offence, found guilty and received at the same time his brother (Reuben Tims) was. [Ledger 45, p. 201]

John Turner [was] convicted of "mule stealing" at the Circuit Court of Hardeman County and sentenced to three years confinement in the Jail and Penitentiary House of the State of Tennessee. Was received into the Penitentiary 10 Dec. 1835. He was born in Pendleton District, South Carolina, and raised to farming in Roane Co., Tenn., on Ten[nessee] River. He married Nancy, daughter of Matthew Hicks, in Hardin Co., Tenn. His wife and two male children are now residing with his father-in-law. His mother, four brothers (two married) and two sisters (both married, one to Nathan Morris and to Moses Overton) reside in Rhea Co., Tenn., near Col. Miles Vernon's. He has two sisters living in Morgan Co., Alabama, married each to Solomon and William Gay. He has several uncles (Turner) and cousins living in Pendleton District, South Carolina. He is 26 years of age, 5' 10" in h[e]ight and weighs one hundred and [blank] lbs. Dark hair, eyes and complexion, full red face and inclined to ballness [sic,]. Stout built and robust man. He has a black mark of nature of the middle finger left hand, on the side next his forefinger. Also a mulberry natural mark on his tongue. A scar on the end and one near his hand on the fore finger of the right hand, and a large scar on the instep of the left foot. He reads and writes a little [original underlined]. *Jno. Turner was discharged on the 26th day of Dec. 1838.* [Ledger 45, pp. 201-2]

Thomas Turner. From Rutherford Co., Tenn. Offence: petty larceny. Sentence: two years. Was received Oct. 28, 1836. He is 27 years old, 5' 5 1/2" high, weighs 133 lbs. Dark hair, blue eyes, sallow complexion, bad countenance, somewhat cross eyed. Has lost some front teeth above and below. A scar above the left knee across the thigh. The beard of the left side of his face white. His father lives in Richmond, Virginia, and one brother. *Thos. Turner was discharged Dec. 5th, 1838.* [Ledger 45, p. 202]

Richard Trimble. From Tipton Co., Tenn. Offence: grand larceny. Sentence: three years. Was received Nov. 1, 1836. He is 24 years old, 5' 8 1/2" high, weighs 155 lbs. Blue eyes, fair hair, sandy beard, fair skin clear of scars. Born and raised in Pittsburgh, Pennsylvania, where his parents now reside. He has lived in Cincinnati, Ohio, Louisville, Kentucky, St. Louis, Missouri and New Orleans. *Richard Trimble was discharged Jan. 15th, 1840. Conduct verry bad. Being detained two months and 16 days for bad conduct.* [Ledger 45, p. 202]

James Tooey. From Giles Co., Tenn. Offence: stabbing. Sentence: five years. He is 26 years old, 5' 5" high and weighs 150 lbs. Dark hair, dark blue eyes, fair skin. A scar on the right arm 1" long and about 4" from the wrist joint. A scar on the right shin 1" long and about the middle. Born in Ireland, has been in the U.S. six years, half of the time in Tennessee. Married Mary, daughter of Saml. Wilson, in Giles Co., Tenn., where he liv[e]d near Brownlaws Mill. Is fond of talking, speaks broken English. [Ledger 45, p. 202]

Tennessee Convicts: Records of the State Penitentiary

James Talton. From Roane County. Offence: grand larceny. Sentence: six years from 30 June 1837. He is 5' 7" high, weighs 160 lbs. Has served one sentence in this prison, this being the second time he has been sentenced for theft. Sentenced by the Circuit Court of Roane County to six years confinement in the Jail and Penitentiary House of the State of Tennessee. Was received July 9, 1837. M.W. J. [Ledger 45, p. 203]

John Thompson. Wayne County. Offence: larceny. Sentence: two years. Rec'd Nov. 12, 1837. He is 22 years of age, 6' high, weighs 192 lbs. Was born in Kentucky, brought up in Tennessee by Anderson Kilpatrick. Now living in Wayne County on the waters [of] Harrisons Creek, three miles from John Raines mill. He is a bright mulatto. Has a scar on his forehead caused he says by having a bonnet burnt on his head. Has a scar on his left cheak, 1 1/2" long. Also one on the under part of his left jaw 1" long. Has followed farming. Sentenced by the Circuit Court of Wayne County to two years in the Penitentiary of the State. *John Thompson discharged Dec. 2, 1839, having been detained 20 d[ay]s for misconduct.* [Ledger 45, p. 203]

H.W. Thomas. From Shelby County. Was received into the Penitentiary June 22, 1839. He is 47 years old, 5' 8" high. Weighs 169 lbs. Born in Shefforshire, England. Served an apprenticeship to the upholstering business in London. Has been in the United States eight years. Has worked in New York, Pittsburgh, New Orleans, Nashville, and etc. He has light gray hair, little inclined to be bald. Fair skin, blue eyes, a good countenance, quick spoken. The said Thomas was found guilty of g[rand] larceny by the Circuit Court of the county of Shelby, held at Raleigh, and sencence [sic,] to undergo confinement in the Jail and Penitentiary House of the State of Tennessee for three years from 22 June 1839. *H.W. Thomas died 31st 1839 [no month given] of peripuemony [sic].* [Ledger 45, p. 203]

Thomas Thompson. From Stewart County. Crime: horse stealing. Sentence: three years from 11 July 1840. Received 14 July 1840. He is 19 years old, 5' 3" high, weighs 132 lbs. Said Thompson was born in Roane Co., Tenn., brought up in McMinn County. He has been a fireman on board the Sd[?] Boat Toledo. He has black hair, gray eyes and fair skin. Has a scar forming a half circle on the fore finger of the left hand. His uncles live in Illinois, he thinks near Beardstown. [Ledger 45, p. 204]

Martin Thaxton. From Rutherford County. Crime: horse stealing. Sentence: three years and six months from 16 July 1840. Received 22 July 1840. He is 22 years old, 5' 9 1/2" high, weighs 128 lbs. Born and brought up in Warren

Co., Tenn., eight miles south of McMinnville near the stage road to Huntsville on the waters of Hickory Creek, where his brother John Thaxton now lives. His father is very old and lives on the same piece of land with his brother. He has one brother in Rhea Co., Missouri, by the name of Thos. Thaxton, and follows farming. One sister in Gibson Co., Tenn., married to a man by the name of Robt. Ellison. Two sisters in Warren County, one married to a man by the name of Elisha Runnels, the other to James Ellison. Said Thaxton has uncles in Kentucky by the name of Brooks, but knows not what county. Said Thaxton has dark hair, dark eyes and dark skin. A tailor by trade. Has a small scar on the wrist joint of the left hand, also a small scar on the joint of the thumb where it joins the hand. He served his apprenticeship with Thos. F. Hicks. [Ledger 45, p. 204]

Wm. Thompson. From Knox County. Crime: horse stealing. Sentence: three years from 3 Aug. 1840. Received 3 Aug. 1840. He is 18 years old, weighs 150 lbs., 5' 9" high. Born and brought up in Buncum [*sic*,, Buncombe] Co., North Carolina. Said Thompson has dark hair, greyish blue eyes, dark skin. He has the end cut of[f] the big toe of the right foot. Has a scar on the right hand just above where the thumb joins it. His father and mother live in Buncum Co., North Carolina, about 30 miles from the county town and five miles from Col. Hodge's mill. There is also a meeting house at Col. Hodge's. Has one uncle by the name of John McAfee living in Warren Co., Tenn., about eight or ten miles from McMinnville. [Ledger 45, p. 205]

Edward Tyler. From Knox County. Crime: forgery. Sentence: three years from 14 July 1840. Rec'd 3 Aug. 1840. He is 54 years old, weighs 132 lbs., 5' 6" high. Born and brought up in North Carolina, Montgomery County. He has dark gray hair, gray eyes, tolerable fair skin. Has had his throat cut, the scar extends from one neck vein to the other. Has one brother in Cherokee Co., Georgia. He has generally followed school teaching. [Ledger 45, p. 205]

Peter W. Tiner. From Montgomery County. Crime: grand larceny. Sentence: three years from 22 Sept. 1840. Rec'd 29 Sept. 1840. He is 27 years old, weighs 153 lbs., 5' 5" high, light complexion, light hair, blue eyes and full face. Has on his forehead a small round scar over his left eye. He was born and brought up in Montgomery County. Married his present wife in Dickson County, her maiden name is Mary Davidson. She has two children, both boys (Jno. and Thomas). She is living with her mother on Cumberland River 12 miles above Clarksville. He has also four sisters married and living in the same county. He has one brother living six miles above Clarksville on the river, his name is Thomas. [Ledger 45, p. 205]

Samuel H. Todd. From Shelby County. Crime: robbery. Sentence: five years from 25 Oct. 1840. Rec'd 25 Oct. 1840. He is 20 years old, born in Augusta Co., Virginia, and brought up in St. Clair Co., Illinois, about four miles from Bellville, where he has two brothers and one half brother. His half brother is names James Pettit. His other connections all live in the above named county except one cousin by the name of Clem Bostick, he lives in Monroe County some 10 miles from Waterloo. He has followed the river as deck hand on several boats. He has dark hair, black eyes and dark skin, weighs 131 lbs., 5' 5" high. [Ledger 45, p. 206]

Larkin Turman. From Giles County. Offence: pettit larceny. Sentence: one year from Oct. 30, 1840. Said Turman is 32 years old, 5' 10" high, weighs about 140 lbs. Born and bro't up in Georgia. Is troubled with fits. Has dark hair, fair skin, a down look. [Ledger 45, p. 206]

Reuben Thompson. From Hardeman County. Crime: larceny. Sentence: three years from 25 Jan. 1841. Rec'd 24 Jan. 1841. He is 26 years old, 5' 5" high, weighs 163 lbs. Born and brought up in Norfolk, Virginia. He has one brother. He has two uncles in Norfolk, one named Wm. Johnston, the other Henry Thompson who was a commission warehouseman. The former (W.J.) is a farmer. He has blue eyes, dark hair and sandy beard. Has had the small pox but few pocks or pits are visible. There is one in the centre of his forehead and one on the right cheek bone. [Ledger 45, p. 206]

Jesse S. Turner. From Fayette County. Crime: horse stealing. Sentence: three years from Oct. 5, 1841, when he was received. He is 19 years old, weighs 144 lbs., 5' 9" high. Has fair hair, blue eyes and fair skin. Was born and brought up in Lunaberg [sic,, Lunenburg] Co., Virginia, near the Brumsey[?] County line about six miles from Brumsey court house. He left Virginia and came to Tennessee with a man by the name of Deaderick Jackson of Fayette. He lived with him three months after which time he lived with a man by the name of Ferris. He has a scar on his left wrist say 3" long, caused by the cut of a knife. [Ledger 45, p. 207]

William A. Timmons. From Coffee County. Crime: rape. Sentence: 10 years from 4 July 1842. Rec'd 4 July 1842. He is 54 years old, 5' 9" high, weighs 161 lbs. Born and brought up in Delaware. His relations live in Ohio and Indiana, but he does not know where. He has grey hair, black eyes, fair skin. Has a wife and six children in the above named county. He has been a regular soldier under Capt. McDaniel, was at siege of Fort Erie under Genl. Brown. [Ledger 45, p. 207]

John Torrance. From Roane County. Crime: passing counterfeit money. Sentence: three years [and] nine months from 6 July 1842. Rec'd 11 July 1842. He is 24 years old, 6' 1 ½" high, weighs 159 lbs. Born in Spartenburg District and brought up in Union District, South Carolina. He has fair hair, pale blue eyes and sallow complexion, large nose. He has a small mole on the chin near the lip, also a mark he calls a strawberry on the back of the neck in the left leader of the neck. His father, W.H. Torrance, has five sons at home with him. He is a night watch in the city of Mobile, Alabama. Has one sister married to a confectioner and lives in Mobile. [Ledger 45, p. 207]

Ratchford Valentine was received in the Penitentiary 8 Sept. 1833. He is 5' 6 ½" in height and weighs 118 lbs. Dark hair hazel eyes, fair complexion, 34 years of age. Born in Naish [sic,, Nash] Co., North Carolina, and brought up there. His parents are dead. He has four brothers and one sister, she is living in North Carolina, married a man by the name of Ball. One of his brothers resides in Weakley Co., W[estern] D[istrict] of Tennessee, the others in North Carolina. He has a scar on the outer edge of each eyebrow, one scar on the ball of the left thumb, a scar on the little toe of the left foot where it joins the foot, and one in the centre of the shin of the right leg. Has worked at rough carpenters business a little. Was found guilty of murder in the second degree at the Circuit Court of Shelby County and sentenced to ten years confinement in the Jail and Penitentiary House of the State of Tennessee. [Ledger 45, p. 209]

Stephen Upton. From Overton County. Crime: manslaughter. Sentence: two years from 11 Mar. 1840. He is 56 years old, 5' 11" high, weighs 168 lbs. Born in Georgia near Augusta, brought up in Overton Co., Tenn. He has grey eyes, fair skin, good countenance. His hair is not very grey for a man of his age. Cooper[?] by trade. Has a wife and two children living seven miles south of Livingston on the head waters of Roaring River. [Ledger 45, p. 209]

John Venable. From Williamson County. Crime: larceny. Sentence: three years from 20 March 1841. Rec'd 23 March 1841. He is 16 years old, 6' high, weighs 149 lbs. Born and brought up [crossed out in original] in Marshall Co., Tenn., near where his father Richard Venable now lives in the settlement of Flat Creek meeting house. Has one sister married to John Shepherd who is overseer for a man by the name of Clinton, seven miles from Bolivar, Tenn. Also one living near Chappel Hill near Rigg's X [Cross] Roads. He has fair hair, blue eyes and fair skin. Has had his right hip injured by a fall from a horse. [Ledger 45, p. 210]

Andrew Vinson. From McMinn County. Crime: larceny. Sentence: two years from 13 Aug. 1841. Rec'd 27 Aug. 1841. He is 16 years old, 5' 6" or 7" high, weighs 142 lbs. Born in Jefferson Co., Alabama, on Cunningham's Creek five miles from David Hainbee's mill. His mother, sister and brothers[?] are now living at Alexr. Baker's on Rogers Creek. He has one uncle in Evington, Alabama, following the tailoring business. Said Vinson has fair hair, fair skin and blue eyes. [Ledger 45, p. 210]

Alexander Vines. From Davidson County. Crime: larceny. Sentence: three years from 15 Oct. 1841. Rec'd Oct. 20, 1841. He is 37 years old, 5' 10" high, weighs 140 lbs. Born and brought up in Hawkins Co., Tenn., on the north fork of Holston. Has two sisters, one by the name of Christopher, the other Elizabeth Young, both living near McGavock's Spring. Has a wife and five children where his sisters live. Said Vines has blue eyes, fair skin and dark hair. [Ledger 45, p. 210]

Hiram Hughs. From Clayburn [sic,, Claiborne] County. Offence: larceny. Rec'd Feb. 7, 1839. Sentence: three years. He is 33 years old, 6' high, weighs 160 lbs. Born and bro't up in Washington, Virginia, 10 miles east of Abbington [sic,] where his father, Nimrod Hughs, now lives. He has a wife and four children in Claiborne County near his sister's, who is married to a man by the name of Abram Andrews. He has sandy hair, fair skin, blue eyes, rough features. Has lost the fore finger of the left hand, the mid[d]le and third finger of the same hand being injured which causes them to be crooked. He is a blacksmith by trade. [Ledger 45, p. 211]

Miflin Hannum. From Robertson County. Convicted of horse stealing. Was received into the Penitentiary 14 May 1839. He is 5' 11" high, weighs 176 lbs and 47 years of age. Born and brought up in Chester Co., Pennsylvania. He has lived in Davidson and Robinson [sic,] counties, Tenn., also in Logan Co., Kentucky. He has a wife and nine children living in Robertson County six miles from Springfield in the direction of Galliton [sic,]. He has a daughter married to Wm. Woodard living within a half mile of his wife's house. The said M. Hannum has dark hair, grey eyes, fair skin, a scar on his left eyebrow caused he sais by the kick of a horse. The fore finger of his left hand has been broken and is still cru̱cked. He has been stab[b]ed in the back below the w̱right shoulder blade by Archibald Bigby of Robertson County. Sentence three years. W.C. Hart, clk, for Wm. McIntosh. [Ledger 45, p. 211]

Lawson Henry. From Knox County. Offence: grand larceny. Sentence: three years. Rec'd Nov. 4, 1839. He is 37 years old, 5' 9" high, weighs 135 lbs. He was born and bro't up in Lincoln Co., Tenn. His father, John Henry, lives in White Co., Tenn. Is married to a Miss Warner. His former wife is yet alive and lives in Lincoln, North Carolina. He has blue eyes, fair skin. He has had his right leg cut off four inches below the knee joint. He has no trade but has followed peddling for a living. [Ledger 45, p. 212]

Eli Hill. From Hamilton County. Offence: horse stealing. Sentence: three years from 1 Apr. 1840. Received 1 April 1840. He is 29 years old, weighs 162 lbs., is 5' 8" high. Born and brought up in Knox Co., Tenn. He was brought up by his grandfather Chambers Hill, two miles south [of] Knoxville. The above named Hill has a wife and three children living in Hamilton County at Ross's Landing on Tennessee River or the town of Chattanooga. He has dark hair, blue eyes, fair skin and what people generally call a good countenance. [Ledger 45, p. 212]

Wm. G. Harrison. From Davidson County. Crime: murder. Sentence: 15 years from 14 Oct. 1840. Received 14 Oct. 1840. He is 24 years old, 5' 9" high, weighs 140 lbs. Born and brought up in Nashville where his father, Wm. Harrison, now lives. Said Harrison has dark hair, blue eyes, fair skin. Has a cut 2 ½" long on the left shoulder blade, a scar on the heel part of the left hand. [Ledger 45, p. 212]

John Heathcock, alias Young. From Davidson County. Crime: maiming. Sentence: two years from 30 Dec. 1840. Rec'd 31 Dec. 1840. He is 26 years old, 5' 9" high, weighs 170 lbs. Born and brought up in Montgomery Co., Tenn., about four miles from New York, where his father, Young Heathcock, now lives. Said Heathcock has a wife and one child at the mouth of Yellow Creek in the above named county. He has black hair, black eyes, very dark skin. Has a large mole on the under jaw on the left side, also a small mole under the right eye. His wife was the widow of Allen Nowlin, the brother of Wm. Nowlin. [Ledger 45, p. 213]

Zachariah Herrol. Claiborne County. Crime: felony. Sentence: one year from 29 May 1841. Rec'd 29 May 1841. He is 40 years old, 5' 10 ½" high, weighs 177 lbs. Born and brought up in Anson Co., North Carolina. Has a wife and eight children living six miles west of Tazwell near the Island Forge. He has dark hair, blue eyes, dark skin, calls himself a farmer. *Died July 19th, 1841, of billious fever.* [Ledger 45, p. 213]

James Hayny. From Maury County. Crime: perjury. Sentence: three years from 3 Sept. 1841, when he was received. He is 27 years old, weighs 159 lbs., 5' 11" high. Born in Robinson [sic,, Robertson] County six miles north of Springfield. Has an half sister married to a man by the name of Elisha Willis and lives in the same settlement. He has a wife and two children living in Limestone Co., Alabama, about 18 miles from Athens and six miles from Gilbertsboro. He has dark hair, hazle eyes and dark skin. Has a small scar on each shin bone made with a broad axe. Has a scar above the right temple, and one in the edge of the hair. [Ledger 45, p. 213]

Peter W. Hendley. From Marshall County. Crime: negro stealing. Sentence: three years from 3 Oct. 1841. Rec'd 3 Oct. 1841. He is 50 years old, weighs 135 lbs., 5' 5" high. Born and brought up [original crossed out] in Wilk[e]s Co., Georgia, and brought up in Tennessee. He has two brothers and two sisters living on Duck River near the Fishing Ford. His sisters are married, one to James Meek, the other to Fitzallen Patterson, and live in the same settlement. He has been married, his wife is dead. He has a son by the name of William living with his brother Micajah Hendley. Said Hendley has grey hair and blue eyes, fair skin, is bald headed. [Ledger 45, p. 214]

Henry Harrell. From Shelby County. Crime: grand larceny. Sentence: five years from Feb. 20, 1842. Rec'd Feb. 20, 1842. He is 33 years old, weighs 162 lbs., 5' 6 ½" high. Born and brought up in the county of Derry, North of Ireland. He has a wife and three children in the city of N[ew] Orleans at the lower Faughbourg. He followed the River and has done some ditching. He has dark hair, blue eyes, fair skin. Has no relations in the United States. [Ledger 45, p. 214]

Herod Bruce. From Henderson County. Crime: bigamy. Sentence: six years from 8 April 1842 when he was received. He is 29 years old, 5' 6" high, weighs 126 lbs. Born in Bunkum [sic,, Buncombe] Co., North Carolina, brought up in Henderson Co., Tenn. His father, Elijah Bruce, lives in Conway Co., Arkansas, 12 miles n[orth] w[est] of Lewisburg. Has four brothers and three sisters married, one to Eliphazo Robinson and lives on the n[orth] fork of Forky [sic,] Deer River eight miles w[est] of Lexington, one half mile of Shady Grove meeting house. One married to Jesse Adams and lives near her father's. One married to J. Avent and lives in Jefferson City, Illinois, five miles w[est] of Mt. Vernon. Said Bruce has been married twice and has one child by his last wife, her name was Cordelia Burchett. He[r] brother Benj. Burchett lives in Independence Co., Arkansas, on White River 10 miles n[orth] e[ast] of

Batesville. (His wife lives with her father.) He has black hair, dark skin and yellowish blue eyes. His right eye has been injured by the bursting of a gun. Has a scar on his left shin bone say 1 ¼" long. [Ledger 45, p. 214]

Joseph Wilson was received in the Penitentiary May 5, 1831. He is 6' 1 ½" high, common weight 200 lbs., 32 years of age. Eyes black, dark skin and hair, heavy beard. Two small scars between the eye brows. A mole on the right side of his face. Born and brought up in Wilson Co., Tenn. Has a sister living in Davidson County and another in Wilson County, also a wife and three children residing near Lebanon. By profession a shoe maker. Was found guilty of murder in the second degree at the Circuit Court of Wilson County, and sentenced to 15 years imprisonment in the Jail or Penitentiary of the State of Tennessee. *Joseph L. Wilson was pardoned (so far as relates to the balance of the imprisonment only) by N. Cannon, Gov. Of Tenn., 10th June 1836.* [Ledger 45, p. 215]

James T. Wilson was received in the Penitentiary 27 Nov. 1831. He is 5' 9" high, weighs 155 lbs., blue eyes, fair skin, light hair, round face. Born in North Carolina, lived in Sumner Co., Tenn., eight years. His mother is dead. His father living in Franklin Co., Missouri. He has one brother older than himself. He has three sisters married, one to Mr. Wideman, one to a Mr. Freeman, and one to John Shannon, all living near his father's near Union Town, four miles from Missouri River. Both his legs sore with an itching humor. Lived on Mansker's Creek, Sumner County. He is 23 years of age. Was found guilty of perjury at the Circuit Court of Maury County and sentenced to three years, two months and 15 days confinement in the Jail and Penitentiary House of the State of Tennessee. *James T. Wilson died of chronic diarrhoea on the 16th November 1833.* [Ledger 45, p. 215]

Thomas Webb was received in the Penitentiary 5 Mar. 1832. He is 19 years old, weighs 143 lbs., is 5' 5 ¼" high, grey eyes, dark hair, fair skin and stout built. He has a small scar on the under part of the left arm, 1 5/8" long. One scar on the right side of the upper lip about ¾" long. Small scar on the third joint of the little finger of the right hand. Further he is clear of scars. He has worked some at the tailoring business. His countenance stern. Born and raised in Wake Co., North Carolina, untill a few years old. Raised after that in Caswell County, same state. His father and mother lives in Knox Co., Tenn., 12 miles from Knoxville, and five miles from Whortleberry Spring meeting house. He has four sisters and three brothers. Has three of his sisters married. His mother has a sister in Wake Co., North Carolina, named Sally Sauls. Was found guilty of grand larceny at the Circuit Court of Knox County and sentenced to three years confinement in the Jail and Penitentiary House of the State of Tennessee. *Thomas Webb was discharged by expiration of sentence 21st Sept. 1835. He was detained two hundred days for bad conduct. He has a wife and three children living in White County near Sparta with her father Berryman Jones. Returned convicted the second time 31 Dec. 1840, rec'd 11 Jan. 1841, came back under the name of John Webster. Crime: larceny. Sentence: one year.* [Ledger 45, p. 215]

John W. Williams was received into the Penitentiary 8 June 1832. He is 5' 8 1/2" in height, weighs 165 lbs. About 20 years of age. Born and brought up in the state of New Jersey near Germantown. Has lived for the last five or six years in the state of Ohio near Cincinnati, one mile on the canal to Dayton, where his mother and one sister now lives. His relations all live in the state of New Jersey, consisting of five uncles, three of the name of Williams and two of the name of Hilderbrence. He has [a] scar under the right jaw on the neck where the jaw joins the neck. He has dark hair and skin, blue eyes, large nose, tolerable good countenance. A small piece cut off of the thumb of the right hand. Has worked some at the carpenter's trade but generally followed farming. Found guilty of petit larceny at the Circuit Court of Davidson County and sentenced to one years confinement in the Jail and Penitentiary House of the State of Tennessee. *John W. Williams was discharged March 29, 1834. He was detained 293 days for bad conduct.* [Ledger 45, pp. 215-6]

Westly Warren was received in the Penitentiary 4 Sept. 1832. He is 18 years of age, 5' 5 1/2" in height and weighs 129 lbs. Light hair, blue eyes, round face, and has a tolerable good countenance. Born in Robertson County and brought up in Giles Co., Tenn., where his father and mother now reside within two miles of John Garner's mill. He has five brothers and eleven sisters. Four of his sisters are married, one to Thomas Cook, one to Lewis Woods, one to Isaac Kidwell and one to Jonathan McMinn. Cook and Woods reside in Laurence County and Kidwell in Giles Co., Tenn. He has a scar on the right hand near the little finger between that and the wrist joint. One on the fore finger of the left hand near the middle joint, it has some resemblance of the letter U. Another on the same hand between the little finger and the wrist joint. He has no trade, generally worked at farming. Was found guilty of petit larceny at the Circuit Court of Laurence County and sentenced to one years confinement in the Jail and Penitentiary House of the State of Tennessee. *Westly Warren was discharged 7th November 1833. He was detained 65 days for bad conduct.* [Ledger 45, p. 216]

Tennessee Convicts: Records of the State Penitentiary

Allen Webster was received in the Penitentiary 13 Oct. 1832. He is 6' 1 ¾" in height and weighs 196 lbs. Blue eyes, dark hair and complexion. Part of the left ear bit of[f]. About 25 years of age. Heavy brow. Was born in Union District, South Carolina. Has a wife and one child living in White Co., Tenn., about eight miles from Sparta and four from Simpson's Mill. His father and mother reside in the same neighbourhood. He has a scar about 1 ½" long over the left eyebrow and a small one on his forehead. Two toes cut off on the left foot next the small one. Was found guilty of stealing shoes at the Circuit of Jackson County and sentenced to one years confinement in the Jail and Penitentiary House of the State of Tennessee. *Allen Webster was discharged by expiration of sentence on the 13th October 1833. His conduct was good.* [Ledger 45, p. 216]

Richard Willis was received in the Penitentiary 26 Oct. 1832. He is 5' 7 ½" in height, weighs 147 lbs. Blue hollow eyes, dark hair and skin, prominent nose. Born in Grainger Co., East Tenn., where his wife and three children now reside about three miles from Clinch River and Hynes's Creek meeting house. His mother lives in the state of Missouri and two brothers in Morgan Co., Alabama, and two in Henderson County. He has a scar on the side of the left knee and several on the cap and shin. One on the right shin about the middle. Has generally followed farming. Was found guilty of stealing whiskey at the Circuit Court of Grainger County and sentenced to three years confinement in the Jail and Penitentiary House of the State of Tennessee. *Richard Willis died of cholera on 17th day of June 1833.* [Ledger 45, p. 217]

William Wilson was received in the Penitentiary 6 Dec. 1832. He is 5' 8" in height and weighs 170 lbs. Dark hair, black eyes, Roman nose and good countenance, 31 years of age. Born in Cumberland Co., North Carolina, where his father and mother now resides. He married a Miss Evans whose parents live in Blount Co., Tenn. He has a small scar on the arm near the wrist, one on the ball of the thumb on the right hand, one on the calf of the left leg caused by a bile, and a mole about ¾" from the left corner of the mouth. A saddler by trade. Was found guilty of voluntary manslaughter and sentenced to six years confinement in the Jail and Penitentiary House of the State of Tennessee at the Circuit Court of Monroe. *William Wilson was pardoned August the 9th, 1838, by Newton Cannon.* [Ledger 45, p. 217]

Davenport Wiseman was received into the Penitentiary 19 Feb. 1833. He is 5' 10 ¾" in height, weighs 155 lbs. Dark grey hair, blue eyes, fair complexion, 40 years of age. Born in Burke Co., North Carolina, near the Yellow Mountains. His wife and five children and mother live at his brother's, Martin

Wiseman, on Boyd's Creek within 10 miles of Athens in McMinn Co., Tenn. His wife's connexions are named Moore and all reside in McMinn Co., Tenn. He has two uncles, Bedford and Giles Wiseman, who reside in Burke Co., North Carolina, and two [other uncles], Robert and James Wiseman, residing in Maury Co., Tenn. He has a scar on the great toe and one between that and his instep of the right foot. A small scar on the shin and a large one on the calf of the left leg caused by a bile. Likewise a large piece bit out of his left ear, similar to a cross[?]. He has generally followed farming. Was found guilty of manslaughter at the Circuit Court of Blount County and sentenced to two years confinement in the Jail and Penitentiary House of the State of Tennessee. *Devenport Wiseman was discharged by expiration of sentence on the 20 day of March 1835. Detained 30 days for bad conduct.* [Ledger 45, pp. 217-8]

John B. Wright was received into the Penitentiary 21 March 1833. He is 6' 1" in height and weighs 172 lbs. Dark hair, grey eyes, long nose, rather dark complexion, 31 years of age. Born in Davidson Co., Tenn. Has a wife and three children living in the same county on Hamilton's Creek about 12 miles from Nashville. He has three brothers, two living in Davidson County and one in Hickman County on Duck River. Wright's wife's maiden name was Cato. Her connexions all reside in the same neighbourhood with his family. He has a scar on the back of the finger next the small finger of the left hand. A scar on the left side of the face running up and down the face very plain when closely examined. Has generally followed farming. Was found guilty of larceny, which sentence was confirmed by the Supreme Court of Davidson County at whose Circuit Court he was first found guilty, and sentenced to three years confinement in the Jail and Penitentiary House of the State of Tennessee. *John B. Wright died of a fit August 17, 1835. His conduct was good.* [Ledger 45, p. 218]

William Walton was received in the Penit'y 10 Nov. 1833. He is 5' 6 ½" in height and weighs 129 lbs. Yellowish eyes, dark hair, fair complexion, 21 years of age. Born in Halifax Co., Virginia, and brought up there. His parents reside in Maury Co., Tenn., within three miles of Bunch's Mill and eight miles of Columbia. He has five brothers and three sisters, all living with his parents. He has a scar between the two outside fingers of the right hand, a scar on the right knee caused by a fall, a scar under the calf of the left leg caused by a bite from a dog, and a large mole on the right side of his neck. He has generally followed farming. Was found guilty of forgery and sentenced to three years confinement in the Jail and Penitentiary House of the State of Tennessee (at the Circuit Court of Maury County.) *William Walton was discharged by the Court of Appeals on the 8th April 1834.* [Ledger 45, pp. 218-9]

Tennessee Convicts: Records of the State Penitentiary

Green White was received in the Penitentiary 17 Dec. 1833. He is 5' 10" in height and weighs 174 lbs. Dark hair, hazel eyes, full face and prominent nose, short forehead, rather dark complexion, 21 years of age. Born in Fayette Co., Kentucky, and brought up in Nashville, Tenn., where his parents now reside. He has an uncle (George White) living near Glasgow in Kentucky. Can give no information on his other connexions. He has two moles on the cheek, one about half way between the corner of the mouth and right eye, and one between (about half way) the corner of the mouth and right ear, and one on the right side of the chin. He has a remarkable place on the right ancle of the right foot where the bone has been broken by a blow from a pound weight. A small scar on the bridge of his nose, a small scar from a cut with a reap hook on the first joint of the little finger of the left hand, a scar on the fore finger of the same hand on the first joint, caused by a felon. He has generally followed boating. Was found guilty of stabbing at the Circuit Court of Davidson County and sentenced to five years confinement in the Jail and Penitentiary House of the State of Tennessee. *Green White died of cholera on the 5th day of July 1835.* [Ledger 45, p. 219]

James Wilson was rec'd in the Penitentiary 7 Nov. 1834. He is 50 years of age, 5' 9" or 10" high, and weighs 135 lbs. Blue eyes, light hair, fair complexion, sharp nose, high forehead. Has a scar on the middle joint of the middle finger of the [blank] hand, and the middle joint of the ring finger of the same hand is enlarged from being knocked out of place. A remarkable scar just above the pit of his stomach, caused by a rising, and a small scar on the muscle of the left arm, caused by a stab from a knife. He has chiefly followed wagon making, but is also a very good blacksmith. He was born in Orange Co., North Carolina. Has lived in Giles and Lincoln counties, Tennessee, for the last 20 years. Has a brother (Hiram Wilson) living near Spring Hill, Murry [sic,, Maury] County and a sister married to James Inscore living near the same place, and another sister married to a man by the name of Brooks (a carpenter) [who?] lives in Florence, Alabama. Has a wife and eleven children living at Richland Furnace near Tennessee River. He was found guilty of forgery at the Circuit Court of Murry County and sentenced to three years confinement in the Jail and Penitentiary House of the State of Tennessee. *James Wilson died of cholera on the 30th day of June 1835.* [Ledger 45, pp. 219-20]

Andrew Wilson was rec'd in the Penitentiary 11 Dec. 1834. He is 34 years of age, 5' 9" or 10" high, and weighs 168 lbs. Grey eyes, dark hair, sharp nose and fair complexion. His left ear very much disfigured by nearly one half of it being bit or cut off. A scar above the left eye (about 1" in length) lying in the edge of the hair, and a large scar on the outside of the left leg caused by a bite from a dog. Has chiefly followed farming. Born and brought up in Pendleton District, South Carolina. Parents dead. Married Sarah Stansill, daughter of John Stansill, who lives in Haversham Co., Georgia. His wife and six children live in Marion or Jefferson Co., Illinois. He has also three daughters, Matilda, Betsy Ann and Amelia, married to John Foster, Wilson Williams and Lewis Orick, residing in said counties in the same neighbourhood. He was found guilty of horse stealing at the Circuit Court of Bedford County and sentenced to five years and six months confinement in the Jail and Penitentiary House of the State of Tennessee. *Andrew Wilson died 22nd Aug. 1836.* [Ledger 45, p. 220]

Thomas M. Watson, convicted of horse stealing at the Circuit Court of Gibson County and sentenced to three years confinement in the Jail and Penitentiary House of the State of Tennessee, was received in the Penitentiary 7 Nov. 1835. He is 24 years of age, 5' 9 3/4" high, and weighs one hundred and [blank] pounds. Born in Burke Co., North Carolina, and raised to farming in Williamson Co., Tenn., near Hardeman's X [Cross] Roads. He married (in Gibson Co., Tenn.) a Miss Keziah Sellers, daughter of Isaac Sellers on Forked Deer River, with whom his wife is now living. A labourer. His father, mother, two brothers (married men), four sisters (two married to two Moseleys) reside in the same neighborhood within six miles of Trenton. Black hair, black beard, black eyes and eye brows, and dark skin. He has a scar about half way between his left eye and fore top. A well formed and well proportioned man. A small scar on his left hand over the fore finger. He can read and write. [Ledger 45, p. 220] [Note this entry is repeated almost verbatim on page 221, not transcribed.]

Peter Walker. Convicted of voluntary manslaughter at the December term of the Circuit Court of Shelby Co., Tenn., and sentenced to two years imprisonment from 4 Jan. 1836 (the time he was received). He is 5' 10 3/4" high, large frame, not fleshy, weighs 172. Hazle eyes, large nose. End of the little finger of the left hand crooked from a bite. A scar on the left cheek a little below the corner of the eye, caused by a blow. He says he has a wife and children living near Memphis, Tenn., and further states he was born in South Carolina. *Peter Walker was discharged Jan. 4th, 1838, having served two years and discharged his duty to the satisfaction of the officers of the prison.* [Ledger 45, p. 221]

Jeremiah Walton. Convicted of petit larceny at the Rutherford County Circuit Court, April term, and sentenced to one year. Was received 18 Apr. 1836. He is 5' 7 3/4" high, 18 years old. Dark hair, eyes and skin. Smooth face and but little beard. Says he was born in Hallifax Co., Virginia. His parents now live in Carroll Co., Western District, Tenn. Has an older brother [and] a sister married to Jonathan Mosely, a farmer in Maury Co., Tenn. *Jeremiah Walton was discharged June 23rd, 1837. Detained two months [and] five days for breach of prison rules.* [Ledger 45, p. 221]

Jesse Warren was convicted o horse stealing [at] a special term of the Circuit Court held for Rutherford County in April 1836, and sentenced to four years imprisonment in the Penitentiary from the time of delivery. He was received 18 Apr. 1836. He is 5' 6 1/4" high, heavy built, inclined to be fleshy. Blue eyes, light hair and eyebrows, fair skin. Two scars above the left eye brow, a verry large scar on the cap of the left knee (cut with a foot adze), a scar on the back of the neck 1 3/4" long running up into the hair, a scar near 3" the navle [sic,]. Broad full face and large mouth and good teeth. Says he was born in Henry Co., Virginia. Is 26 years old and has been 19 years in Tennessee. His parents live in Rutherford Co., Tenn., on Kimbro's land in sight of Rowlacks. Has three brothers married and living in Williamson Co., Tenn. [crossed out in original], four single, and three sisters single. Has an uncle living near Nolandsville, W[illia]mson Co., Tenn. [Ledger 45, p. 222]

Peter Wheeler. From McMinn County. Was received 13 May 1836. He is 25 years old, is 5' 10" high, weighs 160 lbs. Fair skin, hazle eyes, light hair. Born in Blount Co., Tenn., where his father, Wm. Wheeler, now lives. When spoken to has rather a confused down look and slow to answer. Found guilty of horse stealing and sentenced to three years imprisonment in the Jail and Penitentiary of Tennessee from 3 May 1836. *Peter Wheeler was discharged by order of the Governor March 8th, 1839.* [Ledger 45, p. 222]

William Wheeler. From Maury Co., Tenn., was received 17 May 1836. He is 20 years old, 5' 8" high, weighs 165 lbs. Fair skin, light hair and blue eyes, coarse full features and thin beard. His wife and children live seven miles from Columbia in s[ai]d county, Tennessee. Found guilty of petty [sic,] larceny and sentenced to one year imprisonment in the Jail and Penit[entiar]y of Tennessee. *Wm. Wheeler discharged June 2, 1837. Conduct good generally. Detained 16 days for breach of rules.* [Ledger 45, p. 222]

John Williams (man of colour). From Davidson County. Was received 24 May 1836. He is about 28 years old, 5' 8 1/4" high bare foot [underlined in original], weighs 145 lbs. Light copper colour, black eyes, hair and eyelashes and beard. Born and raised in Cumberland Co., North Carolina. The last seven years he has lived in Brownsville, Haywood Co., Tenn., and 12 months in Nashville.

Has a scar from the right ear 3" long and irregular, down under the jaw bone. A scar on the side of the left thumb 2" long, and one on the back of the left wrist. Found guilty of stealing six ducks and sentenced to one year imprisonment in the Penitentiary. *John Williams discharged June 2, 1837. Conduct generally good. Detained nine days for breach of prison rules.* [Ledger 45, p. 223]

James Wright. From Knox Co., Tenn. Was received 1 July 1836. He is 27 years old, 5' 8 ½" high, weighs 155 lbs. Born in Chatham Co., North Carolina, and raised in Knox Co., Tenn. Dark skin and hair, black eyes, short chin, heavy prominent eye brows. A scar on each chin caused by a bite of man, a scar from a burn in front of the left shoulder, a scar on the nose by a bite. The right ankle joint enlarged on the outside. Found guilty of stabbing a negro and sentenced to two years imprisonment in the Tennessee Penitentiary, commencing 20 June 1836. [Ledger 45, p. 223]

Jesse Webb. From Shelby County. Offence: petty [sic,] larceny. Sentence: one year. Was received Jan. 17, 1837. He is 28 years old, 5' 8" high, and weighs 165 lbs. Has grey eyes, full face, has a bloated appearance. A scar on the left side 5" below the arm pit 4 ½" long (cut of a [k]nife). Was born and raised in Giles Co., Tenn., where his father now lives near Zion meeting house, one mile from Buchanan's Mill. *Jesse Webb discharged January 21st, 1838, having served one year and four days. An inoffensive worthless man in or out of a Penitentiary.* [Ledger 45, p. 223]

Isom Watson. Offence: horse stealing. Sentence: five years from [date] rec'd, May 19, 1837. He is 26 years old, 5' 9" high, weighs 165 lbs. Dark hair, yellowish blue eyes, fair skin. Has a wife and one child living with her father, William Thomas, in Sangamond Co., Illinois, on the road leading from Springfield to Galena, six miles from the former. He was born and brought up in Albemarle Co., Virginia, eight miles from Charlott[e]sville on the road leading to Richmond. His father is dead, his mother now lives in Maury Co., Tenn., eight miles south of Columbia. Has one sister married to a man by the name of William Brooks, living in Shelby County, Kentucky. A carpenter by profession. He has a scar over the left eye about half way between the eyebrow and hair. A small scar on the upper lip between the nose and mouth. Sentenced by the Cuircuit Court of Maury County to five years confinement in the Jail and Penitentiary House of the State of Tennessee. [Ledger 45, p. 224]

Saml. Whitesides. From Shelby County. Offence: corn stealing. Sentence: two years. Rec'd 19 Sept. 1837. He is 39 years old, 5' 8" high, weighs 165 lbs.

Dark hair, blue eyes, fair skin. Born and bro't up in Mec[k]lenburg Co., North Carolina. His father Saml. Whitesides lives in Perry Co., Tenn. He has a wife and three children living five miles north east of Rawleigh with her father, Sam'l Berryhill. He has followed shoemaking. Sentenced by the Cuircuit Court of Shelby County to two years confinement in the Jail and Penitentiary House of the State of Tennessee. Samuel Whitesides died May 31st, 1839, of inflamation of the bowels. [Ledger 45, p. 224]

John W. White. From Maury County. He is 24 years old, 5' 8" high, weighs 163 lbs. Dark hair, black eyes, fair skin, large nose. Born in Italy and lived their until he was 14 years old. His father then came to New Orleans where he has been keeping [a] coffee-house. He sayes he has followed the seas as a sailor for five years. Was found guilty of grand larceny at the Cuircuit Court of Maury County and sentence[d] to five years confinement in the Jail and Penitentiary House of the State of Tennessee. [signed] W. McIntosh. [Ledger 45, p. 224]

Joseph Ward. From Lawrence County. Offence: rape. Sentence: 10 years. Rec'd July 17, 1838. He is 18 years old, 5' 8" high, weighs 147 lbs. He has dark hair, fair skin, hazel eyes. Has a scar running up his fore head caused by the cut of an ax. It commences in his eyebrow and runs about 1 ¼". He has lost the bone to the nuckel [sic,] joint of the finger next the little finger of the right hand. It shows where the nail came off. He has a scar running lengthways of his big toe on the right foot. Also a scar on his left knee below the cap occasioned by a fall. He was born in Macklingburg [sic,, Mecklenburg] Co., Georgia. Bro't up in Lawrence Co., Tenn. His mother, Mary Ward, lives in Harden County, 14 miles from Savannah on the waters of Horse Creek. She has six children, three boys and three girls, with her. She is farming. He has two uncles, Leonard and Fredrick Hartwick, living about 12 miles from Lawrenceburg on the waters of Big Buffalo, one of which has a grist mill on Saw Creek. His father run off with his niece some six or seven years ago and he does not know where he is. Her name was Salena Hartwick. Has followed farming and boating. [Ledger 45, p. 225]

Joshua Jones Wilson. From Marrion County. Offence: murder. Sentence: 10 years from 19 July 1838. Rec'd July 24, 1838. He is 68 years old, weighs 140 lbs., 5' 5" high. Born in Culpepper Co., Virginia. Bro't up in Macon Co., North Carolina. He has a wife and two children in Marrion Co., Tenn., seven miles from Jasper on the waters of Battle Creek. He has two brothers in Macon Co., North Carolina. He has grey hair, grey eyes, fair skin. He has a scar across the upper part of the right side of his forehead 2 ½" long. A black smith and gun smith by profession. Sentenced by the Cuircuit Court of Marrion County to ten years confinement in the Jail and Penitentiary House of the State of Tennessee. *Joshua J. Wilson died June 1st, 1839, of general dropsy.* [Ledger 45, p. 225]

Josiah Winters. From Monroe County. He is 19 years old, 5' 9" high, weighs 165 lbs. Dark hair, greyish blue eyes. Has a small scar on the little finger of the right hand. Also a scar on the fore finger of the same hand. Two scars, one on the fore finger and one on the middle finger of the left hand. Born and brought up in Bl[o]unt Co., Tenn., where his mother, Charity Winter now lives. He has three brothers and four sisters, all in Blunt County. Two sisters married, one to Middleton Lain and the other to Jno. Macaslin. He was found guilty of horse stealing at the Sircuit Court of Monroe County and sentenced to three years confinement in the Jail and Penitentiary House of the State of Tennessee, from 21 Sept. 1838. [Ledger 45, p. 226]

Saml. Wyatt. From Davidson County. Offence: grand larceny. Rec'd Feb. 9, 1839. Sentence: three years. He is 28 years old, 5' 9" high, weighs 137 lbs. He has dark hair, hazle eyes and dark skin. Born and bro't up in North Carolina, Martin County, near the Roanoak River. He has six sisters and one half brother in Martin County, North Carolina. He has been overseeing for Thomas Watts in Louisiana, five miles below Vicksburg, for three years, he says. [Ledger 45, p. 226]

John Wilson. From Blount County. Offence: petit larceny. Sentence: one year. Rec'd Feb. 12, 1839. He is 24 years old, 5' 10" high, weighs 140 lbs. Born in Virginia, bro't up in Bl[o]unt Co., Tenn., nine miles east of Merrysville where his mother, Rebecca Wilson, now lives on the waters of Little River. He has dark hair, blue eyes and heavy beard and dark skin. *Discharged 12th Feb. 1840. Conduct good.* [Ledger 45, p. 226]

Washa, alias Pigeon. From Hamilton County. Offence: larceny. Sentence: three years from [date] received, Dec. 5, 1839. He is 23 years old, 5' 8" high, weighs 160 lbs. Born in North Carolina, bro't up in the Cherokee Nation. He has a large Roman nose. He has a scar on the left side of his nose. He has black hair, black eyes. [Ledger 45, p. 226]

Alexander Webb. From Bradley County. Offence: murder. Sentence: 14 years from 7 May 1840. Received 7 May 1840. He is 30 years old, 5' 8" in height, weighs 137 lbs. Born in Warren Co., Tenn., and brought up in Philip [sic,, Phillips] Co., Arkansas, eight miles below Helena, where John Barris now lives who married his aunt. She was formerly married to a man by the name of Sylvanus Philips and lived on the same farm. He has two brothers in Bradley County one mile west of Cleveland, one brother in Marshall County seven miles west of the county town, two brothers in Warren County near the road leading from Sparta to McMinnville. He has dark grey hair, black eyes, dark skin, large nose, heavy beard. He has a large scar on the shin bone of the left leg of dark appearance, two small scars on the shin of the right leg caused by the cut of an axe. His wife and three children live with his brother 13 miles from McMinnville. [Ledger 45, p. 227]

Louis L. Williams. From Montgomery County. [note: page torn, words missing shown as "..."] Offence: malicious shooting. Sentence: three years from 15 May 1840. Received 2 June 1840. He is 23 years old, 5' 6 ½" high, weighs 137 lbs. Born and brought up in Luninburg Co., Virginia, 18 miles west of Luninburg Court House on the waters of Stoney Creek ... Antioch meeting house where his mother Nancy W... now lives. He has a brother in law by the name of ... living with his mother. He has one uncle by the ... John Allen in Montgomery Co., Tenn., one in O... by the name of Wm. Allen, also one aunt by ... Sarah Poindexter in Montgomery Co., Te... followed store keeping in the capacity of sa... Williams has fair hair, fair skin, greyi... countenance, has had the little finger o... [Ledger 45, p. 227]

Isham Walker. From Bedford County. Crime: forgery. Sentence: three years from 15 Aug. 1840. Rec'd 15 Aug. 1840. He is 18 years old, 5' 9" high, weighs 137 lbs. Born and brought up in Bedford Co., Tenn. His father, Robt. Walker, lives in Maury Co., Tenn., at W. Hasley[?] mill on Duck River in the town of Columbia. Said Isham Walker has fair skin, hazle eyes. Has a dark mole directly under the left eye. Has several moles on his neck and face. He has a very large turn of the hair or what is termed by old women a cow lick. [Ledger 45, p. 228]

Thomas Wilson. From Fayette County. [note: page torn, words missing shown as "..."] Crime: grand larceny. Sentence: three years from Oct. 9, 1840. Received Oct. 9, 1840. He is 16 years old, 5' 3 ½" high, weighs 120 lbs. Born and brought up in Wilson County, 11 miles on this side of Lebanon on the stage road. He has one uncle in Wilson County by the name of Richard Perry, living on Cedar Creek near the Cedar lick. His father, James Wilson, is now living in Henderson County seven miles from the town of Lexington near the road leading to Jackson, within one mile of the middle fork ... has three brothers and two sisters, one of h ... man by the name of John Sey ... from Holly

Springs in ... lson has dark hair ... uncles Buck, John ... and Miles Joiner ... [a]ll living in Hen ... [Ledger 45, p. 228]

Samuel Wilson. From Shelby County. Crime: larceny. Sentence: three years from Oct. 23, [18]41, when he was received. He is 47 years old, weighs 161 lbs., 5' 8" high, born in the city of Washington, D.C. Brought up in Baltimore. Had a wife and one child. His wife is dead and his son follows the sea. His business has been selling groceries. Has followed the sea. Has dark hair, hazle eyes and dark skin. Has a scar on the right cheek bone. His wife was the daughter of John Freeberger who lives in Baltimore. Her name is set with Indian Ink on his left arm -- Susan Freeberger was her maiden name. [Ledger 45, p. 229]

Dillard Williams. From Sevier County. Crime: malicious stabbing. Sentence: two years from Dec. 22, 1841. Rec'd Dec. 22, 1841. He is 20 years old, 5' 8" high, weighs 154 lbs. Born in North Carolina, brought up in Cocke C[ount]y on Cansbey's [Cousbey's?] Creek abut six miles from its mouth. Has two sisters married, one to Jesse Kenkins, the other to Wm. McMahan. Also one brother married to the daughter of Elijah Kenkins. All of them are living in Cocke County on the above named creek. His wife was the daughter of Mary Bryant, she is with her mother on Cansby's[?] Creek in Cocke County. She has one child and he thinks will have another. He has fair hair, blue eyes and fair skin. [Ledger 45, p. 229]

[note: page torn, words missing shown as "..."] J... From Shelby County. ... larceny. ... rs from 26 Feb. 1842. ... 160 lbs, 5' 8 $^{1}/_{2}$" in high ... New York where his relations ... he is a sailor and ... first shipped on ... cabin boy ... tters JW ... [Ledger 45, p. 229]

Edward Wyatt. From Wilson County. Crime: larceny. Sentence: one year from June 4, 1842. Rec'd June 6, 1842. He is 37 years old, 5' 2" high, weighs 150 lbs. Born in East Tennessee and brought up in Smith County. Has had a wife and two children but they are all dead. He has worked at the carpenter's trade. Has dark hair, blue eyes and dark skin. [Ledger 45, p. 230]

Richard Wiggins. From Robertson County. [note: page torn, words missing shown as "..."] Crime: larceny. Sentence: one year from 15 June 1842. Rec'd 16 June 1842. He does not know how old he is, says his father never ... him. He is 5' 10" high, weighs 160 lbs. Born ... up in Lancaster District, North

Carolina. Has fair hair ... sallow complexion. Has worked at turning ... bottom chairs. [Ledger 45, p. 230]

[note: page torn, words missing shown as "..."] ...am Walters. From Washington County. ... grand larceny. ... years from 4 Nov. 1842. ... [ye]ars old, 5' 11 1/2" high, weighs 154 lbs. ... and bro't up in Washington Co., Tenn. His ... about three miles on the road to E. Emery's factory ... thers in Missouri but does not know what county ... wes and John Morgan. Has two sisters ... [W]ashington County, one to John Andis ... Walters has dark hair, black eyes, dark, s... ade and currier. [Ledger 45, p. 230]

Peyton T. Phillips. From Jackson County. Crime: murder. Sentenced for life, commuted from hanging. Received Dec. 30, 1845. Is 34 years old, 5' 9 3/4" high, weighs 163 lbs. Born in Smith Co., Tenn., brought up in Jackson Co., Tenn., about 15 miles from Gain[e]sboro near the Cumberland River. His mother's name is Margarett Phillips, his wife lives on the farm of W. Woodfolk in Jackson County. His children are with his relations in Jackson County. Has one uncle by the name of James Phillips living in Smith County on the waters of Peytons Creek. Said Phillips has dark hair, fair skin, blue eyes. Has had his collar bone broken. Has one uncle by the name of Wm. Leuisman, in Mississippi, but does not know where. Has one brother-in-law in Denmark, Madison County, 12 miles from Jackson, on one of the Brownsville roads. Has one brother in Smith County near where his uncle Phillip lives. Is a farmer. *Pardoned by Governor Andrew Johnson, November 3rd, 1857.* [Ledger 87, p. 1]

John Moon. From Montgomery County. Sentenced for life. Crime: murder. Received Nov. 20, 1847. He is 48 years of age, 5' 7 1/2" high, weighs 150 lbs. Was born and brought up in Limerick County, Ireland. Said Moon has one brother in Illinois, does not know his whereabouts. He has fair skin, fair hair, blue eyes. Has a long bark scar on his left shin bone caused by the kick of a horse, also a scar on his chin. Moon is a currier or tanner. *Pardoned by Gov. I.G. Harris, August 23rd, 1858.* [Ledger 87, p. 1]

William McCoy. From Maury County. Crime: rape. Sentence: 15 years. Rec'd Jan. 19, 1848. He is 46 years old, 5' 5", weighs 155 lbs. Was born at sea and brought up in Randolph Co., North Carolina, and has resided in Maury County for the last eight or ten years, and has resided principally with an uncle, Esq. H. Simmons, four miles north of Columbia. He has three sisters in Randolph Co., North Carolina, one of whom married a Mr. Leonard. Said McCoy has dark hair, fair skin, blue eyes. Has had the little finger of the right hand broken, which makes it crooked. *Died of pneumonia Feb. 22, 1860.* [Ledger 87, p. 1]

Marion C. Clark. From Madison County. Crime: murder. Sentence: lifetime. Received May 9, 1848. He is 28 years old, 5' 9" high, and weighs 157 lbs. Was born and brought up in Madison Co., Alabama. He has four sisters and three brothers. Two of his brothers are living in Hardeman Co., Tenn., 18 miles from Bolivar on or near the old State Line road. Three of his sisters are married and are living in the same settlement. One of them married John Smolley, another Wesley Wa... [page torn], the other J.W. Green. Said Clark has been married to the daughter of Smith C. B... [page torn] they have parted. Has one cousin named Simeon Clark somewhere in Madison County, Al... [page torn]. Said Clark has dark hair, hazle eyes and fair skin. Has a scar in the edge of the hair ov[er] the right eye. Has had his collar bone broken. *Pardoned by Governor Andrew Johnson, October 9th, 1857, and discharged October 15th, 1857.* [Ledger 87, page 1]

James Mitchell. From Shelby County. Crime: robbery. Sentence: 15 years. Received Nov. 30, 1848. He is 23 years of age, 5' 9" high, weighs 167 lbs. Was born in Illinois about 26 miles from Edwardsville. Has one sister living in St. Louis, married to a man by the name of James Quirk. Said Mitchell has dark hair, fair skin and hazel eyes. Has a small scar on the right knee, one on the shin of the left leg. Has six scars on his head. *Sent to Insane Asylum.* [Ledger 87, p. 2]

William Davis, alias L.H. Tharp. From Shelby County. Crime: robbery. Sentence: 15 years. Rec'd Nov. 30, 1848. He is 33 years old, 5' 11" high, weighs 143 lbs. Was born in the state of Ohio, 12 miles from Cincin[n]atti. His brother is a carpenter and his sister married a man by the name of William Boggs, a tanner by trade. Said Davis alias Thorp has black hair and eyes and dark skin. Has a female form on his right arm and a male tatt[o]oed on his left, with the letters **S.C.** some 6" above it. The name W. Davis tatto[o]ed with Indian ink just above the left knee. *Gen'l pardon by Gov. I.G. Harris, Oct. 8th, 1861.* [Ledger 87, page 2]

Martin Moore. From Carter County. Crime: murder. Sentence: life time. Received Dec. 26, 1848. He is 38 years of age, weighs 147 lbs., 5' 7 1/4" high, born in North Carolina and raised in East Tennessee. Said Moore has a wife and two children living in Washington County five miles east [of] Jones Boro [*sic,*] on the waters of Cherokee. Said Moore has a small scar in the forehead just above the right eye brow near the nose. Has black gray hair and straight.

By color he is a mulatto boy about half breed and has black eyes. *Died of consumption March 4th, 1859.* [Ledger 87, p. 2]

Carroll King. From Davidson County. Crime: murder. Sentence: lifetime. Rec'd May 3, 1849. He is 19 years old, 5' 7" high, weighs 199 lbs. Was born in Western District, Tenn., and raised in the city of Nashville, where his mother now lives on College Street opposite Miss Sarah King. King has two brothers and one sister all living in Nashville. His eldest brother is a carpenter by trade. He has three uncles living in Knoxville, Tenn. Sally King of Nashville is his aunt. Said King has light hair, fair skin and blue eyes. Has a small scar on the brow of his head in a triangular shape and sunk as if it was fast to the skin. Also a scar near the corner of the head about 1" long. He says they were mad[e] by a fall out of an apple tree. *Pardoned by Gov. Isham Harris, Feb. 8th, 1859.* [Ledger 87, p. 2]

Irvin Hines. From Madison County. Sentence: life time. Rec'd May 12, 1849. Crime: murder. He is 25 years old, 6' 1/4" high, weighs 184 lbs. Born in Gra[i]nger County and bro't up in Hardeman County, West Tenn. Has dark hair, blue eyes. Has one scar in the centre fore head just below the hair, and one in the right side of his fore head. The middle finger of his left hand has had a rising which makes it shorter than the others. Has a mole on his chin, the right side. Say[s] he has had his arm broken just below the shoulder, but is not stiff or crooked from the injury. His father lives in Hardeman County. Has three brothers and one sister, who married a man by the name of Joseph Shepperd, all his [sic] live near his father. *Pardoned by Gov. Isham Harris, Nov. 25, 1858.* [Ledger 87, p. 3]

William A. Estis. From Giles County. Crime: murder. Senten[ce]: lifetime. Received Aug. 20, 1849. He is 26 years of age, 5' 4" high, weighs 115 lbs. Was born and bro't up in Giles Co., Tenn. Has a wife and three children living in said county 5 1/2 miles from Pulaski on the Shelbyville road near where his father T.P[?] Estis now resides. Has one uncle living near Nashville on the N.C. Railroad by the name of Jno. Estis. Has a sister married to a man by the name of Elijah Bell and resides somewhere in Texas. Also one married to a man [named] Wiley Chapman who lives near his father's in Giles County. Said Estis married Miss Eliza Burdan[?]. Said Estis has black hair, fair skin and blue eyes. *Gen'l pardon by Gov. I. G. Harris, Nov. 3, 1859.* [Ledger 87, p. 3]

Anthony Davis. From Knox County. Crime: murder. Sentence: 15 years from 3 Oct. 1849. Rec'd Oct. 26, 1849. He is 30 years old, 5' 4 1/2" high, weigh[s]

145 lbs. Was born in Stafford Shire, England, and bro't up in Pillsbury, England. Has a wife without children living in Troy, New York. Has two sisters and three brothers living in Pittsburg[h], Pennsylvania. Two of his brothers are working at [a] saw mill iron work. The other brother at house painting. His father resides in the suburbs of Pittsburg on the Brownsville road. Said Davis has dark hair, fair skin and blue eyes. Has a scar on the right wrist. Has been raised to work in iron. Is a hammerer and puddler. *Gen'l pardon May 19th, 1861, by Gov. I.G. Harris.* [Ledger 87, p. 3]

John J. Elzey. From Marshall County. Crime: murder. Sentence: 10 years from Dec. 6, 1849. He is 35 years old, 5' 10" high, weighs 145 lbs. Was born and bro't up in Marshal[l] Co., Tenn., near Joel Ewels horse mill. Said Elzey has a wife and seven children living [in] said county. Has one brother and two sisters, one of whom married S.B. Ritters, the other to George H. Craig, all of whom live in the same neighborhood. Said Elzey has dark hair, hazel eyes and dark skin. He is a blacks[mith] by trade. *Disch'gd act of 1836, Apl. 22nd, [18]59.* [Ledger 87, p. 3]

Jefferson Cash. From Davidson County. Crime: grand larceny. Sentence: 11 years. Rec'd Dec. 26, 1849. He is 24 years of age, 5' 11", weighs 155 lbs. Born in Amherst Co., Virginia, brought up in Coffee Co., Tenn. His father William Cash lives in Coffee Co., Tenn., about four [miles from] Pelham and six from Hillsboro on the Jasper and Murfreesboro road. Said Cash has light hair, fair skin and blue eyes. Has lost a part of both thumbs, one from a fellon, the other from the bite of a horse. Has one uncle in Amherst, Virginia, about eight miles from Glasgow near the mountains. The balance of his connexions are in Coffee Co., Tenn. *Pardoned under the act of 1836, April 20th, 1860.* [Ledger 87, p. 4]

Thomas Ellison. From Claiborne County. Crime: murder. Sentence: 10 years. Received Jan. 31, 1850. He is 51 years old, 5' 8" high, weighs 160 lbs. Was born and bro't up in Mason Co., Kentucky, near Mays Lick. Has a wife and 10 children living northwest of Tazewell near Cumberland Gap about eight miles distant. One of his father's sisters married a man by the name of Alex Lewis and lives on the road leading from Cinthiana [sic,] to Paris, Kentucky. Has an uncle living somewhere in Ten[nessee] by the name of Joseph Ellison but does not know where. Said T. Ellison has black hair, black eyes and fair skin. He is a blacksmith by trade. *Pardoned under the act of 1836, June 16th, 1859.* [Ledger 87, p. 4]

Henry Duke, man of color. From Hamilton County. Crime: murder. Sentence: lifetime. Received Apr. 8, 1850. He is 22 years old, 5' 8 ½" high, weighs 162 lbs. Was born in Woodford Co., Kentucky, and brought up in Tuscaloosa, Alabama. Has a wife but no children. She resides in Hamilton County with her brother Saml Carmon about six miles from Harrison on Wolf Clear[?] creek, four miles above Alex McDaniel's mill. He has one brother, a tavern keeper in Tuscaloosa. Also an uncle in Columbia, Georgia, tavern keeping. One brother in Columbus, Mississippi, who has followed stage driving. Said Duke has black hair, hazle eyes and dark skin. Has a scar over his left eye caused by a fall from a horse whilst riding a race. Said scar runs from his brow to the edge of his hair. *Died November 16, 1857, from wounds received in consequence of a rock falling upon him.* [Ledger 87, p. 4]

Samuel Coffman. From Henderson County. Sentence: 10 years. Rec. Aug. 9, [1850]. Crime: murder. He is 24 years old, 5' 6 ½". Was born in Alabama and raised in Hardeman Co., Tenn. His mother, together with six brothers and three sisters, reside in said county about 10 miles north of Lexington. One of his sisters married a man by the name of Wm. Cook. Has a wife living with her father Jackey Stokes in same neighborhood. He has had his right thigh broken making it somewhat shorter than the left one. Has a scar on the ball of the left thumb. Said Coffman has light hair, fair skin and blue eyes. *Pardoned under act of '36, Feb. 14th, 1860.* [Ledger 87, p. 4]

CONVICT REGISTER 1831 - 1850
Tennessee State Penitentiary

Name: George Washington Cook, age 21, born in Kentucky, occupation: tailor. Convicted of stabbing by a court in Madison County, and sentenced to 2 years in the Penitentiary. Received Jan. 21, 1831 and discharged Jan. 21, 1833. Notes: conduct very good. Number in ledger 86: 1.

Name: John Dougan, age 45, born in North Carolina, occupation: cooper. Convicted of manslaughter by a court in Franklin County, and sentenced to 10 years in the Penitentiary. Received Jan. 27, 1831 and discharged June 14, 1833. Notes: died of cholera. Number in ledger 86: 2.

Name: W.H. Crawford, age 21, born in Mississippi, occupation: bricklayer. Convicted of grand larceny by a court in Rhea County, and sentenced to 3 years in the Penitentiary. Received Apr. 6, 1831 and discharged July 4, 1834. Notes: conduct bad. Number in ledger 86: 3.

Name: Beasley Barbee, age 20, born in North Carolina, occupation: tailor. Convicted of shooting by a court in Giles County, and sentenced to 4 years and 8 months in the Penitentiary. Received Apr. 9, 1831 and discharged June 17, 1833. Notes: died of cholera. Number in ledger 86: 4.

Name: Alexander Spears, age 24, born in North Carolina, occupation: laborer. Convicted of horse stealing by a court in Henderson County, and sentenced to 6 years in the Penitentiary. Received Apr. 18, 1831 and discharged Apr. 18, 1837. Notes: conduct good. Number in ledger 86: 5.

Name: David May, age 21, born in Tennessee, occupation: shoemaker. Convicted of petit larceny by a court in Robinson[sic,Robertson] County, and sentenced to 1 year in the Penitentiary. Received Apr. 19, 1831 and discharged Apr. 19, 1832. Notes: conduct very good. Number in ledger 86: 6.

Name: Joseph L. Wilson, age 32, born in Tennessee, occupation: shoemaker. Convicted of murder 2nd degree by a court in Wilson County, and sentenced to 15 years in the Penitentiary. Received May 5, 1831 and discharged June 10, 1836. Notes: pardoned by Gov. Cannon. Number in ledger 86: 7.

Name: Miles Allen, age 45, born in North Carolina, occupation: laborer.

Convicted of larceny by a court in Wilson County, and sentenced to 2 years and 6 months in the Penitentiary. Received May 5, 1831 and discharged June 17, 1833. Notes: died of cholera. Number in ledger 86: 8.

Name: James Counce [Conner?], age 28, born in Virginia, occupation: hatter. Convicted of petit larceny by a court in Murry[sic,Maury] County, and sentenced to 2 years in the Penitentiary. Received May 11, 1831 and discharged May 11, 1833. Notes: conduct generly good. Number in ledger 86: 9.

Name: Jackson Pennel, age 27, born in Maryland, occupation: laborer. Convicted of horse stealing by a court in Davidson County, and sentenced to 8 years in the Penitentiary. Received June 16, 1831 and discharged Jan. 22, 1839. Notes: pardoned by Gov. Cannon. [Published 1839 report shows surname as Penuel.] Number in ledger 86: 10.

Name: John Armstrong, age 35, born in Georgia, occupation: blacksmith. Convicted of horse stealing by a court in Franklin County, and sentenced to 6 years in the Penitentiary. Received July 19, 1831 and discharged July 19, 1837. Notes: conduct generally good. Number in ledger 86: 11.

Name: William Lefevre, age 28, born in South Carolina, occupation: blacksmith. Convicted of fo[r]gery by a court in Franklin County, and sentenced to 3 years in the Penitentiary. Received July 19, 1831 and discharged Nov. 1, 1834. Notes: conduct exceptionable. Number in ledger 86: 12.

Name: James Gibbins, age 18, born in Tennessee, occupation: laborer. Convicted of passing counterfeit coin by a court in Jefferson County, and sentenced to 3 years in the Penitentiary. Received Aug. 1, 1831 and discharged Aug. 25, 1834. Notes: conduct generly good. Number in ledger 86: 13.

Name: George W.R. Rogers, age 32, born in Virginia, occupation: shoemaker. Convicted of horse stealing by a court in Giles County, and sentenced to 5 years and 6 months in the Penitentiary. Received Aug. 27, 1831 and discharged June 11, 1833. Notes: died of cholera. Number in ledger 86: 14.

Name: John Gill, age 42, born in South Carolina, occupation: blacksmith. Convicted of assault with intent to kill by a court in Giles County, and sentenced to 3 years in the Penitentiary. Received Aug. 27, 1831 and discharged Mar. 30, 1833. Notes: pardoned, conduct verry good. Number in ledger 86: 15.

Tennessee Convicts: Records of the State Penitentiary

Name: Abraham Conley, age 21, born in North Carolina, occupation: laborer. Convicted of stealing bacon by a court in Knox County, and sentenced to 1 year in the Penitentiary. Received Aug. 29, 1831 and discharged Aug. 29, 1832. Notes: conduct good. Number in ledger 86: 16.

Name: Silas Conley, age 25, born in North Carolina, occupation: laborer. Convicted of stealing bacon by a court in Knox County, and sentenced to 1 year in the Penitentiary. Received Aug. 29, 1831 and discharged Sept. 23, 1832. Notes: conduct exceptionable. Number in ledger 86: 17.

Name: John Marsh, age 31, born in North Carolina, occupation: laborer. Convicted of petit larceny by a court in White County, and sentenced to 1 year in the Penitentiary. Received Sept. 4, 1831 and discharged Dec. 23, 1832. Notes: conduct bad. Number in ledger 86: 18.

Name: Hugh Moore, age 58, born in South Carolina, occupation: laborer. Convicted of fo[r]gery by a court in Davidson County, and sentenced to 5 years in the Penitentiary. Received Sept. 16, 1831 and discharged June 15, 1833. Notes: died of cholera. Number in ledger 86: 19.

Name: William Sexton, age 25, born in North Carolina, occupation: laborer. Convicted of horse stealing by a court in Roane County, and sentenced to 3 years in the Penitentiary. Received Sept. 29, 1831 and discharged Oct. 18, 1834. Notes: conduct verry good. Number in ledger 86: 20.

Name: William Baldwin, age 24, born in Kentucky, occupation: laborer. Convicted of horse stealing by a court in Overton County, and sentenced to 4 years in the Penitentiary. Received Sept. 30, 1831 and discharged June 10, 1833. Notes: died of cholera. Number in ledger 86: 21.

Name: David Cole, age 38, born in Tennessee, occupation: laborer. Convicted of horse stealing by a court in Lincoln County, and sentenced to 5 years in the Penitentiary. Received Oct. 3, 1831 and discharged July 6, 1835. Notes: died of cholera. Number in ledger 86: 22.

Name: Thomas Haines, age 41, born in Virginia, occupation: laborer. Convicted of petit larceny by a court in Rhea County, and sentenced to 1 year in the Penitentiary. Received Oct. 6, 1831 and discharged Oct. 6, 1832. Notes: conduct good. Number in ledger 86: 23.

Name: Edwin Clark, age 37, born in New Jersey, occupation: hatter. Convicted

Tennessee Convicts: Records of the State Penitentiary

of petit larceny by a court in Robinson [sic] County, and sentenced to 2 years in the Penitentiary. Received Oct. 16, 1831 and discharged Jan. 5, 1834. Notes: conduct exceptionable. Number in ledger 86: 24.

Name: Elisha Cole, age 42, born in Tennessee, occupation: labourer. Convicted of stealing promisory note by a court in Wilson County, and sentenced to 3 years in the Penitentiary. Received Oct. 31, 1831 and discharged Nov. 1, 1834. Notes: conduct bad. Number in ledger 86: 25.

Name: James Wilson, age 23, born in North Carolina, occupation: labourer. Convicted of perjury by a court in Maury County, and sentenced to 3 years and 2 and one-half months in the Penitentiary. Received Nov. 27, 1831 and discharged Nov. 16, 1833. Notes: died of cholera. Number in ledger 86: 26.

Name: Riley Chappell, age 34, born in North Carolina, occupation: labourer. Convicted of stabbing by a court in Maury County, and sentenced to 2 years in the Penitentiary. Received Nov. 27, 1831 and discharged Nov. 27, 1833. Notes: conduct good. Number in ledger 86: 27.

Name: John Batchelor, age 40, born in North Carolina, occupation: labourer. Convicted of perjury by a court in Maury County, and sentenced to 6 years in the Penitentiary. Received Nov. 27, 1831 and discharged Nov. 29, 1837. Notes: conduct good. Number in ledger 86: 28.

Name: Thomas Ferrell, age 35, born in Ireland, occupation: hatter. Convicted of stabbing by a court in Maury County, and sentenced to 2 years in the Penitentiary. Received Nov. 27, 1831 and discharged Nov. 27, 1833. Notes: conduct good. Number in ledger 86: 29.

Name: William B. McCracken, age 23, born in Connecticut, occupation: labourer. Convicted of fo[r]gery by a court in Maury County, and sentenced to 3 years in the Penitentiary. Received Nov. 27, 1831 and discharged June 14, 1833. Notes: died of cholera. Number in ledger 86: 30.

Name: William Swofford, age 30, born in North Carolina, occupation: labourer. Convicted of concealing stolen horses by a court in Monroe County, and sentenced to 3 years in the Penitentiary. Received Dec. 1, 1831 and discharged Jan. 1, 1835. Notes: conduct exceptionable. Number in ledger 86: 31.

Name: Thomas Jackson, age 18, born in Tennessee, occupation: barber. Convicted of petit larceny by a court in Davidson County, and sentenced to 3

Tennessee Convicts: Records of the State Penitentiary

years in the Penitentiary. Received Dec. 6, 1831 and discharged June 9, 1833. Notes: died of cholera. Number in ledger 86: 32.

Name: David Claxton, age 30, born in Tennessee, occupation: waggon maker. Convicted of passing counterfeit money by a court in Bedford County, and sentenced to 3 years in the Penitentiary. Received Dec. 12, 1831 and discharged Jan. 15, 1835. Notes: conduct exceptionable. Number in ledger 86: 33.

Name: John Finley, age 41, born in North Carolina, occupation: labourer. Convicted of petit larceny by a court in Bedford County, and sentenced to 1 year in the Penitentiary. Received Dec. 12, 1831 and discharged Feb. 24, 1833. Notes: conduct bad. Number in ledger 86: 34.

Name: Thompson Jones, age 55, born in Virginia, occupation: labourer. Convicted of horse stealing by a court in David[son] County, and sentenced to 3 years and 8 months in the Penitentiary. Received Dec. 24, 1831 and discharged June 15, 1833. Notes: died of cholera. Number in ledger 86: 35.

Name: John W. Hill, age 27, born in Ohio, occupation: cabinet maker. Convicted of Release prisoner from jail by a court in Fayett[e] County, and sentenced to 5 years in the Penitentiary. Received Dec. 28, 1831 and discharged Dec. 28, 1836. Notes: conduct good. Number in ledger 86: 36.

Name: Baxter A. Powell, age 20, born in Tennessee, occupation: labourer. Convicted of burglary by a court in Robertson County, and sentenced to 15 years in the Penitentiary. Received Jan. 18, 1832 and discharged Oct. 1, 1841. Notes: died of marasmus. Number in ledger 86: 37.

Name: Charles Broughton, age 27, born in New York, occupation: shoe maker. Convicted of petit larceny by a court in Franklin County, and sentenced to 2 years in the Penitentiary. Received Jan. 23, 1832 and discharged Mar. 30, 1834. Notes: conduct exceptionable. Number in ledger 86: 38.

Name: Andrew Stephens, age 18, born in Tennessee, occupation: labourer. Convicted of grand larceny by a court in Blount County, and sentenced to 3 years in the Penitentiary. Received Feb. 13, 1832 and discharged Oct. 21, 1841. Notes: exceptionable. Number in ledger 86: 39. [Published 1837 report shows his discharge as 1835.]

Name: Francis Smith, age 22, born in Tennessee, occupation: labourer. Convicted of grand larceny by a court in Williamson County, and sentenced to

Tennessee Convicts: Records of the State Penitentiary

3 years in the Penitentiary. Received Feb. 29, 1832 and discharged Feb. 28, 1835. Notes: generally good. Number in ledger 86: 40.

Name: Thomas Webb, age 19, born in North Carolina, occupation: labourer. Convicted of grand larceny by a court in Knox County, and sentenced to 3 years in the Penitentiary. Received Mar. 5, 1832 and discharged Sept. 21, 1835. Notes: bad. Number in ledger 86: 41.

Name: John B. Coleman, age 22, born in Virginia, occupation: labourer. Convicted of horse stealiing by a court in Warren County, and sentenced to 3 years in the Penitentiary. Received Mar. 15, 1832 and discharged Mar. 16, 1832. Notes: pardoned. Number in ledger 86: 42.

Name: James R. Tarleton, age 31, born in North Carolina, occupation: labourer. Convicted of grand larceny by a court in Green[e] County, and sentenced to 3 years in the Penitentiary. Received Mar. 18, 1832 and discharged Jun 29, 1835. Notes: generally good. Number in ledger 86: 43.

Name: James Barker, age 17, born in Tennessee, occupation: labourer. Convicted of grand larceny by a court in Roane County, and sentenced to 3 years in the Penitentiary. Received Mar. 18, 1832 and discharged June 9, 1835. Notes: generally good. Number in ledger 86: 44.

Name: Thomas Sherrod, age 23, born in Tennessee, occupation: labourer. Convicted of passing counterfeit money by a court in Sullivan County, and sentenced to 3 years in the Penitentiary. Received Apr. 12, 1832 and discharged July 31, 1835. Notes: conduct exceptionable. Number in ledger 86: 45.

Name: Garland G. Lucas, age 42, born in Virginia, occupation: labourer. Convicted of grand larceny by a court in Sullivan County, and sentenced to 3 years in the Penitentiary. Received Apr. 12, 1832 and discharged June 11, 1833. Notes: died of cholera. Number in ledger 86: 46.

Name: Joseph Thompson, age 25, born in Kentucky, occupation: labourer. Convicted of petit larceny by a court in Robertson County, and sentenced to 3 years in the Penitentiary. Received Apr. 16, 1832 and discharged Apr. 23, 1835. Notes: conduct exceptionable. Number in ledger 86: 47.

Name: John B. Howard, age 31, born in Georgia, occupation: labourer. Convicted of grand larceny by a court in Robertson County, and sentenced to 4 years in the Penitentiary. Received Apr. 16, 1832 and discharged July 7, 1836.

Notes: conduct exceptionable. Number in ledger 86: 48.

Name: James R. Dickerson, age 26, born in Virginia, occupation: labourer. Convicted of petit larceny by a court in Smith County, and sentenced to 1 year in the Penitentiary. Received Apr. 17, 1832 and discharged Apr. 21, 1833. Notes: generally good. Number in ledger 86: 49.

Name: John Delk, age 40, born in Tennessee, occupation: labourer. Convicted of hog stealing by a court in Campbell County, and sentenced to 1 year in the Penitentiary. Received May 4, 1832 and discharged June 20, 1833. Notes: died of cholera. Number in ledger 86: 50.

Name: Robert Yancy, age 27, born in Virginia, occupation: labourer. Convicted of stabbing by a court in Maury County, and sentenced to 2 years in the Penitentiary. Received May 6, 1832 and discharged May 6, 1834. Notes: conduct good. Number in ledger 86: 51.

Name: Henry P. Morgan, age 17, born in South Carolina, occupation: labourer. Convicted of fo[r]gery by a court in McMinn County, and sentenced to 3 years in the Penitentiary. Received May 18, 1832 and discharged June 10, 1835. Notes: conduct good. Number in ledger 86: 52.

Name: Joel Blackwell, age 31, born in South Carolina, occupation: labourer. Convicted of conceilling [sic] stolen horses by a court in Monroe County, and sentenced to 3 years in the Penitentiary. Received June 6, 1832 and discharged July 30, 1835. Notes: conduct good. Number in ledger 86: 53.

Name: Jacob Bradley, age 45, born in Virginia, occupation: waggon maker. Convicted of petit larceny by a court in Davidson County, and sentenced to 2 years and 6 months in the Penitentiary. Received June 8, 1832 and discharged Jan. 12, 1835. Notes: conduct exceptionable. Number in ledger 86: 54.

Name: John W. Williams, age 20, born in New Jersey, occupation: labourer. Convicted of petit larceny by a court in Davidson County, and sentenced to 1 year in the Penitentiary. Received June 8, 1832 and discharged Mar. 29, 1834. Notes: conduct exceptionable. Number in ledger 86: 55.

Name: Daniel Fulward, age 21, born in North Carolina, occupation: labourer. Convicted of petit larceny by a court in Davidson County, and sentenced to 2 years in the Penitentiary. Received June 11, 1832 and discharged June 11, 1834. Notes: conduct good. Number in ledger 86: 56.

Tennessee Convicts: Records of the State Penitentiary

Name: Samuel Keer, age 54, born in Tennessee, occupation: labourer. Convicted of having and concealing c[ounterf by a court in Davidson County, and sentenced to 5 years in the Penitentiary. Received June 13, 1832 and discharged June 18, 1833. Notes: died of cholera. Number in ledger 86: 57.

Name: Eli Adams, age 21, born in Tennessee, occupation: labourer. Convicted of conceiling [sic] stolen horses by a court in Monroe County, and sentenced to 3 years in the Penitentiary. Received July 21, 1832 and discharged Sept. 13, 1835. Notes: conduct generally good. Number in ledger 86: 58.

Name: George Hamden, age 37, born in Virginia, occupation: labourer. Convicted of altering cotton receipts by a court in Franklin County, and sentenced to 3 years in the Penitentiary. Received July 23, 1832 and discharged July 22, 1835. Notes: conduct generally good. Number in ledger 86: 59.

Name: Willis Clement, age 30, born in Georgia, occupation: labourer. Convicted of pas[s]ing counterfeit money by a court in Giles County, and sentenced to 3 years in the Penitentiary. Received Aug. 24, 1832 and discharged Oct. 26, 1833. Notes: died of chronic diar[r]hea. Number in ledger 86: 60.

Name: Westley Warren, age 18, born in Tennessee, occupation: labourer. Convicted of petit larceny by a court in Lawrence County, and sentenced to 1 year in the Penitentiary. Received Sept. 4, 1832 and discharged Nov. 7, 1833. Notes: conduct exceptionable. Number in ledger 86: 61.

Name: Cornelias Bertram, age 24, born in Virginia, occupation: labourer. Convicted of horse stealing by a court in Rhea County, and sentenced to 3 years in the Penitentiary. Received Oct. 3, 1832 and discharged Nov. 17, 1835. Notes: conduct exceptionable. Number in ledger 86: 62. [Published 1837 report spells his name Butram.]

Name: Allen Webster, age 25, born in South Carolina, occupation: labourer. Convicted of petit larceny by a court in Jackson County, and sentenced to 1 year in the Penitentiary. Received Oct. 13, 1832 and discharged Oct. 13, 1833. Notes: conduct generally good. Number in ledger 86: 63.

Name: Henry Horn [or Hone?], age 17, born in Georgia, occupation: labourer. Convicted of petit larceny by a court in Smith County, and sentenced to 3 years in the Penitentiary. Received Oct. 22, 1832 and discharged Feb. 24, 1836. Notes: conduct exceptionable. Number in ledger 86: 64.

Name: Josiah Landers, age 21, born in Tennessee, occupation: labourer. Convicted of burglary by a court in Carroll County, and sentenced to 3 years in the Penitentiary. Received Oct. 23, 1832 and discharged Oct. 16, 1833. Notes: died of chronic diarrhea. Number in ledger 86: 65.

Name: Richard Willis, age 33, born in Tennessee, occupation: labourer. Convicted of burglary by a court in Grainger County, and sentenced to 3 years in the Penitentiary. Received Oct. 26, 1832 and discharged June 17, 1833. Notes: died of cholera. Number in ledger 86: 66.

Name: Gibson Cate, age 32, born in Tennessee, occupation: labourer. Convicted of assault with intent to kill by a court in McMinn County, and sentenced to 9 years in the Penitentiary. Received Nov. 11, 1832 and discharged June 17, 1833. Notes: died of cholera. Number in ledger 86: 67.

Name: William Standifer, age 18, born in Virginia, occupation: labourer. Convicted of petit larceny by a court in McMinn County, and sentenced to 3 years in the Penitentiary. Received Nov. 11, 1832 and discharged Nov. 21, 1835. Notes: [conduct] good. Number in ledger 86: 68.

Name: John J? Green, age 22, born in Virginia, occupation: labourer. Convicted of petit larceny by a court in McMinn County, and sentenced to 2 years in the Penitentiary. Received Nov. 11, 1832 and discharged Jan. 1, 1835. Notes: conduct bad. Number in ledger 86: 69.

Name: Peter Mitchell, age 21, born in South Carolina, occupation: labourer. Convicted of burglary by a court in Harden [sic] County, and sentenced to 5 years in the Penitentiary. Received Nov. 23, 1832 and discharged Jan. 20, 1838. Notes: colored; conduct exceptionable. Number in ledger 86: 70.

Name: Henry Lazenbury, age 22, born in North Carolina, occupation: labourer. Convicted of maiming by a court in Harden [sic] County, and sentenced to 2 years in the Penitentiary. Received Nov. 23, 1832 and discharged Jan. 12, 1835. Notes: conduct exceptionable. Number in ledger 86: 71.

Name: James Campbell, age 22, born in Pennsylvania, occupation: labourer. Convicted of petit larceny by a court in Davidson County, and sentenced to 1 year and 6 months in the Penitentiary. Received Dec. 5, 1832 and discharged Aug. 28, 1834. Notes: conduct exceptionable. Number in ledger 86: 72.

Name: John Morrison, age 54, born in North Carolina, occupation: labourer.

Tennessee Convicts: Records of the State Penitentiary

Convicted of voléntory [sic] manslaughter by a court in Monroe County, and sentenced to 2 years in the Penitentiary. Received Dec. 6, 1832 and discharged June 14, 1833. Notes: died of cholera. Number in ledger 86: 73.

Name: William Wilson, age 31, born in North Carolina, occupation: sad[d]ler. Convicted of volentory [sic] manslaughter by a court in Monroe County, and sentenced to 6 years in the Penitentiary. Received Dec. 6, 1832 and discharged Aug. 9, 1838. Notes: pardoned; conduct good. Number in ledger 86: 74.

Name: Abram Powell, age 27, born in North Carolina, occupation: labourer. Convicted of petit larceny by a court in Henry County, and sentenced to 2 years in the Penitentiary. Received Dec. 15, 1832 and discharged June 16, 1833. Notes: died of cholera. Number in ledger 86: 75.

Name: Robert Hare, age 21, born in Kentucky, occupation: labourer. Convicted of horse stealing by a court in Bedford County, and sentenced to 3 years and 6 months in the Penitentiary. Received Dec. 17, 1832 and discharged June 18, 1836. Notes: conduct verry bad. Number in ledger 86: 76.

Name: Oliver Griffith, age 33, born in Maryland, occupation: gen'l mechanic. Convicted of grand larceny by a court in Shelby County, and sentenced to 4 years and 6 months in the Penitentiary. Received Dec. 31, 1832 and discharged Dec. 4, 1837. Notes: conduct verry exceptionable. Number in ledger 86: 77.

Name: Ambrose A. Norris, age 25, born in Kentucky, occupation: cabinet maker. Convicted of petit larceny by a court in Shelby County, and sentenced to 2 years and 6 months in the Penitentiary. Received Dec. 31, 1832 and discharged Apr. 21, 1836. Notes: conduct verry bad. Number in ledger 86: 78.

Name: Redding R. Hall, age 38, born in South Carolina, occupation: labourer. Convicted of passing count'r bank bills by a court in Tipton County, and sentenced to 3 years in the Penitentiary. Received Jan. 8, 1833 and discharged June 14, 1833. Notes: died of cholera. Number in ledger 86: 79.

Name: Davenport Wiseman, age 40, born in North Carolina, occupation: labourer. Convicted of manslaughter by a court in Blount County, and sentenced to 2 years in the Penitentiary. Received Feb. 19, 1833 and discharged Mar. 20, 1835. Notes: conduct exceptionable. Number in ledger 86: 80.

Name: Wilson Coats, age 37, born in Tennessee, occupation: wheelright [sic]. Convicted of murder pun[?] commuted by a court in Woodford County

[Kentucky?], and sentenced to 21 year in the Penitentiary. Received Feb. 23, 1833 and discharged July 17, 1833. Notes: died of chronic diarrhea. Number in ledger 86: 81.

Name: Isaac Lawrence, age 27, born in North Carolina, occupation: labourer. Convicted of larceny by a court in McNairy County, and sentenced to 3 years in the Penitentiary. Received Feb. 23, 1833 and discharged Mar. 24, 1836. Notes: conduct exceptionable. Number in ledger 86: 82.

Name: William Cassells, age 27, born in Tennessee, occupation: labourer. Convicted of horse stealing by a court in Madison County, and sentenced to 3 years in the Penitentiary. Received Feb. 23, 1833 and discharged Feb. 16, 1836. Notes: conduct verry good. Number in ledger 86: 83.

Name: Isham Conner, age 41, born in South Carolina, occupation: labourer. Convicted of stab[b]ing by a court in Gibson County, and sentenced to 2 years in the Penitentiary. Received Feb. 23, 1833 and discharged Mar. 27, 1835. Notes: conduct exceptionable. Number in ledger 86: 84.

Name: Robt. C. Brogan, age 27, born in Kentucky, occupation: hatter. Convicted of fo[r]gery by a court in Knox County, and sentenced to 3 years in the Penitentiary. Received Mar. 7, 1833 and discharged May 16, 1836. Notes: conduct exceptionable. Number in ledger 86: 85.

Name: Hazard Kesterson, age 52, born in Virginia, occupation: labourer. Convicted of petit larceny by a court in Anderson County, and sentenced to 1 year in the Penitentiary. Received Mar. 8, 1833 and discharged June 16, 1833. Notes: died of cholera. Number in ledger 86: 86.

Name: Peter Seals, age 37, born in Virginia, occupation: labourer. Convicted of ass[ault] & battery w/intent to by a court in Dickson County, and sentenced to 10 years and 8 months in the Penitentiary. Received Mar. 10, 1833 and discharged May 4, 1843. Notes: pardoned by Gov. Jones. Number in ledger 86: 87.

Name: John B. Wright, age 31, born in Tennessee, occupation: labourer. Convicted of larceny by a court in Davidson County, and sentenced to 3 years in the Penitentiary. Received Mar. 21, 1833 and discharged Aug. 17, 1835. Notes: died of a fit. Number in ledger 86: 88.

Name: William Hamilton, age 29, born in Georgia, occupation: cab[inet?] maker. Convicted of passing count[erfeit] money by a court in Rutherford

Tennessee Convicts: Records of the State Penitentiary

County, and sentenced to 3 years in the Penitentiary. Received Apr. 10, 1833 and discharged Sept. 6, 1836. Notes: conduct exceptionable. Number in ledger 86: 89.

Name: John Yates, age 34, born in North Carolina, occupation: waggon maker. Convicted of Ass[ault] w/intent to murder by a court in Marion County, and sentenced to 3 years in the Penitentiary. Received Apr. 18, 1833 and discharged June 10, 1833. Notes: died of cholera. Number in ledger 86: 90.

Name: George W. Morris, age 35, born in South Carolina, occupation: labourer. Convicted of fo[r]gery by a court in Henderson County, and sentenced to 3 years in the Penitentiary. Received Apr. 19, 1833 and discharged Apr. 19, 1836. Notes: conduct good. Number in ledger 86: 91.

Name: John N. Chapman, age 21, born in South Carolina, occupation: labourer. Convicted of petit larceny by a court in McMinn County, and sentenced to 1 year in the Penitentiary. Received May 5, 1833 and discharged May 15, 1834. Notes: conduct generally good. Number in ledger 86: 92.

Name: Bennett A. James, age 35, born in Tennessee, occupation: bl[ac]k smith. Convicted of horse stealing by a court in Wayne County, and sentenced to 3 years in the Penitentiary. Received May 15, 1833 and discharged June 15, 1836. Notes: conduct generally good. Number in ledger 86: 93.

Name: Jackson J. Swaggerty, age 25, born in Tennessee, occupation: labourer. Convicted of petit larceny by a court in Monroe County, and sentenced to 1 year and 3 months in the Penitentiary. Received May 25, 1833 and discharged Sept. 3, 1834. Notes: conduct generally good. Number in ledger 86: 94.

Name: William Tinsley, age 26, born in Kentucky, occupation: cabinett [sic] maker. Convicted of petit larceny by a court in Davidson County, and sentenced to 1 year in the Penitentiary. Received July 6, 1833 and discharged Sept. 29, 1834. Notes: conduct exceptionable. Number in ledger 86: 95.

Name: Hyram Johnson, age 30, born in New York, occupation: shoe maker. Convicted of petit larceny by a court in Williamson County, and sentenced to 1 year in the Penitentiary. Received Aug. 21, 1833 and discharged Nov. 18, 1834. Notes: conduct good. Number in ledger 86: 96.

Name: Ratchford Valentine, age 34, born in North Carolina, occupation: labourer. Convicted of murder 2nd degree by a court in Shelby County, and sentenced to 10 years in the Penitentiary. Received Sept. 8, 1833 and discharged May 5, 1843. Notes: pardoned by Gov. Jones. Number in ledger 86: 97.

Name: John Brandon, age 17, born in Tennessee, occupation: labourer. Convicted of house breaking by a court in Lawrence County, and sentenced to 3 years in the Penitentiary. Received Sept. 10, 1833 and discharged July 1, 1835. Notes: died of cholera. Number in ledger 86: 98.

Name: William Estepp, age 47, born in North Carolina, occupation: labourer. Convicted of petit larceny by a court in Carter County, and sentenced to 2 years in the Penitentiary. Received Oct. 2, 1833 and discharged Nov. 25, 1835. Notes: conduct bad. Number in ledger 86: 99.

Name: John J. Brazeal, age 41, born in Tennessee, occupation: labourer. Convicted of assault & b[attery] intent to k by a court in Henderson County, and sentenced to 21 year in the Penitentiary. Received Oct. 22, 1833 and discharged Nov. 19, 1838. Notes: pardon. Number in ledger 86: 100.

Name: Hamilton Gossett, age 20, born in Tennessee, occupation: labourer. Convicted of horse stealing by a court in Rutherford County, and sentenced to 3 years in the Penitentiary. Received Oct. 28, 1833 and discharged Nov. 17, 1836. Notes: conduct good. Number in ledger 86: 101.

Name: Archibald Porter, age 21, born in North Carolina, occupation: labourer. Convicted of horse stealing by a court in Hamilton County, and sentenced to 4 years in the Penitentiary. Received Oct. 28, 1833 and discharged July 2, 1835. Notes: died of cholera. Number in ledger 86: 102.

Name: John Melton, age 25, born in Tennessee, occupation: labourer. Convicted of petit larceny by a court in Wilson County, and sentenced to 2 years and 6 months in the Penitentiary. Received Nov. 6, 1833 and discharged June 5, 1836. Notes: conduct good. Number in ledger 86: 103. [Published 1837 report spells his name Milton.]

Name: James W. Duncan, age 25, born in South Carolina, occupation: labourer. Convicted of horse stealing by a court in McMinn County, and sentenced to 8 years in the Penitentiary. Received Nov. 8, 1833 and discharged Aug. 12, 1841. Notes: pardoned by Gov. J.K. Polk. Number in ledger 86: 104.

Name: George Corbin, age 37, born in Virginia, occupation: bl[ac]k smith. Convicted of stab[b]ing by a court in Maury County, and sentenced to 2 years in the Penitentiary. Received Nov. 10, 1833 and discharged Nov. 10, 1835.

Tennessee Convicts: Records of the State Penitentiary

Notes: conduct good. Number in ledger 86: 105.

Name: William Walton, age 21, born in Virginia, occupation: labourer. Convicted of fo[r]gery by a court in Maury County, and sentenced to 3 years in the Penitentiary. Received Nov. 10, 1833 and discharged April 8, 1834. Notes: by court of appeals. Number in ledger 86: 106.

Name: Francis McCarpin, age 19, born in Kentucky, occupation: labourer. Convicted of grand larceny by a court in Maury County, and sentenced to 3 years in the Penitentiary. Received Nov. 10, 1833 and discharged June 30, 1835. Notes: died of cholera. Number in ledger 86: 107.

Name: Samuel Cooxey, age 18, born in Virginia, occupation: labourer. Convicted of petit larceny by a court in Henry County, and sentenced to 1 year and 6 months in the Penitentiary. Received Dec. 10, 1833 and discharged April 30, 1836. Notes: conduct bad. Number in ledger 86: 108.

Name: William Brown, age 27, born in Tennessee, occupation: labourer. Convicted of fo[r]gery by a court in Monroe County, and sentenced to 3 years in the Penitentiary. Received Dec. 12, 1833 and discharged Dec. 20, 1836. Notes: conduct good. Number in ledger 86: 109.

Name: Green White, age 21, born in Kentucky, occupation: labourer. Convicted of stabbing by a court in Davidson County, and sentenced to 5 years in the Penitentiary. Received Dec. 17, 1833 and discharged July 5, 1835. Notes: died of cholera. Number in ledger 86: 110.

Name: John Brown, age 28, born in North Carolina, occupation: bl[ac]k smith. Convicted of horse stealing by a court in Davidson County, and sentenced to 3 years in the Penitentiary. Received Dec. 20, 1833 and discharged Dec. 25, 1836. Notes: conduct good. Number in ledger 86: 111.

Name: Ira Olive, age 40, born in North Carolina, occupation: labourer. Convicted of stabbing by a court in Tipton County, and sentenced to 2 years in the Penitentiary. Received Jan. 14, 1834 and discharged Jan. 14, 1836. Notes: conduct good. Number in ledger 86: 112.

Name: Henry Cook, age 25, born in North Carolina, occupation: labourer. Convicted of passing c[ounterfeit] bank note by a court in Tipton County, and sentenced to 3 years in the Penitentiary. Received Jan. 14, 1834 and discharged Jan. 14, 1837. Notes: conduct good. Number in ledger 86: 113.

Tennessee Convicts: Records of the State Penitentiary

Name: Henry K. Redman, age 32, born in Virginia, occupation: bl[ac]k smith. Convicted of passing c[ounterfeit] bank note by a court in Tipton County, and sentenced to 3 years in the Penitentiary. Received Jan. 14, 1834 and discharged Feb. 26, 1837. Notes: conduct generally good. Number in ledger 86: 114.

Name: Joseph Collins, age 28, born in South Carolina, occupation: labourer. Convicted of horse stealing by a court in Franklin County, and sentenced to 6 years in the Penitentiary. Received Jan. 23, 1834 and discharged Sept. 15, 1835. Notes: died of cholera. Number in ledger 86: 115.

Name: Moses A. Nelson, age 34, born in Tennessee, occupation: labourer. Convicted of petit larceny by a court in Co[c]ke County, and sentenced to 1 year in the Penitentiary. Received Jan. 25, 1834 and discharged Jan. 24, 1835. Notes: conduct good. Number in ledger 86: 116.

Name: William Morgan, age 22, born in Virginia, occupation: waggon maker. Convicted of horse stealing by a court in Madison County, and sentenced to 3 years in the Penitentiary. Received Feb. 5, 1834 and discharged Jan. 24, 1836. Notes: died of consumption. Number in ledger 86: 117.

Name: Young Chumney, age 27, born in Tennessee, occupation: labourer. Convicted of larceny by a court in Giles County, and sentenced to 3 years in the Penitentiary. Received Feb. 18, 1834 and discharged Mar. 28, 1837. Notes: conduct generly [sic] good. Number in ledger 86: 118. [Published 1837 report spells his name Chumley.]

Name: John King, age 31, born in Tennessee, occupation: labourer. Convicted of petit larceny by a court in Fentress County, and sentenced to 1 year in the Penitentiary. Received Mar. 11, 1834 and discharged Mar. 15, 1835. Notes: conduct generly [sic] good. Number in ledger 86: 119.

Name: William Miller, age 19, born in Tennessee, occupation: labourer. Convicted of petit larceny by a court in Roane County, and sentenced to 4 years in the Penitentiary. Received Mar. 28, 1834 and discharged June 30, 1835. Notes: died of cholera. Number in ledger 86: 120.

Name: Charles Spears, age 25, born in South Carolina, occupation: labourer. Convicted of petit larceny by a court in Lincoln County, and sentenced to 2 years and 6 months in the Penitentiary. Received Mar. 31, 18334 and discharged Nov. 24, 1836. Notes: conduct generally good. Number in ledger 86: 121.

Tennessee Convicts: Records of the State Penitentiary

Name: James Denton, age 24, born in Tennessee, occupation: labourer. Convicted of petit larceny by a court in Perry County, and sentenced to 2 years in the Penitentiary. Received Apr. 15, 1834 and discharged July 4, 1835. Notes: died of cholera. Number in ledger 86: 122.

Name: John Forgus, age 30, born in North Carolina, occupation: h[ouse] carpenter. Convicted of having c[ounterfeit] bank bills by a court in Rutherford County, and sentenced to 3 years in the Penitentiary. Received Apr. 21, 1834 and discharged May 6, 1837. Notes: conduct generally good. Number in ledger 86: 123.

Name: Franklin McCullough, age 18, born in Tennessee, occupation: bl[ac]k smith. Convicted of negro stealing by a court in Wilson County, and sentenced to 5 years in the Penitentiary. Received May 3, 1834 and discharged May 3, 1839. Notes: conduct generally good. Number in ledger 86: 124.

Name: Alfred Ellis, age 19, born in Tennessee, occupation: moulder. Convicted of volentary [*sic*] manslaughter by a court in County, and sentenced to 5 years in the Penitentiary. Received May 5, 1834 and discharged May 6, 1839. Notes: conduct generally good. Number in ledger 86: 125.

Name: Frances Booby, age 53, born in St. Domingo, occupation: labourer. Convicted of receiving stolen goods by a court in Madison County, and sentenced to 3 years in the Penitentiary. Received May 24, 1834 and discharged May 19, 1835. Notes: died of consumption. Number in ledger 86: 126.

Name: Richard Hankins, age 34, born in Tennessee, occupation: labourer. Convicted of incest by a court in Monroe County, and sentenced to 5 years in the Penitentiary. Received June 5, 1834 and discharged Apr. 3, 1838. Notes: pardoned by Gov. Cannon. Number in ledger 86: 127.

Name: James B. Ivy, age 33, born in Tennessee, occupation: labourer. Convicted of forgery by a court in Monroe County, and sentenced to 3 years in the Penitentiary. Received June 5, 1834 and discharged July 7, 1835. Notes: died of cholera. Number in ledger 86: 128.

Name: James Arp, age 32, born in Virginia, occupation: labourer. Convicted of petit larceny by a court in Monroe County, and sentenced to 1 year and 10 months in the Penitentiary. Received June 5, 1834 and discharged Apr. 15, 1836. Notes: conduct good. Number in ledger 86: 129.

Name: John Mowry, age 43, born in Tennessee, occupation: labourer. Convicted of petit larceny by a court in Monroe County, and sentenced to 1 year and 3 months in the Penitentiary. Received June 5, 1834 and discharged July 1, 1835. Notes: died of cholera. [Name spelled Maury in published report of 1835.] Number in ledger 86: 130.

Name: Lutin McGee, age 21, born in Tennessee, occupation: labourer. Convicted of burglary by a court in Henry County, and sentenced to 5 years in the Penitentiary. Received June 7, 1835 and discharged April 1, 1839. Notes: conduct good, pardoned. Number in ledger 86: 131.

Name: William Phillips, age 47, born in Virginia, occupation: seaman. Convicted of burglary by a court in Bedford County, and sentenced to 5 years in the Penitentiary. Received June 13, 1834 and discharged June 17, 1839. Notes: conduct generally good. Number in ledger 86: 132.

Name: Samuel Chamberlain, age 35, born in Tennessee, occupation: labourer. Convicted of petit larceny by a court in Davidson County, and sentenced to 1 year in the Penitentiary. Received June 17, 1834 and discharged June 20, 1835. Notes: conduct generally good. Number in ledger 86: 133.

Name: Joseph Blackwell, age 36, born in North Carolina, occupation: plasterer. Convicted of petit & grand larceny by a court in Shelby County, and sentenced to 4 years in the Penitentiary. Received June 26, 1834 and discharged July 28, 1838. Notes: coloured, conduct exceptionable. Number in ledger 86: 134.

Name: Basil Bunch, age 23, born in Kentucky, occupation: labourer. Convicted of having & pass[ing] c[ounterfeit by a court in Shelby County, and sentenced to 3 years in the Penitentiary. Received June 26, 1834 and discharged July 1, 1837. Notes: conduct good. Number in ledger 86: 135.

Name: Charles T. Davis, age 20, born in Virginia, occupation: labourer. Convicted of horse stealing by a court in Giles County, and sentenced to 3 years in the Penitentiary. Received Aug. 15, 1834 and discharged June 12, 1835. Notes: escaped. Number in ledger 86: 136.

Name: John A. Murrell, age 28, born in Virginia, occupation: labourer. Convicted of negro stealing by a court in Madison County, and sentenced to 10 years in the Penitentiary. Received Aug. 17, 1834 and discharged Apr. 3, 1844. Notes: conduct generally good, pardoned. Number in ledger 86: 137.

Tennessee Convicts: Records of the State Penitentiary

Name: Robt. Gollihorn, age 33, born in Virginia, occupation: silversmith. Convicted of counterfeiting by a court in Blount County, and sentenced to 3 years in the Penitentiary. Received Aug. 18, 1834 and discharged Sept. 23, 1837. Notes: exceptionable. Number in ledger 86: 138.

Name: John Turner, age 15, born in Tennessee, occupation: labourer. Convicted of grand larceny by a court in Jefferson County, and sentenced to 3 years in the Penitentiary. Received Aug. 19, 1834 and discharged Sept. 4, 1837. Notes: generally good. Number in ledger 86: 139.

Name: Robt. McCall, age 43, born in North Carolina, occupation: millwright. Convicted of volentary [sic] manslaughter by a court in Fayette County, and sentenced to 2 years in the Penitentiary. Received Sept. 8, 1834 and discharged Oct. 18, 1836. Notes: generally good. Number in ledger 86: 140.

Name: John Padgett, age 31, born in Tennessee, occupation: shoe maker. Convicted of petit larceny by a court in Overton County, and sentenced to 1 year in the Penitentiary. Received Sept. 16, 1834 and discharged June 30, 1835. Notes: died of cholera.]Middle initial given as "D" in published report of 1835.] Number in ledger 86: 141.

Name: James Courier, age 15, born in Virginia, occupation: labourer. Convicted of petit larceny by a court in Overton County, and sentenced to 1 year in the Penitentiary. Received Sept. 16, 1834 and discharged Sept. 22, 1835. Notes: conduct bad. Number in ledger 86: 142.

Name: Nickolas Browder, age 21, born in Virginia, occupation: labourer. Convicted of petit larceny by a court in Washington County, and sentenced to 2 years in the Penitentiary. Received Sept. 24, 1834 and discharged July 11, 1835. Notes: died of cholera. Number in ledger 86: 143.

Name: John Minor, age 56, born in Virginia, occupation: labourer. Convicted of volentary [sic] manslaughter by a court in Lincoln County, and sentenced to 8 years in the Penitentiary. Received Sept. 27, 1834 and discharged Feb. 21, 1835. Notes: pardoned. Number in ledger 86: 144.

Name: Henry Minor, age 15, born in Tennessee, occupation: labourer. Convicted of volentary [sic] manslaughter by a court in Lincoln County, and sentenced to 8 years in the Penitentiary. Received Sept. 27, 1834 and discharged Oct. 4, 1838. Notes: pardoned, conduct good. Number in ledger 86: 145.

Tennessee Convicts: Records of the State Penitentiary

Name: John Bond, age 24, born in Kentucky, occupation: labourer. Convicted of petit larceny by a court in Perry County, and sentenced to 1 year in the Penitentiary. Received Oct. 14, 1834 and discharged July 2, 1835. Notes: died of cholera. Number in ledger 86: 146.

Name: John Gage, age 46, born in North Carolina, occupation: labourer. Convicted of counterfeiting by a court in Perry County, and sentenced to 3 years in the Penitentiary. Received Oct. 14, 1834 and discharged Mar. 14, 1836. Notes: died of chronic diar[f]hea. Number in ledger 86: 147.

Name: John W. Moore, age 26, born in North Carolina, occupation: labourer. Convicted of fo[r]gery by a court in Henderson County, and sentenced to 3 years in the Penitentiary. Received Oct. 21, 1834 and discharged Nov. 14, 1837. Notes: conduct exceptionable. Number in ledger 86: 148.

Name: Thos. Ely, age 29, born in Virginia, occupation: labourer. Convicted of horse stealing by a court in Claiborne County, and sentenced to 6 years in the Penitentiary. Received Nov. 5, 1834 and discharged Aug. 9, 1840. Notes: pardoned by Gov. Polk. Number in ledger 86: 149.

Name: Culverson Phillips, age 21, born in North Carolina, occupation: labourer. Convicted of petit larceny by a court in Claiborne County, and sentenced to 1 year in the Penitentiary. Received Nov. 5, 1834 and discharged Dec. 9, 1835. Notes: conduct exceptionable. Number in ledger 86: 150.

Name: James Harris, age 35, born in Pennsylvania, occupation: bl[ac]k smith. Convicted of grand larceny by a court in Maury County, and sentenced to 3 years in the Penitentiary. Received Nov. 7, 1834 and discharged July 1, 1835. Notes: died of cholera. Number in ledger 86: 151.

Name: Elijah Crosen, age 39, born in Virginia, occupation: labourer. Convicted of murder 2nd degree by a court in Maury County, and sentenced to 2 years in the Penitentiary. Received Nov. 7, 1834 and discharged Dec. 12, 1836. Notes: exceptionable. Number in ledger 86: 152. [Published 1837 report spells his name Crosson.]

Name: James Wilson, age 50, born in North Carolina, occupation: wagon maker. Convicted of fo[r]gery by a court in Maury County, and sentenced to 3 years in the Penitentiary. Received Nov. 7, 1834 and discharged June 30, 1835. Notes: died of cholera. Number in ledger 86: 153.

Name: John A. Dean, age 27, born in Pennsylvania, occupation: shoe maker.

Convicted of petit larceny by a court in Campbell County, and sentenced to 3 years in the Penitentiary. Received Nov. 8, 1834 and discharged June 27, 1835. Notes: died of cholera. Number in ledger 86: 154.

Name: George W. Cross, age 20, born in Tennessee, occupation: labourer. Convicted of petit larceny by a court in Monroe County, and sentenced to 1 year in the Penitentiary. Received Dec. 4, 1834 and discharged Feb. 24, 1836. Notes: conduct good. Number in ledger 86: 155.

Name: Samuel Childress, age 23, born in South Carolina, occupation: labourer. Convicted of fo[r]gery by a court in Monroe County, and sentenced to 3 years in the Penitentiary. Received Dec. 4, 1834 and discharged Nov. 22, 1835. Notes: died of chronic diar[r]hea. Number in ledger 86: 156.

Name: John Rhodes, age 24, born in North Carolina, occupation: labourer. Convicted of petit larceny by a court in Monroe County, and sentenced to 1 year in the Penitentiary. Received Dec. 4, 1834 and discharged Jan. 19, 1836. Notes: conduct exceptionable. Number in ledger 86: 157.

Name: Andrew Wilson, age 34, born in South Carolina, occupation: labourer. Convicted of horse stealing by a court in Bedford County, and sentenced to 5 years in the Penitentiary. Received Dec. 11, 1834 and discharged Aug. 26, 1837. Notes: died of chronic diar[r]hea. Number in ledger 86: 158. [Published 1837 report shows his death in 1836.]

Name: James Brown, age 22, born in Tennessee, occupation: shoe maker. Convicted of petit larceny by a court in Bedford County, and sentenced to 1 year in the Penitentiary. Received Dec. 11, 1834 and discharged June 11, 1836. Notes: conduct good. Number in ledger 86: 159.

Name: Moses Park, age 20, born in Tennessee, occupation: labourer. Convicted of assault [with] intent to kill by a court in Davidson County, and sentenced to 3 years in the Penitentiary. Received Dec. 16, 1834 and discharged Dec. 24, 1837. Notes: conduct good. Number in ledger 86: 160.

Name: John Slaughter, age 28, born in Tennessee, occupation: labourer. Convicted of maiming by a court in Fayette County, and sentenced to 2 years in the Penitentiary. Received Dec. 19, 1834 and discharged Dec. 20, 1836. Notes: conduct good. Number in ledger 86: 161.

Name: Hugh Lenox, age 25, born in Tennessee, occupation: labourer. Convicted of horse stealing by a court in Haywood County, and sentenced to 3 years in the Penitentiary. Received Jan. 16, 1835 and discharged July 9, 1835. Notes: died of cholera. Number in ledger 86: 162.

Name: Owen Collins, age 45, born in North Carolina, occupation: labourer. Convicted of assault with intent to kill by a court in Claiborne County, and sentenced to 3 years in the Penitentiary. Received Jan. 17, 1835 and discharged Sept. 19, 1836. Notes: died of chronic diar[r]hea. Number in ledger 86: 163. [Published 1837 report shows his death in 1837.]

Name: Avery Mayfield, age 24, born in Tennessee, occupation: labourer. Convicted of petit larceny by a court in Warren County, and sentenced to 1 year and 6 months in the Penitentiary. Received Feb. 10, 1835 and discharged June 30, 1835. Notes: died of cholera. Number in ledger 86: 164.

Name: Jared B. Millsap, age 25, born in Tennessee, occupation: labourer. Convicted of grand larceny by a court in Blount County, and sentenced to 3 years in the Penitentiary. Received Feb. 17, 1835 and discharged Feb. 22, 1838. Notes: conduct generally good. Number in ledger 86: 165.

Name: George W. Dyer, age 24, born in Tennessee, occupation: sad[d]ler. Convicted of petit larceny by a court in Knox County, and sentenced to 1 year in the Penitentiary. Received Mar. 3, 1835 and discharged Mar. 3, 1836. Notes: conduct generally good. Number in ledger 86: 166.

Name: James Edwards (Fanning), age 30, born in Maryland, occupation: waggon maker. Convicted of horse stealing by a court in Roane County, and sentenced to 5 years in the Penitentiary. Received Mar. 21, 1835 and discharged Apr. 25, 1838. Notes: pardoned. Number in ledger 86: 167.

Name: John Jackson (Gibney), age 35, born in Kentucky, occupation: bl[ac]k smith. Convicted of grand larceny by a court in Humphreys County, and sentenced to 3 years in the Penitentiary. Received Mar. 24, 1835 and discharged Feb. 17, 1838. Notes: conduct good, Gov. Cannon. Number in ledger 86: 168.

Name: Thomas Butcher, age 38, born in Virginia, occupation: plasterer. Convicted of petit larceny by a court in Washington County, and sentenced to 1 year in the Penitentiary. Received Mar. 25, 1835 and discharged July 3, 1835. Notes: colored, died of cholera. Number in ledger 86: 169.

Name: Mic[a]jah Brummet, age 31, born in Tennessee, occupation: labourer. Convicted of horse stealing by a court in Carter County, and sentenced to 4 years in the Penitentiary. Received Apr. 6, 1835 and discharged May 11, 1839. Notes: conduct bad. Number in ledger 86: 170.

Name: James Roberts, age 49, born in Virginia, occupation: labourer. Convicted of keeping counterfeit coin by a court in Perry County, and sentenced to 3 years in the Penitentiary. Received Apr. 15, 1835 and discharged June 30, 1835. Notes: died of cholera. Number in ledger 86: 171.

Name: Thomas Biggs, age 17, born in Tennessee, occupation: labourer. Convicted of involuntary manslaughter by a court in Hawkins County, and sentenced to 1 year in the Penitentiary. Received Apr. 21, 1835 and discharged June 30, 1835. Notes: died of cholera. Number in ledger 86: 172.

Name: Thomas Pruett, age 57, born in North Carolina, occupation: labourer. Convicted of petit larceny by a court in Hawkins County, and sentenced to 1 year in the Penitentiary. Received Apr. 21, 1835 and discharged July 5, 1835. Notes: died of cholera. [Name spelled Prewett in published report of 1835.] Number in ledger 86: 173.

Name: George Maddin, age 62, born in Virginia, occupation: labourer. Convicted of stabbing by a court in Hawkins County, and sentenced to 2 years in the Penitentiary. Received Apr. 21, 1835 and discharged Nov. [?], 1835. Notes: died of chronic diar[r]hea. Number in ledger 86: 174.

Name: Samuel D. Pugh, age 31, born in Tennessee, occupation: cabinett [sic] maker. Convicted of petit larceny by a court in Marion County, and sentenced to 1 year in the Penitentiary. Received Apr. 23, 1835 and discharged June 30, 1835. Notes: died of cholera. Number in ledger 86: 175.

Name: William McNeely, age 30, born in Virginia, occupation: labourer. Convicted of petit larceny by a court in Campbell County, and sentenced to 1 year in the Penitentiary. Received May 11, 1835 and discharged July 4, 1835. Notes: died of cholera. [Name spelled McNeilly in published report of 1835.] Number in ledger 86: 176.

Name: Jeremiah George, age 17, born in South Carolina, occupation: labourer. Convicted of petit larceny by a court in Monroe County, and sentenced to 4 years in the Penitentiary. Received May 28, 1835 and discharged May 28, 1839. Notes: conduct good. Number in ledger 86: 177.

Name: John Ransom, age 23, born in Tennessee, occupation: labourer. Convicted of murder 2nd degree by a court in Davidson County, and sentenced to 20 years in the Penitentiary. Received June 4, 1835 and discharged Jan. 23, 1854. Notes: colored, discharged under act of 1836. Number in ledger 86: 178.

Name: David Brunson, age 37, born in South Carolina, occupation: labourer. Convicted of petit larceny by a court in Henry County, and sentenced to 2 years in the Penitentiary. Received June 4, 1835 and discharged June 14, 1837. Notes: conduct generally good. Number in ledger 86: 179. [Published 1837 report shows his dicharge in 1836.]

Name: Joseph Jackson, age 36, born in Tennessee, occupation: labourer. Convicted of petit larceny by a court in Hardin County, and sentenced to 1 year in the Penitentiary. Received June 6, 1835 and discharged Aug. 14, 1836. Notes: conduct exceptionable. Number in ledger 86: 180.

Name: John Gilbert, age 32, born in North Carolina, occupation: labourer. Convicted of petit larceny by a court in Hardin County, and sentenced to 1 year in the Penitentiary. Received June 6, 1835 and discharged Aug. 14, 1836. Notes: conduct exceptionable. Number in ledger 86: 181.

Name: Asberry Jolly, age 24, born in Kentucky, occupation: bl[ac]k smith. Convicted of grand larceny by a court in Bedford County, and sentenced to 3 years in the Penitentiary. Received June 11, 1835 and discharged July 15, 1838. Notes: conduct good. Number in ledger 86: 182.

Name: William Cox, age 28, born in Tennessee, occupation: labourer. Convicted of petit larceny by a court in Bedford County, and sentenced to 2 years in the Penitentiary. Received June 11, 1835 and discharged July 1, 1835. Notes: died of cholera. Number in ledger 86: 183.

Name: Robt. Andrews, age 20, born in North Carolina, occupation: labourer. Convicted of petit larceny by a court in Bedford County, and sentenced to 1 year in the Penitentiary. Received June 11, 1835 and discharged Aug. 15, 1836. Notes: conduct bad. Number in ledger 86: 184.

Name: Hugh Hoy, age 35, born in Ireland, occupation: baker. Convicted of grand larceny by a court in Shelby County, and sentenced to 3 years in the Penitentiary. Received July 1, 1835 and discharged Sept. 20, 1838. Notes: conduct verry [sic] bad. Number in ledger 86: 185.

Name: Francisco St. John, age 26, born in Cuba, occupation: sailor. Convicted of grand larceny by a court in Shelby County, and sentenced to 9 years in the

Tennessee Convicts: Records of the State Penitentiary

Penitentiary. Received July 1, 1835 and discharged Jan. 9, 1844. Notes: pardoned by Gov. Jones. Number in ledger 86: 186.

Name: Henry Townsend, age 32, born in Georgia, occupation: bl[ac]k smith. Convicted of assau[l]t with intent to kill by a court in Tipton County, and sentenced to 3 years in the Penitentiary. Received July 9, 1835 and discharged Sept. 16, 1838. Notes: conduct verry [sic] bad. Number in ledger 86: 187.

Name: Jacob K. Horton, age 31, born in Ohio, occupation: gun smith. Convicted of grand larceny by a court in Carroll County, and sentenced to 3 years in the Penitentiary. Received July 20, 1835 and discharged Oct. 16, 1838. Notes: conduct verry [sic] bad. Number in ledger 86: 188.

Name: John Elkin, age 23, born in Tennessee, occupation: labourer. Convicted of petit larceny by a court in Co[c]ke County, and sentenced to 1 year in the Penitentiary. Received July 27, 1835 and discharged Aug. 30, 1836. Notes: conduct exceptionable. Number in ledger 86: 189.

Name: Samuel J. Brockwell, age 37, born in North Carolina, occupation: labourer. Convicted of fo[r]gery by a court in Giles County, and sentenced to 3 years in the Penitentiary. Received Aug. 23, 1835 and discharged Dec. 13, 1835. Notes: died of a ruptuer of blood vessel. Number in ledger 86: 190.

Name: James Tipper, age 21, born in Tennessee, occupation: labourer. Convicted of horse stealing by a court in Giles County, and sentenced to 5 years and 6 months in the Penitentiary. Received Aug. 23, 1835 and discharged Apr. 29, 1839. Notes: died of inflamation of the heart & dropsy. Number in ledger 86: 191.

Name: Robt. Henderson, age 21, born in Pennsylvania, occupation: labourer. Convicted of g[rand] larceny by a court in Lawrence County, and sentenced to 4 years and 6 months in the Penitentiary. Received Aug. 30, 1835 and discharged Mar. 2, 1840. Notes: conduct exceptionable. Number in ledger 86: 192.

Name: William J. May, age 45, born in England, occupation: manufacturer. Convicted of horse stealing by a court in Roane County, and sentenced to 3 years in the Penitentiary. Received Sept. 5, 1835 and discharged Aug. 29, 1837. Notes: conduct good, died of apoplexy. Number in ledger 86: 193.

Name: Jones Humes, age 21, born in Tennessee, occupation: labourer. Convicted of p[etit] larceny by a court in Knox County, and sentenced to 3 years in the Penitentiary. Received Sept. 5, 1835 and discharged Oct. 11, 1836. Notes: colored, conduct exceptionable. Number in ledger 86: 194.

Name: Isaac Brumley, age 19, born in Tennessee, occupation: labourer. Convicted of p[etit] larceny by a court in Green[e] County, and sentenced to 1 year in the Penitentiary. Received Sept. 16, 1835 and discharged Feb. 26, 1837. Notes: conduct bad. Number in ledger 86: 195.

Name: Moses Treadway Hopkins, age 45, born in Virginia, occupation: waggon maker. Convicted of horse stealing by a court in Hickman County, and sentenced to 8 years and 6 months in the Penitentiary. Received Sept. 21, 1835 and discharged June 8, 1841. Notes: escaped. Number in ledger 86: 196.

Name: Larkin Timms, age 20, born in South Carolina, occupation: labourer. Convicted of horse stealing by a court in Stewart County, and sentenced to 5 years in the Penitentiary. Received Oct. 5, 1835 and discharged Aug. 9, 1840. Notes: pardoned by Gov. Polk. Number in ledger 86: 197.

Name: Reubins [sic] Timms, age 26, born in South Carolina, occupation: labourer. Convicted of horse stealing by a court in Stewart County, and sentenced to 5 years in the Penitentiary. Received Oct. 5, 1835 and discharged Oct. 7, 1840. Notes: conduct bad. Number in ledger 86: 198.

Name: Samuel Surber, age 39, born in Ireland, occupation: weaver. Convicted of assault with intent to kill by a court in Sullivan County, and sentenced to 3 years in the Penitentiary. Received Oct. 15, 1835 and discharged Oct. 14, 1838. Notes: died of disease of the kidney & bladder. Number in ledger 86: 199.

Name: Daniel McCarty, age 27, born in Tennessee, occupation: bl[ac]k smith. Convicted of p[etit] larceny by a court in Hamilton County, and sentenced to 1 year and 3 months in the Penitentiary. Received Oct. 28, 1835 and discharged Mar. 8, 1837. Notes: conduct exceptionable. Number in ledger 86: 200.

Name: James W. Davis, age 16, born in Tennessee, occupation: labourer. Convicted of p[etit] larceny by a court in Maury County, and sentenced to 1 year in the Penitentiary. Received Nov. 2, 1835 and discharged Dec. 13, 1836. Notes: conduct exceptionable. Number in ledger 86: 201. [Published 1837 report shows his discharge in 1837.]

Name: Thos. M. Watson, age 24, born in North Carolina, occupation: labourer. Convicted of horse stealing by a court in Gibson County, and sentenced to 3 years in the Penitentiary. Received Nov. 7, 1835 and discharged Jan. 12, 1839. Notes: conduct exceptionable. Number in ledger 86: 202.

Name: William Butram, age 24, born in Kentucky, occupation: labourer. Convicted of stealing a free child of colour by a court in Wayne County, and sentenced to 5 years in the Penitentiary. Received Nov. 12, 1835 and discharged Jan. 1, 1841. Notes: conduct good. Number in ledger 86: 203.

Name: John Turner, age 26, born in South Carolina, occupation: labourer Convicted of mule stealing by a court in Hardeman County, and sentenced to 3 years in the Penitentiary. Received Dec. 10, 1835 and discharged Dec. 26, 1838. Notes: conduct generally good. Number in ledger 86: 204.

Name: Mizay Hazlett, age 25, born in South Carolina, occupation: shoe maker. Convicted of receiving stolen goods by a court in Davidson County, and sentenced to 3 years in the Penitentiary. Received Dec. 16, 1835 and discharged Dec. 17, 1838. Notes: conduct exceptionable. Number in ledger 86: 205.

Name: John Allen, age 42, born in Maryland, occupation: bl[ac]k smith. Convicted of passing counterfeit money by a court in Shelby County, and sentenced to 3 years in the Penitentiary. Received Jan. 4, 1836 and discharged May 3, 1839. Notes: alias Jno. Mounts, conduct bad. Number in ledger 86: 206.

Name: Peter Walker, age 45, born in South Carolina, occupation: labourer. Convicted of manslaughter by a court in Shelby County, and sentenced to 2 years in the Penitentiary. Received Jan. 4, 1836 and discharged Jan. 4, 1838. Notes: conduct good. Number in ledger 86: 207.

Name: Eli Sartin, age 23, born in North Carolina, occupation: labourer. Convicted of assault with intent to kill by a court in Jefferson County, and sentenced to 3 years in the Penitentiary. Received Feb. 2, 1836 and discharged Feb. 6, 1839. Notes: conduct generally good. Number in ledger 86: 208.

Name: Michael Lynch, age 55, born in Ireland, occupation: sailer [sic]. Convicted of p[etit] larceny by a court in Lawrence County, and sentenced to 1 year in the Penitentiary. Received Mar. 8, 1836 and discharged Mar. 9, 1837. Notes: conduct generally good. Number in ledger 86: 209.

Name: Silas Brown, age 36, born in Virginia, occupation: labourer. Convicted of volentary [sic] manslaughter by a court in Washington County, and sentenced to 2 years in the Penitentiary. Received Mar. 31, 1836 and discharged Feb. 25, 1838. Notes: conduct good, pardoned by Gov. Cannon. Number in ledger 86: 210.

Name: William McClusky, age 45, born in South Carolina, occupation: labourer. Convicted of manslaughter by a court in Lyncoln [sic] County, and sentenced to 2 years and 3 months in the Penitentiary. Received Apr. 6, 1836 and discharged July 10, 1838. Notes: conduct good. Number in ledger 86: 211.

Name: Jesse Moore, age 45, born in South Carolina, occupation: labourer. Convicted of horse stealing by a court in Lyncoln [sic] County, and sentenced to 3 years in the Penitentiary. Received Apr. 6, 1836 and discharged Mar. 7, 1839. Notes: conduct good, pardoned. Number in ledger 86: 212.

Name: Henry Johnson, age 27, born in New Jersey, occupation: painter. Convicted of horse stealing by a court in Lyncoln [sic] County, and sentenced to 3 years in the Penitentiary. Received Apr. 6, 1836 and discharged Mar. 1, 1839. Notes: conduct generally good, pardomend. Number in ledger 86: 213.

Name: Patrick Here, age 35, born in Ireland, occupation: shoe maker. Convicted of g[rand] larceny by a court in Williamson County, and sentenced to 3 years in the Penitentiary. Received Apr. 11, 1836 and discharged May 21, 1839. Notes: conduct generally good, pardomend. Number in ledger 86: 214.

Name: Redick Sanders, age 28, born in North Carolina, occupation: labourer. Convicted of g[rand] larceny by a court in Bedford County, and sentenced to 3 years in the Penitentiary. Received Apr. 12, 1836 and discharged Apr. 29, 1839. Notes: conduct bad. Number in ledger 86: 215.

Name: William M. Duke, age 30, born in Kentucky, occupation: labourer. Convicted of horse stealing by a court in Perry County, and sentenced to 5 years in the Penitentiary. Received Apr. 13, 1836 and discharged Jan. 29, 1841. Notes: pardoned by Gov. Polk. Number in ledger 86: 216.

Name: Jeremiah Walton, age 18, born in Virginia, occupation: labourer. Convicted of p[etit] larceny by a court in Rutherford County, and sentenced to 1 year in the Penitentiary. Received Apr. 18, 1836 and discharged June 23, 1837. Notes: conduct exceptionable. Number in ledger 86: 217. [Published 1837 report spells his name Watton.]

Name: Jesse Warren, age 26, born in Virginia, occupation: labourer. Convicted of horse stealing by a court in Rutherford County, and sentenced to 4 years in the Penitentiary. Received Apr. 18, 1836 and discharged May 8, 1840. Notes: conduct exceptionable. Number in ledger 86: 218.

Name: Tarleton Poindexter, age 19, born in Virginia, occupation: labourer. Convicted of g[rand] larceny by a court in Hawkin[s] County, and sentenced to 3 years in the Penitentiary. Received Apr. 27, 1836 and discharged June 4, 1839. Notes: conduct generally good. Number in ledger 86: 219.

Name: Edmund Davis, age 42, born in Virginia, occupation: labourer. Convicted of g[rand] larceny by a court in Grainger County, and sentenced to 1 year in the Penitentiary. Received May 3, 1836 and discharged June 6, 1837. Notes: conduct exceptionable. Number in ledger 86: 220.

Name: John Petty, age 21, born in Tennessee, occupation: labourer. Convicted of g[rand] larceny by a court in Frankllin County, and sentenced to 4 years in the Penitentiary. Received May 6, 1836 and discharged May 8, 1840. Notes: conduct good. Number in ledger 86: 221.

Name: James T. Gorham, age 18, born in Tennessee, occupation: tannar [sic]. Convicted of burglary by a court in Robertson County, and sentenced to 5 years in the Penitentiary. Received May 7, 1836 and discharged Sept. 30, 1839. Notes: pardoned by Gov. Cannon. Number in ledger 86: 222.

Name: Burwell Clark, age 18, born in Georgia, occupation: labourer. Convicted of fo[r]gery by a court in Madison County, and sentenced to 3 years in the Penitentiary. Received May 11, 1836 and discharged June 13, 1839. Notes: conduct exceptionable. Number in ledger 86: 223.

Name: Peter Wheeler, age 25, born in Tennessee, occupation: labourer. Convicted of horse stealing by a court in McMinn County, and sentenced to 3 years in the Penitentiary. Received May 13, 1836 and discharged Mar. 8, 1839. Notes: conduct good, pardoned. Number in ledger 86: 224.

Name: Nathaniel Rye (Bradley), age 49, born in Virginia, occupation: waggon maker. Convicted of man stealing & larceny by a court in Maury County, and sentenced to 4 years in the Penitentiary. Received May 17, 1836 and discharged May 17, 1840. Notes: conduct good. Number in ledger 86: 225.

Name: William Wheeler, age 20, born in Tennessee, occupation: labourer. Convicted of p[etit] larceny by a court in Maury County, and sentenced to 1 year in the Penitentiary. Received May 17, 1836 and discharged June 2, 1837.

Notes: conduct generally good. Number in ledger 86: 226.

Name: John Williams, age 28, born in North Carolina, occupation: shoe maker. Convicted of p[etit] larceny by a court in Davidson County, and sentenced to 1 year in the Penitentiary. Received May 24, 1836 and discharged June 2, 1837. Notes: colored, conduct generally good. Number in ledger 86: 227.

Name: Buford Easley, age 30, born in Tennessee, occupation: labourer. Convicted of negro stealing by a court in Fayett[e] County, and sentenced to 6 years in the Penitentiary. Received June 3, 1836 and discharged Aug. 4, 1836. Notes: died of inflamatory fever. Number in ledger 86: 228.

Name: Alexander Cohen, age 50, born in Ireland, occupation: dyer. Convicted of murder 2nd degree by a court in Fayett[e] County, and sentenced to 21 year in the Penitentiary. Received June 3, 1836 and discharged Sept. 20, 1852. Notes: died from a fall. Number in ledger 86: 229.

Name: William E. Felter, age 25, born in New York, occupation: shoe maker. Convicted of horse stealing by a court in Davidson County, and sentenced to 3 years in the Penitentiary. Received June 7, 1836 and discharged Dec. 12, 1836. Notes: discharged by Court of Errors & Appeals. Number in ledger 86: 230.

Name: Robert Ramey, age 48, born in North Carolina, occupation: labourer. Convicted of assault with intent to kill by a court in Henry County, and sentenced to 3 years in the Penitentiary. Received June 9, 1836 and discharged June 13, 1839. Notes: conduct generally good. Number in ledger 86: 231.

Name: James Miller, age 23, born in North Carolina, occupation: labourer. Convicted of horse stealing by a court in Knox County, and sentenced to 6 years in the Penitentiary. Received July 1, 1836 and discharged June 30, 1842. Notes: conduct generally good. Number in ledger 86: 232.

Name: James Wright, age 27, born in North Carolina, occupation: labourer. Convicted of stabbing by a court in Knox County, and sentenced to 2 years in the Penitentiary. Received July 1, 1836 and discharged June 21, 1838. Notes: conduct generally good. Number in ledger 86: 233.

Name: Stokely D. Swaggerty, age 36, born in Tennessee, occupation: labourer. Convicted of receiving stolen goods by a court in Knox County, and sentenced to 1 year in the Penitentiary. Received July 1, 1836 and discharged Mar. 25, 1837. Notes: pardoned by Gov. Cannon. Number in ledger 86: 234.

Tennessee Convicts: Records of the State Penitentiary

Name: Jesse Smith, age 35, born in Tennessee, occupation: labourer. Convicted of horse stealing by a court in Bledsoe County, and sentenced to 3 years in the Penitentiary. Received July 19, 1836 and discharged July 25, 1839. Notes: conduct exceptionable. Number in ledger 86: 235.

Name: Ezekiel Collins, age 34, born in Tennessee, occupation: labourer. Convicted of hog stealing by a court in Hawkins County, and sentenced to 3 years in the Penitentiary. Received Aug. 24, 1836 and discharged July 21, 1839. Notes: conduct good, pardoned. Number in ledger 86: 236.

Name: Andrew Collins, age 28, born in Tennessee, occupation: labourer. Convicted of hog stealing by a court in Hawkins County, and sentenced to 3 years in the Penitentiary. Received Aug. 24, 1836 and discharged July 21, 1839. Notes: conduct good, pardoned. Number in ledger 86: 237.

Name: George Phillips, age 33, born in Tennessee, occupation: labourer. Convicted of p[etit] larceny by a court in Sullivan County, and sentenced to 1 year in the Penitentiary. Received Aug. 18, 1836 and discharged Oct. 23, 1836. Notes: died of marasmus. Number in ledger 86: 238.

Name: Isaac George, age 40, born in North Carolina, occupation: shoe maker. Convicted of g[rand] larceny by a court in McMinn County, and sentenced to 3 years in the Penitentiary. Received Aug. 20, 1836 and discharged Aug. 6, 1839. Notes: conduct generly [sic] good. Number in ledger 86: 239.

Name: William Bailey, age 28, born in North Carolina, occupation: labourer. Convicted of horse stealing by a court in Bradley County, and sentenced to 3 years in the Penitentiary. Received Sept. 19, 1836 and discharged Nov. 28, 1836. Notes: died an invalid when rec[eive]d. Number in ledger 86: 240.

Name: Thomas Morrison, age 16, born in Georgia, occupation: labourer. Convicted of p[etit] larceny by a court in Fayett County, and sentenced to 3 years in the Penitentiary. Received Sept. 30, 1836 and discharged Sept. 30, 1839. Notes: conduct good. Number in ledger 86: 241.

Name: Benjamin Bryant, age 35, born in Virginia, occupation: labourer. Convicted of p[etit] larceny by a court in Warren County, and sentenced to 1 year in the Penitentiary. Received Oct. 3, 1836 and discharged Oct. 24, 1837. Notes: conduct exceptionable. Number in ledger 86: 242.

Name: Richard Gaither, age 23, born in Alabama, occupation: labourer. Convicted of horse stealing by a court in Rutherford County, and sentenced to 3

Tennessee Convicts: Records of the State Penitentiary

years in the Penitentiary. Received Oct. 28, 1836 and discharged Oct. 28, 1839. Notes: conduct exceptionable. Number in ledger 86: 243.

Name: Thomas Turner, age 27, born in Virginia, occupation: sad[d]ler. Convicted of p[etit] larceny by a court in Rutherford County, and sentenced to 2 years in the Penitentiary. Received Oct. 28, 1836 and discharged Dec. 6, 1838. Notes: conduct generally good. Number in ledger 86: 244.

Name: A.B. King, age 19, born in Tennessee, occupation: labourer. Convicted of p[etit] larceny by a court in Knox County, and sentenced to 3 years in the Penitentiary. Received Oct. 28, 1836 and discharged Dec. 2, 1839. Notes: conconduct exceptionable. Number in ledger 86: 245.

Name: Richard Trimble, age 24; born in Pennsylvania, occupation: baker. Convicted of g[rand] larceny by a court in Tipton County, and sentenced to 3 years in the Penitentiary. Received Nov. 1, 1836 and discharged Jan. 15, 1840. Notes: conduct verry [sic] bad. Number in ledger 86: 246.

Name: James McNeese, age 28, born in Tennessee, occupation: labourer. Convicted of assault to kill by a court in Giles County, and sentenced to 3 years in the Penitentiary. Received Nov. 6, 1836 and discharged Jan. 16, 1840. Notes: conduct verry [sic] bad. Number in ledger 86: 247.

Name: William Felts, age 36, born in North Carolina, occupation: shoe maker. Convicted of p[etit] larceny by a court in Roane County, and sentenced to 1 year in the Penitentiary. Received Nov. 14, 1836 and discharged Nov. 6, 1837. Notes: conduct good, pardoned. Number in ledger 86: 248.

Name: John York, age 27, born in North Carolina, occupation: labourer. Convicted of passing counterfeit money by a court in Roane County, and sentenced to 3 years in the Penitentiary. Received Nov. 14, 1836 and discharged June 12, 1839. Notes: died of chronic diar[r]hea. Number in ledger 86: 249.

Name: Nimrod Hooper, age 49, born in Tennessee, occupation: labourer. Convicted of negro stealing by a court in Shelby County, and sentenced to 15 years in the Penitentiary. Received Nov. 16, 1836 and discharged Mar. 3, 1846. Notes: general pardon by A.V. Brown. Number in ledger 86: 250.

Name: Jeremiah Johnson, age 20, born in Tennessee, occupation: labourer. Convicted of p[etit] larceny by a court in Wilson County, and sentenced to 1 year in the Penitentiary. Received Nov. 21, 1836 and discharged Nov. 24,

1837. Notes: conduct good. Number in ledger 86: 251.

Name: Martin Armington, age 56, born in Maryland, occupation: machinist. Convicted of p[etit] larceny by a court in Stewart County, and sentenced to 3 years in the Penitentiary. Received Nov. 25, 1836 and discharged Jan. 15, 1840. Notes: conduct exceptionable. Number in ledger 86: 252.

Name: James Orr, age 22, born in Tennessee, occupation: labourer. Convicted of mare & money stealing by a court in Marshall County, and sentenced to 3 years in the Penitentiary. Received Dec. 2, 1836 and discharged Dec. 4, 1839. Notes: conduct generally good. Number in ledger 86: 253.

Name: Charles Spears, age 28, born in South Carolina, occupation: stone cutter. Convicted of mare stealing by a court in Williamson County, and sentenced to 5 years in the Penitentiary. Received Dec. 9, 1836 and discharged Dec. 9, 1841. Notes: 2nd conviction, conduct fair. Number in ledger 86: 254.

Name: Russell Golorth [Goforth?], age 37, born in Kentucky, occupation: labourer. Convicted of larceny by a court in Hamilton County, and sentenced to 1 year in the Penitentiary. Received Dec. 10, 1836 and discharged Dec. 10, 1837. Notes: conduct good. Number in ledger 86: 255.

Name: Thomas Hudson, age 18, born in Tennessee, occupation: labourer. Convicted of burglary & larceny by a court in Bedford County, and sentenced to 3 years in the Penitentiary. Received Dec. 12, 1836 and discharged Nov. 8, 1839. Notes: pardoned by Gov. Polk. Number in ledger 86: 256.

Name: Joseph Doane, age 18, born in Virginia, occupation: labourer. Convicted of g[rand] larceny by a court in Sullivan County, and sentenced to 3 years in the Penitentiary. Received Dec. 25, 1836 and discharged Jan. 16, 1840. Notes: conductconduct exceptionable. Number in ledger 86: 257.

Name: Lewis D.H. Leger, age 29, born in Pennsylvania, occupation: artist. Convicted of assault to kill by a court in Shelby County, and sentenced to 3 years in the Penitentiary. Received Jan. 17, 1837 and discharged Nov. 19, 1839. Notes: pardoned by Gov. Polk. [Pardon papers show his name as Lewis de St. Leger.] Number in ledger 86: 258.

Name: Jesse Webb, age 28, born in Tennessee, occupation: labourer. Convicted of p[etit] larceny by a court in Shelby County, and sentenced to 1 year in the Penitentiary. Received Jan. 17, 1837 and discharged Jan. 21, 1838. Notes: conduct good. Number in ledger 86: 259.

Tennessee Convicts: Records of the State Penitentiary

Name: Robert C. Brogan, age 30, born in Tennessee, occupation: hatter. Convicted of mare stealing by a court in Maury County, and sentenced to 6 years in the Penitentiary. Received Jan. 18, 1837 and discharged July 1, 1837. Notes: died of dropsy in the brain. Number in ledger 86: 260.

Name: Andrew Baxter, age 40, born in North Carolina, occupation: labourer. Convicted of fellony [sic] by a court in Bradley County, and sentenced to 5 years in the Penitentiary. Received Jan. 19, 1837 and discharged Dec. 16, 1841. Notes: pardoned by Gov. Jones. Number in ledger 86: 261.

Name: Asa S. Ricker, age 31, born in Massachusetts, occupation: hatter. Convicted of p[etit] larceny by a court in Bradley County, and sentenced to 1 year in the Penitentiary. Received Jan. 19, 1837 and discharged Dec. 27, 1837. Notes: conduct good, pardoned by Cannon. Number in ledger 86: 262.

Name: Joseph G. Fogg, age 27, born in Massachusetts, occupation: bl[ac]k smith. Convicted of fo[r]gery by a court in Giles County, and sentenced to 3 years in the Penitentiary. Received Jan. 20, 1837 and discharged Feb. 20, 1840. Notes: conduct generally good. Number in ledger 86: 263.

Name: Guilford Cook, age 48, born in North Carolina, occupation: shoe maker. Convicted of larceny by a court in Dickson County, and sentenced to 3 years in the Penitentiary. Received Feb. 19, 1837 and discharged Jan. 8, 1840. Notes: pardoned by Gov. Polk. Number in ledger 86: 264.

Name: James E. Allen, age 24, born in Virginia, occupation: labourer. Convicted of g[rand] larceny by a court in Dickson County, and sentenced to 5 years in the Penitentiary. Received Feb. 19, 1837 and discharged Feb. 23, 1842. Notes: conduct exceptionable. Number in ledger 86: 265.

Name: James Miller, age 23, born in Tennessee, occupation: farmer. Convicted of horse stealing by a court in White County, and sentenced to 3 years in the Penitentiary. Received Feb. 19, 1837 and discharged July 12, 1837. Notes: died of chronic diar[r]hea. Number in ledger 86: 266.

Name: Uriah Cummings, age 27, born in Virginia, occupation: carpenter. Convicted of p[etit] larceny by a court in Knox County, and sentenced to 2 years and 6 months in the Penitentiary. Received Mar. 3, 1837 and discharged Sept. 4, 1839. Notes: conduct good. Number in ledger 86: 267.

Name: Frederick Barger, age 54, born in Maryland, occupation: Mayland [sic].

Convicted of passing counterfeit money by a court in Knox County, and sentenced to 3 years in the Penitentiary. Received Mar. 3, 1837 and discharged Apr. 3, 1838. Notes: pardoned by Gov. Cannon. Number in ledger 86: 268.

Name: Samuel Holliday, age 37, born in North Carolina, occupation: farmer. Convicted of volentary [sic] manslaughter by a court in Tipton County, and sentenced to 5 years in the Penitentiary. Received Mar. 6, 1837 and discharged Oct. 11, 1839. Notes: pardoned by Gov. Cannon. Number in ledger 86: 269.

Name: Azariah Parks, age 29, born in North Carolina, occupation: labourer. Convicted of negro stealing by a court in Haywood County, and sentenced to 10 years in the Penitentiary. Received Mar. 11, 1837 and discharged Mar. 11, 1847. Notes: conduct verry [sic] bad. Number in ledger 86: 270.

Name: Isaac Hambleton, age 50, born in Virginia, occupation: labourer. Convicted of rape by a court in Lawrence County, and sentenced to 7 years and 6 months in the Penitentiary. Received Mar. 19, 1837 and discharged Apr. 2, 1844. Notes: conduct good, pardoned. Number in ledger 86: 271.

Name: James H. Brown, age 24, born in Kentucky, occupation: labourer. Convicted of g[rand] larceny by a court in Carroll County, and sentenced to 3 years in the Penitentiary. Received Mar. 21, 1837 and discharged Jan. 28, 1840. Notes: pardoned by Gov. Polk. Number in ledger 86: 272.

Name: Aaron F. Jones, age 33, born in Virginia, occupation: steamer doctor. Convicted of mare stealing by a court in Wilson County, and sentenced to 3 years in the Penitentiary. Received Mar. 21, 1837 and discharged May 12, 1840. Notes: conduct bad. Number in ledger 86: 273.

Name: James Tooley, age 26, born in Ireland, occupation: labourer. Convicted of malicious stabbing by a court in Giles County, and sentenced to 5 years in the Penitentiary. Received Mar. 24, 1837 and discharged Mar. 24, 1842. Notes: conduct exceptionable. Number in ledger 86: 274.

Name: Samuel Moran, age 24, born in Tennessee, occupation: labourer. Convicted of p[etit] larceny by a court in Bedford County, and sentenced to 1 year in the Penitentiary. Received Apr. 18, 1837 and discharged Apr. 11, 1838. Notes: conduct generally good. Number in ledger 86: 275.

Name: William Dean, age 45, born in South Carolina, occupation: labourer. Convicted of murder by a court in Bedford County, and sentenced to 15 years in the Penitentiary. Received Apr. 18, 1837 and discharged Apr. 7, 1846. Notes:

died of inflamation of the bladder. Number in ledger 86: 276.

Name: Lewis Sexton, age 25, born in Tennessee, occupation: labourer. Convicted of larceny by a court in Meigs County, and sentenced to 1 year and 6 months in the Penitentiary. Received Apr. 24, 1837 and discharged Oct. 25, 1838. Notes: conduct fair. Number in ledger 86: 277.

Name: Thomas B. Staley, age 22, born in Tennessee, occupation: labourer. Convicted of p[etit] larceny by a court in Hawkins County, and sentenced to 1 year in the Penitentiary. Received Apr. 25, 1837 and discharged July 2, 1838. Notes: conduct bad. Number in ledger 86: 278.

Name: Thomas Mills, age 32, born in Virginia, occupation: labourer. Convicted of receiving stolen good[s] by a court in Shelby County, and sentenced to 1 year in the Penitentiary. Received May 16, 1837 and discharged Apr. 25, 1838. Notes: coloured, conduct good, pardoned. Number in ledger 86: 279.

Name: Isom Watson, age 26, born in Virginia, occupation: carpenter. Convicted of horse stealing by a court in Maury County, and sentenced to 5 years in the Penitentiary. Received May 19, 1837 and discharged June 4, 1841. Notes: pardoned by Gov. Polk. Number in ledger 86: 280.

Name: William Moore, age 58, born in Virginia, occupation: farmer. Convicted of murder 2nd degree by a court in Fayette County, and sentenced to 14 years in the Penitentiary. Received May 26, 1837 and discharged Nov. 10, 1844. Notes: died of old age & emaciation. Number in ledger 86: 281.

Name: Smith Roberts, age 19, born in Tennessee, occupation: labourer. Convicted of p[etit] larceny by a court in White County, and sentenced to 1 year in the Penitentiary. Received June 18, 1837 and discharged June 29, 1838. Notes: conduct exceptionable. Number in ledger 86: 282.

Name: George W. Anderson, age 26, born in Tennessee, occupation: sad[d]ler. Convicted of p[etit] larceny by a court in White County, and sentenced to 1 year in the Penitentiary. Received June 18, 1837 and discharged June 18, 1838. Notes: conduct good. Number in ledger 86: 283.

Name: Samuel West Pew, age 70, born in Virginia, occupation: labourer. Convicted of p[etit] larceny by a court in Lincoln County, and sentenced to 5 years in the Penitentiary. Received June 22, 1837 and discharged Jan. 22, 1842. Notes: conduct exceptionable. Number in ledger 86: 284.

Tennessee Convicts: Records of the State Penitentiary

Name: John Shepperd, age 34, born in North Carolina, occupation: shoe maker. Convicted of receiving stolen goods by a court in Washington County, and sentenced to 3 years in the Penitentiary. Received July 3, 1837 and discharged July 2, 1840. Notes: discharged, conduct fair. Number in ledger 86: 285.

Name: John Rhea, age 31, born in Tennessee, occupation: farmer. Convicted of grand larceny by a court in Washington County, and sentenced to 3 years in the Penitentiary. Received July 3, 1837 and discharged Apr. 25, 1840. Notes: pardoned by J.K. Polk, conduct good. Number in ledger 86: 286.

Name: Parker Everill, age 46, born in Maryland, occupation: hatter. Convicted of malicious stabbing by a court in Grainger County, and sentenced to 5 years in the Penitentiary. Received July 3, 1837 and discharged Apr. 15, 1842. Notes: pardoned by Gov. Jones. Number in ledger 86: 287.

Name: James Tarleton, age 37, born in North Carolina, occupation: cooper. Convicted of grand larceny by a court in Roane County, and sentenced to 6 years in the Penitentiary. Received July 9, 1837 and discharged July 5, 1843. Notes: conduct fair. Number in ledger 86: 288.

Name: David Gawley, age 36, born in South Carolina, occupation: tailor. Convicted of malicious stabbing by a court in Gibson County, and sentenced to 4 years in the Penitentiary. Received July 15, 1837 and discharged July 15, 1841. Notes: conduct tolerably [sic] only. Number in ledger 86: 289.

Name: James Thompson Sampson, age 30, born in Tennessee, occupation: labourer. Convicted of malicious stabbing by a court in Stewart County, and sentenced to 2 years in the Penitentiary. Received July 24, 1837 and discharged July 12, 1839. Notes: conduct good. Number in ledger 86: 290.

Name: William W. Perry, age 58, born in Wales, occupation: shoe maker. Convicted of rape by a court in Stewart County, and sentenced to 12 years in the Penitentiary. Received July 24, 1837 and discharged Oct. 25, 1848. Notes: pardoned under the act of 1836. Number in ledger 86: 291.

Name: William Bunch, age 16, born in Tennessee, occupation: labourer. Convicted of p[etit] larceny by a court in Grainger County, and sentenced to 1 year in the Penitentiary. Received Sept. 6, 1837 and discharged Aug. 11, 1838. Notes: pardoned, conduct good. Number in ledger 86: 292.

Tennessee Convicts: Records of the State Penitentiary

Name: Samuel Moore, age 40, born in North Carolina, occupation: labourer. Convicted of g[rand] larceny by a court in Maury County, and sentenced to 3 years in the Penitentiary. Received Sept. 11, 1837 and discharged Sept. 15, 1840. Notes: conduct generally good. Number in ledger 86: 293.

Name: James Kyle, age 15, born in Tennessee, occupation: mail carrier. Convicted of robbing U[nited] States mail by a court in Davidson County, and sentenced to 1 year and 6 months in the Penitentiary. Received Sept. 15, 1837 and discharged Mar. 15, 1838. Notes: conduct generally good. Number in ledger 86: 294.

Name: Samuel Whitesides, age 39, born in North Carolina, occupation: labourer. Convicted of p[etit] larceny by a court in Shelby County, and sentenced to 2 years in the Penitentiary. Received Sept. 19, 1837 and discharged May 31, 1839. Notes: died of inflamation of the bowels. Number in ledger 86: 295.

Name: John Brown, age 24, born in Pennsylvania, occupation: labourer. Convicted of p[etit] larceny by a court in Montgomery County, and sentenced to 1 year in the Penitentiary. Received Sept. 26, 1837 and discharged Sept. 15, 1838. Notes: discharged, conduct good. Number in ledger 86: 296.

Name: Jacob Calhoun, age 40, born in North Carolina, occupation: labourer. Convicted of murder 2nd degree by a court in Montgomery County, and sentenced to 20 years in the Penitentiary. Received Sept. 26, 1837 and discharged Jan. 14, 1848. Notes: general pardon by N.S. Brown. Number in ledger 86: 297.

Name: Squire Estep, age 32, born in North Carolina, occupation: labourer. Convicted of horse stealing by a court in Blount County, and sentenced to 5 years in the Penitentiary. Received Oct. 15, 1837 and discharged Feb. 15, 1842. Notes: pardoned by Gov. Jones. Number in ledger 86: 298.

Name: Enoch Estep, age 35, born in North Carolina, occupation: labourer. Convicted of horse stealing by a court in Blount County, and sentenced to 5 years in the Penitentiary. Received Oct. 15, 1837 and discharged Feb. 15, 1842. Notes: pardoned by Gov. Jones. Number in ledger 86: 299.

Tennessee Convicts: Records of the State Penitentiary

Name: Tilmon D. Lovell, age 24, born in Tennessee, occupation: labourer. Convicted of stabbing with intent to kill by a court in Sumner County, and sentenced to 2 years in the Penitentiary. Received Oct. 24, 1837 and discharged Sept. 13, 1839. Notes: pardoned, conduct good. Number in ledger 86: 300.

Name: Joseph Hullet, age 23, born in Tennessee, occupation: labourer. Convicted of g[rand] larceny by a court in Sumner County, and sentenced to 3 years in the Penitentiary. Received Oct. 25, 1837 and discharged Sept. 3, 1840. Notes: pardoned, conduct good. Number in ledger 86: 301.

Name: James Henry, age 31, born in North Carolina, occupation: labourer. Convicted of g[rand] larceny by a court in Rutherford County, and sentenced to 3 years and 6 months in the Penitentiary. Received Oct. 31, 1837 and discharged May 29, 1841. Notes: conduct bad. Number in ledger 86: 302.

Name: John Thompson, age 22, born in Tennessee, occupation: labourer. Convicted of g[rand] larceny by a court in Wayne County, and sentenced to 2 years in the Penitentiary. Received Nov. 12, 1837 and discharged Dec. 2, 1839. Notes: colored, conduct generally good. Number in ledger 86: 303.

Name: Harris Evans, age 42, born in South Carolina, occupation: labourer. Convicted of malicious stabbing by a court in Rhea County, and sentenced to 2 years in the Penitentiary. Received Nov. 17, 1837 and discharged Nov. 18, 1839. Notes: discharged, conduct good. Number in ledger 86: 304.

Name: Jones Brown, age 22, born in Kentucky, occupation: labourer. Convicted of fellony [sic] by a court in Gibson County, and sentenced to 3 years in the Penitentiary. Received Nov. 18, 1837 and discharged Sept. 18, 1839. Notes: discharged, conduct good. Number in ledger 86: 305.

Name: James Lively, age 29, born in Virginia, occupation: labourer. Convicted of mare stealing by a court in Wilson County, and sentenced to 5 years in the Penitentiary. Received Nov. 20, 1837 and discharged Sept. 6, 1842. Notes: pardoned by Gov. Jones. Number in ledger 86: 306.

Name: Sherwood Brake, age 57, born in North Carolina, occupation: labourer. Convicted of felony by a court in Bledsoe County, and sentenced to 3 years in the Penitentiary. Received Nov. 23, 1837 and discharged Nov. 19, 1840. Notes: conduct fair. Number in ledger 86: 307.

Name: David S. Cloppe, age 19, born in North Carolina, occupation: labourer. Convicted of volentary [sic] manslaughter by a court in Carroll County, and sentenced to 5 years in the Penitentiary. Received Nov. 23, 1837 and discharged Sept. 17, 1842. Notes: pardoned by Gov. Jones. Number in ledger 86: 308.

Name: Warren Smith, age 18, born in Tennessee, occupation: labourer. Convicted of p[etit] larceny by a court in Anderson County, and sentenced to 1 year in the Penitentiary. Received Nov. 24, 1837 and discharged Dec. 6, 1838. Notes: alias Warren Graham, discharged, conduct gen'l go. Number in ledger 86: 309.

Name: Addison Leath, age 25, born in Tennessee, occupation: labourer. Convicted of stabbing by a court in Anderson County, and sentenced to 3 years in the Penitentiary. Received Nov. 24, 1837 and discharged Nov. 29, 1839. Notes: pardoned by Gov. Polk. Number in ledger 86: 310.

Name: William H. Randolph, age 43, born in Virginia, occupation: labourer. Convicted of horse stealing by a court in Stewart County, and sentenced to 4 years in the Penitentiary. Received Nov. 26, 1837 and discharged Nov. 15, 1841. Notes: conduct generally good. Number in ledger 86: 311.

Name: William Kenneday, age 18, born in North Carolina, occupation: labourer. Convicted of larceny by a court in Morgan County, and sentenced to 1 year in the Penitentiary. Received Nov. 29, 1837 and discharged Dec. 6, 1839. Notes: conduct exceptionable. Number in ledger 86: 312.

Name: William Gragson, age 30, born in North Carolina, occupation: tailor. Convicted of malicious stabbing by a court in Morgan County, and sentenced to 5 years in the Penitentiary. Received Nov. 29, 1837 and discharged Nov. 25, 1842. Notes: conduct fair. Number in ledger 86: 313.

Name: Curtis Manley, age 25, born in North Carolina, occupation: labourer. Convicted of assault with intent to kill by a court in Henderson County, and sentenced to 3 years in the Penitentiary. Received Dec. 6, 1837 and discharged Dec. 15, 1840. Notes: conduct generally good. Number in ledger 86: 314.

Name: Samuel Rogers, age 21, born in Tennessee, occupation: labourer. Convicted of involentory [sic] manslaughter by a court in Washington County, and sentenced to 2 years in the Penitentiary. Received Dec. 6, 1837 and discharged Dec. 31, 1839. Notes: discharged, conduct not good. Number in ledger 86: 315.

Name: William P. Jacobs, age 21, born in Virginia, occupation: labourer. Convicted of fo[r]gery by a court in Franklin County, and sentenced to 3 years in the Penitentiary. Received Dec. 7, 1837 and discharged Oct. 2, 1840. Notes: pardoned by Gov. Polk, cond't good. Number in ledger 86: 316.

Name: John W. White, age 24, born in Italy, occupation: labourer. Convicted of grand larceny by a court in Davidson County, and sentenced to 3 years in the Penitentiary. Received Dec. 11, 1837 and discharged Sept. 17, 1842. Notes: pardoned by Gov. Jones. Number in ledger 86: 317.

Name: Allen Jonagin [Jarnagin?], age 58, born in North Carolina, occupation: labourer. Convicted of malicious stabbing by a court in Davidson County, and sentenced to 3 years in the Penitentiary. Received Dec. 12, 1837 and discharged Oct. 18, 1840. Notes: pardoned by Gov. Polk, cond. good. Number in ledger 86: 318.

Name: Sterling Hindman, age 23, born in New York, occupation: teacher. Convicted of larceny by a court in Perry County, and sentenced to 3 years in the Penitentiary. Received Dec. 13, 1837 and discharged Dec. 26, 1840. Notes: dishcharged, conduct generally good. Number in ledger 86: 319.

Name: Jacob Parkerson, age 24, born in Tennessee, occupation: labourer. Convicted of larceny by a court in Smith County, and sentenced to 1 year in the Penitentiary. Received Dec. 29, 1837 and discharged Dec. 29, 1838. Notes: conduct good. Number in ledger 86: 320.

Name: Ermando Frazier, age 25, born in North Carolina, occupation: labourer. Convicted of horse stealing by a court in Shelby County, and sentenced to 3 years in the Penitentiary. Received Jan. 21, 1838 and discharged Dec. 27, 1840. Notes: conduct bad. Number in ledger 86: 321.

Name: Blake Husky, age 31, born in Virginia, occupation: mill[w]right. Convicted of arson by a court in Shelby County, and sentenced to 4 years and 5 months in the Penitentiary. Received Jan. 21, 1838 and discharged June 21, 1842. Notes: conduct exceptionable. Number in ledger 86: 322.

Name: John Huffman, age 19, born in Virginia, occupation: labourer. Convicted of horse stealing by a court in Fayett[e] County, and sentenced to 3 years in the Penitentiary. Received Jan. 26, 1838 and discharged Dec. 28, 1840. Notes: pardoned by Gov. Polk, conduct good. Number in ledger 86: 323.

Name: Eli Peek [Peck], age 36, born in Connecticut, occupation: labourer. Convicted of larceny by a court in Jefferson County, and sentenced to 1 year and 6 months in the Penitentiary. Received Jan. 26, 1838 and discharged July 20, 1839. Notes: conduct generally good. Number in ledger 86: 324.

Name: John Downing, age 38, born in North Carolina, occupation: labourer. Convicted of horse stealing by a court in Maury County, and sentenced to 5 years in the Penitentiary. Received Jan. 22, 1838 and discharged Nov. 11, 1842. Notes: pardoned by Gov. Jones. Number in ledger 86: 325.

Name: Samuel Virgil, age 21, born in Tennessee, occupation: sad[d]ler. Convicted of grand larceny by a court in Davidson County, and sentenced to 3 years in the Penitentiary. Received Jan. 27, 1838 and discharged Jan. 27, 1841. Notes: alias Sam Yates, conduct generally good. Number in ledger 86: 326.

Name: Isaac Dale, age 62, born in North Carolina, occupation: labourer. Convicted of murder 1st degree by a court in Davidson County, and sentenced to life in the Penitentiary. Received Feb. 5, 1838 and discharged Apr. 27, 1839. Notes: died of rheumatism. Number in ledger 86: 327.

Name: H.B. McCrory, age 18, born in Alabama, occupation: labourer. Convicted of stealing oxen by a court in Davidson County, and sentenced to 3 years in the Penitentiary. Received Mar. 10, 1838 and discharged Mar. 10, 1841. Notes: conduct only tolerably [sic]. Number in ledger 86: 328.

Name: John Posey, age 56, born in South Carolina, occupation: labourer. Convicted of receiving stolen goods by a court in Lawrence County, and sentenced to 4 years in the Penitentiary. Received Mar. 19, 1838 and discharged Mar. 20, 1842. Notes: conduct exceptionable. Number in ledger 86: 329.

Name: Williams Edwards, age 37, born in North Carolina, occupation: farmer. Convicted of involentary [sic] manslaughter by a court in Washington County, and sentenced to 1 year in the Penitentiary. Received Mar. 29, 1838 and discharged Sept. 13, 1838. Notes: died of marasmus. Number in ledger 86: 330.

Name: Levi Goens, age 38, born in Tennessee, occupation: farmer. Convicted of larceny by a court in Hamilton County, and sentenced to 3 years in the Penitentiary. Received Apr. 4, 1838 and discharged Apr. 5, 1841. Notes: conduct fair. Number in ledger 86: 331.

Name: Thomas K. Henson, age 30, born in Tennessee, occupation: bl[ac]k smith. Convicted of volentory [sic] manslaughter by a court in Perry County, and sentenced to 4 years in the Penitentiary. Received Apr. 10, 1838 and discharged Jan. 30, 1842. Notes: pardoned by Gov. Jones. Number in ledger 86: 332.

Name: Joseph Carr, age 15, born in Tennessee, occupation: labourer. Convicted of petit larceny by a court in Monroe County, and sentenced to 1 year in the Penitentiary. Received May 24, 1838 and discharged May 24, 1839. Notes: conduct good. Number in ledger 86: 333.

Name: Riley Alford, age 58, born in Virginia, occupation: labourer. Convicted of fellony [sic] by a court in Grainger County, and sentenced to 2 years in the Penitentiary. Received May 28, 1838 and discharged May 30, 1840. Notes: conduct good. Number in ledger 86: 334.

Name: John Randolph, age 22, born in Georgia, occupation: merchant. Convicted of larceny by a court in Fayett[e] County, and sentenced to 2 years in the Penitentiary. Received June 9, 1838 and discharged July 25, 1840. Notes: conduct good. Number in ledger 86: 335.

Name: Benjamin Springs, age 22, born in Tennessee, occupation: stage driver. Convicted of grand larceny by a court in White County, and sentenced to 3 years in the Penitentiary. Received June 19, 1838 and discharged May 20, 1841. Notes: pardoned by Gov. Polk. Number in ledger 86: 336.

Name: Andrew Swisegood, age 20, born in North Carolina, occupation: labourer. Convicted of horse stealing by a court in Knox County, and sentenced to 3 years in the Penitentiary. Received July 1, 1838 and discharged May 21, 1841. Notes: pardoned by Gov. Polk. Number in ledger 86: 337.

Name: Peyton Elkins, age 36, born in Tennessee, occupation: labourer. Convicted of g[rand] larceny by a court in Knox County, and sentenced to 3 years in the Penitentiary. Received July 1, 1838 and discharged May 21, 1841. Notes: pardoned by Gov. Polk. Number in ledger 86: 338.

Name: John S. Crocker, age 25, born in New York, occupation: clerk.

Convicted of perjury by a court in McMinn County, and sentenced to 3 years in the Penitentiary. Received July 1, 1838 and discharged May 21, 1841. Notes: pardoned by Gov. Polk. Number in ledger 86: 339.

Name: Perry Daniel, age 27, born in South Carolina, occupation: labourer. Convicted of p[etit] larceny by a court in Overton County, and sentenced to 1 year in the Penitentiary. Received July 3, 1838 and discharged July 4, 1839. Notes: conduct generally good. Number in ledger 86: 340.

Name: Cravan C. Butts, age 20, born in North Carolina, occupation: shoe maker. Convicted of p[etit] larceny by a court in Dyer County, and sentenced to 2 years in the Penitentiary. Received July 4, 1838 and discharged June 3, 1840. Notes: pardoned by Gov. Polk. Number in ledger 86: 341.

Name: George Gillimore, age 19, born in Tennessee, occupation: labourer. Convicted of false token by a court in Doane [sic, Roane?] County, and sentenced to 3 years in the Penitentiary. Received July 8, 1838 and discharged July 10, 1841. Notes: conduct fair. Number in ledger 86: 342.

Name: Alexander Plunket, age 23, born in North Carolina, occupation: labourer. Convicted of bigamy by a court in Hickman County, and sentenced to 2 years in the Penitentiary. Received July 16, 1838 and discharged July 17, 1840. Notes: conduct verry [sic] good. Number in ledger 86: 343.

Name: Robert Chappel, age 24, born in North Carolina, occupation: labourer. Convicted of grand larceny by a court in Hickman County, and sentenced to 1 year in the Penitentiary. Received July 16, 1838 and discharged Apr. 16, 1839. Notes: pardoned by the Gov. Number in ledger 86: 344.

Name: Caleb Holley, age 27, born in North Carolina, occupation: labourer. Convicted of petit larceny by a court in Rutherford County, and sentenced to 3 years in the Penitentiary. Received July 16, 1838 and discharged July 16, 1841. Notes: color[e]d, conduct exceptionable. Number in ledger 86: 345.

Name: Joseph Ward, age 18, born in Georgia, occupation: labourer. Convicted of rape by a court in Lawrence County, and sentenced to 10 years in the Penitentiary. Received July 17, 1838 and discharged Feb. 20, 1846. Notes: pardoned (general) by A.V. Brown. Number in ledger 86: 346.

Name: Joseph Brown, age 14, born in Alabama, occupation: labourer. Convicted of larceny by a court in Williamson County, and sentenced to 3 years

Tennessee Convicts: Records of the State Penitentiary

in the Penitentiary. Received July 20, 1838 and discharged July 13, 1841. Notes: col[ore]d, conduct bad dis [*sic*]. Number in ledger 86: 347.

Name: B.M. Gillispie, age 22, born in North Carolina, occupation: labourer. Convicted of horse stealing by a court in Williamson County, and sentenced to 7 years and 6 months in the Penitentiary. Received July 20, 1838 and discharged Aug. 9, 1845. Notes: pardoned under the act of 1836. Number in ledger 86: 348.

Name: Joshua J. Wilson, age 68, born in Virginia, occupation: bl[ac]k smith. Convicted of murder 2nd degree by a court in Marion County, and sentenced to 10 years in the Penitentiary. Received July 24, 1838 and discharged June 1, 1849. Notes: died of general dropsy. Number in ledger 86: 349.

Name: Lacey W. Pickett, age 25, born in Tennessee, occupation: labourer. Convicted of murder 2nd degree by a court in Hardin County, and sentenced to 21 year in the Penitentiary. Received Aug. 4, 1838 and discharged Jan. 16, 1852. Notes: general pardon by Gov. Campbell. Number in ledger 86: 350.

Name: James M. Abbott, age 21, born in North Carolina, occupation: labourer. Convicted of petit larceny by a court in Bedford County, and sentenced to 1 year in the Penitentiary. Received Aug. 21, 1838 and discharged Aug. 14, 1839. Notes: conduct generally good. Number in ledger 86: 351.

Name: Josiah Winters, age 19, born in Tennessee, occupation: labourer. Convicted of mare stealing by a court in Monroe County, and sentenced to 3 years in the Penitentiary. Received Sept. 21, 1838 and discharged Sept. 21, 1841. Notes: conduct fair. Number in ledger 86: 352.

Name: William Harvey, age 32, born in Viryart [*sic*], occupation: shoe maker. Convicted of horse stealing by a court in Monroe County, and sentenced to 4 years in the Penitentiary. Received Sept. 21, 1838 and discharged Aug. 1, 1842. Notes: pardoned by Gov. Jones. Number in ledger 86: 353.

Name: George Mezells, age 32, born in North Carolina, occupation: shoe maker. Convicted of horse stealing by a court in Haywood County, and sentenced to 3 years in the Penitentiary. Received Oct. 12, 1838 and discharged Aug. 18, 1841. Notes: pardoned by J.K. Polk. Number in ledger 86: 354.

Name: John A. Berry, age 25, born in Virginia, occupation: carpenter.

Convicted of grand larceny by a court in Shelby County, and sentenced to 5 years in the Penitentiary. Received Oct. 18, 1838 and discharged June 30, 1843. Notes: pardoned by Gov. Jones. Number in ledger 86: 355.

Name: Josiah Dayton, age 24, born in Pennsylvania, occupation: tailor. Convicted of grand larceny by a court in Shelby County, and sentenced to 5 years in the Penitentiary. Received Oct. 18, 1838 and discharged July 1, 1843. Notes: pardoned by Gov. Jones. Number in ledger 86: 356.

Name: James Read, age 42, born in Rho[de] Island, occupation: shoe maker. Convicted of grand larceny by a court in Knox County, and sentenced to 4 years in the Penitentiary. Received Oct. 28, 1838 and discharged July 31, 1842. Notes: pardoned by Gov. Jones. Number in ledger 86: 357.

Name: Martin Armstrong, age 40, born in New York, occupation: labourer. Convicted of horse stealing by a court in Roane County, and sentenced to 4 years in the Penitentiary. Received Nov. 7, 1838 and discharged Aug. 12, 1842. Notes: pardoned by Gov. Jones. Number in ledger 86: 358.

Name: Joshua Mullins, age 45, born in Tennessee, occupation: labourer. Convicted of petit larceny by a court in Johnson County, and sentenced to 2 years in the Penitentiary. Received Nov. 29, 1838 and discharged Nov. 29, 1840. Notes: conduct verry [sic] good. Number in ledger 86: 359.

Name: Cha[rle]s Donald, age 22, born in France, occupation: doctor. Convicted of petit larceny by a court in Hamilton County, and sentenced to 1 year in the Penitentiary. Received Dec. 7, 1838 and discharged Nov. 30, 1839. Notes: conduct generally good. Number in ledger 86: 360.

Name: Mark Manns [Manus/Marrs?], age 22, born in North Carolina, occupation: labourer. Convicted of grand larceny by a court in Henderson County, and sentenced to 3 years in the Penitentiary. Received Dec. 8, 1838 and discharged Oct. 18, 1841. Notes: pardoned by Gov. Jones. Number in ledger 86: 361.

Name: Richard Ridgeway, age 21, born in Geo. Town D.C., occupation: painter. Convicted of grand larceny by a court in Davidson County, and sentenced to 3 years in the Penitentiary. Received Dec. 14, 1838 and discharged Dec. 14, 1841. Notes: conduct generally good. Number in ledger 86: 362.

Tennessee Convicts: Records of the State Penitentiary

Name: John Dennis [Demis?], age 24, born in North Carolina, occupation: labourer. Convicted of grand larceny by a court in McNairy County, and sentenced to 3 years in the Penitentiary. Received Dec. 20, 1838 and discharged Nov. 4, 1841. Notes: pardoned by Gov. Jones. Number in ledger 86: 363.

Name: Thos. Howard, age 28, born in North Carolina, occupation: labourer. Convicted of grand larceny by a court in Cannon County, and sentenced to 3 years in the Penitentiary. Received Dec. 20, 1838 and discharged Dec. 30, 1841. Notes: conduct exceptionable. Number in ledger 86: 364.

Name: Alfred Anthony, age 38, born in North Carolina, occupation: bl[ac]ksmith. Convicted of murder by a court in Bedford County, and sentenced to life in the Penitentiary. Received Dec. 24, 1838 and discharged July 8, 1849. Notes: died of inflamation of stomach. Number in ledger 86: 365.

Name: Drury Reed, age 20, born in Tennessee, occupation: farmer. Convicted of mare stealing by a court in Bedford County, and sentenced to 3 years in the Penitentiary. Received Dec. 25, 1838 and discharged Aug. 26, 1842. Notes: conduct tolerably good. Number in ledger 86: 366.

Name: Davenport Romines, age 20, born in Virginia, occupation: sad[d]ler. Convicted of fellony [sic] by a court in McMinn County, and sentenced to 3 years in the Penitentiary. Received Dec. 28, 1838 and discharged Nov. 22, 1841. Notes: pardoned by Gov. Jones. Number in ledger 86: 367.

Name: Henry Hood, age 19, born in Tennessee, occupation: book[k]eeper. Convicted of fellony [sic] by a court in McMinn County, and sentenced to 3 years in the Penitentiary. Received Dec. 28, 1838 and discharged Dec. 29, 1841. Notes: conduct exceptionable. Number in ledger 86: 368.

Name: Joseph Gilbert, age 17, born in Virginia, occupation: farmer. Convicted of murder by a court in Warren County, and sentenced to 2 years in the Penitentiary. Received Dec. 31, 1838 and discharged Jan. 29, 1840. Notes: pardoned by Gov. Polk. Number in ledger 86: 369.

Name: William Peoples, age 42, born in North Carolina, occupation: farmer. Convicted of incest by a court in Bradley County, and sentenced to 10 years in the Penitentiary. Received Jan. 4, 1839 and discharged May 29, 1848. Notes: pardoned under the act of 1836. Number in ledger 86: 370.

Tennessee Convicts: Records of the State Penitentiary

Name: Obadiah May, age 60, born in Virginia, occupation: labourer. Convicted of murder by a court in Madison County, and sentenced to life in the Penitentiary. Received Jan. 15, 1839 and discharged June 28, 1850. Notes: died of cholera. Number in ledger 86: 371.

Name: Jeremiah Oakley, age 39, born in North Carolina, occupation: shoe maker. Convicted of petit larceny by a court in Maury County, and sentenced to 2 years in the Penitentiary. Received Jan. 21, 1839 and discharged Jan. 21, 1841. Notes: conduct good. Number in ledger 86: 372.

Name: Nathan G. Johnson, age 22, born in Tennessee, occupation: labourer. Convicted of horse stealing by a court in Maury County, and sentenced to 3 years in the Penitentiary. Received Jan. 21, 1839 and discharged Jan. 27, 1842. Notes: conduct exceptionable. Number in ledger 86: 373.

Name: John McGrew, age 19, born in Georgia, occupation: labourer. Convicted of horse stealing by a court in Franklin County, and sentenced to 3 years in the Penitentiary. Received Jan. 24, 1839 and discharged Jan. 26, 1842. Notes: conduct exceptionable. Number in ledger 86: 374.

Name: Anthony G. Smith, age 50, born in Virginia, occupation: labourer. Convicted of horse stealing by a court in Monroe County, and sentenced to 5 years in the Penitentiary. Received Jan. 30, 1839 and discharged Oct. 20, 1843. Notes: pardoned by Gov. Jones. Number in ledger 86: 375.

Name: Hiram Hughs, age 33, born in Virginia, occupation: bl[ac]k smith. Convicted of grand larceny by a court in Claiborn[e] County, and sentenced to 3 years in the Penitentiary. Received Feb. 7, 1839 and discharged Feb. 15, 1842. Notes: conduct exceptionable. Number in ledger 86: 376.

Name: Samuel Wyett, age 28, born in North Carolina, occupation: raftsman. Convicted of grand larceny by a court in Davidson County, and sentenced to 3 years in the Penitentiary. Received Feb. 9, 1839 and discharged Dec. 24, 1841. Notes: pardoned under the act of 1836. Number in ledger 86: 377.

Name: Parham Strange, age 46, born in Virginia, occupation: carpenter. Convicted of manslaughter by a court in Davidson County, and sentenced to 7 years in the Penitentiary. Received Feb. 11, 1839 and discharged Sept. 15, 1845. Notes: pardoned under the act of 1836. Number in ledger 86: 378.

Tennessee Convicts: Records of the State Penitentiary

Name: Hezekiah Satterfield, age 23, born in South Carolina, occupation: cabinett [sic] mak[er]. Convicted of petit larceny by a court in Blount County, and sentenced to 2 years in the Penitentiary. Received Feb. 12, 1839 and discharged Jan. 13, 1841. Notes: conduct verry [sic] good. Number in ledger 86: 379.

Name: John Wilson, age 24, born in Virginia, occupation: labourer. Convicted of petit larceny by a court in Blount County, and sentenced to 1 year in the Penitentiary. Received Feb. 12, 1839 and discharged Feb. 13, ,1840. Notes: conduct verry [sic] good. Number in ledger 86: 380.

Name: McDaniel Smith, age 24, born in North Carolina, occupation: labourer. Convicted of bigomy [sic] by a court in Wilson County, and sentenced to 4 years in the Penitentiary. Received Feb. 20, 1839 and discharged Dec. 11, 1842. Notes: pardoned by Gov. Jones. Number in ledger 86: 381.

Name: Orin D. Anson, age 32, born in New York, occupation: stage driver. Convicted of bigomy [sic] by a court in Giles County, and sentenced to 3 years in the Penitentiary. Received Mar. 7, 1839 and discharged Mar. 8, 1842. Notes: conduct exceptionable. Number in ledger 86: 382.

Name: Matthew Murphy, age 28, born in South Carolina, occupation: farmer. Convicted of grand larceny by a court in Wayne County, and sentenced to 3 years in the Penitentiary. Received Mar. 27, 1839 and discharged Feb. 12, 1842. Notes: pardoned by Gov. Jones. Number in ledger 86: 383.

Name: Smith Roberts, age 23, born in Tennessee, occupation: labourer. Convicted of grand larceny by a court in Marion County, and sentenced to 3 years in the Penitentiary. Received Mar. 28, 1839 and discharged Mar. 21, 1842. Notes: 2nd conviction, conduct exceptionable. Number in ledger 86: 384.

Name: William Martin, age 29, born in South Carolina, occupation: labourer. Convicted of petit larceny by a court in Hamilton County, and sentenced to 1 year in the Penitentiary. Received Apr. 2, 1839 and discharged Apr. 3, 1840. Notes: conduct good. Number in ledger 86: 385.

Name: Lewis Kirk, age 42, born in Virginia, occupation: labourer. Convicted of petit larceny by a court in Hardin County, and sentenced to 1 year in the Penitentiary. Received Apr. 7, 1839 and discharged Apr. 7, 1840. Notes: conduct simple. Number in ledger 86: 386.

Tennessee Convicts: Records of the State Penitentiary

Name: Alexander Spears, age 29, born in North Carolina, occupation: bl[ac]k smith. Convicted of grand larceny by a court in Bedford County, and sentenced to 4 years in the Penitentiary. Received Apr. 17, 1839 and discharged Jan. 30, 1843. Notes: 2nd conviction, conduct good, pard. by Gov. Jones. Number in ledger 86: 387.

Name: Orlonzo M. D. Bostick, age 35, born in South Carolina, occupation: tailor. Convicted of bigamy by a court in Benton County, and sentenced to 2 years in the Penitentiary. Received May 11, 1839 and discharged May 11, 1841. Notes: conduct good. Number in ledger 86: 388.

Name: Meflin Hannum, age 47, born in Tennessee, occupation: labourer. Convicted of horse stealing by a court in Robertson County, and sentenced to 3 years in the Penitentiary. Received May 14, 1839 and discharged May 14, 1842. Notes: conduct exceptionable. Number in ledger 86: 389.

Name: William Miles, age 32, born in Tennessee, occupation: labourer. Convicted of grand larceny by a court in Franklin County, and sentenced to 3 years in the Penitentiary. Received May 23, 1839 and discharged Apr. 14, 1842. Notes: pardoned by Gov. Jones. Number in ledger 86: 390.

Name: Jackson Lewis, age 21, born in Virginia, occupation: labourer. Convicted of horse stealing by a court in Montgomery County, and sentenced to 3 years in the Penitentiary. Received May 24, 1839 and discharged Apr. 16, 1842. Notes: pardoned by Gov. Jones. Number in ledger 86: 391.

Name: Michael Corley, age 26, born in Ireland, occupation: pedlar [sic]. Convicted of fo[r]gery by a court in Davidson County, and sentenced to 3 years in the Penitentiary. Received June 3, 1839 and discharged Apr. 1, 1842. Notes: pardoned by Gov. Jones. Number in ledger 86: 392.

Name: Thomas Lamsing, age 25, born in Ireland, occupation: tailor. Convicted of stealing money by a court in Davidson County, and sentenced to 1 year in the Penitentiary. Received June 4, 1839 and discharged June 4, 1840. Notes: conduct good. Number in ledger 86: 393.

Name: John Lavender, age 31, born in Kentucky, occupation: stage driver. Convicted of fo[r]gery by a court in Davidson County, and sentenced to 3 years in the Penitentiary. Received June 4, 1839 and discharged Apr. 2, 1842. Notes: pardoned by Gov. Jones. Number in ledger 86: 394.

Name: Simpson Alexander, age 45, born in South Carolina, occupation: stealing [?]. Convicted of horse stealing by a court in Weakley County, and sentenced to 1 year in the Penitentiary. Received June 4, 1839 and discharged June 11, 1840. Notes: conduct good. Number in ledger 86: 395.

Name: Andrew Duncan, age 33, born in North Carolina, occupation: gun smith. Convicted of counterfeiting by a court in Marshall County, and sentenced to 4 years in the Penitentiary. Received June 13, 1839 and discharged June 19, 1843. Notes: conduct exceptionable. Number in ledger 86: 396.

Name: Daniel Doxey, age 33, born in North Carolina, occupation: labourer. Convicted of malicious stabbing by a court in Marshall County, and sentenced to 2 years in the Penitentiary. Received June 13, 1839 and discharged May 20, 1841. Notes: pardoned by Gov. Polk. Number in ledger 86: 397.

Name: John Wakefield, age 63, born in England, occupation: painter. Convicted of fo[r]gery by a court in Haywood County, and sentenced to 3 years in the Penitentiary. Received June 14, 1839 and discharged Apr. 18, 1842. Notes: pardoned by Gov. Jones. Number in ledger 86: 398.

Name: Prestley L. Smith, age 27, born in Tennessee, occupation: merchant. Convicted of receiving stolen property by a court in Wilson County, and sentenced to 4 years in the Penitentiary. Received June 14, 1839 and discharged Aug. 17, 1842. Notes: died of consumption. Number in ledger 86: 399.

Name: John Lawrence, age 47, born in Pennsylvania, occupation: barber. Convicted of grand larceny by a court in Wilson County, and sentenced to 8 years in the Penitentiary. Received June 14, 1839 and discharged Jan. 2, 1846. Notes: col[ore]d, general pardon by A.V. Brown. Number in ledger 86: 400.

Name: Peter Weaver, age 34, born in Tennessee, occupation: bl[ac]k smith. Convicted of volentory [sic] manslaughter by a court in Lincoln County, and sentenced to 5 years in the Penitentiary. Received June 19, 1839 and discharged June 19, 1844. Notes: conduct fair. Number in ledger 86: 401.

Name: H.W. Thomas, age 47, born in England, occupation: upholsterer. Convicted of larceny by a court in Shelby County, and sentenced to 3 years in the Penitentiary. Received June 22, 1839 and discharged July 31, 1839. Notes:

died of peripneumony [*sic*]. Number in ledger 86: 402.

Name: Williams Innes [Immes?], age 21, born in Tennessee, occupation: farmer. Convicted of larceny by a court in Shelby County, and sentenced to 5 years in the Penitentiary. Received June 22, 1839 and discharged June 22, 1844. Notes: dis [*sic*] conduct fair. Number in ledger 86: 403.

Name: Jesse J. McLoad, age 23, born in North Carolina, occupation: well digger. Convicted of horse stealing by a court in Fayett[e] County, and sentenced to 3 years in the Penitentiary. Received July 7, 1839 and discharged May 12, 1842. Notes: pardoned by Gov. Jones. Number in ledger 86: 404.

Name: William Merrill, age 16, born in Tennessee, occupation: labourer. Convicted of stealing money by a court in Stewart County, and sentenced to 3 years in the Penitentiary. Received July 8, 1839 and discharged July 9, 1842. Notes: conduct fair. Number in ledger 86: 405.

Name: Moses Lowe, age 47, born in Tennessee, occupation: shoe maker. Convicted of petit larceny by a court in Bledsoe County, and sentenced to 2 years in the Penitentiary. Received July 17, 1839 and discharged July 11, 1842. Notes: conduct fair. Number in ledger 86: 406.

Name: Daniel Foust, age 55, born in North Carolina, occupation: cooper. Convicted of house burning by a court in Anderson County, and sentenced to 2 years in the Penitentiary. Received July 20, 1839 and discharged Sept. 25, 1839. Notes: pardoned by the Gove[r]nor. Number in ledger 86: 407.

Name: Robt. Bullington, age 28, born in North Carolina, occupation: painter. Convicted of grand larceny by a court in Knox County, and sentenced to 3 years in the Penitentiary. Received July 24, 1839 and discharged June 22, 1842. Notes: pardoned by Gov. Jones. Number in ledger 86: 408.

Name: James W. Grey, age 50, born in Tennessee, occupation: farmer. Convicted of fellony [*sic*] by a court in Knox County, and sentenced to 3 years in the Penitentiary. Received July 24, 1839 and discharged July 14, 1842. Notes: pardoned by Gov. Jones. Number in ledger 86: 409.

Name: Frederick Branstutter, age 28, born in Tennessee, occupation: labourer. Convicted of petit larceny by a court in Sullivan County, and sentenced to 2 years in the Penitentiary. Received Aug. 14, 1839 and discharged Aug. 14, 1841. Notes: conduct good. Number in ledger 86: 410.

Tennessee Convicts: Records of the State Penitentiary

Name: John Moore, age 45, born in New Jersey, occupation: hatter. Convicted of grand larceny by a court in Sullivan County, and sentenced to 3 years in the Penitentiary. Received Aug. 14, 1839 and discharged July 14, 1842. Notes: 2nd conviction, pardoned by Gov. Jones. Number in ledger 86: 411.

Name: James M. Wright, age 21, born in South Carolina, occupation: labourer. Convicted of grand larceny by a court in Co[c]ke County, and sentenced to 3 years in the Penitentiary. Received Aug. 19, 1839 and discharged Aug. 19, 1842. Notes: conduct fair. Number in ledger 86: 412.

Name: John H[?] Davis, age 50, born in South Carolina, occupation: farmer. Convicted of horse stealing by a court in Bradley County, and sentenced to 4 years in the Penitentiary. Received Sept. 9, 1839 and discharged July 17, 1843. Notes: pardoned by Gov. Jones. Number in ledger 86: 413.

Name: James Joyce, age 36, born in Georgia, occupation: farmer. Convicted of shooting by a court in Marshall County, and sentenced to 2 years and 6 months in the Penitentiary. Received Oct. 13, 1839 and discharged Dec. 4, 1841. Notes: pardoned by Gov. Polk. Number in ledger 86: 414.

Name: Jesse Williams, age 47, born in Georgia, occupation: labourer. Convicted of perjury by a court in Lincoln County, and sentenced to 3 years in the Penitentiary. Received Oct. 20, 1839 and discharged Oct. 18, 1842. Notes: conduct fair. Number in ledger 86: 415.

Name: Benjamin F. Glanton, age 18, born in South Carolina, occupation: labourer. Convicted of grand larceny by a court in Tipton County, and sentenced to 3 years in the Penitentiary. Received Oct. 26, 1839 and discharged Oct. 26, 1842. Notes: conduct exceptionable. Number in ledger 86: 416.

Name: William Campbell, age 33, born in Scotland, occupation: sailor. Convicted of grand larceny by a court in Shelby County, and sentenced to 2 years in the Penitentiary. Received Oct. 26, 1839 and discharged Sept. 14, 1841. Notes: pardoned by Gov. Polk. Number in ledger 86: 417.

Name: Wm. Childress, age 30, born in Tennessee, occupation: labourer. Convicted of grand larceny by a court in Knox County, and sentenced to 2 years in the Penitentiary. Received Nov. 4, 1839 and discharged Sept. 7, 1842. Notes: pardoned by Gov. Jones. Number in ledger 86: 418.

Tennessee Convicts: Records of the State Penitentiary

Name: Lawson Henry, age 37, born in Tennessee, occupation: ped[d]ler. Convicted of grand larceny by a court in Knox County, and sentenced to 3 years in the Penitentiary. Received Nov. 4, 1839 and discharged Nov. 8, 1842. Notes: conduct bad. Number in ledger 86: 419.

Name: William Sparks, age 33, born in North Carolina, occupation: labourer. Convicted of petit larceny by a court in Anderson County, and sentenced to 1 year and 3 months in the Penitentiary. Received Nov. 25, 1839 and discharged Feb. 25, 1841. Notes: conduct good. Number in ledger 86: 420.

Name: Ellmore Lindsay, age 30, born in Tennessee, occupation: labourer. Convicted of horse stealing by a court in Williamson County, and sentenced to 3 years in the Penitentiary. Received Nov. 28, 1839 and discharged Oct. 9, 1842. Notes: pardoned by Gov. Jones. Number in ledger 86: 421.

Name: Wasaha, age 23, born in North Carolina, occupation: labourer. Convicted of larceny by a court in Hamilton County, and sentenced to 3 years in the Penitentiary. Received Dec. 5, 1839 and discharged Nov. 30, 1842. Notes: alias Pigeon, conduct fair. Number in ledger 86: 422.

Name: Jesse Killian, age 34, born in North Carolina, occupation: bl[ac]k smith. Convicted of receiving stolen horse by a court in Hamilton County, and sentenced to 4 years in the Penitentiary. Received Dec. 5, 1839 and discharged Sept. 20, 1843. Notes: conduct good, pardoned by Gov. Jones. Number in ledger 86: 423.

Name: James Jones, age 17, born in Virginia, occupation: labourer. Convicted of horse stealing by a court in Sullivan County, and sentenced to 3 years in the Penitentiary. Received Dec. 9, 1839 and discharged Dec. 13, 1842. Notes: conduct good. Number in ledger 86: 424.

Name: Charles C. Mitchell, age 28, born in Kentucky, occupation: shoe maker. Convicted of hog stealing by a court in DeKalb County, and sentenced to 1 year in the Penitentiary. Received Dec. 16, 1839 and discharged Dec. 13, 1840. Notes: conduct good. Number in ledger 86: 425.

Name: Joshua Cresong, age 19, born in North Carolina, occupation: labourer. Convicted of horse stealing by a court in Bradley County, and sentenced to 3 years in the Penitentiary. Received Jan. 8, 1840 and discharged Nov. 11, 1842. Notes: pardoned by Gov. Jones. Number in ledger 86: 426.

Name: James Dalton, age 29, born in Virginia, occupation: labourer. Convicted of p[etit] larceny by a court in Robertson County, and sentenced to 1 year in the Penitentiary. Received Jan. 12, 1840 and discharged Jan. 13, 1841. Notes: conduct good. Number in ledger 86: 427.

Name: Ayres Childress, age blank, born in December [sic], occupation: tailor. Convicted of p[etit] larceny by a court in Madison County, and sentenced to 3 years in the Penitentiary. Received Jan. 21, 1840 and discharged Jan. 21, 1843. Notes: conduct fair. Number in ledger 86: 428.

Name: James Powers, age 20, born in Georgia, occupation: tailor. Convicted of p[etit] larceny by a court in Madison County, and sentenced to 3 years in the Penitentiary. Received Jan. 21, 1840 and discharged Dec. 11, 1842. Notes: pardoned by Gov. Jones. Number in ledger 86: 429.

Name: Noel K. Johnson, age 24, born in South Carolina, occupation: labourer. Convicted of p[etit] larceny by a court in Madison County, and sentenced to 1 year in the Penitentiary. Received Jan. 21, 1840 and discharged Jan. 21, 1841. Notes: conduct good. Number in ledger 86: 430.

Name: John D. Robinson, age 20, born in Tennessee, occupation: labourer. Convicted of p[etit] larceny by a court in Madison County, and sentenced to 3 years in the Penitentiary. Received Jan. 21, 1840 and discharged Dec. 30, 1842. Notes: pardoned by Gov. Jones. Number in ledger 86: 431.

Name: William Kilbuck, age 23, born in Tennessee, occupation: hatter. Convicted of grand larceny by a court in Maury County, and sentenced to 3 years in the Penitentiary. Received Jan. 21, 1840 and discharged Nov. 10, 1842. Notes: pardoned by Gov. Jones. Number in ledger 86: 432.

Name: Jas. W. Payson, age 30, born in Pennsylvania, occupation: hatter. Convicted of grand larceny by a court in Maury County, and sentenced to 3 years in the Penitentiary. Received Jan. 21, 1840 and discharged Nov. 10, 1842. Notes: pardoned by Gov. Jones. Number in ledger 86: 433.

Name: Godfrey R. Romines, age 50, born in Tennessee, occupation: labourer. Convicted of assault with intent to kill by a court in Henry County, and sentenced to 5 years in the Penitentiary. Received Feb. 1, 1840 and discharged Dec. 6, 1844. Notes: pardoned by Gov. Jones. Number in ledger 86: 434.

Tennessee Convicts: Records of the State Penitentiary

Name: Henderson K. Richards, age 20, born in Tennessee, occupation: labourer. Convicted of bigamy by a court in White County, and sentenced to 3 years in the Penitentiary. Received Feb. 13, 1840 and discharged Feb. 18, 1843. Notes: conduct exceptionable. Number in ledger 86: 435.

Name: Leonard Edins, age 25, born in Tennessee, occupation: labourer. Convicted of murder by a court in White County, and sentenced to 2 years in the Penitentiary. Received Feb. 13, 1840 and discharged Feb. 18, 1842. Notes: conduct tolerable. Number in ledger 86: 436.

Name: William Clark, age 19, born in North Carolina, occupation: labourer. Convicted of petit larceny by a court in White County, and sentenced to 1 year in the Penitentiary. Received Feb. 13, 1840 and discharged Feb. 18, 1841. Notes: conduct good. Number in ledger 86: 437.

Name: Stephen Upton, age 56, born in Georgia, occupation: cooper. Convicted of manslaughter by a court in Overton County, and sentenced to 2 years in the Penitentiary. Received Mar. 11, 1840 and discharged Feb. 12, 1842. Notes: pardoned by Gov. Jones. Number in ledger 86: 438.

Name: Henry Blalock, age 37, born in Virginia, occupation: labourer. Convicted of bigamy by a court in Roane County, and sentenced to 2 years in the Penitentiary. Received Mar. 13, 1840 and discharged Mar. 14, 1842. Notes: alias Peter French, conduct exceptionable. Number in ledger 86: 439.

Name: Murdock Bullard, age 45, born in North Carolina, occupation: labourer. Convicted of grand larceny by a court in Gibson County, and sentenced to 1 year and 6 months in the Penitentiary. Received Mar. 18, 1840 and discharged Sept. 18, 1841. Notes: conduct good. Number in ledger 86: 440.

Name: Elvin Kirk, age 24, born in Tennessee, occupation: sad[d]le tree maker. Convicted of malicious stabbing by a court in Anderson County, and sentenced to 2 years and 3 months in the Penitentiary. Received Mar. 21, 1840 and discharged June 14, 1842. Notes: conduct fair. Number in ledger 86: 441.

Name: Eli Hill, age 29, born in Tennessee, occupation: labourer. Convicted of horse stealing by a court in Hamilton County, and sentenced to 3 years in the Penitentiary. Received Apr. 1, 1840 and discharged Feb. 13, 1843. Notes: conduct good, pardoned by Gov. Jones. Number in ledger 86: 442.

Name: Joseph Freeland, age 21, born in North Carolina, occupation: labourer.

Tennessee Convicts: Records of the State Penitentiary

Convicted of horse stealing by a court in Hawkins County, and sentenced to 3 years in the Penitentiary. Received Apr. 15, 1840 and discharged Feb. 15, 1843. Notes: conduct good, pardoned by Gov. Jones. Number in ledger 86: 443.

Name: Henry Webb, age 39, born in Tennessee, occupation: bl[ac]k smith. Convicted of assault with intent to murder by a court in McMinn County, and sentenced to 5 years in the Penitentiary. Received Apr. 26, 1840 and discharged July 7, 1843. Notes: died of inflamation of the brain. Number in ledger 86: 444.

Name: James R. Gray, age 18, born in Georgia, occupation: bl[ac]k smith. Convicted of felony by a court in McMinn County, and sentenced to 3 years in the Penitentiary. Received Apr. 26, 1840 and discharged Apr. 19, 1843. Notes: conduct fair. Number in ledger 86: 445.

Name: Alexander Webb, age 30, born in Tennessee, occupation: bl[ac]k smith. Convicted of murder by a court in Bradley County, and sentenced to 14 years in the Penitentiary. Received May 7, 1840 and discharged Dec. 8, 1846. Notes: conduct good, pardoned by Gov. Brown. Number in ledger 86: 446.

Name: Morris Artist, age 18, born in North Carolina, occupation: bl[ac]k smith. Convicted of shooting by a court in Madison County, and sentenced to 3 years in the Penitentiary. Received May 4, 1840 and discharged May 4, 1843. Notes: conduct fair. Number in ledger 86: 447.

Name: John Mahaffe, age 23, born in Tennessee, occupation: bl[ac]k smith. Convicted of petit larceny by a court in Bradley County, and sentenced to 1 year in the Penitentiary. Received May 7, 1840 and discharged May 7, 1841. Notes: conduct good. Number in ledger 86: 448.

Name: Elvis Bevil, age 24, born in Virginia, occupation: bl[ac]k smith. Convicted of horse stealing by a court in Grainger County, and sentenced to 4 years in the Penitentiary. Received May 12, 1840 and discharged Feb. 22, 1844. Notes: pardoned, conduct good. Number in ledger 86: 449.

Name: William Mercer, age 24, born in North Carolina, occupation: bl[ac]k smith. Convicted of malicious shooting by a court in Carroll County, and sentenced to 2 years in the Penitentiary. Received May 13, 1840 and discharged Mar. 30, 1842. Notes: pardoned by Gov. Jones. Number in ledger 86: 450.

Tennessee Convicts: Records of the State Penitentiary

Name: Lewis L. Williams, age 23, born in Virginia, occupation: store keeper. Convicted of malicious shooting by a court in Montgomery County, and sentenced to 3 years in the Penitentiary. Received June 2, 1840 and discharged June 2, 1843. Notes: conduct fair. Number in ledger 86: 451.

Name: Henry Kelly, age 20, born in Tennessee, occupation: labourer. Convicted of malicious shooting by a court in Hawkins County, and sentenced to 1 year in the Penitentiary. Received June 9, 1840 and discharged June 9, 1841. Notes: conduct fair. Number in ledger 86: 452.

Name: Jacob L. Anderson, age 24, born in Virginia, occupation: labourer. Convicted of larceny by a court in Fayett[e] County, and sentenced to 4 years in the Penitentiary. Received June 9, 1840 and discharged Mar. 13, 1844. Notes: pardoned by Gov. Jones. Number in ledger 86: 453.

Name: Nancy Ann Smith, age 20, born in Tennessee, occupation: labourer. Convicted of larceny by a court in Bledsoe County, and sentenced to 3 years in the Penitentiary. Received June 14, 1840 and discharged May 12, 1842. Notes: col[ore]d, pardoned by Gov. Jones. Number in ledger 86: 454.

Name: James Grooms, age 70, born in South Carolina, occupation: labourer. Convicted of grand larceny by a court in Shelby County, and sentenced to 3 years in the Penitentiary. Received June 16, 1840 and discharged May 3, 1843. Notes: pardoned by Gov. Jones. Number in ledger 86: 455.

Name: David Oment [Osment?], age 40, born in North Carolina, occupation: gun smith. Convicted of fellony [sic] by a court in Haywood County, and sentenced to 3 years in the Penitentiary. Received June 21, 1840 and discharged May 3, 1843. Notes: pardoned by Gov. Jones. Number in ledger 86: 456.

Name: Edward Land, age 32, born in Virginia, occupation: labourer. Convicted of grand larceny by a court in Overton County, and sentenced to 3 years in the Penitentiary. Received July 1, 1840 and discharged May 2, 1843. Notes: pardoned by Gov. Jones. Number in ledger 86: 457.

Name: Thomas Thompson, age 19, born in Tennessee, occupation: labourer. Convicted of horse stealing by a court in Stewart County, and sentenced to 3 years in the Penitentiary. Received July 14, 1840 and discharged July 15, 1843. Notes: conduct fair. Number in ledger 86: 458.

Tennessee Convicts: Records of the State Penitentiary

Name: Martin Thaxton, age 22, born in Tennessee, occupation: tailor. Convicted of horse stealing by a court in Rutherford County, and sentenced to 3 years and 6 months in the Penitentiary. Received July 22, 1840 and discharged July 22, 1844. Notes: resentenced to 6 months. Number in ledger 86: 459.

Name: Martin Scott, age 25, born in Kentucky, occupation: labourer. Convicted of petit larceny by a court in Bledsoe County, and sentenced to 1 year in the Penitentiary. Received July 23, 1840 and discharged July 15, 1841. Notes: conduct good. Number in ledger 86: 460.

Name: Jackson McGuire, age 24, born in Tennessee, occupation: labourer. Convicted of petit larceny by a court in Franklin County, and sentenced to 1 year in the Penitentiary. Received July 29, 1840 and discharged July 29, 1841. Notes: conduct good. Number in ledger 86: 461.

Name: Wesler [sic] McGuire, age 21, born in Tennessee, occupation: labourer. Convicted of petit larceny by a court in Franklin County, and sentenced to 1 year in the Penitentiary. Received July 29, 1840 and discharged July 29, 1841. Notes: conduct good. Number in ledger 86: 462.

Name: William Prumley, age 25, born in Tennessee, occupation: labourer. Convicted of murder by a court in Marion County, and sentenced to 10 years in the Penitentiary. Received July 30, 1840 and discharged Dec. 12, 1849. Notes: pardoned under the act of 1836. Number in ledger 86: 463.

Name: William Thompson, age 18, born in North Carolina, occupation: labourer. Convicted of horse stealing by a court in Knox County, and sentenced to 3 years in the Penitentiary. Received Aug. 3, 1840 and discharged June 9, 1843. Notes: pardoned by Gov. Jones. Number in ledger 86: 464.

Name: Edward Tyler, age 54, born in North Carolina, occupation: teacher. Convicted of fo[r]gery by a court in Knox County, and sentenced to 3 years in the Penitentiary. Received Aug. 3, 1840 and discharged June 9, 1843. Notes: pardoned by Gov. Jones. Number in ledger 86: 465.

Name: John Busbee [Barbee?], age 21, born in Dixon [sic, Dickson Co. TN?], occupation: labourer. Convicted of murder by a court in Henderson County, and sentenced to 2 years in the Penitentiary. Received Aug. 10, 1840 and discharged May 17, 1841. Notes: pardoned by Gov. Polk. Number in ledger 86: 466.

Name: Isham Walker, age 18, born in Bedford [Co. TN], occupation: labourer. Convicted of forgery by a court in Bedford County, and sentenced to 3 years in the Penitentiary. Received Aug. 15, 1840 and discharged Mar. 2, 1843. Notes: pardoned by Gov. Jones. Number in ledger 86: 467.

Name: Peter W. Tiner, age 27, born in Montgomery [Co. TN], occupation: labourer. Convicted of grand larceny by a court in Montgomery County, and sentenced to 3 years in the Penitentiary. Received Sept. 29, 1840 and discharged Sept. 22, 1843. Notes: conduct exceptionable. Number in ledger 86: 468.

Name: Wm. Summerville, age 25, born in Kentucky, occupation: shoe maker. Convicted of stealing notes by a court in Wilson County, and sentenced to 3 years in the Penitentiary. Received Oct. 3, 1840 and discharged Nov. 6, 1840. Notes: pardoned by Gov. Polk. Number in ledger 86: 469.

Name: Haywood Keith, age 25, born in North Carolina, occupation: labourer. Convicted of horse stealing by a court in Marshall County, and sentenced to 3 years in the Penitentiary. Received Oct. 6, 1840 and discharged Oct. 6, 1843. Notes: conduct exceptionable. Number in ledger 86: 470.

Name: Guilford Payne, age 27, born in Tennessee, occupation: labourer. Convicted of grand larceny by a court in Marshall County, and sentenced to 4 years in the Penitentiary. Received Oct. 6, 1840 and discharged July 15, 1844. Notes: pardoned under the act of 1836. Number in ledger 86: 471.

Name: Thomas Wilson, age 16, born in Tennessee, occupation: labourer. Convicted of grand larceny by a court in Fayette County, and sentenced to 3 years in the Penitentiary. Received Oct. 9, 1840 and discharged Aug. 15, 1843. Notes: pardoned by Gov. Jones. Number in ledger 86: 472.

Name: William G. Harrison, age 24, born in Tennessee, occupation: loafer. Convicted of murder 2nd degree by a court in Davidson County, and sentenced to 15 years in the Penitentiary. Received Oct. 14, 1840 and discharged Apr. 18, 1848. Notes: pardoned by Gov. N.S. Brown. Number in ledger 86: 473.

Name: Benjamin Dennis, age 38, born in South Carolina, occupation: waggoner. Convicted of horse stealing by a court in Davidson County, and sentenced to 3 years in the Penitentiary. Received Oct. 14, 1840 and discharged Aug. 12, 1843. Notes: pardoned by Gov. Jones. Number in ledger

86: 474.

Name: Samuel H. Todd, age 20, born in Virginia, occupation: boatsman. Convicted of robbery by a court in Shelby County, and sentenced to 5 years in the Penitentiary. Received Oct. 25, 1840 and discharged July 24, 1845. Notes: pardoned by Gov. Jones. Number in ledger 86: 475.

Name: William W. Ross, age 19, born in North Carolina, occupation: boatsman. Convicted of robbery by a court in Shelby County, and sentenced to 5 years in the Penitentiary. Received Oct. 25, 1840 and discharged Oct. 25, 1845. Notes: conduct exceptionable. Number in ledger 86: 476.

Name: Larkin Turman, age 32, born in Georgia, occupation: boatsman. Convicted of pettit larceny by a court in Giles County, and sentenced to 1 year in the Penitentiary. Received Oct. 30, 1840 and discharged Dec. 8, 1840. Notes: pardoned by Gov. Polk as he was imbicile. Number in ledger 86: 477.

Name: Martin Armington, age 60, born in Maryland, occupation: boatsman. Convicted of horse stealing by a court in Stewart County, and sentenced to 8 years in the Penitentiary. Received Nov. 13, 1840 and discharged Nov. 15, 1848. Notes: 2nd sentence, conduct passable. Number in ledger 86: 478.

Name: Charles Sherman, age 26, born in Vermont, occupation: stage driver. Convicted of stealing a slay [sic] by a court in Giles County, and sentenced to 5 years in the Penitentiary. Received Oct. 30, 1840 and discharged Oct. 30, 1845. Notes: conduct exceptionable. Number in ledger 86: 479.

Name: Joseph C. Cook, age 23, born in Tennessee, occupation: labourer. Convicted of forgery by a court in Franklin County, and sentenced to 3 years in the Penitentiary. Received Nov. 26, 1840 and discharged Nov. 28, 1843. Notes: conduct fair. Number in ledger 86: 480.

Name: Joseph Fuller, age 23, born in Tennessee, occupation: labourer. Convicted of forgery by a court in Rutherford County, and sentenced to 3 years in the Penitentiary. Received Nov. 30, 1840 and discharged Nov. 21, 1843. Notes: conduct fair. Number in ledger 86: 481.

Name: James Scott, age 38, born in North Carolina, occupation: shoe maker. Convicted of negro stealing by a court in Davidson County, and sentenced to 5 years in the Penitentiary. Received Dec. 15, 1840 and discharged Aug. 30, 1845. Notes: pardoned under the act of 1836. Number in ledger 86: 482.

Tennessee Convicts: Records of the State Penitentiary

Name: James Claxton, age 21, born in Tennessee, occupation: boatsman. Convicted of murder by a court in Davidson County, and sentenced to 5 years in the Penitentiary. Received Dec. 21, 1840 and discharged Mar. 18, 1844. Notes: died of marasumus. Number in ledger 86: 483.

Name: John Heathcock, age 26, born in Tennessee, occupation: labourer. Convicted of maiming by a court in Davidson County, and sentenced to 2 years in the Penitentiary. Received Dec. 31, 1840 and discharged Sept. 4, 1841. Notes: alias Young, pardoned by Gov. Polk. Number in ledger 86: 484.

Name: Elizabeth (female) Henderson, age 22, born in Kentucky, occupation: nothing. Convicted of larceny by a court in Bradley County, and sentenced to 3 years in the Penitentiary. Received Jan. 11, 1841 and discharged Aug. 21, 1841. Notes: pardoned by Gov. Polk. Number in ledger 86: 485.

Name: Daniel McCarty, age 33, born in Tennessee, occupation: bl[ac]k smith. Convicted of larceny by a court in Bradley County, and sentenced to 2 years in the Penitentiary. Received Jan. 11, 1841 and discharged Jan. 1, 1843. Notes: 2nd conviction, conduct good. Number in ledger 86: 486.

Name: John Webster, age 27, born in North Carolina, occupation: tailor. Convicted of larceny by a court in Bradley County, and sentenced to 1 year in the Penitentiary. Received Jan. 11, 1841 and discharged Jan. 13, 1842. Notes: alias Thos. Webb, conduct fair. Number in ledger 86: 487.

Name: James Graham, age 20, born in South Carolina, occupation: labourer. Convicted of fellony [sic] by a court in Jefferson County, and sentenced to 3 years in the Penitentiary. Received Jan. 11, 1841 and discharged Jan. 3, 1844. Notes: conduct fair. Number in ledger 86: 488.

Name: John Calvin, age 20, born in Missouri, occupation: boatsman. Convicted of larceny by a court in Henry County, and sentenced to 3 years in the Penitentiary. Received Jan. 24, 1841 and discharged Jan. 25, 1844. Notes: conduct tolerably [sic] only. Number in ledger 86: 489.

Name: Reuben Thompson, age 26, born in Virginia, occupation: boatsman. Convicted of larceny by a court in Hardeman County, and sentenced to 3 years in the Penitentiary. Received Jan. 24, 1841 and discharged Jan. 24, 1844. Notes: conduct exceptionable. Number in ledger 86: 490.

Name: Robert Pendergrass, age 52, born in South Carolina, occupation: labourer. Convicted of larceny by a court in Monroe County, and sentenced to 3 years in the Penitentiary. Received Jan. 24, 1841 and discharged Dec. 21, 1843. Notes: pardoned by Gov. Jones. Number in ledger 86: 491.

Name: William Gatling, age blank, born in blank, occupation: hatter. Convicted of larceny by a court in Davidson County, and sentenced to blank years in the Penitentiary. Received Jan. 28, 1841 and discharged Dec. 6, 1841. Notes: died of chronic rheumatism. Number in ledger 86: 492.

Name: James Arnett, age 42, born in Virginia, occupation: none. Convicted of passing counterfeit money by a court in Davidson County, and sentenced to 3 years in the Penitentiary. Received Feb. 1, 1841 and discharged Dec. 21, 1843. Notes: pardoned by Gov. Jones. Number in ledger 86: 493.

Name: Willis Carlisle, age 43, born in Georgia, occupation: none. Convicted of horse stealing by a court in Davidson County, and sentenced to 5 years in the Penitentiary. Received Feb. 5, 1841 and discharged Mar. 18, 1842. Notes: escaped. Number in ledger 86: 494.

Name: Henry Manley, age 27, born in North Carolina, occupation: labourer. Convicted of petit larceny by a court in Fayette County, and sentenced to 1 year in the Penitentiary. Received Feb. 8, 1841 and discharged Feb. 8, 1842. Notes: conduct good. Number in ledger 86: 495.

Name: Henry Smith, age 20, born in Alabama, occupation: labourer. Convicted of horse stealing by a court in Fayette County, and sentenced to 5 years in the Penitentiary. Received Feb. 8, 1841 and discharged Feb. 9, 1846. Notes: conduct exceptionable. Number in ledger 86: 496.

Name: Jeremiah Barney, age 17, born in Tennessee, occupation: labourer. Convicted of horse stealing by a court in Fayette County, and sentenced to 5 years in the Penitentiary. Received Feb. 8, 1841 and discharged Apr. 20, 1844. Notes: died of consumption. Number in ledger 86: 497.

Name: Isaac Mahaffy, age 39, born in South Carolina, occupation: labourer. Convicted of murder by a court in Wilson County, and sentenced to 10 years in the Penitentiary. Received Feb. 8, 1841 and discharged June 29, 1850. Notes: pardoned under the act of 1836. Number in ledger 86: 498.

Name: James H. Richards, age 22, born in Tennessee, occupation: labourer.

Tennessee Convicts: Records of the State Penitentiary

Convicted of horse stealing by a court in Lauderdale County, and sentenced to 4 years in the Penitentiary. Received Feb. 11, 1841 and discharged Aug. 15, 1844. Notes: died of chronic diarrhae [sic]. Number in ledger 86: 499.

Name: John Bordine, age 27, born in Virginia, occupation: boatsman. Convicted of larceny by a court in Tipton County, and sentenced to 3 years in the Penitentiary. Received Mar. 8, 1841 and discharged Jan. 7, 1844. Notes: pardoned by Gov. Jones. Number in ledger 86: 500.

Name: Cleveland Estep, age 19, born in North Carolina, occupation: labourer. Convicted of larceny by a court in Carter County, and sentenced to 2 years in the Penitentiary. Received Mar. 20, 1841 and discharged Feb. 13, 1843. Notes: conduct good, pardoned by Gov. Jones. Number in ledger 86: 501.

Name: John Venable, age 16, born in Tennessee, occupation: labourer. Convicted of larceny by a court in Williamson County, and sentenced to 3 years in the Penitentiary. Received Mar. 23, 1841 and discharged Feb. 22, 1844. Notes: conduct good, pardoned by Gov. Jones. Number in ledger 86: 502.

Name: Alexander McClennan, age 28, born in North Carolina, occupation: labourer. Convicted of burglary [sic] & larceny by a court in Hamilton County, and sentenced to 5 years in the Penitentiary. Received Apr. 4, 1841 and discharged Jan. 31, 1843. Notes: died of chronic dysentary. Number in ledger 86: 503.

Name: Stephen Snell, age 41, born in North Carolina, occupation: an ex sh[eri]ff. Convicted of forgery by a court in Henderson County, and sentenced to 3 years in the Penitentiary. Received Apr. 23, 1841 and discharged Feb. 22, 1844. Notes: pardoned by Gov. Jones, conduct good. Number in ledger 86: 504.

Name: Henry Norwood, age 16, born in Tennessee, occupation: none. Convicted of buggery by a court in Carroll County, and sentenced to 5 years in the Penitentiary. Received May 12, 1841 and discharged Jan. 31, 1846. Notes: pardoned under the act of 1836. Number in ledger 86: 505.

Name: William Roach, age 24, born in Tennessee, occupation: labourer. Convicted of larceny by a court in Hardiman [sic] County, and sentenced to 3 years in the Penitentiary. Received May 23, 1841 and discharged Mar. 31, 1843. Notes: conduct good, pardoned. Number in ledger 86: 506.

Tennessee Convicts: Records of the State Penitentiary

Name: Uriah Cummings, age 31, born in Virginia, occupation: labourer. Convicted of larceny by a court in Monroe County, and sentenced to 1 year and 9 months in the Penitentiary. Received May 24, 1841 and discharged Feb. 21, 1843. Notes: conduct good, pardoned. Number in ledger 86: 507.

Name: Amos L. Middleton, age 19, born in Tennessee, occupation: labourer. Convicted of horse stealing by a court in Monroe County, and sentenced to 4 years in the Penitentiary. Received May 24, 1841 and discharged May 24, 1845. Notes: died of bilous [sic] fever. Number in ledger 86: 508.

Name: Zachariah Herrill, age 40, born in North Carolina, occupation: farmer. Convicted of fellony [sic] by a court in Claibourne [sic] County, and sentenced to 1 year in the Penitentiary. Received May 29, 1841 and discharged July 19, 1841. Notes: conduct exceptionable. Number in ledger 86: 509.

Name: Patrick O'Brion, age 19, born in Spain, occupation: pedlar [sic]. Convicted of horse stealing by a court in Davidson County, and sentenced to 3 years in the Penitentiary. Received May 29, 1841 and discharged May 30, 1844. Notes: conduct exceptionable. Number in ledger 86: 510.

Name: Archibald Bradfute, age 16, born in Tennessee, occupation: race rider. Convicted of horse stealing by a court in Warren County, and sentenced to 3 years in the Penitentiary. Received June 2, 1841 and discharged Mar. 30, 1844. Notes: conduct good, pardoned. Number in ledger 86: 511.

Name: Bunell Bradley, age 17, born in Tennessee, occupation: labourer. Convicted of horse stealing by a court in Davidson County, and sentenced to 3 years in the Penitentiary. Received June 7, 1841 and discharged Apr. 6, 1844. Notes: conduct exceptionable, pardoned. Number in ledger 86: 512.

Name: David George, age 25, born in South Carolina, occupation: cook. Convicted of horse stealing by a court in Davidson County, and sentenced to 4 years in the Penitentiary. Received Jun 17, 1841 and discharged May 21, 1845. Notes: negro, pardoned under the act of 1836. Number in ledger 86: 513.

Name: John McBride, age 39, born in Tennessee, occupation: labourer. Convicted of counterfeiter by a court in Shelby County, and sentenced to 8 years in the Penitentiary. Received June 26, 1841 and discharged Nov. 11, 1843. Notes: pardoned by Gov. Jones. Number in ledger 86: 514.

Name: Saml. Larkey, age 30, born in Tennessee, occupation: labourer.

Tennessee Convicts: Records of the State Penitentiary

Convicted of larceny by a court in Shelby County, and sentenced to 3 years in the Penitentiary. Received June 26, 1841 and discharged May 1, 1844. Notes: alias Robt. Matlock, pardoned by Gov. Jones. Number in ledger 86: 515.

Name: Joshua Morgan, age 17, born in Tennessee, occupation: labourer. Convicted of larceny by a court in Green[e] County, and sentenced to 1 year and 9 months in the Penitentiary. Received June 29, 1841 and discharged Mar. 29, 1843. Notes: conduct fair. Number in ledger 86: 516.

Name: James H. Oney, age 23, born in Virginia, occupation: wagon maker. Convicted of horse stealing by a court in Giles County, and sentenced to 3 years in the Penitentiary. Received June 30, 1841 and discharged Mar. 18, 1842. Notes: exceptionable. Number in ledger 86: 517.

Name: Riley Sowelle [Souelle?], age 41, born in Tennessee, occupation: mail rider. Convicted of forgery by a court in Henderson County, and sentenced to 4 years in the Penitentiary. Received July 9, 1841 and discharged July 9, 1845. Notes: conduct passable. Number in ledger 86: 518.

Name: Robert Brooks, age 39, born in Tennessee, occupation: labourer. Convicted of petit larceny by a court in Washington County, and sentenced to 1 year in the Penitentiary. Received July 14, 1841 and discharged July 14, 1842. Notes: conduct fair. Number in ledger 86: 519.

Name: William M. Carter, age 19, born in Indiana, occupation: none. Convicted of horse stealing by a court in Rhea County, and sentenced to 3 years in the Penitentiary. Received July 7, 1841 and discharged May 22, 1844. Notes: pardoned under the act of 1836. Number in ledger 86: 520.

Name: Daniel Estep, age 40, born in North Carolina, occupation: thief. Convicted of grand larceny by a court in Carter County, and sentenced to 3 years in the Penitentiary. Received July 23, 1841 and discharged July 25, 1844. Notes: conduct exceptionable. Number in ledger 86: 521.

Name: William Goff, age 46, born in Virginia, occupation: farmer. Convicted of passing counterfeit money by a court in Bledsoe County, and sentenced to 3 years in the Penitentiary. Received July 23, 1841 and discharged May 22, 1844. Notes: pardoned by Gov. Jones by act 1836. Number in ledger 86: 522.

Name: Andrew Vinson, age 16, born in Alabama, occupation: none. Convicted of larceny by a court in McMinn County, and sentenced to 2 years in the

Penitentiary. Received Aug. 27, 1841 and discharged Sept. 2, 1843. Notes: conduct fair. Number in ledger 86: 523.

Name: William Jones, age 22, born in Tennessee, occupation: labourer. Convicted of grand larceny by a court in Jefferson County, and sentenced to 3 years in the Penitentiary. Received Aug. 30, 1841 and discharged June 25, 1844. Notes: pardoned under the law of 1836. Number in ledger 86: 524.

Name: James Haynie, age 27, born in Tennessee, occupation: labourer. Convicted of perjury by a court in Maury County, and sentenced to 3 years in the Penitentiary. Received Sept. 7, 1841 and discharged Aug. 17, 1844. Notes: pardoned by Gov. Jones under the act of '36. Number in ledger 86: 525.

Name: William Roberts, age 37, born in Tennessee, occupation: labourer. Convicted of larceny by a court in Bradley County, and sentenced to 3 years in the Penitentiary. Received Sept. 10, 1841 and discharged Sept. 1, 1843. Notes: conduct fair. Number in ledger 86: 526.

Name: Aaron Mobley, age 27, born in North Carolina, occupation: labourer. Convicted of murder by a court in Grainger County, and sentenced to 21 year in the Penitentiary. Received Sept. 13, 1841 and discharged May 6, 1852. Notes: pardoned by Gov. W.B. Campbell. Number in ledger 86: 527.

Name: Joel Doolen, age 19, born in Tennessee, occupation: labourer. Convicted of larceny by a court in McNairy County, and sentenced to 3 years in the Penitentiary. Received Sept. 15, 1841 and discharged May 16, 1844. Notes: died of chronic diarrhea. Number in ledger 86: 528.

Name: Lewis Shepherd, age 26, born in Ohio, occupation: plasterer. Convicted of grand larceny by a court in Davidson County, and sentenced to 5 years in the Penitentiary. Received Sept. 23, 1841 and discharged June 18, 1846. Notes: alias Calwart, pardoned under the act of 1836. Number in ledger 86: 529.

Name: Peter W. Hendley, age 50, born in Georgia, occupation: labourer. Convicted of negro stealing by a court in Marshall County, and sentenced to 3 years in the Penitentiary. Received Oct. 3, 1841 and discharged Oct. 4, 1844. Notes: conduct fair. Number in ledger 86: 530.

Name: Jesse S. Turner, age 19, born in Virginia, occupation: labourer. Convicted of horse stealing by a court in Fayett[e] County, and sentenced to 3 years in the Penitentiary. Received Oct. 5, 1841 and discharged Oct. 4, 1844.

Tennessee Convicts: Records of the State Penitentiary

Notes: conduct fair. Number in ledger 86: 531.

Name: Stephen Pearson, age 18, born in Tennessee, occupation: tailor. Convicted of forgery by a court in Wilson County, and sentenced to 4 years in the Penitentiary. Received Oct. 11, 1841 and discharged Aug. 2, 1845. Notes: pardoned under the act of 1836. Number in ledger 86: 532.

Name: William R. Doss, age 36, born in Kentucky, occupation: wool carder. Convicted of bigamy by a court in Robertson County, and sentenced to 2 years in the Penitentiary. Received Oct. 13, 1841 and discharged Oct. 11, 1843. Notes: conduct fair. Number in ledger 86: 533.

Name: Riley H. Melton, age 19, born in Tennessee, occupation: labourer. Convicted of petit larceny by a court in Wayne County, and sentenced to 2 years in the Penitentiary. Received Oct. 14, 1841 and discharged Oct. 14, 1843. Notes: conduct fair. Number in ledger 86: 534.

Name: John Collins, age 48, born in South Carolina, occupation: labourer. Convicted of bigamy by a court in Wayne County, and sentenced to 2 years in the Penitentiary. Received Oct. 14, 1841 and discharged Oct. 14, 1843. Notes: conduct fair. Number in ledger 86: 535.

Name: George W. Dickey, age 56, born in North Carolina, occupation: cooper. Convicted of incest [?] by a court in Lawrence County, and sentenced to 15 years in the Penitentiary. Received Oct. 20, 1841 and discharged July 18, 1849. Notes: died of chronic diarrhea. Number in ledger 86: 536.

Name: Alexander Vines, age 37, born in Tennessee, occupation: grocery keeper. Convicted of larceny by a court in Davidson County, and sentenced to 3 years in the Penitentiary. Received Oct. 20, 1841 and discharged Oct. 22, 1844. Notes: conduct exceptionable. Number in ledger 86: 537.

Name: Michael Corroman, age blank, born in Ireland, occupation: boatsman. Convicted of larceny by a court in Shelby County, and sentenced to 1 year in the Penitentiary. Received Oct. 23, 1841 and discharged Oct. 25, 1842. Notes: conduct fair. Number in ledger 86: 538.

Name: Samuel Wilson, age 47, born in D[ist.] of Columbia, occupation: boatsman. Convicted of larceny by a court in Shelby County, and sentenced to 3 years in the Penitentiary. Received Oct. 23, 1841 and discharged Aug. 18, 1844. Notes: conduct good, com[m]uted by Gov. Jones. Number in ledger 86:

539.

Name: John Sapur [?], age 19, born in Virginia, occupation: mail rider. Convicted of stealing letter from US mail by a court in Knox County, and sentenced to 4 years in the Penitentiary. Received Oct. 30, 1841 and discharged Jan. 23, 1845. Notes: died of chronic diarrhea. Number in ledger 86: 540.

Name: Seath [sic] Sears, age 33, born in Ohio, occupation: labourer. Convicted of larceny by a court in Stewart County, and sentenced to 2 years and 6 months in the Penitentiary. Received Nov. 8, 1841 and discharged Mar. 31, 844. Notes: conduct good, pardoned. Number in ledger 86: 541.

Name: William Shadden, age 49, born in Tennessee, occupation: labourer. Convicted of perjury by a court in Jackson County, and sentenced to 3 years in the Penitentiary. Received Nov. 30, 1841 and discharged June 3, 1844. Notes: died of cholera morbus. Number in ledger 86: 542.

Name: John Perdew, age 20, born in Tennessee, occupation: labourer. Convicted of petit larceny by a court in Sullivan County, and sentenced to 2 years in the Penitentiary. Received Dec. 9, 1841 and discharged Dec. 9, 1843. Notes: negro, conduct good. Number in ledger 86: 543.

Name: Francis McAllister, age 30, born in Tennessee, occupation: labourer. Convicted of petit larceny by a court in Henderson County, and sentenced to 3 years in the Penitentiary. Received Dec. 9, 1841 and discharged Oct. 8, 1844. Notes: pardoned under the act of '36. Number in ledger 86: 544.

Name: James Sartin, age 44, born in Georgia, occupation: labourer. Convicted of murder by a court in Coffee County, and sentenced to 6 years in the Penitentiary. Received Dec. 17, 1841 and discharged Sept. 23, 1847. Notes: pardoned under the act of '36. Number in ledger 86: 545.

Name: John Perdue, age 33, born in Virginia, occupation: labourer. Convicted of passing counterfeit money by a court in Coffee County, and sentenced to 3 years in the Penitentiary. Received Dec. 22, 1841 and discharged Dec. 23, 1844. Notes: conduct fair. Number in ledger 86: 546.

Name: Dillard Williams, age 20, born in North Carolina, occupation: labourer. Convicted of malicious stabbing by a court in Sevier County, and sentenced to 2 years in the Penitentiary. Received Dec. 22, 1841 and discharged Dec. 22,

1843. Notes: conduct fair. Number in ledger 86: 547.

Name: Samuel Smith, age 22, born in North Carolina, occupation: labourer. Convicted of horse stealing by a court in McMinn County, and sentenced to 5 years in the Penitentiary. Received Jan. 10, 1842 and discharged Jan. 10, 1847. Notes: conduct fair. Number in ledger 86: 548.

Name: Hardy Smith, age 21, born in North Carolina, occupation: labourer. Convicted of horse stealing by a court in McMinn County, and sentenced to 4 years in the Penitentiary. Received Jan. 10, 1842 and discharged Sept. 26, 1843. Notes: died of chronic[?] digestion[?]. Number in ledger 86: 549.

Name: Isaac Fullerton, age 30, born in Vermont, occupation: boatsman. Convicted of larceny by a court in McNairy County, and sentenced to 1 year in the Penitentiary. Received Jan. 12, 1841 and discharged Dec. 30, 1842. Notes: pardoned by Gov. Jones. Number in ledger 86: 550.

Name: Anderson Masters, age 17, born in Tennessee, occupation: boatsman. Convicted of grand larceny by a court in Carroll County, and sentenced to 3 years in the Penitentiary. Received Jan. 13, 1841 and discharged Nov. 18, 1844. Notes: col[ore]d, pardoned under the act of '36. Number in ledger 86: 551.

Name: John Armstrong, age 54, born in Maryland, occupation: cooper. Convicted of grand larceny by a court in Davidson County, and sentenced to 3 years in the Penitentiary. Received Jan. 27, 1841 and discharged Nov. 27, 1844. Notes: pardoned under the act of '36. Number in ledger 86: 552.

Name: Obediah Norris [Norrie?], age 25, born in Tennessee, occupation: ferryman. Convicted of manslaughter by a court in Claibourn County, and sentenced to 3 years in the Penitentiary. Received Feb. 1, 1842 and discharged Jan. 16, 1845. Notes: pardoned under the act of '36. Number in ledger 86: 553.

Name: Robert Poole, age 60, born in North Carolina, occupation: labourer. Convicted of manslaughter by a court in Marshall County, and sentenced to 6 years in the Penitentiary. Received Feb. 1, 1842 and discharged Apr. 1, 1845. Notes: died of chronic diarrhea. Number in ledger 86: 554.

Name: Robt. L. Montgomery, age 22, born in Tennessee, occupation: bl[ac]ksmith. Convicted of involentary [sic] manslaughter by a court in

Tennessee Convicts: Records of the State Penitentiary

Lincoln County, and sentenced to 1 year in the Penitentiary. Received Feb. 20, 1842 and discharged Feb. 21, 1843. Notes: conduct exceptionable. Number in ledger 86: 555.

Name: Lemuel G. Miles, age 42, born in Tennessee, occupation: bl[ac]ksmith. Convicted of counterfeiting by a court in Lincoln County, and sentenced to 3 years in the Penitentiary. Received Feb. 20, 1842 and discharged Feb. 21, 1848. Notes: conduct exceptionable. Number in ledger 86: 556.

Name: Reubin Johnson, age 40, born in Virginia, occupation: waggoner. Convicted of renams in state 20 drafts [?] by a court in Virginia [sic] County, and sentenced to 1 year in the Penitentiary. Received Feb. 21, 1842 and discharged Feb. 21, 1843. Notes: conduct good. Number in ledger 86: 557.

Name: Henry Harrell, age 33, born in Ireland, occupation: boatsman. Convicted of grand larceny by a court in Shelby County, and sentenced to 5 years in the Penitentiary. Received Feb. 26, 1842 and discharged Feb. 26, 1847. Notes: conduct fair. Number in ledger 86: 558.

Name: John Simpson, age 24, born in New York, occupation: boatsman. Convicted of grand larceny by a court in Shelby County, and sentenced to 4 years in the Penitentiary. Received Feb. 26, 1842 and discharged Feb. 26, 1846. Notes: conduct exceptionable. Number in ledger 86: 559.

Name: James Ward, age 27, born in New York, occupation: jailer. Convicted of grand larceny by a court in Shelby County, and sentenced to 4 years in the Penitentiary. Received Feb. 26, 1842 and discharged Feb. 26, 1846. Notes: conduct exceptionable. Number in ledger 86: 560.

Name: Jesse Norris, age 46, born in Tennessee, occupation: labourer. Convicted of grand larceny by a court in Dickson County, and sentenced to 3 years in the Penitentiary. Received Feb. 26, 1842 and discharged Feb. 26, 1846. Notes: conduct exceptionable. Number in ledger 86: 561.

Name: Thomas Gaddess, age 19, born in Tennessee, occupation: labourer. Convicted of petit larceny by a court in Overton County, and sentenced to 1 year in the Penitentiary. Received Mar. 11, 1842 and discharged Mar. 10, 1843. Notes: conduct exceptionable. Number in ledger 86: 562.

Name: James E. Murry, age 22, born in Tennessee, occupation: sad[d]ler. Convicted of malicous stabbing by a court in Knox County, and sentenced to 2

Tennessee Convicts: Records of the State Penitentiary

years in the Penitentiary. Received Mar. 14, 1842 and discharged Mar. 14, 1843. Notes: pardoned by Gov. Jones. Number in ledger 86: 563.

Name: James Shelton, age 22, born in Tennessee, occupation: labourer. Convicted of petit larceny by a court in Anderson County, and sentenced to 1 year in the Penitentiary. Received Mar. 25, 1842 and discharged Mar. 25, 1843. Notes: conduct fair. Number in ledger 86: 564.

Name: Thomas Daniels, age 23, born in Tennessee, occupation: boatsman. Convicted of ma[i]ming by a court in Davidson County, and sentenced to 2 years in the Penitentiary. Received Mar. 28, 1842 and discharged Feb. 8, 1844. Notes: pardoned under the law of [18]36. Number in ledger 86: 565.

Name: John McNeal, age 26, born in South Carolina, occupation: labourer. Convicted of larceny by a court in Davidson County, and sentenced to 3 years in the Penitentiary. Received Mar. 28, 1842 and discharged Mar. 5, 1845. Notes: pardoned by Gov. Jones. Number in ledger 86: 566.

Name: Richd. C. Pruett, age 40, born in Georgia, occupation: lawyer. Convicted of horse stealing by a court in Franklin County, and sentenced to 7 years in the Penitentiary. Received Mar. 29, 1842 and discharged June 10, 1843. Notes: died of marasmus. Number in ledger 86: 567.

Name: Herod Bruce, age 29, born in North Carolina, occupation: labourer. Convicted of bigamy by a court in Henderson County, and sentenced to 6 years in the Penitentiary. Received Aug. [*sic*, Apr.] 8, 1842 and discharged Dec. 3, 1847. Notes: pardoned under the act of 1836. Number in ledger 86: 568.

Name: George W. Allen, age 18, born in North Carolina, occupation: tailor. Convicted of larceny by a court in Hamilton County, and sentenced to 1 year in the Penitentiary. Received Aug. [*sic*, Apr.] 12, 1842 and discharged Apr. 6, 1843. Notes: conduct good. Number in ledger 86: 569.

Name: John Mayfield, age 28, born in Tennessee, occupation: labourer. Convicted of malicious stabbing by a court in Hamilton County, and sentenced to 2 years in the Penitentiary. Received Aug. [*sic*, Apr.] 12, 1842 and discharged Feb. 22, 1844. Notes: alias Wyatt, conduct good, pardoned. Number in ledger 86: 570.

Name: Bailey Brooks, age 68, born in Virginia, occupation: labourer. Convicted of manslaughter by a court in Madison County, and sentenced to 2 years in the Penitentiary. Received Aug. [sic, Apr.] 21, 1842 and discharged Nov. 1, 1843. Notes: died of old age. Number in ledger 86: 571.

Name: Talton Johnson, age 67, born in Virginia, occupation: bl[ac]k smith. Convicted of stealing a beehive by a court in Van Buren County, and sentenced to 2 years in the Penitentiary. Received Aug. [sic, Apr.] 30, 1842 and discharged Apr. 28, 1844. Notes: conduct good. Number in ledger 86: 572.

Name: Ake Johnson, age 15, born in Tennessee, occupation: none. Convicted of stealing a beehive by a court in Van Buren County, and sentenced to 1 year in the Penitentiary. Received Aug. [sic, Apr.] 30, 1842 and discharged May 1, 1843. Notes: conduct good. Number in ledger 86: 573.

Name: Philip Kasler, age 38, born in Jermany [sic], occupation: tinner. Convicted of larceny by a court in Madison County, and sentenced to 5 years in the Penitentiary. Received May 4, 1842 and discharged May 4, 1847. Notes: conduct fair. Number in ledger 86: 574.

Name: Lewis R. Holeman, age 26, born in North Carolina, occupation: carpenter. Convicted of manslaughter by a court in Bradley County, and sentenced to 2 years in the Penitentiary. Received May 7, 1842 and discharged May 7, 1844. Notes: conduct exceptionable. Number in ledger 86: 575.

Name: Jesse L. Puckett, age 13, born in Kentucky, occupation: ran rules. Convicted of grand larceny by a court in Warren County, and sentenced to 3 years in the Penitentiary. Received May 18, 1842 and discharged May 18, 1845. Notes: conduct fair. Number in ledger 86: 576.

Name: Theodore Deming, age 32, born in New York, occupation: shoe maker. Convicted of grand larceny by a court in Monroe County, and sentenced to 4 years in the Penitentiary. Received May 21, 1842 and discharged Feb. 24, 1846. Notes: pardoned under act of 1836 by Gov. Brown. Number in ledger 86: 577.

Name: William Nun, age 53, born in Virginia, occupation: labourer. Convicted of petit larceny by a court in Claiborn[e] County, and sentenced to 1 year in the Penitentiary. Received May 29, 1842 and discharged May 29, 1843. Notes: conduct good. Number in ledger 86: 578.

Name: Edward Wyett, age 37, born in Tennessee, occupation: carpenter. Convicted of petit larceny by a court in Wilson County, and sentenced to 1 year

Tennessee Convicts: Records of the State Penitentiary

in the Penitentiary. Received June 6, 1842 and discharged June 5, 1843. Notes: conduct good. Number in ledger 86: 579.

Name: Leslie Clark, age 19, born in Kentucky, occupation: labourer. Convicted of perjory [*sic*] by a court in Wilson County, and sentenced to 3 years in the Penitentiary. Received June 6, 1842 and discharged Jan. 20, 1843. Notes: delr. to Sh'ff. of Davidson Co. pr or[der] of Cou. Number in ledger 86: 580.

Name: Fielding Churchwell, age 24, born in Tennessee, occupation: labourer. Convicted of grand larceny by a court in Wayne County, and sentenced to 3 years in the Penitentiary. Received June 14, 1842 and discharged Apr. 21, 1845. Notes: pardoned under the act of 1836. Number in ledger 86: 581.

Name: Richard Wiggers [Wiggins?], age "he don't know", born in North Carolina, occupation: labourer. Convicted of grand larceny by a court in Robertson County, and sentenced to 1 year in the Penitentiary. Received June 15, 1842 and discharged June 15, 1843. Notes: conduct exceptionable. Number in ledger 86: 582.

Name: George Johnston, age 39, born in Vermont, occupation: shoe mane[?]. Convicted of petit larceny by a court in Obion County, and sentenced to 1 year and 5 months in the Penitentiary. Received June 30, 1842 and discharged Nov. 30, 1843. Notes: conduct fair. Number in ledger 86: 583.

Name: Clements Manning, age 20, born in Tennessee, occupation: boatman. Convicted of manslaughter by a court in Stewart County, and sentenced to 2 years and 6 months in the Penitentiary. Received July 2, 1842 and discharged Dec. 6, 1844. Notes: pardoned by Gov. Jones. Number in ledger 86: 584.

Name: William A. Timmans, age 54, born in Delaware, occupation: soldier. Convicted of rape by a court in Coffee County, and sentenced to 10 years in the Penitentiary. Received July 4, 1842 and discharged Dec. 10, 1851. Notes: pardoned under act of 1836. Number in ledger 86: 585.

Name: John Clasure, age 53, born in Kentucky, occupation: farmer. Convicted of grand larceny by a court in Shelby County, and sentenced to 3 years in the Penitentiary. Received July 6, 1842 and discharged May 21, 1845. Notes: pardoned under act of 1836. Number in ledger 86: 586.

Name: John Tarrance [Torrance?], age 24, born in South Carolina, occupation:

labourer. Convicted of passing counterfeit money by a court in Roane County, and sentenced to 3 years and 9 months in the Penitentiary. Received July 6, 1842 and discharged July 13, 1845. Notes: died of marasmus or chronic mental derangement. Number in ledger 86: 587.

Name: William Hosea, age 17, born in North Carolina, occupation: theif [sic]. Convicted of petit larceny by a court in Washington County, and sentenced to 2 years in the Penitentiary. Received July 14, 1842 and discharged July 14, 1844. Notes: conduct exceptionable. Number in ledger 86: 588.

Name: Levi Hosea, age 16, born in North Carolina, occupation: cob[b]ler. Convicted of petit larceny by a court in Washington County, and sentenced to 2 years in the Penitentiary. Received July 14, 1842 and discharged Nov. 22, 1842. Notes: pardoned by Gov. Jones. Number in ledger 86: 589.

Name: James Foster, age 27, born in Tennessee, occupation: harness maker. Convicted of grand larceny by a court in Bledsoe County, and sentenced to 5 years in the Penitentiary. Received July 20, 1842 and discharged July 15, 1847. Notes: conduct verry [sic] bad. Number in ledger 86: 590.

Name: Charles Lapier, age 21, born in Canada, occupation: sailer [sic]. Convicted of p[etit] larceny by a court in Davidson County, and sentenced to 1 year in the Penitentiary. Received Sept. 7, 1842 and discharged Sept. 7, 1843. Notes: discharged, conduct fair. Number in ledger 86: 591.

Name: George Boatman, age 70, born in Virginia, occupation: farmer. Convicted of incest by a court in Grainger County, and sentenced to 5 years in the Penitentiary. Received Sept. 9, 1842 and discharged Jan. 6, 1843. Notes: died of old age, sent to Gregory. Number in ledger 86: 592.

Name: Andrew Curtis, age 20, born in North Carolina, occupation: tailor. Convicted of larceny by a court in Maury County, and sentenced to 3 years in the Penitentiary. Received Sept. 11, 1842 and discharged Sept. 11, 1845. Notes: kept by order of Attorney General. Number in ledger 86: 593.

Name: Robert Myers, age 22, born in Virginia, occupation: labourer. Convicted of manslaughter by a court in Monroe County, and sentenced to 2 years in the Penitentiary. Received Sept. 28, 1842 and discharged Sept. 28, 1844. Notes: conduct fair. Number in ledger 86: 594.

Name: Danl. McVay, age blank, born in blank, occupation: blank. Convicted

Tennessee Convicts: Records of the State Penitentiary

of vol[untary] manslaughter by a court in Claibourn [sic] County, and sentenced to blank years in the Penitentiary. Received Oct. 1, 1842 and discharged Oct. 4, 1842. Notes: pardoned by Gov. Jones. Number in ledger 86: 595.

Name: Thos. Sr. Bragg, age 53, born in Virginia, occupation: farmer. Convicted of murder 2nd degree by a court in Fayett[e] County, and sentenced to 18 years in the Penitentiary. Received Oct. 9, 1842 and discharged Sept. 5, 1844. Notes: died of chronic diarrhea. Number in ledger 86: 596.

Name: Thos. Jr. Bragg, age 23, born in Virginia, occupation: farmer. Convicted of murder 2nd degree by a court in Fayett[e] County, and sentenced to 18 years in the Penitentiary. Received Oct. 9, 1842 and discharged May 14, 1848. Notes: died of chronic inflamation of the bowels. Number in ledger 86: 597.

Name: Jesse Collins, age 17, born in Tennessee, occupation: bl[ac]k smith. Convicted of horse stealing by a court in Lincoln County, and sentenced to 3 years in the Penitentiary. Received Oct. 13, 1842 and discharged Oct. 14, 1845. Notes: conduct exceptionable. Number in ledger 86: 598.

Name: Abram Spears, age 20, born in Tennessee, occupation: labourer. Convicted of murder 2d degree by a court in Shelby County, and sentenced to 21 year in the Penitentiary. Received Oct. 24, 1842 and discharged May 16, 1845. Notes: died of chronic diarrhea. Number in ledger 86: 599.

Name: W.C. Bailey, age 29, born in North Carolina, occupation: painter. Convicted of 2nd conviction h[orse] stealing by a court in Knox County, and sentenced to 4 years in the Penitentiary. Received Oct. 28, 1842 and discharged Oct. 28, 1846. Notes: alias Ernando Frazier, conduct fair. Number in ledger 86: 600.

Name: John Cornwell, age 40, born in Virginia, occupation: labourer. Convicted of keeping & conceiling [sic] c[ou by a court in Green[e] County, and sentenced to 3 years in the Penitentiary. Received Oct. 28, 1842 and discharged July 20, 1844. Notes: died of consumption. Number in ledger 86: 601.

Name: John B. Benham, age 41, born in Tennessee, occupation: farmer. Convicted of passing counterfeit money by a court in Green[e] County, and sentenced to 4 years in the Penitentiary. Received Oct. 28, 1842 and discharged June 5, 1844. Notes: died of chronic diarrhea. Number in ledger 86: 602.

Name: Calvin Manning, age 18, born in Tennessee, occupation: labourer. Convicted of manslaughter by a court in Stewart County, and sentenced to 2 years in the Penitentiary. Received Nov. 8, 1842 and discharged Oct. 29, 1844. Notes: conduct fair. Number in ledger 86: 603.

Name: Blackwood Lyons, age 21, born in Tennessee, occupation: labourer. Convicted of petit larceny by a court in Gibson County, and sentenced to 1 year in the Penitentiary. Received Nov. 17, 1842 and discharged Nov. 17, 1843. Notes: discharged, conduct good. Number in ledger 86: 604.

Name: Wm. L. Johnson, age 26, born in Tennessee, occupation: labourer. Convicted of passing counterfeit money by a court in Ray [sic, Rhea] County, and sentenced to 3 years in the Penitentiary. Received Nov. 20, 1842 and discharged Nov. 20, 1845. Notes: conduct fair. Number in ledger 86: 605.

Name: William Walters, age 23, born in Virginia, occupation: tan[n]er. Convicted of grand larceny by a court in Washington County, and sentenced to 3 years in the Penitentiary. Received Nov. 20, 1842 and discharged Apr. 4, 1844. Notes: died of brain fever. Number in ledger 86: 606.

Name: Spencer Oliver, age 33, born in Tennessee, occupation: labourer. Convicted of grand larceny by a court in Washington County, and sentenced to 3 years in the Penitentiary. Received Nov. 20, 1842 and discharged Nov. 6, 1845. Notes: conduct fair. Number in ledger 86: 607.

Name: James E. Ray, age 18, born in Tennessee, occupation: labourer. Convicted of horse stealing by a court in Williamson County, and sentenced to 3 years and 3 months in the Penitentiary. Received Nov. 30, 1842 and discharged Nov. 17, 1845. Notes: general pardon by A.V. Brown. [Published 1847 report shows surname as Rhea.] Number in ledger 86: 608.

Name: John Mitchell, age 26, born in England, occupation: machinist. Convicted of grand larceny by a court in Williamson County, and sentenced to 3 years in the Penitentiary. Received Nov. 30, 1842 and discharged Nov. 15, 1845. Notes: pardoned under the act of 1836. Number in ledger 86: 609.

Name: George Bean, age 32, born in Tennessee, occupation: bl[ac]ksmith. Convicted of murder 2nd degree by a court in Hamilton County, and sentenced

Tennessee Convicts: Records of the State Penitentiary

to 21 year in the Penitentiary. Received Dec. 17, 1842 and discharged Oct. 27, 1852. Notes: died of chronic diearrhea [sic]. Number in ledger 86: 610.

Name: James Perry, age 26, born in Tennessee, occupation: labourer. Convicted of forgery by a court in Hamilton County, and sentenced to 3 years in the Penitentiary. Received Dec. 17, 1842 and discharged Dec. 13, 1845. Notes: conduct fair. Number in ledger 86: 611.

Name: Elkanah A. Curry, age 18, born in Tennessee, occupation: labourer. Convicted of malicious shooting by a court in Hickman County, and sentenced to 5 years in the Penitentiary. Received Dec. 24, 1842 and discharged July 24, 1848. Notes: conduct pas[s]able. Number in ledger 86: 612.

Name: Franklin Shook, age 20, born in Tennessee, occupation: labourer. Convicted of petit larceny by a court in McMinn County, and sentenced to 1 year in the Penitentiary. Received Dec. 28, 1842 and discharged Dec. 20, 1843. Notes: conduct fair. Number in ledger 86: 613.

Name: Richard Bradford, age 60, born in Georgia, occupation: labourer. Convicted of not specified by Supreme Court by a court in Davidson County, and sentenced to 3 years in the Penitentiary. Received Jan. 4, 1843 and discharged Jan. 4, 1846. Notes: conduct fair. Number in ledger 86: 614.

Name: David Staggs, age 42, born in Tennessee, occupation: labourer. Convicted of not specified by Supreme Court by a court in Davidson County, and sentenced to 1 year in the Penitentiary. Received Jan. 5, 1843 and discharged Jan. 4, 1844. Notes: conduct good. Number in ledger 86: 615.

Name: James Walker, age 20, born in Kentucky, occupation: labourer. Convicted of petit larceny by a court in Macon County, and sentenced to 1 year in the Penitentiary. Received Jan. 7, 1843 and discharged Jan. 7, 1844. Notes: conduct good. Number in ledger 86: 616.

Name: James Allen, age 27, born in Tennessee, occupation: labourer. Convicted of passing counterfeit money by a court in Davidson County, and sentenced to 3 years in the Penitentiary. Received Jan. 17, 1843 and discharged Jan. 17, 1846. Notes: conduct not good. Number in ledger 86: 617.

Name: Littleberry Bostick, age 48, born in South Carolina, occupation: farmer. Convicted of manslaughter by a court in Davidson County, and sentenced to 2 years in the Penitentiary. Received Jan. 18, 1843 and discharged Dec. 7, 1844.

Tennessee Convicts: Records of the State Penitentiary

Notes: pardoned by Gov. Jones, conduct good. Number in ledger 86: 618.

Name: Abraham Briley, age 21, born in Tennessee, occupation: tailor. Convicted of bigamy by a court in Henry County, and sentenced to 2 years and 6 months in the Penitentiary. Received Jan. 26, 1843 and discharged Feb. 28, 1846. Notes: conduct bad. Published 1845 report shows he escaped June 21, 1845 and was retaken Oct. 4, 1845. See also Gaddy, Swaney and Ferguson who escaped with him. Number in ledger 86: 619.

Name: John Burton, age 34, born in South Carolina, occupation: shoe maker. Convicted of larceny by a court in Monroe County, and sentenced to 1 year in the Penitentiary. Received Jan. 27, 1843 and discharged Jan. 27, 1844. Notes: conduct good. Number in ledger 86: 620.

Name: William Andrews, age 38, born in Pennsylvania, occupation: labourer. Convicted of petit larceny by a court in Monroe County, and sentenced to 1 year in the Penitentiary. Received Jan. 27, 1843 and discharged Jan. 27, 1844. Notes: conduct good. Number in ledger 86: 621.

Name: William Whitaker, age 28, born in Tennessee, occupation: labourer. Convicted of petit larceny by a court in White County, and sentenced to 1 year in the Penitentiary. Received Feb. 18, 1843 and discharged Feb. 19, 1844. Notes: conduct good. Number in ledger 86: 622.

Name: James Gaddy, age 19, born in Tennessee, occupation: labourer. Convicted of horse stealing by a court in Smith County, and sentenced to 3 years in the Penitentiary. Received Feb. 19, 1843 and discharged June 21, 1845. Notes: exceptionable. Published 1845 report shows he escaped June 21, 1845. See also Gaddy, Swaney and Ferguson who escaped with him. Number in ledger 86: 623.

Name: Stanislous Smolenski, age 49, born in Poland, occupation: soldier & printer. Convicted of p[etit] larceny by a court in Shelby County, and sentenced to 1 year in the Penitentiary. Received Feb. 24, 1843 and discharged Feb. 25, 1844. Notes: conduct fair. Number in ledger 86: 624.

Name: Richard Hutson, age 28, born in Tennessee, occupation: stone mason. Convicted of horse stealing by a court in Dickson County, and sentenced to 3 years in the Penitentiary. Received Feb. 27, 1843 and discharged Dec. 8, 1846. Notes: conduct fair. Number in ledger 86: 625.

Name: Thornton Brown, age 20, born in Kentucky, occupation: labourer. Convicted of horse stealing by a court in Sumner County, and sentenced to 3 years in the Penitentiary. Received Feb. 28, 1843 and discharged Jan. 13, 1846. Notes: pardoned under the act of 1836. Number in ledger 86: 626.

Name: William Quimby, age 22, born in Tennessee, occupation: loafer & thief. Convicted of mule stealing by a court in Davidson County, and sentenced to 3 years in the Penitentiary. Received Mar. 11, 1843 and discharged Jan. 13, 1846. Notes: pardoned under the act of 1836. Number in ledger 86: 627.

Name: Thos. Wilkerson, age 20, born in Indiana, occupation: boatsman. Convicted of grand larceny by a court in Tipton County, and sentenced to 3 years in the Penitentiary. Received Mar. 11, 1843 and discharged Jan. 13, 1846. Notes: alias Masters, pardoned under the act of 1836. Number in ledger 86: 628.

Name: Nathaniel Austin, age 50, born in South Carolina, occupation: labourer. Convicted of grand larceny by a court in Roane County, and sentenced to 3 years in the Penitentiary. Received Mar. 15, 1843 and discharged July 17, 1846. Notes: pardoned under the act of 1836. Number in ledger 86: 629.

Name: Daniel Burns, age 57, born in North Carolina, occupation: farmer. Convicted of petit larceny by a court in Rhea County, and sentenced to 1 year in the Penitentiary. Received Mar. 16, 1843 and discharged Mar. 17, 1844. Notes: conduct exceptionable. Number in ledger 86: 630.

Name: Irwin Silvers, age 18, born in North Carolina, occupation: labourer. Convicted of grand larceny by a court in Washington County, and sentenced to 4 years in the Penitentiary. Received Mar. 17, 1843 and discharged June 14, 1845. Notes: died of inflamation stomach & bowels. Number in ledger 86: 631.

Name: Willis Ivy, age 17, born in Tennessee, occupation: labourer. Convicted of petit larceny by a court in Bledsoe County, and sentenced to 1 year in the Penitentiary. Received Mar. 16, 1843 and discharged Mar. 29, 1844. Notes: conduct verry [sic] exceptionable. Number in ledger 86: 632.

Name: Oscar S. Coleman, age 37, born in Virginia, occupation: labourer. Convicted of felony by a court in Anderson County, and sentenced to 3 years in the Penitentiary. Received Mar. 25, 1843 and discharged Dec. 30, 1843. Notes: died of consumption. Number in ledger 86: 633.

Tennessee Convicts: Records of the State Penitentiary

Name: George D. Steel, age 26, born in Kentucky, occupation: labourer. Convicted of maiming by a court in Marion County, and sentenced to 2 years in the Penitentiary. Received Mar. 30, 1843 and discharged Mar. 25, 1845. Notes: conduct fair. Number in ledger 86: 634.

Name: Alfred Turley, age 18, born in Tennessee, occupation: labourer. Convicted of grand larceny by a court in Franklin County, and sentenced to 4 years in the Penitentiary. Received Mar. 31, 1843 and discharged Aug. 17, 1844. Notes: died of chronic diarrhea. Number in ledger 86: 635.

Name: Henry Jr. Moorefield, age 16, born in Tennessee, occupation: labourer. Convicted of murder by a court in Johnson County, and sentenced to 10 years in the Penitentiary. Received April 2, 1843 and discharged Apr. 24, 1850. Notes: general pardon by Gov. Trousdale. Number in ledger 86: 636.

Name: Alexander Henry, age 22, born in Tennessee, occupation: labourer. Convicted of felony by a court in Madison County, and sentenced to 3 years in the Penitentiary. Received Apr. 22, 1843 and discharged Feb. 24, 1846. Notes: pardoned under the act of 1836 by A. Number in ledger 86: 637.

Name: Frederick Green, age 20, born in Tennessee, occupation: labourer. Convicted of larceny by a court in McMinn County, and sentenced to 1 year in the Penitentiary. Received Apr. 28, 1843 and discharged April 28, 1844. Notes: conduct good. Number in ledger 86: 638.

Name: Samuel Davis, age 57, born in Virginia, occupation: labourer. Convicted of petit larceny by a court in VanBuren County, and sentenced to 1 year in the Penitentiary. Received May 1, 1843 and discharged May 1, 1844. Notes: conduct good. Number in ledger 86: 639.

Name: James N Stone, age 39, born in North Carolina, occupation: ferryman. Convicted of murder by a court in Obion County, and sentenced to life in the Penitentiary. Received May 1, 1843 and discharged Oct. 11, 1851. Notes: pardoned by Gov. Trousdale. Number in ledger 86: 640.

Name: William Fergeson, age 43, born in Virginia, occupation: shoe maker. Convicted of keeping & passing c[ounterfeit] by a court in Grainger County, and sentenced to 3 years in the Penitentiary. Received May 8, 1843 and discharged May 8, 1846. Notes: discharged, conduct bad. *Nashville Whig* June 21, 1845, offers reward for his recapture. Number in ledger 86: 641.

Name: Lewis Day, age 35, born in Virginia, occupation: shoe maker. Convicted of manslaughter by a court in Claiborne County, and sentenced to 5 years in the Penitentiary. Received May 31, 1843 and discharged Feb. 21, 1844. Notes: died of consumption (sick when recd). Number in ledger 86: 642.

Name: John Dinham, age 37, born in North Carolina, occupation: shoe maker. Convicted of manslaughter by a court in Davidson County, and sentenced to 2 years in the Penitentiary. Received June 13, 1843 and discharged June 13, 1845. Notes: conduct exceptionable. Number in ledger 86: 643.

Name: James Durham, age 40, born in North Carolina, occupation: shoe maker. Convicted of manslaughter by a court in Davidson County, and sentenced to 2 years in the Penitentiary. Received June 13, 1843 and discharged June 13, 1845. Notes: conduct exceptionable. Number in ledger 86: 644.

Name: James Mares, age 25, born in Tennessee, occupation: stone driver. Convicted of grand larceny by a court in Davidson County, and sentenced to 5 years in the Penitentiary. Received June 13, 1843 and discharged Feb. 26, 1848. Notes: pardoned under the act of 1836. Number in ledger 86: 645.

Name: William M. Burke, age 38, born in Georgia, occupation: labourer. Convicted of bigamy by a court in Wayne County, and sentenced to 5 years in the Penitentiary. Received June 16, 1843 and discharged Feb. 26, 1848. Notes: pardoned under the act of 1836. Number in ledger 86: 646.

Name: George Warren, age 30, born in Virginia, occupation: shoe maker. Convicted of murder by a court in Weakley County, and sentenced to life in the Penitentiary. Received June 22, 1843 and discharged May 31, 1853. Notes: general pardon by Gov. Campbell. Number in ledger 86: 647.

Name: Andrew Eddington, age 29, born in Kentucky, occupation: boatsman. Convicted of grand larceny by a court in Shelby County, and sentenced to 5 years in the Penitentiary. Received June 24, 1843 and discharged Oct. 23, 1846. Notes: died of chronic inflamation of stomac[h] & b[owel. Number in ledger 86: 648.

Name: Jacob Fisher, age 33, born in Switzerland, occupation: harness maker. Convicted of grand larceny by a court in Shelby County, and sentenced to 2 years in the Penitentiary. Received June 24, 1843 and discharged May 21, 1845. Notes: pardoned unpardoned under the act of 1836. Number in ledger 86: 649.

Name: Nathaniel Bruce, age 24, born in Illinois, occupation: boatsman. Convicted of grand larceny by a court in Shelby County, and sentenced to 3 years in the Penitentiary. Received June 24, 1843 and discharged Apr. 18, 1846. Notes: pardoned under the act of 1836. Number in ledger 86: 650.

Name: W.H. Caile, age 21, born in North Carolina, occupation: farmer. Convicted of forgery by a court in Haywood County, and sentenced to 5 years in the Penitentiary. Received June 24, 1843 and discharged June 24, 1848. Notes: conduct only tolerable. Number in ledger 86: 651.

Name: John T. Bruce, age 24, born in Tennessee, occupation: labourer. Convicted of larceny by a court in Fentress County, and sentenced to 1 year and 1 month in the Penitentiary. Received June 29, 1843 and discharged July 1, 1844. Notes: conduct fair. Number in ledger 86: 652.

Name: Geoge L. Blawn [Blaron?], age 33, born in South Carolina, occupation: bl[ac]k smith. Convicted of grand larceny by a court in Knox County, and sentenced to 4 years in the Penitentiary. Received July 4, 1843 and discharged Mar. 30, 1847. Notes: pardoned under the act of 1836. Number in ledger 86: 653.

Name: Frederick Carr, age 17, born in Tennessee, occupation: lo[a]fer & thief. Convicted of petit larceny by a court in Knox County, and sentenced to 2 years in the Penitentiary. Received July 4, 1843 and discharged July 4, 1845. Notes: conduct exceptionable. Number in ledger 86: 654.

Name: Daniel Coleman, age 24, born in Tennessee, occupation: shoe maker. Convicted of petit larceny by a court in Knox County, and sentenced to 1 year in the Penitentiary. Received July 4, 1843 and discharged July 4, 1844. Notes: conduct good. Number in ledger 86: 655.

Name: Robt. Wyatt, age 30, born in South Carolina, occupation: labourer. Convicted of malicious shooting by a court in Stewart County, and sentenced to 5 years in the Penitentiary. Received Jully 5, 1843 and discharged Feb. 14, 1846. Notes: died from injury from stone falling on him. Number in ledger 86: 656.

Tennessee Convicts: Records of the State Penitentiary

Name: Spencer Webb, age 43, born in Tennessee, occupation: labourer. Convicted of petit larceny by a court in Roane County, and sentenced to 1 year and 9 months in the Penitentiary. Received July 8, 1843 and discharged Mar. 3, 1845. Notes: pardoned under the act of 1836. Number in ledger 86: 657.

Name: William Shannon, age 38, born in Ireland, occupation: labourer. Convicted of grand larceny by a court in Tipton County, and sentenced to 6 years in the Penitentiary. Received July 9, 1843 and discharged Feb. 15, 1849. Notes: pardoned under the act of 1836. Number in ledger 86: 658.

Name: James Spencer, age 26, born in Pen[n]sylvania, occupation: labourer. Convicted of petit larceny by a court in Tipton County, and sentenced to 3 years in the Penitentiary. Received July 9, 1843 and discharged May 18, 1846. Notes: pardoned under the act of 1836. Number in ledger 86: 659.

Name: George W. Stone, age 23, born in Tennessee, occupation: brickmaker. Convicted of horse stealing by a court in Gibson County, and sentenced to 7 years in the Penitentiary. Received July 16, 1843 and discharged July 16, 1850. Notes: conduct bad. Number in ledger 86: 660.

Name: Bartholomew F. Callan, age 28, born in England, occupation: harness maker. Convicted of grand larceny by a court in Rutherford County, and sentenced to 3 years in the Penitentiary. Received July 26, 1843 and discharged July 25, 1846. Notes: conduct bad. Number in ledger 86: 661.

Name: Henry Baker, age 38, born in North Carolina, occupation: waggon maker. Convicted of horse stealing by a court in DeKalb County, and sentenced to 3 years in the Penitentiary. Received Aug. 15, 1843 and discharged May 31, 1845. Notes: died of dropsey. Number in ledger 86: 662.

Name: William Harris, age 28, born in Tennessee, occupation: tailor. Convicted of passing counterfeit money by a court in DeKalb County, and sentenced to 3 years in the Penitentiary. Received Aug. 15, 1843 and discharged June 18, 1846. Notes: negro, pardoned under the act of 1836. Number in ledger 86: 663.

Name: Andrew J. Wright, age 23, born in Tennessee, occupation: labourer. Convicted of rape by a court in Knox County, and sentenced to 10 years in the Penitentiary. Received Aug. 15, 1843 and discharged Mar. 10, 1843. Notes: conduct only tolerable good. Number in ledger 86: 664.

Tennessee Convicts: Records of the State Penitentiary

Name: Arthur J. Davis, age 71, born in Tennessee, occupation: labourer. Convicted of murder by a court in Knox County, and sentenced to life in the Penitentiary. Received Aug. 15, 1843 and discharged Nov. 19, 1844. Notes: died of old age. Number in ledger 86: 665.

Name: Nelson Majors, age 28, born in Tennessee, occupation: overseer. Convicted of murder by a court in Hardin County, and sentenced to life in the Penitentiary. Received Aug. 26, 1843 and discharged Apr. 10, 1850. Notes: died of consumption. Number in ledger 86: 666.

Name: Charles M. Carrick, age 37, born in Tennessee, occupation: laborer. Convicted of bigamy by a court in Davidson County, and sentenced to 2 years in the Penitentiary. Received Sept. 9, 1843 and discharged Sept. 11, 1845. Notes: conduct fair. Number in ledger 86: 667.

Name: James H. Rucker, age 39, born in Virginia, occupation: farmer. Convicted of malicious shooting by a court in Davidson County, and sentenced to 2 years in the Penitentiary. Received Sept. 14, 1843 and discharged Aug. 8, 1845. Notes: pardoned under the act of 1836. Number in ledger 86: 668.

Name: William Smith, age 20, born in South Carolina, occupation: labourer. Convicted of grand larceny by a court in Carroll County, and sentenced to 5 years in the Penitentiary. Received Sept. 16, 1843 and discharged Sept. 17, 1848. Notes: conduct only tolerably [sic]. Number in ledger 86: 669.

Name: Larkin Turman[?], age 35, born in Georgia, occupation: labourer. Convicted of harboring runaway slave by a court in Carroll County, and sentenced to 3 years in the Penitentiary. Received Sept. 16, 1843 and discharged Sept. 16, 1846. Notes: conduct bad. Number in ledger 86: 670.

Name: Jesse Chavis, age 35, born in Tennessee, occupation: labourer. Convicted of petit larceny by a court in Campbell County, and sentenced to 1 year in the Penitentiary. Received Sept. 18, 1843 and discharged Sept. 22, 1844. Notes: conduct not good. Number in ledger 86: 671.

Name: Elias Grote, age 28, born in Pennsylvania, occupation: labourer. Convicted of negro stealing by a court in Henry County, and sentenced to 5 years in the Penitentiary. Received Sept. 26, 1843 and discharged June 8, 1848. Notes: pardoned under the act of 1836. Number in ledger 86: 672.

Name: Wade Swann, age 23, born in South Carolina, occupation: labourer.

Convicted of murder by a court in Monroe County, and sentenced to life in the Penitentiary. Received Oct.1, 1843 and discharged Oct. 11, 1853. Notes: pardoned by Gov. Campbell. Number in ledger 86: 673.

Name: William Poindexter, age 20, born in Tennessee, occupation: bl[ac]k smith. Convicted of grand larceny by a court in Hawkins County, and sentenced to 3 years in the Penitentiary. Received Oct. 13, 1843 and discharged Aug. 12, 1846. Notes: pardoned under the act of 1836. Number in ledger 86: 674.

Name: David Mainor, age 36, born in Virginia, occupation: ditcher. Convicted of malicious shooting by a court in Stewart County, and sentenced to 7 years and 5 months in the Penitentiary. Received Nov. 2, 1843 and discharged Apr. 2, 1851. Notes: negro, conduct tolerable. Number in ledger 86: 675.

Name: Charles Matthew, age 26, born in North Carolina, occupation: labourer. Convicted of passing counterfeit coin by a court in Coffee County, and sentenced to 3 years in the Penitentiary. Received Nov. 5, 1843 and discharged Sept. 10, 1846. Notes: pardoned under the act of 1836. Number in ledger 86: 676.

Name: Isaac Nelson, age 15, born in Tennessee, occupation: loafer. Convicted of rape by a court in Knox County, and sentenced to 4 years and 6 months in the Penitentiary. Received Nov. 7, 1843 and discharged Apr. 12, 1848. Notes: conduct passable. Number in ledger 86: 677.

Name: Jack Carmichael, age 26, born in Tennessee, occupation: labourer. Convicted of larceny by a court in Washington County, and sentenced to 4 years in the Penitentiary. Received Nov. 22, 1843 and discharged May 27, 1845. Notes: negro, died of consumption. Number in ledger 86: 678.

Name: Paris Russel, age 35, born in Tennessee, occupation: shoe maker. Convicted of recd a stolen calfskin by a court in Washington County, and sentenced to 2 years and 9 months in the Penitentiary. Received Nov. 22, 1843 and discharged July 1, 1846. Notes: conduct good, pardoned under the act of 1836. Number in ledger 86: 679.

Name: Hiram Godsay, age 24, born in Tennessee, occupation: labourer. Convicted of larceny by a court in Bedford County, and sentenced to 3 years in the Penitentiary. Received Nov. 23, 1843 and discharged Sept. 24, 1846. Notes: pardoned under the act of 1836. Number in ledger 86: 680.

Name: Fielding Carter, age 35, born in North Carolina, occupation: labourer. Convicted of malicious stabbing by a court in Johnson County, and sentenced to 3 years in the Penitentiary. Received Nov. 23, 1843 and discharged Sept. 24, 1846. Notes: pardoned under the act of 1836. Number in ledger 86: 681.

Name: Robert Peoples, age 26, born in North Carolina, occupation: labourer. Convicted of obtaining goods under false pre by a court in Johnson County, and sentenced to 5 years in the Penitentiary. Received Dec. 3, 1843 and discharged July 31, 1848. Notes: pardoned under the act of 1836. Number in ledger 86: 682.

Name: Samuel Hughes, age 31, born in Pennsylvania, occupation: carpenter. Convicted of obtaining goods under false pre by a court in Davidson County, and sentenced to 4 years in the Penitentiary. Received Dec. 7, 1843 and discharged Sept. 17, 1847. Notes: pardoned under the act of 1836. Number in ledger 86: 683.

Name: Samuel alias B.B. Willis, age 21, born in N[ew] Hampshire, occupation: labourer. Convicted of grand larceny by a court in Davidson County, and sentenced to 4 years and 6 months in the Penitentiary. Received Dec. 8, 1843 and discharged June 8, 1848. Notes: conduct tolerable only. Number in ledger 86: 684.

Name: James W. Tarlton, age blank, born in Tennessee, occupation: carpenter. Convicted of grand larceny by a court in [H]umphreys County, and sentenced to 10 years in the Penitentiary. Received Dec. 8, 1843 and discharged April 25, 1853. Notes: pardoned under the act of 1836. Number in ledger 86: 685.

Name: George Thomas, age blank, born in Tennessee, occupation: blank. Convicted of grand larceny by a court in Sullivan County, and sentenced to 3 years in the Penitentiary. Received Dec. 9, 1843 and discharged Sept. 24, 1846. Notes: pardoned under the act of 1836. Number in ledger 86: 686.

Name: Robert Thomas, age blank, born in Tennessee, occupation: blank. Convicted of grand larceny by a court in Sullivan County, and sentenced to 3 years in the Penitentiary. Received Dec. 9, 1843 and discharged Sept. 24, 1846. Notes: pardoned under the act of 1836. Number in ledger 86: 687.

Name: Joseph Evans, age 46, born in South Carolina, occupation: labourer. Convicted of passing counterfeit coin by a court in DeKalb County, and sentenced to 3 years in the Penitentiary. Received Dec. 13, 1843 and discharged July 7, 1844. Notes: died of chronic diarrhea. Number in ledger 86: 688.

Name: John Beningfield, age 21, born in Tennessee, occupation: stage driver. Convicted of forgery by a court in Davidson County, and sentenced to 3 years in the Penitentiary. Received Dec. 13, 1843 and discharged Oct. 10, 1846. Notes: pardoned under the act of 1836. Number in ledger 86: 689.

Name: Alfred H. Campbell, age 31, born in Virginia, occupation: cabinett [sic] maker. Convicted of murder by a court in Henderson County, and sentenced to 11 year in the Penitentiary. Received Dec. 18, 1843 and discharged Sept. 24, 1851. Notes: general pardone by Gov. Trousdale. Number in ledger 86: 690.

Name: Joseph C. Stobingh, age 21, born in Tennessee, occupation: tailor. Convicted of burglary & larceny by a court in Henderson County, and sentenced to 3 years in the Penitentiary. Received Dec. 18, 1843 and discharged Dec. 18, 1846. Notes: conduct not good. Number in ledger 86: 691.

Name: James Lee, age 27, born in Tennessee, occupation: shoe maker. Convicted of stabbing & etc.[?] by a court in Giles County, and sentenced to 5 years in the Penitentiary. Received Dec. 18, 1843 and discharged Sept. 1, 1848. Notes: pardoned under the act of 1836. Number in ledger 86: 692.

Name: William Webb, age 19, born in Tennessee, occupation: labourer. Convicted of grand larceny by a court in Giles County, and sentenced to 3 years in the Penitentiary. Received Dec. 18, 1843 and discharged Dec. 15, 1846. Notes: conduct not good. Number in ledger 86: 693.

Name: Eliza Williams, age 36, born in Tennessee, occupation: whore. Convicted of bigamy by a court in Giles County, and sentenced to 2 years and 6 months in the Penitentiary. Received Dec. 18, 1843 and discharged July 27, 1844. Notes: female, pardoned by Gov. Jones. Number in ledger 86: 694.

Name: Priscilla Childress, age 17, born in Tennessee, occupation: whore. Convicted of larceny by a court in Giles County, and sentenced to 1 year and 6 months in the Penitentiary. Received Dec. 18, 1843 and discharged May 28, 1844. Notes: female, pardoned by Gov. Jones. Number in ledger 86: 695.

Name: Henry Harden, age 19, born in Kentucky, occupation: labourer.

Convicted of horse stealing by a court in Carroll County, and sentenced to 5 years in the Penitentiary. Received Jan. 10, 1844 and discharged Oct. 25, 1848. Notes: pardoned under the act of 1836. Number in ledger 86: 696.

Name: James Power, age blank, born in Tennessee, occupation: harness maker. Convicted of passing counterfeit coin by a court in Davidson County, and sentenced to 3 years in the Penitentiary. Received Jan. 16, 1844 and discharged Nov. 16, 1846. Notes: pardoned under the act of 1836. Number in ledger 86: 697.

Name: John Henshaw, age 19, born in Tennessee, occupation: labourer. Convicted of petit larceny by a court in Warren County, and sentenced to 1 year in the Penitentiary. Received Jan. 19, 1843 and discharged Feb. 24, 1845. Notes: conduct good, except attempt to escape. Number in ledger 86: 698.

Name: Saml. B. Kennedy, age 26, born in Tennessee, occupation: shoe maker. Convicted of petit larceny by a court in Cannon County, and sentenced to 1 year and 10 months in the Penitentiary. Received Jan. 24, 1844 and discharged Nov. 24, 1845. Notes: conduct tolerable only. Number in ledger 86: 699.

Name: Bill, a negro , age [blank], born in [blank], occupation: [blank]. Convicted of [blank] by a court in [blank] County, and sentenced to [blank] years in the Penitentiary. Received Feb. 2, 1844 and discharged Feb. 2, 1854. Notes: confined by special act of the Legislature; died,. Number in ledger 86: 700.

Name: Thomas Marshall, age 29, born in Ireland, occupation: labourer. Convicted of petit larceny by a court in Bedford County, and sentenced to 1 year in the Penitentiary. Received Feb. 4, 1844 and discharged Dec. 16, 1844. Notes: conduct nothing extra. Number in ledger 86: 701.

Name: Martin Thaxton, age 26, born in Tennessee, occupation: tailor. Convicted of attempting to escape by a court in Davidson County, and sentenced to 6 months in the Penitentiary. Received Jan. 22, 1844 and discharged July 31, 1844. Notes: conduct bad. Number in ledger 86: 702.

Name: Logan Hanner [Hamner?], age 17, born in Tennessee, occupation: labourer. Convicted of larceny by a court in Robertson County, and sentenced to 3 years in the Penitentiary. Received Feb. 21, 1844 and discharged Jan. 26, 1845. Notes: died of chronic diarrhea. Number in ledger 86: 703.

Tennessee Convicts: Records of the State Penitentiary

Name: John, a negro , age 25, born in Tennessee, occupation: labourer. Convicted of burglary by a court in Sumner County, and sentenced to 10 years in the Penitentiary. Received Feb. 23, 1844 and discharged May 16, 1846. Notes: died of chronic diarrhea. [Published 1849 report shows death date as May 16, 1849.] Number in ledger 86: 704.

Name: Squire H. Pope, age 36, born in Tennessee, occupation: labourer. Convicted of assault with intent to kill by a court in Lawrence County, and sentenced to 3 years in the Penitentiary. Received Feb. 23, 1844 and discharged Dec. 18, 1846. Notes: pardoned under the act of 1836. Number in ledger 86: 705.

Name: Thos. P. Jackson, age 33, born in New York, occupation: boatsman. Convicted of petit larceny by a court in Shelby County, and sentenced to 1 year and 6 months in the Penitentiary. Received Mar. 13, 1844 and discharged Oct. 18, 1844. Notes: died of chronic diarrhea. Number in ledger 86: 706.

Name: John Orr, age 31, born in Scotland, occupation: labourer. Convicted of petit larceny by a court in Shelby County, and sentenced to 1 year in the Penitentiary. Received Mar. 13, 1844 and discharged Mar. 14, 1845. Notes: conduct fair. Number in ledger 86: 707.

Name: Allen Henderson, age 27, born in Tennessee, occupation: labourer. Convicted of grand larceny by a court in Knox County, and sentenced to 3 years in the Penitentiary. Received Mar. 19, 1844 and discharged Dec. 18, 1846. Notes: negro, pardoned under the act of 1836. Number in ledger 86: 708.

Name: William Swaney, age 25, born in North Carolina, occupation: labourer. Convicted of killing bull by a court in Cocke County, and sentenced to 1 year and 6 months in the Penitentiary. Received April 9, 1844 and discharged June 21, 1845. Notes: drowned in attempting to escape. Number in ledger 86: 709.

Name: David Davis, age 30, born in Wales, occupation: boatsman. Convicted of larceny by a court in Madison County, and sentenced to 1 year in the Penitentiary. Received April 22, 1844 and discharged April 22, 1845. Notes: conduct good. Number in ledger 86: 710.

Name: Richard Johnson, age 44, born in South Carolina, occupation: labourer. Convicted of false token by a court in Madison County, and sentenced to 3 years in the Penitentiary. Received April 22, 1844 and discharged July 5, 1845. Notes: pardoned by J.C. Jones. Number in ledger 86: 711.

Tennessee Convicts: Records of the State Penitentiary

Name: Wade H. Trantham, age 35, born in North Carolina, occupation: labourer. Convicted of vol. manslaughter by a court in McMinn County, and sentenced to 3 years in the Penitentiary. Received May 1, 1844 and discharged Mar. 5, 1847. Notes: pardoned under the act of 1836. Number in ledger 86: 712.

Name: John Simpson, age 22, born in Kentucky, occupation: painter. Convicted of larceny by a court in Madison County, and sentenced to 5 years in the Penitentiary. Received May 10, 1844 and discharged May 10, 1849. Notes: conduct fair. Number in ledger 86: 713.

Name: Stephen Pritchard, age 38, born in North Carolina, occupation: labourer. Convicted of rape by a court in Carroll County, and sentenced to 21 year in the Penitentiary. Received May 16, 1844 and discharged May 10, 1852. Notes: died of chronic diarrhea. Number in ledger 86: 714.

Name: William Jones, age 33, born in Tennessee, occupation: cob[b]ler. Convicted of larceny by a court in Warren County, and sentenced to 3 years and 1 month in the Penitentiary. Received May 22, 1844 and discharged April 21, 1847. Notes: pardoned under the act of 1836. Number in ledger 86: 715.

Name: John H. Calhoun, age 62, born in Virginia, occupation: labourer. Convicted of murder by a court in Madison County, and sentenced to life in the Penitentiary. Received May 23, 1844 and discharged Dec. 13, 1849. Notes: general pardon by W. Trousdale. Number in ledger 86: 716.

Name: Jason Cadle, age 43, born in North Carolina, occupation: labourer. Convicted of larceny by a court in Claiborne County, and sentenced to 2 years in the Penitentiary. Received May 31, 1844 and discharged Sept. 22, 1844. Notes: died of chronic diarrhea. Number in ledger 86: 717.

Name: John Crairy, age 18, born in Tennessee, occupation: labourer. Convicted of horse stealing by a court in Marshall County, and sentenced to 2 years in the Penitentiary. Received June 3, 1844 and discharged June 3, 1846. Notes: conduct fair. Number in ledger 86: 718.

Tennessee Convicts: Records of the State Penitentiary

Name: Peter Smith, age 24, born in Virginia, occupation: labourer. Convicted of petit larceny by a court in Blount County, and sentenced to 1 year and 3 months in the Penitentiary. Received June 12, 1844 and discharged Aug. 8, 1845. Notes: pardoned under the act of 1836. Number in ledger 86: 720.

Name: Jacob Collins, age 47, born in North Carolina, occupation: bl[ac]k smith. Convicted of counterfeiting by a court in Lincoln County, and sentenced to 3 years in the Penitentiary. Received June 14, 1844 and discharged Dec. 16, 1844. Notes: died of general dropsy. Number in ledger 86: 721.

Name: John Speck, age 55, born in North Carolina, occupation: labourer. Convicted of assault with intent to kill by a court in Lincoln County, and sentenced to 3 years in the Penitentiary. Received June 14, 1844 and discharged April 8, 1847. Notes: pardoned under the act of 1836. Number in ledger 86: 722.

Name: Leander (W) Speck, age 25, born in Tennessee, occupation: labourer. Convicted of assault with intent to kill by a court in Lincoln County, and sentenced to 3 years in the Penitentiary. Received June 14, 1844 and discharged April 8, 1847. Notes: pardoned under the act of 1836. Number in ledger 86: 723.

Name: William Ballentire, age 30, born in Pennsylvania, occupation: rigger. Convicted of grand larceny by a court in Shelby County, and sentenced to 3 years in the Penitentiary. Received June 23, 1844 and discharged April 22, 1847. Notes: pardoned under the act of 1836. Number in ledger 86: 724.

Name: Jesse B. Kirksey, age 39, born in North Carolina, occupation: butcher. Convicted of grand larceny by a court in Shelby County, and sentenced to 3 years in the Penitentiary. Received July 12, 1844 and discharged July 12, 1847. Notes: conduct passable. Number in ledger 86: 725.

Name: James Sanders, age 27, born in Scotland, occupation: labourer. Convicted of receiving stolen goods by a court in Shelby County, and sentenced to 3 years and 6 months in the Penitentiary. Received July 12, 1844 and discharged Dec. 3, 1847. Notes: pardoned under the act of 1836. Number in ledger 86: 726.

Name: George Vance, age 28, born in Tennessee, occupation: labourer. Convicted of petit larceny by a court in Washington County, and sentenced to 2 years in the Penitentiary. Received July 12, 1844 and discharged July 12, 1846.

Notes: conduct passable. Number in ledger 86: 727.

Name: Cornelius Burrus, age 16, born in Tennessee, occupation: labourer. Convicted of horse stealing by a court in Bledsoe County, and sentenced to 3 years in the Penitentiary. Received July 17, 1844 and discharged June 26, 1847. Notes: pardoned under the act of 1836. Number in ledger 86: 728.

Name: William W. Hancock, age 19, born in Tennessee, occupation: bl[ac]k smith. Convicted of petit larceny by a court in Humphries County, and sentenced to 1 year in the Penitentiary. Received Aug. 11, 1844 and discharged Aug. 8, 1845. Notes: conduct passable. Number in ledger 86: 729.

Name: Aaron W. Gregory, age 22, born in Tennessee, occupation: farmer. Convicted of mare stealing by a court in Bedford County, and sentenced to 4 years in the Penitentiary. Received Aug. 20, 1844 and discharged Aug. 20, 1848. Notes: conduct bad. Number in ledger 86: 730.

Name: Elias M. Walker, age 23, born in Georgia, occupation: labourer. Convicted of felony by a court in McMinn County, and sentenced to 3 years in the Penitentiary. Received Aug. 25, 1844 and discharged June 26, 1847. Notes: pardoned under the act of 1836. Number in ledger 86: 731.

Name: John Davis, age 22, born in South Carolina, occupation: labourer. Convicted of murder by a court in McMinn County, and sentenced to 21 year in the Penitentiary. Received Aug. 25, 1844 and discharged Nov. 25, 1853. Notes: pardoned by Gov. Johnson. Number in ledger 86: 732.

Name: Alexander B. McNickol, age 35, born in Tennessee, occupation: labourer. Convicted of mare stealing by a court in Smith County, and sentenced to 4 years in the Penitentiary. Received Sept. 3, 1844 and discharged Aug. 14, 1846. Notes: died of chronic diarrhea. Number in ledger 86: 733.

Name: Reuben Clark, age 19, born in Tennessee, occupation: labourer. Convicted of horse breaking [sic] by a court in Madison County, and sentenced to 3 years in the Penitentiary. Received Sept. 7, 1844 and discharged Sept. 7, 1847. Notes: conduct fair. Number in ledger 86: 734.

Name: James H. Tucker, age 35, born in New York, occupation: waggon [sic] maker. Convicted of petit larceny by a court in Maury County, and sentenced to 2 years in the Penitentiary. Received Sept. 9, 1844 and discharged Sept. 9, 1846. Notes: conduct passable. Number in ledger 86: 735.

Name: Augustine Torbett, age 30, born in Virginia, occupation: labourer. Convicted of mal[icious] stabbing by a court in Bradley County, and sentenced to 2 years in the Penitentiary. Received Sept. 18, 1844 and discharged July 28, 1846. Notes: pardoned under the act of 1836. Number in ledger 86: 736.

Name: Jacob Oxford, age 50, born in North Carolina, occupation: labourer. Convicted of petit larceny by a court in Bradley County, and sentenced to 1 year in the Penitentiary. Received Sept. 18, 1844 and discharged Sept. 15, 1845. Notes: conduct generally good. Number in ledger 86: 737.

Name: Jacob Lacy, age blank, born in Virginia, occupation: bl[ac]k smith. Convicted of petit larceny by a court in Hardin County, and sentenced to 1 year in the Penitentiary. Received Oct. 2, 1844 and discharged Oct. 2, 1844. Notes: negro, conduct generally passable. Number in ledger 86: 738.

Name: John F. Henderson, age 23, born in Tennessee, occupation: labourer. Convicted of negro stealing by a court in Fayett[e] County, and sentenced to 8 years in the Penitentiary. Received Oct. 3, 1844 and discharged Apr. 3, 1852. Notes: pardoned under the act of 1836. Number in ledger 86: 739.

Name: John Wilson, age 19, born in Tennessee, occupation: labourer. Convicted of petit larceny by a court in White County, and sentenced to 1 year in the Penitentiary. Received Oct. 14, 1844 and discharged Oct. 15, 1845. Notes: alias And. Vinson, conduct fair. Number in ledger 86: 740.

Name: William Reagle [Reayle?], age 37, born in Virginia, occupation: rough carpenter. Convicted of bigamy by a court in Blount County, and sentenced to 5 years in the Penitentiary. Received Oct. 14, 1844 and discharged June 9, 1849. Notes: pardoned under the act of 1836. Number in ledger 86: 741.

Name: John Forest, age 24, born in New York, occupation: spinner[?]. Convicted of petit larceny by a court in Robertson County, and sentenced to 1 year in the Penitentiary. Received Oct. 15, 1844 and discharged Oct. 12, 1845. Notes: conduct fair. Number in ledger 86: 742.

Name: Washington Nixon, age 27, born in Georgia, occupation: cabinett [sic] maker. Convicted of horse stealing by a court in Knox County, and sentenced to 3 years in the Penitentiary. Received Nov. 12, 1844 and discharged Sept. 23, 1847. Notes: pardoned under the act of 1836. Number in ledger 86: 743.

Name: William L. Neal, age 37, born in D[istrict of] C[olumbia], occupation: cabinett [sic] maker. Convicted of petit larceny by a court in Gibson County, and sentenced to 1 year in the Penitentiary. Received Nov. 14, 1844 and discharged Nov. 14, 1845. Notes: conduct good. Number in ledger 86: 744.

Name: Henry Stanmire, age 25, born in Pennsylvania, occupation: boatsman. Convicted of stabbing by a court in Montgomery County, and sentenced to 4 years in the Penitentiary. Received Nov. 15, 1844 and discharged Nov. 15, 1848. Notes: conduct bad. Number in ledger 86: 745.

Name: John S. Alexander, age 19, born in Tennessee, occupation: labourer. Convicted of petit larceny by a court in Rutherford County, and sentenced to 1 year in the Penitentiary. Received Nov. 21, 1844 and discharged Nov. 21, 1845. Notes: conduct fair. Number in ledger 86: 746.

Name: Anderson J. Minton, age 26, born in South Carolina, occupation: tan[n]er. Convicted of burglary by a court in Obion County, and sentenced to 7 years and 6 months in the Penitentiary. Received Nov. 22, 1844 and discharged Dec. 11, 1851. Notes: pardoned under the act of 1836. Number in ledger 86: 747.

Name: William Fasting, age blank, born in Germany, occupation: labourer. Convicted of grand larceny by a court in Shelby County, and sentenced to 3 years in the Penitentiary. Received Nov. 23, 1844 and discharged Sept. 30, 1847. Notes: pardoned under the act of 1836. Number in ledger 86: 748.

Name: James Cross, age 20, born in Tennessee, occupation: labourer. Convicted of petit larceny by a court in Hamilton County, and sentenced to 1 year in the Penitentiary. Received Dec. 10, 1844 and discharged Dec. 4, 1845. Notes: conduct good. Number in ledger 86: 749.

Name: James Gray, age 23, born in Tennessee, occupation: labourer. Convicted of grand larceny by a court in McMinn County, and sentenced to 3 years in the Penitentiary. Received Dec. 24, 1844 and discharged Dec. 23, 1847. Notes: 2nd conviction, conduct fair. Number in ledger 86: 750.

Name: Mehala Brewer, age 18, born in Virginia, occupation: nothing. Convicted of petit larceny by a court in Grainger County, and sentenced to 1 year in the Penitentiary. Received Jan. 14, 1845 and discharged Jan. 1, 1846. Notes: conduct good. Number in ledger 86: 751.

Tennessee Convicts: Records of the State Penitentiary

Name: Narcissa Lemon, age 17, born in Tennessee, occupation: nothing. Convicted of petit larceny by a court in Grainger County, and sentenced to 1 year in the Penitentiary. Received Jan. 14, 1845 and discharged Jan. 1, 1846. Notes: conduct good. Number in ledger 86: 752.

Name: James Pennington, age 25, born in Tennessee, occupation: nothing. Convicted of arson by a court in Grainger County, and sentenced to 5 years in the Penitentiary. Received Jan. 14, 1845 and discharged Dec. 11, 1849. Notes: pardoned under the act of 1836. Number in ledger 86: 753.

Name: Chesley Jones, age 27, born in Georgia, occupation: labourer. Convicted of bigamy by a court in Carroll County, and sentenced to 10 years in the Penitentiary. Received Jan. 17, 1845 and discharged May 23, 1854. Notes: pardoned under the act of 1836. Number in ledger 86: 754.

Name: P.M. Walker, age 32, born in Virginia, occupation: labourer. Convicted of larceny by a court in Davidson County, and sentenced to 2 years in the Penitentiary. Received Jan. 21, 1845 and discharged Dec. 18, 1846. Notes: pardoned under the act of 1836. Number in ledger 86: 755.

Name: John Lackey, age 40, born in North Carolina, occupation: labourer. Convicted of rape by a court in Davidson County, and sentenced to 10 years in the Penitentiary. Received Jan. 23, 1845 and discharged Mar. 1, 1854. Notes: pardoned by Gov. Johnson. Number in ledger 86: 756.

Name: Edward Tyler, age blank, born in North Carolina, occupation: teacher. Convicted of forgery by a court in Bradley County, and sentenced to 3 years in the Penitentiary. Received Jan. 29, 1845 and discharged Nov. 14, 1847. Notes: pardoned under the act of 1836. Number in ledger 86: 757.

Name: Lewis Stewart, age 26, born in Tennessee, occupation: labourer. Convicted of larceny by a court in Claiborne County, and sentenced to 2 years in the Penitentiary. Received Feb. 3, 1845 and discharged Jan. 15, 1847. Notes: conduct fair. Number in ledger 86: 758.

Name: Hiram Pogue, age 25, born in Tennessee, occupation: none. Convicted of petit larceny by a court in Fentress County, and sentenced to 3 years in the Penitentiary. Received Oct. 10, 1845 and discharged Sept. 17, 1847. Notes: pardoned under the act of 1836. Number in ledger 86: 759.

Name: Charles Amos, age 35, born in North Carolina, occupation: cabinett

Tennessee Convicts: Records of the State Penitentiary

[sic] maker. Convicted of petit larceny by a court in Fentress County, and sentenced to 1 year in the Penitentiary. Received Oct. 10, 1845 and discharged Oct. 30, 1845. Notes: conduct fair. Number in ledger 86: 760.

Name: William Lastley, age 17, born in North Carolina, occupation: none. Convicted of petit larceny by a court in Roane County, and sentenced to 2 years in the Penitentiary. Received Nov. 10, 1844 and discharged Oct. 21, 1846. Notes: pardoned under the act of 1836. Number in ledger 86: 761.

Name: Cleveland Lane, age blank, born in North Carolina, occupation: blank. Convicted of petit larceny by a court in Overton County, and sentenced to 1 year in the Penitentiary. Received Nov. 10, 1844 and discharged Nov. 10, 1845. Notes: alias Estep, conduct fair. Number in ledger 86: 762.

Name: Alexander Peck, age 37, born in Tennessee, occupation: labourer. Convicted of petit larceny by a court in Claiborne County, and sentenced to 1 year in the Penitentiary. Received Feb. 3, 1845 and discharged June 12, 1845. Notes: died of inflamation of the brain. Number in ledger 86: 763.

Name: Abraham J. Brewer, age 38, born in Tennessee, occupation: labourer. Convicted of assault with intent to murder by a court in Davidson County, and sentenced to 5 years in the Penitentiary. Received Feb. 4, 1845 and discharged Oct. 10, 1849. Notes: pardoned under the act of '36. Number in ledger 86: 764.

Name: James R. Jonston [Johnston?], age 66, born in North Carolina, occupation: labourer. Convicted of petit larceny by a court in Blount County, and sentenced to 1 year in the Penitentiary. Received Feb. 12, 1845 and discharged Jan. 31, 1846. Notes: conduct fair. Number in ledger 86: 765.

Name: Simon Williams, age 80, born in Virginia, occupation: baker. Convicted of arson by a court in Polk County, and sentenced to 2 years in the Penitentiary. Received Feb. 22, 1845 and discharged Jan. 12, 1847. Notes: negro, pardoned under the act of '36. Number in ledger 86: 766.

Name: Daniel Lemmons, age 22, born in Tennessee, occupation: none. Convicted of murder by a court in Polk County, and sentenced to 5 years in the Penitentiary. Received Feb. 22, 1845 and discharged Jan. 14, 1849. Notes: pardoned by N.S. Brown. Number in ledger 86: 767.

Name: James Brewer, age 39, born in New York, occupation: butcher.

Convicted of grand larceny by a court in Shelby County, and sentenced to 3 years and 6 months in the Penitentiary. Received Feb. 28, 1845 and discharged Aug. 28, 1848. Notes: alias Shaw, conduct only tolerable. Number in ledger 86: 768.

Name: William Bellew, age 27, born in New York, occupation: carpenter. Convicted of larceny & rec'd stolen goods by a court in Madison County, and sentenced to 6 years in the Penitentiary. Received May 3, 1845 and discharged June 26, 1850. Notes: died of cholera. [Published 1851 report shows surname as Ballew.] Number in ledger 86: 769.

Name: Josiah Julany, age 24, born in Tennessee, occupation: bl[ac]k smith. Convicted of petit larceny by a court in Jefferson County, and sentenced to 2 years and 6 months in the Penitentiary. Received May 5, 1845 and discharged Sept. 23, 1847. Notes: pardoned under the act of '36. Number in ledger 86: 770.

Name: David Gillaland, age 47, born in South Carolina, occupation: bl[ac]k smith. Convicted of petit larceny by a court in Jefferson County, and sentenced to 1 year and 6 months in the Penitentiary. Received May 5, 1845 and discharged Nov. 3, 1846. Notes: conduct fair. Number in ledger 86: 771.

Name: George Kinnard, age 32, born in Tennessee, occupation: labourer. Convicted of arson by a court in Hardiman [sic] County, and sentenced to 5 years in the Penitentiary. Received May 18, 1845 and discharged June 18, 1850. Notes: conduct tolerable. Number in ledger 86: 772.

Name: William Rail, age 30, born in Tennessee, occupation: bl[ac]k smith. Convicted of assault with intent to kill by a court in Maury County, and sentenced to 4 years in the Penitentiary. Received May 23, 1845 and discharged Feb. 29, 1849. Notes: pardoned under the act of '36. Number in ledger 86: 773.

Name: William B. Andrews, age 24, born in North Carolina, occupation: labourer. Convicted of malicious stabbing by a court in Maury County, and sentenced to 2 years in the Penitentiary. Received May 23, 1845 and discharged Apr. 17, 1847. Notes: pardoned under the act of '36. Number in ledger 86: 774.

Name: William A. Caldwell, age 24, born in Tennessee, occupation: grog shop keeper. Convicted of assault with intent to kill by a court in Maury County,

Tennessee Convicts: Records of the State Penitentiary

and sentenced to 3 years in the Penitentiary. Received May 23, 1845 and discharged Mar. 29, 1848. Notes: pardoned under the act of '36. Number in ledger 86: 775.

Name: Edmund Napper, age 29, born in Virginia, occupation: labourer. Convicted of petit larceny by a court in Claiborn[e] County, and sentenced to 1 year in the Penitentiary. Received May 31, 1845 and discharged May 21, 1846. Notes: conduct fair. Number in ledger 86: 776.

Name: Elijah Farlee, age 43, born in England, occupation: quack doctor. Convicted of petit larceny by a court in Wayne County, and sentenced to 1 year in the Penitentiary. Received June 12, 1845 and discharged June 12, 1846. Notes: conduct fair. Number in ledger 86: 777.

Name: James Lane, age 28, born in Maryland, occupation: labourer. Convicted of petit larceny by a court in Hawkins County, and sentenced to 1 year and 6 months in the Penitentiary. Received June 12, 1845 and discharged Nov. 28, 1846. Notes: conduct fair. Number in ledger 86: 778.

Name: John Granville Hoolon [Hooton?], age 18, born in North Carolina, occupation: labourer. Convicted of assault with intent to kill by a court in White County, and sentenced to 3 years in the Penitentiary. Received June 12, 1845 and discharged Apr. 8, 1848. Notes: negro, pardoned under the act of '36. Number in ledger 86: 779.

Name: Peter C. Taylor, age 21, born in Tennessee, occupation: labourer. Convicted of petit larceny by a court in Lincoln County, and sentenced to 1 year in the Penitentiary. Received June 12, 1845 and discharged June 12, 1846. Notes: conduct fair. Number in ledger 86: 780.

Name: George W. Brown, age 37, born in New York, occupation: tailor. Convicted of petit larceny by a court in Fentress County, and sentenced to 1 year in the Penitentiary. Received June 25, 1845 and discharged June 25, 1846. Notes: conduct fair. Number in ledger 86: 781.

Name: Elias Rimel, age 45, born in Tennessee, occupation: labourer. Convicted of perjury by a court in Green[e] County, and sentenced to 3 years in the Penitentiary. Received July 3, 1845 and discharged May 5, 1848. Notes: pardoned under the act of '36. Number in ledger 86: 782.

Name: William H. Galaspie, age 48, born in England, occupation: painter tarnerge[?]. Convicted of passing counterfeit money by a court in Roane County, and sentenced to 3 years and 6 months in the Penitentiary. Received July 4, 1845 and discharged Nov. 3, 1848. Notes: pardoned under the act of '36. Number in ledger 86: 783.

Name: Daniel Lickstein, age 25, born in Holland, occupation: moroed[?] dresser. Convicted of grand larceny by a court in Shelby County, and sentenced to 3 years in the Penitentiary. Received July 13, 1845 and discharged Nov. 3, 1848. Notes: alias Buckstein, pardoned under the act of '36. Number in ledger 86: 784.

Name: James Kelly, age 45, born in Ireland, occupation: miller. Convicted of grand larceny by a court in Shelby County, and sentenced to 3 years in the Penitentiary. Received July 13, 1845 and discharged July 13, 1848. Notes: conduct passable. Number in ledger 86: 785.

Name: John Turner, age 44, born in New York, occupation: turner. Convicted of grand larceny by a court in Shelby County, and sentenced to 3 years in the Penitentiary. Received July 13, 1845 and discharged July 13, 1848. Notes: conduct passable. Number in ledger 86: 786.

Name: John Little, age 31, born in Canada, occupation: carpenter. Convicted of grand larceny by a court in Shelby County, and sentenced to 3 years in the Penitentiary. Received July 13, 1845 and discharged May 11, 1848. Notes: pardoned under the act of '36. Number in ledger 86: 787.

Name: Robt. McKay, age 33, born in Scotchman, occupation: moulder. Convicted of petit larceny by a court in Shelby County, and sentenced to 1 year in the Penitentiary. Received July 13, 1845 and discharged July 12, 1846. Notes: conduct fair. Number in ledger 86: 788.

Name: John Galbreath, age 18, born in Tennessee, occupation: thief. Convicted of horse stealing by a court in Washington County, and sentenced to 6 years in the Penitentiary. Received July 16, 1845 and discharged Feb. 28, 1851. Notes: pardoned under the act of '36. Number in ledger 86: 789.

Name: Hugh McCoy, age 33, born in Tennessee, occupation: labourer. Convicted of petit larceny by a court in Gibson County, and sentenced to 1 year in the Penitentiary. Received July 18, 1845 and discharged July 18, 1846. Notes: conduct fair. Number in ledger 86: 790.

Tennessee Convicts: Records of the State Penitentiary

Name: Jesse Thomas, age 23, born in Tennessee, occupation: labourer. Convicted of petit larceny by a court in Gibson County, and sentenced to 1 year in the Penitentiary. Received July 18, 1845 and discharged Oct. 8, 1845. Notes: died of inflamation of the stomach. Number in ledger 86: 791.

Name: Francis Humble, age 18, born in Tennessee, occupation: labourer. Convicted of grand larceny by a court in Gibson County, and sentenced to 3 years in the Penitentiary. Received July 18, 1845 and discharged July 18, 1848. Notes: conduct fair. Number in ledger 86: 792.

Name: John Bennett, age 31, born in Louisiana, occupation: cook. Convicted of negro stealing by a court in Shelby County, and sentenced to 5 years and 10 months in the Penitentiary. Received July 20, 1845 and discharged May 20, 1851. Notes: negro, conduct fair. Number in ledger 86: 793.

Name: John A. McCoy, age 33, born in Kentucky, occupation: labourer. Convicted of negro stealing by a court in Shelby County, and sentenced to 5 years in the Penitentiary. Received July 20, 1845 and discharged Nov. 5, 1847. Notes: general pardon by N.S. Brown. Number in ledger 86: 794.

Name: Jonathan A. Hall, age 23, born in Tennessee, occupation: labourer. Convicted of obtaining goods by false preten by a court in Shelby County, and sentenced to 3 years in the Penitentiary. Received July 20, 1845 and discharged Mar. 27, 1847. Notes: discharged on writ from Supreme Court, Jackson. Number in ledger 86: 795.

Name: John Taggart, age 26, born in Maryland, occupation: stone cutter. Convicted of obtaining goods by false preten by a court in Shelby County, and sentenced to 1 year in the Penitentiary. Received July 20, 1845 and discharged July 20, 1846. Notes: conduct good. Number in ledger 86: 796.

Name: George McElyea, age 21, born in Tennessee, occupation: none. Convicted of petit larceny by a court in Obion County, and sentenced to 1 year and 1 month in the Penitentiary. Received July 24, 1845 and discharged Aug. 24, 1846. Notes: conduct good. Number in ledger 86: 797.

Name: Henry Truett, age 55, born in Tennessee, occupation: thief. Convicted of petit larceny by a court in Williamson County, and sentenced to 1 year in the Penitentiary. Received July 24, 1845 and discharged July 24, 1846. Notes: conduct fair. Number in ledger 86: 798.

Tennessee Convicts: Records of the State Penitentiary

Name: William R. Smith, age 35, born in Tennessee, occupation: labourer. Convicted of counterfeiting by a court in Anderson County, and sentenced to 3 years in the Penitentiary. Received July 26, 1845 and discharged Oct. 23, 1847. Notes: gen'l pardon by Gov. A.V. Brown. Number in ledger 86: 799.

Name: John Qualls, age 23, born in Tennessee, occupation: labourer. Convicted of malicious stabbing by a court in Anderson County, and sentenced to 2 years and 6 months in the Penitentiary. Received July 26, 1845 and discharged Oct. 23, 1847. Notes: gen'l pardon by Gov. A.V. Brown. Number in ledger 86: 800.

Name: Mathias Fresbey, age 23, born in Tennessee, occupation: labourer. Convicted of grand larceny by a court in Johnson County, and sentenced to 4 years in the Penitentiary. Received Aug. 1, 1845 and discharged Apr. 20, 1849. Notes: pardoned under the act of '36. Number in ledger 86: 801.

Name: William Bailey, age 18, born in Tennessee, occupation: labourer. Convicted of petit larceny by a court in Johnson County, and sentenced to 2 years in the Penitentiary. Received Aug. 1, 1845 and discharged July 10, 1847. Notes: conduct good. Number in ledger 86: 802.

Name: Moses Wolf, age 27, born in Germany, occupation: butcher. Convicted of passing counterfeit money by a court in Shelby County, and sentenced to 4 years in the Penitentiary. Received Aug. 10, 1845 and discharged Aug. 10, 1849. Notes: conduct bad. Number in ledger 86: 803.

Name: Baldwin Rowland, age 40, born in Tennessee, occupation: labourer. Convicted of murder by a court in Jackson County, and sentenced to life in the Penitentiary. Received Aug. 31, 1845 and discharged June 13, 1846. Notes: supposed to have died from a ruptured blood vesse. Number in ledger 86: 804.

Name: Robert Hansard, age 17, born in Tennessee, occupation: labourer. Convicted of blank by a court in Franklin County, and sentenced to 1 year in the Penitentiary. Received Sept. 10, 1845 and discharged Sept. 10, 1846. Notes: conduct bad. Number in ledger 86: 805.

Name: William Cunningham, age 18, born in Tennessee, occupation: blank. Convicted of blank by a court in Maury County, and sentenced to 3 years and 6 months in the Penitentiary. Received Sept. 10, 1845 and discharged Mar. 15, 1849. Notes: conduct passable. Number in ledger 86: 806 (number used twice).

twice).

Name: John Jones, age 42, born in Virginia, occupation: bl[ac]k smith. Convicted of grand larceny by a court in Wilson County, and sentenced to 6 years in the Penitentiary. Received Oct. 2, 1845 and discharged May 22, 1851. Notes: pardoned under the act of 1836. Number in ledger 86: 806 (number used twice).

Name: Garland Brown, age 40, born in Virginia, occupation: laborer. Convicted of rec'd stolen goods by a court in Wilson County, and sentenced to 2 years and 6 months in the Penitentiary. Received Oct. 2, 1845 and discharged Feb. 18, 1848. Notes: negro, pardoned under the act of '36. Number in ledger 86: 807.

Name: John Brown, age 22, born in Tennessee, occupation: laborer. Convicted of grand larceny by a court in White County, and sentenced to 4 years in the Penitentiary. Received Oct. 14, 1845 and discharged Oct. 25, 1845. Notes: negro, proven by his master J.D. Neville & deliv'. Number in ledger 86: 808.

Name: George Flippo, age 19, born in Kentucky, occupation: bl[ac]k smith. Convicted of horse stealing by a court in Lincoln County, and sentenced to 5 years in the Penitentiary. Received Oct. 22, 1845 and discharged July 3, 1850. Notes: negro, pardoned under the act of 1836. Number in ledger 86: 809.

Name: A.G. Howard, age 29, born in Tennessee, occupation: bl[ac]k smith. Convicted of grand larceny by a court in Davidson County, and sentenced to 3 years in the Penitentiary. Received Oct. 31, 1845 and discharged Aug. 18, 1848. Notes: pardoned under the act of 1836. Number in ledger 86: 810.

Name: John Durham, age 21, born in Tennessee, occupation: laborer. Convicted of grand larceny by a court in Stewart County, and sentenced to 3 years in the Penitentiary. Received Nov. 2, 1845 and discharged Sept. 1, 1848. Notes: pardoned under the act of 1836. Number in ledger 86: 811.

Name: Allen Emmett, age 22, born in Tennessee, occupation: laborer. Convicted of petit larceny by a court in Knox County, and sentenced to 1 year in the Penitentiary. Received Nov. 3, 1845 and discharged Oct. 25, 1846. Notes: negro, conduct fair. Number in ledger 86: 812.

Name: Robt. F. Crawford, age 24, born in Tennessee, occupation: shoe maker.

Convicted of horse stealing by a court in Knox County, and sentenced to 3 years in the Penitentiary. Received Nov. 3, 1845 and discharged Sept. 1, 1848. Notes: pardoned under the act of 1836. Number in ledger 86: 813.

Name: Jackson M. Blackwell, age 20, born in Tennessee, occupation: laborer. Convicted of arson by a court in Roane County, and sentenced to 3 years in the Penitentiary. Received Nov. 4, 1845 and discharged Aug. 29, 1848. Notes: pardoned under the act of 1836. Number in ledger 86: 814.

Name: Jesse M. Banks, age 30, born in Virginia, occupation: laborer. Convicted of petit larceny by a court in Coffee County, and sentenced to 1 year in the Penitentiary. Received Nov. 10, 1845 and discharged Nov. 10, 1846. Notes: conduct fair. Number in ledger 86: 815.

Name: John Skyler, age 21, born in Tennessee, occupation: laborer. Convicted of grand larceny by a court in Bledsoe County, and sentenced to 3 years in the Penitentiary. Received Nov. 20, 1845 and discharged Sept. 13, 1848. Notes: pardoned under the act of 1836. Number in ledger 86: 816.

Name: William Zachrie, age 18, born in North Carolina, occupation: laborer. Convicted of forgery by a court in Tipton County, and sentenced to 3 years in the Penitentiary. Received Nov. 25, 1845 and discharged Oct. 25, 1848. Notes: pardoned under the act of 1836. Number in ledger 86: 817.

Name: James Clark, age 29, born in New York, occupation: shoe maker. Convicted of petit larceny by a court in Marion County, and sentenced to 1 year and 6 months in the Penitentiary. Received Nov. 28, 1845 and discharged May 26, 1847. Notes: conduct fair. Number in ledger 86: 818.

Name: Armstrong Gaines, age 33, born in Virginia, occupation: laborer. Convicted of harboring a slave by a court in Rutherford County, and sentenced to 3 years and 6 months in the Penitentiary. Received Dec. 6, 1845 and discharged Mar. 27, 1849. Notes: pardoned under the act of 1836. Number in ledger 86: 819.

Name: Jourdan Kiddy, age 30, born in Tennessee, occupation: carpenter. Convicted of petit larceny by a court in Hamilton County, and sentenced to 1 year in the Penitentiary. Received Dec. 8, 1845 and discharged Dec. 1, 1846. Notes: conduct fair. Number in ledger 86: 820.

Name: William King, age 38, born in North Carolina, occupation: laborer.

Tennessee Convicts: Records of the State Penitentiary

Convicted of petit larceny by a court in Hamilton County, and sentenced to 1 year in the Penitentiary. Received Dec. 8, 1845 and discharged Dec. 3, 1846. Notes: conduct fair. Number in ledger 86: 821.

Name: Edward Buchanan, age 48, born in Maryland, occupation: distiller. Convicted of grand larceny by a court in Shelby County, and sentenced to 6 years in the Penitentiary. Received Dec. 14, 1845 and discharged Dec. 14, 1851. Notes: discharged at expiration of sentence. Number in ledger 86: 822.

Name: Benjamin R. Harrison, age 25, born in Kentucky, occupation: printer. Convicted of stealing promisory notes by a court in Shelby County, and sentenced to 3 years in the Penitentiary. Received Dec. 14, 1845 and discharged Dec. 14, 1848. Notes: conduct bad. Number in ledger 86: 823.

Name: Devit Charles, age 42, born in Maryland, occupation: distiller. Convicted of petit larceny by a court in Shelby County, and sentenced to 2 years and 6 months in the Penitentiary. Received Dec. 14, 1845 and discharged Apr. 18, 1848. Notes: pardoned under the act of 1836. Number in ledger 86: 824.

Name: Henry Balduff, age 15, born in Kentucky, occupation: cabin boy. Convicted of petit larceny by a court in Shelby County, and sentenced to 1 year and 6 months in the Penitentiary. Received Dec. 14, 1845 and discharged Dec. 22, 1845. Notes: general pardon by Gov. Brown. [Published 1847 report shows surname as Baldruff.] Number in ledger 86: 825.

Name: Robert Gordon, age 16, born in Kentucky, occupation: cabin boy. Convicted of petit larceny by a court in Shelby County, and sentenced to 1 year and 6 months in the Penitentiary. Received Dec. 14, 1845 and discharged Jan. 8, 1846. Notes: general pardon by Gov. Brown. Number in ledger 86: 826.

Name: Sanlis[?] Spooner, age 43, born in Massachusetts, occupation: farmer. Convicted of petit larceny by a court in Shelby County, and sentenced to 1 year in the Penitentiary. Received Dec. 14, 1845 and discharged Dec. 14, 1846. Notes: conduct good. Number in ledger 86: 827.

Name: John A. Woodruff, age 22, born in Indiana, occupation: laborer. Convicted of petit larceny by a court in Shelby County, and sentenced to 1 year in the Penitentiary. Received Dec. 14, 1845 and discharged Dec. 14, 1846. Notes: conduct good. Number in ledger 86: 828.

Name: Matthew Nebas, age 27, born in New York, occupation: book binder.

Tennessee Convicts: Records of the State Penitentiary

in the Penitentiary. Received Dec. 14, 1845 and discharged Dec. 14, 1846. Notes: conduct good. Number in ledger 86: 829.

Name: Zachariah Owen, age 20, born in Tennessee, occupation: laborer. Convicted of horse stealing by a court in Davidson County, and sentenced to 5 years in the Penitentiary. Received Dec. 24, 1845 and discharged Sept. 10, 1850. Notes: pardoned under the act of 1836. Number in ledger 86: 830.

Name: Peter Tyner, age 32, born in Tennessee, occupation: waggon [sic] maker. Convicted of horse stealing by a court in Davidson County, and sentenced to 10 years in the Penitentiary. Received Dec. 25, 1845 and discharged Aug. 19, 1851. Notes: 2nd conviction, general pardone by Gov. Trousdale. Number in ledger 86: 831.

Name: Thos. Gibson, age 43, born in South Carolina, occupation: shoe maker. Convicted of petit larceny by a court in McMinn County, and sentenced to 2 years in the Penitentiary. Received Dec. 28, 1845 and discharged Nov. 14, 1847. Notes: pardoned under the act of 1836. Number in ledger 86: 832.

Name: Peyton T. Phillips, age 34, born in Tennessee, occupation: farmer. Convicted of murder 1st degree by a court in Jackson County, and sentenced to life in the Penitentiary. Received Dec. 20, 1845 and discharged Nov. 3, 1857. Notes: pardoned by Gov. And. Johnson. Number in ledger 86: 833.

Name: James Templers, age 44, born in Tennessee, occupation: laborer. Convicted of petit larceny by a court in Marion County, and sentenced to 1 year in the Penitentiary. Received Jan. 10, 1846 and discharged Jan. 10, 1847. Notes: conduct not good. Number in ledger 86: 834.

Name: James Fletcher, age 25, born in Kentucky, occupation: laborer. Convicted of passing counterfeit coin by a court in Davidson County, and sentenced to 3 years in the Penitentiary. Received Jan. 12, 1845 and discharged Jan. 12, 1849. Notes: conduct passable. Number in ledger 86: 835.

Name: Henry H. Childress, age 31, born in Tennessee, occupation: tanner. Convicted of grand larceny by a court in Franklin County, and sentenced to 3 years in the Penitentiary. Received Jan. 14, 1845 and discharged Nov. 19, 1848. Notes: pardoned under the act of 1836. Number in ledger 86: 836.

Name: John Petty, age 23, born in Tennessee, occupation: waggon [sic] maker. Convicted of horse stealing by a court in Cannon County, and sentenced to 3

Convicted of horse stealing by a court in Cannon County, and sentenced to 3 years in the Penitentiary. Received Sept. 11, 1845 and discharged July 15, 1848. Notes: alias And[rew] Cartis [Curtis?], pardoned under t. Number in ledger 86: 837.

Name: George R. Langston, age 27, born in South Carolina, occupation: laborer. Convicted of petit larceny by a court in Anderson County, and sentenced to 1 year in the Penitentiary. Received Jan. 17, 1846 and discharged Jan. 18, 1847. Notes: conduct fair. Number in ledger 86: 838.

Name: John Croff, age 37, born in Tennessee, occupation: tanner. Convicted of negro stealing by a court in Davidson County, and sentenced to 5 years in the Penitentiary. Received Jan. 26, 1845 and discharged Jan. 26, 1851. Notes: conduct only tolerable. Number in ledger 86: 839.

Name: Fountain Manning, age 17, born in Tennessee, occupation: laborer. Convicted of petit larceny by a court in Maury County, and sentenced to 1 year in the Penitentiary. Received Jan. 27, 1845 and discharged Jan. 27, 1847. Notes: conduct good. Number in ledger 86: 840.

Name: William Shoemaker, age 35, born in North Carolina, occupation: shoe maker. Convicted of bigamy by a court in Maury County, and sentenced to 2 years and 3 months in the Penitentiary. Received Jan. 27, 1845 and discharged Mar. 13, 1848. Notes: pardoned under the act of 1836. Number in ledger 86: 841.

Name: Josiah Green, age 44, born in North Carolina, occupation: labourer. Convicted of assault with intent to kill by a court in Maury County, and sentenced to 3 years in the Penitentiary. Received Jan. 27, 1846, and discharged Mar. 16, 1848. Notes: general pardon by N.S. Brown. [Published report of 1849 shows given name as Isaiah.] Number in ledger 86: 842.

Name: Thomas C. Gidcomb, age 15, born in Kentucky, occupation: vagabond. Convicted of larceny by a court in Perry County, and sentenced to 3 years in the Penitentiary. Received Jan. 28, 1846, and discharged Jan. 28, 1849. Notes: conduct exceptionable. Number in ledger 86: 843.

Name: Weakley Chick, age 23, born in Alabama, occupation: house painter. Convicted of robbery by a court in Davidson County, and sentenced to 5 years in the Penitentiary. Received Feb. 3, 1846, and discharged Jan. 12, 1847. Notes: general pardon by Gov. Brown. Number in ledger 86: 844.

Name: Thomas Harrison, age 31, born in Davidson [Co., Tenn.?], occupation: carpenter. Convicted of robbery by a court in Davidson County, and sentenced to 5 years in the Penitentiary. Received Feb. 3, 1846, and discharged Jan. 12, 1847. Notes: general pardon by Gov. Brown. Number in ledger 86: 845.

Name: Osenberry Harrison, age 34, born in Davidson [Co., Tenn.?], occupation: fisherman. Convicted of robbery by a court in Davidson County, and sentenced to 5 years in the Penitentiary. Received Feb. 3, 1846, and discharged Jan. 12, 1847. Notes: general pardon by Gov. Brown. Number in ledger 86: 846.

Name: Joseph E. Baldwin, age 24, born in Pennsylvania, occupation: cabinett [sic] maker. Convicted of larceny by a court in Davidson County, and sentenced to 3 years in the Penitentiary. Received Feb. 12, 1846, and discharged Sept. 20, 1847. Notes: general pardon by Gov. Brown. [Published 1847 report shows first name as *James* E.] Number in ledger 86: 847.

Name: William Morton, age 48, born in Virginia, occupation: labourer. Convicted of vol. manslaughter by a court in Wayne County, and sentenced to 2 years in the Penitentiary. Received Feb. 12, 1846, and discharged Jan. 9, 1848. Notes: pardoned under the act of 1836. Number in ledger 86: 848.

Name: Abel Cook, age 28, born in North Carolina, occupation: labourer. Convicted of petit larceny by a court in Green[e] County, and sentenced to 1 year in the Penitentiary. Received Mar. 3, 1846, and discharged Feb. 23, 1847. Notes: conduct good. Number in ledger 86: 849.

Name: Robert Jestice [Justice?], age 31, born in North Carolina, occupation: labourer. Convicted of horse stealing by a court in Shelby County, and sentenced to 4 years in the Penitentiary. Received Mar. 13, 1846, and discharged Dec. 22, 1849. Notes: pardoned under the act of 1836. Number in ledger 86: 850.

Name: James Hunt, age 21, born in Tennessee, occupation: shoe maker. Convicted of petit larceny by a court in Henry County, and sentenced to 2 years in the Penitentiary. Received Mar. 27, 1846, and discharged May 27, 1848. Notes: conduct tolerable. Number in ledger 86: 851.

Name: W. Stephens, age 21, born in Tennessee, occupation: labourer. Convicted of petit larceny by a court in Cocke County, and sentenced to 1 year in the Penitentiary. Received Apr. 14, 1846, and discharged Mar. 27, 1847. Notes: conduct good. Number in ledger 86: 852.

Name: Sterling M. Gott [Jott?], age 28, born in Kentucky, occupation: clerking. Convicted of negro stealing by a court in Shelby County, and sentenced to 8 years in the Penitentiary. Received Apr. 20, 1846, and discharged Oct. 20, 1853. Notes: pardoned under the act of 1836. Number in ledger 86: 853.

Name: James Henry, age 33, born in Ireland, occupation: labourer. Convicted of larceny by a court in Shelby County, and sentenced to 1 year and 1 month in the Penitentiary. Received Apr. 20, 1846, and discharged May 20, 1847. Notes: conduct good. Number in ledger 86: 854.

Name: John Williams, age 36, born in New York, occupation: tailor. Convicted of petit larceny by a court in Shelby County, and sentenced to 1 year in the Penitentiary. Received Apr. 20, 1846, and discharged Apr. 20, 1847. Notes: conduct good. Number in ledger 86: 855.

Name: William Staffle, age 24, born in North Carolina, occupation: labourer. Convicted of horse stealing by a court in Sevier County, and sentenced to 4 years in the Penitentiary. Received May 1, 1846, and discharged Feb. 5, 1850. Notes: pardoned under the act of 1836. Number in ledger 86: 856.

Name: Riley Genoer[?], age 19, born in Tennessee, occupation: carpenter. Convicted of murder in 2nd degree by a court in McMinn County, and sentenced to 20 years in the Penitentiary. Received May 3, 1846, and discharged Mar. 2, 1854. Notes: pardoned by Gov. Johnson. Number in ledger 86: 857.

Name: Matthew Bird, age 60, born in South Carolina, occupation: labourer. Convicted of grand larceny by a court in McMinn County, and sentenced to 3 years in the Penitentiary. Received May 3, 1846, and discharged Feb. 20, 1849. Notes: pardoned under the act of 1836. Number in ledger 86: 858.

Name: James Felts, age 38, born in North Carolina, occupation: labourer. Convicted of petit larceny by a court in McMinn County, and sentenced to 1 year in the Penitentiary. Received May 3, 1846, and discharged Apr. 20, 1847. Notes: conduct good. Number in ledger 86: 859.

Name: William Johnston, age 22, born in Ohio, occupation: clerk. Convicted of counterfeiting by a court in McMinn County, and sentenced to 3 years in the

Penitentiary. Received May 3, 1846, and discharged Feb. 20, 1849. Notes: pardoned under the act of 1836. Number in ledger 86: 860.

Name: Hiram Tacket, age 23, born in Tennessee, occupation: labourer. Convicted of rape by a court in VanBuren County, and sentenced to 10 years in the Penitentiary. Received May 6, 1846, and discharged Feb. 8, 1851. Notes: general pardon by Gov. Trousdale. Number in ledger 86: 861.

Name: James C.D. Slaughter, age 30, born in Kentucky, occupation: labourer. Convicted of murder by a court in Madison County, and sentenced to 4 years and 6 months in the Penitentiary. Received May 11, 1846, and discharged Dec. 13, 1849. Notes: negro, general pardon by Gov. Trousdale. Number in ledger 86: 862.

Name: James Jones, age 30, born in Kentucky, occupation: school teacher. Convicted of counterfeiting by a court in Madison County, and sentenced to 3 years in the Penitentiary. Received May 11, 1846, and discharged Mar. 3, 1849. Notes: pardoned under the act of 1836. Number in ledger 86: 863.

Name: William Price, age 44, born in North Carolina, occupation: cabinett [sic] maker. Convicted of larceny by a court in Robertson County, and sentenced to 3 years in the Penitentiary. Received June 15, 1846, and discharged Aug. 28, 1847. Notes: pardoned by Gov. A.V. Brown. Number in ledger 86: 864.

Name: William Brown, age 37, born in North Carolina, occupation: boatsman. Convicted of horse stealing by a court in Shelby County, and sentenced to 5 years in the Penitentiary. Received May 16, 1846, and discharged Nov. 10, 1849. Notes: died of general dropsy. Number in ledger 86: 865.

Name: William C. Covington, age 23, born in North Carolina, occupation: labourer. Convicted of slave stealing by a court in Shelby County, and sentenced to 5 years in the Penitentiary. Received May 16, 1846, and discharged Apr. 19, 1847. Notes: discharged upon writ of error from Supreme Court, Jackson.. Number in ledger 86: 866.

Name: Robert Marcum, age 40, born in Virginia, occupation: labourer. Convicted of obtaining goods under false prete by a court in Lawrence County, and sentenced to 3 years in the Penitentiary. Received June 16, 1846, and discharged Dec. 4, 1847. Notes: alias J. Toney, general pardon by Gov. N. Brown. Number in ledger 86: 867.

Name: Sanford W. Dunstan, age 26, born in North Carolina, occupation: labourer. Convicted of larceny by a court in Lincoln County, and sentenced to 3 years in the Penitentiary. Received June 16, 1846, and discharged Apr. 11, 1849. Notes: pardoned under the act of 1836. Number in ledger 86: 868.

Name: Wiley Jones, age 23, born in North Carolina, occupation: labourer. Convicted of selling a free man of collour [si by a court in Lincoln County, and sentenced to 5 years in the Penitentiary. Received June 16, 1846, and discharged Feb. 25, 1851. Notes: pardoned under the act of 1836. Number in ledger 86: 869.

Name: Sherrod Jones, age 40, born in North Carolina, occupation: labourer. Convicted of selling a free man of collour [si by a court in Lincoln County, and sentenced to 5 years in the Penitentiary. Received June 16, 1846, and discharged Feb. 25, 1851. Notes: pardoned under the act of 1836. Number in ledger 86: 870.

Name: Jackson Carter, age 20, born in North Carolina, occupation: labourer. Convicted of grand larceny by a court in White County, and sentenced to 5 years in the Penitentiary. Received June 18, 1846, and discharged Feb. 28, 1851. Notes: pardoned under the act of 1836. Number in ledger 86: 871.

Name: James Gideon, age 18, born in Tennessee, occupation: labourer. Convicted of grand larceny by a court in White County, and sentenced to 3 years in the Penitentiary. Received June 18, 1846, and discharged Apr. 21, 1849. Notes: 2nd sentence, pardoned under the act of 1836. Number in ledger 86: 872.

Name: W.H. Seymour, age 17, born in Ohio, occupation: labourer. Convicted of grand larceny by a court in Shelby County, and sentenced to 5 years in the Penitentiary. Received July 26, 1846, and discharged Apr. 9, 1851. Notes: pardoned under the act of 1836. Number in ledger 86: 873.

Name: James Taylor, age 22, born in Pennsylvania, occupation: sailor. Convicted of petit larceny by a court in Shelby County, and sentenced to 3 years in the Penitentiary. Received July 26, 1846, and discharged May 26, 1849. Notes: pardoned under the act of 1836. Number in ledger 86: 874.

Name: Elijah Tomlinson, age 29, born in Kentucky, occupation: [sailor?]. Convicted of malicious stabbing by a court in Shelby County, and sentenced to

2 years in the Penitentiary. Received July 26, 1846, and discharged July 26, 1848. Notes: conduct good. Number in ledger 86: 875.

Name: George Stanton, age 20, born in L. A. [*sic*, Louisiana?], occupation: [sailor?]. Convicted of larceny by a court in Shelby County, and sentenced to 3 years in the Penitentiary. Received July 26, 1846, and discharged May 17, 1849. Notes: pardoned under the act of 1836. Number in ledger 86: 876.

Name: Andrew Hill, age 18, born in North Carolina, occupation: [blank]. Convicted of petit larceny by a court in Rhea County, and sentenced to 1 year in the Penitentiary. Received July 20, 1846, and discharged July 10, 1847. Notes: conduct good. Number in ledger 86: 877.

Name: Johnson Graham, age 25, born in North Carolina, occupation: [blank]. Convicted of burglary by a court in Carter County, and sentenced to 5 years in the Penitentiary. Received July 24, 1846, and discharged Apr. 9, 1851. Notes: pardoned under the act of 1836. Number in ledger 86: 878.

Name: Charles Taylor, age 26, born in Tennessee, occupation: labourer. Convicted of larceny by a court in Decater [*sic*] County, and sentenced to 1 year in the Penitentiary. Received July 29, 1846, and discharged July 29, 1847. Notes: conduct good. Number in ledger 86: 879.

Name: Monroe Roberts, age 17, born in North Carolina, occupation: labourer. Convicted of larceny by a court in Decater [*sic*] County, and sentenced to 1 year in the Penitentiary. Received July 29, 1846, and discharged July 29, 1847. Notes: conduct good. Number in ledger 86: 880.

Name: James Lane, age 26, born in Tennessee, occupation: labourer. Convicted of rape by a court in Hickman County, and sentenced to 10 years in the Penitentiary. Received July 31, 1846, and discharged Jan. 2, 1850. Notes: general pardon by W. Trousdale. Number in ledger 86: 881.

Name: Micham Carrol, age 21, born in Tennessee, occupation: labourer. Convicted of petit larceny by a court in Bedford County, and sentenced to 1 year in the Penitentiary. Received Aug. 15, 1846, and discharged Aug. 13, 1847. Notes: conduct good. Number in ledger 86: 882.

Name: Spencer Keelin, age 23, born in Tennessee, occupation: labourer. Convicted of horse stealing by a court in Carrol[l] County, and sentenced to 3 years in the Penitentiary. Received Sept. 16, 1846, and discharged July 12, 1849. Notes: pardoned under the act of 1836. Number in ledger 86: 883.

Name: Wesley Davis, age 20, born in Tennessee, occupation: labourer. Convicted of grand larceny by a court in Franklin County, and sentenced to 3 years in the Penitentiary. Received Sept. 17, 1846, and discharged July 9, 1849. Notes: pardoned under the act of 1836. Number in ledger 86: 884.

Name: Robert Buckhannon, age 42, born in Tennessee, occupation: labourer. Convicted of giving slaves forged papers by a court in White County, and sentenced to 4 years in the Penitentiary. Received Oct. 22, 1846, and discharged July 23, 1850. Notes: pardoned under the act of 1836. Number in ledger 86: 885.

Name: Clarissa , age 36, born in Virginia, occupation: labourer. Convicted of murder 1st degree by a court in Franklin County, and sentenced to life in the Penitentiary. Received July 6, 1846, and discharged Mar. 2, 1852. Notes: discharged to owner [Capt. Wm. Darwin] by Legislative resolution. Number in ledger 86: 886.

Name: William Jenkins, age 20, born in Tennessee, occupation: labourer. Convicted of rec'd stolen goods by a court in Monroe County, and sentenced to 2 years in the Penitentiary. Received Sept. 26, 1846, and discharged Aug. 18, 1848. Notes: pardoned under the act of 1836. Number in ledger 86: 887.

Name: Thomas Bird, age 21, born in Alabama, occupation: labourer. Convicted of larceny by a court in Hardin County, and sentenced to 1 year in the Penitentiary. Received Oct. 7, 1846, and discharged Oct. 7, 1847. Notes: conduct good. Number in ledger 86: 888.

Name: John N. Handley, age 20, born in Kentucky, occupation: labourer. Convicted of slave stealing by a court in Wayne County, and sentenced to 5 years in the Penitentiary. Received Oct. 15, 1846, and discharged Oct. 15, 1851. Notes: conduct bad. Number in ledger 86: 889.

Name: Thomas E. Goodwin, age 27, born in Kentucky, occupation: gun smith. Convicted of malicious shooting by a court in Dickson County, and sentenced to 4 years and 5 months in the Penitentiary. Received Oct. 25, 1846, and discharged Dec. 14, 1850. Notes: pardoned under the act of 1836. Number in ledger 86: 890.

Tennessee Convicts: Records of the State Penitentiary

Name: George Russel, age 25, born in Tennessee, occupation: farmer. Convicted of malicious shooting by a court in Dickson County, and sentenced to 2 years in the Penitentiary. Received Oct. 25, 1846, and discharged Oct. 25, 1848. Notes: conduct fair. Number in ledger 86: 891.

Name: Jamison W. Duncan, age 38, born in South Carolina, occupation: blank. Convicted of horse stealing by a court in Obion County, and sentenced to 4 years in the Penitentiary. Received Nov. 2, 1846, and discharged July 19, 1850. Notes: alias W. Sneed, pardoned under the act of 1836. Number in ledger 86: 892.

Name: James Irwin, age 36, born in Ireland, occupation: labourer. Convicted of grand larceny by a court in Stewart County, and sentenced to 3 years in the Penitentiary. Received Nov. 6, 1846, and discharged Aug. 23, 1849. Notes: pardoned under the act of 1836. Number in ledger 86: 893.

Name: Franklin Beauchum, age 29, born in Kentucky, occupation: school teacher. Convicted of grand larceny by a court in Overton County, and sentenced to 5 years in the Penitentiary. Received Nov. 6, 1846, and discharged July 18, 1851. Notes: pardoned under the act of 1836. Number in ledger 86: 894.

Name: Jonithon [sic] Richards, age 24, born in Tennessee, occupation: labourer. Convicted of seducing a slave by a court in Overton County, and sentenced to 5 years in the Penitentiary. Received Nov. 6, 1846, and discharged July 18, 1851. Notes: pardoned under the act of 1836. Number in ledger 86: 895.

Name: James Warren, age 31, born in Tennessee, occupation: bl[ac]k smith. Convicted of seducing a slave by a court in Overton County, and sentenced to 3 years in the Penitentiary. Received Nov. 6, 1846, and discharged Sept. 3, 1849. Notes: pardoned under the act of 1836. Number in ledger 86: 896.

Name: Isaac D. Dover, age blank, born in blank, occupation: blank. Convicted of seducing a slave by a court in Roane County, and sentenced to blank years in the Penitentiary. Received Nov. 6, 1846, and discharged Nov. 13, 1846. Notes: died of [blank]. [Published 1847 report shows he died of "spasmodic affection."] Number in ledger 86: 897.

Name: Willis Ivy, age 20, born in Tennessee, occupation: labourer. Convicted of house burning by a court in Bledsoe County, and sentenced to 10 years in the

Tennessee Convicts: Records of the State Penitentiary

Penitentiary. Received Nov. 19, 1846, and discharged Apr. 22, 1856. Notes: negro, pardoned under the act of 1836. Number in ledger 86: 898.

Name: Silas Avery, age 19, born in Tennessee, occupation: labourer. Convicted of bigamy by a court in Gibson County, and sentenced to 2 years in the Penitentiary. Received Nov. 19, 1846, and discharged Nov. 19, 1848. Notes: conduct fair. Number in ledger 86: 899.

Name: William Fin, age 33, born in Tennessee, occupation: labourer. Convicted of counterfeiting by a court in Jackson County, and sentenced to 8 years in the Penitentiary. Received Nov. 26, 1846, and discharged Dec. 3, 1850. Notes: pardoned by Gov. W. Trousdale. Number in ledger 86: 900.

Name: John J. Jackson, age 24, born in Tennessee, occupation: labourer. Convicted of counterfeiting by a court in Jackson County, and sentenced to 3 years in the Penitentiary. Received Nov. 26, 1846, and discharged Sept. 25, 1849. Notes: pardoned under the act of 1836. Number in ledger 86: 901.

Name: James Allcorn, age 45, born in South Carolina, occupation: none. Convicted of counterfeiting by a court in Jackson County, and sentenced to 5 years in the Penitentiary. Received Nov. 26, 1846, and discharged Aug. 23, 1849. Notes: general pardon by Gov. N.S. Brown. Number in ledger 86: 902.

Name: Jefferson Johnson, age 23, born in Tennessee, occupation: none. Convicted of counterfeiting by a court in Jackson County, and sentenced to 3 years in the Penitentiary. Received Nov. 26, 1846, and discharged Sept. 25, 1849. Notes: pardoned under the act of 1836. Number in ledger 86: 903.

Name: David Smith, age 36, born in Tennessee, occupation: none. Convicted of grand larceny by a court in Campbell County, and sentenced to 1 year in the Penitentiary. Received Sept. 18, 1846, and discharged Feb. 24, 1846. Notes: died of inflamation of the brain. Number in ledger 86: 904.

Name: Bryant Tittleton, age 27, born in North Carolina, occupation: none. Convicted of involentary [sic] manslaughter by a court in Henderson County, and sentenced to 1 year in the Penitentiary. Received Dec. 5, 1846, and discharged Dec. 11, 1846. Notes: pardoned by Gov. Brown. Number in ledger 86: 905.

Name: G.W. Brown, age 27, born in Tennessee, occupation: tailor. Convicted of larceny by a court in Davidson County, and sentenced to 3 years in the

Tennessee Convicts: Records of the State Penitentiary

Penitentiary. Received Jan. 13, 1847, and discharged Nov. 6, 1849. Notes: pardoned under the act of 1836. Number in ledger 86: 906.

Name: Joseph Taylor, age 25, born in Tennessee, occupation: tailor. Convicted of grand larceny by a court in Davidson County, and sentenced to 3 years in the Penitentiary. Received Jan. 13, 1847, and discharged Aug. 31, 1847. Notes: pardoned by A.V. Brown, Gov.. Number in ledger 86: 907.

Name: John Prior, age 25, born in Tennessee, occupation: labourer. Convicted of murder by a court in Jackson County, and sentenced to 12 years in the Penitentiary. Received Jan. 13, 1847, and discharged Aug. 27, 1852. Notes: pardoned by W.B. Campbell, Gov.. Number in ledger 86: 908.

Name: John Brewington, age 27, born in Tennessee, occupation: labourer. Convicted of murder by a court in Jackson County, and sentenced to 10 years in the Penitentiary. Received Jan. 13, 1847, and discharged July 20, 1847. Notes: died of billious cholic [*sic*]. Number in ledger 86: 909.

Name: William Brown, age 26, born in Kentucky, occupation: gun smith. Convicted of counterfeiting by a court in Davidson County, and sentenced to 5 years in the Penitentiary. Received Jan. 16, 1847, and discharged Sept. 26, 1851. Notes: pardoned under the act of 1836. Number in ledger 86: 910.

Name: Samuel Barnwell, age 36, born in Tennessee, occupation: labourer. Convicted of counterfeiting by a court in Davidson County, and sentenced to 10 years in the Penitentiary. Received Jan. 16, 1847, and discharged Feb. 10, 1850. Notes: gen'l pardon by Gov. Trousdale. Number in ledger 86: 911.

Name: William Boyd, age 35, born in Virginia, occupation: moulder. Convicted of counterfeiting by a court in Davidson County, and sentenced to 5 years in the Penitentiary. Received Jan. 16, 1847, and discharged Sept. 26, 1851. Notes: pardoned under the act of 1836. Number in ledger 86: 912.

Name: James Spencer, age 48, born in Kentucky, occupation: bl[ac]k smith. Convicted of counterfeiting by a court in Davidson County, and sentenced to 5 years in the Penitentiary. Received Jan. 16, 1847, and discharged Feb. 5, 1851. Notes: pardoned by Gov. Trousdale. Number in ledger 86: 913.

Name: Franklin Hill, age 20, born in Tennessee, occupation: labourer. Convicted of larceny by a court in Franklin County, and sentenced to 2 years in the Penitentiary. Received Jan. 16, 1847, and discharged Jan. 2, 1849. Notes: pardoned under the act of 1836. Number in ledger 86: 914.

Name: Thomas Scott, age 45, born in North Carolina, occupation: stone cutter. Convicted of larceny by a court in Franklin County, and sentenced to 5 years in the Penitentiary. Received Jan. 16, 1847, and discharged Sept. 26, 1851. Notes: pardoned under the act of 1836. Number in ledger 86: 915.

Name: William Owen, age 27, born in Kentucky, occupation: labourer. Convicted of larceny by a court in Grainger County, and sentenced to 4 years in the Penitentiary. Received Jan. 17, 1847, and discharged Jan. 1, 1851. Notes: conduct passable. Number in ledger 86: 916.

Name: A.C. Cook, age 30, born in New York, occupation: copper plate p[?]. Convicted of counterfeiting by a court in Davidson County, and sentenced to 3 years in the Penitentiary. Received Jan. 23, 1847, and discharged Nov. 16, 1849. Notes: pardoned under the act of 1836. Number in ledger 86: 917.

Name: Jarret Watkins, age 47, born in North Carolina, occupation: labourer. Convicted of horse stealing by a court in Monroe County, and sentenced to 4 years in the Penitentiary. Received Jan. 25, 1847, and discharged July 19, 1850. Notes: negro, died of billeous coleramorbus [sic]. Number in ledger 86: 918.

Name: Simpson Millwood, age 23, born in Alabama, occupation: hatter. Convicted of larceny by a court in Tipton County, and sentenced to 3 years in the Penitentiary. Received Feb. 17, 1847, and discharged Dec. 22, 1849. Notes: pardoned under the act of 1836. Number in ledger 86: 919.

Name: Richard Hughes, age 23, born in Tennessee, occupation: labourer. Convicted of counterfeiting by a court in Fentress County, and sentenced to 3 years in the Penitentiary. Received Feb. 25, 1847, and discharged May 14, 1849. Notes: died from a fracture of the leg rec'd at stone quarry. Number in ledger 86: 920.

Name: B.D. Skinner, age 35, born in Virginia, occupation: carpenter. Convicted of bigamy by a court in Fayett[e] County, and sentenced to 10 years in the Penitentiary. Received Feb. 27, 1847, and discharged June 16, 1852. Notes: general pardon by W.B. Campbell. Number in ledger 86: 921.

Tennessee Convicts: Records of the State Penitentiary

Name: John Brigham, age 25, born in Tennessee, occupation: labourer. Convicted of forgery by a court in Stewart County, and sentenced to 3 years in the Penitentiary. Received Mar. 1, 1847, and discharged Feb. 26, 1850. Notes: conduct bad. Number in ledger 86: 922.

Name: Thos. D. Brigham, age 21, born in Tennessee, occupation: labourer. Convicted of forgery by a court in Stewart County, and sentenced to 3 years in the Penitentiary. Received Mar. 1, 1847, and discharged Feb. 26, 1850. Notes: conduct bad. Number in ledger 86: 923.

Name: Jacob Philips, age 49, born in Tennessee, occupation: labourer. Convicted of counterfeiting by a court in Overton County, and sentenced to 3 years in the Penitentiary. Received Mar. 4, 1847, and discharged Apr. 16, 1848. Notes: died from a rupture of a blood vessel. Number in ledger 86: 924.

Name: Joel Thacker, age 41, born in South Carolina, occupation: waggon [sic] maker. Convicted of assault with intent to murder by a court in Coffee County, and sentenced to 3 years in the Penitentiary. Received Mar. 9, 1847, and discharged July 17, 1848. Notes: pardoned by Gov. Brown. Number in ledger 86: 925.

Name: George Freeman, age 45, born in Virginia, occupation: shoe maker. Convicted of petit larceny by a court in Washington County, and sentenced to 2 years and 6 months in the Penitentiary. Received Mar. 10, 1847, and discharged Nov. 9, 1848. Notes: negro slave, pardoned by N.S. Brown. Number in ledger 86: 926.

Name: John Edmans [Edmonds?], age 24, born in Tennessee, occupation: labourer. Convicted of larceny by a court in Bledsoe County, and sentenced to 3 years in the Penitentiary. Received Mar. 18, 1847, and discharged Jan. 17, 1850. Notes: pardoned under the act of 1836. [Name shows as Edwards on published report of 1849.] Number in ledger 86: 927.

Name: William Powell, age 22, born in Tennessee, occupation: overseer. Convicted of petit larceny by a court in Hardeman County, and sentenced to 1 year in the Penitentiary. Received Mar. 20, 1847, and discharged Mar. 20, 1848. Notes: conduct good. Number in ledger 86: 928.

Name: John A. Hughes, age 27, born in Tennessee, occupation: thief. Convicted of horse stealing by a court in Williamson County, and sentenced to

4 years in the Penitentiary. Received Mar. 22, 1847, and discharged Dec. 25, 1850. Notes: pardoned under the act of 1836. Number in ledger 86: 929.

Name: A. Hobbs, age 24, born in Virginia, occupation: clerk. Convicted of forgery by a court in Shelby County, and sentenced to 7 years in the Penitentiary. Received Mar. 30, 1847, and discharged Oct. 20, 1853. Notes: pardoned under the act of 1836. Number in ledger 86: 930.

Name: Isaac Fallick, age 28, born in Ohio, occupation: bl[ac]k smith. Convicted of passing counterfeit money by a court in Shelby County, and sentenced to 3 years in the Penitentiary. Received Mar. 30, 1847, and discharged Feb. 5, 1850. Notes: pardoned under the act of 1836. Number in ledger 86: 931.

Name: William Willis, age 29, born in New York, occupation: labourer. Convicted of grand larceny by a court in Davidson County, and sentenced to 3 years in the Penitentiary. Received Apr. 22, 1847, and discharged Feb. 15, 1850. Notes: 2nd [conviction], pardoned under the act of 1836. Number in ledger 86: 932.

Name: Isham Cagle, age 27, born in Tennessee, occupation: labourer. Convicted of larceny by a court in Sevier County, and sentenced to 1 year in the Penitentiary. Received Apr. 29, 1847, and discharged Apr. 12, 1848. Notes: conduct good. Number in ledger 86: 933.

Name: Mary Finney, age 23, born in North Carolina, occupation: blank. Convicted of larceny by a court in McMinn County, and sentenced to 3 years in the Penitentiary. Received May 3, 1847, and discharged Feb. 26, 1850. Notes: pardoned under the act of 1836. Number in ledger 86: 934.

Name: Wright Benson, age 53, born in North Carolina, occupation: labourer. Convicted of larceny by a court in McNairy County, and sentenced to 2 years in the Penitentiary. Received May 7, 1847, and discharged May 7, 1849. Notes: conduct fair. Number in ledger 86: 935.

Name: James S. Rice, age 42, born in Tennessee, occupation: labourer. Convicted of bigamy by a court in Grainger County, and sentenced to 2 years in the Penitentiary. Received May 11, 1847, and discharged Mar. 15, 1849. Notes: pardoned under the act of 1836. Number in ledger 86: 936.

Name: John Baker, age 28, born in Tennessee, occupation: shoe maker. Convicted of felony by a court in Grainger County, and sentenced to 3 years in the Penitentiary. Received May 11, 1847, and discharged Apr. 30, 1850. Notes: conduct fair. Number in ledger 86: 937.

Name: Daniel Sheets, age 38, born in North Carolina, occupation: labourer. Convicted of murder by a court in Madison County, and sentenced to 1 year in the Penitentiary. Received May 20, 1847, and discharged May 20, 1848. Notes: col[ore]d, 2nd sentence, conduct good. Number in ledger 86: 938.

Name: Francis McCallister, age 35, born in Tennessee, occupation: labourer. Convicted of larceny by a court in Madison County, and sentenced to 1 year in the Penitentiary. Received May 20, 1847, and discharged May 20, 1848. Notes: conduct good. Number in ledger 86: 939.

Name: Elias Jackson, age 31, born in Tennessee, occupation: farmer. Convicted of counterfeiting by a court in Jackson County, and sentenced to 3 years in the Penitentiary. Received May 26, 1847, and discharged Mar. 25, 1850. Notes: pardoned under the act of 1836. Number in ledger 86: 940.

Name: James Wilkins (alias), age 37, born in Virginia, occupation: tailor. Convicted of counterfeiting by a court in Green[e] County, and sentenced to 10 years in the Penitentiary. Received July 1, 1847, and discharged Nov. 16, 1856. Notes: pardoned under the act of 1836. Number in ledger 86: 941.

Name: Burrell Anderson, age 52, born in Tennessee, occupation: labourer. Convicted of murder in 2nd degree by a court in Weakl[e]y County, and sentenced to 15 years in the Penitentiary. Received July 11, 1847, and discharged July 18, 1850. Notes: died of cholera. Number in ledger 86: 942.

Name: Solomon Black, age 33, born in Tennessee, occupation: labourer. Convicted of murder by a court in Washington County, and sentenced to life time years in the Penitentiary. Received July 14, 1847, and discharged Mar. 3, 1854. Notes: pardoned by Gov. Johnson. Number in ledger 86: 943.

Name: Charles Holland, age 18, born in Indiana, occupation: labourer. Convicted of larceny by a court in Macon County, and sentenced to 1 year in the Penitentiary. Received July 19, 1847, and discharged July 19, 1848. Notes: conduct fair. Number in ledger 86: 944.

Tennessee Convicts: Records of the State Penitentiary

Name: Reubin Chick, age 27, born in Kentucky, occupation: loafer. Convicted of crime not specified by court by a court in Davidson County, and sentenced to 2 years in the Penitentiary. Received July 20, 1847, and discharged Dec. 11, 1847. Notes: pardoned by Gov. N.S. Brown. [Pardon papers show his crime was maliciously putting out the eye of William Maxey]. Number in ledger 86: 945.

Name: Ephraim Dunavan, age 25, born in Tennessee, occupation: farmer. Convicted of larceny by a court in Anderson County, and sentenced to 3 years in the Penitentiary. Received July 22, 1847, and discharged May 14, 1850. Notes: pardoned under the act of 1836. Number in ledger 86: 946.

Name: John Knight, age 24, born in Virginia, occupation: carpenter. Convicted of counterfeiting by a court in Anderson County, and sentenced to 3 years in the Penitentiary. Received blank [July 22, 1847], and discharged Aug. 26, 1847. Notes: died of chronic inflamation of the brain. Number in ledger 86: 947.

Name: Absolom Brown, age 29, born in Ohio, occupation: labourer. Convicted of malicious stabbing by a court in Henderson County, and sentenced to 3 years in the Penitentiary. Received Aug. 8, 1847, and discharged May 27, 1850. Notes: pardoned under the act of 1836. Number in ledger 86: 948.

Name: Timothy Hicks, age 44, born in Virginia, occupation: labourer. Convicted of larceny by a court in Co[c]ke County, and sentenced to 1 year in the Penitentiary. Received Aug. 11, 1847, and discharged July 30, 1848. Notes: conduct good. Number in ledger 86: 949.

Name: William G. Mashon, age 25, born in Kentucky, occupation: school teacher. Convicted of petit larceny by a court in McMinn County, and sentenced to 1 year in the Penitentiary. Received Aug. 23, 1847, and discharged Aug. 14, 1848. Notes: conduct good. Number in ledger 86: 950.

Name: B.F. McIntyre, age 14, born in Tennessee, occupation: nothing. Convicted of larceny by a court in Marshal[l] County, and sentenced to 3 years in the Penitentiary. Received Aug. 25, 1847, and discharged Apr. 24, 1850. Notes: general pardon by Gov. Trousdale. Number in ledger 86: 951.

Name: Robert Walker, age 18, born in Tennessee, occupation: thief. Convicted of larceny by a court in Campbell County, and sentenced to 3 years in the

Tennessee Convicts: Records of the State Penitentiary

Penitentiary. Received Sept. 17, 1847, and discharged Feb. 25, 1848. Notes: died with inflamation of the brian. Number in ledger 86: 952.

Name: Washington G. Pass, age blank, born in blank, occupation: no trade. Convicted of horse stealing by a court in Shelby County, and sentenced to 3 years in the Penitentiary. Received Mar. 13, 1846, and discharged Jan. 2, 1849. Notes: pardoned under the act of 1836. Number in ledger 86: 953.

Name: Saml. H. Forbes, age 24, born in South Carolina, occupation: bl[ac]k smith. Convicted of murder in 2nd degree by a court in Shelby County, and sentenced to 15 years in the Penitentiary. Received Sept. 29, 1847, and discharged Feb. 25, 1854. Notes: pardoned by Gov. Johnson. Number in ledger 86: 954.

Name: John Tucker, age 26, born in Virginia, occupation: farmer. Convicted of malicious stabbing by a court in Monroe County, and sentenced to 2 years in the Penitentiary. Received Oct. 2, 1847, and discharged Aug. 18, 1849. Notes: 2nd conviction, pardoned under the act of 1836. Number in ledger 86: 955.

Name: Lucy Witcher, age 47, born in North Carolina, occupation: labourer. Convicted of barn burning by a court in Hawkins County, and sentenced to 3 years in the Penitentiary. Received Oct. 12, 1847, and discharged July 19, 1850. Notes: alias Wm. Walker, pardoned under the act of 1836. Number in ledger 86: 956.

Name: William Neal, age blank, born in blank, occupation: blank. Convicted of [blank] by a court in [blank] County, and sentenced to blank years in the Penitentiary. Received Oct. 16, 1847, and discharged Aug. 17, 1850. Notes: pardoned under the act of 1836. Number in ledger 86: 957.

Name: Isaiah Maidewell, age 35, born in Tennessee, occupation: labourer. Convicted of petit larceny by a court in White County, and sentenced to 2 years in the Penitentiary. Received Oct. 21, 1847, and discharged Sept. 25, 1849. Notes: pardoned under the act of 1836. Number in ledger 86: 958.

Name: Williams Eavans [Evans?], age 33, born in South Carolina, occupation: farmer. Convicted of felony by a court in Polk County, and sentenced to 3 years in the Penitentiary. Received Oct. 23, 1847, and discharged Aug. 17, 1850. Notes: 3rd conviction, pardoned under the act of 1836. Number in ledger 86: 959.

Name: Josiah Chapman, age 57, born in Virginia, occupation: farmer. Convicted of having in posession c[ounterfeit] by a court in Fentress County, and sentenced to 3 years in the Penitentiary. Received Oct. 27, 1847, and discharged Aug. 17, 1850. Notes: pardoned under the act of 1836. Number in ledger 86: 960.

Name: John F. Lewis, age 37, born in Pennsylvania, occupation: labourer. Convicted of petit larceny by a court in Knox County, and sentenced to 1 year in the Penitentiary. Received Nov. 1, 1847, and discharged Oct. 19, 1848. Notes: conduct good. Number in ledger 86: 961.

Name: John Gaddis, age 35, born in Tennessee, occupation: labourer. Convicted of larceny by a court in Overton County, and sentenced to 5 years in the Penitentiary. Received Nov. 4, 1847 and discharged July 10, 1850. Notes: died of cholera. Number in ledger 86: 962.

Name: Samuel King, age 22, born in Tennessee, occupation: tanner. Convicted of larceny by a court in Overton County, and sentenced to 1 year in the Penitentiary. Received Nov. 4, 1847 and discharged Nov. 4, 1848. Notes: conduct good. Number in ledger 86: 963.

Name: Nathan Blackwell, age 48, born in South Carolina, occupation: labourer. Convicted of stealing a sheep by a court in Coffee County, and sentenced to 2 years in the Penitentiary. Received Nov. 4, 1847 and discharged Oct. 4, 1849. Notes: pardoned under the act of '36. Number in ledger 86: 964.

Name: Zachariah Hurt, age 20, born in Tennessee, occupation: machine maker. Convicted of petit larceny by a court in Davidson County, and sentenced to 2 years in the Penitentiary. Received Nov. 11, 1847 and discharged Oct. 4, 1849. Notes: alias Davis, pardoned under the act of '36. Number in ledger 86: 965.

Name: number 966 skipped, age , born in , occupation: Convicted of by a court in County, and sentenced to years in the Penitentiary. Received and discharged . Notes: . Number in ledger 86: 966.

Name: Miller Simmons, age 19, born in Tennessee, occupation: labourer. Convicted of buggery by a court in Washington County, and sentenced to 5 years in the Penitentiary. Received Nov. 16, 1847 and discharged Oct. 4, 1848. Notes: mulatto, died of consumption. Number in ledger 86: 967.

Name: Dempse Johnson, age 26, born in North Carolina, occupation: labourer.

Convicted of petit larceny by a court in Washington County, and sentenced to 3 years in the Penitentiary. Received Nov. 16, 1847 and discharged Nov. 16, 1850. Notes: conduct tolerable good. Number in ledger 86: 968.

Name: John Moon [Moore?], age 48, born in Ireland, occupation: tanner. Convicted of murder by a court in Montgomery County, and sentenced to life in the Penitentiary. Received Nov. 20, 1847 and discharged Aug. 23, 1858. Notes: pardoned by Gov. I.G. Harris. Number in ledger 86: 969.

Name: Gideon Pillow, age 23, born in Tennessee, occupation: labourer. Convicted of petit larceny by a court in Smith County, and sentenced to 1 year in the Penitentiary. Received Nov. 30, 1847 and discharged Nov. 30, 1848. Notes: conduct good. Number in ledger 86: 970.

Name: James Ethridge, age 25, born in Tennessee, occupation: labourer. Convicted of voluntary manslaughter by a court in Humphries County, and sentenced to 3 years in the Penitentiary. Received Dec. 15, 1847 and discharged Oct. 4, 1849. Notes: died of scrof. affec. of the rectum & bladder. Number in ledger 86: 971.

Name: Amos Hampton, age 18, born in Alabama, occupation: labourer. Convicted of horse stealing by a court in Davidson County, and sentenced to 4 years in the Penitentiary. Received Dec. 28, 1847 and discharged Oct. 7, 1851. Notes: pardoned under the act of 1836. Number in ledger 86: 972.

Name: David Priest, age 33, born in Kentucky, occupation: labourer. Convicted of larceny by a court in Davidson County, and sentenced to 1 year in the Penitentiary. Received Dec. 28, 1847 and discharged Dec. 29, 1848. Notes: conduct tolerable good. Number in ledger 86: 973.

Name: John White, age 16, born in Kentucky, occupation: labourer. Convicted of horse stealing by a court in Jefferson County, and sentenced to 3 years in the Penitentiary. Received Jan. 3, 1848 and discharged Jan. 25, 1848. Notes: died of inflamation of the brain. Number in ledger 86: 974.

Name: Daniel Taylor, age 22, born in Tennessee, occupation: labourer. Convicted of larceny by a court in Jefferson County, and sentenced to 1 year in the Penitentiary. Received Jan. 3, 1848 and discharged Dec. 23, 1848. Notes: conduct tolerably good. Number in ledger 86: 975.

Name: Drury Ray, age 17, born in Tennessee, occupation: fisherman.

Convicted of horse stealing by a court in Madison County, and sentenced to 5 years in the Penitentiary. Received Jan. 17, 1848 and discharged Jan. 17, 1853. Notes: conduct tolerably good. Number in ledger 86: 976.

Name: William McCoy, age 46, born in North Carolina, occupation: labourer. Convicted of rape by a court in Maury County, and sentenced to 15 years in the Penitentiary. Received Jan. 19, 1848 and discharged Feb. 22, 1860. Notes: died of pneumonia. Number in ledger 86: 977.

Name: William Smith, age 29, born in Virginia, occupation: soldier. Convicted of obtaining goods under false pre by a court in Shelby County, and sentenced to 4 years in the Penitentiary. Received Jan. 21, 1847 and discharged Dec. 24, 1851. Notes: pardoned under the act of 1836. Number in ledger 86: 978.

Name: Harrison Maidwell, age 24, born in Tennessee, occupation: labourer. Convicted of grand larceny by a court in White County, and sentenced to 4 years in the Penitentiary. Received Feb. 21, 1848 and discharged Nov. 26, 1851. Notes: pardoned under the act of 1836. Number in ledger 86: 979.

Name: Edmund Braudon, age 22, born in Tennessee, occupation: labourer. Convicted of horse stealing by a court in Cannon County, and sentenced to 3 years and 6 months in the Penitentiary. Received Feb. 29, 1848 and discharged June 16, 1851. Notes: pardoned under the act of 1836. Number in ledger 86: 980.

Name: G.W. Brown, age 19, born in Georgia, occupation: labourer. Convicted of grand larceny by a court in Hamilton County, and sentenced to 3 years in the Penitentiary. Received Apr. 9, 1848 and discharged Feb. 8, 1851. Notes: pardoned under the act of 1836. Number in ledger 86: 981.

Name: Lorenzo D. Troxler, age 24, born in Tennessee, occupation: labourer. Convicted of assault & battery / attempt[ed] by a court in Bedford County, and sentenced to 2 years in the Penitentiary. Received Apr. 19, 1848 and discharged Apr. 19, 1850. Notes: conduct tolerably good. Number in ledger 86: 982.

Name: Pleasant Hurst, age 20, born in Tennessee, occupation: labourer. Convicted of attempt to commit rape by a court in Sevier County, and sentenced to 3 years in the Penitentiary. Received Apr. 20, 1848 and discharged Apr. 8, 1851. Notes: conduct tolerably good. Number in ledger 86:

983.

Name: Wesley Brewer, age 20, born in North Carolina, occupation: labourer. Convicted of passing counterfeit money by a court in Shelby County, and sentenced to 3 years in the Penitentiary. Received Apr. 28, 1848 and discharged Apr. 28, 1851. Notes: conduct moderately good. Number in ledger 86: 984.

Name: James Martin, age 45, born in Tennessee, occupation: constable. Convicted of murder by a court in Davidson County, and sentenced to 20 years in the Penitentiary. Received May 4, 1848 and discharged Dec. 28, 1852. Notes: general pardon by Gov. Campbell. Number in ledger 86: 985.

Name: Benjamin Andrews, age 38, born in Virginia, occupation: labourer. Convicted of harbouring & slave stealing by a court in Davidson County, and sentenced to 3 years in the Penitentiary. Received May 5, 1848 and discharged Feb. 24, 1851. Notes: pardoned under the act of 1836. Number in ledger 86: 986.

Name: Jim, a boy of collour , age 40, born in North Carolina, occupation: labourer. Convicted of obtaining goods under false pre by a court in Madison County, and sentenced to 3 years in the Penitentiary. Received May 10, 1848 and discharged Mar. 4, 1851. Notes: pardoned under the act of 1836. Number in ledger 86: 987.

Name: Marian C. Clark, age 28, born in Alabama, occupation: labourer. Convicted of murder by a court in Madison County, and sentenced to life in the Penitentiary. Received May 10, 1848 and discharged Oct. 9, 1857. Notes: pardoned by Gov. A. Johnson. Number in ledger 86: 988.

Name: Robert Logan, age 35, born in New York, occupation: sailor. Convicted of murder by a court in Madison County, and sentenced to 10 years in the Penitentiary. Received May 10, 1848 and discharged Aug. 14, 1849. Notes: died of chronic diahrhea [sic]. Number in ledger 86: 989.

Name: Nathaniel Ussery, age 19, born in Tennessee, occupation: brick mason. Convicted of murder by a court in Madison County, and sentenced to 10 years in the Penitentiary. Received May 10, 1848 and discharged Sept. 25, 1857. Notes: pardoned under the act of 1836. Number in ledger 86: 990.

Name: Wm. G. Jones, age 24, born in Virginia, occupation: shoe maker.

Convicted of horse stealing by a court in Shelby County, and sentenced to 5 years in the Penitentiary. Received May 16, 1848 and discharged Jan. 25, 1853. Notes: pardoned under the act of 1836. Number in ledger 86: 991.

Name: Richard Davis, age 36, born in North Carolina, occupation: farmer. Convicted of petit larceny by a court in Shelby County, and sentenced to 1 year and 6 months in the Penitentiary. Received May 16, 1848 and discharged Nov. 16, 1849. Notes: conduct tolerable good. Number in ledger 86: 992.

Name: John Williams, age 18, born in Virginia, occupation: loafer. Convicted of petit larceny by a court in Maury County, and sentenced to 1 year in the Penitentiary. Received May 25, 1848 and discharged May 25, 1849. Notes: conduct fair. Number in ledger 86: 993.

Name: Saml. G. Ward, age 29, born in Virginia, occupation: merchant. Convicted of obtaining goods under false pre by a court in Tipton County, and sentenced to 3 years in the Penitentiary. Received June 17, 1848 and discharged Sept. 20, 1850. Notes: general pardon by Gov. Trousdale. Number in ledger 86: 994.

Name: Alexander Bowlice, age 29, born in Indiana, occupation: labourer. Convicted of stealing by a court in Lawrence County, and sentenced to 5 years in the Penitentiary. Received June 21, 1848 and discharged Mar. 1, 1853. Notes: conduct good. Number in ledger 86: 995.

Name: J.P. Cheewith[?], age 25, born in Ohio, occupation: preacher. Convicted of bigamy by a court in Sumner County, and sentenced to 2 years in the Penitentiary. Received June 28, 1848 and discharged June 26, 1850. Notes: conduct tolerable only. Number in ledger 86: 996.

Name: James Thomas, age 33, born in Kentucky, occupation: labourer. Convicted of grand larceny by a court in Rhea County, and sentenced to 7 years and 6 months in the Penitentiary. Received July 14, 1848 and discharged July 20, 1850. Notes: died of some disease. Number in ledger 86: 997.

Name: Tobias M. Warford, age 37, born in North Carolina, occupation: carpenter. Convicted of incest by a court in Hardeman County, and sentenced to 21 year in the Penitentiary. Received July 16, 1848 and discharged Aug. 30, 1849. Notes: died of congestive fever. Number in ledger 86: 998.

Name: William B. Needham, age 39, born in Tennessee, occupation:

millwright. Convicted of larceny by a court in Hardeman County, and sentenced to 3 years in the Penitentiary. Received July 16, 1848 and discharged May 27, 1851. Notes: pardoned under the act of 1836. Number in ledger 86: 999.

Name: John Bailey, age 28, born in Pennsylvania, occupation: gambler. Convicted of larceny by a court in Shelby County, and sentenced to 3 years in the Penitentiary. Received July 21, 1848 and discharged July 21, 1851. Notes: discharged at expiration of sentence. Number in ledger 86: 1000.

Name: Felix S. Hall, age 33, born in Kentucky, occupation: cabinet maker. Convicted of larceny by a court in Henderson County, and sentenced to 1 year in the Penitentiary. Received Aug. 3, 1848 and discharged Aug. 3, 1849. Notes: conduct good. Number in ledger 86: 1001.

Name: Pascal Nunn, age 26, born in Tennessee, occupation: farmer. Convicted of assault with intent to commit r by a court in Sevier County, and sentenced to 5 years in the Penitentiary. Received Aug. 5, 1848 and discharged Apr. 15, 1853. Notes: conduct good. Number in ledger 86: 1002.

Name: Andrew McCuistiace, age 38, born in Tennessee, occupation: farmer. Convicted of manslaughter by a court in Jefferson County, and sentenced to 5 years in the Penitentiary. Received Aug. 22, 1848 and discharged May 5, 1853. Notes: pardoned under the act of 1836. Number in ledger 86: 1003.

Name: Solomon Whitlow, age 29, born in North Carolina, occupation: farmer. Convicted of burglary by a court in Grainger County, and sentenced to 5 years in the Penitentiary. Received Sept. 11, 1848 and discharged May 16, 1853. Notes: pardoned under the act of 1836. Number in ledger 86: 1004.

Name: John Shropshire, age 23, born in Tennessee, occupation: farmer. Convicted of petit larceny by a court in Grainger County, and sentenced to 1 year in the Penitentiary. Received Sept. 11, 1848 and discharged Sept. 7, 1849. Notes: conduct good. Number in ledger 86: 1005.

Name: Joel Shropshire, age 37, born in Tennessee, occupation: farmer. Convicted of burglary by a court in Grainger County, and sentenced to 5 years in the Penitentiary. Received Sept. 11, 1848 and discharged May 16, 1853. Notes: pardoned under the act of 1836. Number in ledger 86: 1006.

Name: Alex N. Moore, age 24, born in Tennessee, occupation: bl[ac]k smith.

Convicted of grand larceny by a court in Grainger County, and sentenced to 4 years in the Penitentiary. Received Sept. 11, 1848 and discharged June 2, 1852. Notes: pardoned under the act of 1836. Number in ledger 86: 1007.

Name: E.M.D. Burress, age 28, born in Tennessee, occupation: farmer. Convicted of felinous [sic] assault by a court in Campbell County, and sentenced to 4 years in the Penitentiary. Received Sept. 21, 1848 and discharged June 20, 1852. Notes: pardoned under the act of 1836. Number in ledger 86: 1008.

Name: John Cottrell, age 18, born in Tennessee, occupation: farmer. Convicted of stealing a bank bill by a court in Monroe County, and sentenced to 4 years in the Penitentiary. Received Sept. 30, 1848 and discharged June 30, 1852. Notes: pardoned under the act of 1836. Number in ledger 86: 1009.

Name: John Ellis, age 55, born in New Jersey, occupation: farmer. Convicted of larceny by a court in Monroe County, and sentenced to 2 years in the Penitentiary. Received Sept. 30, 1848 and discharged June 13, 1849. Notes: died of chronic diahrhea [sic]. Number in ledger 86: 1010.

Name: William Turner, age 34, born in Tennessee, occupation: farmer. Convicted of larceny by a court in Knox County, and sentenced to 1 year and 8 months in the Penitentiary. Received Oct. 27, 1848 and discharged Aug. 26, 1849. Notes: died of congestive fever. Number in ledger 86: 1011.

Name: William G. Britt, age 43, born in Kentucky, occupation: farmer. Convicted of felony by a court in Knox County, and sentenced to 3 years in the Penitentiary. Received Oct. 27, 1848 and discharged July 27, 1849. Notes: died of congestive fever. [Published 1849 report shows name as Solomon G. Britt.] Number in ledger 86: 1012.

Name: William Bowles, age 19, born in Tennessee, occupation: farmer. Convicted of mule stealing by a court in Maury County, and sentenced to 3 years in the Penitentiary. Received Nov. 10, 1848 and discharged Sept. 10, 1851. Notes: pardoned under the act of 1836. Number in ledger 86: 1013.

Name: J.M. Hall, age 26, born in Kentucky, occupation: labourer. Convicted of larceny by a court in Overton County, and sentenced to 1 year in the Penitentiary. Received Nov. 11, 1848 and discharged Nov. 11, 1849. Notes: conduct good. Number in ledger 86: 1014.

Name: John Vickars, age 26, born in Tennessee, occupation: labourer. Convicted of larceny by a court in Lincoln County, and sentenced to 3 years in the Penitentiary. Received Nov. 22, 1848 and discharged Aug. 31, 1849. Notes: died of consumption. Number in ledger 86: 1015.

Name: Eli Campbell, age 49, born in Tennessee, occupation: farmer. Convicted of petit larceny by a court in Carter County, and sentenced to 2 years in the Penitentiary. Received Nov. 25, 1848 and discharged Oct. 17, 1850. Notes: pardoned under the act of 1836. Number in ledger 86: 1016.

Name: James Mitchel, age 23, born in Illinois, occupation: labourer. Convicted of robbery by a court in Shelby County, and sentenced to 15 years in the Penitentiary. Received Nov. 30, 1848 and discharged Aug. 21, 1866. Notes: lunatic, transferred to the asylum. Number in ledger 86: 1017.

Name: William Davis, age 33, born in Ohio, occupation: ingineer [sic]. Convicted of robbery by a court in Shelby County, and sentenced to 15 years in the Penitentiary. Received Nov. 30, 1848 and discharged Oct. 8, 1861. Notes: genl. pardon by Gov. I.G. Harris. Number in ledger 86: 1018.

Name: Augustus Finney, age 16, born in Ohio, occupation: labourer. Convicted of arson by a court in Shelby County, and sentenced to 2 years in the Penitentiary. Received Nov. 30, 1848 and discharged Nov. 30, 1850. Notes: conduct tolerable good. Number in ledger 86: 1019.

Name: William Taylor, age 23, born in New York, occupation: boatsman. Convicted of arson by a court in Shelby County, and sentenced to 2 years in the Penitentiary. Received Nov. 30, 1848 and discharged Nov. 30, 1850. Notes: conduct tolerable good. Number in ledger 86: 1020.

Name: Danl. Hoffman, age 23, born in Ohio, occupation: stone mason. Convicted of larceny by a court in Shelby County, and sentenced to 1 year in the Penitentiary. Received Nov. 30, 1848 and discharged Nov. 31, 1849. Notes: conduct good. Number in ledger 86: 1021.

Name: Ransom Elloitt [sic, Elliott], age 48, born in Tennessee, occupation: labourer. Convicted of malicious shooting by a court in Shelby County, and sentenced to 2 years in the Penitentiary. Received Nov. 30, 1848 and discharged Oct. 18, 1850. Notes: parpardoned under the act of 1836. Number in ledger 86: 1022.

Tennessee Convicts: Records of the State Penitentiary

Name: Malinda Brewer, age blank, born in Tennessee, occupation: blank. Convicted of blank by a court in Knox County, and sentenced to 1 year in the Penitentiary. Received Mar. 11, 1848 and discharged Feb. 18, 1849. Notes: 2nd sentence, conduct tolerable good. [Probably same as Mehala Brewer, #757] Number in ledger 86: 1023.

Name: James McMorris, age 17, born in Tennessee, occupation: labourer. Convicted of burglary / attempt to commit ra by a court in Marshall County, and sentenced to 5 years in the Penitentiary. Received Dec. 2, 1848 and discharged Aug. 28, 1853. Notes: pardoned under the act of 1836. Number in ledger 86: 1024.

Name: Nelson Phillip, age 29, born in Tennessee, occupation: labourer. Convicted of rape by a court in Davidson County, and sentenced to 10 years in the Penitentiary. Received Dec. 16, 1848 and discharged Oct. 26, 1856. Notes: died of jaundice. Number in ledger 86: 1025.

Name: Samuel Smith, age 33, born in Illinois, occupation: labourer. Convicted of counterfeiting by a court in Davidson County, and sentenced to 3 years in the Penitentiary. Received Dec. 19, 1848 and discharged Aug. 24, 1851. Notes: died of choler[a]morbus. Number in ledger 86: 1026.

Name: Thomas Davidson, age 34, born in Tennessee, occupation: bl[ac]ksmith. Convicted of assault with intent to kill by a court in Davidson County, and sentenced to 3 years in the Penitentiary. Received Dec. 19, 1848 and discharged Oct. 15, 1850. Notes: general pardon Gov. Trousdale. Number in ledger 86: 1027.

Name: William Flemming, age 25, born in Tennessee, occupation: loafer. Convicted of larceny by a court in Davidson County, and sentenced to 5 years in the Penitentiary. Received Dec. 19, 1848 and discharged Dec. 19, 1851. Notes: general pardon by Gov. Campbell. Number in ledger 86: 1028.

Name: Martin Moore, age 38, born in Tennessee, occupation: labourer. Convicted of murder by a court in Carter County, and sentenced to life in the Penitentiary. Received Dec. 26, 1848 and discharged Mar. 4, 1859. Notes: col[ore]d, died of consumption. Number in ledger 86: 1029.

Name: Andrew Glover, age 32, born in Pennsylvania, occupation: carpenter. Convicted of larceny by a court in Carter County, and sentenced to 3 years in the Penitentiary. Received Dec. 27, 1848 and discharged Oct. 21, 1851. Notes:

pardoned under the act of 1836. Number in ledger 86: 1030.

Name: William Heatherley, age 36, born in Tennessee, occupation: farmer. Convicted of larceny by a court in Jefferson County, and sentenced to 2 years in the Penitentiary. Received Dec. 26, 1848 and discharged Aug. 13, 1849. Notes: died of chronic diarrhea. Number in ledger 86: 1031.

Name: Thomas E. Holmes, age 26, born in Tennessee, occupation: farmer. Convicted of murder by a court in Davidson County, and sentenced to 10 years in the Penitentiary. Received Dec. 28, 1848 and discharged Nov. 15, 1854. Notes: pardoned by Gov. Johnson. Number in ledger 86: 1032.

Name: John Harris, age 23, born in North Carolina, occupation: bl[ac]ksmith. Convicted of petit larceny by a court in Green[e] County, and sentenced to 2 years and 6 months in the Penitentiary. Received Jan. 7, 1849 and discharged Mar. 4, 1848. Notes: pardoned under the act of 1836. Number in ledger 86: 1033.

Name: James W. Kollogg, age 50, born in Virginia, occupation: shoe & boot maker. Convicted of negro stealing by a court in Henry County, and sentenced to 5 years in the Penitentiary. Received Jan. 29, 1849 and discharged Apr. 26, 1850. Notes: committed suicide by cutting his throat. [Published 1851 report shows surname as Kellogg.] Number in ledger 86: 1034.

Name: James Henry, age 25, born in North Carolina, occupation: labourer. Convicted of horse stealing by a court in Henry County, and sentenced to 3 years and 10 months in the Penitentiary. Received Jan. 29, 1849 and discharged Sept. 3, 1852. Notes: pardoned under the act of 1836. Number in ledger 86: 1035.

Name: Lewellen Johnson, age 25, born in North Carolina, occupation: labourer. Convicted of assault with intent to kill by a court in Hardin County, and sentenced to 3 years in the Penitentiary. Received Feb. 9, 1849 and discharged Oct. 18, 1850. Notes: genl. pardon by Gov. Trousdale. Number in ledger 86: 1036.

Name: Azariah Parks, age 41, born in North Carolina, occupation: cooper. Convicted of malicious stabbing by a court in Davidson County, and sentenced to 3 years in the Penitentiary. Received Feb. 2, 1849 and discharged June 26, 1850. Notes: died of cholera. Number in ledger 86: 1037.

Name: John Smith, age 22, born in Georgia, occupation: labourer. Convicted of larceny by a court in Coffee County, and sentenced to 1 year in the Penitentiary. Received Feb. 13, 1849 and discharged Feb. 13, 1850. Notes: conduct good. Number in ledger 86: 1038.

Name: Emander Cotton, age 27, born in Alabama, occupation: labourer. Convicted of larceny by a court in Overton County, and sentenced to 5 years in the Penitentiary. Received Mar. 6, 1849 and discharged Nov. 15, 1853. Notes: pardoned under the act of 1836. Number in ledger 86: 1039.

Name: Joshua Bowman, age 24, born in Tennessee, occupation: labourer. Convicted of assault with intent to kill by a court in Henderson County, and sentenced to 3 years in the Penitentiary. Received Apr. 12, 1849 and discharged Feb. 9, 1850. Notes: genl. pardon by Gov. Trousdale. Number in ledger 86: 1040.

Name: Richard Dillionham, age 26, born in Ohio, occupation: abolitionist. Convicted of negro stealing by a court in Davidson County, and sentenced to 3 years in the Penitentiary. Received Apr. 16, 1849 and discharged June 30, 1850. Notes: died of cholera. [Published 1851 report shows surname as Dillingham.] Number in ledger 86: 1041.

Name: James E. Wray, age 24, born in North Carolina, occupation: cooper. Convicted of murder by a court in Bedford County, and sentenced to 8 years in the Penitentiary. Received Apr. 19, 1849 and discharged Oct. 26, 1856. Notes: 2nd sentence, pardoned under the act of 1836. Number in ledger 86: 1042.

Name: Joseph J. Marshall, age 40, born in Virginia, occupation: shoe maker. Convicted of obtaining goods under false pre by a court in Bedford County, and sentenced to 3 years in the Penitentiary. Received May 3, 1849 and discharged Oct. 19, 1849. Notes: died of inflamation of the bowels. Number in ledger 86: 1043.

Name: Carrol King, age 19, born in Tennessee, occupation: loafer. Convicted of murder by a court in Davidson County, and sentenced to lifetime years in the Penitentiary. Received May 3, 1849 and discharged Feb. 8, 1859. Notes: pardoned by Gov. I.G. Harris. Number in ledger 86: 1044.

Name: W.H. Bryant, age 29, born in North Carolina, occupation: shoe maker. Convicted of horse stealing by a court in Madison County, and sentenced to 6 years in the Penitentiary. Received May 12, 1849 and discharged Feb. 28,

Tennessee Convicts: Records of the State Penitentiary

1854. Notes: pardoned by Gov. Johnson. Number in ledger 86: 1045.

Name: Joseph Bowles, age 48, born in Tennessee, occupation: farmer. Convicted of attempt to kill by a court in Madison County, and sentenced to 5 years in the Penitentiary. Received May 12, 1849 and discharged Mar. 25, 1852. Notes: genl. pardon by Gov. Campbell. Number in ledger 86: 1046.

Name: Irwin Hines, age 25, born in Tennessee, occupation: farmer. Convicted of murder by a court in Madison County, and sentenced to lifetime years in the Penitentiary. Received May 12, 1849 and discharged Nov. 28, 1858. Notes: genl. pardon by Gov. Harris. Number in ledger 86: 1047.

Name: Charles Green, age 23, born in Pennsylvania, occupation: carpenter. Convicted of larceny by a court in Madison County, and sentenced to 5 years in the Penitentiary. Received May 12, 1849 and discharged Jan. 20, 1854. Notes: pardoned under the act of 1836. Number in ledger 86: 1048.

Name: Arnett Purtle, age 23, born in Kentucky, occupation: labourer. Convicted of murder by a court in Madison County, and sentenced to 10 years in the Penitentiary. Received May 12, 1849 and discharged Oct. 12, 1853. Notes: genl. pardon by Gov. Campbell. Number in ledger 86: 1049.

Name: Simpson Hooper, age 33, born in Tennessee, occupation: labourer. Convicted of forgery by a court in Perry County, and sentenced to 4 years in the Penitentiary. Received May 29, 1849 and discharged Mar. 1, 1853. Notes: pardoned under the act of 1836. Number in ledger 86: 1050.

Name: Wright Pearce[?], age 33, born in Tennessee, occupation: farmer. Convicted of rape by a court in Perry County, and sentenced to 10 years in the Penitentiary. Received May 29, 1849 and discharged Apr. 6, 1853. Notes: died of errisyplus [*sic*]. Number in ledger 86: 1051.

Name: John Gatewood, age 19, born in North Carolina, occupation: farmer. Convicted of horse stealing by a court in Hardin County, and sentenced to 3 years in the Penitentiary. Received June 7, 1849 and discharged Apr. 6, 1852. Notes: conduct good. Number in ledger 86: 1052.

Name: David Lyneas, age 24, born in Virginia, occupation: farmer. Convicted of assault with intent to kill by a court in Hawkins County, and sentenced to 3 years in the Penitentiary. Received May 31, 1849 and discharged Feb. 9, 1850. Notes: genl. pardon by Gov. Trousdale. Number in ledger 86: 1053.

Name: Stanford Sutton, age 38, born in Tennessee, occupation: farmer. Convicted of stabbing by a court in Wayne County, and sentenced to 2 years in the Penitentiary. Received June 13, 1849 and discharged Apr. 20, 1850. Notes: genl. pardon by Gov. Trousdale. Number in ledger 86: 1054.

Name: John Wilson, age 26, born in North Carolina, occupation: farmer. Convicted of larceny by a court in Wayne County, and sentenced to 3 years in the Penitentiary. Received June 13, 1849 and discharged Apr. 3, 1852. Notes: pardoned under the act of 1836. Number in ledger 86: 1055.

Name: Bailey Turner [Tunur?], age 55, born in North Carolina, occupation: farmer. Convicted of poligamy [sic] by a court in Warren County, and sentenced to 2 years in the Penitentiary. Received July 4, 1849 and discharged Feb. 10, 1850. Notes: genl. pardon by Gov. Trousdale. Number in ledger 86: 1056.

Name: Jackson M. Blackwell, age 24, born in Tennessee, occupation: stone cutter. Convicted of larceny by a court in Roane County, and sentenced to 3 years in the Penitentiary. Received July 9, 1849 and discharged Apr. 29, 1850. Notes: 2nd sentence, pardoned under the act of 1836. Number in ledger 86: 1057.

Name: Robert A. Prater, age 20, born in Tennessee, occupation: labourer. Convicted of murder by a court in Obion County, and sentenced to 1 year in the Penitentiary. Received July 13, 1849 and discharged Sept. 4, 1849. Notes: genl. pardon by W.S. Brown. Number in ledger 86: 1058.

Name: Danl. Tabor, age 38, born in New York, occupation: smelter. Convicted of persuading slaves from owners by a court in Hardeman County, and sentenced to 7 years and 3 months in the Penitentiary. Received July 13, 1849 and discharged Apr. 30, 1856. Notes: pardoned under the act of 1836. Number in ledger 86: 1059.

Name: David Massingil, age 19, born in Tennessee, occupation: boatsman. Convicted of felony & larceny by a court in Marion County, and sentenced to 3 years in the Penitentiary. Received July 20, 1849 and discharged May 20, 1852. Notes: pardoned under the act of 1836. Number in ledger 86: 1060.

Name: William Bailey, age 22, born in Tennessee, occupation: labourer. Convicted of grand larceny by a court in Johnson County, and sentenced to 3 years in the Penitentiary. Received Aug. 1, 1849 and discharged May 20, 1852. Notes: 2nd conviction, pardoned under the act of 1836. Number in ledger 86: 1061.

Name: George Atkins, age 40, born in Tennessee, occupation: farmer. Convicted of larceny by a court in Grainger County, and sentenced to 3 years in the Penitentiary. Received Jan. 9, 1849 and discharged Nov. 7, 1851. Notes: pardoned under the act of 1836. Number in ledger 86: 1062.

Name: Edward Tyler, age 63, born in North Carolina, occupation: school teacher. Convicted of larceny by a court in McMinn County, and sentenced to 3 years in the Penitentiary. Received Dec. 30, 1848 and discharged July 21, 1850. Notes: 3rd conviction, died of [blank]. Number in ledger 86: 1063. [Also listed under number 1142]

Name: Richard Wilson, age 18, born in Tennessee, occupation: labourer. Convicted of larceny by a court in Coffee County, and sentenced to 1 year in the Penitentiary. Received Oct. 10, 1848 and discharged Oct. 8, 1849. Notes: discharged by expiration of sentence. Number in ledger 86: 1064.

Name: William Edwards, age no description, born in blank, occupation: no description. Convicted of involuntary manslaughter by a court in Wayne County, and sentenced to 1 year in the Penitentiary. Received Oct. 20, 1848 and discharged [Oct. 20, 1848]. Notes: pardoned by Gov. Brown the same [day] received. Number in ledger 86: 1065.

Name: Patia Elom, age 26, born in Tennessee, occupation: blank. Convicted of larceny by a court in Overton County, and sentenced to 1 year in the Penitentiary. Received Nov. 11, 1848 and discharged Oct. 20, 1849. Notes: pardoned under the act of 1836. Number in ledger 86: 1066.

Name: Jas. Jenkins, age blank, born in Tennessee, occupation: blank. Convicted of perjury by a court in Monroe County, and sentenced to 3 years in the Penitentiary. Received May 27, 1848 and discharged May 16, 1849. Notes: died of congestive fever. [Published 1849 report shows William Jenkins received May 27, 1848, age 24, died July 24, 1849. Possibly mixed this prisoners records with William Jenkins, register #887?] Number in ledger 86: 1067.

Name: Thomas Lisenby [*sic*, Lazenby?], age 19, born in North Carolina, occupation: soldier. Convicted of malicious stabbing by a court in Henderson

County, and sentenced to 2 years in the Penitentiary. Received Aug. 7, 1849 and discharged June 27, 1851. Notes: pardoned under the act of 1836. Number in ledger 86: 1068.

Name: Elisha Lindsley, age 25, born in Tennessee, occupation: waggon painter. Convicted of grand larceny by a court in Bedford County, and sentenced to 3 years in the Penitentiary. Received Aug. 17, 1849 and discharged Mar. 9, 1850. Notes: died of congestive fever. Number in ledger 86: 1069.

Name: William A. Estis, age 26, born in Tennessee, occupation: labourer. Convicted of murder 1st degree by a court in Giles County, and sentenced to life in the Penitentiary. Received Aug. 20, 1849 and discharged Nov. 3, 1859. Notes: pardoned by Gov. I.G. Harris. Number in ledger 86: 1070.

Name: Elias Walker, age 28, born in Georgia, occupation: labourer. Convicted of assault & battery / intent to k by a court in McMinn County, and sentenced to 4 years in the Penitentiary. Received Sept. 4, 1849 and discharged Oct. 4, 1851. Notes: 2nd conviction, genl. pardon by Gov. Trousdale. Number in ledger 86: 1071.

Name: George Rooker, age 15, born in Tennessee, occupation: labourer. Convicted of robbing U.S. mail by a court in Davidson County, and sentenced to 5 years in the Penitentiary. Received Sept. 6, 1849 and discharged Oct. 9, 1851. Notes: pardoned by the President of the U.S. Number in ledger 86: 1072.

Name: Galel Scott, age 50, born in Tennessee, occupation: labourer. Convicted of larceny by a court in Davidson County, and sentenced to 3 years and 6 months in the Penitentiary. Received Sept. 7, 1849 and discharged Dec. 17, 1852. Notes: pardoned under the act of 1836. Number in ledger 86: 1073.

Name: Augustus Richter, age 47, born in Prussia, occupation: barber. Convicted of murder by a court in Davidson County, and sentenced to 10 years in the Penitentiary. Received Sept. 7, 1849 and discharged Sept. 21, 1853. Notes: pardoned by Gov. Campbell. Number in ledger 86: 1074.

Name: Sutton McCalester, age 44, born in South Carolina, occupation: labourer. Convicted of larceny by a court in Davidson County, and sentenced to 1 year in the Penitentiary. Received Sept. 7, 1849 and discharged July 23, 1850. Notes: pardoned under the act of 1836. Number in ledger 86: 1075.

Name: James Dooley, age 21, born in Ireland, occupation: labourer. Convicted of larceny by a court in Franklin County, and sentenced to 3 years in the Penitentiary. Received Sept. 8, 1849 and discharged July 2, 1852. Notes: pardoned under the act of 1836. Number in ledger 86: 1076.

Name: John Hite, age 41, born in Tennessee, occupation: carpenter. Convicted of malicious stabbing by a court in Davidson County, and sentenced to 2 years in the Penitentiary. Received Sept. 10, 1849 and discharged July 23, 1850. Notes: pardoned by Gov. Trousdale. Number in ledger 86: 1077.

Name: Miles Jones, age 22, born in South Carolina, occupation: labourer. Convicted of presuading slaves to leave owne by a court in Henry County, and sentenced to 5 years in the Penitentiary. Received Oct. 1, 1849 and discharged June 8, 1854. Notes: discharged under act 1836. Number in ledger 86: 1078.

Name: James Airwood, age 26, born in North Carolina, occupation: labourer. Convicted of bigamy by a court in Blount County, and sentenced to 2 years in the Penitentiary. Received Oct. 7, 1849 and discharged Aug. 28, 1851. Notes: pardoned under the act of 1836. Number in ledger 86: 1079.

Name: John Makelley [McKelley?], age 50, born in North Carolina, occupation: labourer. Convicted of malicious stabbing by a court in Coffee County, and sentenced to 3 years in the Penitentiary. Received Oct. 14, 1849 and discharged Feb. 1, 1853. Notes: pardoned under the act of 1836. Number in ledger 86: 1080.

Name: John Lawrence, age 50, born in North Carolina, occupation: tailor. Convicted of grand larceny by a court in Davidson County, and sentenced to 5 years in the Penitentiary. Received Oct. 14, 1849 and discharged June 23, 1854. Notes: pardoned under the act of 1836. Number in ledger 86: 1081.

Name: John C. Jones, age 25, born in Georgia, occupation: carpenter. Convicted of larceny by a court in Polk County, and sentenced to 5 years in the Penitentiary. Received Oct. 21, 1849 and discharged July 21, 1850. Notes: died of brain fever. Number in ledger 86: 1082.

Name: Anthony Davis, age 30, born in England, occupation: hammerer. Convicted of murder by a court in Knox County, and sentenced to 15 years in the Penitentiary. Received Oct. 26, 1849 and discharged May 19, 1861. Notes: genl. pardon by Gov. I.G. Harris. Number in ledger 86: 1083.

Name: Daniel Martindale, age 47, born in Tennessee, occupation: farmer. Convicted of petit larceny by a court in Overton County, and sentenced to 1 year in the Penitentiary. Received Nov. 4, 1849 and discharged June 25, 1850. Notes: died of cholera. Number in ledger 86: 1084.

Name: John Stowers, age 30, born in Tennessee, occupation: labourer. Convicted of accessary [sic] to murder by a court in Macon County, and sentenced to life in the Penitentiary. Received Nov. 27, 1849 and discharged Apr. 9, 1851. Notes: genl. pardon by Gov. Trousdale. Number in ledger 86: 1085.

Name: Samuel C. Lowe, age 65, born in Maryland, occupation: farmer. Convicted of horse stealing by a court in Smith County, and sentenced to 3 years in the Penitentiary. Received Dec. 2, 1849 and discharged Sept. 23, 1852. Notes: pardoned under the act of 1836. Number in ledger 86: 1086.

Name: Cornelius Dorsey, age 29, born in Tennessee, occupation: [blank]. Convicted of keeping counterfeit coin by a court in Shelby County, and sentenced to 3 years in the Penitentiary. Received Dec. 3, 1849 and discharged Sept. 23, 1852. Notes: pardoned under the act of 1836. Number in ledger 86: 1087.

Name: William Burke, age 22, born in Virginia, occupation: labourer. Convicted of larceny by a court in Shelby County, and sentenced to 2 years in the Penitentiary. Received Dec. 3, 1849 and discharged Oct. 21, 1851. Notes: pardoned under the act of 1836. Number in ledger 86: 1088.

Name: Charles W.H. Jones, age 30, born in Kentucky, occupation: harness maker. Convicted of larceny by a court in Shelby County, and sentenced to 1 year in the Penitentiary. Received Dec. 3, 1849 and discharged Dec. 3, 1850. Notes: conduct good. Number in ledger 86: 1089.

Name: James Butler, age 29, born in Ohio, occupation: boatsman. Convicted of larceny by a court in Shelby County, and sentenced to 3 years in the Penitentiary. Received Dec. 3, 1849 and discharged Sept. 23, 1852. Notes: pardoned under the act of 1836. Number in ledger 86: 1090.

Name: James Brown, age 32, born in New York, occupation: cooper. Convicted of larceny by a court in Shelby County, and sentenced to 4 years and 6 months in the Penitentiary. Received Dec. 3, 1849 and discharged Feb. 20, 1854. Notes: pardoned under the act of 1836. Number in ledger 86: 1091.

Tennessee Convicts: Records of the State Penitentiary

Name: William Popelaski, age 22, born in Poland, occupation: soldier. Convicted of larceny by a court in Shelby County, and sentenced to 3 years and 6 months in the Penitentiary. Received Dec. 3, 1849 and discharged Mar. 15, 1853. Notes: pardoned under the act of 1836. Number in ledger 86: 1092.

Name: Caleb Williams, age 23, born in Pennsylvania, occupation: engineer. Convicted of larceny by a court in Shelby County, and sentenced to 4 years in the Penitentiary. Received Dec. 3, 1849 and discharged July 20, 1850. Notes: alias Fet Williams, cut his own throat. Number in ledger 86: 1093.

Name: James Taylor, age 49, born in Virginia, occupation: labourer. Convicted of circulating counterfeit coin by a court in Shelby County, and sentenced to 3 years in the Penitentiary. Received Dec. 3, 1849 and discharged Sept. 23, 1852. Notes: pardoned under the act of 1836. Number in ledger 86: 1094.

Name: Silas Wilson, age 22, born in Tennessee, occupation: labourer. Convicted of petit larceny by a court in White County, and sentenced to 1 year in the Penitentiary. Received Oct. 20, 1849 and discharged Oct. 21, 1850. Notes: col[ore]d, conduct good. Number in ledger 86: 1095.

Name: John J. Elzey, age 35, born in Tennessee, occupation: bl[ac]k smith. Convicted of murder by a court in Marshall County, and sentenced to 10 years in the Penitentiary. Received Dec. 6, 1849 and discharged Apr. 22, 1859. Notes: act of 1836. Number in ledger 86: 1096.

Name: Nathl. P. Reagan, age 21, born in Tennessee, occupation: school master. Convicted of horse stealing by a court in Sevier County, and sentenced to 5 years in the Penitentiary. Received Dec. 10, 1849 and discharged Oct. 16 [or 10], 1852. Notes: pardoned by Gov. Campbell. Number in ledger 86: 1097.

Name: Allen Williams, age 20, born in Tennessee, occupation: labourer. Convicted of horse stealing by a court in Davidson County, and sentenced to 3 years in the Penitentiary. Received Dec. 10, 1849 and discharged Oct. 6, 1852. Notes: pardoned under the act of 1836. Number in ledger 86: 1098.

Name: Stephen Smith, age 23, born in Tennessee, occupation: farmer. Convicted of larceny by a court in Giles County, and sentenced to 5 years in the Penitentiary. Received Dec. 17, 1849 and discharged Aug. 16, 1854. Notes: pardoned under the act of 1836. Number in ledger 86: 1099.

Tennessee Convicts: Records of the State Penitentiary

Name: Edward Harrell, age 25, born in Tennessee, occupation: farmer. Convicted of negro stealing by a court in Coffee County, and sentenced to 7 years in the Penitentiary. Received Dec. 22, 1849 and discharged July 10, 1856. Notes: pardoned under the act of 1836. Number in ledger 86: 1100.

Name: Thomas Rodgers, age 40, born in Ireland, occupation: labourer. Convicted of larceny by a court in Shelby County, and sentenced to 1 year in the Penitentiary. Received Dec. 24, 1849 and discharged Dec. 24, 1850. Notes: conduct good. Number in ledger 86: 1101.

Name: Jack Herron, age 28, born in New York, occupation: soldier. Convicted of larceny by a court in Shelby County, and sentenced to 1 year in the Penitentiary. Received Dec. 24, 1849 and discharged Dec. 24, 1850. Notes: conduct good. Number in ledger 86: 1102.

Name: John O'Donnell, age 30, born in Scotland, occupation: labourer. Convicted of larceny by a court in Shelby County, and sentenced to 1 year in the Penitentiary. Received Dec. 24, 1849 and discharged Dec. 24, 1850. Notes: conduct good. Number in ledger 86: 1103.

Name: John Ezra Hanna, age 25, born in Massachusetts, occupation: boatsman. Convicted of malicious shooting by a court in Shelby County, and sentenced to 3 years in the Penitentiary. Received Dec. 24, 1849 and discharged Oct. 16, 1852. Notes: pardoned under the act of 1836. Number in ledger 86: 1104.

Name: George Wise, age 33, born in Kentucky, occupation: labourer. Convicted of attempting to pass c[ounterfeit by a court in Shelby County, and sentenced to 3 years in the Penitentiary. Received Dec. 24, 1849 and discharged Oct. 16, 1852. Notes: pardoned under the act of 1836. Number in ledger 86: 1105.

Name: Jefferson Cash, age 24, born in Virginia, occupation: labourer. Convicted of grand larceny by a court in Davidson County, and sentenced to 11 year in the Penitentiary. Received Dec. 26, 1849 and discharged Apr. 20, 1860. Notes: pardoned under the act of 1836. Number in ledger 86: 1106.

Name: John Oagle, age 18, born in Tennessee, occupation: labourer. Convicted of attempt to kill by a court in Davidson County, and sentenced to 2 years and 6 months in the Penitentiary. Received Dec. 29, 1849 and discharged Dec. 21, 1850. Notes: genl. pardon by Gov. Trousdale. Number in ledger 86: 1107.

Tennessee Convicts: Records of the State Penitentiary

Name: W.G. Carlisle, age 30, born in Tennessee, occupation: labourer. Convicted of larceny by a court in Davidson County, and sentenced to 3 years in the Penitentiary. Received Dec. 29, 1849 and discharged Oct. 23, 1852. Notes: pardoned under the act of 1836. Number in ledger 86: 1108.

Name: W. Ford, age 25, born in Kentucky, occupation: loafer. Convicted of larceny by a court in Davidson County, and sentenced to 4 years in the Penitentiary. Received Dec. 29, 1849 and discharged Oct. 14, 1853. Notes: pardoned under the act of 1836. Number in ledger 86: 1109.

Name: Isaac Vaughn, age 25, born in Tennessee, occupation: bl[ac]k smith. Convicted of forgery by a court in Grainger County, and sentenced to 3 years in the Penitentiary. Received Jan. 15, 1850 and discharged Nov. 8, 1852. Notes: pardoned under the act of 1836. Number in ledger 86: 1110.

Name: Robert Drane, age 24, born in Tennessee, occupation: farmer. Convicted of horse stealing by a court in Maury County, and sentenced to 3 years in the Penitentiary. Received Jan. 27, 1850 and discharged Nov. 19, 1852. Notes: pardoned under the act of 1836. Number in ledger 86: 1111.

Name: Thomas Ellison, age 51, born in Kentucky, occupation: bl[ac]k smith. Convicted of murder by a court in Claiborne County, and sentenced to 10 years in the Penitentiary. Received Jan. 30, 1850 and discharged June 16, 1859. Notes: pardoned under the act of 1836. Number in ledger 86: 1112.

Name: Archibald Campbell, age 23, born in Tennessee, occupation: potter. Convicted of horse stealing by a court in Monroe County, and sentenced to 5 years in the Penitentiary. Received Feb. 2, 1850 and discharged Feb. 1, 1854. Notes: pardoned by Gov. Johnson. Number in ledger 86: 1113.

Name: Hugh Goings, age 50, born in Virginia, occupation: labourer. Convicted of bigamy by a court in Monroe County, and sentenced to 2 years in the Penitentiary. Received Feb. 2, 1850 and discharged July 7, 1850. Notes: died of inflamation of the bowels. Number in ledger 86: 1114.

Name: James Shropshire, age 40, born in Tennessee, occupation: farmer. Convicted of grand larceny by a court in Hawkins County, and sentenced to 7 years in the Penitentiary. Received Feb. 14, 1850 and discharged Sept. 7, 1856. Notes: pardoned under the act of 1836. Number in ledger 86: 1115.

Name: John Shropshire, age 25, born in Tennessee, occupation: farmer.

Convicted of grand larceny by a court in Hawkins County, and sentenced to 6 years in the Penitentiary. Received Feb. 14, 1850 and discharged Sept. 21, 1855. Notes: 2nd conviction, pardoned under the act of 1836. Number in ledger 86: 1116.

Name: Francis Shropshire, age 32, born in Tennessee, occupation: farmer. Convicted of petit larceny by a court in Hawkins County, and sentenced to 1 year in the Penitentiary. Received Feb. 14, 1850 and discharged [blank]. Notes: alias Vicca Shropshire, conveyed to lunatic assyl. Number in ledger 86: 1117.

Name: Charles Yates, age 19, born in Tennessee, occupation: labourer. Convicted of horse stealing by a court in Davidson County, and sentenced to 5 years in the Penitentiary. Received Feb. 19, 1850 and discharged Oct. 28, 1854. Notes: pardoned under the act of 1836. Number in ledger 86: 1118.

Name: Seabourn Winters, age 19, born in Tennessee, occupation: labourer. Convicted of murder in 2nd degree by a court in Davidson County, and sentenced to 10 years in the Penitentiary. Received Feb. 19, 1850 and discharged Feb. 8, 1851. Notes: alias S. Durham, genl. pardon by Gov. Trousdale. Number in ledger 86: 1119.

Name: Francis Ballew, age 17, born in South Carolina, occupation: labourer. Convicted of petit larceny by a court in Washington County, and sentenced to 1 year in the Penitentiary. Received Mar. 14, 1850 and discharged Mar. 14, 1851. Notes: conduct tolerable fair. Number in ledger 86: 1120.

Name: Alexander Panther, age 24, born in Tennessee, occupation: labourer. Convicted of murder by a court in Lincoln County, and sentenced to 3 years in the Penitentiary. Received Mar. 20, 1850 and discharged Jan. 13, 1853. Notes: pardoned under the act of 1836. Number in ledger 86: 1121.

Name: William Landrith, age 20, born in North Carolina, occupation: labourer. Convicted of larceny by a court in Lincoln County, and sentenced to 1 year and 8 months in the Penitentiary. Received Mar. 20, 1850 and discharged Aug. 19, 1851. Notes: pardoned under the act of 1836. Number in ledger 86: 1122.

Name: Riley Tucker, age 18, born in Tennessee, occupation: labourer. Convicted of larceny by a court in Lincoln County, and sentenced to 1 year in the Penitentiary. Received Mar. 20, 1850 and discharged Aug. 18, 1850. Notes: died of chronic inflamation of the s[t]omach & bo. Number in ledger

86: 1123.

Name: James Bias, age 22, born in Alabama, occupation: labourer. Convicted of larceny by a court in McNairy County, and sentenced to 1 year in the Penitentiary. Received Mar. 22, 1850 and discharged Aug. 1, 1850. Notes: died of brain fever. [Published 1851 report shows first name as *John*.] Number in ledger 86: 1124.

Name: Elvin Kirk, age 35, born in Tennessee, occupation: saddle tree maker. Convicted of robbery by a court in Anderson County, and sentenced to 5 years in the Penitentiary. Received Mar. 23, 1850 and discharged Nov. 24, 1854. Notes: 2nd sentance [*sic*], pardoned under the act of 183. Number in ledger 86: 1125.

Name: Wiley Allen, age 19, born in Georgia, occupation: labourer. Convicted of larceny by a court in Shelby County, and sentenced to 3 years in the Penitentiary. Received Mar. 30, 1850 and discharged Jan. 25, 1853. Notes: pardoned under the act of 1836. Number in ledger 86: 1126.

Name: Andrew B. Patterson, age 33, born in Tennessee, occupation: labourer. Convicted of murder by a court in Gibson County, and sentenced to 2 years in the Penitentiary. Received Apr. 6, 1850 and discharged Jan. 12, 1852. Notes: genl. pardon by Gov. Campbell. Number in ledger 86: 1127.

Name: Berry (alias Ashberry) Nichols, age 31, born in Tennessee, occupation: labourer. Convicted of counterfeiting by a court in Cocke County, and sentenced to 3 years in the Penitentiary. Received Apr. 8, 1850 and discharged May 20, 1850. Notes: died of congestive fever. Number in ledger 86: 1128.

Name: William Hall, age 14, born in Tennessee, occupation: labourer. Convicted of petit larceny by a court in Cocke County, and sentenced to 2 years in the Penitentiary. Received Apr. 8, 1850 and discharged Feb. 14, 1852. Notes: pardoned under the act of 1836. Number in ledger 86: 1129.

Name: Henry Duker, age 22, born in Kentucky, occupation: stage driver. Convicted of murder by a court in Hamilton County, and sentenced to life in the Penitentiary. Received Apr. 8, 1850 and discharged Nov. 16, 1857. Notes: died from fall of a rock. Number in ledger 86: 1130.

Name: James M. Scott, age 29, born in Tennessee, occupation: labourer. Convicted of fellony [*sic*] by a court in Hamilton County, and sentenced to 3 years in the Penitentiary. Received Apr. 8, 1850 and discharged Feb. 1, 1853. Notes: pardoned under the act of 1836. Number in ledger 86: 1131.

Name: John S. Eads, age 26, born in Tennessee, occupation: labourer. Convicted of negro stealing by a court in Davidson County, and sentenced to 5 years in the Penitentiary. Received Apr. 13, 1850 and discharged July 6, 1850. Notes: died of cholera (always sick). Number in ledger 86: 1132.

Name: William Wray, age 26, born in Tennessee, occupation: labourer. Convicted of horse stealing by a court in Bedford County, and sentenced to 5 years in the Penitentiary. Received Apr. 22, 1850 and discharged Feb. 16, 1853. Notes: pardoned under the act of 1836. Number in ledger 86: 1133.

Name: Green McLenden, age 42, born in Tennessee, occupation: labourer. Convicted of murder by a court in Davidson County, and sentenced to life in the Penitentiary. Received Apr. 26, 1850 and discharged July 24, 1850. Notes: died of fever. Number in ledger 86: 1134.

Name: Paris Marlow, age 35, born in Tennessee, occupation: labourer. Convicted of malicious stabbing by a court in Claibourn [sic] County, and sentenced to 2 years in the Penitentiary. Received May 27, 1850 and discharged Apr. 15, 1852. Notes: pardoned under the act of 1836. Number in ledger 86: 1135.

Name: Henry Sims, age 28, born in Kentucky, occupation: painter. Convicted of grand larceny by a court in Davidson County, and sentenced to 3 years in the Penitentiary. Received Feb. 1, 1850 and discharged Nov. 24, 1852. Notes: alias Henry Simpson, 2nd [conviction], pardoned. Number in ledger 86: 1136.

Name: Elias W. Philps [sic], age 20, born in Kentucky, occupation: cabinett [sic] w.m. Convicted of grand larceny by a court in Weakley County, and sentenced to 5 years in the Penitentiary. Received June 24, 1850 and discharged Mar. 3, 1855. Notes: pardoned under the act of 1836. Number in ledger 86: 1137.

Name: George Williams, age 18, born in Indiana, occupation: labourer. Convicted of grand larceny by a court in Weakley County, and sentenced to 3 years in the Penitentiary. Received June 14, 1850 and discharged Apr. 18, 1853. Notes: conduct only tolerable. Number in ledger 86: 1138.

Name: John Harrison, age 24, born in Tennessee, occupation: labourer.

Convicted of horse stealing by a court in Shelby County, and sentenced to 6 years in the Penitentiary. Received May 19, 1850 and discharged Jan. 4, 1856. Notes: pardoned under the act of 1836. Number in ledger 86: 1139.

Name: John A. Lambert, age 29, born in South Carolina, occupation: labourer. Convicted of forgery by a court in McNairy County, and sentenced to 3 years in the Penitentiary. Received July 19, 1850 and discharged May 16, 1853. Notes: pardoned under the act of 1836. Number in ledger 86: 1140.

Name: Henry Beecham, age 23, born in Alabama, occupation: labourer. Convicted of larceny by a court in McNairy County, and sentenced to 2 years in the Penitentiary. Received July 19, 1850 and discharged June 5, 1852. Notes: pardoned under the act of 1836. Number in ledger 86: 1141.

Name: Edward Tyler, age 70, born in North Carolina, occupation: school teacher. Convicted of larceny by a court in McMinn County, and sentenced to 3 years in the Penitentiary. Received Dec. 30, 1849 and discharged July 21, 1850. Notes: 3rd conviction, died of fever. Number in ledger 86: 1142. [Also listed under number 1063]

Name: John McMahan, age blank, born in Tennessee, occupation: labourer. Convicted of larceny by a court in Shelby County, and sentenced to 1 year in the Penitentiary. Received July 22, 1850 and discharged July 22, 1851. Notes: disch'd at expiration of sentance [sic]. Number in ledger 86: 1143.

Name: Samuel Coffman, age 24, born in Alabama, occupation: labourer. Convicted of murder by a court in Henderson County, and sentenced to 10 years in the Penitentiary. Received Aug. 9, 1850 and discharged Feb. 14, 1860. Notes: dischg'd act of 1836. Number in ledger 86: 1144.

Name: Wm. S. Gurley, age 31, born in North Carolina, occupation: labourer. Convicted of larceny by a court in Bledsoe County, and sentenced to 1 year in the Penitentiary. Received July 9, 1850 and discharged July 9, 1851. Notes: conduct good. Number in ledger 86: 1145.

Name: Gideon Hamby, age 19, born in Tennessee, occupation: labourer. Convicted of mule stealing by a court in Bedford County, and sentenced to 3 years in the Penitentiary. Received Aug. 21, 1850 and discharged June 11, 1853. Notes: pardoned under the act of 1836. Number in ledger 86: 1146.

Name: George Fletcher, age 23, born in Tennessee, occupation: waggon maker.

Tennessee Convicts: Records of the State Penitentiary

Convicted of malicious stabbing by a court in Giles County, and sentenced to 2 years in the Penitentiary. Received Aug. 22, 1850 and discharged May 3, 1851. Notes: genl. pardon by Gov. Trousdale. Number in ledger 86: 1147.

Name: Robt. Burke, age 25, born in Virginia, occupation: labourer. Convicted of house breaking by a court in Jefferson County, and sentenced to 4 years in the Penitentiary. Received Sept. 2, 1850 and discharged May 16, 1854. Notes: alias Geo. Robertson, discharged under the act of. Number in ledger 86: 1148.

Name: William Pearce, age 28, born in Tennessee, occupation: labourer. Convicted of negro & horse stealing by a court in Davidson County, and sentenced to 6 years in the Penitentiary. Received Sept. 16, 1850 and discharged Feb. 3, 1854. Notes: pardoned by Gov. Johnson. Number in ledger 86: 1149.

Name: Robert Clendenning, age 24, born in Tennessee, occupation: labourer. Convicted of horse stealing by a court in Davidson County, and sentenced to 5 years in the Penitentiary. Received Sept. 24, 1850 and discharged Sept. 5, 1855. Notes: discharged under the act of 1836. Number in ledger 86: 1150.

Name: George Hutton, age 18, born in New York, occupation: sailor. Convicted of larceny by a court in Wayne County, and sentenced to 1 year in the Penitentiary. Received Oct. 2, 1850 and discharged Oct. 2, 1851. Notes: conduct good. Number in ledger 86: 1151.

Name: Wm. Griffin, age 22, born in Tennessee, occupation: labourer. Convicted of petit larceny by a court in Davidson County, and sentenced to 2 years in the Penitentiary. Received Oct. 5, 1850 and discharged Aug. 23, 1852. Notes: alias W. Owen, conduct good. Number in ledger 86: 1152.

Name: Peter R. Bowlin, age 51, born in Ohio, occupation: boatsman. Convicted of malicious stabbing by a court in Henry County, and sentenced to 2 years in the Penitentiary. Received Oct. 7, 1850 and discharged Oct. 18, 1850. Notes: genl. pardon by Gov. Trousdale. Number in ledger 86: 1153.

Name: Calvin Coffee, age 30, born in Tennessee, occupation: labourer. Convicted of larceny by a court in Fentress County, and sentenced to 4 years in the Penitentiary. Received Oct. 30, 1850 and discharged July 30, 1854. Notes: discharged under the act of 1836. Number in ledger 86: 1154.

Name: Grandison Napper, age 24, born in Kentucky, occupation: labourer.

Convicted of horse stealing by a court in Sumner County, and sentenced to 4 years in the Penitentiary. Received Oct. 30, 1850 and discharged July 30, 1854. Notes: discharged under the act of 1836. Number in ledger 86: 1155.

Name: J.N. Norville, age 35, born in South Carolina, occupation: labourer. Convicted of negro stealing by a court in Fayette County, and sentenced to 4 years in the Penitentiary. Received Oct. 30, 1850 and discharged July 31, 1854. Notes: pardoned under the act of 1836. Number in ledger 86: 1156.

Name: Benjamin T. Foster, age 51, born in North Carolina, occupation: counterfeiter. Convicted of bigamy by a court in Hickman County, and sentenced to 2 years in the Penitentiary. Received Nov. 4, 1850 and discharged Sept. 20, 1852. Notes: pardoned under the act of 1836. Number in ledger 86: 1157.

Name: Samuel Pattengill, age 19, born in Tennessee, occupation: labourer. Convicted of horse stealing by a court in Dickson County, and sentenced to 3 years in the Penitentiary. Received Nov. 5, 1850 and discharged Aug. 27, 1853. Notes: pardoned under the act of 1836. Number in ledger 86: 1158.

Name: Robert Bird, age 17, born in Tennessee, occupation: mail rider. Convicted of rob[b]ing U.S. mail by a court in Knox County, and sentenced to 10 years in the Penitentiary. Received Nov. 5, 1850 and discharged Oct. 31, 1856. Notes: pardoned by the President U. States. Number in ledger 86: 1159.

Name: Williams Parsons, age 40, born in South Carolina, occupation: labourer. Convicted of grand larceny by a court in Decatur County, and sentenced to 3 years in the Penitentiary. Received Nov. 13, 1850 and discharged Sept. 7, 1853. Notes: pardoned under the act of 1836. Number in ledger 86: 1160.

Name: Mitchel Tallent, age 22, born in Tennessee, occupation: labourer. Convicted of larceny by a court in Roane County, and sentenced to 2 years in the Penitentiary. Received Nov. 15, 1850 and discharged Oct. 6, 1852. Notes: pardoned under the act of 1836. Number in ledger 86: 1161.

Name: Ransom Massey, age 24, born in Tennessee, occupation: farmer. Convicted of larceny by a court in Anderson County, and sentenced to 1 year and 6 months in the Penitentiary. Received Nov. 22, 1850 and discharged Apr. 19, 1852. Notes: conduct tolerable good. Number in ledger 86: 1162.

Name: Alexander Debruce, age 20, born in Tennessee, occupation: labourer.

Convicted of horse stealing by a court in Stewart County, and sentenced to 3 years in the Penitentiary. Received Nov. 25, 1850 and discharged June 29, 1851. Notes: died of brain fever. Number in ledger 86: 1163.

Name: John Hecock, age 21, born in Indiana, occupation: farmer. Convicted of larceny by a court in Shelby County, and sentenced to 1 year in the Penitentiary. Received Nov. 26, 1850 and discharged Nov. 26, 1851. Notes: conduct good. Number in ledger 86: 1164.

Name: Thompson W. Randal, age 38, born in Missouri, occupation: carpenter. Convicted of larceny by a court in Shelby County, and sentenced to 3 years in the Penitentiary. Received Nov. 26, 1850 and discharged Sept. 19, 1853. Notes: pardoned under the act of 1836. Number in ledger 86: 1165.

Name: John Rial, age 35, born in Pennsylvania, occupation: labourer. Convicted of larceny by a court in Shelby County, and sentenced to 2 years in the Penitentiary. Received Nov. 26, 1850 and discharged Oct. 11, 1852. Notes: pardoned under the act of 1836. Number in ledger 86: 1166.

Name: Robert Walter, age 26, born in Virginia, occupation: labourer. Convicted of larceny by a court in Shelby County, and sentenced to 3 years in the Penitentiary. Received Nov. 26, 1850 and discharged Dec. 17, 1852. Notes: genl. pardon by Gov. Campbell. Number in ledger 86: 1167.

Name: Abraham Mitchel, age 26, born in Kentucky, occupation: labourer. Convicted of larceny by a court in Shelby County, and sentenced to 1 year in the Penitentiary. Received Nov. 26, 1850 and discharged Nov. 26, 1851. Notes: colo[red], conduct tolerable. Number in ledger 86: 1168.

Name: William Caldwell, age 30, born in Tennessee, occupation: labourer. Convicted of larceny by a court in Shelby County, and sentenced to 1 year in the Penitentiary. Received Nov. 26, 1850 and discharged Nov. 26, 1851. Notes: 2nd conviction, conduct good. Number in ledger 86: 1169.

Name: R[?] R. McKinley, age 31, born in Tennessee, occupation: labourer. Convicted of harboring a slave by a court in Shelby County, and sentenced to 3 years in the Penitentiary. Received Nov. 26, 1850 and discharged Sept. 19, 1853. Notes: pardoned under the act of 1836. Number in ledger 86: 1170.

Name: Hiram Gould, age 35, born in Vermont, occupation: carpenter. Convicted of larceny by a court in Davidson County, and sentenced to 5 years in the Penitentiary. Received Dec. 5, 1850 and discharged Aug. 13, 1855. Notes: pardoned under the act of 1836. Number in ledger 86: 1171.

Name: Michael Eakin, age 29, born in Ireland, occupation: labourer. Convicted of murder by a court in Franklin County, and sentenced to 3 years in the Penitentiary. Received Dec. 9, 1850 and discharged Oct. 14, 1853. Notes: pardoned under the act of 1836. Number in ledger 86: 1172.

Name: Burrill Perry, age 22, born in Tennessee, occupation: labourer. Convicted of larceny by a court in Davidson County, and sentenced to 3 years in the Penitentiary. Received Dec. 16, 1850 and discharged Oct. 14, 1853. Notes: pardoned under the act of 1836. Number in ledger 86: 1173.

Name: Woodford R. Lester, age 31, born in Kentucky, occupation: labourer. Convicted of malicious stabbing by a court in Davidson County, and sentenced to 2 years in the Penitentiary. Received Dec. 16, 1850 and discharged Jan. 16, 1852. Notes: genl. pardon by Gov. Campbell. Number in ledger 86: 1174.

Name: Joel Bryant, age 26, born in Tennessee, occupation: labourer. Convicted of larceny by a court in Warren County, and sentenced to 2 years in the Penitentiary. Received Dec. 18, 1850 and discharged Nov. 6, 1852. Notes: conduct generally good. Number in ledger 86: 1175.

Name: Phillip Harris, age 27, born in Tennessee, occupation: bl[ac]k smith. Convicted of grand larceny by a court in Bedford County, and sentenced to 5 years in the Penitentiary. Received Dec. 20, 1850 and discharged Aug. 28, 1855. Notes: pardoned under the act of 1836. Number in ledger 86: 1176.

Place Index

AL 070,010-011,017,
   079,084,093,116
AL,Blount Co. 004-005
. Coosa Co. 088
. Evington 144
. Fayette Co. 028
. Florence 051,105,151
. Forsythe 100
. Independence 119
. Jackson Co. 060,081
.   087
. Jefferson Co. 118,144
. Lauderdale Co. 043,051
.   056,085,122
. Limestone Co. 052,078
.   122,146
. Madison Co. 028,044
.   118,137,160
. Marengo Co. 130
. Marion Co. 137
. Mobile 143
. Montgomery Co. 025
. Morgan Co. 139,149
. Randolph Co. 046
. Tallapoosa Co. 100
. Tuscaloosa 021,106,163
. Tuscumbia 133
. Washington Co. 106
AR 002,042,114
AR,Conway Co. 146
. Crittendon Co. 050
. Ft. Smith 117
. Hempstead Co. 128
. Independence Co. 146
. Jackson Co. 046
. Little Rock 042,092
. Napoleon 090
. Phillips Co. 156
. Saline Co. 128
CT,Litchfield Co. 099
Canada,Montreal 072
York 051
Cherokee Nation 079,089
   156
Cuba 123
DC,Georgetown 111
Washington 138
DE 142
District of Columbia 039
England,
  Hampshire Co. 081
. Lancastershire 091
. London 140
. Shefforshire 140
. Staffordshire 162

FL 022
FL,Pensacola 007
Fort Pickering 089
France,Paris 030
GA 014,021,028,048-
   049 062,081,083,110,
   131,142
GA,Albert Co. 102
. Augusta 006,143
. Baldwin Co. 137
. Carroll Co. 006
. Cherokee Co. 141
. Columbia 050,163
. DeKalb Co. 079,087
. Floyd Co. 032,111
. Franklin Co. 037
. Green Co. 014
. Habersham Co. 128
. Hall Co. 047
. Haversham Co. 152
. Henry Co. 079
. Jackson Co. 111
. Jasper Co. 100
. Jefferson Co. 006
. Lawrence Co. 110
. Lincoln Co. 085,114
. Lumpkin Co. 020
. Mecklenburg Co. 155
. Meriwether Co. 037
. Monroe Co. 014
. Murray Co. 032
. Muscogee Co. 037,079
. Pigeon Roost 128
. Rome 032
. Watson Co. 006
. Wilkes Co. 110,146
Germany 066
IL 009,017,093,100,159
IL,Beardstown 140
. Cass Co. 118
. Clark Co. 112
. Edgar Co. 129
. Edwardsville 160
. Franklin Co. 012
. Gallatin Co. 014
. Hamilton Co. 012,019
. Jackson Co. 042
. Jefferson City 146
. Jefferson Co. 152
. Johnson Co. 109
. Lockport 072
. Marion Co. 152
. Morgan Co. 106
. Perry Co. 122
. Pike Co. 127

IL,Pope Co. 007,075
. Saline Lick 056
. Sangamond Co. 154
. St. Clair Co. 142
. Yelconda 075
IN
005,043,048,110,116,143
IN,Bartholomew Co. 020
. Bloomington 101,132
. Bush Co. 127
. Indianapolis 044
. Lawrence Co. 068
. Orange Co. 042,081
. Parke Co. 071,102
. Pike Co. 127
. Terre Haute 132
. Vigo Co. 102
. White River 059
Ireland
024,045,054,123,139
Ireland,Cork 021
. Derry 146
. Entram Co. 051
. Kings Co. 134
. Limerick Co. 159
. Shigo 070
. Waterford Co. 068
Italy 155
Jamaica 007
KY not indexed unless
   county was stated
KY,Adair Co. 031
. Allen Co. 048,050
. Barren Co. 002,028,044
.   049,097
. Bourbon Co. 091
. Bowling Green 002,045
.   070
. Caldwell Co. 001,008
. Callaway Co. 008,010
. Calloway Co. 030
. Clinton Co. 071
. Crab Orchard 043
. Cumberland Co. 071,118
.   129
. Davis Co. 133
. Eddyville 001
. Fayette Co. 095,110
.   115,151
. Fleming Co. 129,136
. Frankfort 136
. Garrett Co. 011
. Glasgow 151
. Hart Co. 015
. Henry Co. 115

Place Index

KY, Hickman Co. 062
. Hopkinsville 054
. Jefferson City 052
. Jefferson Co. 052
. Jessamine Co. 059
. Lexington 007,075
. Logan Co. 017,085,114
.   144
. Louisville 108,139
. Madison Co. 026,063
. Madisonville 114
. Mason Co. 162
. McCracken Co. 008,130
         138
. Monroe Co. 103,115,
         119,134
. Montgomery Co. `099
. Monticello 004
. Ohio Co. 136
. Oldham Co. 070
. Paducah 138
. Pikeville 002`
. Shakertown 085
. Shelby Co. 154
. Spencer Co. 014
. Trigg Co. 102
. Warren Co. 024,042,046
.   070,116
. Wayne Co. 004,073,102
. Whitley Co. 104
. Woodford Co. 012,163,
         174
Kimbrough,Joseph 113
LA   002,047
LA,New Orleans 007,
    091,139-140,146,155
MA,Bellingham 111
    Boston 039,109
MD   034-035,105
MD,Baltimore 001,111,
         158
. Baltimore Co. 041
. Montgomery Co. 001
. Northampton Co. 095
. Reestown? 041
MO 022,066,086,092,
     116,133,149,159
MO,Franklin Co. 147
. Jackson Co. 025
. Jefferson Co. 025
. Madison Co. 114
. Pike Co. 069
. Rhea Co. 141
. Scott Co. 094
. St. Louis 101,139,160

MS not indexed unless
    county was stated
MS,Carrolton 039
. Clayburn Co. 083
. Columbus 163
. Monroe Co. 019
. Natchez 011,039
. Newberry Port 109
. Panola Co. 117
. Tishomingo Co. 102
. Yalobusha Co. 062
NC not indexed unless
    county was given
NC,Anson Co. 145
. Ashe Co. 033,035
. Bertie Co. 29, 81, 83-4
. Buncombe Co. 017,024
.   097,134,141,146
. Burke Co. 066,118,149,
         152
. Cabarrus Co. 037
. Caswell Co. 022,058,
         098,147
. Chatham Co. 088,093
.   154
. Craven Co. 125,131
. Cumberland Co. 149,153
. Davidson Co. 127
. Edgecombe Co. 022,081
. Fayetteville 002
. Franklin Co. 002,022
. Gates Co. 116
. Gold Mines 041
. Granville Co. 036,057,
         108
. Greene Co. 055,105
. Guilford Co. 020,022
.   030,057,067,094-095
. Halifax Co. 087
. Haywood Co. 080
. Iredale Co. 133-134
. Iredell Co. 030,067
. Johnson Co. 007,030,
         061
. Lancaster Co. 158
. Lincoln Co. 055,068
.   129,145
. Macon Co. 155
. Martin Co. 156
. Mecklenburg Co. 037
.   075,096,100,155
. Montgomery Co. 86,141
. Moore Co. 084,087
. Mulberry Dist. 104
NC, Nash Co. 007,037,

NC,Nash Co. 108, 143
. Onslow Co. 037
. Orange Co. 002,010,032
.   039,071,093,095,151
. Pitt Co. 029,086
. Raleigh 006,055,117
. Randolph Co. 006,024
.   073,159
. Richmond Co. 079
. Roane Co. 108
. Rowan Co. 112
. Russel Co. 045
. Rutherford Co. 042
. Stokes Co. 044
. Surry Co. 113
. Wake Co. 014,039,147
. Walker Co. 090
. Wayne Co. 084
. Wilkes Co. 037,039
         107,128
NJ,Newark 132
. Princeton 013
. Salem Co. 060
NJ.Germantown 148
NY,Delaware Co. 003
. Dutchess Co. 056
. Madison Co. 022
. New York 013,022,024
    058,070,094,132,140,
    158
. Oneida Co. 099
. Orange Co. 037
. Rensselaer Co. 032
. Shenango Co. 003,037
. Troy 162
OH   061,142
OH,Adams Co. 048
. Brown Co. 106
. Butler Co. 091
. Cincinnati 052,058,077
.   091,106,136,139,148,
.   160
. Clinton Co. 059
. Hamilton Co. 058
. Jackson Co. 044
. Marybone? 132
. Meigs Co. 131
. Preble Co. 091
. Ravenna 130
. Wilmington C.H. 059
PA,Chambersburg 026
. Chester Co. 144
. Harrisburg 026
. Huntingdon 026
PA,Lancaster Co. 015,

316

Place Index

PA,Lancaster Co. 015,
051
. Montgomery Co.   029
. Philadelphia 041,054
.   060,070,091,104
. Pittsburgh 011,040,139-
140,162
. Schuylkill Co.   104
. Washington Co. 052,136
RI,Providence   111
SC 028,031,043,047,
053,085,089,127,152
SC,Abbeville Dist. 003,
045, 046
. Carhow Co.   087
. Charleston   045,047
. Chester Co. 012,040,
101
. Chesterfield Dist. 079
. Darlington Co.   063
. Edgefield Dist. 010
. Fairfield Dist. 074
. Greenville Co.   020
. Kershaw Dist.   025
. Laurens Dist.   081
. Lawrence Co.   020
. Lawrence Dist. 085
. Marion Co.   029
. Pendleton Co. 035,050
097,107,112,119
122,138-139,152
. Pickens Co.   016
. Richland Dist. 018
. Spartanburg   066
. Spartanburg Co. 043,
055, 106, 073,099,143
. Sumptersville   077
. Sumpterville Dist. 031
. Union Co.   106
.   037,143,149
. York Dist.   083
Scotland,Glasgow 116
Spain,Madrid   094
St. Dominga   007
TN not indexed unless
county was given
TN, Anderson Co. 004-
005 039,064-065,069,126
. 128,132,175,203,215
. 217,219,235,243,265
. 270,284,307,311
. Bedford Co. 002-003
. 008,014,021-022,028
. 037,050,054,060,066
. 083,087,089,096,111

TN,Bedford Co. (cont.)
. 117,124,128,134,137
. 152,157,169,174,181
. 184,187,191,196,198
. 208,210,213,223,249
. 252,256,275,288,296
300,308-309,313
. Benton Co. 8,92,112,213
. Blaine   053
. Bledsoe Co.   040,047
. 065,071,086,105,119
. 124,129,194,202,215
. 221-222,229,238,243
. 256,267,277,281,309
. Bledsoes Lick 062,064
. Blount Co. 018,020,031
. 035,042,045,055,057
. 063,074,080,095,098
. 124,127,149-150,153
. 156,169,174,182,185
. 201,212,255,257,260
. 301,120
. Bradley Co.   031,057
. 086-087,100,112,118
. 125,132,156,194,197
. 210,217,220,225-226
. 230,236,257,259
. Brownsville   013
. Campbell Co. 005,012
. 024,027,080,097,171
. 184,186,248,278,284
. 292
. Campbells Station 012
. Cannon Co. 057,061,088
. 099,210,252,270,288
. Carroll Co.   022,052
. 056,067,083,086,089
. 092,104,153,173,188
. 198,203,220,227,233
. 248,251-252,254,259
. 275
. Carter Co. 009,021,033
. 035-037,053,081,088
. 160,177,185,227,229
. 275,293-294
. Cherokee Purchase 020
. Claiborne Co. 005,020
. 033,092-093,097,110
. 128,132,144-145,162
. 183,185,211,228,233
. 236,239,245,254,259
. 260,262,305,308
. Clinton   005
. Cocke Co. 034,042,068
. 080,092,096,112,121

TN,Cocke Co. (cont.)
. 131,137,158,179,188
. 226,253,271,284,307
. Coffee Co. 061,102,115
. 131,142,162,232,237
. 249,267,281,286,296
299,301,304
. Dandridge   040
. Davidson Co. 001,004
. 006,015,018-019,024
. 026,031-032,037,047
. 053-054,058,064,070
. 072,084,090,093-095
. 097,101-102,108,111
. 113-115,117,127,129
. 130-131,133-134,136
. 140,144-145,147-148
. 150-151,153,156,161
. 162,166-169,171-173
. 175-176,178,181,184
. 186,190,193,201,203
. 204,209,211,213,223
. 224-226,228,230-231
. 233,235,238,241,243
. 245,248,250-252,259
. 260,266,269-271,278
. 279-280,282,284-286
. 287,289,294-296,300
. 301,303-306,308,310
312-313,010,040
. DeKalb Co. 036,116,217
247,250
. Decatur Co.   275,311
. Dickson Co.   022,092
. 103,107,114,121,141
. 175,197,234,242,276
277,311
. Dyer Co.   105,207
. Fayette Co.   001,021
. 034,048,056,078,081
. 083,086-087,111,122
. 130,132,134,137,142
. 157,169,182,184,193
. 194,199,203,206,215
. 221,223,226,230,239
. 257,280,311
. Fayetteville   081
. Fentress Co. 064,117
. 179,246,259-260,262
280,286,310
. Franklin   091
. Franklin Co. 003,017
. 018,024,049,060-061
. 066,081,085-087,098
. 099,102,105,113,119

Place Index

TN,Franklin Co. (cont.)
- 130-131,138,165-166
- 169,172,179,203,211
- 213,222,224,235,244
- 265,269,276,279-280
  301,313.192
- Gallatin 050
- Galloway 036
- Germantown 088
- Gibson Co. 012,044-045
- 48,66,72,104-105,141
- 152,175,189,200,202
- 219,240,247,258,263
  264,278,307
- Giles Co. 002,004-005
- 008,010,014,018-019
- 026,028-029,032,039
- 040,046,049,051,056
- 081,090,094,106,129
- 137,139,148,151,154
- 161,165-166,172,179
- 181,188,195,197-198
- 212,224,229,251,300
  303,310
- Grainger Co. 006,009
- 011,028-029,033,036
- 058,088,090,092,103
- 104,109,117,134,149
- 161,173,192,200,206
- 220,230,238,244,258
- 259,280,282-283,291
  292,299,305,053,045
- Greene Co. 024,042,088
- 097,109,115,122,127
- 134,170,189,229,239
  262,271,283,295
- Hamilton Co. 030,044
- 045,057,065,081,085
- 087,090,092,095,102
- 116-117,125,145,156
- 163,177,189,196,206
- 209,212,217,219,227
- 235,240-241,258,267
  268,288,307
- Hardeman Co. 007,036
- 085,088,118,130,138
- 142,160-161,163,190
- 225,227,261,281,290
  291,298
- Hardin Co. 002,040,042
- 043,059,065,067,074
- 100,115,155,173,187
- 208,212,248,257,276
  295,297
- Hawkins Co. 009,012

TN,Hawkins Co. (cont.)
- 018-019,021-022,039
- 064-067,080,097-098
- 108,110,125,127,144
- 186,192,194,199,220
- 221,249,262,285,297
  306
- Haywood Co. 068,084
- 094,098,153,184,198
  208,214,221,246
- Henderson Co. 004-005
- 043,059,075,079,084
- 089,103,118,130,146
- 149,158,163,165,176
- 177,183,203,209,222
- 227,229,232,235,251
- 278,284,291,296,299
  309
- Henry Co. 010,017,036
- 077,095,109,112,114
- 174,178,181,187,193
- 218,225,242,248,271
  295,301,310
- Hickman Co. 014,022
- 028,041,043,053,060
- 067,100,150,189,207
  241,275,311
- Humphreys Co. 059,081
  095,185,250,011,256
  287
- Jackson Co. 003,012
- 025,048,056,086,119
- 131,149,159,172,232
- 265,269,278-279,283
- Jefferson Co. 015,027
- 035,040,042,045,047
- 048,051,055,063,077
- 078,092,099,118,123
- 131,137,166,182,190
- 204,225,230,261,287
  291,295,310,088
- Johnson Co. 084,209
  244,250,265,298
  Knox Co. 004-005,008
- 012,022,027-028,035
- 036,039,045,053,055
- 057,065,076,081,088
- 090,103,106,111,113
- 115-116,120,124,127
- 131,141,145,147,154
- 161,167,170,175,185
- 188,193,195,197-198
- 206,209,215,217,222
- 226,232,234,239,246
- 247-249,253,257,266

TN,Knox Co. (cont.)
- 267,286,292,294,301
  311,053,106
- Lagrange 001
- Lauderdale Co. 117,227
- Lawrence Co. 004,027
- 032,046,052,055,058
- 066,068,099,148,155
- 172,177,188,190,198
- 204,207,231,253,273
  290
- Lincoln Co. 013,049
- 060,063,067,078,081
- 089,096,099,102,115
- 122,134,145,151,167
- 179,182,191,199,214
- 226,233-234,239,255
- 262,266,274,293,306
- Macon Co. 241,283,302
- Madison Co. 001,007
- 010,012,015,021,062
- 065-066,075,077,081
- 085,092,100,112,115
- 118,133,159-161,165
- 175,179-181,192,211
- 218,220,235-236,244
- 253-254,256,261,273
- 283,288-289,296-297
  138
- Marion Co. 002,079,097
- 103,112,155,176,186
- 208,212,222,244,267
- 269,298
- Marshall Co. 022,030
- 031,062,066,093,101
- 133,143,146,157,162
- 196,214,223,226,230
- 233,255,284,294,303
- Maury Co. 003-005,011
- 016-019,027,029,043
- 046,051,054,061,065
- 070,073-074,078,081
- 083-086,088,093,100
- 108,112,117,122,134
- 146-147,150-151,153
- 154-155,157,159,166
- 168,171,178,183,189
- 192,197,199,201,204
- 211,218,230,238,256
- 261,265,270,288,290
  292,305
- McMinn Co. 015-16,022
- 025,041,044,046-047
- 057,063,074,080,111
- 120,131,140,144,150

Place Index

TN,McMinn Co. (cont.)
. 153,171,173,176-177
. 192,194,207,210,220
. 229,233,241,244,254
. 256,258,269,272,282
 284,299-300,309
. McNairy Co.   026,030
. 032,040,042,058,067
. 068,095,115,175,210
. 230,233,282,307,309
. Meigs Co.   125,199
. Mills Point   112
. Monroe Co. 003,006,020
. 022,029,032-033,043
. 051,057-059,072,074
. 076-077,088,091,101
. 103,107,118-121,127
. 133,142,156,168,171
. 172,174,176,178,180
. 181,184,186,206,208
. 211,226,228,236,238
. 242,249,276,280,285
 292,299,305
. Montgomery Co. 022
 070,081,104,141,145
 157,159,201,213,221
 223,258,287
. Morgan Co. 022,045,055
 203
. Obion Co. 063,090,237
. 244,258,264,277,298
. Overton Co.   002,019
. 029,048,064,071,083
. 089,096,116,129,143
. 167,182,207,219,221
. 234,260,277,281,286
 292,296,299,302,047
. Perry Co. 008,025,027
. 042-043,056,059,107
. 155,180,183,186,191
 203,206,270,297 ,
. Polk Co. 260,285,301
. Powels Valley   073
. Purdy   040
. Rhea Co. 004,011,025
. 035,040,048,063,084
. 086,112,116,127,139
. 165,167,172,202,229
 240,243,275,290 ,
. Roane Co. 003,006,034
. 035,039,045,047,057
. 076-077,081,085,094
. 104,107,112,118,133
. 139-140,143,167,170
. 179,185,188,195,200

TN,Roane Co. (cont.)
. 207,209,219,238,243
. 247,260,262,267,277
 298,311
. Robertson Co. 011,013
. 015,031,044,049,072
. 101,131,136,144,148
. 158,165,168-170,192
. 213,218,231,237,252
 257,273,146
. Rogersville   011
. Roseville   060
. Rowsville   060
. Rutherford Co. 018,031
. 041,044,050,053,056
. 059,069,071,076,089
. 099,109,111,113,116
. 132,139-140,152-153
. 175,177,180,191,194
. 195,202,207,222,224
. 247,258,267
. Sequatchie Valley 029
. 066,092,119
. Sevier Co. 027,041,044
. 079,113,120,158,232
. 272,282,288,291,303
. Sewart Co.   131
. Shelby Co. 007,029,039
. 041,047,052,054,056
. 062,071,083,088,091
. 106,113,115-116,123
. 125,132,140,142,146
. 152,154,158,160,174
. 176,181,187,190,195
. 196,199,201,203,209
. 214-215,221,224,226
. 228-229,231,234,237
. 239,242,245-246,253
. 255,258,260,263-265
. 268-269,271-275,282
. 285,288-291,293,302
. 303-304,307,309,312
 007,059
 Smith Co. 003,014,016
. 025,036,049,071,089
. 099-100,158-159,171
. 172,203,242,256,287
 302
. Somerville   001
TN, Stewart Co.   10,077
. 079,090-091,093,099
. 110,112,117,126,138
. 140,189,196,200,203
. 215,221,224,232,237
. 240,246,249,266,277

TN,Stewart Co. (cont.)
 281,312,001
. Sullivan Co.   009,013
. 022,028,033,058,062
. 064,067,086,102-103
. 120,123,170,189,194
. 196,215,217,226,232
 250
. Sumner Co. 002,037,043
. 045,055,061-062,064
. 065,068,089,113,147
. 202,243,253,290,311
. Tipton Co. 018,034,043
. 046,050,054,093,107
. 132,137,139,174,178
. 179,188,195,198,226
. 227,243,247,267,280
 290
. VanBuren Co.   063,244
 236,273
. Virginia Co. [sic] 234
. Warren Co. 014,036,046
. 050,066,078-079,089
. 102,113,133,141,156
. 157,170,185,194,210
. 228,236,252,254,298
. 313
. Washington Co. 008-009
. 036,057,071,092,094
. 109-110,115,125,133
. 159-160,182,185,190
. 200,203-204,229,238
. 240,243,249,255,263
. 281,283,286-287,306
. Wayne Co. 025,032,058
. 065,085,088-090,100
. 114,117,140,176,190
. 202,212,231,237,245
. 262,271,276,298-299
. 310
. Weakley Co.   012,029
. 104,143,214,245,283
. 308
. White Co. 020,026,028
. 035-036,043,047-048
. 065,072-073,083,086
. 109-110,113,116,126
. 131,137,145,147,149
. 167,197,199,206,219
. 242,257,262,266,274
 276,285,288,303,087
. Williamson Co. 036,054
. 057-058,071,075,077
. 091,105,117,119,126
. 143,152-153,169,176

319

Place Index

TN, Williamson Co.
  (cont.)
. 191,196,208,217,227
  240,264,281,046
. Wilson Co. 004,013-014
. 018,022,041,047,060
. 061,067,069-070,075
. 076,083,087,094,101
. 105,109,114,124,127
. 128-129,147,157,165
. 166,168,177,180,195
. 198,202,212,214,223
. 226,231,236-237,266
  313,158
TX 054,092,101,161
TX, San Jacinto 056
VA, Abingdon 106,123
. Albemarle Co. 019,154
. Amberst Co. 067
. Amherst Co. 83,133,162
. Amhert Co. 064
. Augusta Co. 064,142
. Botetourt Co. 106
. Brumsey [sic] Co. 056
. Brunswick Co. 8,56,104

VA. Buckingham Co.
  042,053,057,071,127
. Charlotte Co. 025
. Culpepper Co. 16,61
  155
. Cumberland 127
. Cumberland Co. 001,106
. Dinwiddie Co. 009
. Faquier Co. 115
. Fredericksburg 058
. Greenbriar Co. 106
. Halifax Co. 004,078
. 098,107,127,150,153
. Hanover Co. 075
. Henrico Co. 001
. Henry Co. 028,047,062
  153
. Lee Co. 033,080,120
. Loudoun Co. 034
. Lunenburg Co. 077,134
. 142,157
. Lynchburg 126
. Mecklenburg 065
. Nelson Co. 069
. Newbern 053

VA, Norfolk 031,142
. Orange Co. 061,067
. Pittsylvania Co. 26,31
  ,49,56,80,98-99
VA, Powhattan Co. 075
. Prince Edward Co.
  106,111
. Prince Wm. Co. 019
. Richmond 039,096,139
. Rockbridge Co. 031
. Rockingham Co. 063
. Shenandoah Co. 011,080
. Smith Co. 094
. Tiger Valley 110
. Washington Co. 022,041
. 048,062,072,091,144
. Wythe Co. 041,093-094
  103
VT, Barry 129
  Bennington 063
. Hartford 040
Wales 099

Name Index

Abbott,James M. 208	Armington,Martin 001,196,224
Ackerson,Perry 132	Armstrong,John 001,166,233
Adams,Eli 172	. Jonathan 098
Jesse 146	. Martin 209
Adkins 024	Arnett,James 001,226
Aikens,Miss 018	Arp,James 180
Airwood,James 301	Artist,Morris 001,220
Alexander 064	Atchela,Moses 117
Alexander,John S. 258	Atkins,George 299
Simpson 214	Austin,Nathaniel 243
Alford,Riley 206	Avent,J. 146
Allcorn,James 278	Avery,Silas 278
Allen,George W. 002,235	Ayres,J. 112
. Jacob Dr. 052	Badget,Peter 098
. James 241	Bailey,John 291
. James E. 197	. W.C. 239
. John 157,190	. Wm. 194,265,298
. Miles 165	Baker,Alexander 144
. Wiley 307	. Henry 247
Allnut,Mr. 047	. James 081
Amos,Charles 259	. John 283
W.W. 101	Baldruff,Henry 268
Anderson,Burrell 283	Balduff,Henry 268
. C.S. 061	Baldwin,James E. 271
. George W. 028,199	. Joseph E. 271
. Hopkins 027	. Wm. 002,167
. Jacob L. 001,221	Ball,Mr. 143
. Miss 013	Ballentire,Wm. 255
. Mr. 013	Ballew,Francis 306
. Polly 027	Wm. 261
Andis,John 159	Banks,Jesse M. 267
Andrews,Abram 144	Barbee,Beasley 002,165
. Benjamin 289	John 222
. Lavicy 123	Barger,Frederick 197
. Mrs. 123	Barker,James 003,170
. Robt. 187	Barney,Jeremiah 132,226
. Wm. 242	Barnwell,Samuel 279
. Wm. B. 261	Barris,John 156
Anson,Orin D. 212	Barton's Creek forge 053
Anthony,Alfred 210	Basker,James 003
Arbaugh,Maryan 042	Bass,Sarah 022

Name Index

Batchellor,John 002-003
Batchelor,John 168
Bates,Capt. 041
  Thomas 056
Baxter,Andrew 197
  Mr. 015
Bays,John 098
Bean,Edmond 117
. George 117,240
. Jesse 117
Beard,Nancy 087
Beauchum,Franklin 277
Beecham,Henry 309
Bell's forge 053
Bell,Elijah 161
Bellew,Wm. 261
Benham,John 134
  John B. 239
Beningfield,John 251
Bennett,John 264
Benson,Wright 282
Benton,Miss 015
Berry,John 106
  John A. 208
Berryhill,Samuel 155
Bertram,Cornelias 172
Bevil,Elvis 103,220
  Howell 103
Bevirt,John 116
Bias,James 307
  John 307
Bicknell,David 025
Bigby,Archibald 144
Biggs,Jno. 009
. Polly 009
. Thomas 009,186
Bill, a negro 252
Binder 037
Bird,Matthew 272
. Robert 311
Bird,Thomas 276

Black,Solomon 283
Blackburn,Wm. 017
Blackman,Miss 062
Blackwell,Jackson M. 267,298
. Joel 003,171
. Joseph 007,181
. Nathan 286
Blair 098
Blair,James 090
Blalock,Henry 104,219
Blanton,Mr. 115
Blaron,George L. 246
Blawn,Geoge L. 246
Bledsoe mill 086
Bledsoe,Polly 104
Boatman,George 134,238
Boggs,Wm. 160
Bohannon,Robert 074
Bond,John 008,183
  Wm. 061
Bone,Miss 008
Booby,Frances 180
  Francis 007
Bootenhammer's mill 090
Booth's Mill 068
Bordine,Benjamin 132
. John 132,227
. Wm. 132
Boss,Daniel 055
Bostick,Clem 142
. Littleberry 241
. Orlonzo M. D. 213
Bowles,Joseph 297
  Wm. 292
Bowlice,Alexander 290
Bowlin,Peter R. 310
Bowman,John 009
  Joshua 296
Boyd,Wm. 279
Boyle,Robert 133
Braden,Mr. 044

Name Index

Bradford, Richard 241
Bradfute, Archibald 133,228
. J.H. 133
Bradfute, Robert 133
Bradley, Bunell 228
. Burrel 133
. Isaac 133
. Jacob 004,108,171
. Nathaniel 192
Bragg, Robert 134
. Thomas 134
. Thos. Jr. 239
. Thos. Sr. 239
Brake, Sherwood 105,202
Brakeville, Peter 072,091
Branan's meeting -
  house 086
Brandon 037
Brandon, John 004-005,177
Branstutter, Frederick 103
  215
Braudon, Edmund 288
Brazeal, John J. 004-005,177
Bremmit, Wm. 005
Brewer, Abraham J. 260
. Elija 084
. James 260
. Malinda 294
. Mehala 258,294
. Wesley 289
Brewington, John 279
Bridges, Nervazene 060
  Wm. 060
Brigham, John 281
  Thos. D. 281
Briley, Abraham 242
Britt, Solomon G. 292
  Wm. G. 292
Brockwell, Samuel J. 010,188
Brogan, Robert C. 004,197
  Robt. C. 175

Bromly, Wm. 079
Brooke, Robert 133
Brooks 141
Brooks, Bailey 133,235
. Christopher 053
. Mr. 037,151
. Robert 229
. Wm. 053,154
Broughton, Charles 003,169
Browder, Nicholas 008
  Nickolas 182
Brown 037
Brown, Absolom 284
. Betty 008
. G.W. 278,288
. Garland 266
. Gen. 001
. Genl. 143
. George W. 262
. Jack 105
. Jacob 104
. James 008,184,302
. James H. 104,198
. John 006,104,178,201,266
. Jonas 105
. Jones 202
. Joseph 207
. R. 129
. Reubin T. 105
. Silas 190
. Thornton 243
. Wm. 006,178,273,279
Brownlaw's mill 139
Bruce, Elijah 146
. Herod 146,235
. John T. 246
. Nathaniel 246
Brumby, Mr. 115
Brumley, Isaac 189
. Margaret 103
. Mr. 115

Name Index

Brumley,Wm. 103
Brummet,Micajah 009,185
Brunson,David 010,187
Bruton,George 093
Bryan,Robert 022
Bryant,Benjamin 194
. Joel 313
. Mary 158
. W.H. 296
Buchanan's mill 102,154
Buchanan,Edward 268
  Widow 031
Buckhannon,Robert 276
Buckstein,Daniel 263
Bullard,Murdock 104,219
Bullington,Robert 106
  Robt. 215
Bunch's mill 150
Bunch,Basil 007,181
. Wm. 104,200
Burchett,Benjamin 146
  Cordelia 146
Burdan,Eliza 161
Burke,Robt. 310
. Wm. 245,302
Burnett's camp ground 113
Burns,Daniel 243
  Thomas 020
Burress,E.M.D. 292
Burrus,Cornelius 256
Burton,John 242
  Thomas 120
Busbee,Cayce 103
  John 103,222
Butcher,Thomas 009,185
Butler,James 302
Butram see Bertram 172
Butram,Cornelius 004
  Wm. 190
Butts,Cravan C. 207
  Craven 105

Byers,Mr. 098
Cadle,Jason 254
Cage,Williamson 066
Cagle,Isham 282
Caile,W.H. 246
Caldwell 063
Caldwell,Wm. 261,312
Calhoun,Jacob 022,201
. John H. 254
. Lemuel 022
Callan,Bartholomew F. 247
Calvin,Alfred 114
. John 114,225
. Lewis 114
Calwart,Lewis 230
Cambel 022
Campbell,Alfred H. 251
. Archibald 305
. Eli 293
. Esqr. 053
. Gov. Wm. B. 100
. James 015,173
. Wm. 116,216
Cannon,Gov. 005-006,039,029
.   055,059,078,095,104,109,
  147,149
. Samuel 088
Carlisle,W.G. 305
  Willis 114,226
Carmichael,Jack 249
Carmon,Samuel 163
Carney,Wm. 114
Carpenter,James 093
Carr,Daniel 029
. Frederick 246
Carr,Joseph 022,029,206
Carrick,Charles M. 248
Carrol,Micham 275
Carter,Fielding 250
. Jackson 274
. Polly 116

Name Index

Carter, Squire 043
. Wm. 116,229
. Wilson 087
Cartis, Andrew 270
Cartright, Wm. 105
Caruthers, Major 078
Cash, Jefferson 162,304
Cassells, Wm. 015,016,033,175
Cate, Gibson 015,173
  Wm. 015
Cato, Miss 150
Chalmes, Mr. 073
Chamberlain, Samuel
  018,019,181
Chambers Mill 024
Chambers, Mr. 015
Chapman, John N. 016,176
. Josiah 286
. Wiley 161
Chappel, Ansel 024
. Eli 024
. Robert 022,024,207
Chappell, Mr. 136
  Riley 014,168
Charles, Devit 268
Chavis, Jesse 248
Cheatham, Thomas 112
Cheewith?, J.P. 290
Chesney, John 092
Chick, Reubin 284
  Weakley 270
Childers, Edmund 021
Childress, Ayres 115,218
. Burton 123
. Henry H. 269
. John 116
. Lem 020
. Loten 115
. Priscilla 251
Childress, Samuel 020,184
. Wm. 020,116,216

Chism, Absalum 085
Christopher, Mrs. 144
Chumley, Young 018,179
Chumney, Young 179
Churchil, H. 067
Churchwell, Fielding 114,237
Clabey's mill 118
Claiborn, Esqr. 122
Clamer, Cain 024
Clapinger's mills 099
Clarissa, a slave 276
Clark, Burwell 021,192
. Edwin 013,086,167
. James 267
. John 021
. Leslie 114,236
. Marian C. 289
. Marion 160
. Reuben 116,256
. Simeon 160
. Wm. 116,219
Clasure, John 115,237
Claxton, David 014,169
. James 113,225
. Joshua 114
Clement, Willis 014-015,172
Clements, Mr. 015
Clendenning, Robert 310
Clift, Wm. 045
Clinton, Mr. 143
Clopinger's mills 099
Cloppe, David 022
  David S. 203
Clopton's mill 013
Closure, John 115
Coats, Wilson 011-012,174
Cockrell, John 108
Coffee, Calvin 310
Coffman, Samuel 163,309
Coggins, Sally 088
Cohen, Alexander 021,193

Name Index

Colbert's reserve 056
Cole, David 013,167
 Elisha 013-014,168
Coleman, John B. 014
. Daniel 246
. John B. 170
. Oscar S. 243
Collins, Andrew 022,194
. Anna 112
. Ezekiel 021,194
. Isaac 115
. Jacob 255
. Jerry 081
. Jesse 239
Collins, John 089,231
. Joseph 018,179
. Lewis 020
. Owen 020,185
. W. 115
Conley, Abraham 167
 Silas 167
Conly, Abraham 012
 Sylas 012
Conner, Isaac 012
. Isham 012,175
. Jacob 012
. James 166
Cook, A.C. 280
. Abel 271
. George W. 010,165
Cook, Guilford 022,197
. Henry 017,037,178
. Joseph C. 113,224
. Thomas 148
. Wm. 133,163
Cooper, Alexander 072
 Matthew 055
Cooxey, Samuel 017,178
Corbin, George 016,177
Corder, Thomas 097
Corley, Michael 024,213

Cornwell, John 115,239
Corroman, Michael 231
Cotton, Emander 296
Cottrell, John 292
Coulter, Alexander 050
 Charles 050
Counce, James 011,166
Courier, James 019,182
Covant, Mr. 128
Covington, Wm. C. 273
Cowin's mill 134
Cox, Isaac 021
 Wm. 021,187
Craig, George 162
 James 103
Crairy, John 254
Crawford, Robt. F. 266
. Thomas 084
. W.H. 165
. Wm. H. 011
Cresong, Joshua 112,217
 Polly 112
Crider's mill 084
Crigmore, Mr. 080
Crocker, John S. 022,206
Crocket's Iron Works 033
Croff, John 270
Crosen, Elijah 019,183
 John 019
Cross, Alfred 020
Cross, Elihu 020
. George W. 019-020,184
. James 258
. Wm. 020
Crosson, Elijah 183
Culps, Adam 021
 Susan 021
Cummings, Uriah 022,197,227
Cunningham, Wm. 265
Curry, Elkanah A. 241
Curtis, Andrew 117,238,270

Name Index

Curtis,E. 117
Dale,Abel 029
  Isaac 029,205
Dalton,James 031,218
Daniel,Dicy 029
. Narcissa 113
. Perry 029,207
. Wm. 029
Daniels,Thomas 032,235
Dann, Levi 080
Darwin,Wm. (Capt.) 276
Davidson,Mary 141
  Thomas 294
Davis's mill 013
Davis,Anthony 161,301
. Arthur J. 248
. Charles T. 026,181
. David 253
. Edmond 028,192
. Henry 008
. James W. 189
. James Wiley 027
. John 256
. John H. 031
. John H? 216
. Mary 137
. Miss 106
. Moses 137
. Mr. 017
. R. 128
Davis,Richard 290
. Samuel 244
. Wesley 276
. Wm. 160,293
  Zachariah 286
Day,Lewis 245
Dayton,Josiah 029,209
Dean,John A. 026,183
Dean, Wm. 028,198
Debruce,Alexander 311
Delany,Daniel 127

Delk,John 024-025,171
Deming,Theodore 236
  Theodore 032
Demis,John 210
Dempsey,George 102
Dennis,Benjamin 031,223
. Daniel 031
. John 030,210
. Joseph 006
. Miss 006
Denton,James 025-026,180
Dew,R. 066
Dickens,Richard 133
Dickenson,James R. 025
Dickerson,James R. 171
Dickey,George M. 032
. George W. 231
. Mr. 027
Dickson, Col. 026
Dicus,Wily 100
Dillihay,Nancy 093
Dillingham,Richard 296
Dillionham,Richard 296
Dinham,John 245
Doan,Joseph 022,028
Doane,Joseph 196
Donald,Cha[rle]s 209
  Charles 030,057
Doolen,Joel 230
Dooley,James 301
Doolin,Joel 032
  Rice 032
Dorsey,Cornelius 302
Doss,Philip 031
. Wm. R. 031,231
Dotson's mill 120
Dotson,Elizabeth 079
  James 079
Dougan,John 024,165
Dover,Isaac D. 277
Dowinng,John 029

Name Index

Downing, John 029,205
Doxey, Daniel 030,124,214
Drake, Richard 022
Drane, Robert 305
Driver, Widow 122
Duke, Henry 163
  Wm. M. 027,191
Duker, Henry 307
Dunavan, Ephraim 284
Duncan 033
Duncan, Andrew 030,214
. J. 071
. James W. 025,177
. Jamison W. 277
Dunlap, John 111
Dunn, James 034
  Mr. 136
Dunstan, Sanford W. 274
Duprice, Nancy 053
Durham, James 245
  John 266
  Seabourn 306
Duval, Miss 030
Dyer, G.W. 028
. George W. 027,185
. Isaac 006
. Patsey 027
. Stewart 027
. Thomas 006
. Wm. 006,106
Eades, Isaac 103
  James 103
Eads, John S. 308
Eagleton, Jno. 098
Eakin, Michael 313
Easley, Buford 193
Easly, Beuford 034
Eavans, Williams 285
Eddington, Andrew 245
Edins, Elizabeth 036
  Leonard 036,219

Edmans, John 281
Edmonds, John 281
Edmunds, Richard 008
Edwards, Delila 036
. Drewry 036
. James 034,185
. Kitty 036
. Wm. 188,299
. Williams 205
Elkin, John 188
Elkins, John 034
. Peyton 036,206
. Saml. 040
Elliott, Ransom 293
Ellis, Alfred 033,180
  John 292
Ellison, James 141
. Joseph 162
. Robert 141
. Thomas 162,305
Elliston, John 094
  Louis 116
Elloitt, Ransom 293
Elom, Patia 299
Ely, Thomas 033-034
  Thos. 183
Elzey, John 162
  John J. 303
Embree, Elijah 110
Emery, E. 159
Emmett, Allen 266
Essray, Miss 005
Estep, Cleveland 036,227,260
. Daniel 037,229
. Enoch 035,037,201
. Squire 035,037,201
. Wm. 032-033,037
Estepp, Wm. 177
Estip, Susan 036
Estis, Jno. 161
Estis, T.P. 161

Name Index

Estis, Wm. 161,300
Ethridge, James 287
  Mr. 049
Evans, Harris 035,202
. Joseph 250
. Miss 121,149
. Williams 285
Everett, Parker 035
  Sylvanus 035
Everill, Parker 200
Ewel, Joel 162
Fallick, Isaac 282
Fanning, James 185
  James E. 034
Farlee, Elijah 262
Fasting, Wm. 258
Felter, Wm. E. 037,193
Felts, James 272
  Wm. 039,195
Fergeson, Wm. 244
Ferrell, Dicy 137
. Smith 064
. Thomas 168
. Wm. 137
Ferris, Mr. 142
Fiddler, Miss 017
Fin, Wm. 278
Finches' mill 105
Findlay, Mr. 078
Finley, John 037,169
Finney, Augustus 293
  Mary 282
Fisher, Jacob 245
Fite 049
Flemming, Wm. 294
Fletcher, George 309
  James 269
Flippo, George 266
Fogg, Joseph G. 039,197
Folly, Sandford 102
Forbes, Saml. H. 285

Ford, Jonathan 004-005
  W. 305
Forest, John 257
Forgus, John 028,037,125,180
Foster 048
Foster, Benjamin T. 311
. James 040,238
. John 152
. Matilda 152
. Rachel 040
. John 113
Foust, Daniel 039,215
  Lewis 039
Fox, Absalom 137
  Elijah 034
Frasier, Ernando 039,239
Frazer, Abner 027
Frazier, Ermando 204
. J. 092
. Samuel 036
Freeberger, John 158
  Susan 158
Freeland, Joseph 039,219
Freeman, Colonel 067
. George 281
. Mr. 147
French, Peter 219
Fresbey, Mathias 265
Frits, Jacob 118
Fry, Jacob 072
Fulks 103
Fuller, Benjamin 006
. Britt 006
. Joseph 113,224
Fullerton, Isaac 040,233
Fulward, Daniel 171
Fulwood, Daniel 037
Furgeson's Furnace 065
Furry, Mr. 033
Gaddess, Thomas 234
Gaddis, John 286

Name Index

Gaddy, James 242
Gaddys, Thomas 048
  Wm. 048
Gage, John 042,183
Gaines, Armstrong 267
  Mrs. 118
Gaither, Richard 044,194
Galaspie, Wm. H. 262
Galbreath, John 263
Gallimore, George 045
Gamble, Esqr. 076
  Mr. 053
Gann, Adam 092
Gardner, Stephen 004-005
Garner, John 002,148
  Miss 037
Garrett 031
Gaskin, Henry 084
Gatewood, John 297
Gatling, Wm. 226
Gawley, David 044,200
  James 045
Gay, John 116
. Solomon 116,139
. Wm. 116,139
Genoer?, Riley 272
Gentry, Allen D. 058
George, Cherry 043
. David 047,228
. Isaac 044,194
. Jeremiah 042,186
Gibbins, James 166
Gibbons, James 040
Gibney, John 059,185
Gibson's mill 061,080
Gibson, Thos. 269
Gidcomb, Thomas C. 270
Gideon, James 274
Gilbert, John 187
. John S. 043
. Joseph 046,210

Giles, Thomas 076
Gill, John 040,166
Gillaland, David 261
Gillespie, Baylum 046
Gillespie, Patrick 046
Gillimore, George 207
Gillispie, B.M. 208
Gillman, Timothy 031
Glanton, Benjamin 046
. Benjamin F. 216
. Margaret 046
Glover, Andrew 294
Godsay, Hiram 249
Goens, Levi 045,205
Goff, Ambrose 047
. Thomas 020
. Wm. 047,229
Goforth, Russell 044,196
Gofourth 062
Goings, Hugh 305
Golden 138
Gollihorn, Robert 042
  Robt. 182
Golorth, Russell 196
Goodman, Martin 106
Goodwin, Thomas E. 276
Gordon's ferry 094
Gordon, Robert 268
Gorham, James 043-044
. James 192
. Thornton 044
Gossett, Hamilton 041-042,177
. Henry 041
Gott, Sterling M. 272
Gould, Hiram 312
Gragson, Wm. 044,055,203
Graham, Benjamin 126
. James 047,225
. Johnson 275
. Mary 113
. Warren 126,203

Name Index

Graves,Patsey 107
  Thomas 107
Gray,Alexander 081
. James 258
. James R. 047,220
. James W. 046
. Jeremiah 047
. Wm. 020
Grayson,Wm 045,055
Green,Bethel 008
. Charles 297
. Frederick 244
. Isaiah 270
. J.W. 160
. John J. 041
. John J? 173
. Joseph 041
. Josiah 270
. Zelpha 008
Greeter,Wm. 006
Gregory,Aaron W. 256
Grey,James W. 215
Griffin,Wm. 310
Griffith,Oliver 041,174
Grooms,James 047,221
Grote,Elias 248
Gunn,Mr. 044
Gurley,Wm. S. 309
Hackwell,Larkin 069
Hadley,Ambrose 086
Hainbee, David 144
Haines ,Thomas 167
Haines,Jeremiah 048
  Thomas 048
Hall,Carter 050
. Felix S. 291
Hall,J.M. 292
. Jonathan A. 264
. Redding 050
. Redding R. 174
. Wm. 307

Halley,Creed 134
Halliday,Samuel 054
Hambleton,Isaac 198
Hamby,Gideon 309
Hamden,George 172
Hameltre,Jere 042
Hamilton 060
Hamilton,Isaac 055
. Wm. 050,175
Hamlett,Richard 089
Hamner,Logan 252
Hampton,Amos 287
Hancock,Wm. W. 256
Handley,John N. 276
Haney's mill 081
Hankins,Richard 051,180
Hanna,John Ezra 304
Hanner,Logan 252
Hannum,Meflin 213
  Miflin 144
Hansard,Robert 265
Harden,Henry 251
Harding,John 130
. Martin 074
. Watkins 074
Hardins ferry 074
Hare,Patrick 054
  Robert 049-050,174
Harley,Sameul 123
Harman's mill 103
Harrell,Edward 304
. Eli 069
. Henry 146,234
Harridon,Genl. 083
Harris,Gov. 159-161
. J. George 113
. James 051,183
Harris,John 295
. Phillip 313
. Wm. 247
Harrison,Benjamin R. 268

331

Name Index

Harrison,John 308
　Osenberry 271
　Thomas 271
　. Wm. 145,233
Hart,Mary 043
. Mrs. 040
. Nancy 059
. Thomas 043,059
. W.C. 144
Hartwick,Fredrick 155
. Leonard 155
. Salena 155
Harvey,Wm. 208
Haskins,John 012
Hasley's mill 157
Hatch,John T. 075
Hawkins 043
Haws,John 085
Hayes,Blackman 031
Haynie,James 230
Hayny,James 146
Hazlett,Mizay 053-054,190
Hearvy,George 057
　Wm. 057
Heathcock,John 145,225
　Young 145
Heatherley,Wm. 295
Hecock,John 312
Hedgecock,Miss 098
Henderson,Allen 253
. Daniel 096
. Elizabeth 225
. Hamilton 052
. Henry 052
. John 052
. John F. 257
. Joseph 131
. Robert 052
Henderson,Robt. 188
Hendley,Micajah 146
. Peter 146,230

Hendley,Wm. 146
Henry's store 124
Henry,Alexander 244
. Arthur 046
. James 055,202,272,295
. John 055,145
. Lawson 145,217
Henshaw,John 252
Henson,Samuel 056
. Thomas 056
. Thomas K. 206
Here,Patrick 054,191
Herndon,George 049
Herrill,Zachariah 228
Herrol,Zachariah 145
Herron,Jack 304
Hesterson,Benjamin 064
. Hazard 064
. Sylvanus 064
. Willis 064
Hetherly,John 080
　Sarah 080
Hewling,Wm. R. 027
Hicks,Matthew 139
. Miss 030
. Nancy 139
. Temperance 048
. Thomas 141
. Timothy 284
Hickson,Mrs. 092
Hignen,Wm. 078
Hilburn,Martin 033
Hilderbrence,Mr. 148
Hill,Andrew 275
. Chambers 145
. Eli 145,219
. Franklin 279
. George 129
　John W. 048,169
. Mr. 073
. Perry 130

Name Index

Hindman,Sterling 056,204
Hines,Irvin 161
Hines,Irwin 297
Hite,John 301
Hobbs,A. 282
Hodge,Col. 141
Hodges,John 088
Hoffman,Danl. 293
Hokimer,Elizabeth 011
Holcomb,W.A. 130
Holeman,Lewis R. 236
Holland's Ferry 068
Holland,Charles 283
. David 022
. Thomas 080
Holley,Caleb 056,207
Holliday,Samuel 055,198
Holmes,Council 084
. Henry 084
. Thomas E. 295
Hone,Henry 172
Hood,Henry 057,210
Hoolon,John Granville 262
Hooper,Dempsey 107
. Nimrod 054,195
. Simpson 297
Hooton,John Granville 262
Hootzell,George 098
Hopkins,Moses T. 053
. Moses Treadway 189
. Ovin 070
Horn,Henry 049,172
Horton's mill 019
Horton,Andrew P. 052
. Jacob K. 052,188
. Margaret 052
Hosea,Levi 238
Wm. 238
Howard,A.G. 266
John B. 048-049,170
. Mr. 047

Howard,Thos. 210
Howerton,Thomas 057
Hoy,Hugh 051-052,187
Huddleston,Sarah 122
Woodson 122
Hudson,Thomas 054,196
Huffines,John 126
Huffman,John 056,204
Michael 056
Hughes mill 074
Hughes,Davis 027
. John 092
. John A. 281
. Mr. 047
. Richard 280
. Samuel 250
. Thomas 095
Hughs,Hiram 144,211
Nimrod 144
Hullet,Joseph 202
Hullett,Joseph 055
Wm. 055
Humble,Francis 264
Humes,Jones 053,188
Humphery,Judge 121
Hunt,James 271
Hunter,John 084
. Mr. 113
. Nancy 059
. Samuel 059
Hurst,Pleasant 288
Hurt,Zachariah 286
Huskey,Blake 056
Husky,Blake 204
Hutchinson,Daniel 039
Hutson,Richard 242
Hutton,George 310
Hynes,Wm. 060
Imes, John 062
Wm. 062
Immes,Williams 215

Name Index

Inman, Elizabeth 043
Innes, Williams 215
Inscore, James 151
Irwin, James 277
Ivey, James B. 058-059
Ivy, James B. 180
  Willis 243,277
Jackson, Deaderick 142
. Elias 283
. John 059,185
. John J. 278
. Joseph 059,187
. Thomas 168
. Thos. P. 253
Jacobs, Nathaniel 061
. Wm. 061,204
James, Bennet 058
. Bennett A. 176
. Wm. 039
Jarnagin, Allen 061,204
Jenkins, Jas. 299
  Wm. 276,299
Jennings, Samuel 043
Jestice, Robert 271
Jim, a negro 289
John, a negro 253
Johnson's mill 076
Johnson, Ake 063,236
. Alexander 124
. Betsey 080
. Danl. 001
. Dempse 286
. Gov. 159-160
. Henry 060,191
. Hiram 041,058
. Hyram 176
. Jacob 063
. Jefferson 278
. Jeremiah 060-061,195
. John 107
Johnson, Lewellen 295

Johnson, Moses 080
. Nathan G. 211
. Nathan S. 061
. Noel K. 062,218
. Peggy 124
. Reuben 063
  Reubin 234
. Richard 110,253
. Sarah 137
. Talton 063,236
. Wm. 137,240
. Wm. Left 063
Johnston, Christenia 090
Johnston, George 063,237
. James R. 260
. Widow 032
. Wm. 142,272
Joiner, Buck 158
. John 158
. Miles 158
Jolly, Asberry 187
. Asbury 060
. Stephen 060
Jonagin, Allen 204
Jones, Aaron F. 061,198
. Berryman 148
. Charles W.H. 302
. Chesley 259
. James 062,217,273
. James J. 081
. James M. 047
. John 266,313
. John C. 301
. Lewis 026
. Miles 301
. Mrs. 040
. Richard 018
. Sherrod 274
. Thompson 058,169
. W. 047
. Wiley 274

Name Index

Jones,Wm. 063,230,254
  Wm. G. 289
Jonston,James R. 260
Jordan's ferry 094
Jott,Sterling M. 272
Joy,Isaac 026
Joyce,James 062,216
Julany,Josiah 261
Justice,Robert 271
Kanaby,James 101
Kasler,Philip 066,236
Kearney,Malinda 006
  Wm. 006
Keeland,Calton 126
Keelin,Spencer 275
Keer,Samuel 172
Keesee,Mr. 128
Keith,Britton 066
. Haywood 066,223
. John 066
Kelley,Henry 066
Kellis ferry 025
Kellogg,James W. 295
Kelly,Henry 221
  James 046,263
Kenkins,Elijah 158
Kenkins, Jesse 158
Kenneday,Wm. 203
Kennedy,Saml. B. 252
  Wm. 022
Kerr,Samuel 064
Kesterson,Hazard 175
Ketchem,Col. 132
Kiddy,Jourdan 267
Kidwell,Isaac 148
Kilbuck,Patience 065
  Wm. 065,218
Kilburn,Martin 033
Killian,Jesse 065,217
Kilpatrick,Anderson 140
Kimbro 153

Kimbro's mill/store 053,137
Kimbrough,Joseph 113
Kincaid,Grace 007
Kindrick, Edmond 083
King 039
King's iron works 133
King,A.B. 195
. Alfred B. 065
King,Carrol 296
. Carroll 161
. F.W. 032
. George 108
. James 108
. John 064,179
. Samuel 286
. Sarah 161
. Wm. 267
Kinnard,George 261
Kirk,Elvin 065,219,307
  Lewis 065,212
Kirksey,Jesse B. 255
Knight,John 284
Kollogg,James W. 295
Kyle,James 065,201
Lackey,John 259
Lacy,Jacob 257
Lain,Middleton 156
Lamb,David 117
Lambert,John A. 309
Lamsing,Thomas 070,213
Lancaster's mill 015
Land,Edward 071,221
Landers,Josiah 067,173
Landerson,Overall 072
Landrith,Wm. 306
Lane 041
Lane,Cleveland 260
. James 262,275
. John 036
Langston,George R. 270
Lapier,Charles 072,238

Name Index

Larkey,Saml. 228
  Samuel 071
Lastley,Wm. 260
Laughmiller see -
  Lockmiller 004
Lavendar,John 070
  Pickens 070
Lavender,John 213
Law,Alexander 134
Lawrence,Isaac 174
. John 070,087,214,301
. Mrs. 040
  see also Lowrance
Lawson,James 014
  Mrs. 040
Lazenbury,Henry 173
Lazenby,Thomas 299
LeMar,James 064
Leath,Addison 069-070,203
. Willis 069
Lee's mill 053
Lee,Augustus 041
. James 251
. Jno. 010
. M. 090
Lefever,Wm. 066
Lefevre,Wm. 166
Leger,Lewis 125
  Lewis D.H. 196
Lemans,Sarah 016
Lemmons,Daniel 260
Lemon,Narcissa 259
Lenox,Hugh 068,184
Leonard,Mr. 159
Lester,Woodford R. 313
Leuisman,Wm. 159
Lewis,Alex 162
. J. 070
. Jackson 213
. James W. 100
. John F. 286

Lickstein,Daniel 263
Liford,John 080
  Katharine 080
Lindsay,Ellmore 217
Lindsey,Ellmore 071
  Wm. 071
Lindsley,Elisha 300
Lisenby,Thomas 299
Lisle,Joseph 077
Little,John 263
Lively,James 069,202
Lively,Robert 069
. Wm. 069
Locke,J.W. 101
Lockmiller,John 004
Loftes,Miss 003
Logan,Robert 289
Long,Milly 127
  Mr. 098
Lovell,Cyrus 069
. Tilman 068-069
. Tilmon D. 202
Lowe,John W.D.F. 071
. Moses 071,215
. Samuel C. 302
Lowrance,Isaac 068
. John 068
. Peter 068
Lucas,Garland 067
  Garland G. 170
Luzenbury,Henry A. 067
Lynch,Michael 068,190
Lyneas,David 297
Lynns Boat Yard 067
Lyons,Blackwood 072,240
  Sally 072
Macaslin,Jno. 156
Mackey 058
Madden,George 080
  John 080
Maddin,George 186

Name Index

Mahaffe, John 086,220
Mahaffy, Isaac 087,226
Maidewell, Isaiah 285
Maidwell, Harrison 288
Mainor, David 249
Majors, Nelson 248
Makelley, John 301
Manghan, Miss 077
Mangrum, James 087
  Joseph 087
Manley, Curtis 084,203
Manley, Elcany 084
. Henry 087,226
Manning, Calvin 240
. Clements 090-091,237
. Fountain 270
. John 090
. John Calvin 091
Manns.Mark 209
Manus, Maloney 084
  Mark 084,209
Marbury, Leonard 068
Marcum, Robert 273
Mares, James 245
Marlow, Paris 308
Marrs, Mark 209
Marsh, John 073,167
Marshall, Joseph J. 296
  Thomas 252
Martin, Elizabeth 085
. James 289
. Mr. 022
. Wm. 085,212
Martindale, Daniel 302
Mashon, Wm. G. 284
Mason's ferry 088,093
Mason, James 103
  Wm. 103
Massey, Ransom 311
Massingil, David 298
Massly 053

Massy 042
Masters, Alexander 089
  Anderson 233
  Thomas 243
Matheny, Lewis 070
Matlock, Gideon 071
Matlock, Refe 071
  Robert 229
. Susan 071
Matthew, Charles 249
Matthews, Nancy 138
  Reuben 138
Maugham, Miss 077
Maury, John 181
Maxfield, Isaac 090
  John 090
Maxwell, John 068
May, David 072,165
. Obadiah 211
. Obediah 085
. Wm. 001,081,188
Mayfield, Avery 079,185
  John 235
McAfee, John 141
McAllister, Francis 089,232
McBride, Andrew J. 088
. John 088,228
. Zekiel 088
McCahin, Dennis 045
McCain, Mr. 120
McCalester, Sutton 300
McCall, Robert 078
  Robt. 182
McCallister, Francis 283
McCarpin, Francis 017,178
McCarty, Daniel 081,087
                189,225
McChaughin, Dennis 055
McChord, Richard 053
McClellan, Alexander 087
McClellen, Esq. 096

Name Index

McClennan, Alexander 227
McCluer, Miss 077
McClure, Henry 069
McCluskey, Wm. 081
McClusky, Wm. 191
McCorkle, Alexr. 017
McCormic, Mr. 099
McCormick, Clayton 035
McCoun, James 081
McCoy, Hugh 263
. John A. 264
. Wm. 159, 288
McCracken, Calvin 027
. John 027
Wm. 073, 168
McCrary, Nancy 063
McCreath, Robert 045
McCrory, H.B. 205
Hiram B. 084
McCuistiace, Andrew 291
McCullouch, Franklin 076
Henry 076
McCullough, Franklin 076, 180
McCutcheon, Mr. 045
McDaniel, Alex 163
. Capt. 143
. Nancy 020
McElyea, George 264
. Henry 081
. Hiram 081
. John 081
McGavock's mill 055
McGavock's spring 144
McGee, Adam 077
. John 121
. Lutin 077, 181
. Thomas 077
McGrew, John 085, 211
McGuire, Jackson 087, 222
. Wesler 222
. Wesley 086

McHenry's ferry 033
McIntosh, W. 099, 126, 155
Wm. 144
McIntyre, B.F. 284
McKay, Robt. 263
McKelley, John 301
McKinley, R? R. 312
McLain's Mill 030
McLenden, Green 308
McLeod, Jesse J. 086
McLoad, Jesse J. 215
McMahan, John 309
Wm. 158
McMillen, Jno. 120
McMinn, Jonathan 148
McMorris, James 294
McNeal, John 090, 235
McNeece, James 083
McNeeley, Wm. 080-081
McNeely, Mr. 071
. Wm. 080, 186
McNeese, James 081, 195
McNeilly, Wm. 186
McNickol, Alexander B. 256
McVay, Danl. 238
Mchord, Richard 053
Measel, George 084
Medlock's mill 004
Meek, James 146
Melton, John 075, 089, 177
. Riley 089
. Riley H. 231
Mendenhall, Marmaduke 050
Mercer, Wm. 086, 220
Merrill, Kitty 036
. Wm. 036, 215
Metcalf's factory 015
Mezells, George 208
Middleton, Abel L. 088
Amos L. 228
Milam, Henry 077

Name Index

Miles, Lemuel G. 234
  Wm. 086,213
Miller, James 081,083,193,197
. John Lock 004
. Jonathan 081
  Mark 076
. Moses 076
. Mrs. 002
. Richard 074
. Robert 076
. Wm. 076,179
Mills, Lemuel J. 089
  Thomas 083,199
Millsap, Jared B. 185
Millwood, Simpson 280
Milsap, Edward 080
  Jared B. 079-080
Milton, John 177
Minor, Henry 078,182
. John 078,182
. Martha 024
Minton, Anderson J. 258
Mirrell, Wm. 036
Mitchel, Abraham 312
  James 293
Mitchell, Charles 116
. Charles C. 217
. James 160
. John 091,240
. Peter 074,173
. R.B. 031
Mobley, Aaron 088,230
Mobly, James 088
Montgomery, Hu 089
. John 098
. Robert L. 089,233
  Moody 090
  Moon, John 159,287
Moore, Alex N. 291
. Hugh 073,167
. Jesse 081,191

Moore, John 041,086,216,287
. John W. 079,183
. Martin 160,294
. Samuel 083,201
. Travis 079
Moore, Wm. 079,083,199
Moorefield, Henry Jr. 244
Mooting Mills 065
Moran, John 083
  Samuel 083,198
Morefield, Henry 085
Morgan, Henry P. 074,171
. James 088
  John 075,159
. Joshua 088,229
. Wm. 075-076,179
Moris, Nathan 139
Mornin, John 001
Morrin, John 001
Morris, Charlotte 051
. George 075,176
. John 057
. Lawrence 031
. Mary Ann 031
. Meshac 019
  Nathan 139
Morrison, John 074,173
  Thomas 081,194
Morton, Wm. 271
Mosely 152
Mosely, Jonathan 153
Moss, Daniel 118
Mounts, Jno. 190
Mowry, John 076-077,181
Mullins, Joshua 084,209
  Wm. 084
Murphey, John 085
  Matthew 085
Murphreys Settlement 068
Murphy, Archibald 095
. Matthew 212

Name Index

Murphy, Wayne 057
Murray, James E. 090
  Thomas D. 090
Murrell, John 077
. John A. 181
. Wm. S. 077
Murry, James E. 234
Myatt, Kendrick 022
Myers, Robert 072,238
Myres, Robert 091
Nandin, John 092
Napper, Edmund 262
  Grandison 310
Nations, Thomas 051
Neal, James P. 020
. Wm. 258,285
Nearing, Quiller 130
Nebas, Matthew 268
Needham, Wm. B. 290
Nelson, Isaac 249
. Moses 092
. Moses A. 179
Newton 091
Nichols, Ashberry 307
  Berry 307
Nixon, Washington 257
Norman 042
Norrie, Obediah 233
Norris, Ambrose 091
. Ambrose A. 174
. Jesse 092,234
. John 091
. Miss 009
. Obadiah 092
. Obediah 233
. Thomas 009
Norvell, Timothy 128
  Wm. 092
Norville, J.N. 311
Norwood, Henry 092,227
Nowlin, Allen 145

Nowlin, Wm. 145
Nun, Wm. 093,236
Nunn, Pascal 291
Nye, N. 002
O'Brien, Patrick 094
O'Brion, Patrick 228
O'Donnell, John 304
Oagle, John 304
Oakley, Jeremiah 093,211
Olive, Ira 093,178
Oliver, John 033,109
  Spencer 094,240
Oment, David 221
Oney, James 094
  James H. 229
Oozele, Elijah 087
Orick, Amelia 152
  Lewis 152
Orr, James 093,196
  John 253
Osment, David 221
Overton, Lane 019
  Moses 139
Owen, Wm. 280,310
  Zachariah 269
Owens 024
Owens, Edwin 122
  Elizabeth 122
Oxford, Jacob 257
Ozment, David 094
  Saml. 094
Padgett, John 096,182
Pannel, Jackson 095
Panther, Alexander 306
Paris, Esq. 096
Park, Moses 184
Parker, Barbary 034
. Mrs. 040
. Nancy 112
Parkerson, Jacob 099,204
Parks, Azariah 098,198,295

Name Index

Parks, John 097
. Moses 097
. Wm. 097
Parsons, Williams 311
Pass, Washington G. 285
Pattengill, Samuel 311
Patterson, Andrew B. 307
  Fitzallen 146
Patty's mill 006
Payne, Dudley 101
. Guilford 101,223
. John 101
. Simpson 101
. Warren 101
Payson, James 100
  Jas. W. 218
Pearce 050
Pearce, Joshua 046
  Wm. 310
Pearce?, Wright 297
Pearson, Mrs. 044
. S.L. 101
. Stephen 231
Peary's mill 076
Peck, Alexander 260
  Eli 099,205
Peek, Eli 205
Pendergrass, Robert 101,226
Pennel, Jackson 166
Pennington, James 259
Pentigrass, Moses 103
Pentigross, Squire 112
Penuel, Jackson 166
Peoples, Robert 250
. Wm. 100,210
Perdew, John 102,232
  Wallace 102
Perdue, John 102,232
Perkins 042
Perowe, Mrs. 007
Perry, Burrill 313

Perry, James 102,240
. Mrs. 003
. Richard 157
. W.W. 099
. Wm. W. 200
Pettit, James 142
Petty, John 098,192,269
Pew, Samuel West 099,199
Phelps' mill 090
Philips, Jacob 281
  Sylvanus 157
Phillip, Nelson 294
Phillips, Culverson 096,183
. Elias W. 308
. George 194
. James 159
. John 086
. Joshua 081
  Margarett 159
. Mrs. 115
. Peyton 159
. Peyton T. 269
. Wm. 096,181
Philps, Elias W. 308
Picket, David 100
Pickett, Lacey W. 208
. Lacy W. 100
. Wm. 100
Pigeon 156,217
Pilchford, Miss 048
Piles, John 130
Pillow, Gideon 287
Plunket, Alexander 100,207
. Dicy 100
Pogue, Hiram 259
Poindexter, Sarah 157
. Talton 098
. Tarleton 097,192
. Wm. 249
Polk, Gov. 022,046,104,109,130
Poole, Robert 233

Name Index

Pope, Daniel 111
  Squire H. 253
Popelaski, Wm. 303
Porter, Archibald 095-096, 177
Posey, John 099, 205
  Sarah Ann 099
Powel, Abram 095
  James 048
Powell, Abram 174
. Baxter 095
. Baxter A. 169
. Wm. 281
Power, James 252
Powers, James 100, 218
  Sarah 100
Prater, Robert A. 298
Prestley, Miss 104
Preston, Samuel 123
Prewett, Thomas 097, 108, 186
Price, Wm. 273
Priest, David 287
Prior, John 279
Pritchard, Stephen 254
Pruett, James 102
. John 102
. Richard 102
. Richd. C. 235
. Thomas 108, 186
Prumley, Wm. 222
Puckett, Jesse 102
. Jesse L. 236
. Sarah 102
. Stokes 102
Pugh, Samuel 097
  Samuel D. 186
Purtle, Arnett 297
Qualls, John 265
Quimby, Wm. 243
Quinn, Mr. 002
Quirk, James 160
Rail, Wm. 261

Raines, John 140
Rains, F.R. 037
Ramey, Robert 109, 193
Randal, Thompson W. 312
Randolph, David 110
. James 110
. John 110-111, 206
. Peyton 111
. Wm. 110, 203
Ransom, Huldia 108
  John 186
Ransum, John 108
Ray, Drury 287
. James E. 240
. John 117
Read, James 209
Reagan, Nathl. P. 303
Reagle, Wm. 257
Reayle, Wm. 257
Redman, Henry K. 106, 179
Reece 032
Reed, Drury 111, 210
. James 111
. Robert 072, 091
. Wm. 111
Reeder, Mr. 028
Reid, James 097
  Mildred 097
Reynolds, Esquire 065
Rhea, Ezekiel 109
. James 109
. James E. 240
. John 071, 106, 109, 200
. Samuel 109
. Thomas 109
Rheuminger, Mrs. 011
Rhodes, John 184
Rial, John 312
Rice, James S. 282
Richard, Isaac 113
Richards, Henderson 113, 219

Name Index

Richardson, James 117,226
. John 117
. Jonithon 277
Richmond 128
Richter, Augustus 300
Ricker, Asa S. 109,197
Ridgeway, Henrietta 111
  Richard 111,209
Ridley's mill 076
Riggs, Sarah 036
Rigsby, James 024
Rimel, Elias 262
Ritchie, Peter 123
Ritters, S.B. 162
Roach, J.L. 045
  Wm. 118,227
Roberts, James 107-108,186
. Monroe 275
. Smith 109-110,112,199,212
. Wm. 118,230
Robertson, George 310
  Mr. 110
Robinson, Benjamin 112
. Eliphazo 146
. James 040
. John D. 112,218
Rockholt's post-office 009
Roddy, Margaret 046
  Mr. 046
Rodes, Elijah 107
. Elizabeth 107
. John 107
. Nancy 107
. Wm. 107
Rodgers, Thomas 304
Rogers 048
Rogers, Gen. John 096
. George W.R. 166
. Reuben 110
. Samuel 110,203
. Washington Rayborn 106

Roland 050
Rolston, Jane 080
  Polly 080
Romines, Davenport 210
. Devenport 111,129
. Godfrey 112
. Godfrey R. 218
Rooker, George 300
Ross, Benjamin 113
. Charles C. 052
. David T. 067
. Mrs. 012
. Wm. N. 113
. Wm. W. 224
Rosses ferry 056
Rotteree, James 010
Rowlack 153
Rowland, Baldwin 265
Ruark, Timothy 102
Rucker's mill 120
Rucker, James H. 248
  Mr. 100
Runnels, Elisha 141
Russel, George 277
. Paris 249
. Sarah 032
Russell, Ephriam 126
  Mrs. 138
Ryan, Harris 012
Rye, Nathaniel 108,192
Ryon, Harris 012
Saffarans, James 052
Sampson, James 126
  James Thompson 200
Sanders, Eliza 076
. James 076,255
. John 076
. Martha 076
. Polly 076
. Reddick 124
. Redick 191

Name Index

Sapur?,John 232
Sartin,Eli 123-124,190
  James 131,232
Sarton,John 040
Sasseen,Elizabeth 131
  John 131
Satterfield,Hezekiah 127,212
Sauls,Sally 147
Savage,R. 040
Scarberry's mill 069
Schuylfield,James 105
Scofield,Ezra 056
Scott's mill 105
Scott,Alexander 037
. Cynthia 129
. Galel 300
. George 033
. James 129,224
. James M. 307
Scott,Martin 129,222
. Robert C. 084
. Thomas 280
Scrimpter,James 103
Scurlock,Thomas 081
Seals,John 121
. Peter 121,175
. Wm. 121
Sears,Seath 232
  Seth 131
Sellers,Dickson 062
. Isaac 152
. Keziah 152
Sexton,Lewis 125,199
Sexton, Wm. 118-119,167
Seymour,W.H. 274
Shadden,Wm. 131,232
Shannon,John 147
  Wm. 247
Sharp's Furnace 033
Shaw,James 261
Shaws ferry road 057

Sheets,Daniel 283
Shell's ford 089
Shelton,James 132,235
Shepherd,John 125,143
  Lewis 130,230
Shepperd,John 200
  Joseph 161
Sherman,Charles 129,224
Sherod,Henry 120
  Thomas 120
Sherrod,Thomas 170
Shoat,James 121
Shoemaker,Wm. 270
Shook,Franklin 241
  Jacob 128
Shropshire,Francis 306
. James 305
. Joel 291
. John 291,305
  Vicca 306
Shugart 032
Silvers,Irwin 243
Simmons,H. 159
. Jane 132
. Miller 286
. Thomas 132
Simms,Miss 131
Simpson's mill 132,149
Simpson,Genl. 003
  Henry 308
. Jane 132
. John 132,234,254
. Wm. Genl. 053
Sims,Henry 308
Singleton,John 105
Skinner,B.D. 280
Skyler,John 267
Slaughter 060
Slaughter,Ann 122
. Branson 122
. Elizabeth 122

Name Index

Slaughter, James 122
. James C.D. 273
. John 122,184
. Sarah 122
. Wm. 122
Smith 022
Smith's mill 003
Smith, Alex 126
. Ambrose 061
  Anthony G. 127,211
. Benjamin 052
Smith, Bird 127
. David 278
. Francis 119,169
. Hardy 131,233
. Henry 130,226
. J? B. 134
. Jarvis 107
. Jesse 124,194
. John 127,296
. John N? 022
. Joseph 128
. Martha 130
. McDaniel 128,212
Smith, Miss 050
. Mrs. 042
. Nancy Ann 129,221
. P.L. 128
. Peter 255
. Prestley L. 214
. Robert 127
. Samuel 131,233,294
. Stephen 303
. Sterling 127
. Thomas 127
. Warren 126,203
. Wm. 248,265,288
. Winniford 080
Smolenski, Stanislous 242
Smolley, John 160
Sneed, W. 277

Snell, Stephen 130,227
Snider 127
Sorton, John 040
Souelle, Riley 229
Sowders 024
Sowelle, Riley 229
Spain, Miss 075
Sparks, Wm. 128,217
Spears, Abraham 132
. Abram 239
. Alexander 118,128,165,213
Spears, Charles 122,179,196
Speck, John 255
  Leander 255
Spence, Brent 108
. Eleanor 093
. Miss 026
Spencer, James 247,279
Spooner, Sanlis? 268
Springs, Abner 127
  Benjamin 126,206
St. John, Francisco 122,187
St. Leger, Lewis 125
  Lewis de 196
Staffle, Wm. 272
Stafford, Ralph 094
Stagg, James 115
  Joseph 115
Staggs, David 241
Staley, Thomas 125
  Thomas B. 199
Standifer, Wm. 120,173
Stanmire, Henry 258
Stansill, John 152
  Sarah 152
Stanton, George 275
Steel, George D. 244
Stephens, Andrew 119-120,169
. Solomon 076
. W. 271
Stewart, Alfred 033

Name Index

Stewart,John 065
. Lewis 259
. Miss 085
Stobingh,Joseph C. 251
Stokes,Jackey 163
  Mrs. 010
Stone,George W. 247
  James N 244
Stout,Robin 051
Stowers,John 302
Strain,Sarah D. 089
Strange,Bird? 127
Strange,Parham 127,211
Stratin,John 035
Stringer's mill 008
Strong,Peyton 115
  Reuben 061
Stubblefield 098
Summerville,Alexander 129
. John 129
. Wm. 129,223
Surber,Samuel 123,189
Suthert,Isaac 033
Suttles 044
Sutton,Joseph 120
Sutton,Oliver 075
. Stanford 298
Swafford,Wm. 119
Swaggarty,Stockley 124
Swaggerty,Jackson 121
. Jackson J. 176
. Stokely D. 193
Swain,W.M. 094
Swan,Mr. 022
Swaney,Wm. 253
Swann,Wade 248
Sweet,John 019
Swisegood,Andrew 127,206
Swofford,Wm. 168
Tabor,Danl. 298
Tacket,Hiram 273

Tafflestreet,Miss 050
Taggart,John 264
Tallent,Mitchel 311
Talton,James 140
Tanner,Roberts 017
Tarleton,James 200
  James R. 170
Tarlton,James R. 134,136
  James W. 250
Tarrance,John 237
Taylor 053
Taylor,Charles 275
Taylor,Daniel 287
. James 274,303
. James Col. 053
. Joseph 278
. Miss 006
. Peter C. 262
. Thomas 045
. Wm. 020,293
Templers,James 269
Terrell,Thomas 134
Thacker,Joel 281
Tharp,L.H. 160
Thaxton,John 141
Thaxton,Martin 140,222,252
. Thomas 141
Thomas,George 250
. H.W. 140,214
. Jackson 134
. James 290
. Jesse 264
. Peter 110
. Robert 110,250
. Wm. 154
Thompson,Charles 136
. Elizabeth 131
. Henry 142
. Jacob 050
. John 140,202
. Joseph 136,170

Name Index

Thompson, Reuben 142,225
. Thomas 140,221
. Wm. 141,222
Thomson, Martin 074
Thornburg, Widow 035
Thorp, L.H. 160
Tilley, Mrs. 138
Timmans, Wm. A. 237
Timmons, Wm. 142
Timms, Larkin 138,189
. Miss 086
. Reubins 189
Tims, Reuben 138
Tiner, Jno. 141
. Peter 141
. Peter W. 223
. Thomas 141
Tinsley, Wm. 136,176
Tipper, James 137,188
  Kinchy 137
Tittleton, Bryant 278
Todd, Samuel 142
  Samuel H. 224
Tollett's mill 071
Tomlinson, Elijah 274
Toney, J. 273
Tooey, James 139
Tooley, James 198
Torbett, Augustine 257
Torrance, John 143,237
  W.H. 143
Totten, Judge 089
Townsend, Henry 137,188
Trainer, Wm. 099
Trammell's rent 080
Trantham, Wade H. 253
Trimble, Richard 057,139,195
Triplett, Jesse 037
Trout, Wm. 004
Troxler, Lorenzo D. 288
Truett, Henry 264

Tucker, Dr. 059
. James H. 256
. John 285
. Riley 306
Turley, Alfred 244
Turman, Larkin 142,224
Turman?, Larkin 248
Turner's mill 102
Turner, Jesse S. 142,230
. John 137-139,182,190,263
. Mary 137
. Mr. 015
. Thomas 139,195
Turner, Wm. 292
Turner?, Bailey 298
Turney, Hopkins 072
Turney, Miss 072
Tyler, Edward 141,222,259
  . 299,309
. John 089
Tyner, Peter 269
Tyson, James 063
Upton, Stephen 143,219
Ussery, Nathaniel 289
Utters mill 119
Valentine, Ratchford 143,176
Van, Jesse 121
Vance, George 255
Vanleer, Anthony 053
Varner, Henry 134
Varnum, Mitchell 032
Vascer, Miss 133
Vasser, John 088
Vaughn, Isaac 305
Venable, John 143,227
  Richard 143
Vernon, Miles 139
Vestal, J. 090
Vickars, John 293
Vines, Alexander 144,231
Vinson, Andrew 144,229,257

Name Index

Virgil, Samuel 205
Wagoner, Mr. 017
Wakefield, John 214
Wakeller, Mr. 037
Walker, Elias 300
. Elias M. 256
. Isham 157, 223
. James 241
. Mr. 130
. Mrs. 040
. P.M. 259
. Peter 152, 190
. Robert 157, 284
 Wm. 285
Wallis's mill 018
Walter, Robert 312
Walters, Jackson 070
. W. 070
. Wm. 240
. Wm? 159
Walton, Jeremiah 152-153, 191
. Wm. 150, 178
Ward Iron Works 085
Ward, Col. 071
. James 234
. Joseph 136, 155, 207
. Mary 155
. Saml. G. 290
Ware, John 004
Ware, Robert 004
Warford, Tobias M. 290
Warner, Miss 145
Warren, George 245
. James 277
. Jesse 153, 191
. Westley 172
. Westly 148
Wasaha, 217
Washa 156
Watkins, Jarret 280
Watson's Iron Works 081

Watson, Isom 154, 199
. Thomas 152
. Thos. M. 189
Watton, Jeremiah 191
Watts, Thomas 156
Weaver's mill 017
Weaver, Peter 214
Webb's mill 079
Webb, Alexander 156, 220
. Henry 220
. Jesse 154, 196
. Spencer 247
. Thomas 147-148, 170, 225
. Wm. 251
Webster, Allen 149, 172
Webster, John 148, 225
Welch's mill 107
West, John 099
Wheeler, Peter 153, 192
. Wm. 153, 192
Wheelock, John 115
Whitaker 048
Whitaker, Wm. 242
White & Co. 056
White's Mill 026
White, George 151
. Green 151, 178
. John 287
. John W. 155, 204
. Richard 037
Whitesides, Samuel 154, 155, 201
Whitford, David 125
Whitlow, Solomon 291
Whitsell, Mrs. 040
Whitson, G. 033
Whitton, Miss 005
Wideman, Mr. 147
Wiggers, Richard 237
Wiggins, Mr. 138
 Richard 158, 237
Wilborn, Mr. 016

Name Index

Wildman, Sarah 059
Wilkerson, Thos. 243
Wilkins, James 283
Wilkinson, James 116
  Wm. 130
Williams, Allen 303
. Betsy 152
. Caleb 303
. Dillard 158, 232
. Eliza 251
. Elizabeth 052
  Fet 303
. George 308
. Henry S. 098
. James 052
  Jesse 216
. John 075, 153-154, 193
.   272, 290
. John W. 148, 171
. Lewis L. 221
. Louis 157
. Mr. 148
. Nancy 157
. Robert 075
. Simon 260
. Stephen 075
. Wilson 152
Williamson's mill 022
Williamson, Mr. 071
Willis, B.B. 250
  Elisha 146
  Richard 149, 173
  Samuel 250
. Sarah 108
. Thomas 108
. Vernon 003
. Wm. 282
Willson, Thomas 071
Wilson, Andrew 151-152, 184
. Hiram 151
. James 095, 151, 157, 168, 183

Wilson, James T. 147
. John 156, 212, 257, 298
. Joseph 147
. Joseph L. 165
. Joshua J. 208
. Joshua Jones 155-156
. Mary 139
. Picker 098
. Rebecca 156
. Richard 299
. Samuel 139, 158, 231
. Silas 303
. Thomas 047, 157, 223
. Wm. 149, 173
Winston, John 122
Winter, Charity 156
Winters, Josiah 156, 208
  Seabourn 306
Wise, George 304
  Joseph 123
Wiseman, Bedford 150
. D. 006
. Davenport 149, 174
. Giles 150
. Martin 149-150
Witcher, Lucy 285
Witt, Mrs. 015
Wolf Meeting House 064
Wolf, Moses 265
Wolfe, Mr. 046
Wollen, Thomas 047
Wood, Delila 107
Wood, James 107
Woodard, Wm. 144
Woodfolk, W. 159
Woodruff, John A. 268
Woods, Lewis 148
Word, Mrs. 013
Wray, James E. 296
  Wm. 308
Wright, Andrew J. 247

Name Index

Wright, James 154, 193
. James M. 216
. John B. 150, 175
Wyatt, Dicy 090
. Edward 158
. John 090, 235
. Robt. 246
. Samuel 156
Wyett, Edward 236
 Samuel 211
Yancy, Robert 171
Yates, Charles 306
 John 104, 176
 Sam 205
York, John 195
Young, Allen 113
. Elizabeth 144
Young, John 225
. Joseph 009
Zachrie, Wm. 267
Zeatman 071

www.ingramcontent.com/pod-product-compliance
Lightning Source LLC
Chambersburg PA
CBHW071144300426
44113CB00009B/1084